SECOND EDITION

# RESEARCH METHODS *in* PSYCHOLOGY

# SECOND EDITION

# RESEARCH METHODS *in* PSYCHOLOGY

## Investigating Human Behavior

**Paul G. Nestor**
*University of Massachusetts Boston*

**Russell K. Schutt**
*University of Massachusetts Boston*

Los Angeles | London | New Delhi
Singapore | Washington DC

Los Angeles | London | New Delhi
Singapore | Washington DC

FOR INFORMATION:

SAGE Publications, Inc.
2455 Teller Road
Thousand Oaks, California 91320
E-mail: order@sagepub.com

SAGE Publications Ltd.
1 Oliver's Yard
55 City Road
London EC1Y 1SP
United Kingdom

SAGE Publications India Pvt. Ltd.
B 1/I 1 Mohan Cooperative Industrial Area
Mathura Road, New Delhi 110 044
India

SAGE Publications Asia-Pacific Pte. Ltd.
3 Church Street
#10-04 Samsung Hub
Singapore 048763

Printed in the United States of America

*Library of Congress Cataloging-in-Publication Data*

Nestor, Paul.
Research methods in psychology : investigating human behavior / Paul G. Nestor, University of Massachusetts, Boston, Russell K. Schutt, University of Massachusetts, Boston.—2nd Edition.

pages cm
ISBN 978-1-4833-4376-1 (pbk.)

1. Human behavior. 2. Human behavior—Research. 3. Psychology—Research. I. Schutt, Russell K. II. Title.

BF199.N37 2014
150.72—dc23          2013046950

This book is printed on acid-free paper.

Certified Chain of Custody
Promoting Sustainable Forestry
www.sfiprogram.org
SFI-01268

SFI label applies to text stock

Acquisitions Editor:   Jerry Westby
Publishing Associate:   MaryAnn Vail
Digital Content Editor:   Rachael Leblond
Production Editor:   Jane Haenel
Copy Editor:   QuADS Prepress (P) Ltd
Typesetter:   C&M Digitals (P) Ltd.
Proofreader:   Kate Peterson
Indexer:   Joan Shapiro
Cover Designer:   Glenn Vogel
Marketing Manager:   Shari Countryman

14 15 16 17 18 10 9 8 7 6 5 4 3 2 1

# Brief Contents

# Detailed Contents

# Preface

A young single woman named Linda is outspoken and very intelligent, committed to social justice, and deeply concerned about problems of discrimination. Which is more probable? (a) Linda is a bank teller or (b) Linda is a bank teller and is active in the feminist movement. Most people answer (b) as more probable. But this is incorrect because it violates the statistical laws of probability—every feminist bank teller is a bank teller; adding a detail, such as "feminist" can only reduce the probability. Yet even experts in probability make this error. As Holt (2011) noted, "The great evolutionary biologist Stephen Jay Gould . . . knew the right answer yet he wrote that 'a little homunculus in my head continues to jump up and down, shout at me—"She can't just be a bank teller; read the description"'" (p. BR16).

The psychologist Daniel Kahneman (2011) showed that we are all naturally inclined to make these kinds of mistakes of reasoning or "cognitive biases," which he described as unconscious errors that distort our perceptions of the world. As Kahneman and others have shown, these errors of intuition are not attributable to disturbed thinking or emotions, but are built into our evolved mental architecture. In this book, we make the case for the scientific method as the best antidote for what have often been described as cognitive illusions, so-called blind spots of the human mind. We start with the work of Kahneman because it, first, provides us with a convincing rationale for the need for the scientific method—the so-called "why" question is at the core of our book. Why research methods? Why statistical reasoning? Why measurement? Why complex research design? For each of these and other related topics of research methodology covered in the book, we explain why we need to know in order for us to understand better the world and ourselves. Along the way, we hope that there will be intellectual surprises for you as well as self-help value as we explore not only the "how's" but more important, the "why's" of research methodology in relation to thinking, remembering, feeling, perceiving, and attending. We hope that our book will convince you, as a member of our jury, of the indispensability of the scientific method.

For us (and we hope for you), the scientific method is not a proverbial ball and chain, shackling creativity, but a set of tools to broaden and build thinking about the world and ourselves. We place research methodology within a broad and rich cultural context of the "public square." To this end, our approach is unique in casting the scientific method widely, in aligning it not only with rigorous testing of ideas but also with the generation of new ideas, spawned by imagination and curiosity. Thus, our aspiration for writing this book is to imbue in you a sense of excitement about psychological research. Far from drudgery, research, as we frame it throughout the text provides the best method for investigating questions that matter to all of us. So in this text, you will learn both to design and to critique research as you explore a diverse array of case examples of how to investigate lively, timeless topics such as happiness and altruism, facial expression of emotion, 9/11 memories, and brain plasticity training.

## ▣ Teaching and Learning Goals

Our purpose in writing this book is to make teaching and learning about research methods in psychology both fun and rewarding. We bring you into the world of psychological research. Here you will find a culture in its own right that is governed by a way of thinking. At center stage is a set of rules and procedures that is collectively known as the scientific method. To engage you, we take you inside various research studies and we ask you to wear alternating hats. With one of these hats, you play the role of the researcher: How does one come up with research ideas? Why must ideas be subjected to the scientific method? How might you design a study to test your ideas? With another hat, you become a research consumer learning how to appraise and critique theory and design.

Our aim is for you to develop a mindset of skepticism without cynicism and more rigorous and disciplined thinking—while still remaining flexible, open-minded, imaginative, innovative, and inventive. With yet another hat that will help you achieve this goal, you will experience research as a participant—that is, as someone who contributes data in the form of answers to a researcher's questions. Do you understand the tasks, measures, and procedures required of participants? Do you think these methods capture what the research intended to study? By playing these alternating roles, we hope to spark your curiosity and creativity and to share with you our passion so that you too learn the joy of conducting sound research.

To accomplish these goals, we employ an approach that is novel and unique in that it melds two distinct yet complementary pedagogical techniques. First, each chapter is designed for *experiential, hands-on, roll-up-the-sleeves* studies that can be customized for both in-class exercises and course projects. Studies are presented from multiple perspectives and can easily be adapted for role-playing exercises with students acting as researchers, participants, or consumers of science. The text is illustrated with examples of study stimuli, such as faces and eyes, to bring to life the actual experimental tasks. In addition, we also include questionnaires and measurement scales that you can take to provide a fuller understanding of the research experience.

Second, we use the findings of cognitive science to guide our text in a way that is most conducive to learning, understanding, and appreciation. We contextualize informational content. For example, statistical reasoning is woven into the text and tied to specific research examples that are chosen to illuminate how the results of any scientific study are probabilistic in nature, a matter of calculating odds via mathematical formulae, which are presented in Chapter 10. Similarly, we emphasize a narrative approach that likens psychological theory to storytelling that can be used in study design and data interpretation. In a nutshell, then, we have used the science of psychology as a guide for writing the text and for accomplishing our teaching and learning goals.

## ▣ Organization of the Book

The way the book is organized reflects our commitment to making research methods interesting. Each chapter is structured around at least one particular published, peer-reviewed study that we selected for innovativeness and inventiveness as well as for impact on our understanding of exciting, cutting-edge topics at the forefront of psychology. Through the lens of these studies, we aim to provide you with a context to stimulate and facilitate learning of various research methods—bringing them to life and infusing them with meaning and practical application. In this sense, our book is anchored in a case-study approach to learning. Using particular published investigations as a storyline, we have tried to provide you with a narrative for learning.

The first three chapters introduce you to the why and how of research in general. Chapter 1 begins with a simple experiment that can easily be done in-class, taken from the pioneering work of Kahneman and Tversky. In Chapter 2, we take you inside the study by Iyengar, Wells, and Schwartz (2006), "Doing Better but Feeling Worse. Looking for the 'Best' Job Undermines Satisfaction." To whet your appetite, Chapter 2 includes Iyengar and colleagues' maximizer/satisficer scale. We encourage you and your classmates to take the maximizer/satisficer scale to help you understand what the participants in their research experienced. Most important, Chapter 2 teaches you how data can be collected, statistically analyzed, and written up in a short research report. Here we demonstrate how maximizer/satisficer test scores can be used for descriptive statistics: What is the average score for the class? What is the range of scores?

In Chapter 2, you then learn how to present these results in a written format of a short research report. This is broken down, step-by-step, illustrated by "right" and "wrong" statements for writing each of the four major sections (Introduction, Method, Results, and Discussion) of a short research report. In addition, you will learn about visually presenting data using graphs. Chapter 3 highlights issues of research ethics. We take you inside the Milgram and Zimbardo studies. We also introduce you to recent cases of scientific misconduct in psychology, which includes a separate piece, set off in a text box, "Scientific Misconduct in Psychology: Is Replication the Answer?"

Chapters 4 and 5 cover essential research techniques of measurement and sampling. In Chapter 4, you learn the meaning of theoretical constructs in psychology, their importance in measuring and building knowledge and for the understanding of our inner and outer worlds. The blending of conceptual and operational modes of thinking in psychological research continues to be highlighted. We compare and contrast two measures of well-being, one of which consists of five simple items that can easily be administered to a class. In Chapter 4, the importance of culture, especially in relation to measurement of intelligence is emphasized. So too are reliability and validity as staples of a school of psychology dedicated to standardized measurement, known as psychometrics. Chapter 5 complements Chapter 4 by using research on happiness to illustrate the process of sampling and the method of survey research based on samples. This chapter extends our review of research about happiness and well-being through review of a major international survey.

In Chapters 6, through 8, you learn about different experimental approaches. Chapter 6 uses the well-known Stroop test as an in-class demonstration of a single-factor experiment. The Stroop can be easily administered, the effect is robust, and the data can be clearly presented both graphically and in written format, all of which can provide a valuable hands-on learning experience. In Chapter 6, we also compare the Stroop experiment with a groundbreaking study that used a randomized clinical trial to examine the effects of computerized cognitive training on memory decline in aging.

Chapter 7 presents complex factorial designs and takes you behind the scenes to learn how eye-gaze and emotional expression of faces interact to influence observers' judgments. The actual experimental stimuli are presented so that students can see first-hand faces that varied in expression (anger, fear) and eye-gaze direction (direct, averted). Chapter 7 also shows how researchers used a multifactorial approach in designing a rather ingenious study to examine the effects of social isolation on intellectual thought. Again the study is deconstructed for you, and you see how the data were collected and analyzed.

Chapter 8 delves into quasi-experiments. This, as you will learn, is a critical research approach in that it offers a much needed experimental methodology for studying those countless topics in human psychology for which key variables cannot be truly controlled and manipulated. In Chapter 8, we create for you the experience of a research participant in a brain imaging study examining "flashbulb" memories of the 9/11 terrorist attacks. We then show you how the researchers created their independent variables, one of which showed that proximity to the World Trade Center influenced intensity of 9/11 memories. Chapter 8 also covers quasi-experiments used in developmental psychology, which include cross-sectional, longitudinal, and cross-sequential approaches. To illustrate, we learn about a developmental study of brain maturation in children with attention deficit hyperactivity disorder.

We devote Chapter 9 to small-*N* design, an important research approach for clinical, behavioral, and counseling psychology. Our examples in this chapter come from research on behavioral change. Chapter 10 brings together many of the statistical and data analytic issues introduced in the prior chapters. Consistent with the earlier chapters, we organize and contextualize statistics and data analysis with reference to a fascinating study published in the prestigious interdisciplinary journal *Science,* "Spending Money on Others Promotes Happiness" by Dunn, Aknin, and Norton (2008). Chapter 11 is dedicated to qualitative methods. These techniques are intended to go beyond numbers, as in the study by Bernadette Sánchez and others (2010) of Latino students' transitions after high school, which we use as an example of qualitative methods.

Finally, in Chapter 12, you will learn about report writing in APA (American Psychological Association) style. We emphasize the general structure of an APA-formatted paper along with the APA rules for citations and referencing. We encourage you to think of APA style not as an obstacle to writing but as a means to help structure your writing. We come full circle in Chapter 12, using as a sample paper of APA report writing the Iyengar and colleagues (2006) study, which we first introduced in Chapter 2.

## ▣ Distinctive Features of the Second Edition

*Expanded and Earlier Coverage of How to Write a Research Report.* In response to instructors' feedback, we introduce the mechanics of research writing in Chapter 2. Using a developmental approach, we focus on the most basic format for writing in scientific research, a short research report, using the maximizer/satisficer scale, which is presented in Chapter 2, which can be easily administered in-class. We concretize the task of composing a short research report, making explicit the "rights" and "wrongs" of scientific writing in psychology and spelling out, step-by-step, the construction of narrative text organized in the Introduction, Method, Results, and Discussion sections. Guidelines for more advanced research writing are presented later in Chapter 10.

*New Feature on Enhanced Learning via Pretesting.* Toward the beginning of each chapter is a new feature that we developed based on research that has shown that students who take a test before studying learn better than students who study without pretesting (e.g., Kornell, Hays, & Bjork, 2009). Chapters thus include a set of 10 pretest questions that, following Roediger and Finn (2010), we call "Testing Before Learning." As an added feature to engage the reader, these pretest questions are written in a jeopardy game-like format based on positive feedback that we have received from our students.

*Streamlined In-Class Demonstrations of Experiments.* We rewrote and reorganized each of the 10 research chapters. We still present simple and direct expositions of the research approach that is the principal focus of each of these chapters. New to the second edition and presented in Chapter 1 are the simple experiments taken from the work of Kahneman and Tversky, which can be easily adapted for both in-class demonstrations and research report writing assignments. Chapter 4 now has extensive coverage of the Satisfaction With Life Scale, which also can be easily incorporated into an engaging in-class demonstration and companion research writing assignment. Hands-on examples about subjective well-being are also used in Chapters 5 and 10. New to Chapter 6 is the Stroop, also introduced for the purposes of providing an in-class demonstration of a famous psychology experiment that effectively teaches the fundamental concepts of independent and dependent variables.

*New Feature on Statistical Reasoning and Probability.* "Stat Corner" is a new feature that we developed based on the research of Kahneman and others. Here we emphasize how to think about statistics by presenting relevant topics in an engaging and nonthreatening manner as, for example, Stat Corner pieces titled "Sample Size Matters,"

"Scientific Misconduct in Psychology: Is Replication the Answer?" and "Story Telling With Numbers and Graphs." Throughout the book, we present the rationale and logic of statistical reasoning first as a countervailing force to what cognitive scientists often refer to as our "probability-blind" minds. We continue in subsequent chapters to build a conceptual understanding of the nature of statistical reasoning and emphasizing—for example, in Chapter 4, the statistical properties of scales of measurement and in Chapter 7, the depiction of correlations via scatter diagrams. Chapter 10 presents descriptive and inferential statistics in the context of real-life studies.

*Updated Development in Research Science and Ethics.* Recent cases of scientific misconduct in psychology research have come to light since the publication of the first edition of this book. Sound research practice and adherence to principles of reliability and validity have been proposed as a "partial cure" for these recent problems of scientific misconduct (e.g., Roediger, 2012). We now draw connections between ethics and research practice in Chapter 3, which includes a separate piece set off in the Stat Corner, "Scientific Misconduct in Psychology: Is Replication the Answer?" In Chapter 4, students will also learn of a new concept in research methods, "replication validity," which may also have direct implications for reducing the risk of scientific misconduct in psychology research. In Chapter 12, we return to the risk of scientific misconduct in reporting results. The "Ethics in Action" activity of Chapter 12 focuses on a July 2010 *Scientific American* piece, "When Scientists Lie" (Shermer, 2010), reviewing a book by the vice provost of the California Institute of Technology David Goodstein titled *On Fact and Fraud: Cautionary Tales From the Front Lines of Science* (2010).

*Cultural and Developmental Perspectives Are Emphasized.* You will learn about research that illuminates how culture shapes our thinking and how our thinking shapes culture. In our coverage of measurement of intelligence (Chapter 4), you will learn the nuts and bolts of experiments on stereotype threat that have provided compelling evidence of the deleterious effects of racial bias on IQ in African American students. You will learn in Chapter 8 of experimental studies of constructivist theories of culture as we highlight the work of Ying-yi Hong, Michael W. Morris, Chi-yue Chiu, and Veronica Benet-Martinez in the *America Psychologist* (2000), "Multicultural Minds: A Dynamic Constructivist Approach to Culture and Cognition." Also in Chapter 8, you learn of different experimental designs used in developmental psychology through the lens of a longitudinal design examining brain maturation in children diagnosed with attention deficit hyperactivity disorder.

*Web-Based Instructional Aids.* The book's study site includes new interactive exercises that link directly to original research articles published by SAGE, on each major research topic. It is important to spend enough time with these exercises to become very comfortable with the basic research concepts presented. The interactive exercises allow you to learn about research on a range of interesting topics as you practice using the language of research. The linked articles now allow the opportunity to learn more about research that illustrates particular techniques.

# Ancillaries

*Instructor Teaching Site.* A password-protected site, available at **www.sagepub.com/nestor2e**, features resources that have been designed to help instructors plan and teach their courses. These resources include an extensive test bank, chapter-specific PowerPoint presentations, lecture notes, sample syllabi, video and web resources, and links to SAGE journal articles with accompanying questions.

*Student Study Site.* An open-access study site is available at **www.sagepub.com/nestor2e**. This site includes mobile-friendly eFlashcards, mid-chapter review web quizzes, and full-chapter web quizzes as well as web resources, video resources, links to SAGE journal articles, and interactive exercises.

# Acknowledgments

Our thanks extend first to Jerry Westby, publisher and senior editor for SAGE Publications. Jerry's consistent support and exceptional vision have made it possible for this project to flourish, while his good cheer and collegiality have even made it all rather fun. Editor extraordinaire Theresa Accomazzo also contributed vitally, while production was managed with great expertise and good cheer by Jane Haenel, assisted by Krishna Pradeep Joghee and his team of copyeditors at QuADS. And we continue to be grateful to work with what has become the world's best publisher in social science, SAGE Publications, and their exceptional marketing manager, Shari Countryman.

We also are indebted to the first-rate psychologists recruited by Jerry Westby to critique our book. Their thoughtful suggestions and cogent insights have helped improve every chapter. They are:

Elizabeth Arnott-Hill, *Chicago State University*

Deborah Baldwin, *University of Tennessee*

Vicki Black Bishop, *Northern Arizona University*

Cynthia Bostick, *California State University–Dominguez Hills*

Mary Jo Carnot, *Chadron State College*

Lawrence Cohen, *University of Delaware*

Chris Goode, *Georgia State University*

Nicholas Herrera, *DePaul University*

Brian Hock, *Austin Peay State University*

Karen Holmes, *Norfolk State University*

Katherine Hooper, *University of North Florida*

Steven Hoover, *St. Cloud State University*

Joel Hughes, *Kent State University*

Amy Hyman, *Florida International University*

Keith Jones, *Texas Tech University*

Sarah Kulkofsky, *Texas Tech University*

James Kuterbach, *Pennsylvania State University*

Sean Laraway, *San Jose State University*

Christopher Leupold, *Elon University*

Susan Lima, *University of Wisconsin*

Donald Loffredo, *University of Houston*

Connie Meinholdt, *Ferris State University*

Padraig O'Seaghdha, *Lehigh University*

Elizabeth Sheehan, *Georgia State University*

L. James Smart, *Miami University*

Carrie Smith, *University of Delaware*

Emily Stark, *Minnesota State University–Mankato*

Seth Surgan, *Worcester State College*

John Wallace, *Ball State University*

Sandra Waters, *North Carolina Central University*

Michael Young, *Southern Illinois University*

The quality of *Research Methods in Psychology: Investigating Human Behavior* benefits increasingly from the wisdom and creativity of our growing SAGE author group. We express our profound gratitude to the following SAGE authors: Ronet Bachman (University of Delaware), Dan Chambliss (Hamilton College), Joe Check (University of Massachusetts Boston), and Ray Engel (University of Pittsburgh). We also thank Sheena Iyengar (Columbia University) for allowing us to use as a stellar example of report writing her pre-publication manuscript (Iyengar, Wells, & Schwartz, 2006) "Doing Better but Feeling Worse. Looking for the 'Best' Job Undermines Satisfaction."

We thank our University of Massachusetts Boston students, including Tory Choate, Dominic Newell, Shaun O'Grady, Eileen Rasmussen, and Ashley Shirai. We greatly appreciate their feedback and assistance in creating the exhibits. We also thank Chris Goldy for his excellent photographs.

No scholarly book project can succeed without good library resources, and for these, we continue to incur a profound debt to the Harvard University library staff and their extraordinary collection. We also have benefited from the resources maintained by the excellent librarians at the University of Massachusetts Boston.

Most important, we thank our families for their love and support. Patti Nestor and Beth Schutt deserve canonization for their loving patience, humor, perspective, and wisdom, for which we are eternally indebted and forever grateful. And to our daughters, Molly Ann Nestor, Bridget Aileen Nestor, and Julia Ellen Schutt, we are blessed by your lives.

*—Paul G. Nestor*
*—Russell K. Schutt*
*Boston, Massachusetts*

# Uncommon Sense and the Scientific Method

## LEARNING OBJECTIVES: FAST FACTS

### Why Scientific Method?

- Pioneering work in cognitive psychology has demonstrated that our minds are susceptible to systematic errors of thinking, reasoning, decision making, and judgment, known as heuristic biases. These deeply ingrained cognitive biases dictate the need for the scientific method.

- The scientific method identifies a set of rules, procedures, and techniques that together form a unified conceptual framework—a formal way of thinking about a problem, idea, or question. The scientific method lays out a foundation for how information is collected, measured, examined, and evaluated.

- Variables are the language of scientific research. The independent variable is defined as an element of a study that is systematically manipulated, changed, or selected. The dependent variable is the observed effect, result, or outcome measured in response to a systematic change in the independent variable.

- The scientific method uses statistics to describe variables and to test the relationships of independent and dependent variables.

## TESTING BEFORE LEARNING

Try your hand at these questions. Don't worry about not knowing the correct response, as you haven't read the chapter yet! But research shows that a pretest such as this can enhance learning (e.g., Kornell, Hays, & Bjork, 2009). So here is the answer. You come up with the question.

1.  A mental shortcut that can lead to systematic errors in reasoning
    a.  What is a parameter?
    b.  What is a heuristic?
    c.  What is a statistic?
    d.  What is a sample bias?

2.  A formal way of thinking that relies exclusively on empirical evidence to create and evaluate knowledge
    a.  What is a heuristic?
    b.  What is a pseudoscience?
    c.  What is scientific method?
    d.  What is probability?

3.  A scientific hypothesis should be open to this kind of evidence.
    a.  What is testimonial?
    b.  What is falsifiable?
    c.  What is intuitive?
    d.  What is authority?

4.  An attribute like height, weight, or happiness that is measurable and that is assigned changing values
    a.  What is a heuristic?
    b.  What is a statistic?
    c.  What is a variable?
    d.  What is a sample?

5.  A variable that is manipulated
    a.  What is a control variable?
    b.  What is a dependent variable?
    c.  What is an independent variable?
    d.  What is a confounding variable?

6.  A variable that measures the effect of a manipulated variable
    a.  What is a control variable?
    b.  What is a dependent variable?
    c.  What is an independent variable?
    d.  What is a confounding variable?

7.  The enemy of the scientific method, the veritable reason for its existence
    a.  What is empiricism?
    b.  What is theory?
    c.  What is measurement?
    d.  What is bias?

8.  Information that is described as empirical because it can be measured and evaluated statistically
    a.  What are data?
    b.  Who are research participants?
    c.  What is error?
    d.  What is description?

9.  A researcher wants to maximize the extent to which findings that are derived from a sample can be applied to a wider population.
    a.  What is generalizability?
    b.  What is sample bias?
    c.  What is probability?
    d.  What is error?

10. "No amount of experimentation can ever prove me right; a single experiment can prove me wrong."—Albert Einstein
    a.  What is the doctrine of falsification?
    b.  What is the doctrine of pseudoscience?
    c.  What is a hypothesis?
    d.  What are data?

**ANSWER KEY:** (1) b; (2) c; (3) b; (4) c; (5) c; (6) b; (7) d; (8) a; (9) a; (10) a

# Biases in Thinking

Imagine that your neighbor asks you to help figure out someone he has just met named Steve: Steve is very shy and withdrawn, invariably helpful but with little interest in people or in the world of reality. A meek and tidy soul, he has a need for order and structure, and a passion for detail.

Your neighbor also explains that Steve was just some random guy, who was picked from the larger population. The neighbor asks you, "Is Steve more likely to be a librarian or a farmer?" How would you answer? Of course, we can't know for sure, but write your best guess here: _____.

## Intuition

If you are like most people, you may have answered that Steve is more likely to be a librarian. Why? His personality seems to be such a natural match with that of a stereotypical librarian, doesn't it? (With apologies to Russ's wife, who is a librarian and is nothing like that stereotype!) Indeed, in reading the above question, this personality resemblance comes to mind immediately, and it is both too striking and too difficult to ignore—the answer just feels right. This is what psychologists define as *intuitive thinking*, that is, judgments and decisions that come to mind automatically, without explicit awareness of the triggering cues and with total acceptance of the accuracy of those cues (Kahneman & Klein, 2009). In our example, the answer of Steve as a librarian reflects intuitive thinking because it arose automatically, without effort and without explicit awareness of the cues that triggered it, namely, the striking resemblance of Steve's personality description with that of a stereotypical librarian.

What likely did not occur to you was a statistical fact that is highly relevant to the question: There are 20 times more male farmers than male librarians in the United States. With so many more farmers than librarians, the likelihood is far greater for "meek and tidy" men to be farmers than librarians. However, studies have consistently shown that when asked about Steve the librarian, most people ignore relevant statistical facts and instead base their answers exclusively on personality resemblance (Kahneman, 2011). We call this reliance on resemblance a **heuristic**, which is defined as a simplifying mental shortcut that people use to make intuitive judgments and predictions (Kahneman & Tversky, 1973). The work of Kahneman and his late colleague Amos Tversky identified some 20 distinct heuristics, each of which causes systematic errors in thinking and judgments, known as cognitive biases.

These biases of intuitive thinking are evident when we judge Steve to be a librarian based exclusively on his personality description, ignoring the statistical fact that we surely know that there are more male farmers than librarians. However, when told the correct answer to questions like this, many research participants expressed strong emotions of disbelief that were comparable with those produced by familiar optical illusions.

What if you had been told in advance how many more farmers there are than librarians? Would that have affected your answer? In another study, Tversky and Kahneman (1974) described Dick as follows: Dick is a 30-year-old man. He is married with no children. A man of high ability and high motivation, he promises to be quite successful in his field. He is well liked by his colleagues.

They then told some research participants that Dick had been drawn from a group of 70 engineers and 30 lawyers and asked them whether Dick was more likely to be a lawyer or an engineer. What would your answer be? _____.

This time there was a twist: Tversky and Kahneman gave some of the research participants the same information that you received (70 engineers, 30 lawyers), but they told the others that the group had 30 engineers and 70 lawyers. We call these proportions the *base rates* for these occupations. But it didn't matter! The research participants in the Tversky and Kahneman studies simply ignored the base rates (Kahneman & Tversky, 1973; Tversky & Kahneman, 1974). Put simply, even if a personality sketch conveys little or no information to help in making a decision like this, people ignore base rates when they decide. Did *you* take the base rate into account?

Do you understand the problem? Consider the optical illusion in Exhibit 1.1. Your visual system deceives you so that the figure in the background seems larger, even though the two figures are exactly the same size. In the same way, **cognitive illusions** occur when our thinking deceives us, and this happens because of curious blind spots, or mental tunnels, in our minds (e.g., Piattelli-Palmarini, 1994). This is what happens when people think about Steve or about Dick.

| Exhibit 1.1 | Cool Brain Trick: In Depth |
|---|---|

### Which monster is larger?

*Note:* To most people, the one in the background seems larger, though in fact they are exactly the same size. But the depth cues in the picture (the receding tunnel) give the 2D (two-dimensional) image a 3D feel. Although both monsters create the same size image in our eyes, our brains take the depth cues into account, which results in a perception of the upper monster as farther away—making it seem larger.

We examine the biases of intuition as a way of setting the stage for learning about a different way of knowing, the **scientific method**. Our intuitive thinking is automatic, effortless, efficient, and often adaptive. But can we count on intuition to produce the right answer? Enter **psychology**, broadly defined as the scientific study of people. The scientific process starts with an idea and then proceeds to a methodology to test that idea. The next step is to statistically analyze the results and draw conclusions from those results. Our goal is to describe the fundamental nature of the topic, to explain how it works, and to predict when it occurs. This is a scientific understanding of the topic of study. Hence, we have fast and frugal versus disciplined and systematic; intuitive judgments versus scientific thinking. Understanding scientific research methods begins with the tale of these two ways of thinking.

What happens when intuitive and scientific thinking clash? Who wins, and why does it matter for us as we learn research methods? As we will see, psychological studies clearly show that intuitive thinking often trumps scientific thinking. In fact, research tells us that we resist particular scientific findings that defy our intuitions and our common sense (Bloom & Weisberg 2007). And we do so naturally without even knowing that our intuitions can deceive us (Kahneman, 2011). In this book, we show you how to think scientifically, that is, to apply scientific research methods to topics in psychology. You will have to decide whether you think the use of scientific research methods helps improve our understanding of human behavior.

## Curiosity and Imagination

However, we do not want to leave you with a negative view of intuition. In fact, there is considerable evidence that a certain type of intuition can be quite effective (Kahneman & Klein, 2009). This intuition is gained through expertise, the most classic example being the ability of chess grand masters to recognize complex patterns and identify the most promising moves. This expert intuition arises from experience and demonstrated skill. Intuition arising from experience and skill is different from the intuition that comes from simplifying heuristics like those evident in the case of "Steve." Intuitions based on simplifying heuristics are likely to be wrong and are prone to predictable, systematic biases (Kahneman & Klein, 2009).

Intuitions can also be important sources of creative thinking. Creative intuitions allow for uncovering patterns and connections of images and ideas that exist, but only a few people can discover them without prompting (Kahneman & Klein, 2009). A prepared yet intuitive and open mind increases the chances of accidentally discovering something fortunate. This is known as the **serendipity** effect. The history of science and technology is marked by a long list of very important but serendipitous discoveries and inventions. For example, in 1954, the Austrian scientist Dr. Leo Sternbach accidentally discovered Librium, the first effective treatment for bipolar disorder ("manic depression"), while cleaning up his lab. The astronomer William Herschel accidentally discovered the planet Uranus while looking for comets, and in fact, he originally identified Uranus as a comet. Lore also has it that the seeds of Isaac Newton's law of universal gravitation can be traced to his observations of the famed apple falling out of a tree. The point of these observations taken from the history and sociology of science is that serendipity teaches us the value of keeping our minds and hearts open to unexpected, unlikely, and counterintuitive events.

# ▣ The Scientific Method

As you will learn throughout the book, the scientific method is the cornerstone of research. We will flesh out various key features of the scientific method throughout the book. But as a starting point, let's think of the scientific method as the veritable rules of the game of research. These rules reflect procedures and techniques for conducting and evaluating psychological research. Together, these rules, procedures, and techniques form a unified conceptual framework—a formal way of thinking about a problem, idea, or question. Just as any game will have a set of rules, procedures, and techniques to govern play, so too does the scientific method lay out a foundation for how information is collected, measured, examined, and evaluated. In this sense, then, the scientific method serves as a playbook or toolbox for psychological research.

The origins of the scientific method may be traced to the school of philosophy known as **empiricism**. Empiricists believe that knowledge is gained through experience, observation, and experiment. In science, the term *empirical* is used to denote information gained from observation or experimentation. This information, commonly referred to as **data**, is described as empirical because it can be measured and evaluated statistically. Data constitute empirical evidence against which all scientific knowledge is tested. Empirical evidence differs from anecdotal evidence, which refers to the subjective impressions of one or more people that are not translated into a quantifiable form. Investigative journalism often uses anecdotal evidence.

Kahneman and Tversky's (1973) approach to studying cognitive illusions provides a simple but elegant example of using the scientific method to investigate a problem. They devised a set of questions, each of which can be viewed as a small experiment. They then tabulated responses to the set of questions; these answers constituted their data. Then, Kahneman and Tversky calculated the percentages of participants who selected either librarian or farmer for Steve's occupation and the percentages of participants who selected either engineer or lawyer for Dick's profession. These percentages are the statistics—the empirical evidence—that Kahneman and Tversky used in answering their scientific question.

## What Is a Scientific Question?

Not every question we can ask is a *scientific question* that can be investigated with empirical evidence. Philosophers often distinguish two types of questions: "is" questions and "ought" questions. This philosophical distinction (known as **is/ought**) may help us understand what is meant by a scientific or "researchable" question. "Is" questions can be answered by facts or empirical data, and these answers are independent of social, cultural, political, and religious preference. These so-called "is" questions, many would argue, are the exclusive domain of scientific research. These are questions that can be best addressed through scientific research.

"Ought" questions call on cultural values and ethical considerations and cannot be answered solely on the basis of scientific evidence. These include questions of religion and faith that fall well beyond the realm of science and for which empiricism would be considered inappropriate. Does God exist? Should capital punishment be overturned? Should same-sex marriage be legalized? Ought questions address the values inherent in laws and customs and are influenced by beliefs that can reflect ideology, politics, and interpretation of rights. Science may contribute to the debate, but science in and of itself certainly cannot provide any direct, definitive answers to these questions. We will leave such questions that are not researchable to philosophers, theologians, and constitutional scholars. The scientific method is really moot for the topics these questions deal with.

The scientific method aims to answer scientific questions. Scientific questions and their answers are commonly framed in reference to a particular theory. In psychology, **theory** is defined as a coherent set of propositions that are used as principles to describe, understand, and explain psychological or behavioral phenomena. Theories often address questions of "how," as in the case of Kahneman and Tversky (1973), who studied the cognitive rules of intuitive reasoning. Ideas for a research study often spring from psychological theories. We use the scientific method to assess the quality of any psychological theory. In psychology, theory often influences all aspects of a study, continuing through the final interpretation of the study's results (Kuhn, 1962).

Thus, Kahneman and Tversky (1973) proposed a general theory of the cognitive processes involved in intuitive predictions and judgments. The major contribution of their approach, called the "heuristic and biases approach," is the discovery of systematic errors in our thinking and reasoning. A sound theory explains psychological or behavioral phenomena. As you have already seen, their theory does just that: It explains a distinct set of mental shortcuts, which are defined as heuristics and which cause systematic errors in probability judgments.

A sound theory also identifies the boundary conditions under which the phenomenon under study does *not* hold. Here too the theory of Kahneman and Tversky (1973) passes with flying colors. For example, consider the base-rate neglect heuristic demonstrated in the question of whether Dick is more likely to be an engineer or a lawyer. Kahneman and Tversky found that this problem does not occur when there is no other descriptive information presented. So if there is no description of Dick's personality, motivation, or ability, people use the base rates to answer the question of whether Dick is more likely to be a lawyer or an engineer. However, the presentation of the slightest inkling of evidence describing Dick's personality leads to ignoring base rates and so to the mistake of judging probability by similarity or resemblance.

## From Theory to Testable Hypothesis

A theory generates testable hypotheses, which are evaluated empirically with the scientific method. A **testable hypothesis** is framed as a statement, often in the form of a prediction that is made prior to the actual collection of data. A testable hypothesis is therefore described as **a priori**, meaning that it is developed before experimentation or observation. A priori hypotheses constitute a key feature of the scientific method. By formulating hypotheses before data collection and analysis, a scientist is less likely to be prone to error and bias by bending the theory to fit the numbers.

In direct contradistinction are hypotheses that are formulated after the data are collected and analyzed. These hypotheses, described as **post hoc** (in Latin, "after this"), pose serious problems for the scientific method. Post hoc hypotheses increase the likelihood of error and bias. The notion is that the more you look the more likely it is you will find something—the more hypotheses you test post hoc, the more likely it is that one of these will by chance be wrongly accepted as true. Formulating hypotheses post hoc is therefore not a good idea; those who use them should at least make statistical adjustments that make it harder to conclude that they have "found something."

Kahneman and Tversky (1973) developed specific, testable a priori hypotheses from their general theory of heuristics and biases in judgment. For example, they hypothesized that the "representativeness heuristic" would cause participants to make systematic errors in evaluating the probability of Steve as a librarian or a farmer. They tested this **hypothesis** by presenting a description of Steve and asking research participants to answer the question of whether Steve is more likely to be a librarian or farmer. Their results were the percentages of participants who judged Steve more likely to be a librarian or farmer. These results provided empirical evidence that could either support or not support their hypothesis; in fact, their hypothesis was supported. Kahneman and Tversky specifically predicted that the representativeness heuristic would cause participants to ignore relevant statistical facts and make their judgment exclusively on the extent to which the personality sketch of Steve as a "meek and tidy soul" meets the stereotypical librarian.

## Variables as the Language of Research

Variables are the language of research. A **variable** is simply defined as any characteristic that can take on different values or that can vary across research participants. Variables can include age, gender, weight, height, education, attitude, income, use of a medication, and virtually any other attribute that can assume multiple values or vary in people. A researcher will identify, often based on theory, key variables to investigate scientifically.

In research, a critical lesson to learn is the concept of independent variable and dependent variable. The **independent variable** is defined as an element of a study that you as a researcher systematically manipulate, change, or select. By contrast, the effects of the manipulation of the independent variable are examined and measured by the **dependent variable**. That is, the dependent variable is the observed effect, result, or outcome that is measured in response to a systematic change of or variation in the independent variable.

Let's illustrate how Kahneman and Tversky (1973) used variables in their work on base-rate neglect with regard to the question of whether Dick is more likely to be an engineer or a lawyer. In this study, participants were assigned to either one of two conditions. In one condition, the participants were told that Dick's personality description had been drawn from a group of 70 engineers and 30 lawyers. In the other condition, they were told that Dick's personality description had been drawn from a group that consisted of 30 engineers and 70 lawyers. So in this study, the researchers manipulated the base rates provided to the research participants for the group from which Dick's personality sketch was drawn: either 70 engineers/30 lawyers or 30 engineers/70 lawyers. So in this study, the independent variable was the base rates presented to the participants, with the two conditions. The effect of variation in this independent variable of base rates was evaluated on the dependent variable, the percentages of participants who predicted Dick to be an engineer or a lawyer.

The same variable can be used differently depending on the study. Take the variable stress at work. In one study, stress at work may be used as an independent variable. For example, let's say employees are selected on the basis of their level of reported stress at work, and then, the brain activity of employees with different stress levels is recorded. Here, the effects of the independent variable "stress at work" on the dependent variable "brain activity" are studied. In a different study, stress at work is used as a dependent variable; for example, a researcher wants to compare the level of stress at work experienced by people who have more and less authoritarian bosses. Here, the experimenter did nothing to alter the number of people at different stress levels in the experiment but, rather, measured the differences in stress at work between the two groups with different types of bosses. So depending on the role it plays in the hypothesized relationship, the same variable can be either independent or dependent.

## Sampling and Populations

Often in research, our observations are collected systematically and quantified by sampling a population. A **population** is defined as any entire collection of people, animals, plants, or things, all of which can be referred to as units, from which we may collect information. Because a population is too large to study in its entirety, a sample is generally selected for study. A **sample** is defined as a group of units selected from a larger group that is known as the *population*.

How a researcher selects a sample from a larger population is critically important for the scientific method. Ideally, a researcher uses a random process to select members from a population. This is known as a **random sample**. It is called "random" to indicate that every member from the larger population has an equal chance of being in the sample. Statistical theory assumes random samples, but in reality, a purely random sample in psychological research is often impractical. We will learn in Chapter 5 that there are specific sampling techniques that can provide an unbiased selection of members from a larger defined group even though they are not purely random. The goal is to use an unbiased method of selecting a sample.

Why is the gold standard for an unbiased sample one that is formed via a random process? The closer the process for creating a sample is to purely random, the greater likelihood that the sample will be representative of a larger group. The objective is to maximize what is referred to as **generalizability**, which means the extent to which findings that are derived from a sample can be applied to a wider population. Remember, a major reason for the scientific method is to combat bias, and a key source of potential bias can originate from how a sample is selected. For example, **case studies**, examining one or only a few, preselected participants, can be seriously if not fatally flawed by selecting only those cases that fit preconceived ideas. This sort of "cherry picking"—that is, deliberately picking only cases that support your view while ignoring those opposing your view—is an anathema to the scientific method. This can lead to a particular form of bias, **sample bias**, which means that some members of the population are less likely than others to be included in the study (Trochim, 2006). Such exclusion of certain members or subgroups of a population under study can sometimes produce misleading results (see Exhibit 1.2).

The issue of sample bias is extremely relevant in heuristic and bias research like Kahneman and Tversky's (1973), which aims to examine the nature and limitations of human thinking. One important question is whether these cognitive biases generalize across different cultures. For example, a researcher in the field of **cultural psychology** studies how culture shapes thinking and how thinking shapes culture (e.g., Nisbett, Peng, Choi, & Norenzayan, 2001). A researcher in the related field of **cross-cultural psychology** studies the universality of psychological processes across different cultures. Researchers in both of these fields of psychology would be interested in sampling persons from different cultures to examine the generalizability of cognitive biases. Overall, then, sampling reminds us of the importance of understanding and appreciating **culture** in research in psychology. Ensuring that our samples of research participants are representative of the diversity of the population is an important consideration in designing research.

| Exhibit 1.2 | Sample and Cross-Population Generalizability |
| --- | --- |

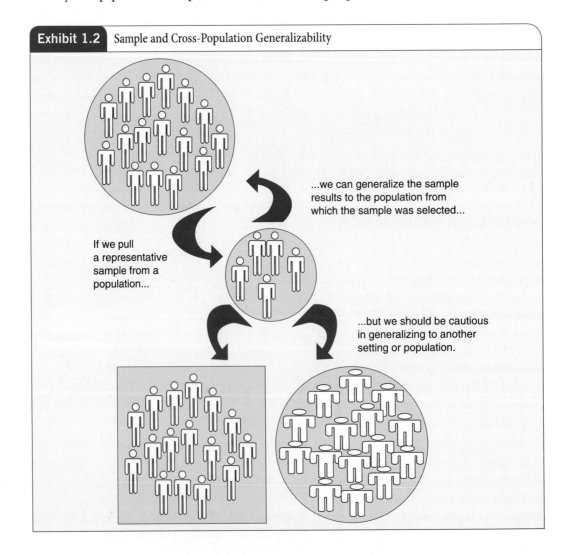

If we pull a representative sample from a population...

...we can generalize the sample results to the population from which the sample was selected...

...but we should be cautious in generalizing to another setting or population.

Sample bias is not a concern in studies of fundamental processes that operate the same across people within and between different populations. For example, Charles Darwin (1859) generated the theory of evolution by natural selection exclusively on the basis of simple observation of species in particular locations. He could not draw a representative sample of species, and he could not compare all different populations of animals. However, he believed that the basic process of evolution by natural selection occurred across all species, and so once he had figured out that process, it could be applied to species and populations that he had not studied. Research after Darwin continued to support this belief. In his later 1872 book, *The Expression of the Emotions in Man and Animals*, and again relying exclusively on observation, Darwin also made the case that all mammals regularly display emotion on their faces. Again, subsequent research supported this conclusion, even though Darwin had not studied a representative sample or examined facial expressions across all populations of mammals.

Test your knowledge of this chapter so far by taking the mid-chapter quiz on the study site: www.sagepub.com/nestor2e

## Evaluating Evidence and Theory

You now know that the scientific method requires the collection of observations, such as responses to questions, test scores, or ratings. These observations are then categorized or quantified systematically, and numeric values are either assigned or computed. These numeric values are the data that constitute empirical evidence. The scientific method uses statistics to test or analyze relationships between and among objective, quantifiable measures of variables that are derived from either experimentation or observation. The sample statistics are assumed to provide estimates of the population. All statistics are based on the logic of **probability**, and they all use the same criterion for evaluation. The question asked and answered by statistical tests may be stated as follows: In light of the data, what is the probability that the obtained results are due to chance? If the statistical analyses of the data show that the obtained results are highly unlikely due to chance, then the predicted relationship is considered to be highly likely. If, on the other hand, the statistical analyses of the data show that the obtained results are likely due to chance, then there is no empirical evidence in support of the expected relationship. The statistical evidence therefore provides a means to test a specific hypothesis and to evaluate a theory.

## Reliability and Validity

All sound research studies rely on the scientific method. However, as we will learn, different areas of psychology often pose and answer scientific research questions differently. Psychologists use a research "toolbox" consisting of a variety of methods and techniques to investigate these questions. Each method and technique has its own advantages and disadvantages, but they all have to meet scientific standards. Not all data are created as equal, as wise psychologists have often noted. Two standards are most important when judging the scientific quality of these methods and techniques as well as the results that they produce.

The first standard is **reliability**, which simply means *consistency*. A reliable study is one that produces data that can be **replicated**, that is, repeated with the same results. Whenever you read about a result of a study, always find out if it has been replicated; if it has, then you can have greater confidence in its reliability.

Equally important in evaluating research is **validity**, which is defined as the extent to which a study provides a true measure of what it is *meant* to investigate. We will learn that there are different types of validity, all of which, however, address the same question: "How true are our conclusions?" or "Are we measuring what we think we are measuring?" In evaluating validity, you will learn to look for what are known as *confounds* or **confounding variables**, which are unwanted sources of influence or variability that can be viewed, much to the dismay of the researcher, as viable alternative explanations for the result of a study. "Those darn confounds" is a damning phrase that can make researchers cringe, as it cuts to the heart or validity of a study. In many studies, researchers use what is referred to as a **control variable** to measure an unwanted source of influence that could invalidate the conclusions of a study (Exhibit 3). The aim is to be able to rule out the effect of a control variable on the results of a study.

**Exhibit 1.3** Three Key Variables

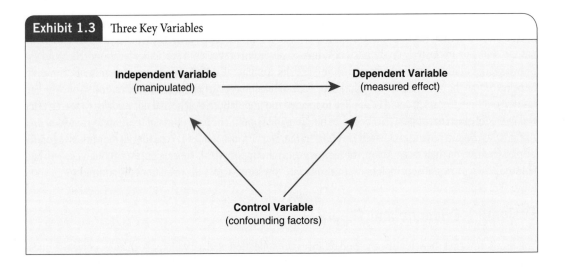

Think of reliability and validity as two related but distinct standards that you should use to evaluate research. A reliable study may not necessarily be valid, but a valid study has to be reliable. As a simple principle, think of reliability as an essential condition for validity. That is, an unreliable finding, which by definition is one that is not reproducible or replicable, cannot be valid. However, the concept of validity extends beyond the idea of reliability. It speaks of the meaningfulness of theoretical conclusions. For example, the findings of heuristics and biases in human thinking have been widely replicated and are extremely reliable. The validity of the theory of systematic errors in cognition is perhaps even more impressive, as evidenced in its impact across so many different fields of study. In fact, this work earned the psychology professor Daniel Kahneman the Nobel Prize in Economics! Scholars have applied the theory of heuristics and biases to a wide variety of fields of study, including medical diagnosis, legal judgment, philosophy, finance, and statistics (Kahneman, 2011).

## Statistical Thinking

The scientific method uses statistics to test relationships between and among objective, quantifiable measures that are derived from either experimentation or observation. Sample statistics provide estimates of population parameters. A **sample statistic** is a quantitative value, such as an average, that is calculated on a subset of observations or data selected from a larger population. A **population parameter** is also a quantitative value, such as an average, but it is typically unknown, and therefore estimated by a sample statistic. In statistics, when you calculate an average of a particular sample of observations, you use this average as an estimate of the overall average in the population from which the sample was drawn. For example, the average height of a sample of American women is used as an estimate of the population average of American women. The aim is to calculate sample statistics to test hypotheses in order to ultimately draw reliable and valid conclusions about the larger group, or population.

## Law of Large Numbers

The *law of large numbers* states that the larger the sample size, the more reliable and valid the sample statistics that are used to estimate population parameters. This is a fundamental principle of statistics. Consider this example taken from Nisbett, Fong, Lehman, and Cheng (1987), in which research participants are asked to explain this simple observation: Why is it that after the first 2 weeks of the major league baseball season the highest batting average is 0.450 but no player in the history of game spanning a century has ever had as higher average than that by the end of the season? The answer to the question is instructive on two grounds. First, 2 weeks provides a relatively small sample of a player's batting ability. Second, extreme values, such as a 0.450 batting average, are more likely in a small sample than in a large sample. To illustrate this second point, consider the following question taken from Tversky and Kahneman (1974):

A certain town is served by two hospitals. In the larger hospital about 45 babies are born each day, and in the smaller hospital about 15 babies are born each day. As you know, about 50% of the babies are boys. However, the exact percentages vary from day to day. Sometimes it may be higher than 50% and sometimes lower. For a period of 1 year, each hospital recorded the days on which more than 60% of the babies born were boys. Which hospital do you think recorded more such days?

According to the law of large number, the smaller hospital should record more such days. However, most people fail to recognize that a deviant ratio of male to female births would be more likely at a hospital with 15 births a day than at a hospital with 45 births a day. Like a 0.450 batting average over the first 2 weeks of a baseball season, the higher are the male births in the smaller hospital with restricted sampling. So as we learn statistical reasoning in relation to the scientific method, the law of large numbers is relatively straightforward to understand yet too often overlooked or ignored.

## Ruling Out Randomness

The work of Kahneman and Tversky (1973) underscores how our thinking is biased toward seeking and seeing patterns where none exists. As such, we misunderstand **randomness**, which simply means a process of chance or luck. Our natural inclination is to believe, albeit incorrectly, that chance events or random patterns are a result of a causal process. In the scientific method, statistics provide a set of quantitative tools that allow us to rule out randomness as an explanation for the phenomenon under study. To use a legal analogy, the burden on the researcher is to prove that the phenomenon under study is unlikely due to chance. A study begins with the assumption of randomness, and statistics allow the researcher to determine the likelihood that an obtained result (e.g., average score) from a sample of research participants is due to chance alone. The researcher aims to reject randomness as an explanation, and does so through the calculation of specific statistical tests (defined by particular computational formulae), some of which we will learn about in following chapters.

So, to recap, all statistics are based on the logic of probability, and particular statistical tests all use the same criterion for evaluation. The question asked and answered by statistical tests may be stated as follows: In light of the data, what is the probability that the obtained results are due to chance? If the statistical analyses of the data show that the obtained results are highly unlikely due to chance, then randomness as an explanation of the obtained results is rejected. The researcher then moves to accepting the hypothesis that the obtained results are consistent with what was predicted on the basis of the theory of the study.

## 🔲 Science Versus Pseudoscience

In philosophical terms, the scientific method represents a specific **epistemology**, or a way of knowing. The scientific way of knowing is exclusively reliant on objective, empirical investigation. Its techniques must be *transparent*, so that the methods, procedures, and data analyses of any study can be easily reproduced. This transparency allows for other researchers to see if the same study can be repeated in a different sample with the same finding. As we have learned in this chapter, when a result is replicated, we have greater confidence that the finding is both reliable and valid. Reliable and valid knowledge is thus knowledge that has a high probability of being true because it has been systematically acquired and empirically tested; that is, it has been produced and evaluated by the scientific method.

Now let us consider knowledge gained not through the scientific method but through other means, such as intuition, impression, gut reactions, or experience. We may be convinced that this knowledge is also true and valid. However, it is not based on empirical evidence generated by the scientific method. Instead, it might be based on authoritarian or expert evidence of what a person tells you to believe, or it might be based on testimonial or anecdotal evidence offered by a person who believes the knowledge to be true because of personal subjective experience.

The crux of the problem arises when the methods of establishing evidence and the body of knowledge generated from these techniques are claimed to represent a legitimate scientific field of study. Consider the well-known case of astrology, which uses horoscopes to predict personality and behavior; many people swear by astrology and believe it to be scientific. However, astrology, along with extrasensory perception, alien-abduction reports, out-of-body experiences, the lunar lunacy effect, rebirthing therapy, and handwriting analysis, are just some of the examples of what is referred to as **pseudoscience**. In popular psychology, pseudoscientific beliefs are dubious but fascinating claims that are touted as "scientifically proven" and bolstered by fervent, public testimonials of believers who have experienced firsthand or who have claimed to have witnessed the phenomenon (Lilienfeld, 2005).

## Recognizing Pseudoscience

History tells us that as knowledge develops over time, some fields of study that initially are seen as scientific come to be seen as pseudoscientific: Today's pseudoscience could be yesterday's science. Take, for example, **phrenology**, a now defunct field of study that was once considered a science in the 19th century. The major, unified belief of phrenology was that bumps and fissures of the skull determined the character and personality of a person. Phrenologists believed that various psychological attributes, including personality traits, intellectual faculties, and moral character, could all be assessed by running their fingertips and palms over the skulls of a patient to feel for enlargements or indentations (see Exhibit 1.4). Advances in neurology would relegate phrenology to the dustbin of pseudoscience.

This porcelain head for sale in a New Orleans antique store shows the sections of the brain, as detailed by 19th-century phrenologists. They believed that each section was responsible for a particular human personality trait. If a section were enlarged or shrunken, the personality would be likewise abnormal. Doctors, particularly those doing entry examinations at American prisons, would examine the new inmate's head for bumps or cavities to develop a criminal profile. For example, if the section of brain responsible for "acquisitiveness" was enlarged, the offender probably was a thief. Criminologist Cesare Lombroso and his school combined phrenology with other models that included external physical appearance traits that they believed could single out criminals from the general population.

Psychology professor Scott Lilienfeld of Emory University has identified "The 10 Commandments of Helping Students Distinguish Science From Pseudoscience in Psychology," and he proposes these rules as a way for us to understand better what science is and what science isn't. Just as we cannot grasp fully the concept of cold without understanding hot, we cannot grasp fully the concept of scientific thinking without an understanding of pseudoscientific beliefs—specifically those beliefs that at first blush appear scientific

| Exhibit 1.4 | Phrenology: Yesterday's Science, Today's Pseudoscience |
| --- | --- |

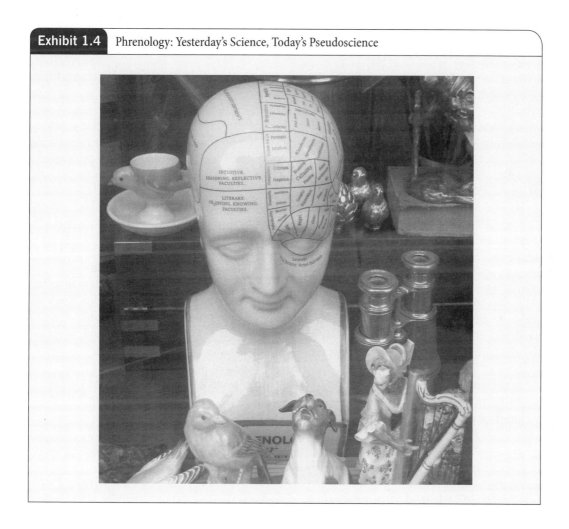

but are not (Lilienfeld, 2005). Among the warning signs of pseudoscience laid out by Lilienfeld (2005) in his "First Commandment" are the following:

1. A tendency to invoke ad hoc hypotheses, which can be thought of as "escape hatches" or loopholes, as a means of immunizing claims from falsification

2. An absence of self-correction and an accompanying intellectual stagnation

3. An emphasis on confirmation rather than refutation

4. A tendency to place the burden of proof on skeptics, not proponents, of claims

5. Excessive reliance on anecdotal and testimonial evidence to substantiate claims

6. Evasion of the scrutiny afforded by **peer review**

7. Absence of "connectivity" (Stanovich, 1997), that is, a failure to build on existing scientific knowledge

8. Use of impressive-sounding jargon whose primary purpose is to lend claims a facade of scientific respectability

9. An absence of boundary conditions (Hines, 2003), that is, a failure to specify the settings under which claims do not hold

Now none of these warning signs alone is sufficient to render a discipline as pseudoscientific. But the more warning signs that are present, the more reason to suspect pseudoscientific machinations are at work.

## Why Pseudoscience?

Why are we so susceptible to pseudoscience? Recall that theories help us understand how a particular phenomenon works. In this case, we want to understand how, in theory, pseudoscience might work. We have learned in this chapter that humans commonly reason with unseen and persistent biases. Pseudoscience preys on these biases. Among the key warning signs of pseudoscience listed by Lilienfeld (2005) is an "emphasis on confirmation rather than refutation." This is known as **confirmatory bias**. We are all subject to this bias to believe and to confirm. It reflects a natural tendency of the human mind to actively seek out and assign more weight to any kind of evidence that favors existing beliefs, expectations, or a hypothesis in hand (Nickerson, 1998). As psychological studies have shown (Gilbert, 1991), believing is always easier than disbelieving and highly evolutionarily adaptive because

> false positives (believing there is a connection between A and B when there is not) are usually harmless, whereas false negatives (believing there is no connection between A and B when there is) may take you out of the gene pool. (Shermer, 2008, p. 42)

In research as well as in real life, other examples of confirmatory bias include preferential treatment of that which supports existing beliefs, looking only or primarily for positive cases, a form of "cherry-picking" and overweighting positive confirmatory instances (Nickerson, 1998). Thus, a common mistake, confirmatory bias reflects both a kind of selective thinking and selective observation—choosing to look only at things that are in line with our preferences or beliefs.

Philosophers of science have long viewed confirmatory bias as a major threat or danger to research. Sir Karl Popper (1959) proposed the **doctrine of falsification**, which often is seen as the holy grail of science. As the Nobel Prize Winner Eric R. Kandel writes in his autobiography, *In Search of Memory* (2006), "Being on the wrong side of an interpretation was unimportant, Popper argued. The greatest strength of the scientific method is its ability to disprove a hypothesis" (p. 96). As we will learn in this book, falsification fits with the **self-correcting** nature of science in which information accumulates with new advances and discoveries. In stark contrast is pseudoscience, which is neither self-correcting nor cumulative in building knowledge (Exhibit 1.5).

Lilienfeld also identified the lure of anecdotal evidence in pseudoscience. And this of course is entirely consistent with what we learned about how personality sketches often lead us to ignore objective base rates and deceive us into making errors in judgment and reasoning (Tversky & Kahneman, 1974).

Developmental psychology also helps us understand the appeal of pseudoscience. Consider that even before the development of language, 1-year-old babies possess a rich understanding of the physical world and the social world, with the former referred to as a "naive physics" and the latter as a "naive psychology" (Bloom & Weisberg, 2007). This evolved adaptation gives children a head start for understanding and learning about objects and people. By the same token, however, it inevitably conflicts with scientific discoveries, sowing the seeds of resistance in children to learning and accepting certain scientific facts. As Carey (2000) noted, the challenge in teaching science to children is "not what the student lacks, but what

| Exhibit 1.5 | Disconfirmation of "All Swans Are White" |
|---|---|

the student *has*, namely alternative conceptual frameworks for the phenomena covered by the theories we are trying to teach" (p. 14). A similar point is made by Bloom and Weisberg (2007), who proposed that people come to "resist certain scientific findings because many of these findings are unnatural and unintuitive" (p. 997). Thus, we can see that pseudoscience can be appealing on many fronts. It often preys on inherent biases in our thinking, capitalizing on our evolved and developed resistance to the uncommon sense of science.

### STAT CORNER

#### Sample Size Matters

Tversky and Kahneman (1974) theorized that people fail to recognize and understand the randomness of truly random events. This is so because people see patterns where there are none and often mistakenly attribute causality to chance occurrences. According to this theory, the human mind does not naturally think statistically but, rather, is "probability blind" (Piattelli-Palmarini, 1994). Tversky and Kahneman (1974) specifically hypothesized that this misunderstanding of randomness would be demonstrated in research participants' responses to the vignette of the deviant male to female ratio of births for the two hospitals—the smaller, 15-daily births versus 45-daily births.

To test this hypothesis, Tversky and Kahneman (1974) had 97 research participants read the vignette and answer the following multiple-choice question by selecting from one of three choices:

*(Continued)*

(Continued)

(a) the larger hospital, (b) the smaller hospital, and (c) about the same (i.e., within 5% of each other). Most people chose "c." Fifty-three of the 97 participants (54.64%) incorrectly selected choice "c," indicating that they believed that each hospital, regardless of the number of births per day, would have about the same number of days of deviant male to female birth ratios. By contrast, only 21 of the 97 (22.16%) research participants correctly chose response "b"—indicating that they understood that the smaller hospital would have the most days of deviant male to female birth ratios.

The question for us to consider relates to whether the study demonstrates statistical or empirical evidence to support the research hypothesis. First, let us look at the size of the sample, denoted by the capital letter $N$, (i.e., $N = 97$). If we apply the law of large numbers to the size of this sample, we ask the question as to whether the sample is of sufficient size to test the hypothesis. We would consider 97 participants as an adequate sample size. Second, let us examine the empirical evidence—the multiple-choice responses of the 97 research participants. Here, we focus on pivotal results: the 54.64% of the 97 participants who incorrectly selected choice "c," versus the 22.16% of the research participants who correctly chose response "b." Thus, we can conclude, as did Tversky and Kahneman (1974), that these results support the hypothesis that most people are insensitive to small sample sizes when judging randomness, or lack thereof.

# Conclusions

The scientific method is a set of procedures and techniques that allows a researcher to ask, study, and answer particular questions about psychology. Scientific questions are commonly framed in reference to a particular theory, which in turn leads to a testable hypothesis that specifies key variables to be investigated. Objective measurement of these variables is critical, because if something in psychology cannot be measured, then it cannot be investigated scientifically. Observations can then be collected systematically and quantified by sampling a population. These observations, translated into numeric values, are what constitute empirical evidence. Statistics are computed to test hypothesized relationships between and among objective, quantifiable measures. Statistics allow the researcher to assess the likelihood that the obtained results are due to chance; a finding that is unlikely due to chance is typically interpreted as supportive of the hypothesis of the study. Reliability and validity are two important standards that are used to judge the scientific quality of any research study.

The scientific method also represents a particular epistemology, that is, a way of knowing that is exclusively reliant on objective, empirical investigation. Its techniques must be transparent so that the methods, procedures, and data analyses of any study can be easily reproduced. Pseudoscience, on the other hand, relies not on empirical evidence but on anecdotal testimonial accounts. Pseudoscientific beliefs are dubious but fascinating claims that are touted as "scientifically proven" and bolstered by fervent, public testimonials of believers who have experienced firsthand or who have claimed to have witnessed the phenomenon. Pseudoscience preys on our naturally evolved and universal tendency for confirmatory bias.

# Key Terms

A priori
Case studies
Cognitive illusions
Cognitive psychology
Confirmatory bias
Confounding variables
Control variable
Cross-cultural psychology
Cultural psychology
Culture
Data
Dependent variable
Doctrine of falsification
Empiricism
Epistemology

Generalizability
Heuristic
Heuristic biases
Hypothesis
Independent variable
Is/ought
Peer review
Phrenology
Population
Population parameter
Post hoc
Probability
Pseudoscience
Psychology
Random sample

Randomness
Reliability
Replicated
Sample
Sample bias
Sample statistic
Scientific method
Self-correcting
Serendipity
Testable hypothesis
Theory
Validity
Variable

# Research in the News

Examples abound of new pseudoscientific disciplines. Perhaps there is no better example than the best-selling tome *The Secret* by television producer Rhonda Byrne (2006). It became a blockbuster, No. 1 on *The New York Times* best-seller list, when it was featured not once but twice by television personality Oprah Winfrey's popular show. What is so evidently alluring about *The Secret* is its central idea, known as the law of attraction, which states that wishing can make things come true, something very young children could resonate to in their beliefs about the Tooth Fairy and Santa Claus. Whether you want money, a new home, or even a regular parking space, just ask, believe you will get it, and you will get it, guaranteed! *The Secret's* mantra is a simple and ancient idea: Ask. Believe. Receive. This is positive thinking with a guarantee, and of course, there are no guarantees in psychology. Explain how *The Secret* meets the nine warning signs of pseudoscience as presented above and outlined by Lilienfeld (2005).

# STUDENT STUDY SITE

Please access the study site at **www.sagepub.com/nestor2e**, where you will find useful study materials such as mobile-friendly eFlashcards and mid-chapter and full chapter web quizzes for each chapter, along with carefully selected articles from research journals that illustrate the major concepts and techniques presented in the book.

## Activity Questions

1. As a cross-cultural psychologist, you have been hired to help researchers design studies that have greater generalizability. What would you recommend in terms of sampling? What kinds of measures might be most helpful? What kind of study design would you recommend?

2. In a May 9, 2010, article in the *Chronicle of Higher Education*, titled "The New War Between Science and Religion," Mano Singham writes about "the new war that pits those who argue that science and 'moderate' forms of religion are compatible worldviews against those who think they are not" [para 1]. The prestigious National Academy of Sciences endorses the position for the compatibility of science and religion. Weigh both the pros and the cons of this debate. Consider how the philosophical distinction between questions of *ought* versus *is* is used to shed light on this debate.

3. Suppose you have been hired as a developmental psychologist to help design a curriculum to teach science and the scientific method to elementary school children. Organize a formal discussion, first addressing people's commonsense intuitive understanding of psychology ("naive psychology") and then why it comes so naturally to us. Address how it could contribute to scientific resistance for understanding the workings of the brain and mind.

## Review Questions

1. Describe the heuristics and biases research approach and its theory. Use the findings of this research to make the case for the scientific method.

2. What is a scientific question? Compare and contrast scientific questions and legal questions.

3. Describe how the scientific method uses statistics to test hypotheses and evaluate theories. Be sure to address statistical reasoning in relation to probability, randomness, sampling, and the law of large numbers.

4. How can you tell the difference between pseudoscience and real science? Why do you think pseudoscience is often so appealing? According to cognitive psychologists, how do our minds make us susceptible to pseudoscience?

5. Describe the relationship of independent variable, dependent variable, and control variable. Be sure to define the function of each in research.

# The Practice of Psychological Research

## LEARNING OBJECTIVES: FAST FACTS

### Reading and Writing Research

- In reading and writing research, always consider the distinction between experimental and non-experimental approaches. Only with an experimental approach can independent variable(s) be directly manipulated, a key point of consideration for establishing causality, the so-called gold standard to which research aspires. Nonexperimental research is correlational in nature, vitally important for studies in psychology that often cannot directly manipulate variables of critical interest, such as exposure to traumatic experiences, as well as individual characteristics of intelligence, personality, or clinical diagnosis.

*(Continued)*

(Continued)

- Writing in psychology is a discipline-specific form of scientific reporting that is based on empirical evidence. Opinions, anecdotes, and personal testimonies, however compelling, are not empirical evidence and, therefore, are "inadmissible" in psychological writing. In writing and reading research, go to the primary sources.

- Statistical analyses serve two principal goals, identified as *descriptive* and *inferential*. Descriptive statistics summarize and present data in a meaningful way but, importantly, do not allow for testing hypotheses and to generalize results to the larger population. By contrast, inferential statistics are a set of techniques that allow for testing of hypotheses about a population from data collected from a sample. Inferential statistics provide the techniques and procedures to determine the probability that the results that you obtained in your analysis of the aggregated data can be generalized to the larger population from which your sample was drawn.

## TESTING BEFORE LEARNING

Try your hand at these questions. Don't worry about not knowing the correct response, as you haven't read the chapter yet! But research shows that a pretest such as this can enhance learning (e.g., Kornell, Hays, & Bjork, 2009). So here is the answer. You come up with the question.

1. A researcher wants to hold constant certain factors that could potentially confound a study's results.
   a. What are control variables?
   b. What are independent variables?
   c. What are dependent variables?
   d. What are heuristic biases?

2. Specifies how a concept will be coded, measured, or quantified
   a. What is a conceptual definition?
   b. What is measurement?
   c. What are inferential statistics?
   d. What is an operational definition?

3. A specific testable statement that can be evaluated by empirical observations or data
   a. What is a variable?
   b. What is a statistic?
   c. What is a sample?
   d. What is a hypothesis?

4. Used to summarize and to present data in a meaningful way
   a. What are data?
   b. Who are research participants?
   c. What are descriptive statistics?
   d. What are inferential statistics?

5. A set of techniques that allows for testing of hypotheses about a population from data collected from a sample
   a. What are data?
   b. Who are the research participants?
   c. What are descriptive statistics?
   d. What are inferential statistics?

6. Provides the strongest evidence of cause-and-effect relationship between independent and dependent variables
   a. What is a correlational approach?
   b. What is a nonexperimental approach?
   c. What is an experimental approach?
   d. What are descriptive statistics?

7. Not empirical evidence and therefore considered "inadmissible" in the court of psychology writing
   a. What are data?
   b. What are anecdotes and personal testimonies?
   c. What are descriptive statistics?
   d. What are inferential statistics?

8. A broad statement that cannot be directly tested but rather needs to be translated into one or more hypotheses
   a. What is an experiment?
   b. What is a generalization?
   c. What is an independent variable?
   d. What is a dependent variable?

9. Unwanted influences of a third variable on the relationship between an independent variable and dependent variable
   a. What are controls?
   b. What are measures?
   c. What are confounds?
   d. What are hypotheses?

10. The extent to which a study or experiment approximates the actual real-life phenomenon under investigation
    a. What is ecological validity?
    b. What is an alternative explanation?
    c. What is temporal precedence?
    d. What is covariation of cause and effect?

**ANSWER KEY:** (1) a; (2) d; (3) d; (4) c; (5) d; (6) c; (7) b; (8) b; (9) c; (10) a

## ARE YOU A MAXIMIZER OR A SATISFICER?

Let's begin this chapter by responding to a set of statements just as you would do if you were completing a survey. How much do you agree or disagree with each of the following 13 statements? Indicate your response by recording a number between 1 and 7 after each statement, where 1 means that you *disagree completely* with the statement and 7 means that you *agree completely* with the statement; of course, a response of 4 would indicate that you *neither agree nor disagree* with the statement.

1. Whenever I'm faced with a choice, I try to imagine what all the other possibilities are, even ones that aren't present at the moment. _____

2. No matter how satisfied I am with my job, it's only right for me to be on the lookout for better opportunities. _____

3. When I am in the car listening to radio, I often check other stations to see if something better is playing, even if I am relatively satisfied with what I'm listening to. _____

4. When I watch TV, I channel surf, often scanning through the available options even while attempting to watch one program. _____

5. I treat relationships like clothing: I expect to try a lot on before finding the perfect fit. _____

6. I often find it difficult to shop for a gift for a friend. _____

7. Renting videos is really difficult. I'm always struggling to pick the best one. _____

8. When shopping, I have a hard time finding clothing that I really love. _____

9. I'm a big fan of lists that attempt to rank things (e.g., the best movies, the best singers, the best athletes, the best novels, etc.). _____

10. I find that writing is very difficult, even if it's just writing a letter to a friend, because it's so hard to word things just right. I often do several drafts of even simple things. _____

11.  No matter what I do, I have the highest standards for myself. _____

12.  I never settle for second best. _____

13.  I often fantasize about living in ways that are quite different from my actual life. _____

Now add up your scores. Congratulations! You have just completed the "Maximization Scale" designed by the psychologist Barry Schwartz (2004).

The Maximization Scale is intended to distinguish people who are "maximizers" from people who are "satisficers." Maximizers always shoot for the best, whereas satisficers are okay with settling for "good enough." When maximizers search for a job, they will shoot for the highest possible income or other rewards; satisficers will be happy with a certain income that's "good enough." From finding a TV channel to picking a restaurant, maximizers generally try to exhaust all possibilities before making their final choice. By contrast, satisficers set standards for themselves and choose the first option that meets that standard. Your responses to each of the statements in the Maximization Scale help determine how close you are to the maximizer or the satisficer end of the continuum.

Schwartz and colleagues gave this set of 13 statements to thousands of people. They considered people to be maximizers if their average score was higher than 52 (the scale's midpoint, determined as the middle item score of 4 multiplied by 13—the number of items). People whose average ratings were lower than the midpoint were considered to be satisficers (Schwartz, 2004). Which category did your score place you in? If you scored above 52 (i.e., the scale's midpoint), Schwartz would consider you to be a person who always has to perform an exhaustive check of all the available choices to make sure you pick the best.

Now let's consider the impact of being a maximizer or a satisficer on the outcomes of job searches. Do you think maximizers or satisficers are more likely to make the "best" choice of a job and be most satisfied with that choice? Sheena Iyengar, Rachael Wells, and Barry Schwartz (2006) investigated this question by categorizing 548 graduating students as either maximizers or satisficers in the fall of their senior year and then following them during the next year as they searched for jobs. When interviewed again the following summer, the maximizers had found jobs that paid 20% more on average than the satisficers' jobs, but the maximizers were less satisfied with the outcome of their job search and were more pessimistic, stressed, tired, worried, overwhelmed, and depressed. The maximizers felt worse even though they had done better than the satisficers! The researchers reasoned that this was because considering so many choices led maximizers to have unrealistic expectations; these unrealistic expectations in turn increased the likelihood of feelings of regret, disappointment, dissatisfaction, and sadness. In fact, the researchers reported that maximizers were more likely to fantasize about jobs that they hadn't applied for and to wish that they had pursued even more jobs than they did.

## ▣ The Research Objective

You have a different objective as a researcher. No longer interested in your individual score, you now focus on the aggregated or group data collected from your class. Let's imagine that your class produced 62 scores on the Maximization Scale, and these constitute our raw data. But from these raw data alone, you would have difficulty in understanding what these scores might mean without performing some kind of statistical analyses.

Statistical analyses serve two principal goals, which are commonly identified as descriptive and inferential. With **descriptive statistics**, the aim is to summarize and present data in a meaningful way. Descriptive statistics reveal important objective features of a set of aggregated data, such as, for example, overall mean score for the class on the Maximization Scale. Descriptive statistics may also point to potentially emerging patterns in the data that could be subjected to further analyses. However, and importantly, we cannot draw conclusions on the basis of descriptive statistics, nor can we test a hypothesis. Rather, descriptive statistics are simply a way to describe your data. A critical limitation of descriptive statistics is that they do not allow you to generalize results to wider general population.

On the other hand, **inferential statistics** are a set of techniques that allow for testing of hypotheses about a population from data collected from a sample. In other words, inferential statistics provide the techniques and procedures to determine the probability that the results that you obtained in your analysis of the aggregated data can be generalized to the larger population from which your sample was drawn.

As a first step in answering our research question, we need to decide on our statistical approach. Because the research question asks only for the percentages of maximizers and satisficers for our class, our data analysis plan can be confined to the use of descriptive statistics. However, descriptive statistics would not be sufficient if the research question asked whether men and women in college differed on their scores on the Maximization Scale. Here, in addition to using descriptive statistics to characterize the distribution of Maximization scores for men and women, you would need inferential statistics to analyze group differences. That is, inferential statistics are required to answer the question as to whether any differences you find between men and women in their Maximization scores are unlikely to be due to chance. We will return to inferential statistics later in this book, but for now let us turn our attention to descriptive statistics.

In the "Stat Corner" you will see how to apply descriptive statistics in our research study on maximization. Descriptive statistics summarize and describe a distribution of values and, in our case, the distribution of scores for the class on the Maximization Scale. Two important features of a distribution are **central tendency** and **variability**. Central tendency is summarized and described with one of three statistics: mode, median, and mean/average. These statistics provide ways of describing the central position for a set of data. Three different descriptive statistics are used to summarize variability of a distribution of numerical values: range, variance, and standard deviation. Each of these three statistical measures of variability provides a quantitative index to summarize the spread of numerical values for a given variable.

In our example, note how stats are used to describe (a) sample size; (b) basic demographics, such as the number of males and females participants, their age, as well as their educational level; (c) group mean and standard deviation on the Maximization Scale; and (d) percentages of maximizers and satisficers. We would encourage you to think of statistics, in general, and these numbers, in particular, as a way a scientist tells a "story." Storytelling and statistics are often thought as two very different intellectual cultures or mind-sets, one literary (storytelling) and the other scientific (statistics) (e.g., Paulos, 2010b). However, for our purposes, you can see in our simple exercise how numbers in the form of descriptive statistics can indeed help us tell the story of our in-class maximization study!

## ▣ Thinking Research

The research methods that you choose depend greatly on the questions asked and the answers you hope to discover. There are two very broad research approaches: **experimental** and **nonexperimental**. The study by Iyengar et al. (2006) used a nonexperimental approach to examine the relationship among three variables: (1) maximizer/satisficer, (2) income, and (3) feeling of well-being. In a nonexperimental approach like this, variables are carefully measured, and the relationship between the variables is examined. Your score on the Maximization Scale measured your value on the maximizer/satisficer variable. If you had been a participant in the research of Iyengar et al. (2006), your job income and feeling of well-being would also have been measured.

A nonexperimental approach is often described as correlational in nature. As we will learn, a *correlation* is a statistic that is computed by a specific formula; this statistic indicates how closely related two variables are. Correlational research allows you to look at the way one set of measurements goes up or down in tandem with another set of measurements. In this way, Iyengar and colleagues could determine that those with higher maximizer scores tended to enter jobs with higher incomes but were less satisfied with those jobs.

The chief advantage of correlational research is that it allows for the quantitative comparison of variables that cannot be manipulated directly. The researcher does not make respondents into maximizers or satisficers; she or he just measures her or his value on the Maximization Scale. In the same way, researchers in correlational research measure the income people receive in a job and their satisfaction with it; they don't take any action to change their income or job satisfaction.

In research that uses an experimental approach, the researcher manipulates the value of cases on the independent variable. That is, the researcher determines which value of the independent variable each research participant is exposed to. To illustrate, consider a study to determine whether a drug is effective. The independent variable is receipt of the drug. The **treatment group**/condition, which is also known as the experimental group/condition, receives the drug under study. The **control group**/condition receives nothing. Often in drug research, there is also a **placebo** group, which receives an inert substance, such as a sugar pill, so that the participants in the placebo group think that they are receiving the drug treatment even though they are not. In many drug studies, the placebo group also serves as the control group or control condition. The control group provides a baseline to compare with the treatment group and, in some studies, with the placebo group. The independent variable, receipt of the drug, therefore has two or three values: (1) receipt of the treatment, (2) receipt of nothing, and, in some studies, (3) receipt of the placebo.

In a true experiment, **random assignment** is used to determine which value of the independent variable each research participant receives. Random assignment ensures that each participant has an equal chance to be assigned to a particular group, condition, or level of an independent variable. Flipping a coin is a simple technique that researchers often use to randomly assign participants. For example, a researcher would assign participants with "heads" to one group and "tails" to the other group. If participants are randomly assigned, the groups exposed to different values of the independent variable should be the same at the outset, on average. This means that any differences between groups on the dependent variable after the participants have been exposed to the independent variable can be directly attributable to the manipulation of the independent variable. This randomized design therefore provides the strongest evidence of a cause–effect relationship between an independent variable and a dependent variable.

In medical research, when research participants are randomly assigned to receive either the drug under investigation or a placebo, the study is referred to as a **randomized clinical trial** (RCT). An RCT also often uses a **double-blind** procedure, whereby both the researcher and the participants are "blind" to who receives the "real" drug and who receives the placebo. Double-blind procedure and placebo are used to control for the potential confound of unwanted effects of expectations of both participants and researchers that might act as unwanted influences on the results of the study. That is why federal regulations require that the value of new drugs be determined in RCTs: This design makes it highly unlikely that the apparent effect of the drug could really be due to something else.

To summarize, in comparison with a nonexperimental approach, an experimental approach allows for rather strict control over the independent variable or variables that are assumed to be the causal agent(s) producing the predicted effect. In the RCT example, the researcher directly manipulates by randomly assigning participants to receive either the real drug or the placebo. The experimental approach of the RCT allows for a direct test of the hypothesis that the drug will cause symptoms to be ameliorated. That is, the hypothesis is that the independent variable of treatment, specifically the drug, will cause the dependent variable, specifically the symptoms of the disease, to be eliminated. On the other hand, a nonexperimental approach cannot establish a cause-and-effect relationship between an independent variable and a dependent variable. Rather, a nonexperimental approach is descriptive in nature, using statistical correlational techniques to quantify relationship among variables. We will cover experimental approaches in Chapters 6 and 7. We cover different nonexperimental approaches in Chapters 4 (psychometrics), 5 (survey design), 8 (quasi-experiments), 9 (single case), and 11 (qualitative). Exhibit 2.1 introduces some of the different types of methods commonly used in psychological research, as well as some of the different types of study design. We likened this to a "research toolbox."

| **Exhibit 2.1** Research Toolbox | |
| --- | --- |
| True experiments | Random assignment of participants to groups and manipulation of one or more independent variables. (Chapters 6 and 7) |
| Quasi-experiments | Experiments in which random assignment is not possible to groups. (Chapter 8) |
| Nonexperimental research | Studies that focus on the distribution of variables, the quantitative association of variables; causation cannot be established. (Chapter 4) |
| Survey design | Research in which information is obtained from a sample of individuals through their responses to specific questions. (Chapter 5) |
| Performance-based measures | Studies of data collected from standardized tests. (Chapter 4) |
| Single-subject designs | Systematic investigation of one or a few cases. (Chapter 9) |
| Qualitative research | Qualitative methods, such as participant observation, intensive interviewing, and focus groups used to study and understand phenomena in terms of the meanings people attach to them. (Chapter 11) |

## Description

The principal objective of research is to provide a scientific understanding of the topic of investigation. Scientific understanding entails two distinct but related processes: description and explanation. We first describe the phenomenon that we intend to study. This may seem obvious, but careful and precise definitions of key concepts and the measures we develop for those concepts are critical for scientific understanding.

Generally, researchers describe and define terms both conceptually and operationally. A **conceptual definition** provides the meaning, often rather broad in scope, of an abstract term, such as *intelligence, anxiety,* or *emotion*. Very similar to what you would find in a dictionary, a conceptual definition demarcates a semantic or linguistic meaning of a psychological term, that is, its usage in words, texts, and language. For example, intelligence as a concept may be defined as the general ability that enables an individual to comprehend the world and to deal effectively with its challenges (Wechsler, 1997).

For the Iyengar et al. (2006) study, maximizer and satisficer represent two key terms that require clear conceptual definitions. How would you define these terms in plain English? How would you categorize them? Borrowing from Schwartz (2004), we define conceptually maximizer and satisficer as two distinct *choice-making strategies*. (1) The choice-making strategy of a maximizer is defined as one that seeks out the absolute best option, usually only after an exhaustive search. (2) The choice-making strategy of a satisficer is defined as one that seeks the "good enough" choice, searching until finding an option that meets a standard of acceptability. Note that the concept is referred to as choice-making strategies. The idea is that choice strategies comes in two types: maximizer and satisficer.

Operational definitions follow from conceptual definitions. An **operational definition** indicates how a concept is coded, measured, or quantified. It may be as simple as an operational definition of gender in which female is coded as 1 and male as 2 (or vice versa). No single operational definition can capture fully the concept it is intended to measure. An operational definition is among several possible objective and measurable indicators of a concept.

For the Iyengar et al. (2006) study, the Maximization Scale provided the key operational definition. Why? Because as we have learned the scale provided an objective score that can range from a low of 13 to a high of 91 ($91 = 13 \times 7$—if you rated each of the 13 statements as *strongly agree*). The operational definition of a maximizer is a score greater than 52. The operational definition of a satisficer is a score less than 52. Thus, we can see that this simple scale of 13 items provided the operational definition of maximizer and satisficer. So now you could describe the choice-making strategies of people in a group by reporting their scores on the Maximization Scale.

## Explanation

Explanation is the other goal of science. In a scientific sense, explaining something means identifying its cause. For example, we might explain people's happiness with their jobs with their maximization score. Variation in maximization, the independent variable, accounts for at least some of the variation in happiness with the job. Maximization has a causal influence; job happiness is the effect. We can also think of explanation as involving prediction: If we know someone's maximization score, we can predict their level of job happiness.

Causality, however, is not a simple matter. In fact, philosophers since the time of Aristotle have debated the true essence of causality. For our purposes, let's think of causality as requiring three kinds of evidence, as described by Cook and Campbell (1979). The first kind of evidence is that of **temporal precedence**. This evidence establishes that the cause *precedes* the effect. Thus, one step toward demonstrating causality is temporal precedence: Smoking cigarettes occurred first, and lung cancer, tragically, followed.

The second type of evidence needed to establish causality is **covariation of the cause and effect**. This means that when the cause is present, the effect is more likely to occur, and when the cause is absent, the effect is less likely to occur. Thus, we need to know that people who smoke cigarettes are more likely to contract lung cancer than those who do not smoke.

Third, causality requires the elimination of **alternative explanations**. In other words, a researcher must show that nothing other than the identified causal variable could be responsible for the observed effect—that is, there is no other plausible explanation for the relationship. In our smoking example, suppose a third variable, such as social class, could explain the relationship of smoking and lung cancer. This alternative explanation could come into play if, for example, people with lower socioeconomic status were more likely to smoke and also were more likely to be victims of cancer. Both the smoking and the cancer could be consequences of lower socioeconomic status; this would lead to a relationship between socioeconomic status and smoking, but that relationship would not reflect a causal effect of smoking on lung cancer.

These three requirements of causality are difficult standards to meet in human psychological research. This holds even with an experimental approach, which ostensibly allows the researcher to test whether changes in an independent variable cause changes in the dependent variable. The problem is that it is impossible in human studies to control for all extraneous, confounding (see Chapter 1), or so-called **third variables** that could account for the observed effect. Consider the often-cited finding that cities with a greater number of churches have a higher crime rate. On the face of it, does this finding mean that having more churches causes higher crime rates? Can you imagine a headline, "Churches Cause More Crimes"?

A classic example of a mistaken causal relationship, you would shout! Why? Because the author of the headline failed to recognize the confounding effects of a third variable, *population size*, on the reported relationship of increased number of churches and elevated rates of crime. More churches do not lead to more crime; instead, the third variable of population leads to *both* more churches and more crime. Note that a third variable is by definition correlated with each member of the pair under study. The confounding arises from the correlation of the third variable with each of the other two variables. In this example, we can see that densely populated areas have more churches and higher crime. To put it in more precise statistical terms, as the density of population areas increases, both the number of churches and the rates of crime also increase. The headline should read "Densely Populated Areas Have More Churches and Higher Crime." But then that would not be newsworthy.

## Practical Knowledge

Scientific understanding through the process of description and explanation often leads to interesting practical applications. Research that is conducted because of potential practical applications is termed **applied research**. By contrast, **basic research** addresses fundamental questions about the nature of abstract psychological processes and ideas, such as emotion, intelligence, reasoning, and social behavior. Applied research addresses important questions that are thought to be of immediate relevance in solving practical problems. What television advertisements are most effective in reducing illicit drug use in children? What is the most effective teaching method for learning math? Do early intervention programs, such as Head Start, lead to better outcomes?

Such questions are investigated and studied in applied research. In fact, a major area of interest and study in applied research is called **program evaluation**. Program evaluation studies the effects on behavior of large-scale policy changes as well as social reforms and innovations occurring in settings such as government agencies, schools, courts, prisons, businesses, health care, and housing. In reality, these distinctions often blur, and the basic and applied research designation is probably most accurately viewed as falling along a continuum. Both basic and applied research are essential and of equal importance, with scientific progress depending on the combined efforts and fruits of basic and applied research. Moreover, basic research often has exceptionally important practical applications that are impossible to predict.

# 🖩 Research Strategies

In conducting research, we are attempting to connect theory with empirical data—evidence we obtained through scientific studies. As we have learned, researchers may make this connection by starting with a psychological theory and testing some of its implications with data. This is the process of **deductive research**; it is most often the strategy used in experimental studies. We deduce a hypothesis from a theory and then collect data with which to test the hypothesis. Alternatively, researchers may develop a connection between psychological theory and data by first systematically collecting data, identifying patterns in the data, and then developing a theory that explains the patterns. This **inductive research** approach is most often used in nonexperimental studies, such as those that use naturalistic observation methods. A particular research study can draw on both inductive and deductive strategies.

So the two most important elements of all scientific research strategies are (1) data and (2) theory. Data are the empirical observations that allow for evaluating a theory. A theory is a set of propositions that explains a variety of occurrences. A theory performs three major functions: (1) organization, (2) explanation, and (3) prediction. A good theory is one that is parsimonious and precise as well as powerful in its breadth and depth of explanation. It can explain a variety of occurrences with the fewest theoretical assertions. Exhibit 2.2 depicts the link between theory and data. As you can see, a deductive research strategy will begin with a theory from which particular statements are drawn and then tested by collecting data. By contrast, an inductive strategy first examines the data and then derives a theory to explain the patterns found in the data.

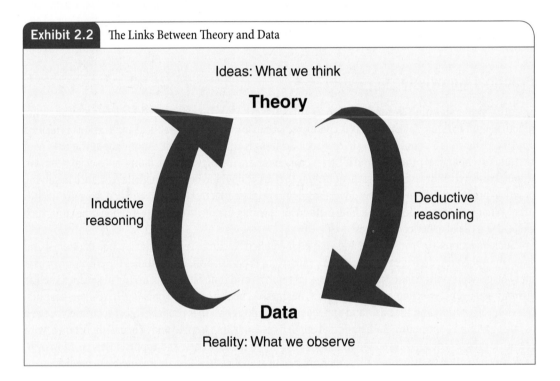

**Exhibit 2.2** The Links Between Theory and Data

Ideas: What we think

**Theory**

Inductive reasoning

Deductive reasoning

**Data**

Reality: What we observe

## Inductive Research

Inductive research entails reasoning from particular data or empirical observations to a general theory. Perhaps the best suited for an inductive research approach is the **naturalistic observation** method. Often used in **qualitative research** (which will be discussed in Chapter 11), a naturalistic observation design studies people in their natural settings so that their behaviors and words can be put into their proper context. Such descriptive study of people is also sometimes referred to as **ethnography**. Here, observation, it is important to emphasize, does not mean the casual "seeing" of everyday life that leads to haphazard impressions. To the contrary, for this research methodology to be effective, observation must be controlled or *systematic*, which means that it must be conducted carefully, with precise description that allows for consistent or reliable cataloging of data and the orderly classification and analysis of that information (Adler & Adler, 1994).

While qualitative researchers use naturalistic observation methods that tend to avoid predetermining categories of action that can be precisely measured, they, like their quantitative counterparts, make sure their studies yield reliable and valid data. In short, the aim of qualitative research is to understand context—the what, how, when, and where of an event or an action. It yields data regarding meanings, concepts, definitions, characteristics, metaphors, symbols, and descriptions of events or actions (Berg, 2004). As such, it is ideally suited for an inductive research approach.

Consider a simple but interesting study by Hussain and Griffiths in the Psychology Division at Nottingham Trent University. Hussain and Griffiths (2009) were interested in the attitudes, experiences, and feelings of online gamers (see Exhibit 2.3). Although MMORPGs (massively multiplayer online role-playing games) have become very popular and there have been some studies of these online gamers, there has been little qualitative research exploring gamers' accounts of their own activities and attitudes. To start to fill this gap, Hussain and Griffiths (2009) recruited 71 online gamers through posts on online gaming forums and in World of Warcraft games. The researchers "interviewed" these 71 participants online, either through online chat or by e-mail. Most of the interview questions were open-ended. The researchers explained why they used this approach:

> The unstructured nature of the interviews allowed gamers to develop their own narrative by exploring their experiences of MMORPGs. The researcher allowed gamers to speak for themselves (i.e., the emergent themes were participant led rather than researcher led). This allowed gamers to take control of the interview process and prevented researchers' subjective bias entering the analytic stage. (p. 748)

The researchers read through the interviews and identified the main themes that were expressed in them. For example, many comments had to do with the psychosocial impact of online gaming. Although the "vast majority" of the gamers highlighted positive effects of the activity, some pointed to potentially adverse effects:

> I've lost my IRL [in real life] friends because I couldn't find the time to be with them; I quit school. Whenever someone asks me to do something on the weekends, I always think "ooh, but we're raiding, I really shouldn't go out," and that's a way of thinking which I really dislike. (Hussain & Griffiths, 2009, p. 750)

The researchers conclude by noting not only how gamers use gaming to alleviate negative feelings but also how they may experience personal problems due to the online gaming. They raise questions about the difference between socializing online and offline, and they focus attention on the problem of addiction. Although Hussain and Griffiths do not attempt to develop their own theory of online gaming, the patterns that they find and the questions that emerge from their research provide a foundation that others could use in developing such a theory. The researchers urge more generalizable research about online gamers using quantitative methods, and they recommend policies that could reduce the likelihood of problems due to online gaming.

To recap, using the Hussain and Griffiths (2009) study as an example illustrates two important points. First, an inductive approach starts with data and then develops a theory that explains the patterns in the data. Note that Hussain and Griffiths first systematically collected and then analyzed their data—comments by the gamers about their attitudes and experiences, and from these data, offered some theoretical inferences the interests and motives of gamers. The second point is to call your attention to this new approach to collecting interesting information on psychological processes through the Internet! This we would recommend as a convenient, accessible methodology for perhaps a study that you can conduct as part of your research methods course (see Activity Questions at the end of this chapter). It is a good example of how adopting a scientific perspective can address interesting questions about everyday activities and add value to them.

**Exhibit 2.3**  Interviewing Online Gamers

## Deductive Research

In deductive research, reasoning proceeds from a general theory to particular data. Theories, however, are not directly testable. Thus, hypotheses must be derived from a theory. These hypotheses are then tested, and the ensuing results are used to evaluate how well the theory works—that is, how well it describes, explains, and predicts the nature of the phenomenon under study. A hypothesis is defined as a specific testable statement that can be evaluated by empirical observations or data. It is different from generalizations that are embedded in a theory. A **generalization** is a broad statement that cannot be directly tested but rather needs to be translated into one or more hypotheses. That is, a theory will consist of a host of generalizations, and each generalization can lead to one or more hypotheses.

Only hypotheses are directly testable. This is so because a hypothesis proposes a specific relationship between two or more variables that must be measurable. And as we know, one of these variables will be the independent variable that is hypothesized to predict, influence, or cause variation in the dependent variable. In deductive research, then, the investigators formulate one or more hypotheses and develop particular methods and procedures of measurement and/or experimentation. This yields data that serve as a direct test of a given hypothesis.

Let us examine the Iyengar et al. (2006) maximization study as an example of deductive research. As we learned earlier in this chapter, Iyengar et al. designed their study to examine the theory originally proposed by Herbert Simon (1956) that maximizer and satisficer represent two distinct decision-making strategies. Iyengar and colleagues tested the hypothesis that in comparison with satisficers, maximizers would make more money but be less happy. Their study therefore measured three key variables: (1) maximization/satisficer score, (2) salary, and (3) well-being. In this study, there is one independent variable, the maximization/satisficer score, and two dependent variables, salary and well-being. And the hypothesis is that that these two decision-making strategies, maximizers versus satisficers, would influence both salary and happiness but in opposite directions.

The lesson here for us is twofold. First is the question as to why the Iyengar et al. (2006) study is a good example of deductive research. The answer is because the study began with the Simon theory of the two decision-making strategies, followed by the testing of the specific hypothesis that maximizers would make more money but be less happy than satisficers. That is, in deductive research the sequence is theory, followed by hypothesis, and then data collection.

The second lesson to be gleaned here pertains to understanding the key variables of the study and their predicted relationships between them. Why is the score on the Maximization Scale used as the independent variable? Why are salary and well-being used as the two dependent variables? The answer is because the independent variable, decision-making strategy of either maximizer or satisficer, was predicted to influence the two dependent variables, salary and well-being. That is, the researchers used the scores on the Maximization Scale to categorize participants as either maximizers or satisficers. They then compared satisficers and maximizers on the two dependent variables of salary and well-being.

We plead guilty to belaboring this point, but learning the distinction between independent and dependent variables is critical for understanding research in psychology. Recall from Chapter 1 that we likened variables to the language of research. Exhibit 2.4 provides additional practice for learning the distinction between independent and dependent variables. As you can see in Exhibit 2.4, hypotheses can be worded in several different ways, and identifying the independent and dependent variables is sometimes difficult. When in doubt, try to rephrase the hypothesis as an "if–then" statement: "If the independent variable increases (or decreases), then the dependent variable increases (or decreases)." Exhibit 2.4 (examples of hypotheses) presents several hypotheses with their independent and dependent variables and their "if–then" equivalents.

Exhibit 2.4 demonstrates another feature of hypotheses: **direction of association**. When researchers hypothesize that one variable increases as the other variable increases, the direction of the association is positive (Hypotheses 1 and 2). When one variable decreases as the other variable decreases, the direction of association is also positive. But when one variable increases as the other decreases, or vice versa, the

| Exhibit 2.4 | Hypotheses Predict Associations Between Independent and Dependent Variables | | | |
|---|---|---|---|---|
| *Original Hypothesis* | *Independent Variable* | *Dependent Variable* | *IF-THEN Hypothesis* | *Direction of Association* |
| 1. Deeper encoding of words, better memory | Levels of encoding | Recall of words | IF encoding level increases, THEN memory increases | + |
| 2. Older age, reduced motor speed | Age | Motor speed | IF age increases, THEN, motor speed decreases | – |
| 3. Higher SAT scores, better GPAs | SAT | GPA | IF SATs are higher, THEN GPAs are higher | + |
| 4. Exam grades are higher for students who study in the library versus dorm | Place of study | Exam grade | IF place of study is the library THEN exam grades are higher compared with those who study in dorm | NA |

Test your knowledge of this chapter so far by taking the mid-chapter quiz on the study site: www.sagepub.com/nestor2e

direction of the association is negative or inverse. Hypothesis 2 states a negative or inverse association between increased age and reduced motor speed. Hypothesis 4 is a special case in which the independent variable is categorical (which we will discuss in Chapter 4), as in this example, where students study for an exam, either in the library or in their dorms. This qualitative variable cannot be said to increase or decrease. In this case, the concept of direction of association does not apply, and the hypothesis simply states that one category or level of the independent variable is associated with higher values of the dependent variable.

## The Research Circle

In reality, the process of conducting research designed to test explanations for psychological phenomena involves a dynamic interplay of moving from theory to data and then back to theory. This process can be characterized as a **research circle**. As Exhibit 2.5 shows, deductive and inductive research processes can be closely intertwined. With deductive research, theory gives birth to hypotheses, which are then tested by data. With inductive research, data give birth to an **empirical generalization**—a statement that describes patterns found in the data, from which a theory is formulated. The goals of inductive and deductive research approaches are identical: to develop and formulate theories, a set of general propositions that serve to organize and interpret data or to generate predictions for events and actions for which no data have yet to be obtained. We will know break down the research circle into specific steps using our maximization study as an example.

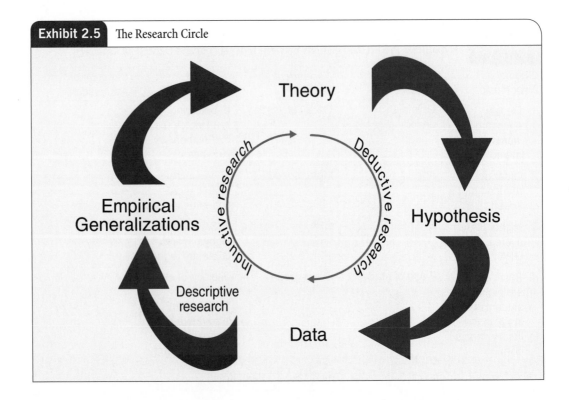

**Exhibit 2.5** The Research Circle

## Getting Started

Getting started in research is tough. Often what works is to find a research study that interests you. In this book, we have introduced several research studies, all of which we hope you find interesting. We selected these studies because of the simplicity of their methods and their potential teaching value. So, for example, we covered the Kahneman studies in Chapter 1, and now in Chapter 2, we have delved into research of Iyengar and collaborators (2006). In so doing, we have reviewed the research pertaining to these particular topics, whether heuristic biases of the Kahneman ilk, online gaming by Hussain and Griffiths (2009), or the maximization study by Iyengar and colleagues (2006). So the first step in the research process is to identify a topic of interest. But how, you may ask.

Psychology is a staple of contemporary culture. And your interests may be piqued through various media accounts of psychological research (e.g., a "Research in the News" of this book). We suggest that a potential wealth of inspiration for new ideas may be found in the **popular science** literature, often written by eminent scientists who aim to explain science for a general audience. An example of an outstanding work of popular science is the 2011 book by the psychologist and winner of the Nobel Prize in economic science, Daniel Kahneman, *Thinking, Fast and Slow*.

Closely related to popular science is **science journalism**, which often focuses on recent developments in science that are judged newsworthy. Pieces in both popular science and science journalism are often exceptionally well-written works of literary distinction: lively, clear, and engaging and free of technical jargon. The downside is that some popular literature (not *Thinking, Fast and Slow*) can sometimes lack the critical sense of proportionality, cautiousness, and tentativeness that is fundamental to the scientific method. In the popular press, scientific findings can be oversold, if not downright sensationalized.

We emphasize these works of journalism only as a source of ideas that might inspire and motivate you to pursue a formal line of investigation using the scientific method. These journalistic pieces represent important **secondary sources**, that is, secondhand media accounts of scientific work. They are best used as clues to lead you to the **primary source**, the firsthand report published in a peer-reviewed journal.

In research, you must go to the primary source. In our example, you would read the Iyengar et al. (2006) study published in *Psychological Science*. You will find that *Psychological Science* is considered a top-tier peer-reviewed periodical. For a study to be published in *Psychological Science*, it must past the muster of reliability and validity as evaluated through the rigors of peer review. So your first general criterion for evaluating a study is to *consider the source*: where an empirical report such as the Iyengar et al. study is published. A credible source requires peer review. In reading a primary source, the goals of the study should be clearly defined and articulated, and the methods and design of the study should be sufficient to achieve its goals. Ask yourself, "If I had to design this study to test this hypothesized relationship, what would I do?" In other words, you want to evaluate whether the study provides the best method for achieving the goals of the research. Here, a mental template might be helpful: Begin with the broad distinction of whether you would classify a study as either experimental or nonexperimental. Consider whether the research question can be adequately addressed by either an experimental or a nonexperimental approach.

## Staking Out the Research Literature

The formal research literature can also serve as a fountain for new ideas. These ideas may come to us when we consider empirical findings of various peer-reviewed studies that are published in scientific **journals**. These journals constitute the scientific literature. Exhibit 2.6 presents a partial list of major peer-reviewed publications in psychology. In looking at this list, you see that the peer-reviewed publications fall into one of two categories: (1) **empirical articles** and (2) **review articles**. An empirical article reports on a particular study and is written in a certain format divided into sections: Abstract, Introduction (which will contain a review of the relevant literature that is the focus of the study), Method, Results, and Discussion (see Chapter 12).

A review article examines several studies of a particular phenomenon, such as heuristics and biases (Tversky & Kahneman, 1974). It evaluates the methodology used across different studies; examines the degree to which findings are **robust** across various conditions, settings, and procedures; and comments on the extent to which the empirical findings allow for general theoretical conclusions.

| Exhibit 2.6 | Some Important Peer-Reviewed Journals for Psychological Research | |
|---|---|
| **Empirical Articles** | **Review Articles** |
| *Behavior Therapy* | *American Psychologist* |
| *Child Development* | *Annual Review of Psychology* |
| *Cognitive Psychology* | *Psychological Bulletin* |
| *Developmental Psychology* | *Psychological Review* |
| *Journal of Abnormal Psychology Science* | |
| *Journal of Applied Psychology* | |
| *Journal of Educational Psychology* | |
| *Journal of Experimental Child Psychology* | |
| *Journal of Experimental Psychology: General* | |
| *Journal of Experimental Psychology: Learning, Memory, and Cognition* | |
| *Journal of Experimental Psychology: Human Perception and Performance* | |
| *Journal of Personality and Social Psychology* | |
| *Proceedings of the National Academy of Sciences* | |
| *Psychological Assessment* | |
| *Psychological Science* | |
| *Neuropsychology* | |
| *Science* | |

## The Power of Observation

Suppose you have no formal experience in research but you have always been curious about the human face. In many ways, you have chosen a wonderful topic for research that can be studied by the power of simple *observation*. Science often begins with simple observation, which can serve as a source of both evidence and ideas. Charles Darwin, for example, generated the theory of evolution by natural selection exclusively on the basis of simple observation. In his later book *The Expression of the Emotions in Man and Animals*, and again relying exclusively on observation, Darwin (1872/1988) would make the case that all mammals regularly display emotion on their faces. For us mere mortals, we might look for the "agony of defeat and the thrill of victory" etched on the faces of the athletes when watching our favorite sport.

Paul Ekman is a world-renowned psychologist who has devoted his career to studying facial expressions of emotions (see Exhibit 2.7). Inspired by Darwin, Ekman began his research by observing facial expressions of emotions of people from various cultures. Malcolm Gladwell, in a delightful 2002 *New Yorker* piece of science journalism, described how Ekman first traveled to places like Japan, Brazil, and Argentina, carrying photographs of men and women posing various distinctive faces. As recounted by Gladwell, everywhere Ekman went in the developed world, people agreed on what those expressions meant. But because these people all lived in developed countries, they, Ekman knew, could have picked up the same cultural rules watching the same movies and televisions shows. The indefatigable Ekman, armed with his trusty photographs, next traveled to the most remote villages in the jungles of Papua New Guinea, and there he found, lo and behold, that these tribe folk also had no problem interpreting various facial expressions of emotions. In this very important sense, then, as you recall from Chapter 1, Ekman began his work as a true *cultural psychologist*.

| Exhibit 2.7 | Universal Expression of Seven Major Categories of Facial Emotions |
| --- | --- |

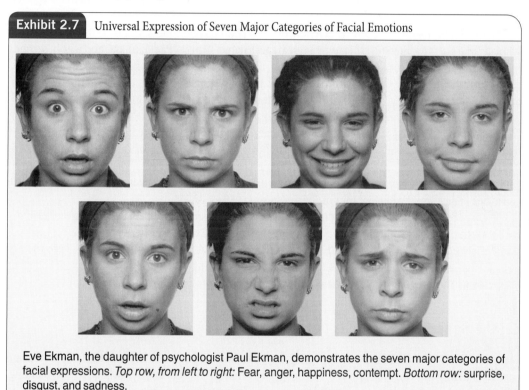

Eve Ekman, the daughter of psychologist Paul Ekman, demonstrates the seven major categories of facial expressions. *Top row, from left to right:* Fear, anger, happiness, contempt. *Bottom row:* surprise, disgust, and sadness.

Over the next half-century, Paul Ekman would build a program of psychological research around his breakthrough discovery that facial expressions of emotions were not socially learned but rather are the universal products of evolution. His nonexperimental studies of facial expression across cultures, which began with naturalistic observations, would be extended to elegant experimental studies by him and other researchers (see also, e.g., Leppanen & Nelson, 2009; Mandal & Ambady, 2004). Together, this research established the human face as an exquisite and efficient organ of emotional communication.

Also important is that observations often act to restrict our attention, and oftentimes they may be subject to bias. However, sometimes with our observant eye, we might stumble on an important discovery that may not have been of primary interest to us. This is why we want to emphasize that during the earlier phases of research when we are trying to generate ideas, narrowing the focus of observation may be counterproductive, stifling perhaps our imagination and creativity. Here you might be better served by a frame of mind in which your attention and observation act not so much as a narrow spotlight of illumination of a particular area of interest but as a lantern casting a diffuse radiance over the panoply of experience (Lehrer, 2009b).

## Searching the Literature

The Internet has been described as a godsend for researchers and scholars, especially for those who like to work in their pajamas (Tuhus-Dubrow, 2008)! Tracking down a published peer-reviewed article on the Internet can often be done in a matter of seconds, all from the comfort of your home. In addition, many researchers have very accessible and highly informative websites that include articles that can be identified by typing their name into a search engine, such as Google, and then easily downloaded free of charge. Internet traveling, so to speak, from hyperlink to hyperlink may also lead to an *online serendipity* of stumbling onto an unexpected article that could add a new dimension to your thinking or perhaps lead you down a very different path from your original idea.

A branch of Google called Google Scholar (http://scholar.google.com) specializes in searches of the scholarly and scientific literature: Just type a researcher's name, such as "Paul Ekman," and within seconds you will have access to a corpus of scholarly and scientific work on facial expression of emotion. Two excellent websites for major psychological organizations are American Psychological Association (www.apa.org) and Association for Psychological Science (www.psychologicalscience.org). **PsycINFO** and **PsycLIT** are specialized, noncommercial search engines sponsored by the American Psychological Association (APA) to serve as databases for citations and abstracts of the world's literature in psychology and related fields. So too is the **Social Sciences Citation Index (SSCI)**, which includes articles from not only psychology but also related fields, such as sociology and criminology. With SSCI, you can identify a "key article" on your topic. SSCI will then provide you with a list of articles that have cited your key article. This list will give you a start in developing a bibliography of articles relevant to your topic.

These websites are not free and are **proprietary**, open only to subscribers. For example, websites of scientific journals are generally proprietary, meaning that only paid subscribers can access their contents of peer-reviewed articles. Most college and university libraries have subscriptions to a number of proprietary websites that can be accessed through the library system. Consulting with the library staff of your college or university will help you learn how to access proprietary websites of scholarly information.

## Let the Searcher Beware!

Elizabeth Kirk (2002) offers some excellent guidelines for evaluating information from the Internet that are available on the Johns Hopkins University webpage: www.library.jhu.edu/researchhelp/general/evaluating. Kirk's main take-home point is that you should never use information that cannot be verified by other independent sources. To make her point about the dangers of accepting Internet information as gospel, she cites the famous Latin phrase *caveat lector*: Let the reader beware. She lists several criteria against which all information should be evaluated. Among these are authority (e.g., Who wrote it?), publishing body (e.g., Who is the sponsor of the site?), point of view or bias (e.g. Does the website advocate a point of view or sell media products, such as books, pamphlets, videos, etc.?), connection to the scientific literature (e.g., Does it cite references to peer-reviewed articles?), verifiability and transparency (e.g., Is the methodology open to public scrutiny and able to be reproduced?), and timelines (e.g., What is the date, and does the information get updated?).

Keep in mind that general search engines such as the family of Google search tools can be very useful, but they are commercially based and derive a portion of their revenues through advertisement. As such, they may shape scholarship in unforeseen ways (Evans, 2008). Other scholars, such as the anthropologist Alex Bentley of Durham University in England, quoted in the *Boston Sunday Globe* of November 23, 2008, by the journalist Rebecca Tuhus-Dubrow, have warned that the Internet "makes academic research a popularity contest" dominated by search engines that order or prioritize information in ways that may have little to do with scientific merit or impact.

The common lesson is that the tremendous benefits of the Internet, especially in the early phases of generating ideas, may also come with some potential costs. As we know from Chapter 1, we are all prone to confirmatory bias, which may lead us to only search for information on the Internet that supports our positions and ideas. We should always remain cognizant that the Internet and the search tools used to navigate the electronic world have limitations that may affect how we search and gather information in ways we may not fully appreciate.

## Reading the Research Literature

Once you have a topic of interest, the next step is to review the research literature relevant to your topic. For our purposes, think of the relevant research literature as consisting of primary sources, that is peer-reviewed empirical articles and review articles (see Exhibit 2.6). It is easy to become overwhelmed by the breadth and depth of the research literature on any given topic. Thus, an important challenge is to narrow your focus and to demarcate the boundaries of your literature review.

To illustrate, let us use the Iyengar et al. (2006) study on maximization. Let us imagine that we learned about the study through a science journalism piece. In fact, this is pretty much what happened when we came across this headline of a science journalism piece summarizing the study: "Are you a grumpy maximizer or a happy satisficer?" (Jarrett, 2006). So now we have a topic—maximization and its relationship to well-being. With appetites whetted, we are off to find the primary source, published in *Psychological Science*, authored by Iyengar et al. (2006) titled "Doing Better but Feeling Worse: Looking for the 'Best' Job Undermines Satisfaction."

We carefully read the seven-page article. Included in the article is a reference list of 20 citations. These 20 citations form the Iyengar et al. (2006) literature review. Which of those citations do you think would be relevant to your literature review? Go to those primary sources, meaning read those articles that you have deemed relevant to your literature review. You are now on your way to developing a relevant research review. So a very simple tactic is as follows. Find a key article—in this example, Iyengar et al.—and read it carefully. Check the article's reference page, found at end of the manuscript. Think of the reference page as the "blueprint" for the research literature review; that is, it defines the scope of the research reviewed for that article.

You have now assembled a set of articles to review. Now the question is how to review them. In reading the research literature, adopt a skeptical mind-set. With a skeptical mind-set, all knowledge is constantly questioned, and all empirical evidence is subjected to rigorous scrutiny. What does this mean in practice? It means simply that you want to develop a set of benchmarks against which you can review the literature.

Let's begin with our first benchmark, which pertains to the principles of reliability and validity introduced in Chapter 1. A reliable study, as we learned in Chapter 1, is one that can be replicated; the findings can be consistently demonstrated across independent research studies. For a useful reminder, think of the headline borrowed from Kosslyn and Rosenberg (2001): "Reliability: You Can Count on It!" For validity, a useful headline reminder might read, "Validity: What Does It Really Mean?" (Kosslyn & Rosenberg, 2001). So the lesson is clear: Apply these principles of reliability and validity as benchmarks in reviewing the literature.

A second benchmark pertains to the theoretical underpinnings of the research under review. Ask yourself, "Is there a dominant theory that ties the various reviewed studies, and if so how do the researchers define it?" This is no easy task. But for clues as to how to do this, let's look again at the Iyengar et al. (2006) study. They described their work as emanating from the seminal theory of Herbert Simon (1956), which identified two distinct decision-making strategies, maximizer and satisficer.

We have learned earlier in this chapter the importance of conceptual definitions that come from a specific theory. Now we can apply this to our literature review. To wit, ask yourself, "Are conceptual definitions provided for key terms, and do I consider these as theoretically sound?" So now we have a second benchmark for you to apply in reviewing the literature: the clarity and quality of the theory. In short, be mindful of these theoretical considerations in evaluating research literature; if absent or not clearly defined, a different topic might be in order!

In this book, you will learn about various research designs (see Exhibit 2.1). What this means is that different studies use different kinds of methods. These methods generally follow the experimental/nonexperimental division that we presented earlier in this chapter. In reading the scientific literature, you may find that researchers have used different methods to investigate your topic of interest. And in some studies, the researcher may have even combined both experimental and nonexperimental methods to investigate a given topic. Overall, be mindful of the diversity of methods used within a particular study as well as across different studies. Do different methods of investigation yield similar results?

For example, Dunn and colleagues, in a 2008 study published in *Science*, combined both experimental and nonexperimental methods to address the age-old question as to whether money can buy happiness. For their nonexperimental study, Dunn, Aknin, and Norton (2008) conducted a nationally representative survey study asking 632 Americans about their happiness, charitable donations, and annual incomes. For their experimental study, research participants were given either 5 or 10 dollars, which they were instructed either to spend on themselves or to donate to charity.

Results from both the national survey and the experiment painted a similar picture: On the survey, happier people reported donating more money to others. Similarly, research participants who were randomly assigned in the experiment to spend money on others also experienced greater happiness than those assigned to spend money on themselves.

Thus, we see that Dunn and colleagues employed two different methodologies: (1) nonexperimental survey of a nationally representative sample of Americans and (2) experimental manipulation of randomly assigning participants to spend money on others or themselves. Both methodologies yielded similar results. These similar results offer *converging* evidence. The lesson for reading and reviewing research literature with a critical, scientific eye is clear. We can now also state clearly our third benchmark for how to review scientific literature as follows: Look for diversity in the methods used to investigate a given topic and whether these yield converging results.

To recap, use prior studies listed in the reference section of a peer-reviewed paper to help demarcate a body of relevant literature. Adopt a skeptical mind-set in reading and reviewing the relevant literature, that is, the set of studies that you have assembled based on prior research. Read and review the literature against three benchmarks for evaluating research: (1) reliability and validity, (2) theoretical underpinnings, and (3) converging evidence.

## Communication of Research Products

There is perhaps no more difficult task for both students and professors alike than writing a research paper in psychology. To do so requires psychological writing, a discipline-specific form of scientific reporting that is based on APA publication style. The most recent version of the *APA Style Manual* (discussed in detail in Chapter 12) is widely recognized as the gold standard for scientific writing in psychology. It articulates the principles of *clarity*, *concise wording*, and *accuracy*, with the aim of producing writing that will facilitate the flow of communication from author to reader (Carson, Fama, & Clancy, 2008).

In psychological writing, our main objective is to produce a scholarly paper that describes and explains psychological concepts. The goal of description and explanation is to provide an understanding of psychological concepts within the context of empirical investigation (Thaiss & Sanford, 2000). We rely exclusively on peer-reviewed primary sources for gathering empirical evidence (see Exhibit 2.6).

Empirical evidence is the cornerstone of psychology and psychological writing (e.g., Bem, 2003; Carson et al., 2008). As we have learned, empirical evidence is derived from observation or experimentation conducted under controlled conditions. As Carson et al. (2008) describe in *Writing for Psychology*, different academic disciplines have different views on what is considered evidence. For example, the humanities, but not psychology, consider logic and rhetoric as evidence. In a similar vein, psychology writing does not consider opinions as evidence, regardless of whether these personally held convictions are based on controlled observation. Nor, as we recall from our discussion of pseudoscience, would anecdotes and personal testimonies, however compelling, be considered as evidence in psychological writing.

You should also consider the *quantity* of the empirical evidence in your psychological writing (Carson et al., 2008). In psychology, as in all sciences, you will find empirical studies that report contradictory results. Your writing should take into account these contradictory results, as you aim to provide an accurate description as concisely as possible of the research literature. And as you have learned in the above sections on reading and critiquing research, make clear in your writing whether findings have been replicated; converging evidence is more convincing than results from a single study, and this should be communicated in concise wording to your reader.

In addition to the quantity of empirical evidence cited in support of a conclusion, you must also evaluate the *quality* of that evidence gathered from primary sources (Carson et al., 2008). Always remember that the highest value sources of empirical evidence are peer-reviewed journals (Carson et al., 2008). As shown in Exhibit 2.6, review articles and empirical journal articles are the two most important primary sources of evidence that are used in psychological writing. Each type of article calls on a different critical eye: For a review article, you want to discern the author's major argument and how other empirical studies are used to support that argument; for an empirical article, your evaluation is more directly targeted to specific elements of the reported study, such as theoretical rationale, hypothesis, methodology, statistical analyses, and conclusions (Carson et al., 2008).

## Writing a Literature Review

All psychological research presented in peer-reviewed journals generally begins with a literature review. Some psychology journals are exclusively devoted to publishing literature reviews of particular topics of interest. Consider, for example, what the prestigious *Psychological Bulletin* seeks to publish, as described on their webpage:

> Integrative reviews or research syntheses focus on empirical studies and seek to summarize past research by drawing overall conclusions from many separate investigations that address related or identical hypotheses. A research synthesis typically presents the authors' assessments of the (a) state of knowledge concerning the relations of interest; (b) critical assessments of the strengths and weaknesses in past research; and (c) important issues that research has left unresolved, thereby directing future research so it can yield a maximum amount of new information. (APA, n.d.)

As you can see from this description, literature reviews serve an extremely important function in developing a scientific understanding of a topic. A sound literature review creates and evaluates a body of knowledge that is drawn from a synthesis of empirical findings across independent studies.

A critical reading of any literature review, however, should pay close attention to several factors. First, how were the empirical studies selected for review? A major limitation is that authors of reviews are relatively free to select studies and can choose on their own those empirical findings viewed as relevant. Two independent reviewers of the very same topic could reach very different conclusions. We know from Chapter 1 the problems of confirmatory bias. It is not hard to imagine how confirmatory bias may influence a reviewer to seek only empirical findings that fit with a certain school of thought.

Second, most traditional reviews lack an objective benchmark to evaluate the strength of different empirical findings gleaned across various studies. How does one weigh the importance of one empirical finding over the other? Third, literature reviews are limited by **publication bias**. That is, reviews are based on studies that have been published. Studies often are unpublished because of negative findings, such as failing to replicate a certain phenomenon or effect. A review generally does not take into consideration unpublished studies, instead focusing exclusively on empirical findings that have been reported in peer-reviewed journals. Publication bias can be a particular problem for studies examining the effectiveness of a particular drug. In fact, all drug studies, often referred to as "trials," must now be filed with the Food and Drug Administration, including negative trials in which the drug failed to show the predicted effect. The Food and Drug Administration requires this to limit the effects of publication bias in its reviews of drug studies.

Because of these difficulties reviews now often incorporate **meta-analysis** as a method to provide a more unbiased evaluation of the literature. Meta-analysis is a statistical tool that provides an objective metric to weigh the strength of results from individual studies. The metric used provides an estimate of **effect size** (strength or magnitude of the demonstrated findings) for the results of each study included in the review. The effect size statistic allows for studies to be directly and objectively compared with each other. The average effect size across studies can be computed to provide an objective indicator of the overall strength of the empirical findings. This, in turn, might also provide an index of the degree generalizability of the empirical findings, as the review includes many studies varying in settings, samples, procedures, and time periods. Meta-analysis provides a statistical means to combat the biases of any reviewer.

In summary, keep in mind that a large portion of the research process requires evaluating prior studies with a thoughtful skepticism that is informed by the scientific method. Keep in mind writing your literature review, the importance of including both negative and positive studies, and the problem of publication bias.

## Writing an Empirical Paper

Writing an empirical paper represents one of the major academic challenges for students in research methods courses. The eminent research psychologist Daryl Bem (2003) used the shape of an hourglass as a metaphor for how an empirical paper be composed. That is, visualize the shape of an hourglass with its two connected vertical glass bulbs fused together at their common "neck" (see Exhibit 2.8). Now apply that same image to the shape of your empirical paper. Like the outline of an hourglass, the contour of your paper will begin broadly, become progressively narrow in the middle sections, and then broaden out again by the latter parts.

In other words, an empirical paper is organized into the following sections: Abstract, Introduction, Method, Results, Discussion, and References (see Exhibit 2.9). The top of the hourglass in Exhibit 2.8 shapes the introduction with its broad beginning, followed by its neck in the narrowing down to specifics in the method and results, and then with the lower bulb reflecting the broadening out again in the discussion. Bem (2003) made clear this analogy to the hourglass when he explained that an empirical paper "begins with broad statements, progressively narrows down to the specifics of your study, and then broadens out again to more general considerations" (p. 4).

| Exhibit 2.8 | Hourglass Shape of a Research Report |
| --- | --- |

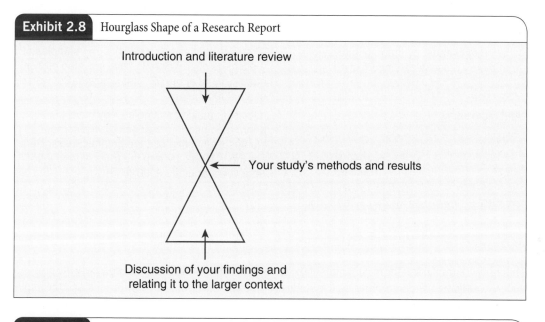

| Exhibit 2.9 | The Key Ingredients of a Short Research Report |
| --- | --- |

| The *introduction* begins broadly with an opening topical statement: | "Individuals differ considerably from one and another in the strategies they use in making decisions." |
| --- | --- |
| It quickly becomes specific by presenting the theory that provides the conceptual framework of the study: | "Schwartz (2004) identified two distinct decision- or choice-making strategies: (1) satisficer and (2) maximizer." |
| It gets more specific with clear conceptual definitions: | "The choice strategy of a maximizer is defined as one that seeks out the absolute best option, usually only after an exhaustive search. The choice strategy of a satisficer is defined as one that seeks the 'good enough' choice, searching until finding an option that meets a standard of acceptability." |
| Close introduction by describing your study in conceptual terms: | "In this pilot study, we examined the percentages of maximizers and satisficers in a college student sample." |
| The *method* and *results* sections are the most specific—the "neck" of the hourglass: | Method: "Sixty-two UMB college students (23 males/39 females) ranging in ages from 18 to 38 years completed the 13-item Maximization Scale." Results: "In the current pilot study, 13 of the 62 students (21%) scored higher than 61.75 and were classified as maximizers. Forty-nine of the 62 (79%) students scored lower than 61.75 and were classified as satisficers." |
| The *discussion* section leads with statement of major findings: | "In the current pilot study, the principal results revealed that 79% of the students were classified as satisficers and 21% were classified as maximizers." |

*(Continued)*

(Continued)

| It becomes broader by drawing implications from theory presented in introduction: | "Previous studies using much larger samples of thousands of participants have reported higher base rates of about 33% maximizers (Schwartz et al., 2004)." |
|---|---|
| And more so: | "Decision-making strategies may have a bearing on people's well-being, with some studies suggesting that the greatest maximizers are the least happy with the fruits of their labor (e.g., Iyengar et al., 2006)." |

*Note:* UMB = University of Massachusetts Boston.

## Abstract

The abstract summarizes the major points of the study. In writing an abstract, state concisely the problem under investigation, the procedures used to study the problem, the results, the conclusions, and the implications of the research findings.

## Introduction

The introduction identifies the problem to be investigated and why it is important. Be sure to cast the problem and rationale in a psychological theory, which should serve as a framework for the study, defining its key concepts and terms. Two general questions are helpful guides for reading an introduction: What is the study about, and why does it matter? More formal questions are as follows: What is the theory and the hypothesis, and how are they related?

## Method

The empirical paper differs from the literature review in organization. That is, the empirical paper must have a method section and a results section. The method section details the operations and procedures that the researcher used in the study.

Two helpful hints in writing the method: First, the method section should provide sufficient detail so that another researcher can reproduce the study. Second, you as a reader should be able to put yourself in the shoes of a participant and understand exactly what the participant actually was instructed to do in the study. How participants were recruited and how the study sample was formed should be clearly stated in the method. Was the sample generated via a random process? In reading the method, look for any signs of sample bias that occur when participants are not randomly selected. Also, consider how representative the sample is, as this will affect the generalizability of the study results. Last, the method section should make clear operational definitions for both independent and dependent variables. What was the experimental task? Was random assignment used to create the independent variable?

## Results

The results section presents the major statistical findings of the study. The results include both descriptive statistics and inferential statistics. Descriptive statistics summarize the data, usually in the form of averages/means and standard deviations (a statistical measure of variability or range of scores). Inferential statistics in the form of tests of significance tell the probability of whether the observed differences found in the study were produced by random, or chance, factors. Also important for inferential statistics is an estimate of what is known as effect size. The effect size refers to the strength of the predicted or hypothesized relationship between the independent variable and the dependent variable.

## Discussion

In the discussion section, the major findings of the study are often restated, but typically only in narrative form, and the theoretical meaning of the results is discussed. Important questions to consider in reading the discussion are as follows: Do the empirical findings support the inferences and explanations? Does the discussion section duly express tentativeness and exercise cautiousness, which are essential to the scientific method? Are alternative interpretations carefully considered?

Perhaps the most important question for the discussion section is whether the limitations of the study are thoughtfully and explicitly discussed. These limitations may be related to the extent to which the operations and procedures adequately capture the intended phenomena. Is the experiment too unrealistic, too contrived—clever but lacking any real application to life? The extent to which a study or experiment approximates the actual real-life phenomenon under investigation refers to **ecological validity**. Related to but different from questions of ecological validity are those that pertain to the generalizability of the study and how representative or culturally diverse is the sample. These considerations fall under the general or broader category of **external validity** (ecological validity is one particular aspect of external validity, which is covered in Chapter 4).

---

### STAT CORNER

### Story Telling With Numbers and Graphs

Our in-class exercise generated a distribution of scores on the Maximization Scale based on a sample of 62 students. In your short research report, descriptive statistics are included in both method and results sections. In the method section, the descriptive statistics summarize key features of your sample, including number of participants, their age, years of education, as well as number of males and females. For example, in our method section, we described the age and education of our sample.

> Participants had a mean age of 22.71 years (SD = 4.50) and a mean education completed of 14.17 years (SD = 1.10).

Often in the results, a graph plotting key data can be very instructive. For the sake of illustration, let us consider two figures that were routinely used in plotting descriptive data. First, the frequency distribution on the Maximization Scale represents continuous data that can be appropriately and effectively depicted in a histogram (see Exhibit 2.10). The results are also well suited for a bar chart (see Exhibit 2.11). A bar chart is similar to a histogram. But whereas a histogram is used for continuous data that can take on any value within a range, the bar chart is used for data that are in categories. In other words, a histogram is used for continuous data that can be quantified or measured, such as scores on a test; a bar chart (also known as a bar graph) is used for data that can be counted, such as number of women in a study. As you see, a histogram is used to plot scores for the Maximization Scale that can range from a low of 13 to a high of 91 (see Exhibit 2.10). By contrast, for plotting the frequency or number of students classified as either a maximizer or a satisficer, a bar chart is used (see Exhibit 2.11). Refer to the following websites for instructional videos on constructing bar graphs and histograms in Microsoft Excel: *bar graph:* http://www.youtube.com/watch?v=aBV2vvTFI84; *histogram:* http://www.youtube.com/watch?v=UASCe-3Y1to.

*(Continued)*

(Continued)

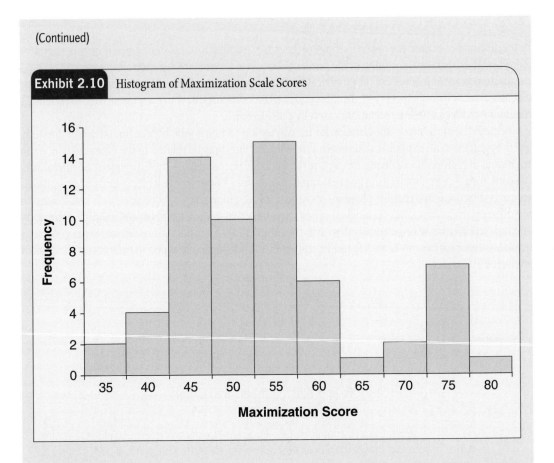

**Exhibit 2.10** Histogram of Maximization Scale Scores

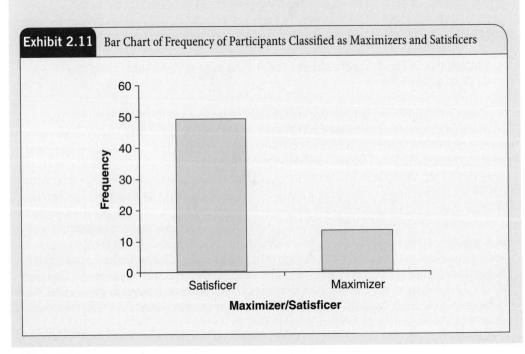

**Exhibit 2.11** Bar Chart of Frequency of Participants Classified as Maximizers and Satisficers

## A Short Research Report

Exhibit 2.9 provides an outline for writing a short research report (laboratory report). In this pilot study, students first served as research participants, completing the Maximization Scale, and then they switched hats and became investigators, analyzing the data and producing a short research report. The research question for this pilot study is simply this: What are the percentages of maximizers and satisficers in the class sample? The sample consists of their fellow classmates.

Note that our rationale for this in-class exercise is to engage you in psychological writing. We choose a laboratory report/short research report format as our starting point. Our main learning objective is to introduce you to the organization, content, and style of an empirical paper via this short research report format. In Chapter 12, we cover in detail the APA-style formatting rules used in writing research reports. But for now let us focus on organization and content in writing a short research report titled "Base Rates of Maximizers and Satisficers in a Research Methods Course."

## Introduction

1.  Introduce the reader to the nature of the problem being investigated. The following opening statement is intended to be broad, written in plain English, without psychological jargon.

    *Right:* Individuals differ considerably from one and another in the strategies that they use in making decisions.

    By contrast, the following as an opening statement would be too technical, and the information is presented too soon. Avoid plunging into technical research in your opening statement. It is better to present research findings later in the introduction. As a general rule, your opening statement should be about people, not psychologists or their research (Bem, 2003). The following is a perfectly appropriate sentence for the introduction but not for an opening statement.

    *Wrong:* Simon (1956) was the first to distinguish two types of decision-making strategies, maximizers and satisficers.

2.  Move to more specificity by presenting a theoretical background of your research report.

    *Right:* Schwartz (2004) identified two distinct decision- or choice-making strategies: (1) satisficer and (2) maximizer.

    By contrast, the following statement would be wrong on at least two counts. First, it is presented in the first person as an opinion. Although accurate, the wording of the statement is inappropriate for our short research report. Also, do not write in the first person. Second, the statement does not present the particular theory (i.e., Schwartz, 2004) that provides the conceptual framework for our pilot study.

    *Wrong:* I think that some people always aim to make the best possible decision whereas other people aim for "good enough" decisions.

3.  Provide conceptual definitions of key terms.

    *Right:* The choice strategy of a maximizer is defined as one that seeks out the absolute best option, usually only after an exhaustive search. The choice strategy of a satisficer is defined as one that seeks the "good enough" choice, searching until finding an option that meets a standard of acceptability.

*(Continued)*

(Continued)

By contrast, the following statement is wrong because it provides operational definitions of the key terms. It belongs in the method section. The reader at this point has not been presented with enough information for this sentence to be informative.

*Wrong:* Based on the averages from thousands of subjects, a total score of 61.75 or greater is classified as a maximizer, and a score lower than 61.75 is classified as a satisficer.

4. Close the introduction by describing your study in conceptual terms.

*Right:* In this pilot study, we examined the percentages of maximizers and satisficers in a college student sample.

By contrast, the following statement would be wrong for the introduction because it defines the study sample. It belongs in the method section.

*Wrong:* A total of 62 college students completed the Maximization Scale, the 13-item scale presented at the beginning of this chapter.

## Method

The method section of the empirical report is divided into separate subsections. For our short research report, our method section has three subsections: (a) Sample, (b) Measures, and (c) Procedure.

1. *Sample:* The sample subsection should include the number of research participants, their key demographics, and how participants were recruited.

   a. The following simple statement informs the reader of the exact sample size and key demographics.

      *Right:* Sixty-two University of Massachusetts, Boston, college students (23 males/39 females) ranging in ages from 18 to 38 years participated in this pilot study.

      By contrast, the following statement would be wrong because it is too vague; size of sample and key demographics (e.g., age, gender breakdown) must be presented in the method section.

      *Wrong:* Students in my research methods class participated in our study.

   b. The method should present specific statistics to describe important characteristics of the study sample.

      *Right:* Participants had a mean age of 22.71 years ($SD = 4.50$) and a mean education completed of 14.17 years ($SD = 1.10$).

      By contrast, the following statement is wrong because age and education need to be quantified.

      *Wrong:* Our sample consisted of college-age students.

   c. A summary statement is helpful to close the sample subsection of the method.

      *Right:* Participants were students enrolled in an introductory research methods course. All students participated as part of an in-class exercise.

      By contrast, the following statement would be wrong because it is too imprecise and too casual or colloquial.

      *Wrong:* Anyone who came to class that day participated in the study.

2. *Measures:* This subsection describes the key measures used in the study, including operational definitions.

   a. The following statement describes the Maximization Scale used in the pilot study as consisting of 13 statements that participants were instructed to rate from 1 to 7, *completely disagree* to *completely agree.*

      *Right:* Participants completed the Maximization Scale. The scale consists of 13 statements designed to measure satisficer/maximizer decision-making strategies. Participants were instructed to read each statement and rate themselves from 1 to 7, *completely disagree* to *completely agree*, on each statement.

      By contrast, the following statement would be wrong because it is too vague.

      *Wrong:* Participants rated 13 statements from 1 to 7, *completely disagree* to *completely agree.*

   b. The measurement subsection identifies the Maximization Scale as the tool used to define operationally the variable of decision-making strategy.

      *Right:* The 13-item scale provided the operational definition to measure choice strategies of maximizer and satisficer.

      By contrast, the following statement would be wrong for the measures subsection of the method because it provides a conceptual definition (see above; already provided in the introduction) instead of an operational definition.

      *Wrong:* The choice strategy of a maximizer is defined as one that seeks out the absolute best option, usually only after an exhaustive search. The choice strategy of a satisficer is defined as one that seeks the "good enough" choice, searching until finding an option that meets a standard of acceptability.

   c. It is important to specify the criterion, specifically the exact cutoff score, used to categorize participants as either maximizers or satisficers.

      *Right:* Based on the averages from thousands of participants who had taken the Maximization Scale, a total score of 61.75 or greater is classified as a maximizer, and a score lower than 61.75 is classified as a satisficer.

      By contrast, the following statement would be wrong because it fails to specify how the Maximization Scale was used to categorize participants as either maximizers or satisficers.

      *Wrong:* Research participants completed the Maximization Scale.

## Procedure

1. The procedure subsection describes what exactly the research participants did.

   *Right:* Participants enrolled in an introductory research methods course at the University of Massachusetts Boston completed the Maximization Scale during class.

   By contrast, the following statement would be uninformative.

   *Wrong:* My classmates and I filled out a questionnaire about lots of different things.

*(Continued)*

(Continued)

**Results**

1. The results section presents the data and the statistics used to address the research question of the percentages of maximizers and satisficers in this sample.

   a. The following statement presents in numerical form the scores on the Maximization Scale.

   *Right:* The mean Maximization Scale score for the sample of 62 students was 55.35 ($SD$ = 10.19), ranging from a low of 35 to a high of 80.

   By contrast, the following statement would not belong in the results section because it both is in the first-person and lacks quantification, that is, exact percentages of satisficers and maximizers.

   *Wrong:* As I predicted, there were more satisficers than maximizers.

   b. The results section must include the data bearing on the research question.

   *Right:* In the current pilot study, 13 of the 62 students (21%) scored higher than 61.75 and were classified as maximizers. Forty-nine of the 62 (79%) students scored lower than 61.75 and were classified as satisficers.

   By contrast, the following statement would not be appropriate for the results section (or for the paper in general).

   *Wrong:* I thought my score on the 13-item Maximization Scale was not valid.

**Discussion**

1. The discussion begins with a restatement of the major findings of the study. You want to avoid redundancies in your writing. However, a restatement of the major findings helps you stick to the empirical facts and to prioritize for the reader the relevance of the obtained findings in reference to the research question.

   *Right:* In the current pilot study, the principal results revealed that 79% of the students were classified as satisficers and 21% were classified as maximizers.

   By contrast, the following statement would be wrong for an empirical report, in general, and the discussion section, in particular. Opinions are not "admissible" in the court of psychological writing!

   *Wrong:* As both research participant and research investigator, I learned a lot from our in-class exercise using the Maximization Scale.

2. The discussion is the section of the paper where you provide an interpretation of the results of your study. Set the stage for interpretation by returning to previous research reviewed in the introduction.

   *Right:* Previous studies (Schwartz, 2004) using much larger samples of thousands of participants have reported higher percentages with about 33% versus the current 21% of participants classified as maximizers in this investigation.

   The following statement would be wrong because it offers an interpretation that goes well beyond the current study, which did not address (measure) differences between maximizers and satisficers in the *quality of their decisions.*

   *Wrong:* Our results showed that maximizers make better decisions than satisficers.

3. In the discussion section, your interpretation always needs to be tempered by the limitations of the study. Always exercise caution in your interpretation. Maintaining your skeptical mind-set is especially important when you are writing up your own research!

   *Right:* The current study had several limitations, all of which may have contributed to the lower percentage of maximizers we found in relation to prior research. Foremost among these limitations are that the current study had a smaller sample size and was conducted as part of an in-class exercise in an introductory course on research methods; students served first as participants and then as investigators responsible for analyzing the data collected from their class and producing a laboratory report. Thus, the participants were fewer in number and recruited in a decidedly nonrandom manner. As such, any interpretation of the current results is constrained by the fact that the participants may not have constituted a representative sample. Other limitations . . .

   The following statement would be wrong because it is too informal and does not at all explain the idea of how limitations of the study could specifically constrain any interpretation of the results.

   *Wrong:* No study is perfect, and we did this as part of our class, and so I wouldn't offer any interpretation of the results.

4. Conclude by placing your results, notwithstanding the limitations of the study within a broader theoretical context.

   *Right:* The current results added to growing empirical evidence in support for distinguishing maximizers and satisficers, with recent studies suggesting that these two decision-making strategies may in turn play an important role in emotional well-being and vocational achievement (Iyengar et al., 2006; Schwartz, 2004).

# Conclusions

Research can be divided into approaches: experimental and nonexperimental. An experimental approach provides the strongest evidence for a cause-and-effect relationship between an independent variable and a dependent variable. By contrast, a nonexperimental approach is often described as correlational; it cannot establish causality because the independent variable(s) cannot be directly manipulated. In reality, causality is difficult to establish for any theory in psychology, as even highly controlled experiments cannot rule out all potential confounding factors. Evidence for causality should establish (a) temporal precedence, (b) covariation of cause and effect, and (c) elimination of alternative explanations. For both experimental and nonexperimental research, always consider the so-called third-variable problem before concluding that there is evidence of a correlation between a pair of measures. Likewise, variables are defined both conceptually and operationally in experimental and nonexperimental research.

Both inductive and deductive reasoning can figure prominently in theory formation and explanatory research. We have likened this process to a research circle in which deductive reasoning goes from theory to hypotheses to data, whereas inductive reasoning goes from data to empirical generalizations to theory. Ideas, as the so-called grist for the mill for research aimed toward building scientific theory, can come from many sources. The most important of these is the psychological literature, which consists of studies that have met the rigors of peer review. Scientific journalism and popular science literature can be two other potential sources for ideas, but articles and reports appearing in these two venues are not subject to peer review. As such, these secondary sources can best serve as clues to lead you to the primary source, the first-hand empirical report published in a peer-reviewed journal.

Writing in psychology is a discipline-specific form of scientific reporting that is based on the APA *Publication Style Manual* (2009). Empirical evidence is the cornerstone of psychology and psychological writing. Opinions, anecdotes, and personal testimonies, however compelling, are not empirical evidence and therefore are "inadmissible" in psychological writing. In writing and reading research, go to primary sources. In both reading a primary source of an empirical article and writing an empirical report, pay close attention as to whether the abstract summarizes the study, the introduction defines key concepts, the method specifies operations and procedures, the results present descriptive and inferential statistics, and the discussion covers interpretation of the findings as well as limitations of the research.

Last, descriptive statistics are distinguished from inferential statistics. The goal of descriptive statistics is to summarize and present numerical information in a manner that is instructive and helpful. Measures of central tendency (e.g., mean) and variability (e.g., standard deviation) can be computed to provide objective statistics that are used to describe the distribution of values. Descriptive data can be graphed. For example, a bar chart graphs the frequency distribution of a categorical variable, and a histogram graphs the frequency distribution of a continuous, quantitative variable. However, and importantly, you can neither draw conclusions on the basis of descriptive statistics nor test a hypothesis or generalize results to the larger population. On the other hand, inferential statistics are a set of techniques that allow for testing of hypotheses about a population from data collected from a sample. Critically, inferential statistics can do what descriptive statistics cannot. Inferential statistics can provide a direct test of a research hypothesis. That is, inferential statistics provide the techniques and procedures to determine the probability that the results that you obtained in your analysis of the aggregated data can be generalized to the larger population from which your sample was drawn.

# Key Terms

| | | |
|---|---|---|
| Alternative explanation | Experimental | PsycINFO |
| Applied research | External validity | PsycLIT |
| Bar chart | Frequency distribution | Publication bias |
| Basic research | Generalization | Qualitative research |
| Central tendency | Histogram | Random assignment |
| Conceptual definition | Inductive research | Randomized clinical trial |
| Control group | Inferential statistics | Research circle |
| Covariation of the cause and effect | Journals | Review articles |
| Deductive research | Meta-analysis | Robust |
| Descriptive statistics | Naturalistic observation | Science journalism |
| Direction of association | Nonexperimental | Secondary sources |
| Double blind | Operational definition | Social Sciences Citation Index (SSCI) |
| Ecological validity | Placebo | Temporal precedence |
| Effect size | Popular science | Third variables |
| Empirical articles | Primary source | Treatment group |
| Empirical generalization | Program evaluation | Variability |
| Ethnography | Proprietary | |

# Research in the News

1. Consider an interesting newspaper article by the journalist Javier Zarracina that appeared in the April 4, 2010, *Boston Globe*, titled "A Life Lesson From the Majors. Smile, You'll Live Longer." The newspaper account describes an empirical study published in the peer-reviewed journal *Psychological Science* by researchers Ernest L. Abel and Michael Kruger (2010) titled "Smile Intensity in Photographs Predicts Longevity." Read the Abel and Kruger (2010) paper, and provide a critique as both an educated consumer of psychological research and a professional reviewer of the study.

2. In the online *Time* January 16, 2009, article "How to Lift Your Mood? Try Smiling," John Cloud tells the story of how he was coaxed during his workouts by his personal trainer: "Relax your face." Cloud writes that he remained skeptical about his trainer's advice until he read a January 2009 *Journal of Personality and Social Psychology* study by Matsumoto and Willingham (2009), which compared facial expressions in two groups of judo athletes—blind and sighted competitors from the 2004 Olympics in Athens. This study prompted Cloud to discover one of the oldest questions in the study of emotion as to whether we all learn facial expression through our culture or they are genetically coded for everyone. By the end of his enjoyable piece, Cloud concludes,

> The emotional train does run in two directions between your brain, which may be screaming from the pain that your trainer is causing, and your face, which can—if you draw it into a relaxed expression—inform your brain that it shouldn't be protesting so much. So next time you're working out and grimacing push your facial muscles into submission. Look blank. You will find it's easier to get through one more rep. (http://content.time.com/time/health/article/0,8599,1871687,00.html)

What makes this piece an example of science journalism? How would you describe the reporting methods used in this article? How do the style, organization, and content of science journalism compare with the scientific method of peer-reviewed studies? Do you think Cloud's conclusions are supported by the scientific literature?

## STUDENT STUDY SITE

Please access the study site at **www.sagepub.com/nestor2e,** where you will find useful study materials such as mobile-friendly eFlashcards and mid-chapter and full chapter web quizzes for each chapter, along with carefully selected articles from research journals that illustrate the major concepts and techniques presented in the book.

# Activity Questions

1. Researchers in psychology "play" with ideas that require conceptual and operational definitions, such topics as maximization, happiness, intelligence, anxiety, impulsivity, attention, and emotion. For each of these, provide conceptual and operational definitions.

2. Independent, dependent, and control variables also fall under the "must know" category. To understand them requires practice. Here are some study situations that demonstrate each of these three variables.

a. You want to see if different instructional sets influence performance on a cognitive test. One instructional set presents the cognitive test as an ability-diagnostic measure of intelligence, and the other instructional set presents the cognitive test as an ability-nondiagnostic laboratory measure of problem solving unrelated to intelligence.

Independent (what you change/manipulate) variable: instructional set.

Dependent (what you observe/measure) variable: scores on cognitive test.

Control (what you hold constant) variable: cognitive test, same test given under the two instructional sets

b. You want to see if facial expressions can influence perception. You decide to have subjects look at cartoons and rate them on a funniness scale either while holding a pen between their lips, which makes it impossible to contract either of the two smiling muscles, or while holding a pen clenched between their teeth, which has the opposite effect of making them smile.

Independent (what you change/manipulate) variable: facial expression induced by holding a pen either between lips or clenched between teeth

Dependent (what you observe/measure) variable: funniness scores/ratings

Control (what you hold constant) variable: cartoons, same whether viewed while holding a pen between lips or clenched between teeth; funniness scale

c. You have been hired to evaluate the effectiveness of two diets: South Beach versus Atkins. You want to make sure both dieting groups weigh about the same before starting either the South Beach or the Atkins diet. So you weigh everyone before the diet and at the completion of the diet 6 weeks later.

Independent (what you change/manipulate) variable: diet (South Beach vs. Atkins).

Dependent (what you observe/measure) variable: difference in weight before and after.

Control (what you hold constant) variable: pre-diet weight; length of time (6 weeks) on respective diets

d. You want to study the influence of Alzheimer's disease on memory while controlling for age. What this means is that you will have two groups of people of about the same age; one group will be diagnosed with Alzheimer's disease, and the other group will be your control group of healthy persons.

Independent (what you change/manipulate) variable: group (Alzheimer's disease vs. control).

Dependent (what you observe/measure) variable: scores on memory test.

Control (what you hold constant) variable: age, memory test, same given to both groups.

3. Transform each of the following statements or problems into at least two testable hypotheses.

a. Talking on cell phones while driving should be against the law.

b. Listening to Mozart will make people smarter.

c. Steroids increase home runs in baseball.

d. Eating a vegetarian diet increases your grade-point average.

e. Money can buy you happiness.

4. In virtually all experiments, there is a degree of deception as researchers need to avoid creating bias by providing too much information before subjects have completed a study. What do you think about the ethics of deception in psychological research?

5. High school yearbooks can be used to study faces. Consider the Kniffin and Wilson (2004) study, in which participants rated photographs of people they knew taken from their high school yearbooks. Then these same photographs were rated by another person of the same age and sex as the yearbook owner who did not know the people in the photographs. This would be a rather straightforward exercise to do in class, provided students have their high school yearbooks! Students rate the attractiveness of photographs of graduates they knew from their own yearbook, and then these same photographs are rated by another student of the same age and sex as the yearbook owner who does not know the people in the photographs. You can collect data and then combine them with ratings from other students who participated in the exercise. What are your independent and dependent variables? What is your hypothesis and why? What are your expected results and why?

6. Consider the following "thought experiment" taken from the psychologist Paula M. Niedenthal's (2007) review published in *Science*, "Embodying Emotion": A man goes into a bar to tell a new joke. Two people are already in the bar. One is smiling and one is frowning. Who is more likely to "get" the punch line and appreciate his joke? (p. 1002)

You probably could easily guess correctly that the smiling person would get the joke. But describe how the research of Ekman and colleagues could be used as evidence for your answer.

# Review Questions

1. Why is a naturalistic observational methodology considered to be a nonexperimental study? What are the strengths and limitations of nonexperimental studies?

2. Describe how Paul Ekman's studies of facial expression of emotions addressed cross-cultural differences.

3. Compare and contrast deductive and inductive research strategies.

4. Identify and explain the three criteria for establishing cause and effect.

5. Describe how a researcher develops and uses conceptual and operational definitions.

6. Describe how there are the three kinds of evidence that are needed to establish causality. Why should a psychological researcher always be skeptical about interpreting evidence of causality?

7. How might a third variable serve to confound the interpretation of results? What should a researcher do when concerned about third variables?

8. Explain how it is that a theory cannot be directly tested. If this is so, how does a researcher go about evaluating a theory?

9. When obtained results achieve statistical significance, what does that mean precisely?

10. External validity and ecological validity are two important considerations in evaluating research.

What do they mean? How are they related? How are they different?

11. What considerations should you keep in mind when using popular search engines, such as Google Scholar?

12. Science journalism and popular science represent two interesting sources for developing thoughts and ideas about research. How would you use these sources as leads in pursuing a research question?

13. How might confirmatory bias on the part of the researcher contaminate a literature review? What can be done to reduce confirmatory bias in literature reviews?

14. What is peer review, and why is it important?

15. How would you review each of the sections of an empirical article?

16. What is the purpose of a control group?

17. Explain how an obtained result could achieve statistical significance but be of a small effect size.

18. Explain the fundamental truism that you cannot infer causality on the basis of correlation.

19. Explain how a correlation coefficient contains two critical pieces of information about the relationship of two variables: (a) the strength of the relationship and (b) the direction of the relationship.

20. How does publication bias influence a literature review?

CHAPTER 3

# Ethics in Behavioral Research

## LEARNING OBJECTIVES: FAST FACTS

- Stanley **Milgram's obedience experiments** led to intensive debate about the extent to which deception could be tolerated in psychological research and how harm to subjects should be evaluated.

- Egregious violations of human rights by researchers, including scientists in Nazi Germany and researchers in the Tuskegee syphilis study, led to the adoption of federal ethical standards for research on human subjects.

- The 1979 Belmont Report developed by a national commission established three basic ethical standards for the protection of human subjects: respect for persons, beneficence, and justice. The American Psychological Association added two other principles. The Department of Health and Human Services adopted in 1991 the Federal Policy for the Protection of Human Subjects. This policy requires that every institution seeking federal funding for biomedical or behavioral research on human subjects have an institutional review board (IRB) to exercise oversight.

## TESTING BEFORE LEARNING

Try your hand at these questions. Don't worry about not knowing the correct response, as you haven't read the chapter yet! But research shows that a pretest such as this can enhance learning (e.g., Kornell, Hays, & Bjork, 2009). So here is the answer. You come up with the question.

1. Used to reduce risk of harm due to deception in an experiment
   a. What is informed consent?
   b. What is debriefing?
   c. What is beneficence?
   d. What is justice?

2. Respect for persons, beneficence, and justice
   a. What is an institutional review board (IRB)?
   b. What is the Health Insurance Portability and Accountability Act (HIPAA)?
   c. What are the three basic ethical standards of the 1979 Belmont Report for the protection of human subjects?
   d. What is the Certificate of Confidentiality?

3. Required by federal regulations for every institution that seeks federal funding for biomedical or behavioral research on human subjects
   a. What is an IRB?
   b. What is the Health Insurance Portability and Accountability Act (HIPAA)?
   c. What is the Office for Protection From Research Risks?
   d. What is the 1979 Belmont Report?

4. Achieving valid results is the necessary starting point for ethical research practice.
   a. What is the principle of justice?
   b. What is the principle of confidentiality?
   c. What is the principle of beneficence and nonmaleficence?
   d. What is the principle of fidelity and responsibility?

5. Protection of research participants
   a. What is the most important ethical principle?
   b. What is an optional research practice?
   c. What is the least important ethical principle?
   d. What is an aspirational ethical principle?

6. An important document that should explain in plain language the risks and benefits of participating in a research study
   a. What is the Certificate of Confidentiality?
   b. What is the Federal Policy for the Protection of Human Subjects?
   c. What is the informed consent form?
   d. What is the Health Insurance Portability and Accountability Act (HIPAA)?

7. Applies to ethical standards that are set by federal regulations
   a. What is the APA Ethical Code of Conduct?
   b. What is an IRB?
   c. What is peer review?
   d. What is confidentiality?

8. In the famous Zimbardo prison simulation study, the psychologist Phillip Zimbardo served as both "warden" in the simulated prison and the principal investigator who was responsible for deciding whether the study should be continued as planned.
   a. What is a valid research design?
   b. What is staged manipulation?
   c. What is an ethical conflict of interest?
   d. What is random assignment?

9. This is the most important ethical criticism of the Milgram study.
   a. Why were more measures not taken to avoid harming participants?
   b. Why were the participants not randomly assigned to study conditions?
   c. Why did Milgram conduct his study at Yale University?
   d. Why were the participants debriefed?

10. Voluntary nature of participation in a study should be made explicitly clear.
    a. What is obtaining confidentiality?
    b. What is random assignment?
    c. What is obtaining informed consent?
    d. What is debriefing?

**ANSWER KEY:** (1) b; (2) c; (3) a; (4) d; (5) a; (6) c; (7) b; (8) c; (9) a; (10) c

# Obedience to Authority

Let's begin with a thought experiment (or a trip down memory lane, depending on your prior exposure to this example). One spring morning as you are drinking coffee and reading the newspaper, you notice a small ad for a psychology experiment at the local university. "Earn money and learn about yourself," it says. Feeling a bit bored with your job as a high school teacher, you call and schedule an evening visit to the lab.

**WE WILL PAY YOU $45 FOR ONE HOUR OF YOUR TIME**

*Persons Needed for a Study of Memory*

You arrive at the assigned room at the university, ready for an interesting hour or so, and are impressed immediately by the elegance of the building and the professional appearance of the personnel. In the waiting room, you see a man dressed in a lab technician's coat talking to another visitor—a middle-aged fellow dressed in casual attire. The man in the lab coat turns and introduces himself and explains that, as a psychologist, he is interested in the question of whether people learn things better when they are punished for making a mistake. He quickly convinces you that this is a very important question for which there has been no adequate answer; he then explains that his experiment on punishment and learning will help answer this question. Then he announces, "I'm going to ask one of you to be the teacher here tonight and the other one to be the learner." "The experimenter" (as we'll refer to him from now on) says he will write either "teacher" or "learner" on small identical slips of paper and then asks both of you to draw one. Yours says "teacher." The experimenter now says, in a matter-of-fact way, "All right. Now, the first thing we'll have to do is to set the learner up so that he can get some type of punishment."

He leads you both behind a curtain, sits the learner down, attaches a wire to his left wrist, and straps both of his arms to the chair so that he cannot remove the wire (Exhibit 3.1). The wire is connected to a console with 30 switches and a large dial on the other side of the room. When you ask what the wire is for, the experimenter says he will demonstrate. He then asks you to hold the end of the wire, walks back to the control console, flips several switches, and focuses his attention on the dial. You hear a clicking noise, see the dial move, and then feel an electric shock in your hand. The shock increases, and the dial registers more current when the experimenter flips the next switch on the console.

"Oh, I see," you say. "This is the punishment. Couldn't it cause injury?" The experimenter explains

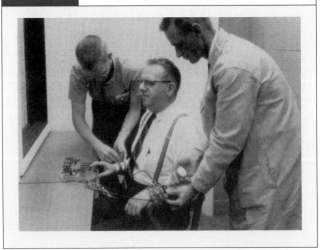

**Exhibit 3.1** Learner Strapped in Chair With Electrodes

that the machine is calibrated so that it will not cause permanent injury but acknowledges that when it is turned up all the way it is very, very painful and can result in severe, although momentary, discomfort.

Now you walk back to the other side of the room (so that the learner is behind the curtain) and sit before the console (Exhibit 3.2). The experimental procedure has four simple steps. (1) You read aloud a series of word pairs, like *blue box, nice day, wild duck,* and so forth. (2) Next, you read one of the first words from those pairs and a set of four words, one of which contains the original paired word. For example, you might say, "blue: sky ink box lamp." (3) The learner states the word that he thinks was paired with the first word you read (*blue*). If he gives a correct response, you compliment him and move on to the next word. If he makes a mistake, you flip

**Exhibit 3.2**  Milgram's "Shock Generator"

a switch on the console. This causes the learner to feel a shock on his wrist. (4) After each mistake, you are to flip the next switch on the console, progressing from left to right. You note that there is a label corresponding to every 5th mark on the dial, with the 1st mark labeled "slight shock," the 5th mark labeled "moderate shock," the 10th "strong shock," and so on through "very strong shock," "intense shock," "extreme-intensity shock," and "danger: severe shock."

You begin. The learner at first gives some correct answers, but then, he makes a few errors. Soon you are beyond the 5th mark ("slight shock") and are moving in the direction of more and more severe shocks. You recall having heard about this experiment, and so you know that as you turn the dial, the learner's responses increase in intensity from a grunt at the 15th mark ("strong shock") to painful groans at higher levels, to anguished cries to "get me out of here" at the "extreme-intensity shock" levels, to a deathly silence at the highest level. You also know that as you proceed and indicate your discomfort at administering the stronger shocks, the experimenter will tell you, "The experiment requires that you continue" and, occasionally, "It is absolutely essential that you continue." Please mark on the console below the most severe shock that you would agree to give the learner (Exhibit 3.3).

You may very well recognize that this thought experiment is a slightly simplified version of the famous "obedience" experiments by Stanley Milgram begun at Yale University in 1960. Did you know that Milgram also surveyed Yale undergraduates and asked them to indicate at what level they would terminate their "shocks"? The average (mean) maximum shock level predicted by the Yale undergraduates was 9.35, corresponding to a "strong" shock. Only one student predicted that he would provide a stimulus above that level, but only barely so, for he said that he would stop at the "very strong" level. Responses were similar from nonstudent groups who were asked the same question.

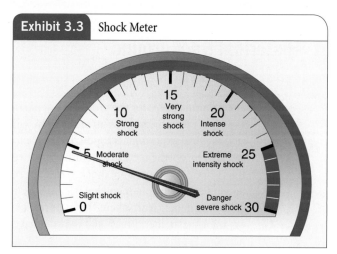

**Exhibit 3.3**  Shock Meter

What was the actual average level of shock administered by the 40 New Haven adults who volunteered for the experiment? It was 24.53, or a level higher than "extreme-intensity shock" and just short of the "danger: severe shock" level. Twenty-five (62.5%) of Milgram's original 40 subjects complied with the experimenter's demands all the way to the top of the scale (originally labeled simply as "XXX"). And lest you pass this result off as simply the result of the subjects having thought that the experiment wasn't real, we hasten to point out that there is abundant evidence from the subjects' own observed high stress and their subsequent reports that many subjects really believed that the learner was receiving actual, hurtful shocks.

Are you surprised by the subjects' responses? By the Yale undergraduates' predictions of so many compassionate responses? By your own response? (We leave it to you to assess how accurately you predicted the response you would have given if you had been an actual subject.)

Of course, our purpose in introducing this little "experiment" is not to focus attention on the prediction of obedience to authority; instead, we want to introduce the topic of research ethics by encouraging you to think about research from the standpoint of the people who are the subjects of behavioral research. We refer to Milgram's research on obedience throughout this chapter, since it is fair to say that this research ultimately had as profound an influence on the way psychologists think about research ethics as it had on the way psychologists understand obedience to authority.

Every psychologist needs to consider how to practice the discipline ethically, whether that practice involves clinical care about personal problems, research to learn about human behavior, or a combination of both. Although the 15 ethical standards in the "research and publication" category are but a fraction of the 83 standards in the entire 2002 **Code of Conduct, American Psychological Association** (APA), it is not possible to draw a clear dividing line between ethics applicable to clinical and to research practice: Whenever we interact with other people as psychologists, we must give paramount importance to the rational concerns and emotional needs that will shape their responses to our actions. It is here that ethical research practice begins, with the recognition that our research procedures involve people who deserve as much respect for their well-being as we do.

# Historical Background

Formal procedures for the protection of participants in research grew out of some widely publicized abuses. A defining event occurred in 1946, when the **Nuremberg War Crime Trials** exposed the horrific medical experiments conducted by Nazi doctors and others in the name of "science." Milgram's research on obedience also generated controversy about participant protections (Perry, 2013, p. 37). In the 1970s, Americans were shocked to learn that researchers funded by the U.S. Public Health Service had followed 399 low-income African American men in the **Tuskegee syphilis study** in the 1930s, collecting data to learn about the "natural" course of the illness (Exhibit 3.4). Many participants were not informed of their illness and were denied treatment until 1972, even though a cure (penicillin) was developed in the 1950s.

| **Exhibit 3.4** | Tuskegee Syphilis Experiment |

Egregious violations of human rights like these resulted in the United States in the creation of the National commission for the Protection of Human Subjects of Biomedical and Behavioral Research. The commission's 1979 **Belmont Report** (U.S. Department of Health, Education, and Welfare, 1979) established three basic ethical principles for the protection of human subjects (Exhibit 3.5):

1. **Respect for persons:** Treating persons as autonomous agents and protecting those with diminished autonomy

2. **Beneficence:** Minimizing possible harms and maximizing benefits

3. **Justice:** Distributing the benefits and risks of research fairly

The Department of Health and Human Services and the Food and Drug Administration then translated these principles into specific regulations that were adopted in 1991 as the **Federal Policy for the Protection of Human Subjects**. This policy has shaped the course of social science research ever since, and you will have to take it into account as you design your own research investigations. Professional associations like the APA, university review boards, and ethics committees in other organizations also set standards for the treatment of human subjects by their members, employees, and students, although these standards are all designed to comply with the federal policy. This section introduces these regulations.

Federal regulations require that every institution that seeks federal funding for biomedical or behavioral research on human subjects have an **institutional review board (IRB)** that reviews

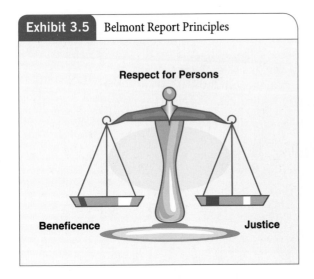

**Exhibit 3.5** Belmont Report Principles

research proposals. IRBs at universities and other agencies apply ethical standards that are set by federal regulations but can be expanded or specified by the IRB itself (Sieber, 1992). To promote adequate review of ethical issues, the regulations require that IRBs include members with diverse backgrounds. The Office for Protection from Research Risks, National Institutes of Health, monitors IRBs, with the exception of research involving drugs (which is the responsibility of the federal Food and Drug Administration).

The APA started the process of developing an ethics code in 1938, when it formed a committee to consider the issue (Korn, 1997). Work on a formal APA ethics code then began in 1947 (Fisher, 2003). A committee reviewed more than 1,000 descriptions of "critical incidents" in which practicing psychologists had been confronted by ethical issues, deliberated about the ethical principles that should guide decisions in such incidents, and sought feedback from APA members. The resulting ethics code was published in 1953 and has subsequently been revised nine times (Fisher, 2003).

## Ethical Principles

The 2002 APA Ethics Code, the most recent version, contains 151 enforceable ethical standards as well as five general principles. The general principles are meant to be general "aspirational" values that capture the discipline's "moral vision" and are consistent with the Belmont Report's three ethical principles, while the ethical standards are meant to apply to all APA members and to be enforced by the APA Ethics Committee. In addition, more than half of the state boards that license psychologists as well as numerous other bodies stipulate that psychologists must comply with the APA Ethics Code. Violations of the code can be investigated by the APA Ethics Committee and can lead to sanctions ranging from a reprimand to expulsion. (Detailed procedures are available at http://www.apa.org/ethics/code/index.aspx.) Of course, legal actions by aggrieved parties are also a possibility, but violations of the code are not in and of themselves legal violations (Fisher, 2003).

Fifteen of the code's 151 enforceable standards pertain specifically to research and publication, but many others—on competence, human relations, privacy and confidentiality, and assessment—have direct implications for research practice. The APA's general principles for ethical practice reflect this view of research ethics as part of a commitment to overarching ethical principles across all areas of psychological practice. We present these principles first as a foundation for our own discussion of specific ethical standards (APA, 2010b).

*Principle A. Beneficence and Nonmaleficence:* Psychologists strive to benefit those with whom they work and take care to do no harm. In their professional actions, psychologists seek to safeguard the welfare and rights of those with whom they interact professionally and other affected persons and the welfare of animal subjects of research. When conflicts occur among psychologists' obligations or concerns, they attempt to resolve these conflicts in a responsible fashion that avoids or minimizes harm. Because psychologists' scientific and professional judgments and actions may affect the lives of others, they are alert to and guard against personal, financial, social, organizational, or political factors that might lead to misuse of their influence. Psychologists strive to be aware of the possible effect of their own physical and mental health on their ability to help those with whom they work.

*Principle B. Fidelity and Responsibility:* Psychologists establish relationships of trust with those with whom they work. They are aware of their professional and scientific responsibilities to society and to the scientific communities in which they work. Psychologists uphold professional standards of conduct, clarify their professional roles and obligations, accept appropriate responsibility for their behavior, and seek to manage conflicts of interest that could lead to exploitation or harm. Psychologists consult with, refer to, or cooperate with other professionals and institutions to the extent needed to serve the best interests of those with whom they work. They are concerned about the ethical compliance of their colleagues' scientific and professional conduct. Psychologists strive to contribute a portion of their professional time for little or no compensation or personal advantage.

*Principle C. Integrity:* Psychologists seek to promote accuracy, honesty, and truthfulness in the science, teaching, and practice of psychology. In these activities, psychologists do not steal, cheat, or engage in fraud, subterfuge, or intentional misrepresentation of fact. Psychologists strive to keep their promises and to avoid unwise or unclear commitments. In situations in which deception may be ethically justifiable to maximize benefits and minimize harm, psychologists have a serious obligation to consider the need for, the possible consequences of, and their responsibility to correct any resulting mistrust or other harmful effects that arise from the use of such techniques.

*Principle D. Justice:* Psychologists recognize that fairness and justice entitle all persons to access to and benefit from the contributions of psychology and to equal quality in the processes, procedures, and services being conducted by psychologists. Psychologists exercise reasonable judgment and take precautions to ensure that their potential biases, the boundaries of their competence, and the limitations of their expertise do not lead to or condone unjust practices.

*Principle E. Respect for People's Rights and Dignity:* Psychologists respect the dignity and worth of all people and the rights of individuals to privacy, confidentiality, and self-determination. Psychologists are aware that special safeguards may be necessary to protect the rights and welfare of persons or communities whose vulnerabilities impair autonomous decision making. Psychologists are aware of and respect cultural, individual, and role differences, including those based on age, gender, gender identity, race, ethnicity, culture, national origin, religion, sexual orientation, disability, language, and socioeconomic status and consider these factors when working with members of such groups. Psychologists try to eliminate the effect on their work of biases based on those factors, and they do not knowingly participate in or condone activities of others based upon such prejudices.

Did Milgram respect these principles in the obedience experiments? Perhaps it is unfair to judge his research in light of principles adopted 40 years later, but it is still instructive to ask the question. No doubt you already want to know more of the details in order to evaluate whether Milgram took "care to do no harm" and established "relationships of trust" with his subjects. We will report many of these details in this chapter. But do you also see that we have to convert these abstract principles into concrete standards before we can hope to evaluate the degree of harm, trust, and other features of a research project, no matter how current that project is or what details we have learned about it?

We have organized our discussion of ethical standards for research under four headings that reflect the five APA principles:

1. To achieve valid results

2. To maintain professional integrity

3. To protect research subjects

4. To encourage appropriate application

Each of these principles became a focus of debate about Milgram's experiments, so we will return frequently to that debate to keep our discussion realistic. We will also refer frequently to the 2002 APA Ethics Code to keep our treatment current. You will soon realize that there is no simple answer to the question of what is (or isn't) ethical research practice or, more generally, which practices are consistent with the APA's general principles. The issues are just too complicated and the relevant principles too subject to different interpretations. But we do promise that by the time you finish this chapter, you will be aware of the major issues in research ethics and be able to make informed, defensible decisions about the ethical conduct of psychological research.

Bear in mind that no specific ethical standard can implement fully the intent of an abstract principle. In addition, you will soon realize that most of the specific standards help implement more than one of the five principles. So as you read about the standards in each of the following sections, ask yourself two questions: (1) Do these standards capture the intent of the general principle? (2) Do these standards help implement any other general principles?

## Achieving Valid Results (Principle B: Fidelity and Responsibility)

Commitment to achieving valid results is the necessary starting point for ethical research practice. Simply put, we have no business asking people to answer questions, submit to observations, or participate in experimental procedures if we are simply seeking to verify our existing prejudices or convince others to take action on behalf of our personal interests. It is the pursuit of objective knowledge about human behavior—the goal of validity—that motivates and justifies our investigations and gives us some claim to the right to influence others to participate in our research. Knowledge is the foundation of human progress as well as the basis for our expectation that we, as behavioral scientists, can help people achieve a brighter future. If we approach our research projects objectively, setting aside our personal predilections in the service of learning a bit more about human behavior, we can honestly represent our actions as potentially contributing to the advancement of knowledge.

Milgram made a strong case in his 1963 article and 1974 book on the obedience experiments that he was committed to achieving valid results—to learning how and why obedience influences behavior. He tied his motivations directly to the horror of the Holocaust, to which the world's attention had been drawn once again by the capture and trial of Hitler's mastermind of that genocide, Adolf Eichmann (Perry, 2013, p. 210). In Milgram's (1963) own words,

It has been reliably established that from 1933–45 millions of innocent persons were systematically slaughtered on command. . . . Obedience is the psychological mechanism that links individual action to political purpose. It is the dispositional cement that binds men to systems of authority . . . for many persons obedience may be a deeply ingrained behavior tendency. . . . Obedience may [also] be ennobling and educative and refer to acts of charity and kindness, as well as to destruction. (p. 371)

Milgram (1963) then explains how he devised experiments to study the process of obedience in a way that would seem realistic to the subjects and still allow "important variables to be manipulated at several points in the experiment" (p. 372). According to Milgram, every step in the experiment was carefully designed—and documented—to ensure that subjects received identical and believable stimuli and that their responses were measured carefully. The experiment's design reflected what had become in the preceding 30 years a social psychology research tradition of laboratory experiments in which participants were deceived by manipulations that seemed realistic (Perry, 2013, pp. 31–35).

Milgram (1963) made every effort to convince readers that "the particular conditions" of his experiment created the conditions for achieving valid results (p. 377). These particular conditions included the setting for the experiment at Yale University, its purported "worthy purpose" to advance knowledge about learning and memory, and the voluntary participation of the subject as well as the learner—as far as the subject knew. Milgram then tested the importance of some of these "particular conditions" (e.g., the location at Yale) in replications of the basic experiment (Milgram, 1965).

However, not all psychologists agreed that Milgram's approach could achieve valid results. Milgram's first article, on the research, "Behavioral Study of Obedience," was published in 1963 in the *Journal of Abnormal and Social Psychology*. In the next year, the *American Psychologist* published a critique of the experiment's methods and ethics by the psychologist Diana Baumrind (1964). Her critique begins with a rejection of the external validity—the generalizability—of the experiment, because

the laboratory is unfamiliar as a setting and the rules of behavior ambiguous. . . . Therefore, the laboratory is not the place to study degree of obedience or suggestibility, as a function of a particular experimental condition.

[And so,] the parallel between authority-subordinate relationships in Hitler's Germany and in Milgram's laboratory is unclear. (p. 423)

Milgram (1964) quickly published a rejoinder, in which he disagreed with (among other things) the notion that it is inappropriate to study obedience in a laboratory setting: "A subject's obedience is no less problematical because it occurs within a social institution called the psychological experiment" (p. 850).

Milgram (1974) also argued in his later book that his experiment had been replicated in other places and settings with the same results, that there was considerable evidence that the subjects had believed that they actually were administering shocks, and that the "essence" of his experimental manipulation—the request that subjects comply with a legitimate authority—was also found in the dilemma faced by people in Nazi Germany, soldiers at the My Lai massacre in Vietnam, and even the cultists who drank poison in Jonestown, Guyana, at the command of their leader, Jim Jones (Miller, 1986).

Baumrind (1985) was still not convinced. In a follow-up article in the *American Psychologist*, she argued that "far from illuminating real life, as he claimed, Milgram in fact appeared to have constructed a set of conditions so internally inconsistent that they could not occur in real life" (p. 171). Although Stanley Milgram died in 1984, a recent review of the transcripts and other original data from his research raises additional concerns about its validity. Milgram never publicized one condition in which most subjects refused to give strong shocks when the "learner" was a friend (Perry, 2013, p. 177). More of the subjects than Milgram acknowledged resisted the command that they continue with the shocks, and even those who were classified as "obedient" "were all looking for a way to get out of the experiments" (Perry, 2013, p. 296).

Do you agree with Milgram's assumption that obedience could fruitfully be studied in the laboratory? Do you find merit in Baumrind's criticism? Are you troubled by the new evidence that Milgram may have presented his evidence selectively to make his conclusions as convincing as possible? Will your evaluation of the ethics of Milgram's experiments be influenced by your answers to these questions? Should our ethical judgments differ depending on whether we decide that a study provides valid information about important social-psychological processes?

We can't answer these questions for you, but before you dismiss them as inappropriate when dealing with ethical standards for the treatment of human subjects, bear in mind that both Milgram and his strongest critic at the time, Baumrind, buttressed their ethical arguments with assertions about the validity (or invalidity) of the experimental results. It is hard to justify *any* risk for human subjects, or even *any* expenditure of time and resources, if our findings tell us nothing about human behavior.

## Maintaining Professional Integrity (Principle C: Integrity)

How can you assess the validity of an experiment or other research method? The scientific concern with validity requires in turn that scientists be open in disclosing their methods and honest in presenting their findings (APA Ethics Code). By contrast, research distorted by political or personal pressures to find particular outcomes or to achieve the most marketable results is unlikely to be carried out in an honest and open fashion. To assess the validity of a researcher's conclusions and the ethics of their procedures, you need to know exactly how the research was conducted. This means that articles or other reports must include a detailed methodology section, perhaps supplemented by appendices containing the research instruments or websites or other contact information where more information can be obtained.

Milgram presented his research in a way that would signal his adherence to the goal of honesty and openness. His initial 1963 article included a detailed description of study procedures, including the text of the general introduction to participants, the procedures involved in the learning task, the "shock generator," the administration of the "sample shock," the shock instructions and the preliminary practice run, the standardized feedback from the "victim" and from the experimenter, and the measures used. Many more details, including pictures, were provided in Milgram's (1974) subsequent book (Exhibit 3.6).

| Exhibit 3.6 | Diagram of Milgram Experiment |

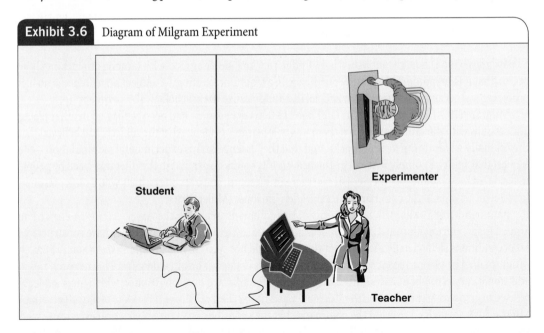

The act of publication itself is a vital element in maintaining openness and honesty. Others can review and question study procedures and so generate an open dialogue with the researcher. Although Milgram disagreed sharply with Baumrind's criticisms of his experiments, their mutual commitment to public discourse in journals widely available to psychologists resulted in a more comprehensive presentation of study procedures and more thoughtful discourse about research ethics. Almost 50 years later, this commentary continues to inform debates about research ethics.

The latest significant publication in this open dialogue about Milgram's work actually calls into question his own commitment to the standard of openness and honesty. In *Behind the Shock Machine: The Untold Story of the Notorious Milgram Psychology Experiments*, Perry (2013) presents evidence from research records and participant interviews that Milgram's publications contained misleading statements about participants' postexperiment **debriefing**, about adherence to the treatment protocol, about the extent of participants' apparent distress, and about the extent of support for his favored outcome.

Openness about research procedures and results thus goes hand in hand with honesty in research design and in research reporting. In spite of this need for openness, some researchers may hesitate to disclose their procedures or results to prevent others from building on their ideas and taking some of the credit or, as may have occurred with Milgram, to make their procedures seem more acceptable or their findings more impressive. You may have heard of the long legal battle between a U.S. researcher, Dr. Robert Gallo, and a French researcher, Dr. Luc Montagnier, about how credit for discovering the AIDS virus should be allocated. Although a public dispute such as this one is unusual—even more unusual is its resolution through an agreement announced by the then president Ronald Reagan and the then prime minister Jacques Chirac (Altman, 1987)—concerns with priority of discovery are common. Scientists are like other people in their desire to be first. Enforcing standards of honesty and encouraging openness about research are the best solutions to these problems (as exemplified by the chronology of discovery that Gallo and Montagnier jointly developed as part of the agreement).

Test your knowledge of this chapter so far by taking the mid-chapter quiz on the study site: www.sagepub.com/nestor2e

## Protecting Research Participants (Principle A: Beneficence and Nonmaleficence)

Protection of research participants is the most important ethical principle, so you will probably not be surprised to learn that several specific ethical standards in the APA Ethics Code pertain to it. We will again focus attention on the obedience experiments, since the most serious charge leveled against the ethics of Milgram's study was that he had harmed his subjects. We will organize our discussion of the APA ethical standards in this area into four subcategories:

1. Avoid harming research participants (Standard 3.04)

2. Obtain informed consent (Standards 3.10, 8.02–8.06)

3. Avoid deception in research, except in limited circumstances (Standards 8.07, 8.08)

4. Maintain privacy and confidentiality (Standards 4.01–4.07)

### Avoid Harming Research Participants

Although this standard may seem straightforward, it can be difficult to interpret in specific cases and harder yet to define in a way agreeable to all behavioral scientists. Does it mean that subjects should not be at all harmed psychologically as well as physically? That they should feel no anxiety or distress whatever during the study nor after their involvement ends? Should the possibility of any harm, no matter how remote, deter research?

Before we address these questions with respect to Milgram's experiments, a verbatim transcript of one session will give you an idea of what participants experienced (Milgram, 1965, p. 67):

*150 volts delivered.* You want me to keep going?

*165 volts delivered.* That guy is hollering in there. There's a lot of them [questions] here. He's liable to have a heart condition. You want me to go on?

*180 volts delivered.* He can't stand it! I'm not going to kill that man in there! You hear him hollering? He's hollering. He can't stand it. . . . I mean who is going to take responsibility if anything happens to that gentleman?

*[The experimenter accepts responsibility.]* All right.

*195 volts delivered.* You see he's hollering. Hear that. Gee, I don't know. *[The experimenter says: "The experiment requires that you go on."]* I know it does, sir, but I mean—hugh—he don't know what he's in for. He's up to 195 volts.

*210 volts delivered.*

*225 volts delivered.*

*240 volts delivered.*

This experimental manipulation generated "extraordinary tension" (Milgram, 1963):

Subjects were observed to sweat, tremble, stutter, bite their lips, groan and dig their fingernails into their flesh. . . . Full-blown, uncontrollable seizures were observed for 3 subjects. [O]ne . . . seizure so violently convulsive that it was necessary to call a halt to the experiment [for that individual]. (p. 375)

An observer (behind a one-way mirror) reported, "I observed a mature and initially poised businessman enter the laboratory smiling and confident. Within 20 minutes he was reduced to a twitching, stuttering wreck, who was rapidly approaching a point of nervous collapse" (Milgram, 1963, p. 377).

From the critic Baumrind's (1964) perspective, this emotional disturbance in subjects was "potentially harmful because it could easily effect an alteration in the subject's self-image or ability to trust adult authorities in the future" (p. 422). Milgram (1964) quickly countered that

momentary excitement is not the same as harm. As the experiment progressed there was no indication of injurious effects in the subjects; and as the subjects themselves strongly endorsed the experiment, the judgment I made was to continue the experiment. (p. 849)

When Milgram (1964) surveyed participants in a follow-up, 83.7% endorsed the statement that they were "very glad" or "glad" "to have been in the experiment," 15.1% were "neither sorry nor glad," and just 1.3% were "sorry" or "very sorry" to have participated. Interviews by a psychiatrist a year later found no evidence "of any traumatic reactions" (p. 849)—although of the 780 initial participants, only 140 were invited for an interview and only 32 accepted the invitation (Perry, 2013, p. 217). Subsequently, Milgram (1977) argued that "the central moral justification for allowing my experiment is that it was judged acceptable by those who took part in it" (p. 21).

Milgram (1963) also reported that he attempted to minimize harm to subjects with postexperiment procedures "to assure that the subject would leave the laboratory in a state of well being" (p. 374). "A friendly reconciliation was arranged between the subject and the victim, and an effort was made to reduce any tensions that arose as a result of the experiment" (p. 374). In some cases, the "dehoaxing" (or "debriefing") discussion was extensive, and Milgram (1964) claimed that all subjects were promised (and later received) a comprehensive report.

Professor Baumrind (1964) was unconvinced, writing, "It would be interesting to know what sort of procedures could dissipate the type of emotional disturbance just described" (p. 422; citing Milgram, 1964). In a later article, Baumrind (1985) dismissed the value of the self-reported "lack of harm" of subjects who had been willing to participate in the experiment—although noting that still 16% did *not* endorse the statement that they were "glad" they had participated in the experiment. Baumrind (1985) also argued that research indicates that most introductory psychology students who have participated in a deception experiment report a decreased trust in authorities as a result—a tangible harm in itself.

Many social scientists, ethicists, and others concluded that Milgram's procedures had not harmed the subjects and so were justified for the knowledge they produced, but others sided with Baumrind's criticisms (Miller, 1986; Perry, 2013, p. 269). Perry's (2013) recent investigation found even more evidence of psychological harm, including feelings of shame that had persisted since the experiment (pp. 77–78). The experimental records also reveal that debriefing never occurred for some participants and was very limited for almost all (pp. 76–84). Most were not told after the experiment that the shocks were fake; the usual "dehoaxing" consisted of the "learner" reassuring the "teacher" that the shocks he had received were not harmful.

What is your opinion of the possibility for harm at this point? Does Milgram's debriefing process relieve your concerns? Are you as persuaded by the subjects' own endorsement of the experiment as was Milgram?

What about possible harm to the subjects of **Zimbardo's prison simulation study** at Stanford University (Haney, Banks, & Zimbardo, 1973)? The study was designed to investigate the impact of social position on behavior—specifically, the impact of being either a guard or a prisoner in a prison, a "total institution." The researchers selected apparently stable and mature young male volunteers and asked them to sign a contract to work for 2 weeks as a guard or a prisoner in a simulated prison. Within the first 2 days after the prisoners were incarcerated by the guards in a makeshift basement prison, the prisoners began to be passive and disorganized, while the guards became sadistic—verbally and physically aggressive (Exhibit 3.7). Five prisoners were soon released for depression, uncontrollable crying, fits of rage, and, in one case, a psychosomatic rash. Instead of letting things continue for 2 weeks as planned, Zimbardo and his colleagues terminated the experiment after 6 days to avoid harming the subjects.

Through discussions in special postexperiment encounter sessions, feelings of stress among the participants who played the role of prisoner seemed to be relieved; follow-up during the next year indicated no lasting negative effects on the participants and some benefits in the form of greater insight.

Would you ban such experiments because of the potential for harm to subjects? Does the fact that Zimbardo's and Milgram's experiments seemed to yield significant insights into the effect of a social situation on human behavior—insights that could be used to improve prisons or perhaps lessen the likelihood of another Holocaust—make any difference (Reynolds, 1979)? Do you believe that this benefit outweighs the foreseeable risks?

Well-intentioned researchers may also fail to foresee all the potential problems. Milgram (1974) reported that he and his colleagues were surprised by the subjects' willingness to carry out such severe shocks. In Zimbardo's prison simulation, all the participants signed consent forms, but how could they have been fully informed in advance? The researchers themselves did not realize that the study participants would experience so much stress so quickly, that some prisoners would have to be released for severe negative reactions within the first few days, or that even those who were not severely stressed would soon

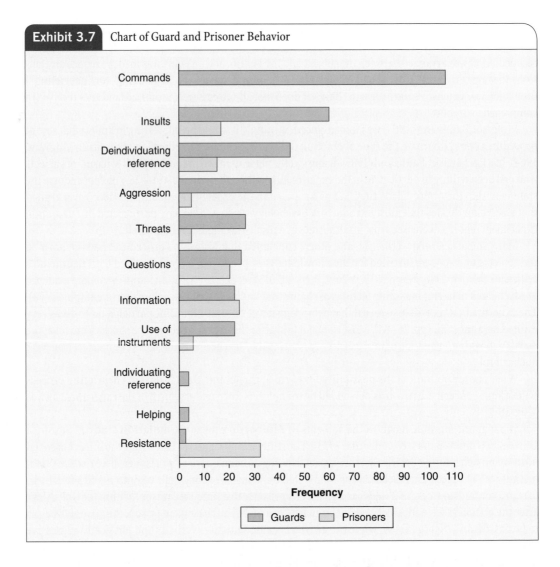

**Exhibit 3.7** Chart of Guard and Prisoner Behavior

be begging to be released from the mock prison. If this risk was not foreseeable, was it acceptable for the researchers to presume in advance that the benefits would outweigh the risks? And are you concerned, like Arthur Miller (1986), that real harm "could result from *not doing* research on destructive obedience" (p. 138) and other troubling human behaviors?

### Obtain Informed Consent

The requirement of informed consent is also more difficult to define than it first appears. To be informed, consent must be given by persons who are competent to consent, have consented voluntarily, are fully informed about the research, and have comprehended what they have been told (Reynolds, 1979). Yet you probably realize, like Baumrind (1985), that due to the inability to communicate perfectly, "full disclosure of everything that could possibly affect a given subject's decision to participate is not possible, and therefore cannot be ethically required" (p. 165).

Obtaining informed consent creates additional challenges for researchers. The researcher's actions and body language should help convey his verbal assurance that consent is voluntary. The language of the consent form must be clear and understandable to the research participants and yet sufficiently long and detailed to explain what will actually happen in the research. Exhibits 3.8 and 3.9, from the authors' own research, illustrate two different approaches to these trade-offs. The consent form in Exhibit 3.8 was approved by a university for a psychology experiment with undergraduate students. It is brief and to the point but leaves quite a bit to the imagination of the prospective participants. The consent form in Exhibit 3.9 reflects the requirements of an academic hospital's IRB. Because the hospital is used to reviewing research proposals involving drugs and other treatment interventions with hospital patients, it requires a very detailed and lengthy explanation of procedures and related issues, even for a simple survey. You can probably imagine that the requirement that prospective participants sign such lengthy consent forms can reduce their willingness to participate in research and perhaps influence their responses if they do agree to participate (Larson, 1993).

---

**Exhibit 3.8**  UMB Consent Form

University of Massachusetts at Boston
Department of Psychology
100 Morrissey Boulevard
Boston, MA 02125-3393

Consent Form for the Project: "Examining Gaze Evoked Inhibition of Return and Its Implications for Social Communication"

*Introduction and Contact Information*

You have been asked to take part in a research project as described below. The researcher will explain the project to you in detail. You should feel free to ask questions. If you have further questions later, Paul Nestor, the person mainly responsible for this study, will discuss them with you. His telephone number is 617-287-6387.

*Description of the Project*

You have been asked to take part in a research study on eye gaze. This research seeks to improve our understanding of gaze processing as a key component underlying social communication, which will provide researchers with a better understanding of how problems associated with gaze processing are relevant for certain disorders, including schizophrenia and autism. The results of this study will be especially beneficial to the fields of psychology, medicine, and computer vision.

If you decide to take part in this research study, here is what will happen:

You will first fill out a few questionnaires that will ask you some background questions about yourself and also some questions about your thinking and beliefs. Then, you will sit in front of a computer screen, and the experimenter will mount the headset of an eye tracker device on your head. This device will determine your gaze position throughout the experiment. Prior to the experiment, a calibration procedure will be performed in order to maximize the system's precision of measurement. In this procedure, a dot will appear at nine different positions on the screen. You will be asked to track that dot, that is, to keep looking at it wherever it appears.

*(Continued)*

(Continued)

Afterwards, there will be a number of experimental trials. Before each trial, the experimenter will verbally explain to you the task that you have to complete. The tasks will require you to respond to a target either by pressing a button on a joystick or by shifting your eyes to the target. Your button press or eye movement will indicate your response. The first few trials will be practice trials that allow you to familiarize yourself with the interface. In the subsequent trials, you will be asked to perform as quickly and accurately as possible. The time from completing the questionnaires to the completion of the experiment will be approximately one hour and a half.

After the experiment, the experimenter will ask you some questions about your experience with the interface. She will ask you about the difficulty of each task and what you liked or disliked about it.

*Risks or Discomforts*

The equipment is not harmful to the eyes. It may happen that you feel discomfort after wearing the headset for some time. In that case, you should inform the experimenter, who will remove the headset immediately. After a break of a few minutes you can decide whether you want to continue your participation or quit the experiment.

By participating in this study, you will be part of the scientific effort to understand the importance of eye gaze processing in social communication. You will actively participate in the ongoing research by performing in the experimental tasks and delivering your feedback. Moreover, you will receive $10 for your participation.

*Confidentiality*

All information you provide throughout your assessment is confidential. None of the information will identify you by name. All information will be given a code number, and access to the data will be limited to the research team. The data will be stored in a locked file and destroyed after the research has been concluded.

*Participation and Rights*

The decision whether or not to take part in this research study is voluntary on your part. You do not have to participate. If you do decide to take part in this study, you may terminate your participation at any time. If you wish to terminate your participation in the research study, you simply inform Kristy Klein (617-319-7056) of your decision. Whatever you decide will in no way penalize you or affect your grade or status as a student.

You may also write or call a representative of the Institutional Review Board (IRB), at the University of Massachusetts at Boston, which oversees research involving human subjects. The Institutional Review Board may be reached at the following address: IRB, Office of Research and Sponsored Programs, Quinn Administration Building-2-015, University of Massachusetts at Boston, 100 Morrissey Boulevard, Boston, MA 02125-3393. You can contact the Board by telephone at (617) 287-5370 or at human. subjects@umb.edu.

I HAVE READ THE CONSENT FORM. MY QUESTIONS HAVE BEEN ANSWERED. MY SIGNATURE ON THIS FORM MEANS THAT I UNDERSTAND THE INFORMATION AND I CONSENT TO PARTICIPATE IN THIS STUDY. I ALSO CERTIFY THAT I AM 18 YEARS OF AGE OR OLDER.

_____     _____     _____
Signature of Participant              Date              Signature of Researcher

_____                        _____
Printed Name of Participant                      Printed Name of Researcher

**Exhibit 3.9** BIDMC Consent Form

**Research Consent Form for Social and Behavioral Research**

Dana-Farber/Harvard Cancer Center

BIDMC/BWH/CH/DFCI/MGH/Partners Network Affiliates OPRS 11-05 | OPRS 11-05

---

**Protocol Title:** ASSESSING COMMUNITY HEALTH WORKERS' ATTITUDES AND KNOWLEDGE ABOUT EDUCATING COMMUNITIES ABOUT CANCER CLINICAL TRIALS

**DF/HCC Principal Research Investigator / Institution:** Dr. Russell Schutt, Ph.D. / Beth Israel Deaconess Medical Center and Univ. of Massachusetts, Boston

**DF/HCC Site-Responsible Research Investigator(s) / Institution(s):**

Lidia Schapira, M.D. / Massachusetts General Hospital

**Interview Consent Form**

---

## A. INTRODUCTION

We are inviting you to take part in a research study. Research is a way of gaining new knowledge.

A person who participates in a research study is called a "subject." This research study is evaluating whether community health workers might be willing and able to educate communities about the pros and cons of participating in research studies.

It is expected that about 10 people will take part in this research study.

An institution that is supporting a research study either by giving money or supplying something that is important for the research is called the "sponsor." The sponsor of this protocol is National Cancer Institute and is providing money for the research study.

This research consent form explains why this research study is being done, what is involved in participating in the research study, the possible risks and benefits of the research study, alternatives to participation, and your rights as a research subject. The decision to participate is yours. If you decide to participate, please sign and date at the end of the form. We will give you a copy so that you can refer to it while you are involved in this research study.

If you decide to participate in this research study, certain questions will be asked of you to see if you are eligible to be in the research study. The research study has certain requirements that must be met. If the questions show that you can be in the research study, you will be able to answer the interview questions.

If the questions show that you cannot be in the research study, you will not be able to participate in this research study.

Page 1 of 6

| DFCI Protocol Number: 06-085 | Date DFCI IRB Approved this Consent Form: January 16, 2007 |
|---|---|
| Date Posted for Use: January 16, 2007 | Date DFCI IRB Approval Expires: August 13, 2007 |

*(Continued)*

(Continued)

**Research Consent Form for Social and Behavioral Research**

Dana-Farber/Harvard Cancer Center

BIDMC/BWH/CH/DFCI/MGH/Partners Network Affiliates OPRS 11-05                    OPRS 11-05

We encourage you to take some time to think this over and to discuss it with other people and to ask questions now and at any time in the future.

## B. WHY IS THIS RESEARCH STUDY BEING DONE?

Deaths from cancer in general and for some specific cancers are higher for black people compared to white people, for poor persons compared to nonpoor persons, and for rural residents compared to non-rural residents. There are many reasons for higher death rates between different subpopulations. One important area for changing this is to have more persons from minority groups participate in research about cancer. The process of enrolling minority populations into clinical trials is difficult and does not generally address the needs of their communities. One potential way to increase particpation in research is to use community health workers to help educate communities about research and about how to make sure that researchers are ethical. We want to know whether community health workers think this is a good strategy and how to best carry it out.

## C. WHAT OTHER OPTIONS ARE THERE?

Taking part in this research study is voluntary. Instead of being in this research study, you have the following option:

- Decide not to participate in this research study.

## D. WHAT IS INVOLVED IN THE RESEARCH STUDY?

**Before the research starts (screening):** After signing this consent form, you will be asked to answer some questions about where you work and the type of community health work you do to find out if you can be in the research study.

   If the answers show that you are eligible to participate in the research study, you will be eligible to participate in the research study. If you do not meet the eligibility criteria, you will not be able to participate in this research study.

**After the screening procedures confirm that you are eligible to participate in the research study:**
You will participate in an interview by answering questions from a questionnaire. The interview will take about 90 minutes. If there are questions you prefer not to answer we can skip those questions. The questions are about the type of work you do and your opinions about participating in research. If you agree, the interview will be taped and then transcribed. Your name and no other information about you will be associated

Page 2 of 6

| DFCI Protocol Number: | 06-085 | Date DFCI IRB Approved this Consent Form: | January 16, 2007 |
| Date Posted for Use: | January 16, 2007 | Date DFCI IRB Approval Expires: | August 13, 2007 |

**Research Consent Form for Social and
Behavioral Research**

Dana-Farber/Harvard Cancer Center

BIDMC/BWH/CH/DFCI/MGH/Partners Network Affiliates          OPRS 11-05

---

with the tape or the transcript. Only the research team will be able to listen to the tapes. Immediately following the interview, you will have the opportunity to have the tape erased if you wish to withdraw your consent to taping or participation in this study. You will receive $30.00 for completing this interview.

**After the interview is completed:** Once you finish the interview there are no additional interventions.

...

**N. DOCUMENTATION OF CONSENT**

My signature below indicates my willingness to participate in this research study and my understanding that I can withdraw at any time.

_____          _____

Signature of Subject                                           Date
or Legally Authorized Representative

_____          _____

Person obtaining consent                                  Date

---

**To be completed by person obtaining consent:**

The consent discussion was initiated on _____ (date) at _____ (time.)
☐ A copy of this signed consent form was given to the subject or legally authorized representative.

**For Adult Subjects**

☐ The subject is an adult and provided consent to participate.
☐ The subject is an adult who lacks capacity to provide consent and his/her legally authorized representative:
　☐ gave permission for the adult subject to participate
　☐ did not give permission for the adult subject to participate

---

Page 6 of 6

| DFCI Protocol Number: 06-085 | Date DFCI IRB Approved this Consent Form: January 16, 2007 |
| Date Posted for Use: January 16, 2007 | Date DFCI IRB Approval Expires: August 13, 2007 |

As in Milgram's study, experimental researchers whose research design requires some type of subject deception try to get around this problem by withholding some information before the experiment begins but then debriefing subjects at the end. In the debriefing, the researcher explains to the subject what happened in the experiment and why and responds to questions. A carefully designed debriefing procedure can help research participants learn from the experimental research and grapple constructively with feelings elicited by the realization that they were deceived (Sieber, 1992). However, even though debriefing can be viewed as a substitute, in some cases, for securing fully informed consent prior to the experiment, debriefed subjects who disclose the nature of the experiment to other participants can contaminate subsequent results (Adair, Dushenko, & Lindsay, 1985). Apparently for this reason, Milgram provided little information in his "debriefing" to participants in most of his experiments. It was only in the last 2 months of his study that he began to provide more information, while still asking participants not to reveal the true nature of the experimental procedures until after the study was completely over (Perry, 2013, pp. 76, 84). Unfortunately, if the debriefing process is delayed, the ability to lessen any harm resulting from the deception is also reduced.

For a study of the social background of men who engage in homosexual behavior in public facilities, Laud Humphreys (1970) decided that truly informed consent would be impossible to obtain. Instead, he first served as a lookout—a "watch queen"—for men who were entering a public bathroom in a city park with the intention of having sex. In a number of cases, he then left the bathroom and copied the license plate numbers of the cars driven by the men. One year later, he visited the homes of the men and interviewed them as part of a larger study of social issues. Humphreys changed his appearance so that the men did not recognize him. In *Tearoom Trade* (1970), his book on this research, Humphreys concluded that the men who engaged in what were viewed as deviant acts were, for the most part, married, suburban men whose families were unaware of their sexual practices. But debate has continued ever since about Humphreys's failure to tell the men what he was really doing in the bathroom or why he had come to their homes for the interview. He was criticized by many, including some faculty members at the University of Washington who urged that his doctoral degree be withheld. However, many other professors and some members of the gay community praised Humphreys for helping normalize conceptions of homosexuality (Miller, 1986).

If you were to serve on your university's IRB, would you allow this research to be conducted? Can students who are asked to participate in research by their professor be considered to be able to give informed consent? Do you consider "informed consent" to be meaningful if the true purpose or nature of an experimental manipulation is not revealed?

The process and even possibility of obtaining informed consent must take into account the capacity of prospective participants to give informed consent. Children cannot legally give consent to participate in research; instead, they must in most circumstances be given the opportunity to give or withhold their *assent* to participate in research, usually by a verbal response to an explanation of the research. In addition, a child's legal guardian must give written informed consent to have the child participate in research (Sieber, 1992). There are also special protections for other populations who are likely to be vulnerable to coercion—prisoners, pregnant women, mentally disabled persons, and educationally or economically disadvantaged persons. Would you allow research on prisoners, whose ability to give informed consent can be questioned? What special protections do you think would be appropriate?

## Avoid Deception in Research, Except in Limited Circumstances

Deception occurs when subjects are misled about research procedures to determine how they would react to the treatment if they were not research subjects. Deception is a critical component of many psychological experiments, in part because of the difficulty of simulating real-world stresses and dilemmas in a laboratory setting. The goal is to get subjects "to accept as true what is false or to give a false impression" (Korn, 1997, p. 4). In Milgram's (1964) experiment, for example, deception seemed necessary because the subjects could not be permitted to administer real electric shocks to the "stooge," yet it would not have made sense to order the subjects to do something that they didn't find to be so troubling. Milgram (1992) insisted that the deception was absolutely essential, although the experimental records indicate that some participants figured out the deception (Perry, 2013, pp. 128–129).

The results of many other psychological and social psychological experiments would be worthless if subjects understood what was really happening to them while the experiment was in progress. The real question is "Is this sufficient justification to allow the use of deception?"

Gary Marshall and Philip Zimbardo (1979) sought to determine the physiological basis of emotion by injecting student volunteers with adrenaline so that their heart rate and sweating would increase and then placing them in a room with a student "stooge" who acted silly. But the students were told that they were being injected with a vitamin supplement to test its effect on visual acuity (Korn, 1997). Piliavin and Piliavin (1972) staged fake seizures on subway trains to study helpfulness (Korn, 1997). Would you vote to allow such deceptive practices in research if you were a member of your university's IRB? What about less dramatic instances of deception in laboratory experiments with psychology students like yourself?

Do you believe that deception itself is the problem? Aronson and Mills's (1959) study of the severity of initiation to groups is a good example of experimental research that does not pose greater-than-everyday risks to subjects but still uses deception. This study was conducted at an all-women's college in the 1950s. The student volunteers who were randomly assigned to the "severe initiation" experimental condition had to read a list of embarrassing words. We think it's fair to say that even in the 1950s, reading a list of potentially embarrassing words in a laboratory setting and listening to a taped discussion was unlikely to increase the risks to which students were exposed in their everyday lives. Moreover, the researchers informed the subjects that they would be expected to talk about sex and could decline to participate in the experiment if this requirement would bother them. None dropped out.

To further ensure that no psychological harm was caused, Aronson and Mills (1959) explained the true nature of the experiment to the subjects after the experiment. The subjects did not seem perturbed: "None of the Ss expressed any resentment or annoyance at having been misled. In fact, the majority were intrigued by the experiment, and several returned at the end of the academic quarter to ascertain the result" (p. 179).

Are you satisfied that this procedure caused no harm? Do you react differently to the debriefing by Aronson and Mills than you did to Milgram's debriefing? The minimal deception in the Aronson and Mills experiment, coupled with the lack of any ascertainable risk to subjects plus a debriefing, satisfies the ethical standards for research of most psychologists and IRBs, even today.

What scientific or educational or applied value would make deception justifiable, even if there is some potential for harm? Who determines whether a nondeceptive intervention is "equally effective"? Baumrind (Miller, 1986) suggested that personal "introspection" would have been sufficient to test Milgram's hypothesis and has argued subsequently that intentional deception in research violates the ethical principles of self-determination, protection of others, and maintenance of trust between people and so can never be justified (Baumrind, 1985). How much risk, discomfort, or unpleasantness might be seen as affecting willingness to participate? When should a postexperimental "attempt to correct any misconception" due to deception be deemed sufficient? Can you see why an IRB, representing a range of perspectives, is an important tool for making reasonable, ethical research decisions when confronted with such ambiguity?

## Maintain Privacy and Confidentiality

Maintaining privacy and confidentiality is another key ethical standard for protecting research participants, and the researcher's commitment to that standard should be included in the informed consent agreement (Sieber, 1992). Procedures to protect each subject's privacy—such as locking records and creating special identifying codes—must be created to minimize the risk of access by unauthorized persons. However, statements about confidentiality should be realistic: Laws allow research records to be subpoenaed and may require reporting of child abuse; a researcher may feel compelled to release information if a health- or life-threatening situation arises and participants need to be alerted. Also, the standard of confidentiality does not apply to observation in public places and information available in public records.

There is one exception to some of these constraints: The National Institutes of Health can issue a **Certificate of Confidentiality** to protect researchers from being legally required to disclose confidential information. Researchers who are focusing on high-risk populations or behaviors, such as crime, substance abuse, sexual activity, or genetic information, can request such a certificate. Suspicions of child abuse or neglect must still be reported, and in some states, researchers may still be required to report crimes such as elder abuse (Arwood & Panicker, 2007).

The **Health Insurance Portability and Accountability Act (HIPAA)** passed by Congress in 1996 created much more stringent regulations for the protection of health care data. As implemented by the U.S. Department of Health and Human Services in 2000 (and revised in 2002), the HIPAA Final Privacy Rule applies to oral, written, and electronic information that "relates to the past, present or future physical or mental health or condition of an individual" (Cava, Cushman, & Goodman, 2007). The HIPAA rule requires that researchers have valid authorization for any use or disclosure of "protected health information" from a health care provider. Waivers of authorization can be granted in special circumstances (Cava et al., 2007).

## Encouraging Appropriate Application
## (Principle D: Justice; Principle E: Respect for People's Rights)

Scientists must also consider the uses to which their research is put. Although many scientists believe that personal values should be left outside the laboratory, some feel that it is proper—even necessary—for scientists to concern themselves with the way their research is used.

Milgram made it clear that he was concerned about the phenomenon of obedience precisely because of its implications for people's welfare. As you have already learned, his first article (Milgram, 1963) highlighted the atrocities committed under the Nazis by citizens and soldiers who were "just following orders." In his more comprehensive book on the obedience experiments (Milgram, 1974), he also argued that his findings shed light on the atrocities committed in the Vietnam War at My Lai, slavery, the destruction of the American Indian population, and the internment of Japanese Americans during World War II. Milgram makes no explicit attempt to "tell us what to do" about this problem. In fact, as a dispassionate psychological researcher, Milgram (1974) tells us, "What the present study [did was] to give the dilemma [of obedience to authority] contemporary form by treating it as subject matter for experimental inquiry, and with the aim of understanding rather than judging it from a moral standpoint" (p. xi).

Yet it is impossible to ignore the very practical implications of Milgram's investigations, which Milgram took pains to emphasize. His research highlighted the extent of obedience to authority and identified multiple factors that could be manipulated to lessen blind obedience (e.g., encouraging dissent by just one group member, removing the subject from direct contact with the authority figure, and increasing the contact between the subject and the victim). It is less clear how much Milgram's laboratory manipulation can tell us about obedience in the very different historical events to which he generalized his conclusions.

A widely publicized experiment on police response to domestic violence provides an interesting cautionary tale about the uses of science. Lawrence Sherman and Richard Berk (1984) arranged with the Minneapolis police department for the random assignment of persons accused of domestic violence to be either arrested or simply given a warning. The results of this field experiment indicated that those who were arrested were less likely subsequently to commit violent acts against their partners. Sherman (1993) explicitly cautioned police departments not to adopt mandatory arrest policies based solely on the results of the Minneapolis experiment, but the results were publicized in the mass media and encouraged many jurisdictions to change their policies (Binder & Meeker, 1993; Lempert, 1989). Although we now know that the original finding of a deterrent effect of arrest did not hold up in many other cities where the experiment was repeated, Sherman (1992) later suggested that implementing mandatory arrest policies might have prevented some subsequent cases of spouse abuse (pp. 150–153). In particular, in a follow-up study in Omaha, arrest warrants reduced repeat offenses among spouse abusers who had already left the scene when the police arrived. However, this Omaha finding was not publicized, so it could not be used to improve police policies. So how much publicity is warranted, and at what point in the research should it occur?

Social scientists who conduct research on behalf of specific organizations may face additional difficulties when the organization, instead of the researcher, controls the final report and the publicity it receives. If organizational leaders decide that particular research results are unwelcome, the researcher's desire to have the findings used appropriately and reported fully can conflict with contractual obligations. Researchers can often anticipate such dilemmas in advance and resolve them when the contract for research is negotiated—or they may simply decline a particular research opportunity altogether. But often, such problems come up only after a report has been drafted, or the problems are ignored by a researcher who needs to have a job or needs to maintain particular personal relationships. These possibilities cannot be avoided entirely, but because of them, it is always important to acknowledge the source of research funding in reports and to consider carefully the sources of funding for research reports written by others.

## STAT CORNER

### Scientific Misconduct in Psychology: Is Replication the Answer?

Zimbardo and Milgram have long been considered classics for teaching us the importance of ethics in psychological research. Their historical lesson is clear and direct: All researchers must ensure the protection of human subjects. More recently, however, two troubling cases of scientific misconduct have shaken psychological research, both of which raise critical yet very different ethical questions from those of the Zimbardo and Milgram studies. In the first of these two cases, the Office of Research Integrity of the National Institutes of Health found that the psychologist Marc Hauser of Harvard University had committed scientific fraud by fabricating data, falsifying data, and inaccurately describing the methods and procedures of his studies (U.S. Department of Health and Human Services, Office of Research Integrity, 2012). Then, following the Hauser affair, came a major fraud case involving the psychologist Diederik Stapel of Tilburg University in the Netherlands. Not surprisingly, these very high-profile cases of fraud, each involving acclaimed professors, have generated considerable outcry among both scientists and the public at large. This outrage is perhaps best captured by the headline of a *New York Times* November 2, 2012, article by Benedict Carey, which read, "Fraud Case Seen as a Red Flag for Psychology Research."

In the aftermath of these cases, several prominent researchers in psychology have weighed in on how future cases of scientific misconduct might be prevented. The problem is of course quite complicated, one that has historically plagued all kinds of scientific endeavors since ancient times (Gross, 2012). Moreover, in a July 2010 *Scientific American* piece "When Scientists Lie," the essayist Michael Shermer writes that in many instances of scientific fraud and deceit the perpetrators fool themselves into believing that their finding or discovery will turn out to be true when subsequent investigators perform the proper studies (see also Goodstein, 2010). One partial solution, as Roediger (2012) as well as others (Frank & Saxe, 2012) have proposed, is replication of results, which as we know is defined as the "repetition of the experimental methods that led to a reported finding by a researcher unaffiliated with the original result" (Frank & Saxe, 2012, p. 600). How might independent replication help solve the ethical problem of scientific misconduct? Put simply, the idea is that a fabricated result will fail to meet the independent replication test. This, of course, does not mean that failure to replicate means that the original results were fabricated. As we know, there are a variety of methodological, design, and statistical issues that could influence whether a given finding can be replicated. However, the moral of the story is that a scientific culture that values and encourages replication may be one in which the lure of fabricating data or falsifying data is seriously diminished.

# 🔲 Conclusions

The extent to which ethical issues are a problem for researchers and their subjects varies dramatically with the type of research design. Much survey research, in particular, creates few ethical problems. In fact, researchers from Michigan's Institute for Survey Research interviewed a representative national sample of adults some years ago and found that 68% of those who had participated in a survey were somewhat or very interested in participating in another; the more times respondents had been interviewed, the more willing they were to participate again. Presumably they would have felt differently if they had been treated unethically (Reynolds, 1979). On the other hand, some experimental studies in the social sciences that have put people in uncomfortable or embarrassing situations have generated vociferous complaints and years of debate about ethics (Reynolds, 1979; Sjoberg, 1967).

The evaluation of ethical issues in a research project should be based on a realistic assessment of the overall potential for harm and benefit to research subjects rather than just an apparent inconsistency between any particular aspect of a research plan and a specific ethical guideline. For example, full disclosure of "what is really going on" in an experimental study is unnecessary if subjects are unlikely to be harmed. The requirement that subjects give signed, informed consent to participate in research can be waived when their participation is anonymous and the research procedures do not involve any increase in risk beyond what they normally experience. To make such realistic and balanced assessments, researchers must make every effort to foresee all possible risks and to weigh the possible benefits of the research against these risks. They should consult with individuals having different perspectives to develop a realistic risk/benefit assessment, and they should try to maximize the benefits to, as well as minimize the risks for, potential research subjects (Sieber, 1992).

Ultimately, these decisions about ethical procedures are not just up to you, as a researcher, to make. Your university's IRB sets the human subjects protection standards for your institution and will require that researchers—and even, in most cases, students—submit their research proposal to the IRB for review. So we leave you with the instruction to review the APA guidelines, consult your university's procedures for the conduct of research with human subjects, and then proceed accordingly.

# Key Terms

Belmont Report
Beneficence
Certificate of Confidentiality
Code of Conduct, American
  Psychological Association
Debriefing

Federal Policy for the Protection of
  Human Subjects
Health Insurance Portability and
  Accountability Act (HIPAA)
Institutional review board (IRB)
Justice
Milgram's obedience experiments

Nuremberg War Crime Trials
Office for Protection from Research
  Risks, National Institutes of Health
Respect for persons
*Tearoom Trade*
Tuskegee syphilis study
Zimbardo's prison simulation study

# Research in the News

"You need subjects and they're hard to get" (Belluck, 2009, p. 1). The developmental psychologist Deborah Linebarger made this statement in an article about scientists who use their own children in their research. Since Jonas Salk injected his children with polio vaccine, researcher-parents have studied their children's response to tickling, tested their children's cognition, scanned their brains, and recorded their children's every verbal utterance and visible behavior. But Robert M. Nelson at Philadelphia's Children's Hospital Center for Research Integrity is troubled. "The role of the parent is to protect the child. Once that parent becomes an investigator, it sets up an immediate potential conflict of interest" (Belluck, 2009, p. 1). Even Dr. Linebarger acknowledges that "when you mix being a researcher with being a parent, it can put your kids in an unfair place" (Belluck, 2009, p. 1). What is your opinion? What are the advantages and disadvantages to researchers of using their own children as research participants? What are the advantages and disadvantages to their children? Do you think that this approach to research is good for science?

## STUDENT STUDY SITE

Please access the study site at **www.sagepub.com/nestor2e,** where you will find useful study materials such as mobile-friendly eFlashcards and mid-chapter and full chapter web quizzes for each chapter, along with carefully selected articles from research journals that illustrate the major concepts and techniques presented in the book.

# Activity Questions

1. Should psychologists be permitted to conduct replications of Milgram's obedience experiments? Of Zimbardo's prison simulation? Can you justify such research as permissible within the current APA ethical standards? If not, do you believe that these standards should be altered so as to permit Milgram-type research?

2. How do you evaluate the current APA ethical code? Is it too strict, too lenient, or just about right? Are the enforcement provisions adequate? What provisions could be strengthened?

3. Does debriefing solve the problem of subject deception? How much must researchers reveal after the experiment is over as well as before it begins?

4. Investigate the standards and operations of your university's IRB. Interview one IRB member and one researcher whose research has been reviewed by the IRB (after receiving the appropriate permissions!). How well do typical IRB meetings work to identify the ethical issues in proposed research? Do researchers feel that their proposals are treated fairly? Why or why not?

5. The Collaborative Institutional Training Initiative offers an extensive online training course in the basics of human subjects protections issues. Go to the public access site at https://www.citiprogram.org/rcrpage.asp?affiliation=100, and complete the course in social and behavioral research. Write a short summary of what you have learned.

6. Read the entire APA Ethics Code at the website of the APA Ethics Office, http://www.apa.org/ethics/. Discuss the difference between the aspirational standards and the enforceable standards.

# Review Questions

1. Describe the history of egregious violations of human rights in the United States that prompted the creation of the National Commission for the Protection of Human Subjects of Biomedical and Behavioral Research.

2. Describe the three basic ethical principles for the protection of human subjects established in the 1979 Belmont Report (U.S. Department of Health, Education, and Welfare, 1979).

3. How did the Belmont Report set the stage for the 1991 Federal Policy for the Protection of Human Subjects and the creation of IRBs?

4. What were the major ethical issues raised by the *Tearoom Trade* study?

5. How would you weigh Milgram's explanations in defense of the ethics of his research on obedience against Baumrind's criticisms and Perry's new evidence?

6. What should a researcher do to ensure that participants are truly informed?

7. Under what circumstances, if any, is deception in research ever justified?

8. Describe a thoughtful and comprehensive debriefing. What is the objective? What should you do if a participant becomes upset with the study? What are the pros and cons of debriefing subjects immediately following their participation or waiting until the completion of data collection?

9. Compare and contrast the ethical violations in the Milgram study with those of the Zimbardo prison simulation study.

10. What is a Certificate of Confidentiality? How and why might a researcher request it, and who would issue it?

11. What are the safeguards a researcher must put in place to protect the confidentiality and privacy of research participants?

# Ethics in Action

Now that we have formally introduced the critical topic of ethics in research, we begin a new exercise that is intended to highlight fascinating yet all too common ethical dilemmas and challenges in science.

The April 21, 2010, *New York Times* article by Amy Harmon titled "Tribe Wins Fight to Limit Research of Its DNA" reverberates with ethical and cultural ramifications for all researchers to take to heart. The article states that beginning in 1990, researchers from Arizona State had enrolled members of the Havasupai Indians of the Grand Canyon as participants in studies that they hoped might reveal genetic clues to the tribe's devastating rate of diabetes.

> But they learned that their blood samples had been used to study many other things, including mental illness and theories of the tribe's geographical origins that contradict their traditional stories. The geneticist responsible for the research has said that she had obtained permission for wider-range genetic studies. Acknowledging a desire to "remedy the wrong that was done," the university's Board of Regents . . . agreed to pay $700,000 to the 41 of the tribe's members, return the blood samples and provide other forms of assistance to the impoverished Havasupai—a settlement that legal experts said was significant because it implied that *the rights of research subjects can be violated when they are not fully informed about how their DNA might be used* [italics added].

As you can see, this case raises substantial ethical issues. First and foremost is the question of informed consent. How would you improve the informed consent form for these studies? Dr. Markow, the geneticist and principal investigator of the studies, described in the article as defending her actions as ethical, is quoted as saying, "I was doing good science." The tribal council member Carletta Tilousi countered, "I'm not against scientific research. I just want it to be done right. They used our blood for all these studies, people got degrees and grants, and they never asked our permission."

What do you think about these two different positions and opinions? How might these issues of misuse of data apply to psychological research? The case also underscores the ethical obligation, emphasized in the APA Ethics Code, for psychological researchers to exercise cultural sensitivity in their work. For example, many members of the tribe expressed concern that they had unknowingly participated in research that could potentially damage the tribe, perhaps calling into question their sacred cultural beliefs and even sovereign rights to tribal land. How might a researcher become culturally sensitive in working with ethnic and racial minorities?

# Conceptualization and Measurement

## LEARNING OBJECTIVES: FAST FACTS

### Measurement in the Testing of Ideas

- A construct is simply an idea, concept, or theoretical abstraction that has multiple referents, which in psychology are known as measurable variables.

- To "play" with theoretical constructs such as intelligence, happiness, and personality requires objective instruments of measurement. No one measurement can fully capture a construct.

- A tool of measurement is judged by the extent to which it provides reliable (consistent) and valid (meaningful) scores.

- The correlation coefficient statistic is used to assess reliability and validity.

- A reliable instrument is internally consistent and stable over time, as reflected by high interitem and test–retest reliability coefficients.

- An instrument has convergent validity when it correlates with other measures of the same construct, and it has discriminant validity when it does not correlate with the measures of a different construct.

## TESTING BEFORE LEARNING

Try your hand at these questions. Don't worry about not knowing the correct response, as you haven't read the chapter yet! But research shows that a pretest such as this can enhance learning (e.g., Kornell, Hays, & Bjork, 2009). So here is the answer. You come up with the question.

1. Best described as a theoretical abstraction
   a. What is a variable?
   b. What is a hypothesis?
   c. What is a sample?
   d. What is a construct?

2. No single variable can fully capture the breadth and depth of my meaning.
   a. What is a variable?
   b. What is a hypothesis?
   c. What is a sample?
   d. What is a construct?

3. Tells you how consistent your measure is, both internally and over time
   a. What is reliability?
   b. What is validity?
   c. What is bias?
   d. What is a construct?

4. Tells you how good your measure is, that is, the extent to which it captures the concept (e.g., intelligence) for which it was designed
   a. What is reliability?
   b. What is validity?
   c. What is bias?
   d. What is a construct?

5. Especially important for statistical analyses
   a. What is a construct?
   b. What is a variable?
   c. What is level of measurement?
   d. What is a hypothesis?

6. A good example of a ratio level of measurement because I have an absolute zero point with fixed measuring units
   a. What is income?
   b. What is intelligence?
   c. What is personality?
   d. What is anxiety?

7. A level of measurement that is used with categorical data, such as gender, team membership, geographical location, yes/no responses, etc.
   a. What is a nominal level of measurement?
   b. What is an ordinal level of measurement?

c. What is an interval level of measurement?
d. What is a ratio level of measurement?

8. A school of psychology that focuses on the use of objective tests to measure mental processes
   a. What is positive psychology?
   b. What is psychometrics?
   c. What is psychoanalysis?
   d. What is physiological psychology?

9. For the measurement of many human traits, such as height, weight, or intelligence, that are collected from a large sample, most observations fall near the center, with gradually fewer scores as you move to the extremes.
   a. What is a construct?
   b. What is a variable?
   c. What is a statistic?
   d. What is a normal curve?

10. A test "looks like" it measures what it is supposed to measure.
   a. What is discriminant validity?
   b. What is convergent validity?
   c. What is face validity?
   d. What is construct validity?

ANSWER KEY: (1) d; (2) d; (3) a; (4) b; (5) c; (6) a; (7) a; (8) b; (9) d; (10) c

What Is Happiness?

Imagine that you have been asked to measure something that is dear and close to all our hearts—our happiness! To whet your appetite, please read each of the following five statements, and indicate the degree to which you agree with each statement by recording a number between 1 (*strongly disagree*) and 7 (*strongly agree*).

1. In most ways, my life is close to my ideal.
2. The conditions of my life are excellent.
3. I am satisfied with my life.
4. So far, I have gotten the important things I want in life.
5. If I could live my life over, I would change almost nothing.

Now compute your total score by adding up your five responses. The psychologist Ed Diener and his colleagues have given this test, known as the Satisfaction With Life Scale (SWLS), to thousands of people (Diener, Emmons, Larsen, & Griffin, 1985; Pavot & Diener, 1993). Their results indicated that people tend to report being generally satisfied with their lives. In fact, as Pavot and Diener (1993) reported, most samples fall in the range on the SWLS of 23 to 28, meaning that the average response in most groups to the individual questions was about 5 or 6 on the 7-point scale, which Pavot and Diener interpreted as indicating *slightly satisfied* to *satisfied*.

The SWLS is used as a **measurement** tool by psychologists to investigate the age-old question "What is happiness?" Long the interest of philosophers and wise laypersons, the question of what is happiness has emerged as a fertile area of research in psychology. Indeed, the past 20 years have witnessed the emergence of a school of psychology known as positive psychology. Defined as the scientific study of ordinary human strengths and virtues, **positive psychology** seeks to learn about human thriving, flourishing, optimism, resilience, joy, and capabilities (Seligman, 1991; Sheldon & King, 2001). In short, positive psychology is interested in studying happiness.

# 🔲 Theoretical Constructs

In positive psychology, *subjective well-being* is the term used for what we refer to in everyday language as happiness (Diener, 2000). Subjective well-being is what is called a theoretical construct. A **construct** is an idea, concept, or abstraction that has multiple referents, which in psychology are known as measurable variables. A construct does not exist as a material entity; it is not concrete as, say, a table is concrete; it cannot be held or touched; it cannot be hit, kicked, or scratched.

A psychological construct such as "subjective well-being" can be measured by a variety of techniques or operations. For example, anxiety is a psychological construct that can be measured in several different ways. It can be measured by objective self-report tests that ask questions about specific behaviors, feelings, or thoughts that are theorized to be indicators of anxiety. It can be measured when a researcher uses observational techniques to code particular behaviors. It can also be measured physiologically by recording galvanic skin response, that is, changes in the electrical properties of the skin.

A construct is cast in a psychological theory. Let's imagine that the SWLS you just completed piqued your interest. You now have become passionate about studying the question "What is happiness?" In your research, you discover the construct of subjective well-being. You learn about the psychological theory that describes, defines, and explains the construct of subjective well-being. The idea, perhaps to your surprise, is quite simple. You learn that subjective well-being is defined conceptually as the extent to which people view themselves as living good lives (Diener, 2000). In other words, each person is the final arbiter or judge of the quality of his or her life (Diener, 2000). With this subjective definition in mind, you can surely see why the SWLS is such a widely used tool in studies of happiness. Indeed, from your experience from taking the test, you no doubt know that the SWLS is all about having people evaluate their own lives using their own individual standards.

Note how theory provides a conceptual framework to study a particular topic. Let's think of a different theoretical approach to the question of well-being. Perhaps you find the SWLS to be too subjective. Well-being, you theorize, goes beyond simple personal satisfaction that is measured with the SWLS. Your theoretical approach is more clinical than that of the subjective well-being studies pioneered by Diener and colleagues. Instead of subjective well-being, your research leads you to the construct of mental health. You discover the work of the social scientist Corey Keyes (2007), who offers a conceptual definition of mental health that you find intriguing: "a state of successful performance of mental function, resulting in productive activities, fulfilling relationships with people, and the ability to adapt to change and cope with adversity" (U.S. Public Health Service, 1999, p. 4).

Thus, here we have two approaches from the same school of psychology, each essentially researching the question "What is happiness?" For Diener and colleagues, their theoretical approach is organized around the psychological construct of subjective well-being. For Keyes, it is the construct of mental health for which he adopted a clinical perspective, and in fact developed a classification system of mental health that parallels the *Diagnostic and Statistical Manual*, used for mental illness.

## Methods of Measurement

Variables are intimately connected to constructs. Think of a variable as derived from a construct; that is, SWLS is a variable derived from the construct of subjective well-being (Pavot & Diener, 1993). However, no one variable alone can fully capture a theoretical construct. In other words, no single tool of measurement can by itself fully capture a construct.

To underline this point, consider the *experience sampling method* (ESM), another tool that is used to assess subjective well-being (Csikszentmihalyi & Csikszentmihalyi, 1988; Csikszentmihalyi & Larson, 1987; Krueger & Schkade, 2008). The ESM provides a record of current circumstances and feelings as they are experienced in real time. Its main objective is to measure the subjective experiences of persons as they are engaged in their everyday lives. Let's imagine that you are a participant in a study that uses ESM. Typically, you would be prompted or signaled by an electronic device such as a cell phone at irregular times within a defined period (e.g., between 9:00 a.m. and 9:00 p.m.). In response to the prompt, you would record what you are experiencing and feeling at that time.

For example, the sample of 2,250 adults in an ESM study by Killingsworth and Gilbert (2010) received a signal on their iPhone at random times; the signal asked them to respond to three simple questions: a happiness question ("How are you feeling right now?"); an activity question ("What are you doing right now?"); and a mind-wandering question ("Are you thinking about something other than what you are currently doing?"). Their results indicated that people spend considerable time mind wandering, which in turn caused them to feel unhappy. The researchers concluded that "a human mind is a wandering mind, and a wandering mind is an unhappy mind" (p. 932).

Notwithstanding the exciting prospects of the marriage of ESM with smart phone technology, there have also been developments in more traditional, low-tech, pencil-and-paper measures of subjective well-being. Enter the *day reconstruction method* (DRM). Here, you would be asked to reconstruct the experiences that you had yesterday (Kahneman et al., 2004). That is, participants are instructed to think about the preceding day, which is divided into episodes, and to describe each episode. Kahneman and colleagues wanted to know how the DRM stacked up against the gold standard of the EMS. Their results were very encouraging for the use of the DRM. In particular, they found that DRM reports from 909 employed women corresponded with the results previously established with research using the ESM.

## Operationalizing and Measuring Constructs

Each of these three approaches, the SWLS, the ESM, and the DRM, provides a distinct operational definition for the construct of subjective well-being. As you know, the SWLS is quick, easy to administer, and easy to take. By contrast, the DRM takes between 45 and 75 minutes to complete, but it provides data beyond what is collected using the five-item SWLS, including how much time respondents spend doing certain activities and how they feel when they are engaged in these activities. In fact, the DRM is intended to reproduce the information that the ESM captures in real time. Its key advantage over the ESM is that instead of providing only a sampling of moments, DRM offers an assessment of contiguous episodes over a full day (Kahneman et al., 2004). Now let us see how to use scores from the SWLS and the DRM to operationalize subjective well-being.

First for the SWLS, take your score along with your classmates' scores. This would give you a sample of scores. Scores can range as low as 5 and as high as 35. As you can see by the items, a lower score would indicate dissatisfaction with life, and a higher score would indicate satisfaction with life. In particular, a score of 20 represents the neutral point on the scale, meaning that the respondent is about equally satisfied and dissatisfied with life. Pavot and Diener (1993) provided a useful descriptive classification for SWLS scores: 26 to 30 = *satisfied*, 21 to 25 = *slightly satisfied*, 15 to 19 = *slightly dissatisfied*, and 5 to 9 = *very dissatisfied* with life.

And as we know from Chapter 2, sample scores can be summarized using descriptive statistics of central tendency (e.g., mean) and variation or range (e.g., standard deviation). In fact, as Pavot and Diener (1993) reported, most samples fall in the range on the SWLS of 23 to 28, meaning that most groups range from *slightly satisfied* to *satisfied*. For the SWLS, you could collect the scores and then tabulate the class average and standard deviation. You could compare your summary statistics with those reported by Pavot and Diener (1993). How does the level of life satisfaction for your class compare with the findings of Pavot and Diener (1993)? And yes, by the way, congratulations, you have successfully operationalized subjective well-being using the SWLS!

The DRM also provides a means to operationalize subjective well-being. It assesses "experienced well-being," in contrast to the SWLS, which measures general life satisfaction. These two methods highlight two aspects of well-being. The DRM hopes to capture the well-being that people experience as they live their lives (Kahneman, 2011). The other aspect, for which the SWLS is designed, relates to the issue of how people evaluate their lives, that is, the judgment that they make when asked to evaluate their lives (Kahneman, 2011). The important point is that *experienced well-being* and *life evaluation* each represent two components of the construct of subjective well-being. That each is assessed and operationalized using different methods of measurement underscores the critical point that no one variable can fully capture the meaning of a construct.

Kahneman (2011) recently reflected on the roles of experienced well-being, as measured by DRM, and life evaluation, as indexed by SWLS. He noted that life evaluation and experienced well-being can be influenced by different events. For example, educational achievement is associated with greater life satisfaction but not with greater experienced well-being. In fact, Kahneman (2011) noted that in the United States, educational achievement may be linked to higher reported levels of stress. In a similar vein, adverse health detracts more from experienced well-being than from life evaluation. As Kahneman (2011) concluded, experienced well-being and life evaluation are related but different aspects of happiness. And we will give Kahneman the last word on what is the good life, as he put it best: "It is only a slight exaggeration to say that happiness is the experience of spending time with people you love and who love you" (p. 395).

## Advantages of Multiple Methods

Overall, keep in mind that the variables and particular measurement operations chosen for a study should be consistent with the research question. For example, Keyes chose variables and particular measurement operations that were aimed toward investigating and addressing the question of whether mental health reflects more than simply the absence of mental illness. To address these questions, he used two kinds of methods of measurement: objective self-report adjective checklists and the interview. These two methods of measurement provided him with data to demonstrate that mental health means more than the absence of mental illness. As an example, adults with mental illness had higher levels of positive functioning with regard to life goals, resilience, and friendships than adults without mental illness but who were classified as "pure languishing." On the basis of these findings, Keyes (2007) concluded that languishing could often be worse than the presence of a diagnosable mental illness.

Multiple methods of measurement are thus essential for us to develop a complete understanding of a phenomenon, such as the relationship between mental health and mental illness, or for distinguishing different aspects of happiness, such as life satisfaction and experienced well-being. Keep in mind the importance of using different forms of measurement of the same construct. By doing so, you can test whether these multiple methods of measurement are related, and the degree to which they are adds to our understanding of a given construct. We will discuss more on this later in the chapter.

# ▣ Levels of Measurement

Measurement is the foundation of psychological research. It is defined as the process by which numbers are used to designate objects or events according to some objective rule. By *rule*, we mean, the way numbers are used to represent a particular **scale** or **level of measurement**. A variable can have one of four scales of measurement: (1) nominal, (2) ordinal, (3) interval, or (4) ratio (see Exhibit 4.1). The operational definition of a variable specifies the particular level of its measurement. Knowing the level of measurement of a variable dictates the mathematical and statistical procedures that can be computed. As such, levels of measurement are important to understand, particularly for data analysis.

| Exhibit 4.1 | Four Levels of Measurement |
|---|---|
| Nominal | Categorical, including dichotomies, no ranking |
| Ordinal | Ranks on a scale, numerical degrees, distances unequal |
| Interval | Ranks with equal distance, but no true zero point |
| Ratio | Ranks with equal distance, true zero point means absence of the quantity |

## Nominal Level of Measurement

The **nominal level of measurement** (also called the categorical or qualitative level) identifies variables whose values have no mathematical interpretation; they vary in kind or quality but not in amount. In fact, it is conventional to refer to the values of nominal variables as "attributes" instead of values. "State" (referring to the United States) is one example. The variable has 50 attributes (or categories or qualities). We might indicate specific states with numbers, so California might be represented by the value 1 and Oregon with the value 2 and so on, but these numbers do not tell us anything about the difference between the states except that they are different. Oregon is not one unit more of "state" than California, nor is it twice as much "state." Nationality, occupation, religious affiliation, and region of the country are also variables measured at the nominal level. Put simply, a categorical variable is one that uses a nominal scale of measurement (see Exhibit 4.2).

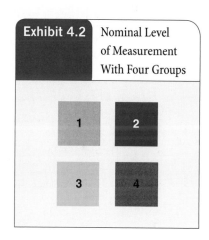

Exhibit 4.2 Nominal Level of Measurement With Four Groups

Although the attributes of categorical variables do not have a mathematical meaning, they must be assigned to cases with great care. The attributes we use to measure, or categorize, cases must be mutually exclusive and exhaustive:

- A variable's attributes or values are **mutually exclusive** if every case can have only one attribute.

- A variable's attributes or values are **exhaustive** when every case can be classified into one of the categories.

When a variable's attributes are mutually exclusive and exhaustive, every case corresponds to one, and only one, attribute. We know this sounds pretty straightforward, and in many cases it is. However, what we think of as mutually exclusive and exhaustive categories may really be so only because of social convention; when these conventions change, or if they differ between the societies in a multicountry study, appropriate classification at the nominal level can become much more complicated.

## The Special Case of Dichotomies

**Dichotomies**, variables having only two values, are a special case from the standpoint of levels of measurement. The values or attributes of a variable such as gender clearly vary in kind or quality but not in amount.

Thus, the variable is categorical—measured at the nominal level. Yet we can also think of the variable as indicating the presence of the attribute "female" (or "male") or not. Viewed in this way, there is an inherent order: A female has more of the "female" attribute (it is present) than a male (the attribute is not present). So what do you answer to the test question "What is the level of measurement of 'gender'?" "Nominal," of course, but you'll find that when a statistical procedure requires that variables be quantitative, a dichotomy can be perfectly acceptable. As we can see from the graphs (see Exhibit 4.3), changing the number assigned to "male" and "female" does not change the number of men and women participants in a study. We still have the same number of men and women in the data set.

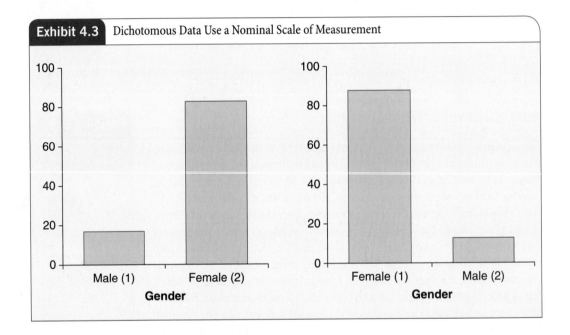

**Exhibit 4.3** Dichotomous Data Use a Nominal Scale of Measurement

In Chapter 2, we created a dichotomous variable when we categorized participants as either maximizers or satisficers. As you recall, we categorized respondents based on their scores on the measure of maximization. Note that the scores on the maximization measure represent quantitative data that we used to create these two qualitative categories. Scores that fell below the cutoff on the maximization measure were categorized as satisficers and those above the cutoff on the maximization measure were categorized as maximizers.

Now let's imagine that we want to compare maximizers and satisficers on grade point average. We would create a dichotomous variable that we call "decision-making style," which would have two attributes, satisficer (made up of all respondents who scored below the cutoff) and maximizer (made up of all respondents who scored about the cutoff). We could code "1" for satisficer and "2" for maximizer. These numbers have no arithmetical meaning, but the numerical code needs to be consistent, for this example, all satisficers must be coded with "1" and all maximizers must be coded with "2." Once we have our dichotomous code in place to categorize maximizers and satisficers, we could then use software-based statistical analyses to compare the two groups on grade point average.

## Ordinal Level of Measurement

The first of the three quantitative levels is the **ordinal level of measurement**. At this level, the numbers assigned to response choices allow for "greater than" and "less than" distinctions. And because this level of measurement allows for a ranking of responses, such as degree of agreement or frequency of occurrence, ordinal level of measurement is sometimes referred as a ranking scale.

Oftentimes, research participants are asked to rank the frequency of occurrence of a particular emotion or behavior on a numerical scale. For example, Keyes asked participants to rate how frequently in the past 30 days they felt (a) cheerful, (b) in good spirits, (c) extremely happy, (d) calm and peaceful, (e) satisfied, and (f) full of life. For each of these positive emotions, participants rated how frequently they had experienced each on a scale by selecting only one of the five numbered responses (typically presented from left to right) with 1 = *none of the time*, 2 = *a little of the time*, 3 = *some of the time*, 4 = *most of the time*, or 5 = *all of the time.*

Researchers commonly referred to this metric as a **Likert scale**, named after its originator, psychologist Rensis Likert (Likert, 1932). Keyes used another ordinal scale when he asked participants to "rate their life overall these days" on a scale ranging from 0 = *worst possible life overall* to 10 = *best possible life overall.*

A simple depiction of an ordinal scale of measurement is presented in Exhibit 4.4. Here imagine that the respondents participated in a driving test in which they rank ordered four different cars on a 1 to 4 scale, with 1 = *most favorite* and 4 = *least favorite*. Exhibit 4.5 simply shows that ranking always involves an ordinal scale, such as that used by Olympic judges. Other common examples of an ordinal level of measurement are letter grades, military rank, and socioeconomic status.

| **Exhibit 4.4** | Ordinal Level of Measurement for Car Preference |
| --- | --- |

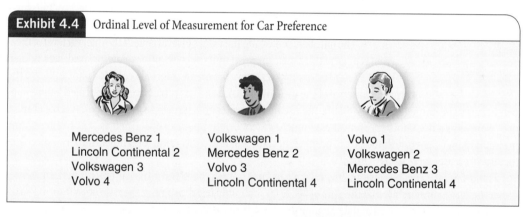

| | | |
| --- | --- | --- |
| Mercedes Benz 1 | Volkswagen 1 | Volvo 1 |
| Lincoln Continental 2 | Mercedes Benz 2 | Volkswagen 2 |
| Volkswagen 3 | Volvo 3 | Mercedes Benz 3 |
| Volvo 4 | Lincoln Continental 4 | Lincoln Continental 4 |

As with nominal variables, the different values of a variable measured at the ordinal level must be mutually exclusive and exhaustive. They must cover the range of observed values and allow each case to be assigned no more than one value. Often, instruments that use an ordinal level of measurement simply ask respondents to rate their responses to some questions or statements along a continuum of, for example, strength of agreement, level of importance, or relative frequency.

A key limitation of the ordinal level of measurement is that you cannot assume that respondents perceive the differences between response scale points as equidistant. For example, you cannot assume that the

| **Exhibit 4.5** | Always Ordinal, Ranking |
| --- | --- |

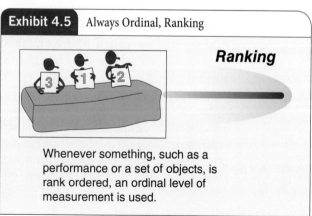

Whenever something, such as a performance or a set of objects, is rank ordered, an ordinal level of measurement is used.

distance or difference between "all of the time" and "most of the time" is equal to the distance or difference between "a little of the time" and "none of the time." While these points on the response scale are intended to

| Exhibit 4.6 | Fahrenheit Temperature Uses an Interval Level of Measurement |
|---|---|

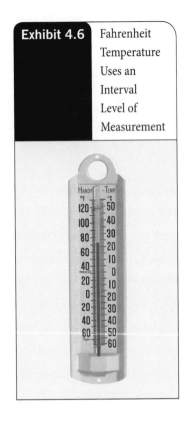

reflect an order of frequency ("all of the time" to "none of the time"), the numbers that you would assign to each of the response scale points (e.g., *all of the time* = 5, *most of the time* = 4, *some of the time* = 3, *a little of the time* = 2, and *none of the time* = 1) do not indicate the magnitude of difference between any two points on this ordinal response scale.

For instance, say you answered "all of the time," which is assigned and coded with a value of 5 for how frequently you felt cheerful in the past 30 days, and another participant responded with "none of the time," which we coded with a value of 1. You cannot say that the "all of the time" response is five times greater than the "none of the time" response just because you decided to code these responses as 5 and 1, respectively. The SWLS that you took at the beginning of this chapter uses an ordinal scale of measurement.

## Interval Level of Measurement

An **interval level of measurement** has all the characteristics of nominal and ordinal scales of measurement. That is, like a nominal scale, it gives a name or category for each observation, with the number serving as a code for a label (e.g., 1 = *females*, 2 = *males*). As in an ordinal scale, responses are numerically ordered or ranked from lowest to highest on some particular characteristic. But in addition, an interval level of measurement by definition uses a scale on which the distances between any two points are of known size. The numbers indicating the values of a variable at the interval level of measurement represent fixed measurement units but have no absolute, or fixed, zero point.

What this means is that a zero value on an interval scale does not indicate the complete absence of the measured variable. This is true even if the scaled values happen to carry the name "zero." The Fahrenheit scale illustrates this issue (see Exhibit 4.6). A temperature of 0° Fahrenheit does not represent the complete absence of temperature, defined as the absence of any molecular kinetic energy. Rather, 0° Fahrenheit became a handy convention for temperature measurement for largely accidental reasons of history.

The key point is that because an interval scale has no true zero point, ratio measurements make no sense. For example, we cannot state that the ratio of 40° to 20° Fahrenheit is the same as the ratio of 100° to 50°. After all, if the "zero" degree applied at the temperature that Fahrenheit happens to measure as 10°, the two ratios would instead be 30 to 10 and 90 to 40, respectively, and would no longer be equivalent. For this reason, that is, the absence of a true zero point in an interval scale, we cannot say that 80° is "twice as hot" as 40°. Such a claim would assume a true zero point, which an interval scale lacks. Remember, as with all interval scales, that decision about where to "start" the Fahrenheit temperature scale is arbitrary and is not tied to an underlying physical reality of atmospheric climate.

In psychology, standardized measures of intelligence, personality, and aptitude typically use an interval level of measurement, just as do education tests such as the SAT (Scholastic Assessment Test) and GRE (Graduate Record Examination). That is, these standardized measures use an arbitrary zero point, as there is, for example, no such thing as no intelligence, no personality, and the like. Likewise, as with our example of temperature, you cannot say an IQ (Intelligence Quotient) score is twice as large as another IQ score. So while an IQ of 130 is 65 scaled points greater than an IQ of 65, it is not twice as great.

## Ratio Level of Measurement

The numbers indicating the values of a variable at the **ratio level of measurement** represent fixed measuring units and an absolute zero point (zero means absolutely no amount of whatever the variable indicates).

Income is measured on a ratio scale, as no income equals zero dollars and cents! Weight is also measured on a ratio scale, as the scale of ounces and pounds has a genuine zero point. Kelvin temperature is another example of a ratio scale because in classical physics, zero on the Kelvin scale means absolute zero, the case in which all motion stops. Speed in terms of time in track and field races would also be considered to be measured on a ratio scale (see Exhibit 4.7).

For most statistical analyses in social science research, the interval and ratio levels of measurement can be treated as equivalent, but there is an important difference: On a ratio scale, 10 is 2 points higher than 8 and is also two times greater than 5. Ratio numbers can be added and subtracted, and because the numbers begin at an absolute zero point, they can be multiplied and divided (so ratios can be formed between the numbers). For example, people's ages can be represented by values ranging from 0 years (or some fraction of a year) to 120 or more. A person who is 30 years old is 15 years older than someone who is 15 years old (30 − 15 = 15) and is twice as old as that person (30/15 = 2). Of course, the numbers also must be mutually exclusive and exhaustive so that each case can be assigned one and only one value.

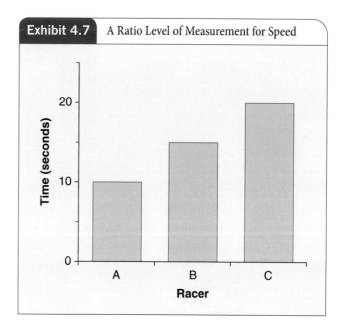

**Exhibit 4.7** A Ratio Level of Measurement for Speed

## Comparison of Levels of Measurement

Exhibit 4.8 summarizes the types of comparisons that can be made with different levels of measurement as well as the mathematical operations that are legitimate. All four levels of measurement allow researchers to assign different values to different cases. Scores obtained on ordinal, interval, or ratio scales of measurement all allow for mathematical operations and are thus often referred to as quantitative variables.

**Exhibit 4.8** Properties of the Four Different Levels of Measurement

| Examples of Comparison Statements | Appropriate Math Operations | Relevant Level of Measurement | | | |
|---|---|---|---|---|---|
| | | Nominal | Ordinal | Interval | Ratio |
| A is equal to (not equal to) B | = (≠) | XX | XX | XX | XX |
| A is greater than (less than) B | > (<) | | XX | XX | XX |
| A is three more than (less than) B | + (−) | | | XX | XX |
| A is twice (half) as large as B | × (/) | | | | XX |

By contrast, a nominal level of measurement involves classifying observations using an arbitrary number as a code for group membership (e.g., *females* = 1, *males* = 2). Thus, a nominal level of measurement does not allow for mathematical operations and is used for what are often referred to as qualitative variables. Keep in mind that researchers choose levels of measurement in the process of creating operational definitions for their variables; the level of measurement is not inherent in the variable itself. Many variables can be measured at different levels with different procedures.

| Exhibit 4.9 | Levels of Measurement and Statistical Approaches |

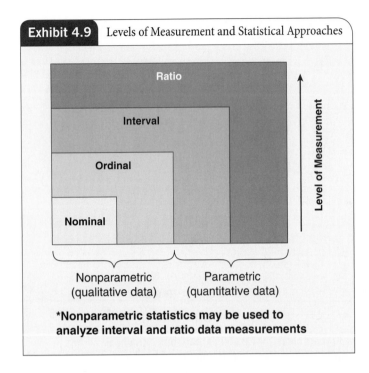

Nonparametric (qualitative data) — Parametric (quantitative data)

**\*Nonparametric statistics may be used to analyze interval and ratio data measurements**

## Why Measurement Level Matters

Levels of measurement are especially important for statistical analyses that we will cover in depth in Chapter 10. We will learn in Chapter 10 that different types of statistical procedures require different levels of measurement of variables. For example, **nonparametric statistics** test hypotheses for variables that use either a nominal or an ordinal scale of measurement.

A commonly used nonparametric statistical procedure that will be covered in Chapter 10 is the *chi-square* test. Let's imagine for a moment that you are interested in the question of whether there are more women than men majoring in psychology. To answer this question, you could perform a chi-square statistic test comparing percentages of female and male psychology majors. You would use the nonparametric chi-square test because gender is a categorical variable, meaning that it is measured on a nominal scale that can only be analyzed using nonparametric statistics.

Test your knowledge of this chapter so far by taking the mid-chapter quiz on the study site: www.sagepub.com/nestor2e

On the other hand, **parametric statistics** are used with variables that are measured on either an interval or a ratio scale. A commonly used parametric statistical procedure that will be covered in Chapter 10 is the *t-test statistic*. Imagine you wanted to compare the SATs of female and male college applicants. A *t* test would allow you to compare the average SATs of these two groups. The SAT would be considered a variable that is measured on an interval scale and thus suitable to be analyzed with parametric statistics, such as the *t* test.

In general, parametric statistics are preferable because they provide a more powerful test than do nonparametric statistics of a research hypothesis. That is, parametric statistics provide the best chance of establishing whether there is a relationship between independent and dependent variables. Exhibit 4.9 depicts the relationship of levels of measurement and parametric and nonparametric statistics.

## The Special Case of Psychometrics

**Psychometrics** is a school of psychology that studies the application of psychological tests as objective measures of the mind and mental processes. The word *psychometric* literally means "to measure the mind." At the heart of the psychometric approach is that people have certain levels of **psychological traits**, such as those related to intelligence, personality, or attitudes, and that these presumed enduring and stable dispositions can be measured by objective tests. Equally important for the psychometric approach are competencies, such as those related to scholastic aptitude or academic achievement, which can also be measured by objective pencil-and-paper tests, such as the SAT (see Exhibit 4.10).

Psychometrics provides us with the most powerful set of tools and concepts for the measurement of human traits. These measurement tools or tests are used to operationalize constructs, such as

| Exhibit 4.10 | Psychometrics of Educational Testing |

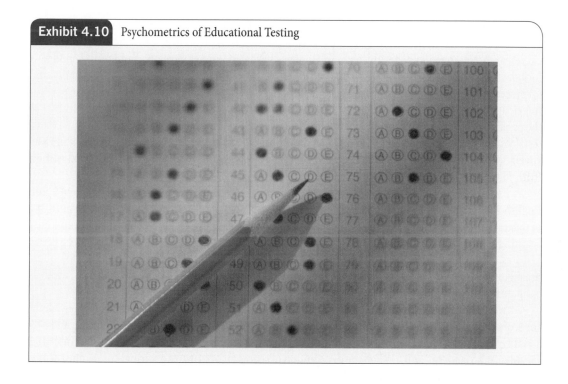

psychological traits. In psychometrics, a specific set of procedures is used to operationalize a construct. These procedures are quite extensive and represent a field of study in and of itself in psychology and in education, known as *test construction* or *tests and measurements* (see Kline, 1986).

The psychometric approach to creating operational definitions uses the principle of **standardization** of both test administration and test scoring. Standardization simply means that testing, scoring, and interpretation procedures are uniform across all administrations of the test. In constructing a psychometric test, a researcher identifies a **standardization sample**, which is defined as a random selection of people drawn from a carefully defined population. As we will study in Chapter 5, random sampling simply means that each person of the targeted or defined population has an equal chance of being selected to be part of the standardization sample.

The tests, administered uniformly to the standardization sample, are then scored according to the same specified and objective criteria for each examinee. From the standardization sample, the **norms** of the test are calculated. The norms of a test involve two measures. The first is the mean or average score for the standardization sample. The second measure is the **standard deviation**, which indicates the degree to which an individual score deviates from the sample mean (see Chapter 10 for details).

In psychology, psychometrics has long been the dominant approach to the study of the construct of intelligence. Let us consider a widely used standardized test of IQ known as the Wechsler Adult Intelligence Scale–Fourth Edition (WAIS-IV; Wechsler, 2008). Test construction begins with a conceptual definition of the construct under study. In this case, Wechsler (1944) provided the original conceptual definition for the construct of intelligence as the "capacity of the individual to act purposely, to think rationally, and to deal effectively with his environment" (p. 3). This conceptual definition represents one of the earliest formulations of intelligence, but one that has remain controversial in psychology and in society in terms of its measurement of cultural meaning (see, e.g., Brown, 1992; Lemann, 1999; Neisser et al., 1996; Nisbett et al., 2012).

The most recent revision in 2008 of the Wechsler measure of intelligence offers a text book example of the psychometric approach to test construction. First, based on an ever-growing body of empirical research, the conceptual definition of intelligence has been further developed and refined and now includes four distinct factors: (1) verbal comprehension, (2) perceptual reasoning, (3) working memory, and (4) processing speed. Test questions and tasks have been revised. Second, and in keeping with the psychometric approach, norms were updated for the WAIS-IV. Creating norms for a test is a defining feature of the psychometric approach. Norms help to standardize a test, and they require frequent updating, so that a test does not become obsolete. For the WAIS, updating test norms requires a new standardization sample. Given the rapid changes in society, the WAIS is updated approximately every 10 years. The next edition (fifth edition) of the test is due in 2018.

In "norming" the WAIS-IV, the developers gave the IQ test to a standardization sample of 2,200 English-speaking people who were randomly selected from a carefully defined population. The norming of the test came from a stratified sampling of the population. A **stratified sample** is formed by randomly selecting from relatively uniform subpopulations called strata. Strata are defined along specified, objective features. As part of the standardization process, the test scores generated from a standardization sample are plotted or graphed. The graph shows the range of scores as well as the distribution of scores, which is simply a tally of the number of examinees who obtained a certain score.

As we had covered in Chapter 2, this kind of graph (histogram) provides a frequency distribution for the scores generated from a sample. For many human traits, from height to weight to intelligence and personality predispositions, scores are distributed along a **normal curve** that is represented in Exhibit 4.11 (Kosslyn & Rosenberg, 2001). When the distribution of scores approximates a normal curve, most scores fall near the center, with gradually fewer scores as you move toward either extreme. In general, the larger the sample, the more closely will the distribution of scores resemble the normal curve, which is also known as the *bell curve*, due its bell shape—bilaterally symmetrical with a single peak in the middle.

Exhibit 4.11 shows the normal curve for WAIS-IV IQ scores. WAIS-IV raw scores are converted by a specific statistical formula to standard scores, with a mean of 100 and a standard deviation of 15. As you can see in Exhibit 4.11, about two thirds of the scores from the standardization sample fall within 1

**Exhibit 4.11** Normal Distribution of IQ Scores

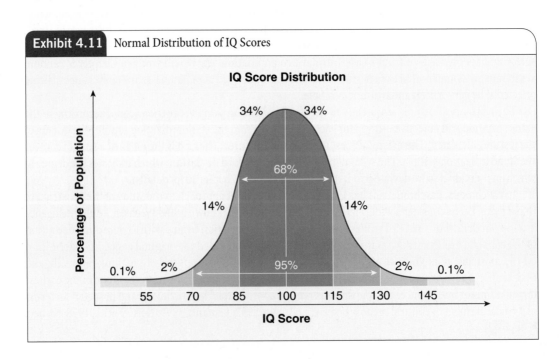

standard deviation above and below the mean of 100. In other words, two thirds of all scores fall within the range of 85 to 115. What this means is that a person with an IQ of 115 earns a score that falls 1 standard deviation unit above the mean of 100. In qualitative terms, an IQ of 115 would be classified as falling in the *high average* range. Thus, you can see how a person's score on a standardized test can be compared and interpreted relative to others in the standardized sample.

# Evaluating Measures

For a test to be meaningful or useful, it must be both *reliable* and *valid*. As we learned in Chapter 1, *reliability* refers to consistency, as for example, the extent to which a research finding can be replicated. In measurement, reliability reflects the consistency of a test. There are two types of reliability of a measure. One is test–retest reliability, which is used to assess the stability of scores over time on a measurement. Internal consistency of a measure is another type of reliability, which can be used when you want to assess, for example, the extent to which the items of a test cohere. This type of reliability can be very useful because high internal consistency could mean that the test is measuring a unitary trait. *Validity*, on the other hand, is different from reliability and refers to the meaning of what is measured. Validity can be evident by what a measure might predict, for example, IQ scores predict school success.

Multiple methods of measurement in the form of reliable and valid tests are essential for understanding a theoretical construct. Consider the construct of well-being. Recall the two measures, SWLS and DRM, used to assess well-being. Note that these two different measurements revealed important insights about well-being. To wit, findings from studies that have employed these measurements indicated that life satisfaction and experienced well-being may represent two distinct aspects of happiness. In large part, we owe this advancement in our understanding of happiness to the development and use of these two different measures that researchers have employed to assess the construct of well-being. This represents an example of good research practice, namely, the use of multiple, reliable, and valid measures. Now let us learn how we too can practice good research using reliable and valid measures.

## Measurement Reliability

A reliable test yields consistent scores when the construct being measured is not changing (or the measured scores change in direct correspondence to actual changes in the construct). If a test is reliable, it is affected less by measurement error or chance variation than if it is unreliable. Reliability is a prerequisite for measurement validity: We cannot really measure a construct if the tests we are using give inconsistent results. In fact, because it usually is easier to assess test reliability than test validity, you are more likely to see an evaluation of measurement reliability in a research report than an evaluation of measurement validity.

## Stability Over Time

In the "Stat Corner," we show how the correlational statistic provides a clear and direct assessment of the reliability of a measure. This statistic is used to compute a reliability coefficient of a measure. The stability of a measure over time is assessed by what is referred to as the **test–retest reliability** coefficient. The test–retest reliability coefficient provides a quantitative index of the precision of the measurement, with a higher correlation coefficient indicative of smaller measurement error. For example, a construct such as intelligence is presumed to remain stable over time. In fact, the actual test–retest reliability for the WAIS-IV full-scale IQ is a remarkable .96 (Wechsler, 2008).

A major shortcoming of test–retest reliability is the "practice effect," whereby respondents' familiarity with the questions from the first administration of the test affects their responses to the subsequent administration of the same test. As a result, many standardized tests have alternate forms, which come in very handy when an examinee might need to be retested over a relatively short period of time.

Think of a study that is investigating the effects of a new drug on memory. Participants are tested before and after a 60-day treatment trial. A control group that receives a placebo is also tested on two occasions, before and after receiving the inert substance. To control for practice effects that could influence test scores, alternate forms of the memory measurement would need to be administered. In selecting your memory measure, then, you would look at the **alternate-forms reliability** of the test. Alternate-forms reliability reflects the degree of agreement between two slightly different tests comprising different sets of questions or items of the same construct.

In a similar vein, often research involves different raters coding the same behavior. Here, consistency among raters needs to be established so that the same behavior is coded reliably. This type of reliability is referred to as **interobserver reliability**, which indexes the degree to which raters consistently code the same observed behavior. That is, interobserver reliability measures the degree of agreement among raters.

With two raters, the same correlation statistic used with test–retest reliability is acceptable for assessing interobserver reliability. However, with more than two raters, the *intraclass correlation coefficient* (ICC) is used to assess interobserver reliability. The statistical formula for the ICC is different from that for the correlation used for test–retest reliability. Yet the ICC is equivalent to what would be the average of the test–retest correlations between all pairs of tests (Shrout & Fleiss, 1979).

## Internal Consistency

Tests usually consist of many items, all of which are typically intended to measure the same construct, whether IQ, a personality trait, or reading comprehension. When researchers use multiple items to measure a single construct, they must be concerned with **interitem reliability** (or interitem or internal consistency). The idea is that if the items of a test are all measuring the same construct, the correlation among these items should be high. The goal is to have consistency across items within a test.

One frequently used measure of internal consistency is the **split-half reliability** coefficient. Here, you randomly divide all items that are supposed to measure the same trait or construct into two sets. Calculate the total score for each randomly divided half. The correlation between the two total scales is the split-half reliability coefficient. **Cronbach's alpha** is another **reliability measure** commonly used to assess interitem reliability. Very similar to split-half reliability, Cronbach's alpha is computed by several iterations of randomly dividing a scale of items into sets of split halves. You (or the computer program) compute the reliability coefficient, recomputing on the next set, and so on until you have computed all possible split-half estimates of reliability.

## Increasing Reliability

One rather simple and straightforward way to increase the internal consistency of an instrument is to make it longer! In other words, by adding more related items to your test, you will increase the internal consistency of the test. Why is this so?

In any response, there is **random error of measurement**—variation due to multiple little factors that have nothing to do with the construct you are trying to measure. Perhaps an answer is influenced by a story in that morning's newspaper, by the noise of a truck passing by, and on and on. Any given response to a question will therefore contain a large component of random error of measurement. But as you increase the number of items in a test, the random error involved in each answer to each particular question will be cancelled out by the random error associated with the responses to the other questions. The more you add questions related to the concept of interest, the more the random error will wash out in this way.

Exhibit 4.12 compares test–retest reliabilities for three indexes commonly used to assess subjective well-being: (1) a single-item measure of general satisfaction, (2) the five-item SWLS, and (3) ESM-generated real-time reports of emotional state (Krueger & Schkade, 2008).

As you can see, the differences in test–retest reliabilities between the single-item measure and the five-item SWLS are striking. The single-item SWLS showed moderate reliabilities, falling between .40 and .66 (Krueger & Schkade, 2008). However, the longer, five-item SWLS had reliabilities as high as .84. In addition, as reported by Krueger and Schkade (2008), Eid and Diener (2004) used a powerful statistical technique known as structural equation modeling and estimated the stability of the five-item SWLS to be very high, around .90.

| Exhibit 4.12 | Reliability of Subjective Well-Being Measures | | | |
|---|---|---|---|---|
| | Coefficient Alpha | Test–Retest | Time Interval | Construct |
| Single-item measures | | | | |
| Andrews and Whithey (1976) | | .40–.66 | 1 hour | Life satisfaction |
| Kammann and Flett (1983) | | .50–.55 | Same day | Overall happiness, satisfaction |
| Multiple-item measures | | | | |
| Alfonso and Allison (1992) | .89 | .83 | 2 weeks | SWLS |
| Pavot, Diener, Colvin, and Sandvik (1991) | .85 | .84 | 1 month | SWLS |
| Blais, Vallerand, Pelletier, and Briere (1989) | .79–.84 | .64 | 2 months | SWLS |
| Diener et al. (1985) | .87 | .82 | 2 months | SWLS |
| Yardley and Rice (1991) | .80 | .50 | 10 weeks | SWLS |
| Magnus, Diener, Fujita, and Pavot (1993) | .87 | .54 | 4 years | SWLS |
| ESM | | | | |
| Steptoe, Wardle, and Marmot (2005) | | .65 | Weekend– weekday | Experienced happiness |

*Note:* SWLS = Satisfaction With Life Scale; ESM = Experience Sampling Method.

The take-home point is straightforward. Increasing the number of items of a measure improves test–retest reliability. In addition, Exhibit 4.12 also presents estimates of internal consistency (coefficient alpha) for the SWLS. As Exhibit 4.12 shows, the SWLS had highly internal consistency reliability, with coefficient alpha values ranging from .79 to .89.

## STAT CORNER

### Correlation and Measurement Reliability

The correlation coefficient is one of the most useful statistical tests in psychological research. Computed by a specific formula, this statistic provides an index of how closely related two variables are. This statistic, known as the correlation coefficient (symbolized as $r$), can range from .00 to +1.00 and .00 to −1.00. If there is no relationship between two variables, that is, the variation in one variable has nothing to do with the variation in the other variable, then the correlation value will be .00 or close to .00. The closer a correlation between two variables is to 1.00, either +1.00 or −1.00, the stronger is the relationship between the two variables. The positive and negative signs of the correlation coefficient tell the direction of the relationship between the two variables. A positive correlation coefficient (a "plus" sign) means that there is a positive linear relationship—as scores on one variable increase, so do scores on the other variable. A negative correlation coefficient (a "minus" sign) means that there is an inverse linear relationship—as scores on one variable increase, scores on the other variable decrease.

Researchers often use **scatter diagrams** to graph correlations. A scatter diagram is a graph of a correlation. A correlation always involves two variables. Let's call one variable $x$ and the other $y$. Let us say a participant had a score of 5 on one variable, labeled $x$, and a score of 10 on another variable, labeled $y$. Make a two-dimensional graph with a horizontal $x$-axis and a vertical $y$-axis. Now plot the participant's scores of 5, 10 (5 to the right and 10 up). Each participant can be represented by a point on the graph, in this example, 5, 10, which represents scores on the $x$ and $y$ variables. So if there are 12 participants, there should be 12 points. The direction of the points on the graph will signify whether the correlation between the two variables across all participants is either positive or negative. For a positive correlation, the graph will depict points that fall on an imaginary line that tilts upward to the right. For a negative correlation, the graph will depict points that fall on an imaginary line that tilts downward to the right.

The correlation coefficient is also used to quantify reliability. For example, test-retest reliability is the statistical correlation computed between scores on the same measures across two time periods for the same respondents. The correlation value or coefficient between the two sets of scores is used as the quantitative measure of test–retest reliability. Ideally, if the scores remained identical across the two testing intervals for all respondents, then the correlation coefficient would be 1.00. This would indicate perfect agreement between the scores for respondents across the two testing intervals. In reality, however, the scores of respondents vary if the test is administered again. As such, correlation coefficients of .70 to .80 are considered satisfactory values for test–retest reliability. The test–retest reliability correlation also reflects the extent to which the rank order of respondents' scores is consistent across the two testing periods. Rank order simply means where or in which position in the class a respondent's score falls in relation to the other test takers. If the rank order of scores for Test 1 is reproduced for Test 2, then the test–retest reliability will be high. By contrast, if the rank order of scores for respondents is all mixed up across the two testing sessions, then the test–retest correlation coefficient will be low.

Exhibit 4.13 presents a hypothetical set of scores for the same test given 1 year apart for the same nine respondents. The correlation between the two sets of scores is .95, which indicates very high test–retest reliability. This indicates that the scores on this test remained extremely stable over the 1-year period between Time 1 and Time 2. The scatterplot plots the scores for Time 1 and Time 2 for each of the nine respondents. As you can see, the imaginary line tilts upward, indicative of the strong positive correlation of .95.

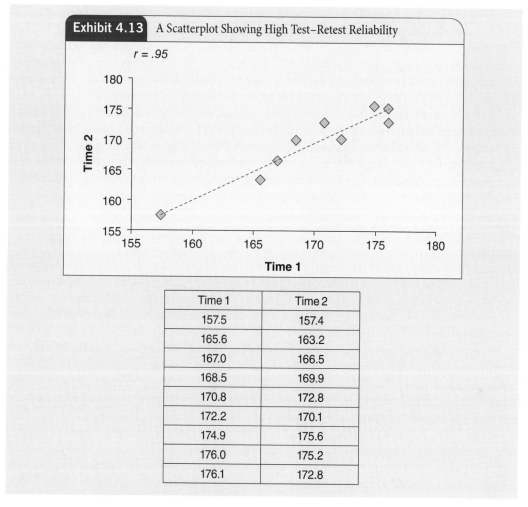

**Exhibit 4.13**  A Scatterplot Showing High Test–Retest Reliability

$r = .95$

| Time 1 | Time 2 |
|--------|--------|
| 157.5 | 157.4 |
| 165.6 | 163.2 |
| 167.0 | 166.5 |
| 168.5 | 169.9 |
| 170.8 | 172.8 |
| 172.2 | 170.1 |
| 174.9 | 175.6 |
| 176.0 | 175.2 |
| 176.1 | 172.8 |

## The Logic of Measurement Validity

How do we know whether a test measures what it says it measures? Does the WAIS-IV measure intelligence? Does the SWLS measure well-being? In psychological measurement, these are questions about the validity of an instrument or a test.

A valid instrument is one that taps the construct we intend to tap. Put simply, a valid measure does what it is supposed to do—the WAIS-IV measures intelligence, the SWLS measures subjective well-being, and so on. Note that questions of validity are not the same as questions of reliability: Reliability and validity are not synonymous. An instrument may be very reliable because it provides a highly consistent measure of a construct, but it may be invalid because it measures the wrong construct.

To illustrate the difference between validity and reliability, consider the following example. Imagine you gave a standard IQ test like the WAIS-IV in English to a group of Swahili-speaking high school students in Kenya. You may find high test–retest reliability for the WAIS-IV, but would you have a valid measure of those students' intelligence? No, you would have a measure of their knowledge of English, but you would not have a valid measure of their intelligence. For these Swahili-speaking students of Kenya, the WAIS-IV in English is a measure of English proficiency rather than a measure of intelligence.

Giving an English-language IQ test to assess the intelligence of Swahili-speaking Kenyan students is, of course, an obvious example of measuring a construct other than the one intended. However, in most instances in psychological measurement, the question of validity is subtler yet always present. Indeed, to a certain extent, all measures in psychology share this problem with validity. This, as we have learned, is because operational definitions of a construct are imperfect. Operational definitions inevitably include elements that are not supposed to be included, while portions of the underlying construct that should be measured are excluded.

This is why we need multiple measures of the same construct. We also need multiple indicators or outcome measures to assess the quality of a construct, such as the extent to which it explains and predicts certain phenomena. In other words, we need to assess the validity of a construct. Ultimately, we evaluate the validity of a construct by determining whether its multiple indicators cohere into predictable and logical patterns of relationships. In so doing, we consider various kinds of validity. We start with the simple question of face validity of an instrument.

## Face Validity

The question of face validity asks whether a test "looks like" it measures what it is supposed to measure (Anastasi, 1988). Face validity is essentially a matter of opinion and lacks a firm scientific or empirical basis. It adds little or nothing to the validation of a test. In fact, if anything, problems can arise when what a psychological test is supposed to measure looks too obvious. Such an instrument may be subjected to **social desirability bias**, in which examinees respond defensively to test items based on how they wish to be perceived rather than openly and genuinely.

Other test-taking strategies, such as examinees "faking bad" or "faking good," may also threaten the validity of an instrument whose measurement objective appears to be too transparent. Face validity is similar to the legal term *prima facie*, a Latin expression meaning "on its first appearance," or "at first sight." However, in law, prima facie evidence is an essential element of jurisprudence, whereas in psychology the face validity of an instrument is inconsequential.

For subjective well-being research, social desirability bias has long been viewed as a major concern. After all, well-being is a highly desirable state, and people may be inclined to be overly favorable in their judgments of life satisfaction, either, unconsciously, in order to preserve a positive self-image or, consciously, in order to project a good impression on others, including the researcher administering the SWLS.

Social desirability has long been considered a serious threat to the validity of any self-report measure. It is often measured using the Marlowe-Crowne Social Desirability Scale, which consists of 33 true/false items (Crowne & Marlowe, 1960). Consider two scale items: "I like to gossip at times" and "I am always willing to admit when I make a mistake." Endorsing "false" for liking gossip and choosing "true" for always admitting a mistake are scored as socially desirable. A higher score raises the question of sociality desirability bias in the self-report. Good research practice is to include a measure of social desirability bias whenever self-reports are the critical source of data or evidence, as is indeed the case for subjective well-being research.

## Content Validity

A valid test needs to provide a full measure of a construct. For example, the WAIS-IV includes 10 core subtests, each of which is presumed to measure a distinct aspect of intelligence, such as verbal reasoning or constructional abilities of working with your hands. Thus, **content validity** refers to the extent to which test items have sufficient breadth to capture the full range of the construct intended to be measured.

In this regard, Keyes (2007) went to great lengths to make sure that his measures provided the full range of the meaning of the construct of mental health. Recall that he used multiple measures to capture what he conceptualized to be the multidimensional nature of mental health. In so doing, his measurement of mental health as well as his *DSM* measure of mental illness would be considered to be valid from the standpoint of content validity.

## Criterion Validity

The validity of a test can also be measured against a certain criterion or outcome. For example, a measure of blood alcohol concentration or a urine test could serve as the criterion for validating a self-report measure of drinking, as long as the questions we ask about drinking refer to the same period of time. Thus, **criterion validity** addresses the extent to which test scores agree with an objective criterion that follows logically from the measured variable. The criterion that researchers select can be measured either at the same time as the variable to be validated or after that time.

**Concurrent validity** exists when a measure yields scores that are closely related to scores on a criterion measured at the same time. A store might validate a test of sales ability by administering it to sales personnel who are already employed and then comparing their test scores with their actual sales performance. **Predictive validity** is the ability of a measure to predict scores on a criterion measured in the future. For example, SAT scores might be predictive of college grade point averages.

## Construct Validity

As we have learned, psychological constructs exist not as material entities but as ideas inferred on the basis of empirical relationships among measured variables. The question then becomes, how does one demonstrate the validity of a construct? Enter the **multitrait–multimethod matrix**, a table of correlations that is used to assess **construct validity** (Campbell & Fiske, 1959). Today, we view the multitrait–multimethod matrix as the gold standard for testing the validity of new ideas and new measurements in psychology. It tells you both how good your idea is and whether your idea is new and different.

In understanding the logic of a multitrait–multimethod approach, it is helpful to recall the advantages of using multiple methods of measurement. Now with a multitrait–multimethod matrix, you use not only two or more methods of measurement, but you also identify two or more theoretical constructs or traits to investigate. To simplify, let's consider two traits, intelligence and extraversion; each is measured with two different methods of measurement: (1) behavioral observations and (2) tests of intelligence (e.g., WAIS-IV) and extraversion (e.g., NEO Five-Factor Personality Inventory; Costa & McCrae, 1985).

Within a single multitrait–multimethod matrix, two fundamental aspects of construct validity can be empirically evaluated. First is **convergent validity**, which is established by examining whether the same trait measured by two different methods yields similar results. In our example, intelligence measured by the WAIS-IV and behavioral observations should be related and so should extraversion measured by the NEO and behavioral observations. If different measures (e.g., behavioral observations, test scores) of the same trait correlate, then this would be considered strong empirical evidence for convergent validity. Second, the matrix provides a format to examine **discriminant validity**, which is demonstrated when different traits using the same form of measurement are unrelated. In our example, intelligence and extraversion should be unrelated, whether measured using tests or by behavioral observations. Thus, construct validity requires both convergent and discriminant validity, which can be most effectively empirically evaluated via the multitrait–multimethod matrix.

Exhibit 4.14 depicts a multitrait–multimethod matrix of our hypothetical example of two traits, intelligence and extraversion, and two methods of measurement, objective tests and behavioral observation. The psychometric methods of measurement are the WAIS-IV IQ test for the construct of intelligence and the NEO Five Factor Personality Inventory test for the construct of extraversion. There are three important points regarding the multitrait–multimethod matrix of correlational values presented in Exhibit 4.14. First, the correlational values presented in the diagonal (in parentheses) of the matrix are the Cronbach alpha reliability coefficients. This is a correlational statistic that indicates the degree of internal consistency for each of the four measurements; higher values reflect stronger reliability of the measure. As shown in the matrix, each of the four measurements had reliability coefficients of .90. Correlation values of this magnitude indicate highly reliable, internally consistent measures.

| Exhibit 4.14 | Multitrait–Multimethod Matrix of Correlations Between Intelligence and Extraversion | | | |
|---|---|---|---|---|
| | Psychometric Measures | | Behavior Observations | |
| | Intelligence | Extraversion | Intelligence | Extraversion |
| Psychometric measures | | | | |
| Intelligence | (.90) | .30 | | |
| Extraversion | .30 | (.90) | | |
| Behavior observations | | | | |
| Intelligence | .70 | .10 | (.90) | .30 |
| Extraversion | .10 | .70 | .30 | (.90) |

Second are the same-trait/different-method correlation coefficient values. Here, we see a .70 correlation coefficient between scores on the WAIS-IV IQ test and behavioral observation recordings for the construct of intelligence. We also see an identical .70 value for the correlation between scores on the NEO Five Factor Inventory test of extraversion and behavioral observation recordings for the construct of extraversion. Thus, the same-trait/different-method comparisons revealed high correlation values of .70 for intelligence and for personality. We therefore can conclude that our results demonstrated convergent validity for the each of these constructs of intelligence and extraversion. Third, the different-traits/same-method pairs for tests of intelligence and extraversion revealed a very low value of .30, as did the different-traits/same-method pairs for behavioral observations of intelligence and extraversion. For discriminant validity, there should be no relationship between two different constructs, such as intelligence and extraversion, that are tested with the same form of measurement, such as a psychometric instrument or behavioral observation.

Exhibit 4.15 presents the three important correlations generated from a multitrait–multimethod matrix. First is the reliability correlation of internal consistency of a trait measure (i.e., same trait/same method of measurement). Second is the convergent validity correlation of the same trait measured by two different methods, such as behavioral observations and test scores (i.e., same trait/different methods of measurement). A high correlation of two different methods of measurement of the same trait indicates high convergent validity. Third is the discriminant validity correlation of two different constructs measured by the same method. Here, a low correlation indicates high discriminant validity. Last are the nonsense correlations of different traits and different measures.

| Exhibit 4.15 | Correlation Coefficients in a Multitrait–Multimethod Matrix | |
|---|---|---|
| Coefficients | Constructs/Traits | Methods/Measurements |
| 1. Reliability correlation | Same | Same |
| 2. Convergent validity correlation | Same | Different |
| 3. Discriminant validity correlation | Different | Same |
| 4. Nonsense correlation | Different | Different |

## Latent Variable Models

Constructs can be inferred, developed, and evaluated through the use of a set of specialized statistical techniques that are referred to as **latent variable models** (Heinen, 1996). Perhaps the most well-known of these models is **factor analysis**, which can be used when a researcher wants to identify the distinct dimensions or "factors" of a given construct (DeCoster, 1998). For example, let us consider factor analyses of intelligence that were used in constructing the WAIS-IV. In this model, the construct of intelligence has been shown to encompass four distinct factors: (1) verbal comprehension, (2) perceptual reasoning, (3) working memory, and (4) processing speed.

How, you may ask, did this model come to be? Essentially, the model is a product of factor analyses, which may be viewed as a "bottom up" inductive procedure that investigates patterns of correlations among responses to a very large set of measurable indicators or variables. In this example, these indicators or variables are objective responses to an extensive sample of thousands of IQ test items. Factor analysis as a statistical technique uncovers what items coalesce or the extent to which participants respond similarly across various items. The more similar the scores, the more likely it is that this set of items taps a particular factor, such as working memory.

Note that the researcher labels a factor such as working memory based on what the interrelated items appear to be measuring. That is, the researcher infers the factor on the basis of the content of the interrelated items. Labeling and inferring factors are thus based on interpretation of the content that is measured. It is subjective, even though it is based on empirical findings, and as a result, it often needs to be confirmed on a second independent sample of participants given the same test items. This is referred to as **confirmatory factor analysis**, which is used to determine whether the same set of factors can be replicated in a new independent sample.

Constructs and factors are often used interchangeably. For our example, however, we used factor analysis to test the underlying structure of IQ. The four factors—working memory, processing speed, perceptual reasoning, and verbal comprehension—may be viewed as distinct dimensions of the construct of intelligence.

## Culture and Measurement

Culture matters greatly in psychological measurement. Our measurements can be biased against certain cultures and ethnicities. For example, numerous studies have shown an **outcome bias** in IQ testing that places African Americans as a group at an approximately 15-point disadvantage in comparison with white groups (Neisser et al., 1996). Imagine flipping a coin that consistently comes up heads for any reason. In probability theory, the coin would be considered to be biased, regardless of any consequences that the outcome may or may not have. By analogy, an IQ test for which the black mean falls approximately 1 standard deviation (about 15 points) or less below the mean of whites would also be considered ipso facto evidence of outcome bias (Neisser et al., 1996).

In 1995, the social psychologists C. M. Steele and J. Aronson demonstrated how negative stereotypes (e.g., "genetic deficit") that have been traditionally used to explain racial IQ differences detract from actual test performance of African Americans. This phenomenon is referred to as **stereotype threat**, and its deleterious effects on intelligence in African American students are shown in Exhibit 4.16. These data provide strong evidence that the racial disparity in IQ is due to environmental and social factors, not to a genetic deficit.

To understand how the disparity in IQ between racial groups has been erroneously interpreted as evidence of genetic inferiority, consider the following well-known plant analogy developed by the evolutionary biologist Richard Lewontin (1976), which is depicted in Exhibit 4.17. Imagine having a packet of virtually identical seeds, half of which you plant in a pot containing fertile soil and the other half in a pot of barren soil. The group of seeds planted in the poor soil will inevitably grow, but their growth will be stunted in comparison with the group of seeds planted in the rich soil.

**Exhibit 4.16** Stereotype Threat in IQ Performance in African Americans

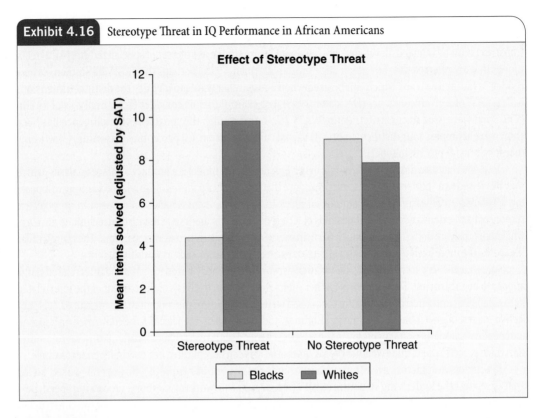

**Effect of Stereotype Threat**

Blacks    Whites

**Exhibit 4.17** The Plant Analogy Used to Explain Why Group Differences in IQ Are Determined by the Environment

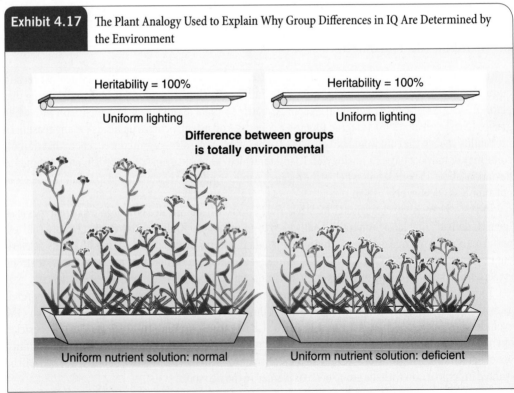

Keep in mind that because the two groups of seeds are genetically identical, any differences in growth *between* the two potted plants are entirely due to the *environment,* which in this case is the soil. By the same token, *within* each group of seeds, some plants will grow larger than others. In contradistinction to the group differences observed between the two pots, the differences in plant heights within each pot are due to genetic variation within each group of seeds.

Now to apply this analogy to race/ethnic differences in IQ, we know that genetic variation can produce individual differences in IQ within a group (e.g., Bouchard & McGue, 1981), yet we also know that the average IQ difference between groups can still only be determined by the environment (e.g., Gray & Thompson, 2004). That is, genes along with environmental factors will influence individual differences in IQ, but only culture and environment will determine group differences in IQ. The critical lesson to take from this analogy is that any interpretation for racial/ethnic differences in IQ cannot use within-group genetic variation to account for between-group differences (Gray & Thompson, 2004). And the larger lesson for research methods in general is the importance of cultural considerations in any measurement in psychology (Na et al., 2010).

## Conclusions

Researchers in psychology "play" with constructs. A construct is simply an idea, concept, or theoretical abstraction that has multiple referents, which in psychology are known as measurable variables. A construct is defined conceptually, a variable operationally. A theory unites a construct with its corresponding variables and their distinct forms of measurements. It does so by translating abstract concepts into particular measurable variables, each of which will include a form of objective measurement.

Research in psychology may thus be viewed as a dynamic interplay between conceptual and operational modes of thinking. On the one hand are theoretical constructs that exist as abstract formulations in need of empirical validation. On the other hand are operational definitions that act as recipes for specifying how constructs will be produced and measured. An operational definition specifies the scale of measurement that will be used to score a variable. A dependent variable can be scored by either one of four scales of measurement: nominal, ordinal, interval, or ratio. These scales of measurement are especially important when considering arithmetic calculations and statistical tests. Recall, for example, that a nominal scale reflects simple categorization for which any arithmetic calculations beyond basic counting are impossible. Knowing the scale of measurement of a variable is thus critical for what mathematical and statistical procedures are allowed to be computed. Measurement in the form of standardized tests is a field of study in and of itself and is known as psychometrics. Psychometrics is based on the principles of standardization of test construction, test administration, and test scoring.

A tool of measurement is judged by the extent to which it is a reliable and valid instrument. Reliability speaks to the consistency of a measurement, in terms of internal cohesiveness of its items and the stability of its scores over time. Validity speaks to whether the instrument measures what it is supposed to—the WAIS-IV measures intelligence, the SWLS measures subjective well-being, and so on. Questions of validity are not the same as questions of reliability: Reliability and validity are not synonymous. An instrument may be very reliable because it provides a highly consistent measure of a construct, but it may be invalid because it measures the wrong construct. The multitrait–multimethod matrix is a table of correlation coefficient values that can be calculated to compare and evaluate the reliability and validity of two or more psychological constructs. Last, measurement does not occur in a vacuum. The outcome bias of IQ testing underscores the importance of cultural considerations in any measurement in psychology.

# Key Terms

Alternate-forms reliability
Concurrent validity
Confirmatory factor analysis
Construct
Construct validity
Content validity
Convergent validity
Criterion validity
Cronbach's alpha
Dichotomy
Discriminant validity
Exhaustive
Face validity
Factor analysis
Interitem reliability
Interobserver reliability

Interval level of measurement
Latent variable models
Level of measurement
Likert scale
Measurement
Multitrait–multimethod matrix
Mutually exclusive
Nominal level of measurement
Nonparametric statistics
Normal curve
Norms
Ordinal level of measurement
Outcome bias
Parametric statistics
Positive psychology
Predictive validity

Psychological traits
Psychometrics
Random error of measurement
Ratio level of measurement
Reliability measure
Scale
Scatter diagram
Social desirability bias
Split-half reliability
Standard deviation
Standardization
Standardization sample
Stereotype threat
Stratified sample
Test–retest reliability

# Research in the News

In a May 13, 2010, *New York Times* piece "Metric Mania," the mathematics professor John Allen Paulos (2010a) writes, "The problem isn't with statistical tests themselves but with what we do before and after we run them." Let's imagine that you have been assigned to write a similar piece for the *New York Times*, which you cleverly title "The Rule of Measurement." In your piece, you want to explain to the reader that all statistics depend on reliable and valid measurements. That is, you want to explain why reliable and valid measurement is the lifeline of statistics as well as a vital component of all research. In so doing, describe the four different levels of measurement and how each can be applied to investigate a research question.

## STUDENT STUDY SITE

Please access the study site at **www.sagepub.com/nestor2e**, where you will find useful study materials such as mobile-friendly eFlashcards and mid-chapter and full chapter web quizzes for each chapter, along with carefully selected articles from research journals that illustrate the major concepts and techniques presented in the book.

# Activity Questions

1. Richard E. Nisbett (2009) argues in his book *Intelligence and How to Get It: Why Schools and Culture Count* that the disparity in average IQ between Americans of European and of African descent is "purely environmental." Explain how

the Lewontin (1976) analogy shows that the racial disparities in IQ are best understood in terms of environmental factors.

2. Role-play what it would be like being a research participant assigned to either the stereotype threat or the nonstereotype threat condition of the Steele and Aronson (1995) study. Perhaps hand out exam blue books and read the two different sets of instructions to give your students a feel of what it would be like to be in either the stereotype threat or the nonstereotype threat condition.

3. The Implicit Association Test (IAT) is among the most widely researched web-based measures of covert thoughts and feelings. Go to https://implicit.harvard.edu/implicit/, and investigate the IAT, and take one of the IAT measures. Evaluate the IAT in terms of reliability and validity. What are the pros and cons of this relatively new technology for assessing covert thoughts and feelings? What are the cultural implications?

4. Are important constructs in psychological research always defined clearly? Are they defined consistently? Search the literature for six research articles that focus on "mental illness," "mental health," "happiness," or some other construct suggested by your instructor. Is the construct defined clearly in each article? How similar are the definitions? Write up what you have found in a short report.

5. Two important human traits—intelligence and happiness—have attracted your curiosity. You are interested in construct validation of these two traits. You have at your disposal two methods of measurement: psychometric tests and behavioral observations. Show how you would use a multitrait–multimethod matrix to evaluate the construct validity of intelligence and happiness using these two different methods of measurement. Make sure to address both convergent validity and discriminant validity.

6. Imagine that you have been asked by a political consultant to devise a measure to assess whether people agree or disagree with a set of positions regarding a particular policy or political position. Describe how you would use a *nominal* level of measurement to gauge people's opinions. What statistic would you use to summarize your hypothetical data that you plan to collect using a nominal level of measurement? What statistical test would you use to analyze your nominal data? Now describe how you would use an *ordinal* level of measurement to gauge people's opinions. Again, identify the statistic you would use to summarize your ordinal data, and also indicate the best statistical approach for your data analysis. Finally, compare and contrast your nominal and ordinal levels of measurement.

7. Stereotype threat creates a significant problem in psychometric testing of cognitive abilities. Imagine that you wanted to study the effect of stereotype threat on high-level mathematics performance in women. Explain the stereotype threat and how it is theorized to detract from women's performance in mathematics, especially at higher levels of complexity. What staged manipulation would you devise to create or operationalize stereotype threat in this study? How might stereotype threat be reduced so that people are judged by their abilities rather than by stereotype?

8. The construct of intelligence extends well beyond what is measured by IQ tests. For example, the psychologist Howard Gardner (1983, 1993) proposed the existence of multiple intelligences ranging from musical to logical-mathematical to interpersonal ability. What do you think intelligence means? What would your construct of intelligence entail? Would you include, as Howard Gardner does, the *bodily kinesthetic intelligence* that is shown by gifted athletes, surgeons, or dancers?

# Review Questions

1. Think of a construct such as subjective well-being. How was it developed? How is it operationalized?

2. Why does a Likert scale use an ordinal level of measurement?

3. What are the advantages of using multiple methods or multiple forms of measurement such as behavioral observations and psychophysiological recordings?

4. Why is face validity inadequate? How would social desirability bias and face validity be related?

5. Why is IQ measured with an interval scale and income with a ratio scale?

6. Why can only the mode be used with data measured with a nominal scale? Why can't the arithmetic mean and standard deviation be used with the nominal level of measurement?

7. What IQ score equals $1\frac{1}{3}$ standard deviation below the mean of 100?

8. What percentages of cases are expected to fall within $\pm 1$ standard deviation of the mean of the normal curve?

9. How would you stratify a sample of 2,000 people ranging in ages from 16 to 90 years?

10. How would you demonstrate that a test provides an internally consistent measure of a construct?

11. Why is discriminant validity important for construct validation?

12. Describe the relationship between the four levels of measurements and parametric/nonparametric statistics.

13. Describe the research design used in stereotype threat studies.

14. How does research on stereotype threat help explain the IQ disparity between Americans of European and of African descent?

15. Discuss the ethics of using staged manipulations in research.

16. Explain the principles of construct validity. Show how to construct a multitrait–multimethod matrix.

17. Why would alternate-forms reliability be important when comparing people's memory before and after receiving a treatment drug?

18. What is outcome bias?

19. What kind of evidence would you cite to demonstrate the predictive validity of IQ?

# Ethics in Action

1. What are the ethical implications of the erroneous conclusion that racial group differences in IQ are hardwired, fixed, and genetically immutable? How does such a mistaken claim lead to the ethically dubious argument that enrichment programs are of little or no benefit because of immutable group IQ differences?

2. Recall from Chapter 3 ("Research in the News") the importance of fully informed consent for research participants with regard to how data collected from them in a given study will be used. Now consider informed consent for research participants in a study of racial differences in group IQ. What are the major ethical obligations a researcher has in ensuring that participants are fully informed as to the purpose of a study examining racial differences in group IQ?

3. In the stereotype threat studies by Steele and colleagues (1995) participants are given the same test, but some participants are essentially told that it is an IQ measure and other participants are told that it is a nondiagnostic measure of problem solving (i.e., not an IQ test). How would you justify this deception as ethical? How is it in keeping with the principle elucidated in the APA Ethical Code (see Chapter 3): *Avoid deception in research, except in limited circumstances*?

# Sampling and Survey Research

## LEARNING OBJECTIVES: FAST FACTS

### Sampling and Survey Design

- Sampling theory focuses on the generalizability of descriptive findings to the population from which the sample was drawn. Researchers must also consider whether statements can be generalized from one population to another.

- Probability sampling methods rely on a random selection procedure to ensure that there is no systematic bias in the selection of elements. In a probability sample, the odds of selecting elements are known, and the method of selection is carefully controlled.

- The likely degree of error in an estimate of a population characteristic based on a probability sample decreases when the size of the sample and the homogeneity of the population from which the sample was selected increase. Sampling error is not affected by the proportion of the population that is sampled except when that proportion is large. The degree of sampling error affecting a sample statistic can be estimated from the characteristics of the sample and knowledge of the properties of sampling distributions.

- Survey designs must minimize the risk of errors of observation (measurement error) and errors of nonobservation (errors due to inadequate coverage, sampling error, and nonresponse). The likelihood of both types of error varies with the survey goals. A survey questionnaire or interview schedule should be designed as an integrated whole, with each question and section serving some clear purpose and complementing the others.

- Questions must be worded carefully to avoid confusing the respondents, encouraging less than honest responses, or triggering biases.

## TESTING BEFORE LEARNING

Try your hand at these questions. Don't worry about not knowing the correct response, as you haven't read the chapter yet! But research shows that a pretest such as this can enhance learning (e.g., Kornell, Hays, & Bjork, 2009). So here is the answer. You come up with the question.

1. The process through which individuals or other entities are selected to represent a larger population of interest
   a. What is a census?
   b. What is sampling?
   c. What is probability?
   d. What is a population?

2. Used to study the entire population of interest
   a. What is a census?
   b. What is sampling?

   c. What is probability?
   d. What is a population?

3. A random selection procedure to ensure that there are no systematic biases in the selection of elements
   a. What is nonprobability sampling?
   b. What is sampling?
   c. What is probability sampling?
   d. What is sampling error?

4. Needed in assessing whether we can compare the results obtained from samples of different populations
   a. What is sampling error?
   b. What is the sampling frame?
   c. What is probability sampling?
   d. What is cross-population generalizability?

5. The entire set of individuals or other entities to which study findings are to be generalized
   a. What is probability sampling?
   b. What is sampling?
   c. What is a population?
   d. What are elements?

6. A major problem because it reflects a less representative sample and thus less generalizable findings obtained from that sample
   a. What is sampling error?
   b. What is probability sampling?
   c. What is chi-square?
   d. What are inferential statistics?

7. A set of mathematical procedures used to estimate how likely it is that, given a particular sample, the true population value will be within some range of the sample statistics
   a. What is chi-square?
   b. What are inferential statistics?
   c. What is probability sampling?
   d. What is sampling error?

8. Differences between the population and the sample, which can be estimated statistically, are due only to chance factors (random error), not to systematic sampling error.
   a. What is a contingency table?
   b. What are inferential statistics?
   c. What is chi-square?
   d. What is random sampling error?

9. One of the most common analytic approaches in survey research to show how responses to one question (the dependent variable) are distributed within the responses to another question (the independent variable)
   a. What is a contingency table?
   b. What are inferential statistics?
   c. What is chi-square?
   d. What is random sampling error?

10. An inferential statistic used to test hypotheses about the relationships between variables in a contingency table
    a. What is random sampling error?
    b. What is probability sampling?
    c. What is chi-square?
    d. What are elements?

**ANSWER KEY:** (1) b; (2) a; (3) c; (4) d; (5) c; (6) a; (7) b; (8) d; (9) a; (10) c

# How Happy Are You?

Please imagine a ladder with steps numbered from 0 at the bottom to 10 at the top. Suppose we say that the top of the ladder represents the best possible life for you and the bottom of the ladder represents the worst possible life for you. On which step of the ladder would you say you personally feel you stand at this time, assuming that the higher the step the better you feel about your life and the lower the step the worse you feel about it. Which step comes closest to the way you feel?

This question dates back to surveys by the psychologist Hadley Cantril at the Institute for International Social Research (Geer, 2004, p. 390). In his 1965 book, *The Pattern of Human Concerns*, Cantril reported the results of surveys using this question—he called it the "Self-Anchoring Striving Scale"—in countries around the world. Since that time, Cantril's question has been included in hundreds of surveys and has been the focus of much research into the bases of human happiness and, more generally, what came to be called "quality of life."

The Gallup Organization included Cantril's question in its 2005–2006 Gallup World Poll (GWP) of adults in 132 countries. As a result of this international survey, we know that the average response in the United States was 7.0; Norway had one of the highest average scores (7.7) and Sudan one of the lowest (3.6). By comparison, where did your score fall? If you are reading this book in the United States and had a score more like the average adult in Norway, you might now feel even a bit happier, whereas if your score was much lower than the U.S. average, you might start to wonder why. Thanks to Ed Diener (Diener, Ng, Harter, & Arora, 2010) and other psychologists (e.g., Aknin et al., 2013), we now know that the average responses to this Self-Anchoring Striving Scale question vary much more between countries than they do among groups within countries, and we also know quite a bit about why different people feel more or less happy.

We hope it keeps you feeling happy about studying research methods to return to research about happiness in this chapter, but we use happiness research in this chapter to illustrate a very different methodological issue: sampling. You will therefore learn much more about happiness research throughout this chapter as we study the logic of sampling and the design of surveys.

If you and your classmates answered the Cantril question, you are probably already thinking about the logic of sampling and the design of surveys. Have you calculated the average response for the class and compared it with the average reported by Gallup for your own country? Because you and your classmates are a sample of students, you may be asking yourselves whether your responses are likely to be typical for students at your school, for college students throughout your country, or perhaps for all adults. These are the types of questions we can answer if we understand the logic of sampling. Did every student answer the question? Would they have given the same answer if the question had been included in a longer survey about intimate partners? Would it have mattered if someone asked students the question face-to-face? These are issues about survey design.

We first discuss why it is important to consider the key sampling question: Can findings from a sample be generalized to the population from which the sample was drawn? We then review different sampling methods and some of the associated statistical issues. Next, we explain the major steps in designing questions and combining them in surveys. We also describe four different survey designs and then give examples of some basic statistics that are useful in analyzing data obtained in survey research. We conclude with a discussion of ethical issues in survey research. By the chapter's end, you should be well on your way to becoming an informed critic of sample surveys and a knowledgeable creator of surveys—and you will also have expanded your knowledge about happiness. We hope *that* makes you happy!

## ▣ Selecting Research Participants

Your classmates probably varied in their scores on the Striving Scale. No doubt your own happiness has been higher at some times and lower at others. You also have just learned that the average Striving Scale scores vary between nations. We can't simply assume that what people tell us about their happiness or any feelings or behaviors at one point in time will hold for other people or at different times. This is why researchers have to be concerned with sampling—the selection of individuals or other entities to represent a larger population of interest.

Of course, if we can study the entire population of interest—that is, conduct a **census**—we can avoid the problem. This is what the federal government tries to do every 10 years with the U.S. Census. But the census approach is not likely to be feasible with a large population. To conduct the 2010 Census, the U.S. Bureau of the Census spent more than $5.5 billion and hired 3.8 million people to have one person in about 134 million households answer the 10 census questions (U.S. Bureau of the Census, 2010a, 2010b). Up to six follow-ups and 565,000 temporary workers were used to contact the 28% of households that did not return their census form in the mail, at a cost of $57 per nonrespondent (compared with just 42 cents for those who mailed in the form) (U.S. Bureau of the Census, 2010a, 2010c). Even after all that, we know from the 2000 U.S. Census that some groups are still likely to be underrepresented (Armas, 2002; Holmes, 2001), including minority groups (Kershaw, 2000), impoverished cities (Zielbauer, 2000), well-to-do individuals in gated communities and luxury buildings (Langford, 2000), and even college students (Abel, 2000). The number of persons missed in the 2000 U.S. Census was estimated to be between 3.2 and 6.4 million (U.S. Bureau of the Census, 2001).

For most survey purposes, it is much better to survey only a limited number from the total population so that there are more resources for follow-up procedures required to locate respondents and overcome their reluctance to participate. This is the logic of the American Community Survey (ACS), a survey conducted by the U.S. Bureau of the Census every year with a sample of 3 million households (U.S. Bureau of the Census, 2010d). The ACS includes 60 questions rather than just the 10 in the decennial census.

# Sample Planning

To plan a sample or to assess the quality of a sample selected by another researcher, you need to answer two questions:

1. From what population will you select cases?
2. What method will you use to select cases from this population?

## Define the Population

Let's focus first on defining the population, since everything else in a sample survey depends on that. Behavioral researchers have administered happiness surveys to samples of many different populations. Some have surveyed students, some have surveyed other groups in the United States, while others have surveyed samples of the entire U.S. population as well as samples in other countries—as the GWP did. The results of these surveys demonstrate the importance of the population we study, for there are some surprising consistencies and some unexpected differences. Students, disabled persons, the elderly, and adult samples tend to report similar, although not identical, levels of happiness, as do men and women, African Americans, and whites (Diener & Diener, 1996; Myers & Diener, 1995). However, Diener and his colleagues' analysis of the GWP found marked variation in happiness between countries, confirming a pattern revealed in earlier research (Diener, Diener, & Diener, 1995). In addition, satisfaction with different life domains varies across cultures (Biswas-Diener, Vitterso, & Diener, 2005).

The key lesson here is that we must define clearly the population that we actually have studied and not give the impression that we collected data about some larger or different aggregation that we really wish we could have studied. We need to know if we can safely *generalize* the findings from a study of one population to other populations; to the extent that findings can be generalized to other populations, we have achieved **cross-population generalizability** (external validity). The psychologist Lara B. Aknin and her collaborators (2013) used the GWP to investigate whether "prosocial spending" (using your financial resources to help others) is related to being happier in countries around the world. The consistent results across the 136 countries in the poll led them to conclude that this relationship is a real psychological universal (although, of course, we only know for sure that it held in the period of the survey, 2006–2008). This is unusually strong evidence of cross-population generalizability, but even if we have studied people in just one country, or in one state or one group, we need to consider whether our findings are likely to apply to other populations.

When the psychological process being studied is really a "psychological universal," findings should be similar no matter what the sample we use to study it. For example, college students in a psychologist's laboratory can yield important insights about human behavior when that behavior reflects basic human propensities. Facial expressions used to display emotions? Similar around the world (Ekman, 2003). Production of stress hormones in response to perceived threats? Similar around the world (University of Maryland, 2013). And you now know that prosocial spending is associated with more happiness around the world. But you can only be as confident of cross-population generalizability as the evidence that has been obtained for it.

## Define Sample Components

Defining the population(s) of interest is only the first step in most research. Unless we can conduct a census or we are confident that we are studying attitudes or behaviors that are the same among all people, we have to be concerned with how we draw a sample from the population. But before we introduce different methods for sampling from a population, we need to learn a few more terms (Exhibit 5.1).

| Exhibit 5.1 | Representative and Unrepresentative Samples |
| --- | --- |

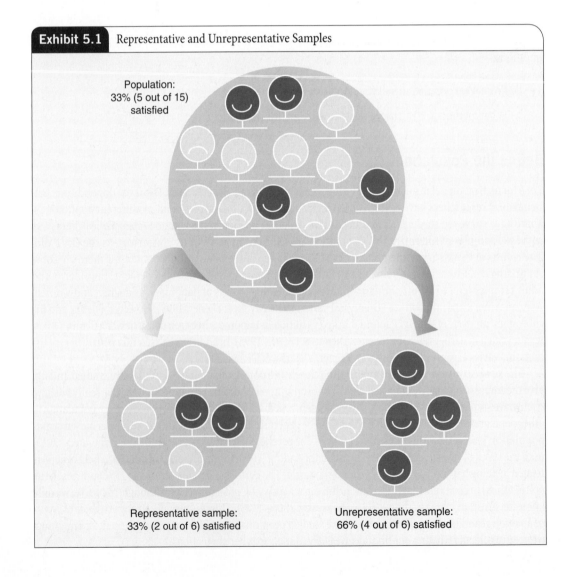

Population:
33% (5 out of 15) satisfied

Representative sample:
33% (2 out of 6) satisfied

Unrepresentative sample:
66% (4 out of 6) satisfied

Our goal is to use procedures leading to a sample that is representative of the population of interest. If the sample is representative of the population, our findings can be generalized to the population. So our goal is **sample generalizability**. In many studies, we sample directly from the cases, or **elements**, or elementary units, in the population of interest. For a survey about mental health among students at a large Midwestern public university, Eisenberg, Gollust, Golberstein, and Hefner (2007) obtained from the registrar's office a list of the entire population of students at the school. This list, from which the elements of the population are selected, is termed the **sampling frame**. The students who are selected and interviewed from that list are the cases, or elements.

# Sampling Methods

Sampling methods can be distinguished as either "nonprobability" or "probability." **Nonprobability sampling methods** result in a sample in which the **probability of selection** of any case, or element, is unknown. **Probability sampling methods** are selected in a way so that we know the probability of selection of the cases or elements. Probability sampling is the preferred method of sampling in most **survey research** because it leads to much greater confidence in sample representativeness. However, we will start with a brief discussion of nonprobability sampling methods because they are very common, relatively easy to use, and often preferred when psychologists study processes that they assume to be common across people.

## Nonprobability Sampling Methods

**Availability sampling** is the simplest type of nonprobability sampling method. If you were invited to participate in an experiment in your Introductory Psychology course, it was because you and other students were "available" (and willing). Behavioral research with samples of students who are simply "available" for experiments or surveys has shown that this sampling method can lead to great insights about human behavior and psychological processes. However, because such availability sampling does not result in a **representative sample** of the student population, it is risky to assume that the results from one study can be generalized to other students, much less to all adults. It takes many repetitions of such studies with such small-scale "samples" to give us some confidence in their generalizability.

Cases (elements) are selected for availability sampling because they're available or easy to find. Thus, this sampling method is also known as haphazard, accidental, or convenience sampling. There are many ways to select elements for an availability sample, such as inviting interested students to come to an on-campus lab, including a survey inside a magazine (with the plea to subscribers to complete and return it), or asking questions of available students at campus hangouts. Many happiness researchers have used availability samples of students who volunteer to participate in a research project.

## Quota Sampling

**Quota sampling** is intended to overcome the most obvious flaw of availability sampling: that the sample will just consist of whomever or whatever is available, without any concern for its similarity to the population of interest. The distinguishing feature of a quota sample is that quotas are set to ensure that the sample represents certain characteristics in proportion to their prevalence in the population.

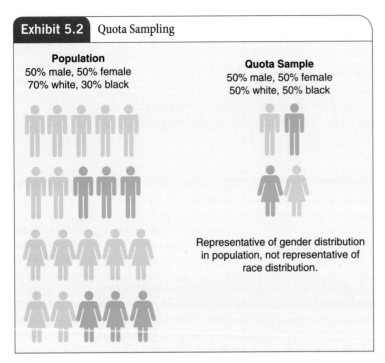

**Exhibit 5.2** Quota Sampling

**Population**
50% male, 50% female
70% white, 30% black

**Quota Sample**
50% male, 50% female
50% white, 50% black

Representative of gender distribution
in population, not representative of
race distribution.

Suppose that you wish to sample the adult residents of a town in a study of support for placing a group home in the town. You know from the town's annual report that 48% of the town's adult residents are men and 52% are women, and that 60% are employed, 5% are unemployed, and 35% are out of the labor force. Let's say that you believe that gender and employment status are important factors in shaping support for group homes. You might then decide that you want to ensure that your sample represents the population accurately in terms of gender and employment status, and so these percentages become the quotas for the sample (Exhibit 5.2). If you plan to include a total of 500 residents in your sample, 240 must be men (48% of 500), 260 must be women, 300 must be employed, and so on. With the quota list in hand, you (or your research staff) can now go out into the community looking for the right number of people in each quota category. You may go door to door, bar to bar, or just stand on a street corner until you have surveyed 240 men, 260 women, and so on.

There are several other types of nonprobability sampling methods. **Snowball sampling** involves asking a small number of people in some population of interest for referrals to others like themselves. You might start a snowball sample by asking a few students you know who have used illicit drugs in the past to suggest others they know who have the same type of history. Your sample size grows as you repeat this process. This is a good way to develop a sample from a relatively inaccessible population.

Methodologists use the term **purposive sampling** to refer to selecting a sample of people because they fulfill a specific purpose of the researcher. For example, if you want to study the psychology of political officials, you may draw a purposive sample of the leading political figures in your town. They are selected because they are "the" opinion leaders.

## Probability Sampling Methods

When psychologists seek to survey a sample of people in order to develop a description that can be generalized to a larger population, they use a probability sampling method. Probability sampling methods are those in which the probability of selection of any case is known and that probability is not zero (so there is some chance of selecting each element). These methods randomly select elements and therefore have no **systematic bias**; nothing but chance determines which elements are included in the sample. This feature of probability samples makes them much more desirable than nonprobability samples when the goal is to generalize to a larger population. The GWP used such a random selection method (Diener et al., 2010).

Probability sampling methods rely on a random, or chance, selection procedure. To go back to the example of a coin toss, heads and tails are equally likely to turn up when the coin is tossed; their probability of selection is 1 out of 2, or .5.

There is a natural tendency to confuse the concept of **random sampling**, in which cases are selected only on the basis of chance, with a haphazard method of sampling. On first impression, "leaving things up to chance" seems to imply not exerting any control over the sampling method. But to ensure that nothing but chance influences the selection of cases, the researcher must proceed methodically, leaving nothing to chance except the selection of the cases themselves. The researcher must follow carefully controlled procedures if a purely random process is to be the result.

The four most common methods for drawing random samples are (1) simple random sampling, (2) systematic random sampling, (3) stratified random sampling, and (4) cluster sampling.

## Simple Random Sampling

**Simple random sampling** requires some procedure that generates numbers or otherwise identifies cases strictly on the basis of chance. As you know, flipping a coin or rolling a die can be used to identify cases strictly on the basis of chance, but these procedures are not very efficient tools for drawing a sample. When a large sample must be generated, a computer program can easily generate a random sample of any size. Organizations that conduct phone surveys often draw random samples using another automated procedure, called **random-digit dialing**. A machine dials random numbers within the phone prefixes corresponding to the area in which the survey is to be conducted. The GWP used random-digit dialing to select random samples for telephone surveys in the nations in which telephones are widespread (Diener et al., 2010).

The probability of selection in a true simple random sample is equal for each element. If a sample of 500 is selected from a population of 17,000 (i.e., a sampling frame of 17,000), then the probability of selection for each element is 500/17,000, or .03. Every element has an equal chance of being selected, just like the odds in a toss of a coin (1/2) or a roll of a die (1/6).

## Systematic Random Sampling

**Systematic random sampling** is a variant of simple random sampling. The first element is selected randomly from a list or from sequential files, and then, every $n$th element is selected. This is an efficient method for drawing a random sample when the population elements are arranged sequentially, such as in folders in filing cabinets. The one problem to watch out for is **periodicity**—that is, the sequence varies in some regular, periodic pattern. For example, the houses in a new development with the same number of houses on each block (e.g., eight) may be listed by block, starting with the house in the northwest corner of each block and continuing clockwise. If the **sampling interval** is 8, the same as the periodic pattern, all the cases selected will be in the same position (see Exhibit 5.3). In this situation, the starting point needs to be changed for each block. But in reality, periodicity and the sampling interval are rarely the same.

## Stratified Random Sampling

**Stratified random sampling** uses information known about the total population prior to sampling to make the sampling process more efficient. First, all elements in the population (i.e., in the sampling frame) are distinguished according to their value on some relevant characteristic. That characteristic forms the sampling strata. Next, elements are sampled randomly from within these strata. For example, race may

**Exhibit 5.3** The Effect of Periodicity on Systematic Random Sampling

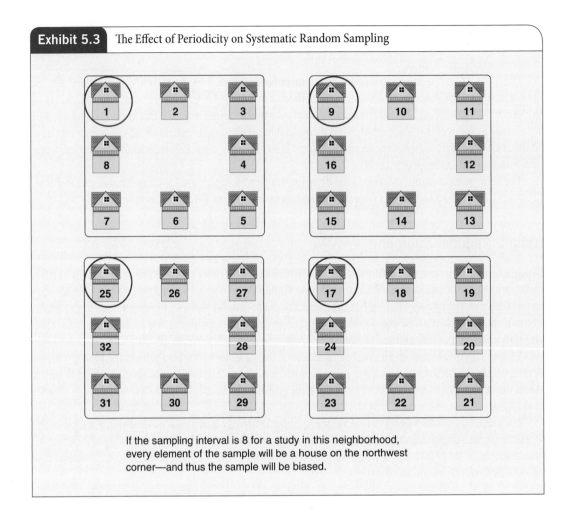

If the sampling interval is 8 for a study in this neighborhood, every element of the sample will be a house on the northwest corner—and thus the sample will be biased.

be the basis for distinguishing individuals in some population of interest. Within each racial category, individuals are then sampled randomly. Of course, using this method requires more information prior to sampling than is the case with simple random sampling. It must be possible to categorize each element in one, and only one, stratum, and the size of each stratum in the population must be known.

This method is more efficient than drawing a simple random sample because it ensures the appropriate representation of elements across strata. It is commonly used in national surveys. Yang's (2008) study of happiness over time in the United States used the General Social Survey, a multistage stratified probability sample of noninstitutionalized adults of ages 18 and older. Recall from Chapter 4 that for the WAIS-IV, the test developers used data gathered in October 2005 by the U.S. Bureau of Census to stratify their standardization sample along the following variables: age, sex, race/ethnicity, self or parent educational level, and geographic region.

Stratified sampling can be either proportionate or disproportionate. **Proportionate stratified sampling** ensures that the sample is selected so that the distribution of characteristics in the sample matches the distribution of the corresponding characteristics in the population. So, for example, if the population ratio of undergraduates to graduates is 2 to 1, the number of students sampled in both strata can be set so as to replicate this ratio (Exhibit 5.4). Eisenberg and his colleagues (2007) used a slightly different sampling design—**disproportionate stratified sampling**—in a survey of student mental health at a large Midwestern university. The registrar's list distinguished undergraduate and graduate students, so Eisenberg et al. were able to sample these two groups separately, as different strata. They knew that the mental health of graduate and professional students "has been particularly understudied," so they selected a higher fraction of graduate students than undergraduate students from the list provided by the registrar. This disproportionate sampling procedure enabled them to calculate separate statistical estimates for graduate as well as for undergraduate students.

| Exhibit 5.4 | Stratified Random Sampling |
|---|---|

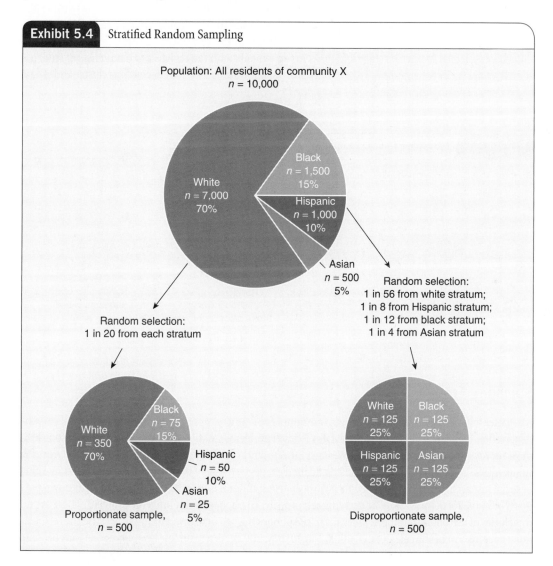

## Cluster Sampling

**Cluster sampling** is useful when a sampling frame of elements is not available, as often is the case for large populations spread out across a wide geographic area or among many different organizations. A **cluster** is a naturally occurring, mixed aggregate of elements of the population, with each element appearing in one, and only one, cluster. Schools could serve as clusters for sampling students, blocks could serve as clusters for sampling city residents, counties could serve as clusters for sampling the general population, and businesses could serve as clusters for sampling employees. In the GWP, cluster sampling was used to generate a representative sample in poorer countries without widespread phone ownership. As reported by Diener et al. (2010), Gallup first randomly selected geographical units for their sample, and then, they randomly selected residences within those geographic units (clusters).

Drawing a cluster sample is, at least, a two-stage procedure. First, the researcher draws a random sample of clusters (Exhibit 5.5). A list of clusters should be much easier to obtain than a list of all the individuals in each cluster in the population. Next, the researcher draws a random sample of elements within each selected cluster. Because only a fraction of the total clusters are involved, obtaining the sampling frame at this stage should be much easier. For example, in a cluster sample of students, a researcher could contact the schools selected in the first stage and make arrangements with the registrar to obtain lists of students at each school (Levy & Lemeshow, 1999). Many professionally designed surveys combine cluster and stratified probability sampling methods.

| Exhibit 5.5 | Multistage Cluster Sampling |
|---|---|

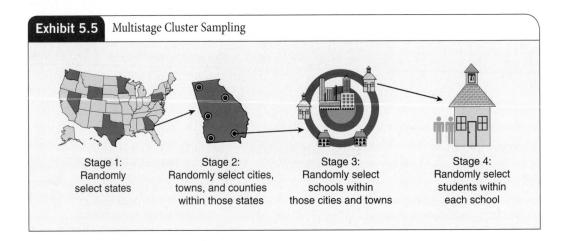

Stage 1:
Randomly
select states

Stage 2:
Randomly select cities,
towns, and counties
within those states

Stage 3:
Randomly select
schools within
those cities and towns

Stage 4:
Randomly select
students within
each school

## Sampling Error

No matter what type of sample you draw, your sample will be less representative if more potential respondents refuse to participate. Unfortunately, this is a real problem in national surveys. The rate of response to most surveys in the United States and Western Europe has been declining since the early 1950s (Groves & Couper, 1998). Growing popular cynicism and distrust of government have undermined trust in the value of social research. More recently, people have been using caller IDs to screen out calls from unknown parties (Dillman, 2000, pp. 8, 28). The growing reliance on cell phones compounds the problem. There are no directories of cell phone numbers, and calls to cell phones may go unanswered simply because the recipient must pay the cost of the call (Keeter, 2008; Nagourney, 2002). As a result of these changes, it has become increasingly challenging for survey researchers to achieve the 70% response rate that most consider necessary if their survey results are to represent the surveyed population. Between 1979 and 2003, the average phone survey response rate declined from more than 75% to about 60% (Tourangeau, 2004, pp. 781–783) (Exhibit 5.6).

Even if there is a very high rate of response to a probability sample, there will still be some **sampling error**—some difference in the characteristics of the sample compared with those of the population from which it is selected. Selection on the basis of chance ensures that there is no systematic bias in the sampling method, but there will still be some differences from the population just on the basis of chance. If you toss a coin twice, it's quite possible that it will come up heads both times even though only one side of

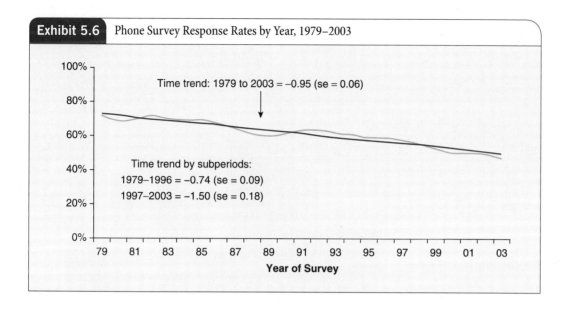

**Exhibit 5.6** Phone Survey Response Rates by Year, 1979–2003

the coin is "heads." The same thing can happen if you toss it four times, although then it is quite a bit less likely that you will have four heads. And so on. Sample generalizability depends on the amount of sampling error—that is, on how large the difference is between the characteristics of a sample and the characteristics of the population from which it was selected. The larger the sampling error, the less representative the sample—and thus the less generalizable the findings obtained from that sample. Of course, representation in a sample is never perfect, but it's important to provide information about how representative a given sample is.

*Estimating Sampling Error*

After we have drawn our sample and obtained our data, we can estimate the confidence we can place on the sample statistic as being representative of the population—that is, we can calculate the likely amount of sampling error. The tool for calculating sampling error is called inferential statistics.

To understand inferential statistics, we need to think of our sample as one possible sample of the many we could have selected from the population. Imagine drawing a great many samples from a population and calculating the average (mean) happiness level for each one. Some of the sample means would be higher, and some would be lower; some would be right about at the actual mean for the entire population. If we plot the mean values for all these samples, the chart would form a **sampling distribution**, like that displayed in Exhibit 5.7.

Sampling distributions for many statistics, including the mean, have a "normal" shape. The graph of a normal distribution, like that in Exhibit 5.8, looks like a bell, with one "hump" in the middle—centered on the population mean—and the number of cases tapering off on both sides of the mean. A normal distribution is symmetric: If you fold it in half at its center (at the population mean), the two halves match perfectly. This shape is produced by **random sampling error (chance sampling error)**—variation owing purely to chance. The value of a sample statistic varies from sample to sample because of chance, so higher and lower values are equally likely.

The properties of a sampling distribution facilitate the process of statistical inference. In the sampling distribution, the most frequent value of the sample statistic—the statistic (e.g., the mean) computed from the sample data—is identical to the population parameter—the statistic computed for the entire population. In other words, we can have a lot of confidence that the value at the peak of the bell curve represents

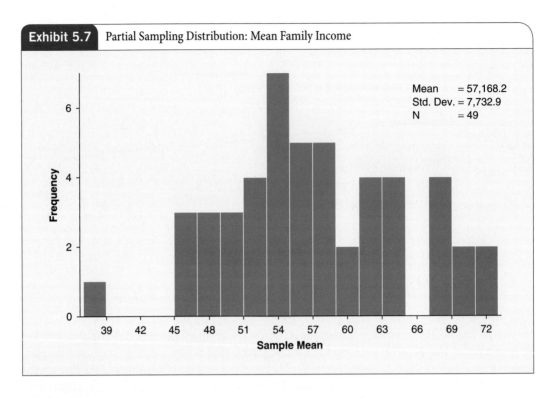

**Exhibit 5.7** Partial Sampling Distribution: Mean Family Income

Mean = 57,168.2
Std. Dev. = 7,732.9
N = 49

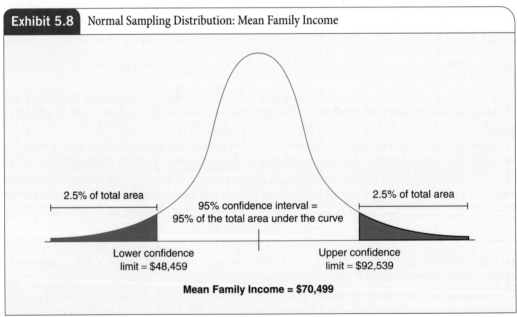

**Exhibit 5.8** Normal Sampling Distribution: Mean Family Income

2.5% of total area

95% confidence interval =
95% of the total area under the curve

2.5% of total area

Lower confidence
limit = $48,459

Upper confidence
limit = $92,539

**Mean Family Income = $70,499**

the norm for the entire population. A population parameter also may be termed the *true value* for the statistic in that population. A sample statistic is an estimate of a population parameter.

In a normal distribution, a predictable proportion of cases fall within certain ranges. Inferential statistics takes advantage of this feature and allows researchers to estimate how likely it is that, given a particular sample, the true population value will be within some range of the statistics. For example, a statistician might conclude from a sample of 30 students that *we can be 95% confident that the true mean family income in the total population is between 20.1 and 25.7*. The interval from 20.1 to 25.7 would then be called the "95% confidence interval for the mean." The lower (20.1) and upper (25.7) bounds of this interval are termed the *confidence limits*. Exhibit 5.8 marks such confidence limits, indicating the range that encompasses 95% of the area under the normal curve; 95% of all sample means would fall within this range, as does the mean of our hypothetical sample of 30 cases. The more cases in the randomly selected sample, the more confident we can be in a given sample estimate (the confidence limits will be smaller). There were 136,839 respondents in the GWP used by Diener et al. (2010) to study happiness. As a result of this huge sample size, the 95% confidence limits around the sample statistics that they calculated were very, very tiny (.006 for the sample average of 5.36 on Cantril's Self-Anchoring Striving Scale). Even when they examined the averages within individual countries, the average sample size of 1,061 meant that these estimates would likely be very close to the true population value.

Don't make the mistake of thinking that a larger sample is better because it includes a greater proportion of the population. Even the huge sample in the GWP is really only a miniscule fraction of the world's population. In fact, it is the number of cases that is most important; the proportion of the population that the sample represents does not affect the sample's representativeness—unless that proportion is large (Sudman, 1976). Other things being equal, a random sample of 1,000 from a population of 1 million (with a sampling fraction of 0.001, or 0.1%) is much better than a random sample of 100 from a population of 10,000 (although the sampling fraction is 0.01, or 1%, which is 10 times higher).

Test your knowledge of this chapter so far by taking the mid-chapter quiz on the study site: www.sagepub.com/ nestor2e

## ▣ Writing Survey Questions

Once you have chosen a population to study and a method for sampling from that population, you must decide what questions to ask in your survey. Presenting clear and interesting questions in a well-organized **questionnaire** is a critical task. All hope for achieving measurement validity is lost unless the questions in a survey are clear and convey the intended meaning to respondents.

Adherence to a few basic principles will go a long way toward ensuring clear and meaningful questions.

### Avoid Confusing Phrasing

Try to answer the following question, one used in a 1980 National Priorities Survey, United States Space Program by the Planetary Society:

> The Moon may be a place for an eventual scientific base, and even for engineering resources. Setting up a base or mining experiment will cost tens of billions of dollars in the next century. Should the United States pursue further manned and unmanned scientific research projects on the surface of the Moon?
>
> Yes ☐          No ☐          No opinion ☐

Does a "yes" response mean that you favor spending tens of billions of dollars for a base or for a mining experiment? How should you answer if you favor further research projects on the Moon but oppose funding a scientific base or engineering? How do you answer if you favor unmanned scientific research projects but oppose manned projects?

In most cases, a simple direct approach to asking a question minimizes confusion. Try to use shorter rather than longer words and sentences and keep the total number of words to 20 or fewer and the number of commas to three or fewer (Peterson, 2000). Here's a good, clear question used in the General Social Survey to measure happiness: "Taken all together, how would you say things are these days—would you say that you are very happy, pretty happy, or not too happy?" A sure way to muddy the meaning of a question is to use **double negatives**: "Do you *disagree* that rich people are *not* happy?" Respondents have a hard time figuring out which response matches their sentiments. To be safe, it's best just to avoid using negative words like "don't" and "not" in questions.

So-called **double-barreled questions** are also guaranteed to produce uninterpretable results because they actually ask two questions but allow only one answer. For example, during the Watergate scandal, Gallup poll results indicated that when the question was "Do you think President Nixon should be impeached and compelled to leave the presidency, or not?" only about a third of Americans supported impeaching President Richard M. Nixon. But when the Gallup organization changed the question to ask respondents if they "think there is enough evidence of possible wrongdoing in the case of President Nixon to bring him to trial before the Senate, or not," more than half answered "yes." Apparently, the first "double-barreled" version of the question confused support for impeaching Nixon—putting him on trial before the Senate—with concluding that he was guilty before he had had a chance to defend himself (Kagay & Elder, 1992).

Be sure that each question is asked of only the respondents who have the information needed to answer. If you include a question about job satisfaction in a survey of the general population, first ask respondents whether they have a job. These **filter questions** create **skip patterns**. For example, respondents who answer "no" to one question are directed to skip ahead to another question, but respondents who answer "yes" go on to the **contingent question**. Skip patterns should be indicated clearly with arrows or other marks in the questionnaire, as demonstrated in Exhibit 5.9.

| **Exhibit 5.9** | Filter Questions and Skip Patterns |
|---|---|

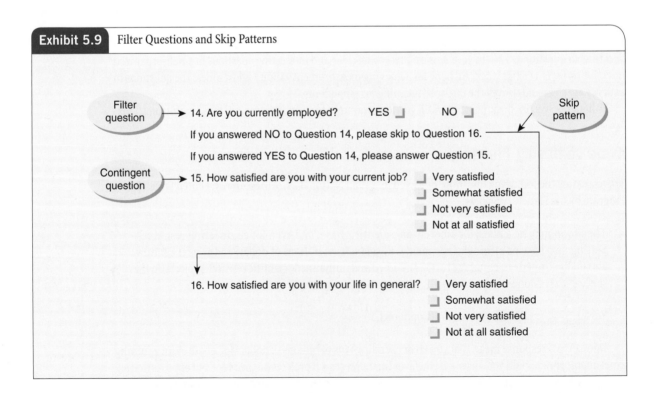

## Minimize the Risk of Bias

Specific words in survey questions should not trigger biases unless that is the researcher's conscious intent. Answers can be biased by subtle problems in phrasing that make certain responses more or less attractive to particular groups, so researchers have to test reactions to the phrasing of a question. When Ross (1990) was seeking to determine respondents' interest in household work rather than formal employment in her survey of stress and mental health, she took special care to phrase her questions in a balanced, unbiased way. For example, she asked, "If you could choose, would you rather do the kind of work people do on jobs or the kind of work that is done around the house?" Her response options were "Jobs," "House," "Both," "Neither," "Don't care," and "Don't know." She could easily have biased the distribution of responses to this question by referring to housework as "the kind of work that women traditionally have done around the house" or by simply referring to housework as "staying home during the day." The explicit gender typing would probably have made men less likely to choose housework as their preference.

## Avoid Making Either Disagreement or Agreement Disagreeable

People often tend to agree with a statement just to avoid seeming disagreeable. When an illegal or socially disapproved behavior or attitude is the focus, we have to be concerned that some respondents will be reluctant to agree that they have ever done or thought such a thing. In this situation, the goal is to write a question and response choices that make agreement seem more acceptable. For example, Kilpatrick and colleagues (2003) prefaced their questions about childhood sexual victimization with a statement that began as follows:

> Sometimes a person may do sexual things to a young person that the young person doesn't want. These unwanted sexual things can happen to boys as well as girls and to young men as well as young women. People who try to do unwanted sexual things to young people are not always strangers. . . . They can even be a family member.

Asking about a variety of behaviors or attitudes that range from socially acceptable to socially unacceptable will also soften the impact of agreeing with those that are socially unacceptable.

## Minimize Fence-Sitting and Floating

Two related problems in question writing also stem from people's desire to choose an acceptable answer.

**Fence-sitters**, people who see themselves as being neutral, may skew the results if you force them to choose between opposites. In most cases, about 10% to 20% of such respondents—those who do not have strong feelings on an issue—will choose an explicit middle, neutral alternative (Schuman & Presser, 1981). Adding an explicit neutral response option is appropriate when you want to find out who is a fence-sitter.

Even more people can be termed **floaters**: respondents who choose a substantive answer when they really don't know. A third of the public will provide an opinion on a proposed law that they know nothing about if they are asked for their opinion in a closed-ended survey question that does not include "Don't know" as an explicit response choice (Exhibit 5.10). However, 90% of these persons will select the "Don't know" response if they are explicitly given that option. On average, offering an explicit response option increases the "Don't know" responses by about a fifth (Schuman & Presser, 1981). It's a good idea to omit the "No opinion" or "Don't know" category when you feel that people have an opinion but are reluctant to express it.

**Exhibit 5.10** The Effect of Floaters on Public Opinion Polls

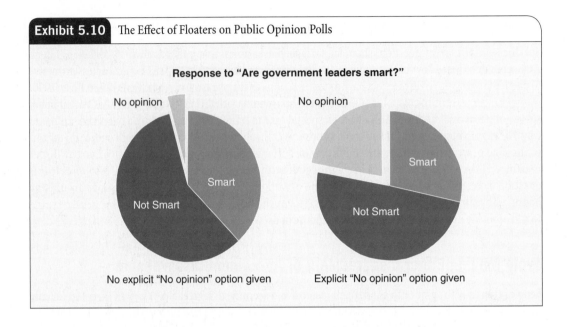

**Response to "Are government leaders smart?"**

No explicit "No opinion" option given

Explicit "No opinion" option given

Conducting a **survey pretest** should be the final step to check question wording. For a pretest, draw a small sample of individuals from the population you are studying, or one very similar to it, and try out the survey procedures with them. You may include in the pretest version of a written questionnaire some space for individuals to comment on each key question, or with in-person interviews, you may audiotape the test interviews for later review. Revise any questions that respondents do not seem to interpret as you had intended or that are not working well for other reasons.

# Combining Questions in Indexes and Scales

Writing single questions that yield usable answers is a challenge. Even though they may seem simple, single questions are prone to error due to **idiosyncratic variation**, which occurs when individuals' responses vary because of their reactions to particular words or ideas in the question. Differences in respondents' backgrounds, knowledge, and beliefs almost guarantee that some will understand the same question differently.

The guidelines in this chapter for writing clear questions should help reduce idiosyncratic variation caused by different interpretations of questions. The fascinating findings obtained from research using the Self-Anchoring Striving Scale shows just how much insight into human feelings can be gained with a very clear and straightforward survey question (Diener et al., 2010). But the best option is often to develop multiple questions about a concept and then to average respondents' answers to these questions in a composite measure termed an **index**.

The idea is that idiosyncratic variation in response to particular questions will average out, so the main influence on the combined measure will be the concept that all the questions focus on. The index can be considered a more complete measure of the concept than can any one of the component questions.

Creating an index is not just a matter of writing a few questions that seem to focus on a concept. Questions that seem to you to measure a common concept might seem to respondents to concern several different issues.

The only way to know that a given set of questions does, in fact, form an index is to administer the questions to people like those you plan to study. If a common concept is being measured, people's responses to the different questions should display some consistency. In other words, responses to the different questions should be correlated. Diener et al.'s (1985, p. 72) Satisfaction With Life Scale (SWLS) is an example of a well-tested index.

| Rating | Statement |
|---|---|
| _____ | 1. In most ways, my life is close to my ideal. |
| _____ | 2. The conditions of my life are excellent. |
| _____ | 3. I am satisfied with my life. |
| _____ | 4. So far, I have gotten the important things I want in life. |
| _____ | 5. If I could live my life over, I would change almost nothing. |

Try it out: Enter your answers (from 1 = *strongly disagree* to 7 = *strongly agree*) on each blank line and add them up. Were your responses to the five questions generally consistent? Were there some idiosyncratic reasons that you answered one or more questions differently than the others?

Special statistics called reliability measures help researchers decide whether responses are consistent across the questions asked of a sample. Psychologists have developed a great many indexes that have proved to be reliable in a range of studies and are available for subsequent researchers, like the SWLS Scale. It usually is much better to use such an index to measure a concept than to try to devise questions to form a new index. Use of an existing index both simplifies the work involved in designing a study and facilitates comparison of findings with those obtained in other studies.

## ▣ Organizing Surveys

Now that you have your questions prepared, you must decide what type of survey to conduct. There are five basic survey designs: mailed, group administered, phone, in-person, and electronic. Exhibit 5.11 summarizes the typical features of the five different survey designs. Each design differs from the others in one or more important features.

*Manner of Administration.* The five survey designs differ in the manner in which the questionnaire is administered. Mailed, group, and electronic questionnaires are completed by the respondents themselves. During phone and in-person interviews, however, the researcher or a staff person asks the questions and records the respondent's answers.

*Questionnaire Structure.* Survey designs also differ in the extent to which the content and order of the questions are structured in advance by the researcher. Most mailed, group, phone, and electronic surveys are highly structured, fixing in advance the content and order of the questions and most response choices. In-person interviews are often highly structured, but they may include many questions without fixed response choices. Extra questions are added as needed to clarify or explore answers to the most important questions.

**Exhibit 5.11** Typical Features of the Five Survey Designs

| Design | Manner of Administration | Setting | Questionnaire Structure | Cost |
|---|---|---|---|---|
| Mailed survey | Self | Individual | Mostly structured | Low |
| Group survey | Self | Group | Mostly structured | Very low |
| Phone survey | Professional | Individual | Structured | Moderate |
| In-person interview | Professional | Individual | Structured or unstructured | High |
| Electronic survey | Self | Individual | Mostly structured | Very low |

The order is a particularly important part of questionnaire structure. The order in which questions are presented will influence how respondents react to the questionnaire as a whole and how they may answer some questions. Both the major sections in the questionnaire and the questions within the sections must be organized in a logical order that would make sense in a conversation.

Question order can lead to **context effects** (also called **priming effects**) when one or more questions influence the responses to subsequent questions (Schober, 1999). Strack, Martin, and Schwartz (1988) identified the importance of context effects in happiness surveys. They asked students two questions:

1. How happy are you with your life in general?

2. How happy are you with your dating?

The students were asked to rate their happiness in response to each question on an 11-point scale, ranging from *not so happy* to *extremely happy*.

But here's the catch. Some of the questionnaires presented the questions in the order used above, on successive pages, while other questionnaires presented the questions in the reverse order, on successive pages. Can you guess the results? When students were asked the dating question first, they tended to report that they were happier with their "life in general." This is a context or priming effect. Similarly, married people tend to report that they are happier "in general" if the general happiness question is preceded by a question about their happiness with their marriage (Schuman & Presser, 1981). Focusing respondents' attention on something specific they felt happy about caused them to think more about that when they responded to the next question about their general happiness (Kahneman, Krueger, Schkade, Schwarz, & Stone, 2006). We can also refer to context effects as a focusing illusion (see Chapter 1, "Activity Questions").

When you design a survey, you should be aware of the potential for problems due to question order and evaluate carefully the likelihood of context effects (Labaw, 1980).

*Setting.* Most surveys are conducted in settings where only one respondent completes the survey at a time; most mail and electronic questionnaires and phone interviews are intended for completion by only one respondent. The same is usually true of in-person interviews. On the other hand, a variant of the standard survey is a questionnaire distributed simultaneously to a group of respondents, who complete the survey while the researcher (or assistant) waits. Students in classrooms are often the group involved, although this type of group distribution also occurs in surveys of employees and members of voluntary groups.

*Cost.* As mentioned earlier, in-person interviews are the most expensive type of survey. Phone interviews are much less expensive, but surveying by mail is cheaper yet. Electronic surveys are now the least expensive method because there are no interviewer costs, no mailing costs, and, for many designs, almost no costs for data entry. Of course, extra staff time and expertise are required to prepare an electronic questionnaire.

## Mailed, Self-Administered Surveys

A **mailed survey** is conducted by mailing a questionnaire to respondents, who then administer the survey themselves. The central concern in a mailed survey is maximizing the response rate. Even an attractive questionnaire full of clear questions will probably be returned by no more than 30% of a sample unless extra steps are taken to increase the rate of response. It's just too much bother for most potential recipients; in the language of social exchange theory, the costs of responding are perceived to be much higher than any anticipated rewards for doing so. Of course, a response rate of 30% is a disaster; even a response rate of 60% represents so much nonresponse error that it is hard to justify using the resulting data. Fortunately, the conscientious use of a systematic survey design method can be expected to lead to an acceptable 70% or higher rate of response to most mailed surveys (Dillman, 2000).

Sending follow-up mailings to **nonrespondents** is the single most important requirement for obtaining an adequate response rate to a mailed survey. The follow-up mailings explicitly encourage initial nonrespondents to return a completed questionnaire; implicitly, they convey the importance of the effort. Dillman (2000) has demonstrated the effectiveness of a standard procedure for the mailing process: (a) sending a brief announcement to respondents a few days before the questionnaire is mailed; (b) sending the questionnaire itself with a well-designed, personalized **cover letter** (see the next section), a self-addressed stamped return envelope, and, if possible, a token monetary reward; (c) sending a reminder postcard thanking respondents and reminding nonrespondents 2 weeks after the initial mailing; (d) sending a replacement questionnaire with a new cover letter and self-addressed stamped return envelope only to nonrespondents 2 to 4 weeks after the initial questionnaire mailing; and (e) sending another replacement questionnaire 6 to 8 weeks after the initial survey mailing—by priority or special delivery, if possible.

The cover letter for a mailed questionnaire is critical to the success of a mailed survey. This statement to respondents sets the tone for the questionnaire. The cover letter or introductory statement must show that the researcher is credible, it should be personalized for the respondent (Dear Tom, *not* Dear Student), it should interest the respondent in the contents of the questionnaire, and it should reassure the respondent that the information will be treated confidentially (Exhibit 5.12).

If Dillman's (2000) procedures are followed and the guidelines for cover letters and questionnaire design also are adhered to, the response rate is almost certain to approach 70%. One review of studies using Dillman's method to survey the general population indicates that the average response to a first mailing will be about 24%; the response rate will rise to 42% after the postcard follow-up, to 50% after the first replacement questionnaire, and to 72% after a second replacement questionnaire is sent by certified mail (Dillman, Christenson, Carpenter, & Brooks, 1974).

## Group-Administered Surveys

A **group-administered survey** is completed by individual respondents assembled in a group. The response rate is not usually a major concern in surveys that are distributed and collected in a group setting because most group members will participate. The real difficulty with this method is that it is seldom feasible because it requires what might be called a captive audience. With the exception of students, employees, members of the armed forces, and some institutionalized populations, most populations cannot be sampled in such a setting. A standard introductory statement should be read to the group that expresses appreciation for their participation, describes the steps of the survey, and emphasizes that the survey is voluntary and that the results will be treated as confidential.

**Exhibit 5.12** Sample Questionnaire Cover Letter

**University of Massachusetts at Boston**
**Department of Sociology**
**May 24, 2013**

Jane Doe
AIDS Coordinator
Shattuck Shelter

Dear Jane:

AIDS is an increasing concern for homeless people and for homeless shelters. The enclosed survey is about the AIDS problem and related issues confronting shelters. It is sponsored by the Life Lines AIDS Prevention Project for the Homeless—a program of the Massachusetts Department of Public Health.

As an AIDS coordinator/shelter director, you have learned about homeless persons' problems and about implementing programs in response to those problems. The Life Lines Project needs to learn from your experience. Your answers to the questions in the enclosed survey will improve substantially the base of information for improving AIDS prevention programs.

Questions in the survey focus on AIDS prevention activities and on related aspects of shelter operations. It should take about 30 minutes to answer all the questions.

Every shelter AIDS coordinator (or shelter director) in Massachusetts is being asked to complete the survey. And every response is vital to the success of the survey: The survey report must represent the full range of experiences.

You may be assured of complete confidentiality. No one outside of the university will have access to the questionnaire you return. (The ID number on the survey will permit us to check with nonrespondents to see if they need a replacement survey or other information.) All information presented in the report to Life Lines will be in aggregate form, with the exception of a list of the number, gender, and family status of each shelter's guests.

Please mail the survey back to us by Monday, June 4, and feel free to call if you have any questions.

Thank you for your assistance.

Yours sincerely,

*Russell K. Schutt*

Russell K. Schutt, PhD

Project Director

*Stephanie Howard*

Stephanie Howard

Project Assistant

## Telephone Surveys

In a **phone survey**, interviewers question respondents over the phone and then record their answers. Most telephone surveys use random-digit dialing at some point in the survey process (Lavrakas, 1987). A machine calls random phone numbers within designated exchanges, whether or not the numbers are published. When the machine reaches an inappropriate household (e.g., a business in a survey that is directed to the general population), the phone number is simply replaced with another. However, when the households are contacted, the interviewers must ask a series of questions at the start of the survey to ensure that they are speaking to the appropriate member of each household.

*Maximizing Response to Phone Surveys*

Phone surveying has traditionally been the method of choice for relatively short surveys of the general population. Response rates in phone surveys used to be very high—often above 80%—because few individuals would hang up on a polite caller or suddenly stop answering questions in the middle of a call (at least within the first 30 minutes or so). However, several social changes have made it increasingly difficult to obtain a high rate of response in a phone survey (Dillman, 2000): (a) the growing use of caller IDs to screen out calls from unknown callers, (b) the use of cell phones (which often do not have exchanges based on geographic area), and (c) people's getting accustomed to "just saying no" to calls from telemarketers.

Because people often are not at home, multiple callbacks will be needed for many sample members. The number of callbacks needed to reach respondents by telephone has increased greatly in the past 20 years, with increasing numbers of single-person households, dual-earner families, and out-of-home activities. Survey research organizations have increased the usual number of phone contact attempts from just 4 to 20.

In addition to these problems, response rates can be much lower in harder-to-reach populations. In a recent phone survey of low-income women in a public health program (Schutt, Cruz, & Woodford, 2008), the University of Massachusetts Center for Survey Research achieved a 55.1% response rate from all eligible sampled clients after a protocol that included up to 30 contact attempts, although the response rate rose to 72.9% when it was calculated as a percentage of clients the center was able to locate (Roman, 2005).

## In-Person Interviews

Face-to-face social interaction between interviewer and respondent is the unique feature of **in-person interviews**. If money is no object, in-person interviewing is often the best survey design.

In-person interviewing has several advantages: (a) responses rates are higher than with any other survey design; (b) questionnaires can be much longer than with mailed or phone surveys; (c) the questionnaire can be complex, with both open-ended and closed-ended questions and frequent branching patterns; (d) the order in which questions are read and answered can be controlled by the interviewer; (e) the physical and social circumstances of the interview can be monitored; and (f) respondents' interpretations of questions can be probed and clarified.

But researchers must be alert to some special hazards due to the presence of an interviewer. Respondents should experience the interview process as a personalized interaction with an interviewer who is very interested in the respondent's experiences and opinions. At the same time, however, every respondent should have the same interview experience—asked the same questions in the same way by the same type of person, who reacts similarly to the answers. Therein lies the researcher's challenge—to plan an interview process that will be personal and engaging and yet consistent and nonreactive (and to hire interviewers who can carry out this plan). Careful training and supervision are essential, because small differences in intonation or emphasis on particular words can alter respondents' interpretations of the meaning of a question (Groves, 1989; Peterson, 2000). Without a personalized approach, the rate of response will be lower and answers will be less thoughtful—and potentially less valid. Without a consistent approach, information obtained from different respondents will not be comparable—it will be less reliable and less valid.

As with phone interviewing, computers can be used to increase control of the in-person interview. In a **computer-assisted personal interviewing (CAPI)** project, interviewers carry a laptop computer that is programmed to display the interview questions and to process the response that the interviewer types in, as well as to check that these responses fall within allowed ranges. Interviewers seem to like CAPI, and the data obtained are comparable in quality to data obtained in a noncomputerized interview (Shepherd, Hill, Bristor, & Montalvan, 1996). A CAPI approach also makes it easier for the researcher to develop skip patterns and experiment with different types of questions for different respondents without increasing the risk of interviewer mistakes (Couper et al., 1998).

## Electronic Surveys

The widespread use of personal computers and the growth of the Internet have created new possibilities for survey research. In October 2003, more than half of American households were connected to the Internet (Cooper & Victory, 2002). As the proportion of the population that is connected increases, the Internet may become the preferred medium for survey research on many topics.

**Electronic surveys** can be prepared in two ways (Dillman, 2000, pp. 352–354). **E-mail surveys** can be sent as messages to respondents' e-mail addresses. Respondents then mark their answers in the message and send them back to the researcher. This approach is easy for researchers to develop and for respondents to use. However, it is cumbersome for surveys that are more than four or five pages in length. By contrast, **web surveys** are made available to Internet users on a remote server. Respondents are asked by e-mail (or regular mail) to visit the website and respond to the web questionnaire by checking answers.

Web surveys are becoming the more popular form of Internet survey because they are so flexible (see Exhibit 5.13). Web surveys can be quite long, with questions that are inapplicable to a given respondent hidden from the respondent, so that the survey may actually seem much shorter than it is. The questionnaire's design can feature many graphic and typographic elements. Respondents can view definitions of words or instructions for answering questions by clicking on linked terms. Lengthy sets of response choices can be presented with pull-down menus. Pictures and audio segments can be added when they are useful. Because answers are recorded directly into the researcher's database, data entry errors are almost eliminated and results can be reported quickly.

You can learn more about the features of the popular SurveyMonkey web survey program at http://www.surveymonkey.com/mp/take-a-tour/.

| **Exhibit 5.13** | SurveyMonkey Web Survey Example |
|---|---|

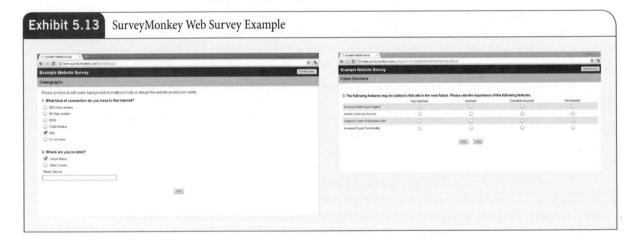

When the population to be surveyed has a high rate of Internet use, the web makes possible fast and effective surveys (Dillman, 2000). A skilled web programmer can generate a survey layout with many attractive features that make it more likely that respondents will give their answers—with a clear understanding of the questions (Smyth, Dillman, Christian, & Stern, 2004). To ensure that the appropriate people respond to a web-based survey, researchers may require that respondents enter a PIN (personal identification number) to gain access to the web survey (Dillman, 2000).

Eisenberg et al. (2007) used a web-based survey in their survey of university students' mental health. Sample members were first mailed an introductory letter along with $2 as a token of appreciation. They then received up to four e-mail reminders with a link to the survey. They were also told they had been entered into a cash sweepstakes.

# A Comparison of Survey Designs

Which survey design should be used and when? Group-administered survéys are similar, in most respects, to mailed surveys, except that they require the unusual circumstance of having access to the sample in a group setting. We therefore don't need to consider this survey design by itself; what applies to mailed surveys applies to group-administered survey designs, with the exception of sampling issues. The features of **mixed-mode surveys** depend on the survey types that are being combined. Thus, we can focus our comparison on the four survey designs that involve the use of a questionnaire with individuals sampled from a larger population: (1) mailed surveys, (2) phone surveys, (3) in-person surveys, and (4) electronic surveys. Exhibit 5.14 summarizes their strong and weak points.

**Exhibit 5.14**  Advantages and Disadvantages of the Four Survey Designs

| Characteristics of Design | Mail Survey | Phone Survey | In-Person Survey | Web Survey |
|---|---|---|---|---|
| Representative sample | | | | |
| Opportunity for inclusion is known | | | | |
|     For completely listed populations | High | High | High | Medium |
|     For incompletely listed populations | Medium | Medium | High | Low |
| Selection within sampling units is controlled (e.g., specific family members must respond) | Medium | High | High | Low |
| Respondents are likely to be located | | | | |
|     If samples are heterogeneous | Medium | Medium | High | Low |
|     If samples are homogeneous and specialized | High | High | High | High |
| Questionnaire construction and question design | | | | |
|     Allowable length of questionnaire | Medium | Medium | High | Medium |
| Ability to include | | | | |
|     Complex questions | Medium | Low | High | High |
|     Open questions | Low | High | High | Medium |
|     Screening questions | Low | High | High | High |
|     Tedious, boring questions | Low | High | High | Low |
| Ability to control question sequence | Low | High | High | High |
| Ability to ensure questionnaire completion | Medium | High | High | Low |
| Distortion of answers | | | | |
|     Odds of avoiding social desirability bias | High | Medium | Low | High |
|     Odds of avoiding interviewer distortion | High | Medium | Low | High |
|     Odds of avoiding contamination by others | Medium | High | Medium | Medium |
| Administrative goals | | | | |
|     Odds of meeting personnel requirements | High | High | Low | Medium |
|     Odds of implementing quickly | Low | High | Low | High |
|     Odds of keeping costs low | High | Medium | Low | High |

The most important consideration in comparing the advantages and disadvantages of the four methods is the likely response rate they will generate. Because of the great weakness of mailed surveys in this respect, they must be considered the least preferred survey design from a sampling standpoint. However, researchers may still prefer a mailed survey when they have to reach a widely dispersed population and don't have enough financial resources to hire and train an interview staff or to contract with a survey organization that already has an interview staff available in many locations.

Contracting with an established survey research organization for a phone survey is often the best alternative to a mailed survey. The persistent follow-up attempts that are necessary to secure an adequate response rate are much easier over the phone than in person. A phone survey limits the length and complexity of the questionnaire but offers the possibility of very carefully monitoring the interviewers (Dillman, 1978; Fowler, 1988).

In-person surveys are clearly preferable in terms of the possible length and complexity of the questionnaire itself, as well as the researcher's ability to monitor conditions while the questionnaire is being completed. Mailed surveys often are preferable for asking sensitive questions, although this problem can be lessened in an interview by giving respondents a separate sheet to fill out on their own. Although interviewers may themselves distort results, either by changing the wording of questions or by failing to record answers properly, survey research organizations can reduce this risk through careful training of interviewers and through ongoing monitoring of interviewer performance. Some survey supervisors may have interviews tape-recorded so that they can review the dialogue between interviewers and respondents and provide feedback to interviewers to help improve their performance.

The advantages of electronic surveys are increasing as Internet usage spreads and personal computer capacity improves, but what matters is computer usage among the population to be surveyed. There must be evidence of a reasonably high rate of Internet usage before one makes a decision to conduct an Internet survey.

These various points about the different survey designs lead to two general conclusions. First, in-person interviews are the strongest design and generally preferable when sufficient resources and a trained interview staff are available; telephone surveys have many of the advantages of in-person interviews at much less cost, but response rates are an increasing problem. Second, the "best" survey design for any particular study will be determined by the study's unique features and goals rather than by any absolute standard of what the best survey design is.

# Analyzing Surveys

Survey researchers, like researchers using other methods, can use a variety of statistics to test their hypotheses. One of the most common analytic approaches in survey research is **contingency table** analysis. A contingency table shows how responses to one question (the dependent variable) are distributed within the responses to another question (the independent variable). That is, we construct a contingency table to determine whether values of cases on the dependent variable are contingent on the values of those cases on the independent variable. In our "Stat Corner," we discuss how data presented in a contingency table are commonly analyzed.

## STAT CORNER

### Vagaries of Sampling

Even when the association between two variables is consistent with the researcher's hypothesis, it is possible that the association was just due to the vagaries of sampling on a random basis. It is conventional in statistics to avoid concluding that an association exists in the population from which the sample was drawn unless the probability that the association was due to chance is less than 5%. In other words, a statistician normally will not conclude that an association exists between two variables unless he or she can be at least 95% confident that the association was not due to chance. In a contingency table, estimation of the probability that an association is not due to chance can be based on the **chi-square** ($\chi^2$) statistic. The probability is customarily reported in a summary form such as "$p < .05$," which can be translated as "The probability that the association was due to chance is less than 5 out of 100 (5%)."

When the analyst feels reasonably confident (at least 95% confident) that an association was not due to chance, it is said that the association is statistically significant. Recall from Chapter 2 that **statistical significance** means that an association is not likely to be due to chance, according to some criterion set by the analyst. Convention (and the desire to avoid concluding that an association exists in the population when it doesn't) dictates that the criterion be a probability less than 5%.

But statistical significance is not everything. You might recall from the sampling section that sampling error decreases as sample size increases. For this same reason, an association is less likely to appear on the basis of chance in a larger sample than in a smaller sample. In a table with more than 1,000 cases, the odds of a chance association are often very low indeed. For example, in the table in the Kahneman et al. (2006) article, with a sample size of 1,173 individuals, the probability that the association between happiness and family income was due to chance was less than 1 in 1,000 ($p < .001$)! In a large sample, even a weak association may be statistically significant ($p < .05$), but it will still be too weak to be substantively important.

Exhibit 5.15 shows how responses to the happiness question varied by family income in the study reported by Kahneman and his colleagues (2006). The numbers in the table have been converted to percentages of the total number in each income category. This conversion to percentages standardizes the distributions in each column, so that they each add up to 100. To begin to read the table, you can compare the distribution of percentages in the first column with those in the second column. You can see that the percentage of respondents in the "very happy" category is higher for the respondents making $20,000 to $49,999 (30.2%) than it is for those making less than $20,000 (22.2%). You can also see that the percentage of "very happy" respondents is even higher (41.9%) in the $50,000 to $89,999 category but about the same for those making $90,000 and more. Overall, you can see that as income increases, the percentage of respondents in the "not too happy" category declines and the percentage in the "very happy" category increases.

| Exhibit 5.15 | Distribution of Self-Reported Global Happiness by Family Income, 2004 | | | |
|---|---|---|---|---|
| *Response* | *Under $20,000* | *$20,000–$49,999* | *$50,000–$89,999* | *$90,000 and over* |
| Not too happy | 17.2 | 13.0 | 7.7 | 5.3 |
| Pretty happy | 60.5 | 56.8 | 50.3 | 51.8 |
| Very happy | 22.2 | 30.2 | 41.9 | 42.9 |

# ▣ Conclusions

Sampling is a powerful tool for behavioral science research. Probability sampling methods allow a researcher to use the laws of chance, or probability, to draw samples from which population parameters can be estimated with a high degree of confidence. A sample of just 1,000 or 1,500 individuals can be used to estimate reliably the characteristics of the population of a nation comprising millions of individuals.

But researchers do not come by representative samples easily. Well-designed samples require careful planning, some advance knowledge about the population to be sampled, and adherence to systematic selection procedures—all so that the selection procedures are not biased. And even after the sample data are collected, the researcher's ability to generalize from the sample findings to the population is not completely certain. The best that he or she can do is to perform additional calculations that state the degree of confidence that can be placed in the sample statistic.

Surveying a sample of the population of interest is an exceptionally efficient and productive method for investigating a wide array of research questions. Considerations of time and expense can make a survey the preferred data collection method for contributing to psychological science.

But there is an important trade-off in survey research. The relative ease with which survey data can be collected from large and often representative samples allows us to develop findings that can be generalized to the population from which the sample was drawn with a known degree of confidence. Psychologists can use survey data to test many hypotheses about the relations between independent and dependent variables, such as "Higher income is associated with more happiness."

What survey research does not allow us to do is to test to see if providing people with more income causes an increase in their happiness. Survey research does not allow "manipulation" of the values of cases on the independent variable (income, in this case). Survey research is called "correlational research" because it only allows us to determine whether variables are associated with each other—by creating contingency tables, calculating correlation coefficients, or using other statistics. If we want to vary exposure to the independent variable and see what happens to the dependent variable as a result, we need to turn to an experimental research design.

In brief, survey research is strong with respect to generalizability of findings but weak with respect to establishing causality in relationships. Have you ever heard the expression "Correlation does not prove causation"? That is the problem, and that is why we will introduce experimental design in the next chapter.

# Key Terms

Availability sampling
Census
Chi-square ($\chi^2$)
Cluster
Cluster sampling
Computer-assisted personal interview (CAPI)
Context effects (also called priming effects)
Contingency table
Contingent question
Cover letter
Cross-population generalizability
Disproportionate stratified sampling
Double-barreled question
Double negative
Electronic survey
Elements
E-mail survey
Fence-sitters
Filter question

Floaters
Group-administered survey
Idiosyncratic variation
Index
In-person interview
Interview schedule
Mailed survey
Mixed-mode survey
Nonprobability sampling method
Nonrespondents
Periodicity
Phone survey
Probability of selection

Probability sampling method
Proportionate stratified sampling
Purposive sampling
Questionnaire
Quota sampling
Random-digit dialing
Random sampling
Random sampling error (chance
    sampling error)
Representative sample
Sample generalizability
Sampling distribution
Sampling error

Sampling frame
Sampling interval
Simple random sampling
Skip patterns
Snowball sampling
Statistical significance
Stratified random sampling
Survey pretest
Survey research
Systematic bias
Systematic random sampling
Web survey

# Research in the News

1. *The Boston Globe*'s Stan Grossfeld (2007) reported on the problem of steroid drug use by professional athletes. It is hard to determine the scope of the problem because many athletes refuse to talk about it. Do you think your classmates would respond honestly to questions in a confidential survey about recent drug use? What about professional athletes? Why might their orientation to a survey about drug use differ?

2. A recent survey found that 4 in 10 college students endure stress often (Fram & Tompson, 2008). Propose a probability sampling design to study this issue that combines stratification and clustering. What challenges would a survey research organization confront in implementing your design?

## STUDENT STUDY SITE

Please access the study site at **www.sagepub.com/nestor2e**, where you will find useful study materials such as mobile-friendly eFlashcards and mid-chapter and full chapter web quizzes for each chapter, along with carefully selected articles from research journals that illustrate the major concepts and techniques presented in the book.

# Activity Questions

1. Response rates to phone surveys are declining even as phone usage increases. Part of the problem is that lists of cell phone numbers are not available and wireless service providers do not allow outside access to their networks. Cell phone users may also have to pay for incoming calls. Do you think regulations should be passed to increase the ability of survey researchers to include cell phones in their random-digit-dialing surveys? How would you feel about receiving survey calls on your cell phone? What problems might result from "improving" phone survey capabilities in this way?

2. In-person interviews have for many years been the "gold standard" in survey research because the presence of an interviewer increases the response rate, allows better rapport with the interviewee, facilitates clarification of questions and instructions, and provides feedback about the interviewee's situation. However, researchers who design in-person

interviewing projects are now making increasing use of technology to ensure consistent questioning of respondents and to provide greater privacy while answering questions. But having a respondent answer questions on a laptop while the interviewer waits is a very different social process from actually asking the questions verbally. Which approach would you favor in survey research? What trade-offs can you suggest there might be in terms of quality of information collected, rapport building, and interviewee satisfaction?

3. Select a random sample using the table of random numbers in Appendix I. Compute a statistic based on your sample, and compare it with the corresponding figure for the entire population. Here's how to proceed:

   a. First, select a very small population for which you have a reasonably complete sampling frame. One possibility would be the list of asking prices for houses advertised in your local paper. Another would be the listing of some characteristic of states in a U.S. Census Bureau publication, such as average income or population size.

   b. The next step is to create your sampling frame, a numbered list of all the elements in the population. If you are using a complete listing of all elements, as from a U.S. Census Bureau publication, the sampling frame is the same as the list. Just number the elements (states). If your population is composed of housing ads in the local paper, your sampling frame will be those ads that contain a housing price. Identify these ads, and then number them sequentially starting with 1.

   c. Decide on a method of picking numbers out of the random number table in Appendix I, such as taking every number in each row, row by row (or you may move down or diagonally across the columns). Use only the first (or last) digit in each number if you need to select 1 to 9 cases or only the first (or last) two digits if you want fewer than 100 cases.

   d. Pick a starting location in the random number table. It's important to pick a starting point in an unbiased way, perhaps by closing your eyes and then pointing to some part of the page.

   e. Record the numbers you encounter as you move from the starting location in the direction you decided on in advance, until you have recorded as many random numbers as the number of cases you need in the sample. If you are selecting states, 10 might be a good number. Ignore numbers that are too large (or small) for the range of numbers used to identify the elements in the population. Discard duplicate numbers.

   f. Calculate the average value in your sample for some variable that was measured—for example, population size in a sample of states or housing price for the housing ads. Calculate the average by adding up the values of all the elements in the sample and dividing by the number of elements in the sample.

   g. Go back to the sampling frame, and calculate this same average for all the elements in the list. How close is the sample average to the population average?

   h. Estimate the range of sample averages that would be likely to include 90% of the possible samples.

4. Consider how you would design a split-ballot experiment to determine the effect of phrasing a question or its response choices in different ways. Check recent issues of the local newspaper for a question used in a survey of attitudes about some social policy or political position. Propose some hypothesis about how the wording of the question or its response choices might have influenced the answers people gave, and devise an alternative that differs only in this respect. Distribute these different questions to two halves of a large class (after your instructor makes the necessary arrangements) to test your hypothesis.

# Review Questions

1. Discuss how cross-population generalizability would be essential for cultural studies in psychology.

2. What is sampling error? How does it affect sample generalizability?

3. Compare and contrast probability sampling and nonprobability sampling.

4. What is a sampling distribution? Discuss the relationship of sampling distributions and inferential statistics, particularly in relation to statistical significance.

5. What is the difference between sample statistic and population parameter?

6. What is a contingency table? What inferential statistic is used to analyze contingency table data?

7. Describe two types of errors that can occur in survey designs. How can they be minimized?

8. Discuss how social exchange theory can be used in survey designs.

9. What are the advantages of in-person interviews over other types of surveys?

10. What considerations are important in deciding which survey design to use?

# Ethics in Action

1. How much pressure is too much pressure to participate in a probability-based sample survey? Is it okay for the U.S. government to mandate legally that all citizens participate in the decennial census? Should companies be able to require employees to participate in survey research about work-related issues? Should students be required to participate in surveys about teacher performance? Should parents be required to consent to the participation of their high school–age students in a survey about substance abuse and health issues? Is it okay to give monetary incentives for participation in a survey of homeless shelter clients? Can monetary incentives be coercive? Explain your decisions.

2. Federal regulations require special safeguards for research on persons with impaired cognitive capacity. Special safeguards are also required for research on prisoners and on children. Do you think special safeguards are necessary? Why or why not? Do you think it is possible for individuals in any of these groups to give "voluntary consent" to research participation? What procedures might help make consent to research truly voluntary in these situations? How could these procedures influence sampling plans and results?

CHAPTER **6**

# Causation and Experimentation
## Single-Factorial Designs

## LEARNING OBJECTIVES: FAST FACTS

### Causation and Experimentation

- A true experiment provides the best test of whether manipulation of an independent variable causes changes in a dependent variable. A true experiment uses random assignment to form equivalent control and experimental groups before treatment (pretest) that can be directly compared on the dependent variable following treatment (posttest).

- The internal validity of an experiment is defined as the extent to which the systematic manipulation of one or more independent variables produces the predicted or hypothesized effect on the dependent variable. The goal is to design an internally valid experiment that will allow the researcher to establish causal relationships among the key variables under study.

- Sample generalizability, replication of findings, and real-world impact of the results (ecological validity) increase external validity of experiments.

- We should exercise caution (in the spirit of the scientific method) in drawing any causal conclusion that an independent variable caused a change in a dependent variable.

## TESTING BEFORE LEARNING

Try your hand at these questions. Don't worry about not knowing the correct response, as you haven't read the chapter yet! But research shows that a pretest such as this can enhance learning (e.g., Kornell, Hays, & Bjork, 2009). So here is the answer. You come up with the question.

1. Provides the strongest empirical evidence of causality
   a. What is a correlational study?
   b. What is a quasi-experiment?
   c. What is an independent variable?
   d. What is a true experiment?

2. When extraneous factors complicate the results of an experiment
   a. What are confounds?
   b. What are independent variables?
   c. What are matched pairs?
   d. What are descriptive statistics?

3. Held constant to control for potential confounds
   a. What are independent variables?
   b. What are dependent variables?
   c. What are control variables?
   d. What are experimental errors?

4. The "great equalizer" used in research design for assigning participants to control and experimental groups before the introduction of the independent variable
   a. What is internal validity?
   b. What is external validity?
   c. What is random assignment?
   d. What is random sampling?

5. Can be used to check the effectiveness of random assignment in creating control and treatment groups
   a. What is a posttest?
   b. What is a pretest?
   c. What is a manipulation check?
   d. What is a paired $t$ test?

6. Used for data analysis to assess the probability of whether the observed differences found in the study were produced by random or chance factors
   a. What are inferential statistics?
   b. What are descriptive statistics?
   c. What are selection biases?
   d. What are null results?

7. The main reason for conducting the study, yet it cannot be tested directly, and can only be accepted if the results are statistically significant
   a. What is the null hypothesis?
   b. What is the research hypothesis?

*(Continued)*

(Continued)

c. What is level of significance?
d. What is experimental control?

8. This research design is used when participants are assigned to different conditions of the independent variable.
   a. What is a repeated-measures design?
   b. What is an independent-groups design?
   c. What is a Latin square design?
   d. What is a correlational design?

9. This research design is used when all participants are to receive all levels of the independent variable.
   a. What is a repeated-measures design?
   b. What is an independent-groups design?
   c. What is a Latin square design?
   d. What is a correlational design?

10. It is a threat to internal validity.
    a. What is statistical significance?
    b. What is a confound?
    c. What is an effect size?
    d. What is statistical power?

ANSWER KEY: (1) d; (2) a; (3) c; (4) c; (5) b; (6) a; (7) b; (8) b; (9) a; (10) b

# The Stroop Test: Calisthenics for the Brain?

See the full-color Word Lists on the inside back cover of this book to complete this exercise.

Now let's begin with a simple exercise. All you need is a stopwatch. Please refer to the full-color Word Lists on the inside back cover of this book (the lists are provided here in gray shades for your reference). For each word in the first Word List, say aloud the color of the *print* of each word. Do not read the words. Just say what color they are printed in. For example, for the word *red*, you should say "Red." Start from the top row and go from left to right, as you do when you read a page. Go as fast as you can without making mistakes. Are you ready? Begin timing and go.

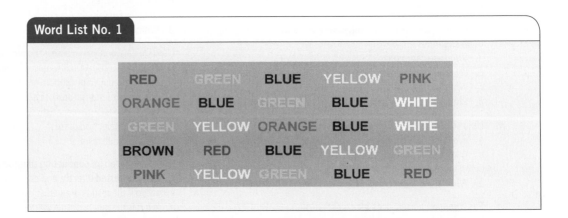

**Word List No. 1**

| | | | | |
|---|---|---|---|---|
| RED | GREEN | BLUE | YELLOW | PINK |
| ORANGE | BLUE | GREEN | BLUE | WHITE |
| GREEN | YELLOW | ORANGE | BLUE | WHITE |
| BROWN | RED | BLUE | YELLOW | GREEN |
| PINK | YELLOW | GREEN | BLUE | RED |

Now let's continue. Remember, the same thing—just say the color of the ink of the word. Begin timing and go.

**Word List No. 2**

| | | | | |
|---|---|---|---|---|
| RED | GREEN | BLUE | YELLOW | PINK |
| ORANGE | BLUE | GREEN | BLUE | WHITE |
| GREEN | YELLOW | ORANGE | BLUE | WHITE |
| BROWN | RED | BLUE | YELLOW | GREEN |
| PINK | YELLOW | GREEN | BLUE | RED |

No doubt you found the second set of words more difficult than the first. This can be seen in your slower response times. Were you surprised by the difference in your response times for the first and second set of words? What do you think caused the difference? As you likely noticed, in the first set of color words, the font color and its corresponding color word name matched. For example, the term "red" is printed in red. In the second set of words, the font color and its corresponding color word name do not match. For example, the word "red" is printed in green ink.

What you experienced in reading the second list of words is known as the Stroop effect, named after the psychologist John Ridley Stroop who first reported this curious phenomenon in 1935. The Stroop effect occurs when we respond more slowly to a color word whose font color name does not match. These color words, which are called *incongruent*, create interference, so response times are invariably slower because the font and corresponding color word do not match. And as you can see, when the font color and color word name match, these words, which are called *congruent*, are much easier for us, and our response times are much faster.

## ▣ Basics of Experimentation

What causes the Stroop effect? Note that the research question is one of cause and effect, and as such, it requires an experimental design known simply as a **true experiment**. As you know, variables differ in the degree to which they can be controlled or manipulated. In a true experiment, a researcher has complete control over the manipulation of the independent variable. Such **experimental control** allows for testing whether systematically varying the independent variable causes changes in the dependent variable.

In many areas of science, such as chemistry and physics, true experiments are de rigueur, the standard approach to establishing causality. In these sciences in which all other extraneous sources can be controlled, a true experiment can provide the empirical ammunition for a causal explanation often formulated in terms of a particular theoretical model. In psychology, different circumstances and challenges prevail, yet here too, true experiments are quite common. However, causal explanations are much more difficult to establish than in chemistry or physics and certainly much trickier, even when a true experiment is performed.

In an experiment, independent variables are often referred to as **factors**. An experiment must have at least one independent variable with at least two levels or **conditions** that are manipulated by the experimenter; otherwise, it would not be an experiment. An experiment with just one independent variable is called a **single-factor experiment**. This is the simplest and most basic experiment with two variables, one independent variable and one dependent variable. As we will see in Chapter 7, experiments with more than one independent variable are often referred to as **multifactorial designs**.

The Stroop task is an example of a single-factor experiment. The one independent variable, which we call word type, has two levels or conditions: congruent (Word List No. 1) and incongruent (Word List No. 2). Word type is therefore the independent variable that is manipulated across two types of color words, congruent (Word List No. 1) and incongruent (Word List No. 2). Thus, we say that word list is systematically varied when congruent and incongruent sets of words are each presented.

The defining feature of an experiment is the degree of control a researcher exercises over all aspects of the study design. In a true experiment, the researcher controls with whom, with what, and how the study is conducted. In this chapter, we learn about true experiments—their basic ingredients as well as how to design and conduct them. We examine true experiments in light of the difficulties of establishing causality in psychology.

## Selecting Research Participants

A researcher selects a sample, deciding who will be included in the study and who will be excluded. For example, our Stroop task presented color words in English. So in this instance, a researcher would include as participants only people who speak and read English as their first language and would exclude those who do not. This is referred to as the inclusion and exclusion criteria of a study.

In practical terms, inclusion and exclusion criteria of a study are very important to consider for at least two reasons. One reason is ethical. Think of a treatment study. Here ethics require us to be mindful not to exclude people from the potential benefit of a **treatment**. Likewise, inclusion and exclusion criteria can also determine whether particular groups such as ethnic minorities are underrepresented in research or not. Underrepresentation also poses an important scientific problem. Thus, our second reason is scientific and one with which you are now quite familiar—namely, that a researcher aims to generate a sample that will maximize generalizability.

As we know from Chapter 5, the generalizability of a study depends greatly on the representativeness of its sample to the larger population. In Chapter 5, we also learned that research participants may be selected from the population using probability or nonprobability sampling. We learned that probability sampling is essential to accurately describe a population, for example, when conducting scientific polls.

However, in experimental psychology, probability sampling is not often possible nor is it considered as crucial in large part because the focus is on testing hypotheses about behavior involving processes that are presumed to be similar across people. Here nonprobability sampling is the common standard used to select research participants. This as we know has the potential to create bias, which we should recognize as an important limitation of the experimental approach for generalizing findings to other populations and situations.

A researcher also decides on the number of research participants for a study. As we know, sample size is important, and the general rule is the larger the better. Recall the law of large numbers from Chapter 1. Larger sample sizes offer greater statistical power to detect an effect if it is real and present in the population. However, often researchers rely on intuition and judgment, which we know can be flawed, in deciding the size of a sample. The unfortunate result is that they select too small a sample, which leaves their studies unduly exposed to chance and bias.

As we will learn, a sample that is too small does not provide sufficient power to test a research hypothesis. It can be said that researchers "shoot themselves in the foot" when they select a sample that is too small to find a hypothesized effect. Fortunately, a relatively straightforward statistical computation known as **power analysis** can be used to determine the size of a sample needed to discover an effect if one truly exists. So the take-home message is that researchers should not rely on the luck of the draw in choosing a sample size. Indeed, deciding on the size of a sample is too important to leave it to pure whimsy.

## Randomly Assigning Research Participants

A true experiment also uses **randomization** in assigning participants to groups or to different conditions of an independent variable. For example, as shown in Exhibit 6.1, if we have two groups or two conditions, we could simply flip a coin with heads being assigned to one group and tails to the other.

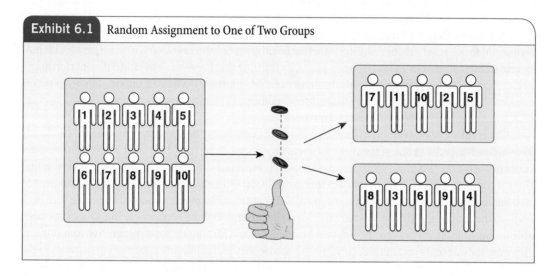

| Exhibit 6.1 | Random Assignment to One of Two Groups |

A table of random numbers (Appendix I) can also be used to assign participants to groups. To generate odd and even numbers, we would select a row of numbers in the table. Simply proceed across the row, noting whether the number is odd or even. If you reach the end of one row, continue; just select a different row of numbers and proceed until all participants have been assigned to a group. Use a simple decision rule: If the random number is even, assign the next participant to Group 1, and if the random number is odd, assign the next participant to Group 2.

This process of **random assignment** ensures that any extraneous influence is just as likely to affect one group as the other group. At the outset of an experiment, before the introduction of the independent variable, there should be no systematic differences between **treatment/experimental** and **control groups**; that is, groups should be roughly equivalent at the beginning of an experiment so that systematic differences between groups emerge only in response to the direct manipulation of the independent variable. Random assignment cannot guarantee that the groups are equivalent, but it does ensure that any preexisting differences between the groups are not systematic but rather are due to chance. With random assignment, each person selected from a target population has an equal chance of being assigned to either a treatment or a control group.

In this sense, random assignment acts to "level the playing field" before the application of the independent variable. As such, random assignment helps minimize a form of **selection bias**, which is defined as a systematic error in sampling resulting in some member of a target population being less likely to be included in the study than others. This type of selection bias is known as sample bias (see Chapter 1). For example, a researcher makes the error of selection bias when high-income individuals are assigned to one group and low-income individuals to the other group.

In principle, then, if a study effectively randomly assigns participants to treatment and control groups, any preexisting differences between the groups prior to the introduction of the independent variable are due to chance. Fortunately, we can estimate the likelihood of that chance difference, and primarily by including enough participants, we can design our experiment so that the likelihood of a chance difference is very low. And if in this way we reduce the likelihood of chance variation to a very low level, we can say that any subsequent difference between groups on the dependent variable is caused by the direct manipulation of the independent variable—with only that very low probability that the difference is due to chance. We say that such a difference that is unlikely to be due to chance is "statistically significant."

To illustrate, let us consider an influential article published in the prestigious *Proceedings of the National Academy of Sciences* titled "Memory Enhancement in Healthy Older Adults Using a Brain Plasticity-Based Training Program: A Randomized, Controlled Study." In this study, Merzenich and colleagues (Mahncke et al., 2006) examined whether healthy participants aged 60 years or older would show improved mental abilities following brain plasticity training that involved "working out"—performing a prescribed 5-day-a-week regimen of cognitive exercises on their home computers. The researchers randomly assigned participants to one of the three conditions: (1) brain plasticity computer-based training, (2) active computer-based training, and (3) no training.

Why is this study a true experiment? It is a true experiment because the researchers randomly assigned participants to one of the three different conditions. Why would random assignment be especially important in this study? Random assignment is especially important here because we know that there is considerable variation in people's mental abilities. With a nonrandom sampling technique, the risk would have been so great that one group could, for example, be overrepresented by people with high levels of the mental abilities being studied. This could be fatal, and the researchers would not have been able to conclude, as they correctly did, that brain plasticity training improved cognitive functioning. However, they were correct in their conclusion because they had randomly assigned participants to the training conditions. Thus, the researchers could make the strong argument that brain plasticity training caused improved mental abilities.

To recap, the defining feature of a true experiment is random assignment either to groups or to the levels/conditions of the independent variable created by the researcher. Random assignment allows a true experiment to demonstrate a cause-and-effect relationship between the independent variable and the dependent variable. By using random assignment, a true experiment can test whether systematically varying the independent variable causes changes in the dependent variable.

## Theater of Independent Variables

Independent variables are created and studied for their impact on a dependent variable. Recall that an independent variable must have at least two levels. Each level of the independent variable needs to be sufficiently distinct. Let us say you reward small children with either one treat or two treats for correct answers on a task. To your surprise, however, performance of children who receive one treat did not differ from those who received two treats.

This represents a **null result**, which occurs when an independent variable fails to produce an effect on the dependent variable. The most likely reason for a null result in this hypothetical scenario is that manipulation of one treat versus two treats represented much too small a range to produce the desired effect on the dependent variable of test performance. The take-home lesson for experimental design is to devise levels of an independent variable that are truly distinct so that its effect on the dependent variable can be objectively assessed and clearly interpreted (Underwood, 1957).

Below we cover different types of independent variables. In reading about these different independent variables, keep in mind two questions. First, does the independent variable reliably produce the desired effect? Here, think of whether other researchers can replicate the effect. The second question to keep in mind is how does the independent variable relate to the psychological theory that is being examined?

## Simple and Direct Manipulations

In many instances, an independent variable provides a simple, direct, and straightforward manipulation, as in a Stroop experiment. For example, compare the color words for Word List No. 1 and Word List No. 2. The colors words (red, blue, etc.) themselves are held constant. What is varied is the color of the font of the word. So in Word List No.1, the congruent condition, the color term red is printed in red font. But in Word List No. 2, the incongruent condition, the same color term, red, is printed in green font.

Thus, in our Stroop experiment, we call our independent variable, word type, which is systematically varied when congruent and incongruent sets of words are each presented. We can quantify the impact of our independent variable, word type, on our dependent variable, response time. You can do so by comparing your response times for the two lists. Calculate the difference in time between the two lists. Subtract your average response time for Word List No. 1 from your average response time for Word List No. 2. Bingo! This numerical value quantifies the Stroop effect of processing incongruent color words in comparison with congruent words.

How big is this effect? How reliable is this effect? These are two questions that are always important to consider in evaluating the results of a true experiment. For our simple Stroop experiment, response times tend to be on average twice as slow for incongruent words as for congruent words. So we can say that the Stroop effect is quite robust. It is also quite reliable, as the effect is extremely replicable, consistently shown across various samples and studies. Moreover, the effect holds for different variants of the Stroop task. For example, on an emotional Stroop test, researchers have found that participants are slower to name the color of a negative emotional word, such as "war," "kill," and "cancer," than a neutral word, such as "clock," "chair," and "windy" (Gotlib & McCann, 1984; McKenna & Sharma, 2004).

You might think of the Stroop effect, in and of itself, as cute but a bit too contrived and wonder what it actually tells us. In other words, what is the theoretical impact of the Stroop effect? We might counter by saying that the Stroop test is an excellent example to use in learning how a true experiment provides the best test of causality. You agree, but you still are wondering (based on what you learned in Chapter 4) about a theoretical framework for the Stroop effect. A thoughtful question, we would respond enthusiastically, complimenting you for posing a question that highlights an important teaching point for us; that is, experimentation should be closely connected to theory in psychological research.

What does this mean for the Stroop experiment? In layperson terms, we can learn a lot about how we pay attention and concentrate from the Stroop. For example, we can read words automatically with little or no attention. But identifying the font of a word requires a little more attention, and identifying the fonts of color words that conflict with their color names requires a lot of attention. Now to translate this psychological phenomenon into formal terms, we ask what theoretical construct might be examined by the Stroop.

Enter the theoretical construct of attention. This theoretical construct can be traced to William James, one of the founding figures in psychology, who first described "varieties of attention" more than a century ago (James, 1890; Nestor & O'Donnell, 1998; Parasuraman, 1998; Rees, Frackowiak, & Frith, 1997). Today, research in psychology and cognitive neuroscience continues to be inspired by James's seminal idea of the varieties of attention. And the Stroop task often sits center stage in much of this research. For example, we have combined the Stroop task and functional magnetic resonance imaging of brain activity to examine the neuropsychology of attention in people with schizophrenia. And of course, another line of research as illustrated in the Merzenich study uses the Stroop and related phenomena to examine the efficacy of cognitive exercises—whether so-called mental calisthenics actually work.

## Covert and Indirect Manipulations

We know that a good theory generates a testable hypothesis that can be framed as a statement often in the form of a prediction that is made prior to the actual collection of data. For example, the **facial feedback**

**hypothesis** states that facial movements by themselves can reenact particular emotional feelings and that these emotional feelings can be created by simply "tricking" a person into making specific facial contractions (Niedenthal, 2007; Strack, Martin, & Stepper, 1988).

The million-dollar question is how this could be done in the laboratory. Sometimes, it is necessary to use a covert or indirect manipulation to create the desired variation in the independent variable. Enter Strack and colleagues, who developed a very simple but ingenious method to create an independent variable based on holding a pen between either the teeth or between the lips. Try this and see what you think. Did holding a pen between your teeth covertly induce you to smile? Did holding a pen between your lips covertly induce you to frown?

Strack and colleagues found that this was indeed the case for their research participants and that these covert facial expressions influenced participants' funniness ratings of comic strips; that is, Strack, Martin, and Stepper (1988) found significantly higher funniness ratings for participants who rated cartoons with a pen between their teeth than for those who rated the same cartoon with a pen between their lips (Exhibit 6.2). Neither group reported that they were aware that the position of the pen in the mouth made facial muscle contractions intended to induce either a smile or a frown.

| Exhibit 6.2 | Participants in the Strack, Martin, and Stepper (1988) Study Either Held a Pen Between the Lips to Inhibit Smiling, as in the Left Panel, or Else Held the Pen Between the Teeth to Facilitate Smiling |
| --- | --- |

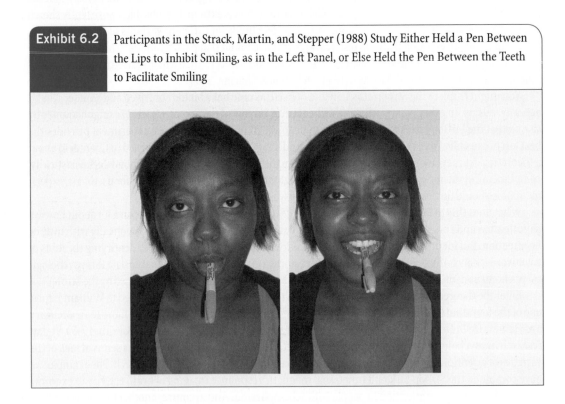

In addition, the study included a control condition, in which a third group of participants rated the funniness of cartoons while holding a pen in their nondominant hand that they would not normally use for writing. As it turned out, participants rated the control condition as most difficult, yet their funniness ratings were higher than those of the covert frown condition. This finding with the control condition ruled out that the findings were confounded by unrecognized differences in difficulty between covert smiling and covert frowning.

## Treatment Manipulations

A treatment outcome study poses some interesting research design challenges. First, a large number of participants are needed to be enrolled in the study. This is because a different group of participants must be assigned to the treatment and control groups. In addition, most treatment studies will need to have a group of participants who are assigned to a placebo group condition. This design feature is most often associated with drug studies in which a control group is administered a pharmacologically inert preparation or placebo drug.

A placebo condition helps address the problem of **demand characteristics**. Demand characteristics occur when participants form expectations as to the true purpose of the study and then alter their responses in the experiment to fit with their preconceived notions of the study. An experimenter may also send signals unwittingly as to how a research participant is expected to respond, usually in ways to confirm the researcher's hypothesis, such as showing the predicted beneficial effect for treatment. If the placebo group improves as much as the treatment group, this improvement would be attributable to the demand characteristics participants develop from simply being administered a druglike substance.

Placebo effects are also not just limited to drug studies. For example, Merzenich and colleagues controlled for placebo-like effects in their brain training study by having their active control (comparison) group engaged in computer use following the same schedules (60 minutes/day, 5 days/week, for 8 to 10 weeks) as the experimental group (Mahncke et al., 2006). The researchers could thus investigate placebo effects by comparing cognitive outcome measures for the active computer-based **comparison group** with the no-contact control group.

To rule out the possibility of placebo effects, both groups—the computer-based comparison group and the no-contact control group—should show similar responses on outcome measures. Also to combat expectancies of both participants and researchers, *double-blind* procedures are often added as a standard design feature of an experiment, particularly in a drug trial study (see Chapter 2). A double-blind feature of a study means that both the experimenter and the participant are deliberately kept blind to (unaware of) or kept in the dark as to whether the participant is receiving the treatment or the placebo.

The Merzenich study demonstrated a cognitive training effect on mental abilities of older people. It has received considerable attention in both popular (e.g., "brain games") press and scientific literature. The reliability of the effect remains an active area of research. So too does the extent to which the effect transfers to real-life improvement in everyday cognition. And finally, theoretically, the study provides a window on an important concept in neuroscience of plasticity, which highlights the brain as a dynamic organ whose pathways and synapses can be modified by cognitive training.

## Staged Manipulations

At times, experimental independent variables can be quite clever and creative. Think of the Zimbardo prison study and the Milgram study covered in Chapter 3 on ethics. Here manipulations of an independent variable can be much more complicated. In these studies, the independent variable is created via what is referred to as a **staged manipulation**. The goal of a staged manipulation is to fashion the psychological state or social situation that is the topic of investigation.

With a staged manipulation, there is frequently a confederate who typically is presented as another participant in an experiment but is actually an accomplice of the researcher. As you may recall, the famous Milgram study discussed in Chapter 3 employed confederates to create a psychological state of obedience. As you learned in Chapter 3, these kinds of studies raise serious ethical concerns that need to be reviewed by an institutional review board before one ever even attempts a **pilot study** (Knapp & VandeCreek, 2006). If your study is approved by an institutional review board, then, pilot a **manipulation check** to measure directly whether the independent variable manipulation creates the intended effect on people.

As a more recent example of a staged manipulation, consider the Bushman and Baumeister (1998) laboratory studies of interpersonal violence. In these studies, undergraduate participants received either positive ("No suggestions. Great essay!"), or negative ("This is one of the worst essays I have ever read!") feedback about essays that they had written. Next, the participants competed in a game against the person they believed had marked their essays. The researchers rigged the game so that all participants, regardless of whether they had been either insulted or praised, always won. When they won, the research participants were told that they could blast their opponent with a loud noise with the decibel level set by them. However, reminiscent of the Milgram study (see Chapter 3), there was no actual opponent and no one actually received the blast. Researchers recorded the exact decibel level at which the participants blasted their fictitious opponent as the dependent measure of interpersonal violence.

Before we get to their interesting findings, let's take a moment to think about the actual manipulation used in Bushman and Baumeister's (1998) study. Put yourself in these researchers' shoes. Their challenge was to design an experiment to simulate conditions that lead to violence in the real world. No small task, first and foremost, since is it *ethically* ever right to create conditions that cause people to believe that they responded aggressively toward another person, even if in reality that person exists only as a fictitious character?"

Apart from these critical ethical considerations, the research question of *ecological validity* looms large. Simply stated, is insulting people with negative feedback a realistic simulation of real-life triggers of violence? Is the degree to which a participant retaliates against a presumed target with a noise blaster a valid dependent variable to measure propensity for interpersonal violence?

These are questions for you to consider in evaluating the ecological validity of what is often referred to as a *laboratory analog* study. In this example, Bushman and Baumeister (1998) developed a laboratory analog study of interpersonal violence. And their study produced a novel and interesting finding whereby only people with certain personality traits known as narcissism (i.e., extremely egotistical) responded aggressively when faced with an opponent whom they believed had insulted them. They interpreted their results as support for the theory of "threatened egotism" as one pathway to interpersonal violence in the real world.

## Measuring Dependent Variables

All true experiments have as the dependent variable a **posttest**—that is, measurement of the outcome in both groups after the experimental group has received the treatment. Many true or randomized experiments also have **pretests** that measure the dependent variable prior to the experimental intervention. A pretest can be exactly the same as a posttest, just administered at a different time. Pretest scores permit a direct measure of how much the experimental and comparison groups changed over time, such as a change in memory among elderly persons.

Oftentimes, however, using identical pre- and posttests is to be avoided, especially if performance is likely to be influenced by practice in taking the same measure twice. This creates problems because a researcher wants to ensure that any observed pre- and posttests changes are attributable to the independent variable and not to practice effects. Here the use of pre- and posttest measures that have alternate forms would be wise, and as you may recall from Chapter 4, you can check to see if your pre- and posttest measures have good *alternate-forms reliability*.

As we also know from Chapter 4, how a dependent variable is measured has a direct bearing on how data can be statistically analyzed. For example, in our Stroop experiment, the dependent measure is response time. Response time constitutes a ratio scale of measurement with a true zero point with fixed measuring units and equal intervals. What this means is, we can say a response time of 10 seconds for congruent words is twice as fast as a response time of 20 seconds for incongruent words. Again only a dependent variable scaled on a ratio level of measurement allows us to make exact mathematical statements such as this.

For the Merzenich study, their dependent variables were posttest measures of mental abilities (Mahncke et al., 2006). Their research participants completed psychometric tests of cognition at posttest following training. These psychometric tests use an interval level of measurement. As you may recall, interval and ratio constitute the two most precise levels of measurement, which allow for parametric statistics. Parametric statistics, in turn, are considered the most powerful statistics for discovering an effect if one truly exists.

## Controlling Confounds

A true experiment aims to establish a causal relationship between the independent variable and the dependent variable. However, other factors might also influence this relationship. These factors may be extraneous, peripheral, or unimportant to the goal of the study. These factors can **confound** the results of an experiment. There are three techniques that are often used to control confounds.

Randomization is one technique to address the problem of confounds. Think about a common memory experiment that studies how many trials are needed for participants to learn a list of words that vary in terms of visual imagery. Here our independent variable is visual imagery of words. However, we know that irrespective of imagery, words presented at the beginning and the end of a list tend to be remembered better than words in the middle of a list. The position of the word on a list, whether at the beginning, known as the *primacy effect*, or at the end, known as the *recency effect*, can confound the results of an experiment that may be examining visual imagery and recall. To control for this position effect, an experimenter could randomize the order of presentation of the words so that each list would present the same words in a different order.

Another technique is to hold constant a variable or feature of an experiment that could influence the results. These factors that are held constant are known as control variables. For example, in the Stroop experiment, the number of words in each list is a control variable that is held constant. As you can see, Lists 1 and 2 each consisted of 25 color words. Each list also contains identical color words. These color words themselves are held constant across both lists.

The great challenge is, of course, in identifying or selecting which variables are to be controlled for or held constant, as there are more control variables than a researcher could ever desire to hold constant in practice. Some variables are rather straightforward to hold constant, such as the time of the day the study is conducted, temperature of the room, and the instructions introducing the study. These can be easily incorporated in the study design so that all participants are tested at the same time of day under the same room temperature and receive the same instructions introducing the experiment.

A third technique is to quantify the effects of a variable known to be strongly related to the independent variable as well as the dependent variable but thought to be extraneous. In the Merzenich study, let's imagine we found out that the experimental group differed from the comparison and the control groups on an important variable that could affect both the treatment and the outcome (Mahncke et al., 2006). For the sake of illustration, let's consider what it would mean if the experimental group as a whole had lower blood pressure, which in turn could influence both responses to the brain plasticity training as well as performance on the cognitive outcome measures. In this hypothetical example, any result pointing to a brain plasticity training effect on memory would be considered confounded, or influenced by a *third variable*—in this case, blood pressure.

Thus, the basic idea of this third technique known as **statistical control** is to quantify the effects of variables that cannot be randomized but are known to be strongly related to the dependent variable and the independent variable. These are control variables for which an experimenter collects data. In the example, blood pressure readings would be collected, because it could serve as a third variable or alternative explanation of age-related changes in memory; that is, blood pressure could confound the relationship of age and memory. As such, blood pressure would be used as a control variable to statistically adjust the dependent variable of scores on tests of memory.

There are different statistical techniques available to compare groups on a dependent variable, such as memory, while controlling for group differences on a control variable, such as blood pressure. The most well-known of these statistical techniques is **analysis of covariance**, which allows the researcher to test whether a difference on a dependent measure exists, even after controlling or covarying for the effects of specific control variables. Analysis of covariance is beyond the scope of this book (see, e.g., Kirk, 1994, for description). However, the principle to keep in mind is that a dependent measure can be adjusted statistically, which in effect eliminates the confounding influence of a specified third variable. This statistical test allows the experimenter to conclude that observed group differences on a dependent variable could not be attributable to unwanted effects of a third variable that has been statistically controlled for.

# 🔲 Basic Experimental Designs

Now we are faced with the interesting challenge of designing an experiment. We have the basic ingredients—independent, dependent, and control variables. The task is how to arrange these basic elements to design an effective experiment. As you know, the most basic experimental design has one independent variable, with two levels: (1) an experimental (treatment) group and (2) a control group. Your principal aim as a researcher is to design an experiment in which the only difference between the groups is the manipulated variable. This means that you want to make sure that all other factors are held constant via control variables, randomization, and statistical control. A simple basic experiment can come in two forms: (1) posttest-only design and (2) pretest–posttest design.

## Posttest-Only Design

What researchers call a *posttest-only design* is what we would commonly call a simple true experiment. A posttest-only design must have these three features: (1) random assignment of participants to treatment and control conditions, (2) manipulation of the independent variable, and (3) measurement of the effects of the independent variable on the dependent variable.

First, as you know, random assignment is an important technique that we use to control for selection bias. Our goal is to make our groups equivalent prior to the introduction of the independent variable. With random assignment, we can say that any preexisting differences between the groups prior to the introduction of the independent variable are due to chance.

Second, in a posttest-only design, the independent variable must have two or more levels, for example, an experimental group that receives a treatment and a control group that does not. Note that the group of participants who received the level of independent variable that is the focus of the study is called the *experimental* or *treatment group*. Note also that the group that received no training is called the *control group*. Do not confuse a control group with a control variable, which is defined as a variable that is held constant. The control group provides a means to determine changes that might occur naturally in the absence of treatment. The control group thus provides a **baseline** against which the treatment or experimental group can be compared.

In the Merzenich study, for example, the experimental group received the treatment of brain plasticity training and the control group did not (Mahncke et al., 2006). A posttest-only design can also be used in studies that want to vary the amount of the independent variable. Perhaps, you want to compare 5 versus 10 hours of brain plasticity training: 5- and 10-hour training would be the two conditions of the independent variable. You would randomly assign participants to each, and then, you could compare their responses. Last, the effects of the independent variable are measured on the dependent variable, which is also known as the posttest. The dependent variable should be identical for both groups. The same posttest allows for a direct comparison between groups, and this, of course, is crucial for any experimental design.

The selection of the dependent variable is also important. Here you want to make sure your dependent variable is sufficiently sensitive as a measure so that it can capture a range of performance. A dependent variable can often be problematic because it has a restricted range of performance. For example, when a dependent variable fails to discriminate various degrees of poor performance, meaning that all scores are confined to the very low end of the range, this is referred to as a **floor effect**. Think of a test in which all items are failed as an illustration of a floor effect. The opposite circumstance is called a **ceiling effect** in which the dependent variable is seriously restricted in range by very high scores. Think of getting 100% correct on a test as an illustration of a ceiling effect.

## Pretest–Posttest Design

You can probably guess the only difference between a posttest-only design and a *pretest–posttest* design. Yes, the only difference between the two is that a pretest–posttest design includes a pretest! A pretest–posttest design is also referred to as a **randomized comparative change design**, or a **pretest–posttest control group design**.

A pretest is given prior to the introduction of the independent variable. It can serve two principal functions. One important function is that a pretest can provide a baseline measure to compare the effects of the independent variable. Pretest scores permit a direct measure of how much the treatment and control groups changed over time up to the posttest, such as a change in memory among elderly persons. A pretest can be exactly the same as a posttest, just administered at a different time. However, as we know, in some instances, identical pre- and posttest should be avoided especially if performance is likely to be influenced by practice in taking the same measure twice. In these studies, a researcher should use pre- and posttest measures that have alternate forms.

Another important function is that a pretest can be used as a check on how well random assignment worked in making groups equivalent. Ideally, there should not be significant group differences on the pretest. If there are group differences, then, we would conclude that random assignment failed to create equivalent groups. Thus, a pretest measure before treatment is often used to evaluate whether random assignment was successful (that sampling or selection biases did not lead to an initial difference between the groups).

## Multiple Pretests and Posttests

An experiment may have multiple posttests and perhaps even multiple pretests. Multiple posttests can identify just when the treatment has its effect and for how long. This is particularly important when treatments are delivered over a period of time (Rossi & Freeman, 1989). However, strictly speaking, an experiment does not require a pretest. Random assignment is thought to equate experimental and comparison groups before the intervention is administered to the experimental group so that in principle a pretest is unnecessary. Any subsequent difference in outcome between the experimental and comparison groups is therefore likely to be due to the intervention (or to other processes occurring during the experiment), and the likelihood of a difference just on the basis of chance can be calculated.

This is fortunate, because the dependent variable in some experiments cannot be measured in a pretest. For example, if you want to test the effect of class size on student reactions to a teacher, you can't

Test your knowledge of this chapter so far by taking the mid-chapter quiz on the study site: www.sagepub.com/ nestor2e

measure their reactions to the teacher until they have been exposed to the experimental treatment—the classes of different size. There can also be a disadvantage to having a pretest, even when it is possible to do so. The act of taking the pretest can itself cause participants to change.

# ▣ Two Options in Assigning Participants

In designing a research study, you are faced with an important procedural decision about assigning participants to control and experimental conditions. You have two options. In one procedure, participants are randomly assigned to the different conditions of the study. This means each participant receives only one condition of the experiment. Thus, with this procedure, your sample is divided into groups, with each group receiving only one condition or level of the independent variable.

This procedure gives birth to what is called an **independent-groups design**. It is also known as a **between-subjects design** (see Exhibit 6.3). Independent-groups design and between-subjects design are synonymous and are used interchangeably. Technically, you can combine the terms and use the label *independent-groups, between-subjects design*. What a mouthful! In the other procedure, all research participants receive all levels of the independent variable. This is called a **repeated-measures design**, also known as a **within-subjects design**. Again, you can combine these terms and use the label *repeated measures, within-subjects design*.

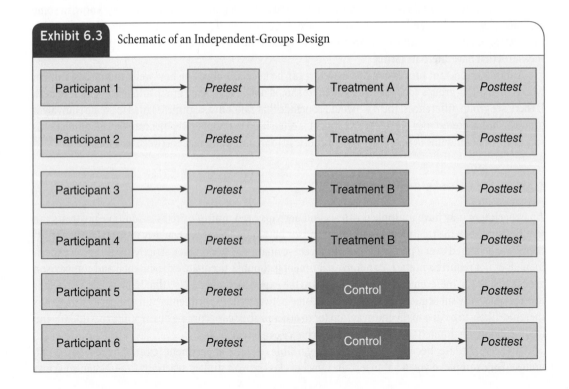

| **Exhibit 6.3** | Schematic of an Independent-Groups Design |

| Participant 1 | → | Pretest | → | Treatment A | → | Posttest |
| Participant 2 | → | Pretest | → | Treatment A | → | Posttest |
| Participant 3 | → | Pretest | → | Treatment B | → | Posttest |
| Participant 4 | → | Pretest | → | Treatment B | → | Posttest |
| Participant 5 | → | Pretest | → | Control | → | Posttest |
| Participant 6 | → | Pretest | → | Control | → | Posttest |

So to simplify, there are two basic ways of allocating participants to experimental conditions. Allocating participants via a between-subjects procedure creates an independent-groups design. Allocating participants via a within-subjects procedure creates a repeated-measures design. Now we will examine each of these designs below.

## Independent-Groups Design

In an independent-groups design, research participants are randomly assigned to each of the experimental conditions. With this design, each participant in each group experiences only one condition of the independent variable. And because the same participants never receive all conditions of the independent variable, a different group of participants must be assigned to each condition of the independent variable. For this reason, independent-group designs require a large number of people to be enrolled in a study.

An independent-groups design is commonly the preferred design for outcome studies. Here a researcher may want to compare different types of treatment and to isolate their effects. Likewise, an educational researcher may want to compare the relative benefits of different curricula or teachers. And in these studies, having the same participants experience each of the different treatments or different educational curricula would be counterproductive. The obvious problem is that experience in one condition could very well spill over and influence responses in subsequent conditions.

As an illustration, consider the Merzenich study, an independent-groups design that used a between-subjects allocation: Participants assigned to the experimental group received only brain plasticity training, and those assigned to the comparison group received only the educational DVD. If somehow experimental and comparison groups became exposed to each other's training, then the experimenter would not be able to attribute the improved memory to brain plasticity training.

Exhibit 6.3 provides a simple schematic of the between-subjects procedure of assigning participants used in an independent-groups design. As in the Merzenich study, Exhibit 6.3 shows that participants are randomly assigned to one of the three levels of the independent variable labeled A, B, and Control, with all receiving both pre- and posttests.

## Matched-Pairs Design

**Matching** is another procedure sometimes used to equate groups, but by itself, it is a poor substitute for randomization. Matching of individuals in a treatment group with those in a control group might involve pairing persons on the basis of similarity of gender, age, year in school, or some other objective characteristic. The basic problem is that, as a practical matter, individuals can only be matched on a few characteristics; unmatched characteristics between the experimental and control groups may still influence the results of the study. When matching is used as a substitute for random assignment, the research becomes *quasi-experimental* instead of being a true experiment (see Chapter 8).

Matching can be combined with random assignment. This is referred to as a **matched-pairs design**, which for between-subjects studies provides a better bet that the groups are equivalent before the introduction of the independent variable manipulation. In a matched-pairs design, we first create pairs of participants that are matched on a variable that is strongly related to the dependent variable. We then randomly assign one of the pairs to the experimental condition and the other to the control condition; that is, each member of the pair is assigned to *different* levels of the independent variable (see Exhibit 6.4). In short, an effective matched-pairs design provides a degree of experimental control of between-subject **individual differences** that is comparable with that of a repeated-measures design. As such, a matched-pairs design provides greater power to detect statistical significance than simple random assignment of an independent-groups design.

| Exhibit 6.4 | Matched-Pairs Design Combines Matching and Random Assignment |

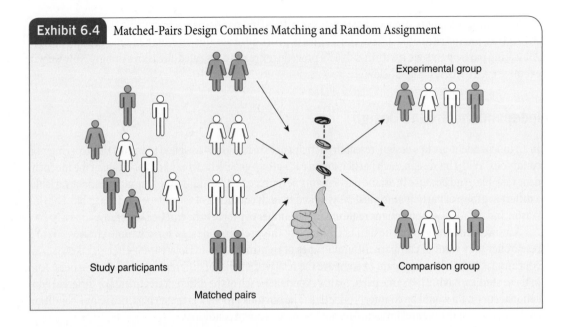

## Repeated-Measures Design

When individuals are presumed to vary widely on a dependent variable, a repeated-measures design is often the preferred choice for testing a research hypothesis. Under these circumstances, within-subjects comparisons may be more sensitive than between-subjects comparisons. As we know, a repeated-measures design compares the performance of the same individual across all of the different experimental conditions.

In our Stroop experiment, for example, you as a participant received both the congruent and incongruent word lists, and your response times for each word list was measured (if you carried out all the instructions). As we will learn shortly, this is known as a repeated measure because the same measure (e.g., response time) is repeated for the same participant for each of the two conditions of the experiment. This allows you to compare the responses of the same participant to each of the two conditions. This is known as a within-subjects comparison. It provides a very effective technique, different from random assignment, to control for individual differences.

Another important advantage of a repeated-measures design is that fewer research participants are needed because all participants will receive all treatments. A repeated-measures design is also desirable when an experimenter is sure that the effect of one treatment will not carry over to, or contaminate, the other condition or conditions of the experiment.

Finally, a repeated-measures design is essential for longitudinal studies, which will be discussed in Chapter 8. In a longitudinal study, the same research participants are followed over time, for example, when the same child is tested at age 6, then at age 10, and then again at age 13. Widely used in developmental psychology, a **longitudinal research design** can collect data for decades, as participants might be followed over their life spans, and these data are ordered in time so that developmental trajectories or courses can be examined.

## Carryover Effects

An important source of experimental error for a repeated-measures design is the problem of **carryover effects** from one treatment or condition to the next (Elmes, Kantowitz, & Roedinger, 2006). This of course is not a source of experimental error for an independent-groups design, since the participants are only exposed to one treatment. But a major concern for any within-subjects manipulation arises if performance in one condition affects performance in a subsequent condition.

If carryover effects are not controlled, any results will be confounded by the order of presentation of the conditions. Under these circumstances, a researcher will not be able to attribute the results of a study to a particular treatment or condition. True differences in treatment, or true differences between or among levels of the independent variable, may be masked by the order in which the levels of the independent variable were presented. Carryover effects can also arise from rather routine factors, such as fatigue participants might experience by the end of an experiment, or from familiarity or practice effects participants might experience over the course of a study. Thus, these carryover effects are considered to be confounding variables that present major challenges for within-subjects manipulations.

## Randomizing

Randomizing the order in which participants receive treatments is a way to combat carryover effects. Here the principle and objective are the same as when random assignment is used to form groups for a between-subjects design. A random order can be generated by using a table of random numbers or by as simple a task as writing the different orders of treatment on slips of paper and then drawing them out of a hat. Randomization ensures that any differences in treatment orders are due to chance only. However, generally there are fewer treatment orders compared with the number of participants, and for this reason, randomization is really not an effective technique for equating order of treatments.

## Counterbalancing

A more commonly used technique to control for the order of treatments is known as **counterbalancing**. Counterbalancing the order of treatments tends to be more effective than randomizing the order of treatments because it ensures that each treatment or level of the independent variable occurs in each time period of the experiment. That way, every treatment has the same chance of being influenced by confounding variables related to a treatment coming before and after it.

Complete counterbalancing begins by calculating all possible treatment orders. For two treatments, this will be very straightforward. For example, let's say your two treatments are computer-based neural plasticity training and computer-based educational training. You would have only two orders of administering the treatment: Half the participants receive computer-based neural plasticity training and then computer-based educational training, and half receive computer-based educational training and then computer-based neural plasticity training.

As the number of treatments, conditions, or levels of the independent variable increases, so too does the number of possible orders. For five treatments, you have 120 different orders. This is calculated as follows: $5! = 5 \times 4 \times 3 \times 2 \times 1$. Four treatments have 24 different orders ($4! = 4 \times 3 \times 2 \times 1$). Three treatments have six different orders ($3! = 3 \times 2 \times 1$). As you can see, in experimental design, fewer levels of the independent variables are easier to manage and require fewer research participants. Overall, however, even with as few as four treatments, complete counterbalancing becomes unwieldy and impractical.

With complete counterbalancing often untenable, researchers will frequently use what is called a **Latin-square design** as a way to combat confounds of carryover effects in within-subjects experiments. A Latin-square design is an *incomplete* counterbalancing arrangement in which each possible order of treatments occurs equally often across research participants.

For example, consider a Latin square for counterbalancing the order of three treatment conditions: memory (M), reasoning (R), and processing speed (PS). As shown in Exhibit 6.5, in this arrangement, memory will be administered first, second, or third equally often, as will the treatment of reasoning and processing speed. This arrangement is presented in a Latin square with rows representing the participants in the study and columns representing the order of these treatments—that is, Participant 1 receives memory first, followed by reasoning, and then processing speed; Participant 2 receives reasoning first, following by processing speed, and then memory; and Participant 3 receives processing speed, memory, and then reasoning. The same order of treatments is presented for Participants 4 through 6.

| Exhibit 6.5 | A Latin Square for Counterbalancing the Order of Three Treatments Across Six Research Participants | | | |
|---|---|---|---|---|
| | | | Order | |
| | Participant Number | 1st | 2nd | 3rd |
| Square 1 | 1 | M | R | PS |
| | 2 | R | PS | M |
| | 3 | PS | M | R |
| Square 2 | 4 | M | R | PS |
| | 5 | R | PS | M |
| | 6 | PS | M | R |

*Note:* M = memory; R = reasoning; PS = processing speed.

Usually, however, a researcher will need to use more research participants than treatments. What this means is that a researcher will need to use some number in calculating sample size that is a multiple of the number of the treatments in the Latin square. So if there are three treatments, then a researcher could use sample sizes of 3, 6, 9, 12, 15, and so on, as long as the sample size can be divided by 3 (the number of treatments for this example) with no remainder. A Latin-square design thus provides a practical remedy to the problem of carryover effects. The constraint it places on sample size is not too burdensome. And keep in mind that an advantage of a repeated-measures design is that it requires fewer subjects than an independent-groups design.

However, an important cautionary note is to be kept in mind: Because the same Latin-square arrangement can be used over and over (see Exhibit 6.5), there is a possibility that somehow the order of the treatments becomes confounded with the effects of the treatments. In other words, just as random assignment can fail in an independent-groups design, so can a Latin square for counterbalancing order of treatments in a repeated-measures design. There is a statistical test for square uniqueness that will determine whether the Latin square proved effective in counterbalancing order of treatments (please refer to Kirk, 1994, as the statistical test for square uniqueness is beyond the scope of this book). In the final analysis, complete counterbalancing remains the safest technique for repeated-measures designs.

## Selecting Between- or Within-Subjects Allocation

As you can see, there are pros and cons to weigh when considering whether to manipulate an independent variable between subjects or within subjects. For between-subjects allocation, there is always the threat that random assignment will fail to neutralize individual differences and that groups will not be equal prior to treatment or manipulation of the independent variable. Remember, randomization procedures deal in probability, which means that groups formed by random assignment could still differ by chance. On the other hand, if carryover effects are to be avoided at all cost, then an independent-groups design will certainly be favored over a repeated-measures design.

There is an additional interesting question that extends beyond the pros and cons of a between- and within-subjects allocation of participants to experimental conditions. Let's imagine that we take the *same* independent variable, and in one experiment, we use a repeated-measures design and in the other experiment, we use an independent-groups design. How would these two experiments fare? Greene (1996) designed a project to answer this question using a well-studied memory experiment. His results gave the advantage to the repeated-measures design over the independent-groups design; that is, his within-subjects manipulation replicated findings of prior studies, his between-subjects manipulation did not.

## Validity and Experimentation

Ideally, we want to design an experiment in which all extraneous factors are sufficiently controlled so that changes in the dependent variables result solely from changes in the independent variable. How then might independent, dependent, and control variables be optimally arranged for us to demonstrate causality? To put it simply, the objective is to design an internally valid experiment that works! By "works," we mean whether an experiment will have sufficient sensitivity to detect the effects it purports to investigate.

### Internal Validity

The concept of **internal validity** speaks to the logic of experimental design—the extent to which procedures and methods are optimally arranged so that the effects of the independent variable on the dependent variable can be "evaluated unambiguously" (Underwood, 1957, p. 86); that is, the internal validity of an experiment is defined as the extent to which our conclusion about the effect of the systematic manipulation of one or more independent variables on the dependent variable reflects what actually happened. The goal is to design experiments with high internal validity that will allow the researcher to identify causal relationships among the key variables under study.

We use the term **design sensitivity** when thinking about the extent to which a researcher has constructed the best possible study to evaluate the topic under investigation. Some questions to consider when evaluating internal validity are as follows: Are the levels of the independent variable sufficiently distinct? Are the experimental conditions effectively designed to create the hypothesized effect? Is the manipulation strong enough to create an effect? Does the dependent variable provide enough precision of measurement to pick up the effects of the independent variable? How are participants assigned to the experimental conditions? Did the randomization procedures provide adequate control? Should all participants receive all levels of the independent variable? Or is the hypothesis of the study best addressed by random assignment to different conditions so that each participant receives only one level of the independent variable?

We aim to design an internally valid experiment or study that minimizes **experimental error**. Experimental error is broadly defined as any influence on the dependent variable that is not due solely to the systematic change in the independent variable. You have already learned that there are many potential sources of experimental error, and these are all considered threats to the internal validity of an experiment. Experimental error produces confounds, whereby the unwanted influences of so-called nuisance variables make the results very difficult to interpret unambiguously.

Threats to internal validity can be addressed via experimental control, as when the order or stimulus presentation is randomized or by control variables that hold constant potential influences that could confound results. Statistical control can also play an important role in internal validity—that is, in ruling out alternative explanations of results. As we learned, this can be done by quantifying the effects of a so-called third variable that cannot be randomized but are known to be strongly related to the dependent variable, independent variable, or both. In a specific statistical procedure, known as analysis of covariance, the measurements of a dependent variable can be adjusted by taking into account these influences. In so doing, analysis of covariance provides a statistical control for the confounding influence of a specified third variable.

## Causality and Chance

Internal validity is about evaluating causality. Does the internal design of an experiment allow the researcher to draw causal conclusions about the effect of the independent variable on the dependent variable? Does the internal strength of the experimental design support a causal interpretation of the results? These are questions about causality and internal validity.

On the other hand, statistics, used to test the relationship between the independent and dependent variable, asks about the probability of the results of an experiment being due to chance alone; that is, the question for statistical analysis is framed simply: Are the results of an experiment statistically significant?

To answer this question, inferential statistics provide a test of statistical significance. Statistical significance testing tells us the likelihood or probability that the observed effect revealed by data analysis could be due to chance alone. Statistical probabilities are set at levels of significance in the form of *probability (p) values*. Traditionally, *p* values of .05 or less indicate that an obtained finding is statistically significant, meaning that there is a 5% likelihood or less that the obtained results are due to chance alone. Thus, *statistical significance* simply means that a finding is unlikely due to chance at a certain level of probability, usually .05 or less.

Statistical significance is used to test what is referred to as the **null hypothesis.** The null hypothesis is defined as the hypothesis of no difference or no relationship, which the researcher tries to reject, nullify, or disprove. The alternative hypothesis, the **research hypothesis** predicts a specific relationship between the independent variable and the dependent variable. Statistics do not directly test a research hypothesis; that is, a significance level of less than 5% allows for the rejection of the *null* hypothesis of no difference between the groups, but *in principle*, it does not allow for the acceptance of the research hypothesis. In practice, however, if our statistical analysis allows us to reject the null hypothesis, then the research hypothesis is indeed accepted.

Statistics and experimental design go hand in hand. Statistics determine whether the obtained results of an experiment are significant, that is, the likelihood that the results are due to chance alone. If the results achieved statistical significance, the next question is one of interpretation. Now the major issue to weigh is the internal validity of the experimental design. And here the degree of internal validity of an experiment will determine whether a causal relationship between the independent variable and the dependent variable is properly identified (see "Stat Corner").

## Type I and Type II Errors

Two types of errors must be weighed in making decisions about whether to reject or accept the null hypothesis. **Type I error** occurs when the null hypothesis is wrongly rejected. To use a legal analogy, the maxim that "all defendants are innocent until proven guilty" is akin to a null hypothesis. A jury makes a Type I error when it wrongly convicts an innocent defendant. In science, what is the likelihood of a Type I error, that is, rejecting the null hypothesis when in fact it is true? The answer is the level of statistical significance stated as a probability (i.e., $p$ value). A probability of a Type I error is the significance level. So if statistical analysis of the results showed a $p$ value of less than .03, then the chances are less than 3% that the obtained results are due to chance alone; there is less than 3% chance of a Type I error of incorrectly rejecting the null hypothesis (see Chapter 10).

**Type II error** occurs when the null hypothesis is incorrectly accepted. A jury makes a Type II error when it fails to convict a guilty defendant. When you as a researcher commit a Type II error, you have in effect shot yourself in the foot! You have missed a significant result because your research design lacked sensitivity. In psychological research, Type II errors are difficult to gauge in terms of how often they may occur. This is likely because studies that are plagued by Type II errors have by definition failed to achieve statistical significance and therefore are seldom reviewed for publication. This helps explain the problem of *publication bias* in the psychological literature that we discussed in Chapter 2.

How might Type I and Type II errors bear on the internal validity of an experiment? First, a Type I error may occur because of a design flaw, for example, a failure to randomize the order of stimulus presentation in a test of memory of high-imagery words. Here the significant results may be confounded by the order of stimulus presentation. For example, because a disproportionate number of high-imagery words happened to occur near the end of the list, these were more readily recalled. Thus, the significant effect of better recall for high-imagery words would be confounded by order of the presentation of the words.

Type II errors are typically understood as a problem of *statistical power,* which as you know means the extent to which a study is adequately designed to find the predicted significant effect. In other words, the likelihood of a Type II error decreases as internal validity of an experiment increases. And as internal validity of an experiment increases, so does its statistical power.

Sample size is a major factor related to statistical power. Sample size, of course, refers to the number of research participants/observations/data points that are expected to be collected and analyzed. In general, larger samples provide greater statistical power. The idea is that if only a handful of research participants are tested, then a negative finding of no difference or no relationship may arise simply because not enough people were tested.

## External Validity

Whenever we hear of a new research finding, one of our first questions is, To whom do the results of the study apply? Doctors, for example, may fail to pursue for their patients a treatment, which has been demonstrated to be effective in experiments, if they think the results have limited applicability and relevance. Relevance and applicability depend on external validity.

As we know, external validity addresses the extent to which results of a particular study that involves a sample of subjects will generalize to the wider population. The need for generalizable findings can be thought of as the Achilles' heel of randomized experimental design. The design components that are essential for a randomized experiment and that minimize the threats to internal validity make it more difficult to achieve external validity in the form of sample generalizability (being able to apply the findings to some clearly defined larger population), cross-population generalizability (generalizing across subgroups and to other populations and settings, conditions, and outcomes), and *ecological validity* (discussed in Chapter 2) or the real-world impact of research (see Exhibit 6.6).

| Exhibit 6.6 | Greater Generalizability and Applicability, Greater External Validity |

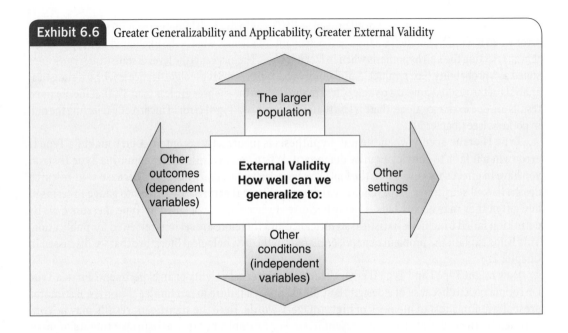

## Sample Generalizability

Research participants, who can be recruited for a laboratory experiment, randomly assigned to a group, and kept under carefully controlled conditions for the study's duration, are unlikely to be a representative sample of any large population of interest to social scientists. Can they be expected to react to the experimental treatment in the same way as members of the larger population? The generalizability of the treatment and of the setting for the experiment also must be considered (Cook & Campbell, 1979). The more artificial the experimental arrangements are, the greater the problem will be (Campbell & Stanley, 1966).

A researcher can take steps both before and after an experiment to increase a study's generalizability. The Merzenich study is likely to yield more generalizable findings than are laboratory experiments that rely on college students as research participants (Mahncke et al., 2006). In studies like the Merzenich and colleagues' investigation as well as some field experiments, participants can even be selected randomly from the population of interest, and thus, the researchers can achieve results that are generalizable to that population. For example, some studies of the effects of income supports on the work behavior of poor persons have *randomly sampled* persons within particular states before randomly assigning them to experimental and comparison groups. When random selection is not feasible, the researchers may be able to increase generalizability by selecting several different experimental sites that offer marked contrasts on key variables (Cook & Campbell, 1979).

Note that the random assignment of research participants to groups is not the same as random sampling of individuals from some larger population (see Exhibit 6.7). In fact, random assignment (randomization) does not help at all to ensure that the research participants are representative of some larger population; instead, representativeness is the goal of random sampling. What random assignment does—create two or more equivalent groups—is useful for maximizing the likelihood of internal validity, not generalizability. As sketched in Exhibit 6.7, random sampling and random assignment are vital in constructing sensitive and valid designs. Random sampling by maximizing generalizability increases the external validity of the results of a study. Similarly, random assignment by equating treatment and control groups prior to the manipulation of the independent variable enhances the ability of an experiment to generate internally valid results.

| Exhibit 6.7 | Random Sampling and Random Assignment Increase External and Internal Validity, Respectively |

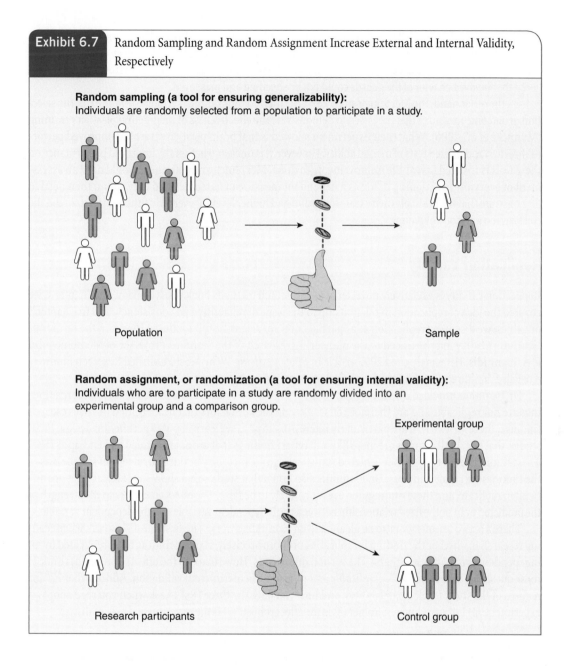

**Random sampling (a tool for ensuring generalizability):**
Individuals are randomly selected from a population to participate in a study.

Population

Sample

**Random assignment, or randomization (a tool for ensuring internal validity):**
Individuals who are to participate in a study are randomly divided into an experimental group and a comparison group.

Experimental group

Research participants

Control group

# Ecological Validity

As we touched on in Chapter 2, ecological validity is a form of external validity that is concerned with the real-life impact of results generated from research studies. We have already learned that ecological validity is especially important in studies that want to investigate whether some form of training or treatment can improve real-life functioning. Ecological validity rests largely on the extent to which the researchers select the proper outcome measures.

In general, laboratory experiments often fall short on ecological validity. The researcher tries to balance experimental control and internal validity, on one hand, with general applicability of ecological validity, on the other hand. As we have seen, for example, the Stanford Prison Experiment described in Chapter 3 is thought of as an experiment with considerable ecological validity. However, it lacked experimental control and internal validity in that many of the particular features of the environment that triggered the abusive behavior of the guards could not be specified and measured.

On the other hand, the Merzenich study can be criticized for its limited ecological validity in the selection of outcome measures that they used to demonstrate the effectiveness of their neural plasticity training (Mahncke et al., 2006). What their experiment showed is that brain plasticity training improved performance on standardized tests of mental ability. However, it is unclear whether the improved performance on these tests translated to real-life improvement. To do so, Merzenich and colleagues would need an assessment of everyday functioning in life as a dependent measure of outcome , and they would then need to demonstrate that the brain plasticity training group had higher levels of everyday functioning than did the comparison and control groups.

## Replication Validity

Replication validity is a relatively novel term for a research methods book in psychology. (In Chapter 1, we covered the idea of replication in relationship to the issue of reliability and consistency, and in Chapter 3 on ethics, we discussed replication as a "partial cure" for scientific misconduct.) However, the term **replication validity** may be traced to the pioneering research of the Stanford Professor of Medicine John P. A. Ioannidis. His widely cited 2005 article in *PLoS Medicine* "Why Most Published Research Findings Are False" has direct implications for psychological experiments.

Dr. Ioannidis provided convincing quantitative simulation evidence that most scientific research findings are not replicable and are therefore false. Among the key factors that he identified in false research findings, there are two that are particularly interesting to us as we learn about experimental design. First, studies that use small samples are more likely to report findings that are not replicated and end up as false. These findings, even though they achieved statistical significance, may be due to inadvertent sample bias— the flukiness of small numbers. Dr. Ioannidis also noted that studies that show small effect sizes are difficult to replicate, and these findings too are more likely to be false. The effect size refers to the strength of the predicted or hypothesized relationship between the independent variable and the dependent variable.

There are two lessons for us to be gleaned from Ioannidis's work. The first question to ask when reading research is whether the finding is replicable, or more precisely, Has the finding been replicated by an independent group of researchers? The second question is, How robust is the effect? You might think of these questions as the two "Rs"—*replicable* and *robust*—of experimental validation. Add another "R" for realism of the study (ecological validity), and now you have the three "Rs" to ask when you read about an experiment: (1) Is the finding replicable? (2) Is the effect robust? (3) Is the experimental task realistic?

---

### STAT CORNER

### Statistical Significance

Now let us apply statistical significance testing to the results of the Merzenich study. Exhibit 6.8 presents the pre- and posttest scores on memory (mean ± standard deviation) for experimental brain plasticity training ($n = 53$), comparison with DVD educational ($n = 53$), and control ($n = 56$) groups. As you can see, in relation to their pretest scores, the experimental brain plasticity training group showed an improvement of 2.3 points in posttest memory scores. By contrast, neither the comparison nor the control group showed a significant improvement in posttest memory scores. The key question is whether the 2.3 point improvement for the experimental brain plasticity training group is statistically significant, that is, whether this gain in memory is unlikely due to chance.

To answer this question, the researchers used a specific statistical test, known as a **paired-sample** *t* test (see Chapter 10), to compare pre- and posttest memory scores for each of the three groups. The pre- and posttest memory scores are submitted to a paired-sample *t* test, which calculates a specific statistical value with a corresponding significance level. Here what is actually being tested is the mean difference in improvement against zero. So for the experimental group, the value being tested is 2.3 against zero. Is this 2.3 gain in memory a large number or a small number? Is this difference in pre- and posttest memory scores a real one or one that could be reasonably expected due to chance alone? The answer is found in the *p* value of .019 (1.9%). This means that the probability or likelihood that a difference of 2.3 points in memory would occur by chance alone is about 1.9%. This level of significance allows for the null hypothesis to be rejected in favor of the research hypothesis that brain training improves memory.

Note a potential problem in these results pertains to the pretraining memory scores: As you can see in Exhibit 6.8, the brain plasticity group had the lowest pretest memory scores. This raises concerns as to whether the subsequent posttest improvement for the brain plasticity training group was confounded by their relatively low pretest scores. Here, analysis of covariance could be used to statistically equate the three groups on pretest memory scores. This would adjust the scores on the dependent variable—the posttest outcome measure—for the initial differences on the pretest measure. If the results still remain significant, then we would have more confidence in concluding that neural plasticity training improved memory, even after controlling for the relatively lower pretest scores for the experimental group. In the absence of this statistical control, however, the beneficial effect of brain plasticity training on memory can be questioned.

| Exhibit 6.8 | Training Improves Global Memory Score | | | |
|---|---|---|---|---|
| Group | Pretest | Posttest | Difference | p Value |
| Experimental | 48.9 ± 1.3 | 51.2 ± 1.2 | 2.3 ± 0.9 | .019 |
| Comparison | 50.2 ± 1.2 | 51.2 ± 1.2 | 1.0 ± 0.9 | .29 |
| Control | 51.2 ± 1.0 | 52.3 ± 1.1 | 1.1 ± 0.9 | .22 |

## Can Causality Be Established?

As we see in the "Stat Corner," the results of the Merzenich study indicated that the experimental computer-based training group showed a statistically significant improvement on the outcome measure of memory as assessed by standardized neuropsychological tests. The experimental group sustained its improved memory at a 3-month follow-up. By contrast, neither the active computer-based training group nor the no-contact control group showed any significant change on the outcome measure of memory at the end of the study or at the 3-month follow-up. The comparison and control groups had similar responses on the outcome measures. Merzenich and colleagues concluded that their brain plasticity–based program significantly improved memory in mature adults (Mahncke et al., 2006). Was this causal conclusion justified? How confident can we be in this conclusion? Do you think that this effect is likely to generalize to other people and settings?

We can say that brain plasticity improved cognition in the Merzenich study because only participants who received this training showed improved performance on the outcome measures of memory (Mahncke et al., 2006). This improvement occurred after the treatment. This is important because causality requires demonstrating that the predicted effect followed treatment. This time order criterion (or, as we learned in Chapter 2, *temporal precedence*) of causality is clearly demonstrated in the Merzenich study.

However, two aspects of their data raise concern as to whether a causal relationship can be concluded between their demonstrated association of brain plasticity training and improved memory. The first aspect concerns preexisting differences among the three groups on the pretest memory measure, with the experimental group showing the lowest scores prior to receiving brain plasticity training. The second concern centers on the strength of the brain plasticity training on the posttest outcome measure of memory. The Merzenich results pointed to a rather small effect for the brain plasticity training on memory scores for the experimental group (Mahncke et al., 2006).

Both aspects of their data—pretest differences and small effect size—pose major problems for drawing a causal connection between brain plasticity training and memory improvement. Also important to remember is that our statistics test the null hypothesis, not the research hypothesis. A statistically significant finding tells us that the obtained results are unlikely due to chance, but this is a far cry from establishing a causal prediction formulated in the research hypothesis. We can therefore safely conclude that the Merzenich data pointed to an empirical association of treatment and better memory scores for the experimental group, but we should exercise caution (in the spirit of the scientific method) in drawing any causal conclusion that brain plasticity training by itself produced memory improvement in the experimental group.

In addition, we must be mindful of the multiple influences at work in any psychological study—only the influence of a sole independent variable is studied in a single-factor experiment. As we will learn in Chapter 7, most psychological experiments involve more than one independent variable. There are many advantages of manipulating two or more independent variables simultaneously within the same experiment. Chief among these is that so-called multifactorial experiments allow us to examine an important issue of validity—that is, whether results generalize across several independent variables.

And as we will also learn in Chapter 7 that *interactions* between and among independent variables can be tested in these multifactorial experiments. In this sense, then, multifactorial experiments offer a more realistic chance of arriving at a causal explanation. As a preview to Chapter 7, we will learn how two independent variables interact, meaning the effects produced by one independent variable are not the same across levels of a second independent variable. For now, however, we end this chapter looking at some common errors in reasoning that can lead to invalid causal explanations.

## Mistakes in Reasoning About Causality

Recall that in Chapter 1, we learned that we are naturally prone to making certain errors of reasoning, such as when confirmatory bias influences our collection and interpretation of evidence. These errors of reasoning, or *heuristic biases* (see Chapter 1), come in many different forms, including those that predispose us to infer causation on the basis of correlation.

Consider the old adage, "Correlation does not prove causation." This maxim is meant to remind us that a correlation between two variables might be caused by something other than an effect of the presumed independent variable on the dependent variable—that is, it might be a **spurious relationship**. If we measure children's shoe sizes and their academic knowledge, for example, we will find a positive association. However, the association results from the fact that older children have larger feet as well as more academic knowledge. Shoe size does not cause knowledge, or vice versa.

Researchers should make sure that their causal conclusions reflect the unit of analysis in their study. Experiments involve investigating group differences. As such, the group is the proper unit of analysis. What this means is that conclusions about group-level processes should be made based on experimental data collected from groups, and conclusions about individuals should be based on individual-level data. Ignoring this individual versus group level of analysis distinction can give rise to two kinds of errors in making causal conclusions.

First, an error of reasoning known as the **ecological fallacy** occurs when you make conclusions about an individual based only on analyses of group data. For example, a research participant who received the computerized cognitive training will have better memory than a person who did not participate in the study. Essentially, the mistake is taking the average for the group and blindly applying it to an individual member of the group.

However, don't be too quick to reject all the conclusions about individual processes based on group-level data; just keep in mind the possibility of an ecological fallacy. If we don't have individual-level data, we can't be sure that patterns at the group level, often summarized by the arithmetic average or mean, will hold at the individual level. Second, when data about individuals are used to make inferences about group-level processes, a problem occurs that can be thought of as the mirror image of the ecological fallacy: the **reductionist fallacy**, also known as reductionism or individualist fallacy (see Exhibit 6.9).

| **Exhibit 6.9** | Errors in Causal Conclusion |
| --- | --- |

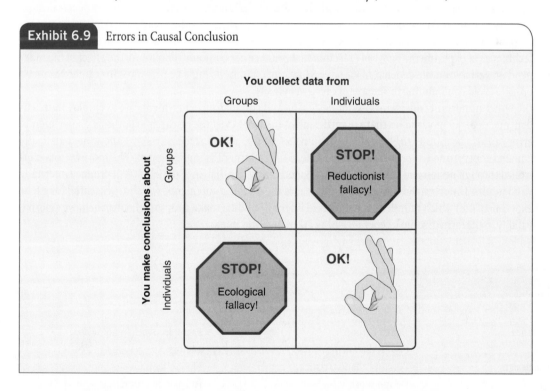

In summary, the fact that errors in causal reasoning can be made should not deter you from carrying out experiments or make you unduly critical of researchers who make inferences about individuals on the basis of group data. However, just because a person is a member of a group with a certain average, such as a high memory score, does not mean you can conclude that the person will have a strong memory!

# ▣ Conclusions

We have learned about a particularly well-controlled and powerful research design known simply as a true experiment. In a true experiment, a researcher has complete control over the manipulation of the independent variable. Such experimental control allows for testing whether systematically varying the independent variable causes changes in the dependent variable; that is, a researcher aims to design an internally valid experiment that will identify causal relationships among the key variables under study.

A pivotal question in designing a true experiment is how participants will be allocated to control and experimental conditions. There are two basic procedures for assigning participants to treatment conditions. In a between-subjects procedure, participants are randomly assigned to control and experimental groups. This procedure gives birth to what is called an independent-groups design, also known as a between-subjects design. Random assignment is critical in forming equivalent control and experimental groups before the introduction of the independent variable. We use this design to ensure that participants are exposed to only one level of the independent variable, for example, a particular treatment, and not to any other types of treatment.

In a within-subjects procedure, all participants receive all conditions of the experiment. This procedure gives birth to what is called a repeated-measures design, also known as a within-subjects design. Each participant serves as his or her own control. As such, a repeated-measures design requires fewer participants than a between-subjects design. A repeated-measures design provides one of the most powerful techniques of experimental control of factors that could either confound or obscure the effect of the independent variable on the dependent variable. However, conditions must be presented in counterbalanced order to avoid confounding influences of carryover effects.

Other important considerations for designing and conducting experiments are to employ independent and dependent variables that are sufficiently sensitive to test the research hypothesis. Experimental error can also be minimized by statistical control in the use of pretest measures that allow for statistically equated control and experimental groups before the treatment is implemented. The more factors controlled through design and statistical tools, the more likely it is that an experiment will produce internally valid results. Unfortunately, often it is the case that the design components, which are essential for a true experiment and which minimize the threats to internal validity, make it more difficult to achieve external validity in the form of sample generalizability and real-world impact.

# Key Terms

Analysis of covariance

Baseline

Between-subjects design

Carryover effects

Ceiling effect

Comparison group

Condition

Confounds

Control group

Counterbalancing

Demand characteristics

Design sensitivity

Ecological fallacy

Experimental control

Experimental error

Experimental group

Facial feedback hypothesis

Factors

Floor effect

Independent-groups design

Individual differences

Internal validity

Latin-square design

Longitudinal research design

Manipulation check

Matched-pairs design

Matching

Multifactorial design

Null hypothesis

Null result

Paired-sample *t* test

Pilot study

Posttest

Power analysis

Pretest

Pretest–posttest control group design

Randomization

Randomized comparative change
    design

Reductionist fallacy

Repeated-measures design

Replication validity

Research hypothesis

Selection bias

Single-factor experiment

Spurious relationship

Staged manipulation

Statistical control

Treatment

True experiment

Type I error

Type II error

Within-subjects design

## Research in the News

1. The April 27, 2009, issue of the *New Yorker* contains a lengthy article by Margaret Talbot titled "Brain Gain: The Underground World of 'Neuroenhancing' Drugs." Talbot addresses the use of psychiatric drugs as brain boosters or cognitive enhancers by healthy adults. She details cases of healthy college students with stellar grades seeking even better academic results by using stimulants that are prescribed for the treatment of attention deficit hyperactivity disorder. This "off-label" use (meaning that the drug has neither its manufacturer's nor the FDA's [U.S. Food and Drug Administration] approval) has become increasingly popular not only among students but also with many other professionals, including scientists and researchers. In fact, the psychologist Martha Farah of the University of Pennsylvania and her colleagues (Greely et al., 2008) reviewed the empirical evidence for the use of cognitive enhancers from 40 laboratory studies involving healthy research participants. In their review appearing in *Nature*, "Towards Responsible Use of Cognitive Enhancing Drugs by the Healthy," they concluded that cognitive enhancers may help people who don't meet diagnostic criteria for any kind of cognitive impairment (Greely et al., 2008). Discuss the scientific evidence for the use of "neuroenhancers" and the kind of study you would design to investigate their effectiveness.

## STUDENT STUDY SITE

Please access the study site at **www.sagepub.com/nestor2e,** where you will find useful study materials such as mobile-friendly eFlashcards and mid-chapter and full chapter web quizzes for each chapter, along with carefully selected articles from research journals that illustrate the major concepts and techniques presented in the book.

## Activity Questions

1. "The Problem With Prozac" headlines the column written by the science journalist Martin Enserink (2008) in *ScienceNOW*, a website devoted to daily news about research. Enserink reports on a controversial new study that claims that Prozac and other so-called selective serotonin reuptake inhibitors, which are widely used to treat depression, are largely ineffective for the vast majority of patients who take them. Design a true experiment to examine the effectiveness of Prozac. Your design must contain each of these six features:

a. Experimental or treatment group is the group that will receive the experimental treatment, manipulation of the variable under study.

b. Control group is used to produce comparisons. The treatment of interest is deliberately withheld or manipulated to provide a baseline performance with which to compare the experimental or treatment group's performance.

c. Independent variable is the variable that you as an experimenter manipulate to determine its influence on the dependent variable.

d. Dependent variable is what you will measure in the study.

e. Random assignment is how you will form your treatment and control groups. When you use random assignment, each participant has an equal probability of being selected for either the treatment or control group.

f. Double-blind means that neither the participant nor the experimenter knows whether the research participant is in the treatment or the control condition.

2. You have found a statistically significant result but one that is of a very small effect size. How would you interpret these results, and what implications might these findings have in designing future studies, especially in regard to sample size?

# Review Questions

1. How would you define a true experiment? How does a true experiment compare with other study designs of the "research toolbox" presented in Chapter 2?

2. Compare and contrast between-subject designs and within-subjects designs.

3. Compare and contrast experimental control and statistical control.

4. Describe the relationship between statistical significance and Type I error and the relationship between statistical power and Type II error.

5. What is the main objective or purpose of randomly assigning research participants in a between-subjects design?

6. How does a matched-pairs design increase the likelihood that experimental and control groups will be similar before the treatment is employed?

7. How does counterbalancing reduce the likelihood of confounds related to carryover effects?

8. What is a Latin-square design and when would you consider using it?

9. What is a null hypothesis? What is a research hypothesis?

10. Why is it important to understand that statistics allow for the rejection of the null hypothesis but do not provide a direct test of the research hypothesis?

11. Why is causality so difficult to establish even with a true experiment?

12. What are ceiling effects? What are floor effects? What kinds of problems do these pose for the researcher?

13. What are individual differences? Compare how between-subjects designs and within-subjects designs address the problem of individual differences.

14. What is a null result? How might experimental error and design sensitivity contribute to a null result?

15. What does *statistical significance* mean? What does *effect size* mean? How are statistical significance and effect size similar? How are they different?

16. What is external validity? What is internal validity? What is the relationship between external validity and internal validity?

17. Explain staged manipulation as a device to create an independent variable.

18. Describe the design of the study by Merzenich and colleagues (Mahncke et al., 2006). How did these researchers arrange the independent and dependent variables and control variables?

19. Discuss some of the alternative explanations for the findings of the Merzenich study (Mahncke et al., 2006).

20. Under what circumstances would you recommend the use of double-blind procedures?

# Ethics in Action

1. Randomization and double-blind procedures are key features of experimental design that are often used by studies to investigate the efficacy of new treatments for serious and often incurable, terminal diseases. What ethical issues do these techniques raise in studies of experimental treatments for incurable, terminal diseases?

2. What about the random assignment used in the Merzenich study (Mahncke et al., 2006)? What are the ethical concerns that two thirds of their research participants were not given the opportunity to receive the treatment? How could a similar study be designed so that all participants eventually receive the desired treatment?

3. Are cognitive enhancers described in *Research in the News* a form of cheating, and will they add to inequality of opportunity and contribute to an uneven playing field?

# CHAPTER 7

# Complex Research Designs
## Multifactorial Experiments

## LEARNING OBJECTIVES: FAST FACTS

- Researchers often aim to design experiments to capture the complexity of the topic under study. Such complex research designs are known as multifactorial designs because two or more independent variables (factors) are manipulated at the same time within the same experiment.

- A multifactorial experiment allows for the testing of effects of all possible combinations of the independent variables on the dependent variable. Of particular importance is that these designs provide a means to investigate the interactions between independent variables.

- Such experiments can vary the independent variables between subjects, others can vary them within subjects, and still others can combine between-subjects and within-subjects manipulation of the independent variables.

- The analysis of variance (ANOVA), also known as the $F$ test, is a general statistical procedure used to analyze the results of a multifactorial experiment. The larger the $F$ ratio, the more likely it is that the results of the experiment are statistically significant and not due to chance alone.

## TESTING BEFORE LEARNING

Try your hand at these questions. Don't worry about not knowing the correct response, as you haven't read the chapter yet! But research shows that a pretest such as this can enhance learning (e.g., Kornell, Hays, & Bjork, 2009). So here is the answer. You come up with the question.

1. Used when two or more independent variables are manipulated at the same time within the same experiment
   a. What is a single-factor experiment?
   b. What is a multifactorial experiment?
   c. What is a nonexperimental study?
   d. What is a control condition?

2. The simplest design of a multifactorial experiment
   a. What is a 1 × 1 design?
   b. What is a 1 × 2 design?
   c. What is a 2 × 1 design?
   d. What is a 2 × 2 design?

3. A multifactorial design that has two independent variables, with three levels for one of the independent variables and four levels for the other independent variable
   a. What is a 2 × 2 design?
   b. What is a 3 × 4 design?
   c. What is a 2 × 3 design?
   d. What is a 3 × 4 design?

4. A research design to test for the interaction between independent variables
   a. What is a single-factor experiment?
   b. What is a nonexperimental study?
   c. What is a multifactorial experiment?
   d. What is a control condition?

5. In a multifactorial design, the effect an independent variable exerts on a dependent variable
   a. What is a main effect?
   b. What is an interaction effect?
   c. What is a simple main effect?
   d. What is the effect size?

6. When the results show that the influence of an independent variable differs depending on the level of a second independent variable
   a. What is a main effect?
   b. What is an interaction effect?
   c. What is a simple main effect?
   d. What is the effect size?

7. The mean values for each of the conditions in a multifactorial experiment
   a. What is a main effect?
   b. What is an interaction effect?
   c. What is a simple main effect?
   d. What is the effect size?

*(Continued)*

(Continued)

8. These values are plotted to see if there is visual indication of an interaction.
   a. What are simple main effects?
   b. What are main effects?
   c. What are control variables?
   d. What are statistics?

9. Interpret these effects first in a multifactorial experiment.
   a. What are the main effects?
   b. What are the simple main effects?

   c. What are the interaction effects?
   d. What are the control effects?

10. A graph of the simple main effects shows two lines that cross over each other.
    a. What is additivity?
    b. What is a crossover interaction?
    c. What is a main effect?
    d. What is a regression line?

**ANSWER KEY:** (1) b; (2) d; (3) d; (4) c; (5) a; (6) b; (7) c; (8) c; (9) a; (10) b

# Facial Expressions of Emotions

Let us imagine that you are a research participant in a study and you are asked to recognize facial expressions of emotions. Below are two photographs of the same person (Exhibit 7.1). We want to see how quickly you can identify each facial expression of emotion. In the first photograph, what emotion is he showing? _____ And in the second photograph, what emotion is he showing? _____

**Exhibit 7.1** Name That Emotion as Quickly as You Can

 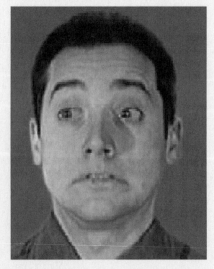

You probably had no difficulty identifying anger for the first photograph and fear for the second photograph. We can recognize these basic emotions almost automatically. Our ease and efficiency are no doubt a remnant of our evolutionary past, as recognizing these emotions would have been important for both survival and cooperation.

But let's take another look at these photographs. Note that each photograph is of the same person but shows two distinct facial expressions of emotions. So we can see that facial identity does not change, yet the facial expression does. What makes the facial expressions different? Try making an angry face, and then a fearful face. Or try imitating the anger and fear expressions of these two photographs. Note the different facial muscle contractions in the lip and mouth area that you use for anger versus fear. Also note that your eye gaze is direct for anger but averted for fear.

Now let us think of these two photographs as stimuli used in an experiment to study how quickly people can identify different facial expressions of emotions. Think of these two photographs in relation to the now familiar concept of the independent variable, which is also referred to as a *factor*. You have already learned about single-factor experiments, which by definition have one independent variable, with two or more levels. But here we have photographs of faces that vary on two important features: (1) emotional expression and (2) direction of eye gaze. These features are clearly distinct from the other and vary across two levels. As such, each can be represented as an independent variable, each with two levels: (1) anger versus fear for emotion expression and (2) direct versus averted for eye gaze direction. Also important to note is that the actual identity of the person is the same in both photographs. Identity is therefore a *control variable* that is held constant across both photographs.

In this chapter, we will learn about experiments in which two or more independent variables are manipulated at the same time within the same study. As you might guess, these experimental designs can become quite complex. These complex experimental designs are referred to as factorial designs. We use the term multifactorial for experiments that vary two or more independent variables. We will learn that multifactorial experiments have two important advantages over single-factor experiments. First, with a multifactorial experiment, the effects of each independent variable on the dependent variable can be isolated and tested. Second, a multifactorial experiment allows the researcher to isolate and test what are referred to as the *interaction effects* of the independent variables on the dependent variable. As such, multifactorial experiments provide a powerful and economical research design to begin to disentangle the intricacies of human experience.

## ▣ Multifactorial Designs

Psychological research aims to understand the complexity of reality and the multiple factors influencing human behavior through reliable and valid experimentation. Controlled investigations in the form of multifactorial experiments provide procedures and techniques necessary for understanding the nature of the phenomenon under study. They are by definition complex because reality is complex. Complex experimental designs are more realistic, as we will see, in part because they allow a researcher to examine how independent variables interact with each other and also because they tell us how these interactions influence the dependent variable.

The study of human emotions may at first appear experimentally intractable, meaning that it does not lend itself to controlled laboratory research. Indeed, how can a researcher manipulate emotions in the laboratory? And would these laboratory manipulations provide a realistic depiction of true human emotional experience? But as you know, elegant experimental studies by Paul Ekman and other researchers (e.g., Strack, Martin, & Stepper, 1988) have indeed shown that emotions can be covertly induced (without a person even knowing) and reliably manipulated by specific facial muscle contractions.

The principal idea behind this research is that the emotional salience of the human face reflects an intricate interaction among distinct features of the face. Note the term *interaction*, which, we will learn in this chapter, has a specific meaning. But before we learn about interactions, an analogy might be helpful. Different drugs are known to interact to produce harmful or beneficial effects. Consider the effects of valium and alcohol, which when taken together can interact to produce feelings of depression. Using each alone, however, may produce a very different emotional effect. Similarly, two drugs may work together or synergistically to enhance or magnify one or more effects. In other words, elements interact to generate effects that otherwise would not have occurred with each drug alone.

To understand the meaning of interaction in a multifactorial experiment, let's look at the four photographs below, which vary on two factors: (1) emotional expression and (2) eye gaze direction. Let's say we found that emotional expression and eye gaze direction interacted to influence our responses to these photographs (Exhibit 7.2). What could this mean? Say we had a single-factor experiment with only one independent variable—emotional expression—and we found a faster response to anger faces than to fear faces. But now in our multifactorial experiment, we add a second independent variable: eye gaze direction. We again find the effect of a faster response to anger faces. However, we also find that the effect of emotional expression is influenced by the direction of eye gaze of the faces in the photograph. That is, we find that responses to emotional facial expression depended on the eye gaze direction: Direct eye gaze sped responses to an anger face but slowed responses to a fear face. For a fear face, the pattern reversed, with faster responses for averted eye gaze than direct eye gaze.

This would be an example of how the interaction of emotion expression and gaze direction joined to influence the responses to these photos. We define an **interaction** as occurring when the effects of one level of the independent variable depend on the particular level of the other independent variable. In our example, emotion expression and eye gaze direction interacted, meaning the influence of the independent variable of emotional expression differed depending on the level of the second independent variable—that is, whether the eyes of the faces gazed directly or were averted. The crucial take-home message is as follows: Had we studied each of these two independent variables separately using two single-factor experiments, we would not have been able to test for this interaction of eye gaze and emotional expression.

| Exhibit 7.2 | Example of Experimental Stimuli Used in the Adams, Gordon, Baird, Ambady, and Kleck (2003) Study |
| --- | --- |

## Notations and Terms

The simplest multifactorial experimental design contains two independent variables, each with two levels or values. Factorial experiments are typically designated or identified by a numbering notation. For example, a **2 × 2 factorial design** has two independent variables, with two levels or values. In this notation, the *number of numbers* tells us how many factors or independent variables there are, and the *number* values indicate the number of levels of the independent variables. A 3 × 4 (spoken as "three by four") factorial design indicates two independent variables: one with three levels and the other with four levels. The order of the numbers makes no difference, so that a 3 × 4 factorial design could be just as easily identified as a 4 × 3.

In a factorial design, every level of each independent variable is combined. For a 3 × 4 design, this means that the 3 levels of one independent variable are combined with the 4 levels of the other independent variable for a total of 12 levels or treatments. Thus, the number of treatment groups that we have in any factorial design can be calculated by simply multiplying through the number notation. In our 2 × 2 example, we have 2 × 2 = 4 groups. In a 3 × 4 factorial design, we have 3 × 4 = 12 groups. A factorial experiment allows us to examine all these combinations.

## Theory and Experimentation

How might complex experimental designs be applied to fascinating theoretical questions? Theory serves as the starting point for all investigations, and it provides a conceptual framework for how particular psychological phenomena might work in real life. Theory and experimentation are closely intertwined. To wit, theory guides how an experiment is designed, how independent variables are developed and manipulated, how dependent variables are measured, and what specific hypotheses are tested.

For complex multifactorial designs, the role of theory may be even more prominent than for single-factor experiments. After all, developing and creating two or more independent variables and specifying how they may interact are certainly advanced when a researcher has a well-developed theoretical model. A researcher begins, however, with the important task of defining conceptually and operationally all the key variables under study. For example, consider research studies of facial expressions of emotion. As we know, the ground-breaking research of Ekman and others has shown the universality of facial expressions of emotions (see also, e.g., Leppanen & Nelson, 2009; Mandal & Ambady, 2004). This research established the human face as an exquisite and efficient organ of emotional communication.

For Ekman, and other researchers, the term *emotions* represents another key concept that he defines broadly as a rapid and coordinated response system that evolved to enable humans to react quickly and effectively to events that affect their welfare (Ekman, 2003). In this conceptual definition of emotions as a response system, facial expressions are a critical medium of communication. As we know, operational definitions follow from conceptual definitions. In the Ekman (1992, 2003) work, the Facial Action Coding System provides the operational definition of various facial expressions of emotions. The coding system defines specific combinations of facial muscle movements that are universally and discretely generated when certain emotions are elicited (see Exhibit 7.3).

Through the use of the Facial Action Coding System, Ekman (1992, 2003) identified seven discrete emotional expressions that humans in different cultures develop a similar capacity to recognize: (1) happiness, (2) sadness, (3) fear, (4) anger, (5) surprise, (6) disgust, and (7) contempt. The generalizability of such findings was especially impressive. You will find descriptions of the particular combinations of facial action units for each expression in Exhibit 7.3.

| Exhibit 7.3 | Operational Definitions for Producing Seven Major Categories of Facial Expressions of Emotions |
|---|---|

| *Seven Major Categories of Facial Expressions of Emotions* |
|---|
| *Sadness:* The eyelids droop as the inner corners of the brows rise and, in extreme sadness, draw together. The corners of the lips pull down, and the lower lip may push up in a pout. |
| *Surprise:* The upper eyelids and brows rise, and the jaw drops open. |
| *Anger:* Both the lower and the upper eyelids tighten as the brows lower and draw together. Intense anger raises the upper eyelids as well. The jaw thrusts forward, the lips press together, and the lower lip may push up a little. |
| *Contempt:* This is the only expression that appears on just one side of the face: One half of the upper lip tightens upward. |
| *Disgust:* The nose wrinkles, and the upper lip rises, while the lower lip protrudes. |
| *Fear:* The eyes widen and the upper lids rise, as in surprise, but the brows draw together. The lips stretch horizontally. |
| *Happiness:* The corners of the mouth lift in a smile. As the eyelids tighten, the cheeks rise, and the outside corners of the brows pull down. |

## Design Questions

As we learned with single-factor experiments, there are two basic ways of assigning participants to experimental conditions. In a multifactorial experiment that uses a between-subjects allocation, participants are randomly assigned to the different conditions of the independent variables. So with two independent variables with two conditions, participants will be randomly assigned to only one of four conditions. In other words, there will be four groups of participants, randomly assigned to one of the four experimental conditions. In a multifactorial experiment that uses a within-subjects allocation, each participant is measured after receiving each level of each of the independent variables.

A multifactorial experiment can also use a between-subjects allocation of participants to one independent variable and a within-subjects allocation of participants to the other independent variable. This is called a **mixed-factorial design** because it has both between-subjects and within-subjects independent variables. For example, imagine that you randomly assigned participants to either a control or a treatment group. This variable, would be your between-subjects independent variable. All participants are then administered an experimental task such as the Stroop test, which has two conditions. This would be your within-subjects, repeated measures independent variable.

## Adding an Independent Variable

All single-factor experiments must incorporate one and *only one* independent variable with two or more levels. So in the Merzenich group study of Chapter 6, the single-factor experiment had one independent variable, which we called "cognitive treatment," with groups of participants randomly assigned to one of three treatment conditions: (1) brain plasticity training, (2) educational DVD, and

(3) no treatment. Thus, in a single-factor experiment, a researcher can always add a new level to an existing independent variable, as, for example, when a baseline, no-treatment group is incorporated into the study design.

By contrast, in a multifactorial experiment, an altogether new independent variable is devised and incorporated into the research design. It is therefore important to understand the difference between adding a level to an existing independent variable, as is done in a single-factor experiment, versus devising an entirely new and distinct independent variable altogether, as is done in a multifactorial experiment.

How then does a researcher add a second independent variable? Exhibit 7.4, adapted from a study by Rowe, Hirsh, and Anderson (2007), illustrates a multifactorial design with two independent variables. As shown in Exhibit 7.4, there are two independent variables: (1) mood induction, with two levels, happy or sad, and (2) cognitive exercise, also with two levels, verbal or visual. Note that the two independent variables—mood induction and cognitive exercises—are *qualitatively* different from each other. Note also that we have not simply added a new level to an existing independent variable, but rather, we have devised two distinct independent variables—one *mood* and the other *cognition*—that are each manipulated within the same multifactorial experiment.

Exhibit 7.4 illustrates a 2 × 2 between-subjects factorial design. Four groups of participants were randomly assigned to one of the four experimental conditions: (1) happy mood/verbal, (2) happy mood/visual, (3) sad mood/verbal, and (4) sad mood/visual. That is, some participants would receive the happy mood induction followed by the verbal task, some would receive the happy mood induction followed by the visual task, others would receive the sad mood induction followed by the verbal task, and still others would receive the sad mood induction followed by the visual task.

What do we gain from this design? In this particular study, the results showed that mood influences performance in different ways depending on the cognitive task. That is, a happy mood improved performance for generating remote verbal associations, a test of creative problem solving, but it detracted from performance on a visual task that requires attention to detail (see Rowe et al., 2007). In this sense, then, these results showed that mood and cognition *interact*, and this as we know means that the influence of the independent variable of mood induction differs depending on the level of the second independent variable—that is, whether the cognitive exercise involves verbal creativity or visual attention to fine details. Again, the important point to emphasize is that a multifactorial experiment provides unique information that cannot be generated by a single-factor experiment. Indeed, had we studied each of these two independent variables separately using two single-factor experiments, we would not have discovered this interaction of mood and cognition.

| Exhibit 7.4 | Independent Variables (IV) of Mood Induction and Cognitive Tests, Each With Two Levels | |
|---|---|---|
| **Mood Induction (IV) Level** | **Cognitive Exercises (IV)** | |
| | *Verbal* | *Visual* |
| Happy | Improved verbal–word associations | Diminished visual attention |
| Sad | Diminished verbal–word associations | Improved visual attention |

# 🔲 Within-Subjects Experiment

As we know, the 2 × 2 factorial design has two independent variables, each with two levels. It is the simplest multifactorial design. Oftentimes, researchers use a 2 × 2 within-subjects (also known as repeated measures) factorial design instead of a 2 × 2 between-subjects factorial design. This is because fewer participants are needed for a within-subjects design than for a between-subjects design. A within-subjects design also automatically controls for individual differences, as each participant serves as his or her own control. Thus, a 2 × 2 within-subjects design is generally considered one of the most efficient and economical multifactorial designs.

| Exhibit 7.5 | Fearful Eye Whites Are Larger Than Happy Eye Whites |
|---|---|

17ms          17ms

Fearful          Happy

## A 2 × 2 Within-Subjects Design

We naturally and automatically perceive facial expressions of emotion holistically as messages (e.g., "That person is mad about something"). These facial expressions are nonetheless complex stimuli, configurations of more basic elementary features. Consider, for example, the eye region of the face, one of the key sources of information for decoding emotional expression (e.g., Whalen, 1998). Exhibit 7.5, taken from Whalen et al. (2004), compares the "eye whites," known as the sclera, of standardized (Ekman, 1992, 2003) fearful and happy faces (see Chapter 2). Note in Exhibit 7.5 the larger size of fearful eye whites in comparison with that of happy eye whites. In an ingenious brain-imaging study, Whalen et al. (2004) recorded neural activity while the participants viewed a series of slides, each with either fearful eye whites or happy eye whites (see Exhibit 7.5). Whalen et al. found the amygdala of the human brain to be especially sensitive to fearful white eyes but not to happy white eyes. These scientific findings give credence to the "wide-eyed" fear shown by actors in horror movies!

Now, let us return to the photographs of fear and happy faces (Exhibit 7.2). These photographs were used in the 2003 article published in *Psychological Science* titled "Perceived Gaze Direction and the Processing of Facial Displays," by the researchers Reginald B. Adams and Robert E. Kleck (see Appendix C). Adams and Kleck theorized that eye gaze direction and facial expressions represent two distinct and isolable features of the human face, which, among others, may be especially important in conveying social information. According to their theory, eye gaze direction and facial expressions can each be understood in terms of **approach avoidance motivation**. That is, both can share informational value as signals of approach, propelling behavior forward, setting the stage for direct expression, confrontation, or "fight"; conversely, they may fuel avoidance, triggering inhibition, culminating in "flight" from negative stimuli of potential danger and threat (see Adams & Kleck, 2003; Elliot, 2006).

## Operationalizing Independent Variables

To test their theory, Adams and Kleck (2003) designed a 2 × 2 within-subjects experimental design. They sought to manipulate two aspects of the face that they thought would be particularly important for emotional expression. These were (1) facial muscle contractions that form different emotional expressions, such as anger or fear, and (2) gaze direction, such as direct or averted eyes. Their challenge was to devise a way to separate gaze direction and facial expression so that the effects of each on perception could be studied.

Their literature review indicated that different emotional expressions can be perceived more readily if associated with certain directions of the eyes. They were particularly interested in studies that showed anger expression to be more quickly perceived when accompanied by a direct gaze in contrast to fear faces being more quickly perceived when coupled with an averted gaze. Based on these studies, Adams and Kleck (2003) formulated a two-prong hypothesis: (1) anger faces with direct gaze would be more readily perceived than anger faces with averted gaze and (2) fear faces with averted gaze would be more readily perceived than fear faces with direct gaze.

To test their hypothesis, the researchers had to first create experimental stimuli—that is, to construct facial stimuli that varied in expression and gaze direction. They did so by using Adobe Photoshop to doctor the gaze direction of faces of anger and fear, some of which were taken from the Ekman series (see Chapter 2). They created four types of faces: (1) anger with direct gaze, (2) anger with averted gaze, (3) fear with direct gaze, and (4) fear with averted gaze.

Next, the researchers had to organize their four types of faces into an experimental task for participants to perform. The experimental task they constructed had participants view one at a time on a computer monitor a face that had an expression of either anger or fear and a gaze direction of either direct or averted. For each face, participants made a speedy judgment as to whether the face displayed anger or fear by responding via a right or left mouse click. The participants were instructed to label each face (for fear or anger) as quickly and accurately as possible.

The final step in their factorial design centered on whether to use a within-subjects or a between-subjects manipulation. They opted for a within-subjects design. What this meant is that all participants received all four types of faces. This allowed for the comparison of participants' response times in emotional judgment for the aforementioned four different kinds of faces. In doing so, with a within-subjects design, individual differences that could figure very prominently in processing emotions are automatically controlled. In other words, people may vary greatly in their responses to emotional faces. Because in a within-subjects design each participant serves as his or her own control, these individual differences are effectively held constant.

The second advantage is that within-subject designs are more economical than between-subjects designs. That is, fewer participants are needed to perform the experimental task. However, having fewer participants requires that you collect more observations per participant. Here, for a point of clarification, let us suppose that observations are analogous to the items of a test. The reliability of a test can often be increased by simply adding more items. It is good to keep the same principle in mind in light of the reduced number of participants commonly seen in within-subjects designs. For example, Adams and Kleck (2003) had a sample size of 32 participants. Yet their experimental task had 240 slides consisting of 60 anger/direct gaze, 60 anger/averted gaze, 60 fear/direct gaze, and 60 fear/averted eye gaze. The 240 slides were presented in a random order. The large number of items or slides of their experimental task provided a sufficient number of observations to reliably measure emotional perception.

## The 2 × 2 Design

The experiment manipulated two independent variables: (1) emotional expression and (2) gaze direction. Each independent variable had two levels, with anger or fear faces as the two levels of emotional expression and directed or averted eyes as the two levels of gaze direction. In other words, each face varied in expression (anger or fear) and gaze direction (direct or averted). The 2 × 2 factorial design produced four

| Exhibit 7.6 | Mean Response Times in Milliseconds to Correctly Labeled Anger and Fear Expressions, as a Function of Gaze Direction |

| Type of Emotional Expression (Independent Variable B) | Eye Gaze Direction (Independent Variable A) | | Row Means (Main Effect of Emotional Expression) |
|---|---|---|---|
| | Direct (A1) | Averted (A2) | |
| Anger (B1) | 862.3 A1B1 | 914.1 A2B1 | 888.2 |
| Fear (B2) | 944.5 A1B2 | 891.2 A2B2 | 917.9 |
| Column means (main effect of eye gaze direction) | 903.4 | 902.7 | |

combinations of conditions: (1) anger/direct-gaze faces, (2) anger/averted-gaze faces, (3) fear/direct-gaze faces, and (4) fear/averted-gaze faces. The dependent measure was response time in milliseconds for judging faces as expressions of either anger or fear

Now, let us make a diagram of the Adams and Kleck (2003) 2 × 2 factorial experiment with their two independent variables: (1) gaze direction with two levels (direct/averted) and (2) facial expression with two levels (anger/fear). Let us call *direction of eye gaze* Factor A and *type of emotional expression* Factor B. Exhibit 7.6 shows the four combinations: (1) direct gaze/anger (A1B1), (2) averted gaze/anger (A2B1), (3) direct gaze/fear (A1B2), and (4) averted gaze/fear (A2B2). The number presented in the upper left cell of Exhibit 7.6 is the mean response time to correctly judge faces displaying anger expressions with direct gaze (mean = 862.3). The number presented in the upper right cell of Exhibit 7.6 is the mean response time to correctly judge faces displaying anger expressions with averted gaze (mean = 914.1). The number presented in the bottom left cell of Exhibit 7.6 is the mean response time to correctly judge faces displaying fear expressions with direct gaze (mean = 944.5). The number presented in the bottom right cell of Exhibit 7.6 is the mean response time to correctly judge faces displaying fear expressions with averted gaze (mean = 891.2).

You can see that the numbers in the two left cells are the response times for Condition A1: direct gaze/anger and direct gaze/fear. The numbers in the two right cells are the response times for Condition A2: averted gaze/anger and averted gaze/fear. We can average the numbers in the two left cells and find the average response time to faces with direct gaze to be 903.4, as shown in the bottom left column. Likewise, we can average the numbers in the two right cells and find the average response time to faces with averted gaze to be 902.7. These response times to faces with direct gaze (903.4) and averted gazes (902.7) are called the *column means* because they are calculated by averaging the columns of the table. Looking at the column means shows us that faces with direct gaze were responded to as quickly as faces with averted gaze. The less than 1-millisecond difference between these two conditions tells us that gaze direction by itself had no effect on response times for emotional judgments.

The effect of type of facial expression on response time can be examined by looking at the rows of Exhibit 7.6. The numbers in the two upper cells are the response times for Condition B1: anger/direct gaze and anger/averted gaze. The numbers in the two lower cells are the response times for Condition B2: fear/direct gaze and fear/averted gaze. We can average the numbers in the two upper cells and find the average response time to facial expressions of anger to be 888.2, as shown in the end of the upper right row. Likewise, we can average the numbers in the bottom right row and find the average response times to facial expressions of fear to be 917.9, as shown in the end of the bottom right row. These response times to anger expression (888.2) and fear expression (917.9) are called *row means* because they are calculated by averaging the rows of the table. The row means shows us that anger faces were responded to more quickly than were fear faces.

## Main Effects

There are two factors or independent variables presented in Exhibit 7.6. We are interested in the effects of each of these factors on the dependent variable. What effect does gaze direction have on mean response times? What effect does the type of emotional expression of the face have on mean response times? In a factorial experiment, the effects of each independent variable on a dependent variable are referred to as the **main effect** of that independent variable. A main effect can be calculated for each independent variable. In the Adams and Kleck (2003) study, because there are two independent variables, two main effects can be calculated. We have already done so in Exhibit 7.6 when we calculated column means and row means. The column means tell us the main effect of gaze direction. These values were 903.4 for faces with direct gaze and 902.7 for faces with averted gaze (averaging over whether the faces displayed anger or fear expressions). For the main effect of gaze direction, we compared the average response times for faces with direct gaze with those with averted gaze. We can see that the column means are nearly identical—there's less than a 1-millisecond difference. We therefore conclude that the main effect of gaze direction of the faces does not significantly influence the dependent variable of response time.

For the main effect of type of facial emotional expression, we look at the row means in Exhibit 7.6. These values are 888.2 milliseconds for angry faces versus 917.9 milliseconds for fearful faces. We can see that the participants responded faster to angry faces than to fearful faces, regardless of whether these emotional expressions were displayed in conjunction with either direct or averted eye gaze. The difference of 29.7 milliseconds in response time between facial expressions of anger versus facial expressions of fear is statistically significant, meaning that it was not likely due to chance. We can therefore conclude that the main effect of type of facial expression of emotion did influence the dependent variable of response time. In the Adams and Kleck (2003) study, the participants made faster judgments in correctly labeling angry facial expressions than fearful facial expressions.

## Interactions

So far we have based our conclusion on the main effects of the two independent variables: (1) gaze direction and (2) emotional expression. We concluded that the main effect of gaze direction did not influence the response rates to the facial expressions: Regardless of their emotional expression, faces with direct gaze were labeled as quickly as faces with averted gaze. In contrast, the main effect of emotional expression did influence the response rates: Regardless of their gaze direction, anger faces were correctly labeled more quickly than were fear faces. However, before interpreting the main effect of emotional expression, we must first look to see if there is a statistical interaction between the two independent variables. A statistical interaction occurs when the effects of one level of the independent variable depend on the particular level of the other independent variable.

In the Adams and Kleck (2003) study, as shown in Exhibit 7.6, we see that direct gaze decreased the response time in judging anger faces (from 914.1 to 862.3 milliseconds) but increased the response time in judging fear faces (from 891.2 to 944.5 milliseconds). Exhibit 7.6 also shows that averted gaze reduced the response time in judging fear faces (from 944.5 to 891.2 milliseconds) but increased the response time in judging anger faces (from 862.3 to 914.1 milliseconds). This pattern reflects an interaction between type of emotional expression and gaze direction. The interaction means that the effect of emotional expression depended on the gaze direction of the face. In simple words, we can describe the interaction as follows: On the one hand, direct gaze led to faster judgment of anger faces but slower judgment of fear faces. On the other hand, averted gaze led to faster judgment of fear faces but slower judgment of anger faces.

## Interpreting Results

Thus, factorial designs provide two distinct sources of information: (1) the main effect of each independent variable by itself and (2) any interaction effect of the independent variables. Keep in mind that main effects are statistically independent of interaction effects. That is, you can have no significant main effects but still have significant interaction effects, or vice versa.

How then do we interpret results generated from a multifactorial 2 × 2 experiment that produces significant main and interaction effects? We always begin by looking to see if there is an interaction between the independent variables, and if so, we interpret the interaction first, before the main effects.

An interaction indicates that any interpretation of a main effect of an independent variable by itself will be misleading. This is because the interaction tells us that the effects of the independent variable depend on the particular level of the other independent variable. We therefore cannot interpret a main effect of an independent variable without first taking into consideration whether that effect interacts with another independent variable.

In the Adams and Kleck (2003) study, for example, we would be wrong to conclude on the basis of the main effect of emotional type that response times are faster for anger faces than fear faces. Why? Because the data showed that this main effect is qualified by the significant interaction of emotion type and gaze direction. The main effect of emotion type depended on the gaze direction of the faces—direct gaze, faster response to anger faces, and averted gaze, faster response times to fear faces.

We often graph main effects and interactions as a way to help us understand and interpret our data. Exhibit 7.7 depicts the absence of the main effect for the independent variable of gaze direction on the dependent variable of response time. The values plotted in this figure are the column means from Exhibit 7.6. Similarly, Exhibit 7.8 plots the row means from Exhibit 7.6 and shows the main effect for the other independent variable of emotional expression. Exhibit 7.8 shows graphically what we have already noted about the effect of faster response times for anger faces than for fear faces.

However, in Exhibit 7.9, we plot the interaction of emotion type and gaze direction. To do this, we plot the values in each of the four cells of Exhibit 7.6. Each cell value reflects what is referred to as a **simple main effect**. A simple main effect compares the influence of one level of an independent variable at a given level of another independent variable.

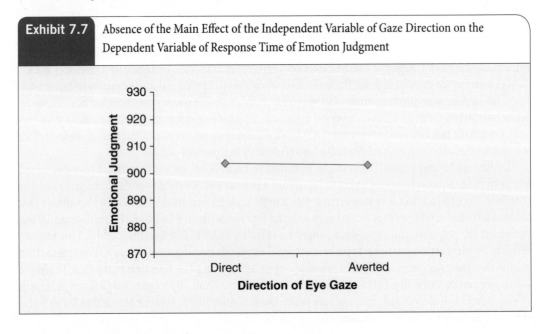

**Exhibit 7.7** Absence of the Main Effect of the Independent Variable of Gaze Direction on the Dependent Variable of Response Time of Emotion Judgment

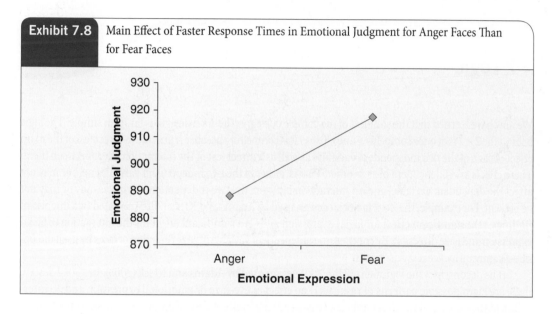

**Exhibit 7.8** Main Effect of Faster Response Times in Emotional Judgment for Anger Faces Than for Fear Faces

To interpret an interaction, we need to look at the simple main effects. The simple effects in Exhibit 7.6 reveal a pattern of a classic **crossover interaction**. In Exhibit 7.9, the two lines cross over, depicting the interaction of emotional expression and gaze direction. That is, Exhibit 7.9 shows the interaction, characterized on one line by faster response times for anger faces with direct gaze than for anger faces with averted gaze and on the other line by faster response times for fear faces with averted gaze than for fear faces with direct gaze.

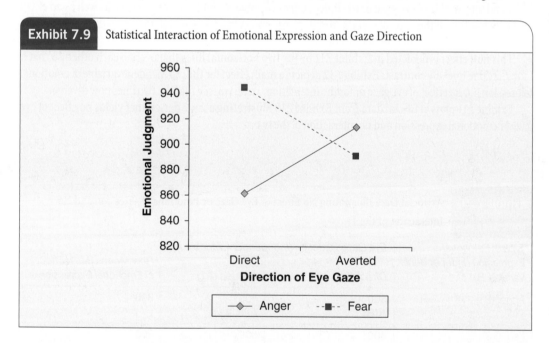

**Exhibit 7.9** Statistical Interaction of Emotional Expression and Gaze Direction

Finally, if, on the other hand, the lines in Exhibit 7.9 did not cross over and in fact were parallel to each other, we would conclude that no interaction occurred between the independent variables. For example, if there were no interaction between the independent variables, the horizontal lines in Exhibit 7.9 would appear on visual inspection to be parallel.

Test your knowledge of this chapter so far by taking the mid-chapter quiz on the study site: www.sagepub.com/nestor2e

# ▣ The 2 × 2 Logic

We now have learned that the simplest of the complex designs, the 2 × 2 design, is far from simple! The logic behind the 2 × 2 is at once compelling and elusive. It is compelling because it provides a direct test of the main effect of each of the two independent variables as well as a direct test of the interaction effect between them. These effects are independent of each other. That is, either of the two independent variables may or may not affect the dependent variable, and an interaction between the two independent variables may or may not be present. For example, the 2 × 2 factorial design used by Adams and Kleck (2003) revealed two important findings: (1) a significant effect for facial expression and (2) a significant effect for the interaction of facial expression and gaze direction. By contrast, the independent variable of gaze direction of faces by itself did not significantly influence response times.

Let us deconstruct the logic behind the 2 × 2 design used by Adams and Kleck (2003). In a 2 × 2 design, there are eight possible patterns of results: (1) no effect of eye gaze or emotional expression and no interaction of the two; (2) main effect only of eye gaze; (3) main effect only of emotional expression; (4) main effects of eye gaze and emotional expression but no interaction of the two; (5) interaction effect only of eye gaze and emotional expression; (6) main effect of eye gaze and interaction of eye gaze and emotional expression; (7) main effect of emotional expression and interaction of eye gaze and emotional expression; and (8) main effects of eye gaze and emotional expression plus interaction effect.

Exhibit 7.10 presents artificial data of the most disappointing pattern of findings of no effect for the independent variable of eye gaze or the independent variable of emotional expression, as well as no effect of the interaction of the two. We set the simple main effects to a value of 800 to demonstrate a pattern of results of no main effects or interaction effect.

This null effect is depicted in Exhibit 7.11 by the two horizontal lines that overlap each other (so that it looks like one line). By contrast, Exhibit 7.12 depicts a main effect for the independent variable of emotional expression but no effect of eye gaze or for the interaction. Here, you see that the two lines now diverge.

Exhibit 7.11 plots artificial data from Exhibit 7.10 illustrating a 2 × 2 design that yields no effect of eye gaze or emotional expression and no interaction of the two.

| Exhibit 7.10 | Artificial Data Illustrating No Effect of Eye Gaze or Emotional Expression and No Interaction of the Two | | |
|---|---|---|---|
| *Type of Emotional Expression (Independent Variable B)* | *Eye Gaze Direction (Independent Variable A)* | | *Row Means (Main Effect of Emotional Expression)* |
| | *Direct (A1)* | *Averted (A2)* | |
| Anger (B1) | 800 A1B1 | 800 A2B1 | 800 |
| Fear (B2) | 800 A1B2 | 800 A2B2 | 800 |
| Column means (main effect of eye gaze direction) | 800 | 800 | |

Now, let us consider a pattern of results from our 2 × 2 design that yields main effects of eye gaze and emotional expression but no interaction of the two. These artificial data are presented in Exhibit 7.13. As you can see in the row and cell means, there is a main effect for eye gaze and for emotional expression, but these variables do not interact.

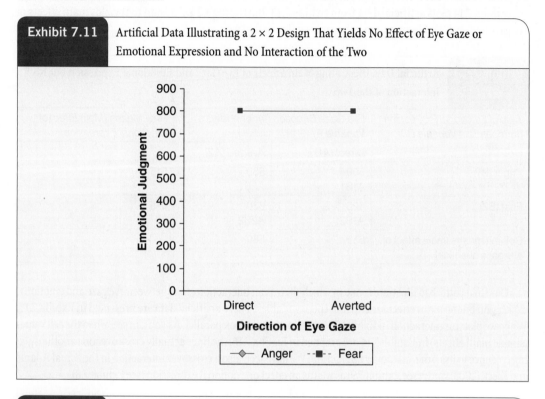

**Exhibit 7.11** Artificial Data Illustrating a 2 × 2 Design That Yields No Effect of Eye Gaze or Emotional Expression and No Interaction of the Two

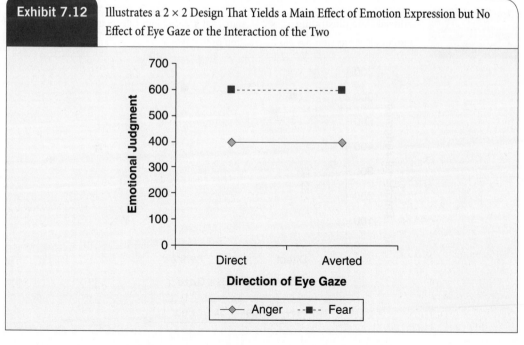

**Exhibit 7.12** Illustrates a 2 × 2 Design That Yields a Main Effect of Emotion Expression but No Effect of Eye Gaze or the Interaction of the Two

Experimentalists often use the term **additivity** to indicate the absence of interaction between independent variables. In fact, we can think of *additivity* and *no interaction* as synonymous. For example, if you have two main effects but no interaction, we can say that the values of one independent variable exert a similar, *additive* effect on the values of the other independent variable. This can be seen in Exhibit 7.12.

Exhibit 7.14 plots artificial data from Exhibit 7.13 illustrating a 2 × 2 design that yields main effects of eye gaze and emotional expression but no interaction of the two.

| Exhibit 7.13 | Artificial Data Illustrating Main Effects of Eye Gaze and Emotional Expression but No Interaction of the Two | | |
|---|---|---|---|
| *Type of Emotional Expression (Independent Variable B)* | *Eye Gaze Direction (Independent Variable A)* | | *Row Means (Main Effect of Emotional Expression)* |
| | *Direct (A1)* | *Averted (A2)* | |
| Anger (B1) | 500 A1B1 | 530 A2B1 | 515 |
| Fear (B2) | 600 A1B2 | 630 A2B2 | 615 |
| Column means (main effect of eye gaze direction) | 650 | 580 | |

Our final pattern to illustrate is one in which there is an interaction effect between eye gaze and emotional expression but no main effect for either of these variables. These artificial data are presented in Exhibit 7.15. When we plot this interaction in Exhibit 7.16, the lines do not look parallel. As you can see, when the cell values (simple main effects) in Exhibit 7.15 are graphed in Exhibit 7.16, the lines actually cross over one another, giving credence to its name, crossover interaction. We have seen also a crossover interaction in the actual Adams and Kleck (2003) study (see Exhibit 7.9) as well as an effect of emotional expression (see Exhibit 7.8).

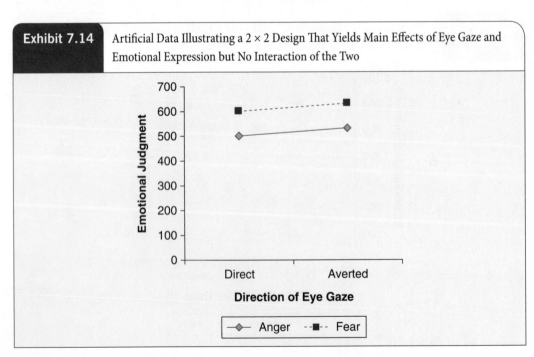

| Exhibit 7.14 | Artificial Data Illustrating a 2 × 2 Design That Yields Main Effects of Eye Gaze and Emotional Expression but No Interaction of the Two |
|---|---|

Exhibit 7.16 provides a clear depiction of how the crossover interaction can also be referred to as an **antagonistic interaction**. This is because as you can see in the values presented in Exhibit 7.15, the two independent variables of eye gaze and emotional expression show opposite effects on the dependent variable of response time. To wit, direct eye gaze led to faster responses to anger faces but slower responses to fear faces, whereas averted gaze led to faster responses to fear faces but slower responses to angry faces.

| Exhibit 7.15 | Artificial Data Illustrating Interaction of Eye Gaze and Emotional Expression but No Main Effect of Eye Gaze or Emotional Expression | | |
|---|---|---|---|
| *Type of Emotional Expression (Independent Variable B)* | *Eye Gaze Direction (Independent Variable A)* | | *Row Means (Main Effect of Emotional Expression)* |
| | *Direct (A1)* | *Averted (A2)* | |
| Anger (B1) | 500 A1B1 | 600 A2B1 | 650 |
| Fear (B2) | 600 A1B2 | 500 A2B2 | 650 |
| Column means (main effect of eye gaze direction) | 650 | 650 | |

| Exhibit 7.16 | Artificial Data Illustrating a 2 × 2 Design That Yields Interaction Effect of Eye Gaze and Emotional Expression but No Main Effects |
|---|---|

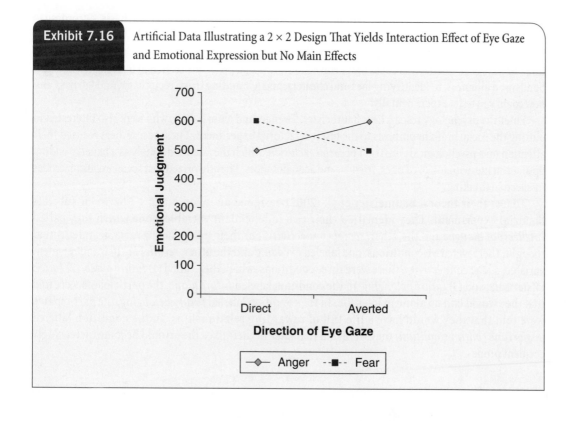

Exhibit 7.16 plots artificial data from Exhibit 7.15 illustrating a 2 × 2 design that yields interaction effect of eye gaze and emotional expression but no main effects.

# Between-Subjects Experiment

In a between-subjects factorial experiment, each combination of the independent variables is administered to a separate group of research participants. These combinations are the experimental conditions. So in a 2 × 2 between-subjects factorial experiment, there are four combinations of the two independent variables, or four experimental conditions. Participants are randomly assigned to one of these four experimental conditions, so that each participates in only one of the four experimental conditions. A 2 × 2 between-subjects factorial experiment therefore compares responses on a dependent variable across four separate groups of subjects, each group receiving only one of the four experimental conditions.

# A 2 × 3 Between-Subjects Design

Let us consider an idea taken from evolutionary psychology of the **social brain hypothesis**. According to this theoretical perspective, intelligent thought is shaped by our "social connectivity"—the degree to which we enjoy friendships, love, companionship, and intimacy. You might think what an interesting idea it is that our advanced intellectual capacities evolved to solve social problems related to forming friendships, bonds, and alliances; to identifying foes and cheaters; and to building trust, reciprocity, and fairness. But how could you test it experimentally?

Enter the psychology researchers Baumeister, Twenge, and Nuss (2002), who were also interested in putting the social brain hypothesis to the test in a factorial experiment. These researchers focused their attention on a psychological construct of *social exclusion*, which they defined simply as a belief of ending up alone in life, without loved ones, friends, and acquaintances. They theorized that social exclusion erodes intellectual thinking.

To test their theory, Baumeister et al. (2002) designed an ingenious 2 × 3 between-subjects factorial experiment. They identified their two independent variables, one which they called *intellectual thought* and the other, *social connectivity*. For their independent variable, intellectual thought, there were two conditions: one labeled *encoding* and the other, *recall*. For their independent variable, social connectivity, there were three conditions, which they called (1) *future alone*, (2) *future misfortune*, and (3) *future belonging*. In the condition labeled *future alone*, the participants were told that they would end up alone in later life. In the condition labeled *future belonging*, the participants were told that they would have a life full of rewarding relationships. In the condition labeled *misfortune control condition*, they were told that later in their lives they would become increasingly accident prone.

The 2 × 3 factorial design produced six combinations of conditions. These were (1) encoding/future alone, (2) encoding/future belonging, (3) encoding/future misfortune, (4) recall/future alone, (5) recall/future belonging, and (6) recall/future misfortune. The researchers randomly assigned participants to one of these six experimental conditions. They made the obvious choice of a between-subjects design.

A within-subjects design would definitely not work for this study: You can't tell the same people in one condition that their futures will be lonely and bereft of social contact and then in another condition that they will have lives full of rich social relationships! Baumeister et al. (2002) thus used a between-subjects design controlling for individual differences in Graduate Record Examination (GRE) performance by randomly assigning participants to one of the six experimental conditions. As we know, a between-subjects design requires more participants than a within-subjects design. Baumeister had a sample size of 65 undergraduates. Compare that with the sample of 32 undergraduates used in the within-subjects experiment of Adams and Kleck (2003) discussed previously.

## ▣ Operationalizing Independent Variables

For the experimental task, the participants read passages from the GRE verbal section. Then, following a specified time delay, they answered questions about these passages. Baumeister et al. (2002) considered crucial the comparison of test scores for the *encoding/future alone* versus *recall/future alone* conditions. They hypothesized that social exclusion would lower scores for only those participants in the recall/future alone condition but not for those assigned to the encoding/future alone or any of the other conditions. In other words, test scores would not be reduced even for participants in the encoding/future alone condition. These persons read the GRE passages after being told that they would end up alone later in life, but *before* answering the multiple-choice questions, they had learned from the experimenter that the forecast of their lonely demise was bogus. By contrast, in the recall/future alone condition, the participants read or encoded the GRE passages under normal conditions, but they were tested on recall of the passage information under the influence of the personality feedback that described their futures as those of aloneness.

Exhibit 7.17 provides a schematic outline of the experiment. Research participants could be randomly assigned to either the encoding or the recall condition. In the *encoding condition*, the participants received the feedback about their futures first, read the GRE passages, and were then told that the feedback was not true, followed by their answering recall questions about the GRE passages. Thus, in the encoding condition, the participants read or encoded the passages after receiving "news" that that they would end up alone in later life (future alone), become increasingly accident prone in later life (future misfortune), or have a life full of rewarding relationships (future belonging). However, they were then told that their future horoscopes were wrong, before they completed the recall test of the passages.

For the *recall condition*, the participants received the same experimental events as for the encoding condition but in a different sequence. That is, they read the GRE passages, received one of the three kinds of feedback information about their futures, and then after completing the recall questions for the GRE passages were told that the forecasts about their futures were wrong.

**Exhibit 7.17** Schematic Outline of Sequence of Experimental Events for Baumeister et al. (2002)

*Sequence of Experimental Events*

*Group*

Recall    Read GRE Passages →    Future Forecast either: 2. Future Alone    →    Complete GRE Passage Questions    →    Told forecast was bogus

1. Future Misfortune →

3. Future Belonging →

Encoding    Future forecast either:

1. Future Misfortune →

2. Future Alone    →    Read GRE Passages → Told forecast was bogus    →    Complete GRE Passage Questions

3. Future Belonging →

## ▣ Manipulation Check

Baumeister et al. (2002) took several steps to increase the believability of the bogus feedback in forecasting a future alone life. As they wrote,

> Because this feedback was randomly assigned and would therefore be given to at least some people who presumably have rich networks of friends, several steps were taken to enhance credibility. First, each participant was given accurate feedback about his or her level of extraversion, on the basis of an accurate scoring of the trait scale. Second, the experimenter added that the participant may well have many friends and acquaintances at present, which is common in young people in university settings. The experimenter went on to say, however, that once the person is past the age at which people are constantly forming new friendships, the current friends will tend to drift apart and not be replaced, so that the individual will spend more and more time alone. (p. 819)

At this point, you might still be a bit skeptical about the staged manipulation of the Baumeister et al. (2002) study. Did it effectively create the psychological state of future loneliness, future belonging, or future misfortune in the participants randomly assigned to any one of these feedback conditions? Perhaps reading exactly what these descriptions entailed might be helpful. Participants randomly assigned to the crucial "future alone" condition heard the following personality description:

> You're the type who will end up alone later in life. You may have friends and relationships now, but by your mid-20s most of these will have drifted away. You may even marry or have several marriages, but these are likely to be short-lived and not continue into your 30s. Relationships don't last, and when you're past the age where people are constantly forming new relationships, the odds are you'll end up being alone more and more. (p. 819)

Participants randomly assigned to the "future belonging" condition heard the following personality description:

> You're the type who has rewarding relationships throughout life. You're likely to have a long and stable marriage and have friendships that will last into your later years. The odds are that you'll always have friends and people who care about you. (Baumeister et al., 2002, p. 819)

Participants randomly assigned to the "nonsocial future misfortune" condition heard the following personality description:

> You're likely to be accident prone later in life—you might break an arm or a leg a few times, or maybe be injured in car accidents. Even if you haven't been accident prone before, these things will show up later in life and the odds are you will have a lot of accidents. (Baumeister et al., 2002, p. 819)

As a research participant, would you be convinced? Or would you dismiss these predictions as meaning nothing more or less than a horoscope from a fortune teller? Fortunately, as researchers, we don't need to assume the role of a movie critic in assessing the extent to which the staged manipulations actually worked. As we learned in Chapter 6, sound experimental design often includes a manipulation check. In the Baumeister et al. (2002) study, a simple questionnaire provided at the end of the study as part of the debriefing would have helped determine the degree to which the participants actually bought the bogus feedback. Unfortunately, the study did not include any manipulation check that might have helped determine objectively that the participants believed the fake feedback.

# Main Effects and Interactions

Exhibit 7.18 presents the results for the Baumeister experiment. The 2 × 3 multifactorial design provides a test for the main and interaction effects of social connectivity. Let us begin, as we always should, by first examining for a statistical interaction for the independent variables of social connectivity and intelligent thought. We do so by looking at each of the six simple main effects presented in each of the six cells in Exhibit 7.18. What value stands out? As shown in Exhibit 7.18, the readings scores are markedly lower for the recall/future alone condition. Otherwise, the scores are essentially the same across the other five conditions.

| Exhibit 7.18 | Scores for Graduate Record Examination Reading Passages Comprehension | | |
|---|---|---|---|
| *Social Connectivity (Independent Variable B)* | *Intelligent Thought (Independent Variable A)* | | *Row Means (Main Effect of B)* |
| | *Encoding* | *Recall* | |
| Future alone | 4.78 | 2.75 | 3.76 |
| Future misfortune | 4.60 | 4.58 | 4.59 |
| Future belonging | 4.40 | 4.75 | 4.57 |
| Column means (main effect of A) | 4.59 | 3.02 | |

*Note:* Higher scores indicate better performance.

The researchers specifically predicted that reading scores would be significantly reduced for this condition only. In other words, they predicted a statistical interaction in which the effects of social exclusion would affect only those participants who took the reading test believing that they would end up alone in life. The effect depended exclusively on the interaction of aloneness and having to recall information to answer questions. The effect did not occur for participants who read the passages believing that they would end up alone in life but who later took the recall testing knowing, if not relieved, that they were not doomed to a life of aloneness. By ostensibly removing the social aloneness effect, the experimenters showed that reading scores recovered to the levels seen in the future belonging and future misfortune conditions.

Exhibit 7.19 depicts the interaction of social connectivity and intelligent thought. To do so, we graph the simple main effects for each of the six conditions presented in Exhibit 7.18. For ease of illustration, we use a line graph, which is commonly used to depict statistical interaction. As Exhibit 7.19 shows, all but the recall/future alone condition have similar reading scores.

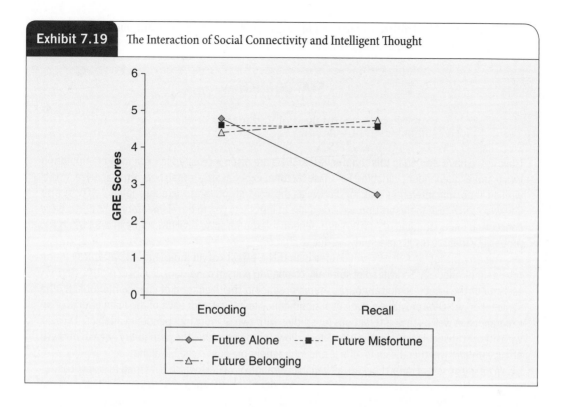

**Exhibit 7.19** The Interaction of Social Connectivity and Intelligent Thought

We run into the same pattern of findings in the Baumeister et al. (2002) study as we did in the Adams and Kleck (2003) study. That is, in both studies, had we only looked at the main effects, we would have made erroneous interpretations and drawn false conclusions from the results. Keep in mind that multifactorial experiments provide a powerful research design to investigate interactions. Arguably, the ability to test interactions is the primary reason we pursue such a complex research design. The lesson is by now familiar: Statistical interactions should be examined by graphing simple main effects. Consider any main effect in a multifactorial experiment of two or more independent variables only after examining for interactions.

## Interpreting Results

The results of the Baumeister et al. (2002) study revealed a statistical interaction between social connectivity and intellectual thought. As these researchers hypothesized, intellectual processes related to the recall but not to the encoding of passages declined in participants who were told that they would end up alone in life.

The findings pointed to a specific effect that could not be attributable to the general effects of hearing bad news. If the latter were the case, we would have expected the future misfortune condition to also show reductions in intellectual thought. This, of course, did not materialize, as only the recall/future alone condition showed reduced scores.

As you can see, the Baumeister et al. (2002) study was well designed, incorporating a misfortune future condition that effectively served to rule out a general effect of receiving bad news for their findings. However, as with all studies, there were limitations. As we discussed earlier, the researchers failed to include a manipulation check for their rather elaborate staged event.

Also, as we have learned, between-subjects designs are at the mercy of random assignment to control for or neutralize individual differences. Individuals differ in their reading comprehension, which is the dependent variable used in this study. A pretest measure (see Chapter 6) would have provided additional control for any individual differences that might have occurred by chance but still could have influenced the findings. Finally, a sample of college students is of limited generalizability.

---

**STAT CORNER**

### Analysis of Variance

Now, as we have learned in this chapter, researchers are often interested in varying or manipulating two or more independent variables. For these factorial experiments, researchers often analyze results with an important inferential statistic, known as the analysis of variance (abbreviated ANOVA), also known as the $F$ test. In this section, we would like to introduce you to the elementary logic and a basic conceptual understanding of ANOVA as a general inferential statistical procedure in evaluating the probability that the results of a study are due to chance.

The advantage of ANOVA procedures is that the effects of all independent variables can be tested simultaneously. So instead of statically comparing pairs of conditions, levels, or groups, ANOVA tests *all* of the effects simultaneously, thereby reducing the likelihood of chance findings. By the same token, ANOVA provides a statistical significance test ($F$ test) for each of the main effects of an experiment as well as their interactions for studies with two or more independent variables. Thus, as with other statistical tests, an ANOVA/$F$ test allows us to determine the probability of each of these effects—that is, whether the main effects and interactions are due to chance alone.

In nearly all sets of data, there will be variability (range of values), which is referred to statistically as variance. ANOVA provides statistical procedures for identifying the sources of this variability (hence the name *analysis of variance*). For each main effect and interaction effect, ANOVA computes an $F$ statistic, which is a ratio of two types of variance: systematic and error variance. Ideally, a researcher hopes to design an experiment that maximizes systematic variance and minimizes error variance. Systematic variance is also referred to as *between-groups variance* and error variance as *within-group variance*. The $F$ statistic can then be stated as the ratio of between-group variance to within-group variance.

$$F \text{ ratio} = \text{between-group variance}/\text{within-group variance}$$

Recall that statistics provide a direct test of the null hypothesis. Under the null hypothesis, the $F$ ratio should be 1, meaning that the between-group variance should be the same as the within-group variance. The greater the ratio of between-group variance to within-group variance, the more likely it is that the null hypothesis is false and therefore should be rejected. Thus, the larger the $F$ ratio, the more likely it is that the results of the experiment are statistically significant and not due to chance alone (see Chapter 10).

---

## 🔲 Conclusions

We examined in depth two examples of multifactorial experiments. We learned that the Adams and Kleck (2003) study employed a within-subjects manipulation of two independent variables, each with two levels: (1) facial expression and (2) gaze direction. This $2 \times 2$ factorial design tested main effects for facial expression and gaze direction as well as the interaction of these two independent variables. The results showed a very interesting interaction of facial expression and gaze direction: Anger faces were more readily recognized when coupled with direct gaze, whereas fear faces were more readily recognized when coupled with averted gaze. The Baumeister et al. (2002) study illustrated a 2 × 3 factorial design with between-subjects manipulations of two independent variables: (1) intelligent thought with two levels: encoding or recall and (2) social connectivity with three levels: future alone, future belonging, or future misfortune. Here too, the results showed a very interesting interaction of intelligent thought and social connectivity: Passage recall but not passage encoding was negatively affected by thoughts of a future alone. Both studies reveal that multifactorial designs allow us to test both main and interaction effects, and we learned that interaction effects always take precedence over main effects. In other words, we always consider interaction effects before looking at main effects. We also learned that within-subjects designs can be limited by small sample size, but this problem can be addressed by making sure to use a sufficient number of observations per participants. For between-subjects designs, our concerns center on the degree to which random assignment can control or neutralize individual differences. Overall, multifactorial experiments provide a powerful research design to help us understand the rich and complex influences that shape psychology.

## Key Terms

2 × 2 factorial design

Additivity

Analysis of variance (ANOVA)

Antagonistic interaction

Approach avoidance motivation

Crossover interaction

Error variance

Experimental stimuli

Experimental task

Factorial designs

*F* test

Interaction

Main effect

Mixed-factorial design

Simple main effect

Social brain hypothesis

Systematic variance

## Research in the News

The December 26, 2006, *New York Times* editorial, "Exercise for Your Aging Brain" reports on a study published in the *JAMA* (*Journal of American Medical Association*) on cognitive training in the elderly. The editorial reads in part,

> When tested five years later, these participants had less of a decline in the skill they were trained in than did a control group that received no cognitive training. The payoff from mental exercises seemed far greater than we are accustomed to getting for physical exercise—as if 10 workouts at the gym were enough to keep you fit five years later.

The *JAMA* study by Willis et al. (2006) is titled "Long-Term Effects of Cognitive Training on Everyday Functional Outcomes in Older Adults." Imagine that you have been asked to design a multifactorial experiment to compare the effects of physical exercise and cognitive exercise on everyday functioning for older adults. Your two independent variables are physical exercise and cognitive exercise, and each will have two levels, high intensity and low intensity. High-intensity physical exercise involves increasingly demanding aerobics, and high-intensity cognitive exercise involves increasingly demanding problem-solving tasks. Low-intensity physical exercise involves breathing exercises, and low-intensity cognitive exercise involves simple puzzles. For your dependent variable, you will use the measure of functional everyday outcomes borrowed from Willis et al. In developing your experiment, choose between a complex within-subject designs and a complex between-subjects design. Explain your choice. What is your research hypothesis? Present artificial data in a 2 × 2 table that you think might be consistent with your hypothesis.

## Activity Questions

1. As a researcher, you are interested in pursuing the Rowe et al. (2007) study described earlier in the chapter. As you recall, the Rowe et al. (2007) study demonstrated an interaction between mood and cognition. Based on this finding, you also hypothesize an interaction between mood and cognition. State precisely the hypothesis—that is, the specific nature of the interaction. Exhibit 7.20 has the mean scores (ranging from 0 to 100; higher score means better performance) for the artificial data. Do these results suggest an interaction between mood and cognition? If so, describe the nature of the interaction. Draw a figure showing these results.

| Exhibit 7.20 | Expected Results Based on Rowe et al. (2007) | |
| --- | --- | --- |
| | *Cognitive Exercises (IV)* | |
| *Mood Induction (IV) Level* | *Remote Association Test* | *Selective Attention Test* |
| Happy | 85 | 60 |
| Sad | 67 | 89 |

2. Cognitive psychologists often theorized about a mental dictionary in which words are organized in networks of associates of varying degrees of "connectivity" (Carmazza, 1996; Nelson, Schrieber, & McEvoy, 1992; Nestor et al., 1998). Exhibit 7.21 illustrates this model of network connectivity. As you can see in Exhibit 7.21, DINNER and DOG each belong to high- and low-connected networks of associates, respectively. Notice also in Exhibit 7.21 the size of the two networks (number of associates). Nelson et al. (1992) have shown that pairs of words belonging to high-connected yet small-in-size networks are easiest to remember. They have developed a large normative data base consisting of four distinct types of words: (1) high connectivity/small network size (e.g., MONKEY/ZOO), (2) low connectivity/small network size (e.g., BEE/HIVE), (3) high connectivity/large network size (e.g., WHISKEY/DRUNK), and (4) low connectivity/large network size (e.g., BIRTHDAY/PARTY). In support of the Nelson et al. model, we (Nestor et al., 1998) have reported the highest rates of recall for words of high connectivity/small network size, followed by words of low connectivity/small network size, then by words of high connectivity/large network size, and finally by words of low connectivity/large network size. Identify the independent variables and their levels that are used to test the network model of memory. Present, in a 2 × 2 table, artificial data that would be consistent with the pattern of recall demonstrated by Nestor et al. (1998). Describe what you would expect an analysis of these artificial data to yield in terms of main effects and interaction. Draw a figure showing these results.

**Exhibit 7.21** High Connectivity (*Upper Panel*) and Low Connectivity (*Lower Panel*) Among the Associates of Two Different Words

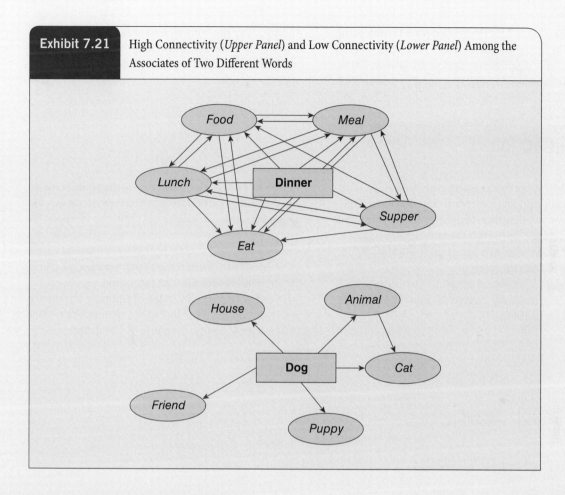

## Review Questions

1. Compare and contrast single-factor experiments with multifactorial experiments. Discuss the implications of adding a new level to an existing and sole independent variable of a single-factor experiment versus devising an altogether new independent variable in a multifactorial experiment.

2. Among the many advantages of multifactorial experiments is testing for interactions between and among independent variables. First, discuss the meaning of interaction and why it is so important in multifactorial experiments. Second, describe the crossover interaction covered in this chapter. Last, be sure to explain why it is crucial in interpreting results that interactions be examined before looking at any main effects.

3. When there is no interaction between independent variables present, the results are considered to be additive. What are the implications of additivity when interpreting main effects of independent variables?

4. Compare and contrast the advantages of using between-subjects complex (or factorial) designs and within-subjects complex (or factorial) designs. When would you choose one over the other?

5. As you may have surmised from this chapter as well as other chapters, experimental design and statistics are intimately connected. Experimental design deals with devising independent variables, measuring dependent variables, staging events or manipulations, and deciding on a within-subjects or between-subjects strategy to test research participants. Statistics, on the other hand, deals with calculating odds, probabilities, and mathematical

quantities: It provides the tools necessary for us to evaluate the likelihood that the results of our experiments are statistically significant and not due to chance. Think about the relationship of experimental design and statistics. Can you think of some analogies to explain this relationship to an educated person? Would a sport analogy work? For example, is experiment design the game and statistics the referee?

# Ethics in Action

1. Critique the ethics of the Baumeister et al. (2002) study. What are some of the ethical considerations and risks in deceiving participants by telling them that they will have lonely and unhappy futures? Do you think debriefing participants is effective? Refer to the APA Ethics Code, Standard 8.07b, Deception in Research, covered in Chapter 3, which states, "Psychologists do not deceive prospective participants about research that is reasonably expected to cause physical pain or severe emotional distress."

2. College students in psychology classes often fulfill a course requirement by participating in a research study. Discuss some of the ethical dilemmas and challenges this poses for researchers and professors. In your discussion, take into consideration APA Ethics Code, Standard 8.04b (see Chapter 3), which states, "When research participation is a course requirement or opportunity for extra credit, the prospective participant is given the option of equitable alternative activities." Do you think this standard provides a student sufficient protection and leverage in the research process?

# CHAPTER 8

# Quasi-Experimental and Nonexperimental Designs

## LEARNING OBJECTIVES: FAST FACTS

- Subject variables and natural-treatment are quasi-independent variables because they cannot be directly manipulated.

- The most common quasi-experiment is a nonequivalent control group design in which experimental and control groups have been predetermined or predesignated by either an existing subject characteristic or an already occurred natural treatment and are not created by random assignment.

*(Continued)*

(Continued)

- Matching individuals or groups on a variable that is highly related to the dependent variable is commonly used to equate participants before the study. However, matching on a pretest measure can present confounds related to regression to the mean for interpreting posttest results.

- A quasi-experimental design is needed to study the psychological effect of the September 11, 2001, terror attacks (9/11) because we cannot directly control or manipulate via random assignment exposure to 9/11.

- Age used as a subject variable is confounded with numerous other factors that pose a serious threat to internal validity. In developmental studies, a cross-sequential design helps control for confounds related to age. A cross-sequential design increases the internal validity of developmental research.

## TESTING BEFORE LEARNING

Try your hand at these questions. Don't worry about not knowing the correct response, as you haven't read the chapter yet! But research shows that a pretest such as this can enhance learning (e.g., Kornell, Hays, & Bjork, 2009). So here is the answer. You come up with the question.

1. Research participants are selected on the basis of a particular characteristic, such as age, gender, or diagnosis.
   a. What is a natural treatment?
   b. What is attrition?
   c. What is a subject variable?
   d. What is a dependent variable?

2. Independent variables that are selected but cannot be directly manipulated
   a. What is a Latin-squares design?
   b. What is a quasi-experimental design?
   c. What is a true experimental design?
   d. What is a single-factor design?

3. A type of independent variable that is used when exposures to events, situations, or settings that emanate from the "real world" define how participants are selected
   a. What is a natural treatment?
   b. What is attrition?
   c. What is a subject variable?
   d. What is a dependent variable?

4. Experimental and control groups are not created by random assignment but have been predetermined or predesignated by either a preexisting subject characteristic or an already occurred natural treatment.
   a. What is a nonequivalent control group design?
   b. What is a before-and-after-design?
   c. What is an ex post facto control group design?
   d. What is a Latin-squares design?

5. Individuals in the control group are selected on the basis of some characteristics of individuals in the treatment group that if uncontrolled could confound the results.
   a. What is aggregate matching?
   b. What is individual matching?
   c. What is random assignment?
   d. What is a random sample?

6. A control group is selected that is similar to the treatment group in the distributions of key variables: the same average age, the same percentage of females, and so on.
   a. What is aggregate matching?
   b. What is individual matching?
   c. What is random assignment?
   d. What is a random sample?

7. A threat to internal validity when participants are matched on the basis of pretest scores
   a. What is random assignment?
   b. What is attrition?
   c. What is regression to the mean?
   d. What is design sensitivity?

8. A source of internal invalidity can occur when preexisting characteristics of participants influence the formation of treatment and comparison groups.
   a. What is response bias?
   b. What is heuristic bias?
   c. What is item bias?
   d. What is selection bias?

9. In this nonexperimental design, individuals may decide themselves whether to enter the "treatment" or "control" group.
   a. What is a nonequivalent-control-group design?
   b. What is a before-and-after-design?
   c. What is an ex post facto control group design?
   d. What is a Latin-squares design?

10. The same research participants are followed over time, as for example, when the same child is tested at age 6 years, then at age 10 years, and then again at age 13 years.
    a. What is a cross-sectional method?
    b. What is a cross-sequential method?
    c. What is a time-lag method?
    d. What is the longitudinal method?

**ANSWER KEY:** (1) c; (2) b; (3) a; (4) a; (5) b; (6) a; (7) c; (8) d; (9) c; (10) d

# Flashbulb Memories of 9/11

Let's travel back in time to 9/11, and imagine that you were living in Manhattan in the vicinity of the World Trade Center. Three years later, in 2004, you have been recruited to participate in a **functional magnetic resonance imaging (fMRI)** study of your memories of that day. You agree to participate in the study, in which fMRI records your brain activity as you recall your personal memories of the terrorist attacks of 9/11 in New York City. To collect your data, the researcher places you in an fMRI scanner, and you view a screen that presents 60 words, one at a time. Your task is to use each word as a cue for you to recollect your personal memories of that tragic day (see Exhibit 8.1).

| **Exhibit 8.1** | Word Cues Used as Experimental Stimuli in the Study by Sharot, Martorella, Delgado, and Phelps (2007) | |
|---|---|---|
| Hands | Reading | Sleep |
| Circle | Reporter | Weather |
| Classes | Evening news | Breakfast |
| Drink | Lunch | New York City |
| Evening | Radio | Teacher |
| Street corner | Homework | Writing |
| Building | Greed | Work |
| E-mail | Exam | Food |
| Quiet | Morning | Noise |
| Walking | Transportation | Mail |
| Boredom | Red | Dream |
| Thought | Afternoon | Clothes |
| Cool | Phone | Photograph |
| Mom | Office | Weekday |
| Airplane | Sibling | Music |
| Hearing | Weekend | Paper |
| Coffee | Moral | Sidewalk |
| Shopping | Dad | Significant other |
| Stair | Money | University |
| Hot | Family | Friend |

Now let us look at Sharot et al. (2007)'s influential fMRI study, which used these very same word cues to examine personal recollections of 9/11 in 24 research participants, all of whom had been in Manhattan on the day of the 9/11 terrorist attacks. Participants, tested approximately 3 years after the terrorist attacks, viewed these word cues, presented one at a time, on a screen while fMRI recorded their brain activity. Sharot and colleagues designed this study for the purpose of studying *flashbulb memory*, a term first introduced by Brown and Kulik (1977), "to describe the recall of consequential events such as hearing news of a presidential assassination" (p. 389). Sharot et al. sought to address two key research questions: (1) the neural basis of flashbulb memories of the 9/11 terrorist attacks in New York City and (2) how emotion influences these personal recollections.

However, to research these questions, Sharot and colleagues (2007) could not use a "true" experiment. Why? Because as you recall, an experiment can only be "true" if participants are randomly assigned to different experimental conditions (between-subjects design) or if all participants receive all experimental conditions in a randomized or counterbalanced order (within-subjects design). For the Sharot et al. study, participants could not be randomly assigned to a 9/11 group. So Sharot et al. devised what is known as a quasi-experiment. Quasi-experiments are commonly used in psychology research when random assignment is impossible. In these instances, quasi-experiments aim to investigate the effects of independent variables that cannot be directly manipulated. As we will learn in this chapter, the Sharot et al study is one example of a quasi-experimental study.

# ▣ Quasi-Experimental Designs

In many instances, we cannot directly manipulate an independent variable. Gender, race, age, ethnicity, socioeconomic status, locale, diagnosis, personality traits, and personal history are just some examples of independent variables that are not possible for an experimenter to directly manipulate. Rather, for these kinds of variables, an experimenter either *selects* participants who have a particular characteristic or studies participants who have been exposed to specified events, such as war or trauma, or might live in certain settings or situations, such as a neighborhood or a geographic region.

When particular individual characteristics are used as the bases of selecting research participants, an experimenter is often interested in studying the effects of these **subject variables** on a dependent measure. Here, a subject variable such as gender is treated as a type of independent variable. Similarly, when exposure to events, situations, or settings that emanate from the "real world" defines how participants are selected, we refer to this type of independent variable as a **natural treatment**. In studies of the effects of a natural treatment on a dependent variable, exposure and nonexposure would form the two levels of the independent variable.

Note the difference in the type of independent variable we focus on in quasi-experiments. Whereas in experimental designs, the independent variable is controlled and directly manipulated by the experimenter, in a quasi-experiment, the independent variable is likely to be a naturally occurring "treatment" or even a subject characteristic.

Many behavioral researchers consider naturally occurring treatments and subject characteristics to be a distinct class of independent variables that can be termed "quasi-independent." You could then define a quasi-experiment as one that investigates the effects of a **quasi-independent variable** on a dependent variable. The word *quasi* means "as if" or "to a degree." A quasi-experiment resembles a true experiment except for the degree to which an experimenter can directly control and manipulate one or more of the independent variables and the assignment of participants to treatments defined by the independent variable(s). In other words, in a true experiment, the experimenter can randomly assign participants to experimental and control conditions (between-subjects design) or assign all participants to all experimental conditions in a randomized or counterbalanced order (within-subjects design).

The label *quasi* unfortunately often takes on a negative connotation. It often implies a second-class citizenship status for a quasi-experiment in relation to a true experiment. This, however, is not how we want to think about a quasi-experimental research design. For many vital problems in psychology, a quasi-experiment provides us with the most practical and ethical research option. Indeed, a researcher who studies child abuse cannot randomly assign participants to victimized and nonvictimized groups. A researcher who studies gender differences in cognition cannot randomly assign people to male and female groups. A researcher who studies schizophrenia cannot assign persons to mentally ill and healthy groups.

The list could go on and on, but the point is simple: Quasi-experiments offer a fertile research design for investigating some of the most important and creative questions in psychology. Thus, as to the often asked question of which is the best research design, the answer depends solely on the type of question under investigation. In this chapter, we will learn how natural treatments and subject variables can be arranged in quasi-experimental designs. We also need to point out that some behavioral researchers restrict use of the term *quasi-experimental design* to studies in which groups are compared that differ in terms of natural treatments, but others also consider designs involving subject variables as "quasi-experimental." We will discuss both types of quasi-experiments in this chapter. Specifically, we will discuss two major types of quasi-experimental designs involving natural treatments as well as subject variables as independent variables (other types can be found in Cook & Campbell, 1979; Mohr, 1992):

- *Nonequivalent control group designs:* **Nonequivalent control group designs** have experimental and comparison groups that are designated before the treatment occurs and are not created by random assignment.

- *Before-and-after designs:* **Before-and-after designs** have a pretest and posttest but no comparison group. In other words, the participants exposed to the treatment serve, at an earlier time, as their own controls.

It is important to recognize that the key advantage of a quasi-experiment is that it allows us to study the effects of an independent variable that cannot be directly manipulated as would be the case in a true experiment. As such, a quasi-experiment can be very interesting, offering a more realistic rendition of the phenomenon under study. As we know, greater realism of an experiment may lead to greater impact. In this sense, a quasi-experiment is often judged as having greater *ecological validity* than a true experiment. Nonetheless, a quasi-experiment lacks the control features of a true experimental design. This comes at a very high cost of internal validity, because whenever an experimenter does not have direct control over the variables, cause-and-effect relationships become extremely problematic. That is, one cannot infer a causal relationship between independent and dependent variables for a quasi-experiment that by definition selects but does not directly manipulate these variables. The key design questions for us are what are some of the specific limitations of a quasi-experimental approach and how these problems might be minimized. We will consider these limitations in the following sections.

## Nonequivalent Control Group Designs

Recall that in Chapter 6, we learned the importance of using random assignment in creating experimental and control groups. We learned that random assignment provides us with the best chance of ensuring that the groups would be equivalent at the beginning of the experiment before the treatment or the manipulation of the independent variable. The logic, now so familiar to us, can be simply stated as follows: If groups formed by random assignment subsequently differed on the dependent variable, then such difference, in principle, would be attributable to the treatment or the independent variable—since the groups should have been equivalent at the outset. Now with quasi-experiments, we know that our control and experimental groups are not formed by random assignment. Rather, the groups are selected on the basis of preexisting, immutable subject characteristics or exposure to some kind of natural treatment. As a result, the control group cannot be considered to be equivalent to the experimental group. Their preexisting differences are not equalized by random assignment, as would be the case in a true experiment.

One of the most powerful types of quasi-experimental design is referred to as a nonequivalent control group design. Nonequivalent control group designs have experimental and control groups that have been predetermined by an already occurred natural treatment and are not created by random assignment. However, what makes this type of design "quasi-experimental" is that the individuals could not select themselves for the treatment in a way that would mean that they were likely to differ at the outset from those in the "control group."

Consider a study by Ruth Wageman (1995) that used a quasi-experimental design to investigate how the organization of work tasks and rewards affected work team functioning. Her research question was whether it was preferable to organize work and work rewards in a way that stressed either interdependence or individual autonomy. More than 800 Xerox service technicians in 152 teams participated. Wageman allowed district managers to choose which intervention they would implement in their work team. Thus, management of some teams stressed interdependence; others, autonomy; and still others, a hybrid model in which members worked part of the time as an interdependent team and part of the time as autonomous individuals (see Exhibit 8.2).

| Exhibit 8.2 | Quasi-Experimental Design | | | |
|---|---|---|---|---|
| **Nonequivalent Control Group Design** | | | | |
| **Experimental Group:** | | $O_1$ | $X_a$ | $O_2$ |
| **Comparison Group 1:** | | $O_2$ | $X_b$ | $O_2$ |
| **Comparison Group 2:** | | $O_3$ | $X_c$ | $O_2$ |
| | | **Pretest** | **Treatment** | **Posttest** |
| Team interdependence | Group | Team performance | Interdependent tasks | Team performance |
| | Hybrid | Team performance | Mixed tasks | Team performance |
| | Individual | Team performance | Individual tasks | Team performance |

*Note:* O = Observation (pretest or posttest); X = Experimental treatment.

Notice that Wageman (1995) did not use random assignment to determine which team received which management style. And while she did compare pretest and posttest team performance, her three groups likely differed considerably regardless of whether their district managers stressed interdependence, individual autonomy, or a combination of the two. Also important to keep in mind is that her research design could not disentangle the effects of the intervention itself from the effects of the district manager, who not only implemented the strategy but also decided which one to use.

In this regard, there may be important *interactions* among the characteristics of the managers and the intervention they chose to apply to their work teams. For example, the hybrid model may be effective with a certain management personality, whereas emphasizing work team interdependence might be better suited for managers with a different personality style. And this, as we know from Chapter 7, would constitute an interaction whereby the effect of one variable, in this case management intervention, differs depending on the effect of another variable, in this case personality style of manager. However, employees could not themselves choose the type of management style for the group in which they worked.

These confounds clearly limit the extent to which we can draw internally valid conclusions from this study. Wageman reported a surprising finding: Team performance improved more for the hybrid model of management than with either interdependence or autonomy (see Exhibit 8.3). Such a finding would no doubt be of great interest to those who might study management or organizational psychology. Indeed, they may have a more sanguine take on the study as resonating with realism and practicality, which might be otherwise lacking in a design with strong experimental controls, such as random assignment. In this regard, then, we can see that quasi-experimental studies with nonequivalent control or comparison groups often receive high marks for their external validity in general and their *ecological validity* in particular. That is, they are often high in generalizability and high in realism.

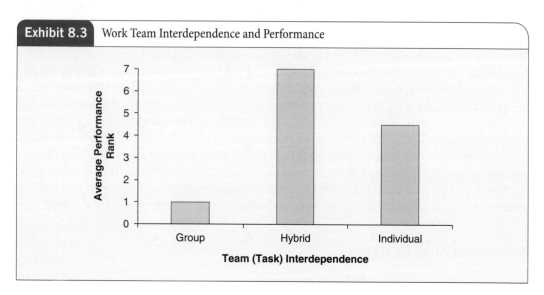

**Exhibit 8.3**  Work Team Interdependence and Performance

*Note:* 7 = high rank, 1 = low rank.

## Matching

In a nonequivalent control group design, the comparability of the treatment group and the control group is improved by individual matching or aggregate matching. Each technique serves as an attempt to control for confounding factors related to failure to use randomization in forming treatment and control groups. In **individual matching**, individual cases in the treatment group are matched with similar individuals in the control group. In some situations, this can create a control group that is very similar to the treatment group, as when Head Start participants were matched with their siblings to estimate the effect of participation in Head Start (Currie & Thomas, 1995). However, in many studies, it may not be possible to match on the most important variables.

In most situations with a nonequivalent control group design for which, by definition, random assignment is not possible, the second method of matching makes more sense: identifying a comparison group that matches the treatment group in the aggregate rather than trying to match individual cases. This is referred to as **aggregate matching**. It means finding a comparison group that has similar distributions on key variables: the same average age, the same percentage of females, and so on. For this design to be considered quasi-experimental, however, individuals must not have been able to choose whether to be in the treatment group or in the control group.

Matching, however, is not without problems. A researcher matches on a variable that is highly related to the dependent variable. Oftentimes, a researcher can collect pretest measures and then match participants either individually or in the aggregate on pretest scores. For example, suppose you are studying the effects of two different teaching methods on reading comprehension. Because you could not randomly assign students to one of the two different teaching methods, you might decide to administer a pretest measure of reading competence before the study begins. You would then match the participants on their pretest reading scores. This would allow you to determine the effects of the two different teaching methods on the posttest of reading comprehension while controlling for pretest reading competence.

How could this kind of matching on pretest measures become problematic for interpreting posttest scores? Let us examine a curious statistical phenomenon known as **regression artifact**. It can occur anytime a pretest measure is used for matching. In our example, suppose we calculated the mean pretest reading comprehension score for the two student groups. There are 20 students in each class, so we would sum all of their pretest scores and divide by 20 to get the mean or average for each group. We could then identify students with extreme pretest scores (i.e., very high or very low) and compare with their posttest scores. What often occurs, regardless of any kind of intervention, is that people who received extreme scores on a test of ability when retested on that same ability, earn scores that are closer to the mean of their group than were their original pretest scores. This statistical phenomenon is known as **regression to the mean**.

In our example, we selected participants on the basis of a pretest measure, reading competence, and then matched them on the basis of their pretest scores. Any subsequent differences in posttest measures may have been related to the effect of the teaching method or may have been due to regression to the mean. In other words, regression to the mean may be a confounding factor for interpreting results of studies that match groups on pretest measures. It represents a threat to the internal validity in a nonequivalent group design that uses a pretest measure for matching. Indeed, regression to the mean is important to consider whenever random assignment is not or cannot be used and groups are matched on a pretest measure.

## Before-and-After Designs

The common feature of before-and-after designs is the absence of a comparison group. Because all cases are exposed to the experimental treatment, the basis for comparison is provided by comparing the pretreatment with the posttest measures. These designs are thus useful for studies of interventions that are experienced by virtually every case in some population, for example, total coverage programs such as Social Security or studies of the effect of a new management strategy in a single organization. Of course, there are often many reasons why participants' pretest and posttest scores may differ, so a simple before-and-after design with just one pretest and one posttest is not considered to be quasi-experimental. Before-and-after designs can be called quasi-experimental when they involve multiple pretests and posttests and/or more comparison groups.

## Time-Series Designs

In a **time-series design**, you compare the trend in the dependent variable up to the date of the intervention or event whose effect is being studied and the trend in the dependent variable after the intervention. A substantial disparity between the preintervention trend and the postintervention trend is evidence that the intervention or event had an impact (Rossi & Freeman, 1989).

Time-series designs are particularly useful for studies of the impact of new laws or social programs that affect everyone and that are readily assessed by some ongoing measurement. For example, Paul A. Nakonezny, Rebecca Reddick, and Joseph Lee Rodgers (2004) used a time-series design to identify the impact of the Oklahoma City terrorist bombing in April 1995 on the divorce rate in Oklahoma. They hypothesized that people would be more likely to feel a need for support in the aftermath of such a terrifying event and thus be less likely to divorce.

Nakonezny et al. (2004) first calculated the average rate of change in divorce rates in Oklahoma's 77 counties in the 10 years prior to the bombing and then projected these rates forward to the 5 years after the bombing. As they hypothesized, they found that the actual divorce rate in the first years after the bombing was lower than the prebombing trend would have predicted, but this effect diminished to nothing by the year 2000 (see Exhibit 8.4).

| Exhibit 8.4 | Divorce Rates in Oklahoma Before and After the Oklahoma City Bombing |
|---|---|

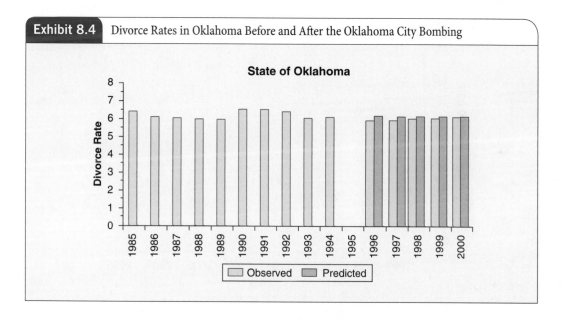

The **interrupted-time-series design** is often used in quasi-experimental research to examine observations before and after a naturally occurring treatment. In the simplest time-series design, there is a single experimental group for which we have obtained multiple observations before and after a naturally occurring treatment. Such a design might be used to examine the effects of a public policy change on a particular behavior, such as the influence of changing the age of legal drinking on car accidents in young drivers. Here, you would look at accident rates over several years, and you would need to know when the time series is interrupted by the natural treatment, which in this example would be when the public policy or law changed. You could compare accidents before and after the new law went into effect.

Consider the study done by Robert D. Gibbons and colleagues (2007) as an example of an interrupted-time-series design to examine the effects of a naturally occurring treatment. These researchers investigated the effect of public health warnings about the safety of antidepressant drugs issued by U.S. and European regulators in 2003 and 2004. The warnings, which discouraged the use of antidepressants in children and adolescents, coincided with a sharp jump in suicide rates in children and adolescents (ages 5–19 years). The researchers wanted to know whether the policies that discouraged the use of antidepressants in treating children and adolescents had inadvertently led to untreated depression in the young that, which in turn contributed to the jump in suicide rates.

In this quasi-experimental research, then, the naturally occurring treatment is the policy change discouraging the use of antidepressants in children and adolescents. Thus, Gibbons et al. (2007) compared the suicide rates of children and adolescents before and after the regulators issued their warnings. As you can see in Exhibit 8.5, they plotted suicide rates before and after the warnings from 1998 to 2005 in the Netherlands. Over a 3-year period between 2003 and 2005, after the regulators issued the warnings, antidepressant prescription rates showed a 22% decline, and the suicide rate showed a 49% increase for children and teens. The United States showed a similar pattern of lower antidepressant prescription rates and higher suicide rates for children and adolescents.

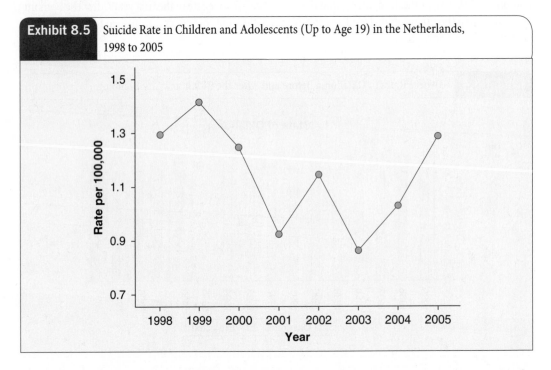

**Exhibit 8.5** Suicide Rate in Children and Adolescents (Up to Age 19) in the Netherlands, 1998 to 2005

Gibbons and colleagues interpreted these findings as showing that regulatory policies discouraging the use of antidepressants in children and adolescents may have inadvertently increased the suicide rates for these groups. The results have remarkable ecological validity as they suggested that antidepressants may help reduce suicide rates in children, adolescent, and adults across counties and states. These findings are also consistent with those of prior studies (Bramness, Walby, & Tverdal, 2007; Gibbons, Hur, Bhaumik, & Mann, 2005; Grunebaum, Ellis, Li, Oquendo, & Mann, 2004; Isacsson, 2001; Ludwig & Marcotte, 2005). Together, these studies may be viewed as quasi-experiments of the effects of a natural treatment (public health warnings) on a dependent variable or outcome measure (suicide rates).

## Before-and-After Design With Multiple Groups

David P. Phillips's (1982) study of the effect of TV soap-opera suicides on the number of actual suicides in the United States illustrates a powerful **multiple-group before-and-after design.** In this type of quasi-experimental design, several before-and-after comparisons are made involving the same independent and dependent variables but with different groups. Exhibit 8.6 represents this design in a simple diagram.

| Exhibit 8.6 | Before-and-After Design: Soap-Opera Suicide and Actual Suicide | | |
|---|---|---|---|
| Experimental group | $O_{11}$ | $X_1$ | $O_{21}$ |
| | $O_{12}$ | $X_2$ | $O_{22}$ |
| | $O_{13}$ | $X_3$ | $O_{23}$ |
| | $O_{14}$ | $X_4$ | $O_{24}$ |
| | *Pretest* | *Treatment* | *Posttest* |
| | Suicide rate | Soap-opera suicides | Suicide rate |

*Note:* O = observation (pretest or posttest); X = experimental treatment.

Phillips identified 13 soap-opera suicides in 1977 and then recorded the U.S. suicide rate in the weeks prior to and following each TV story. In effect, the researcher had 13 different before-and-after studies, one for each suicide story. In 12 of these 13 comparisons, deaths due to suicide increased from the week before each soap-opera suicide to the week after (see Exhibit 8.7).

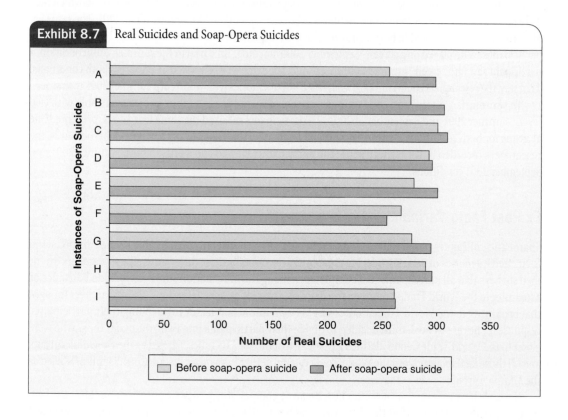

Exhibit 8.7   Real Suicides and Soap-Opera Suicides

Another type of before-and-after design involves multiple pretest and posttest observations of the same group. For example, a **repeated-measures panel design** includes several pretest and posttest observations. Repeated-measures panel designs are stronger than simple before-and-after panel designs because they allow the researcher to study the process by which an intervention or treatment has an impact over time.

# ▣ A Quasi-Experiment of Memories of 9/11

How does the brain remember emotional events such as 9/11? Do flashbulb memories exist? As mentioned earlier in this chapter, Sharot and colleagues (2007) recruited participants who had been in the vicinity (Manhattan) of the World Trade Center on the morning of 9/11 when the terrorist attacks occurred. Three years after witnessing the attacks, the participants underwent fMRI studies of their personal recollections of 9/11. The fMRI is a widely used technique that records the brain at work, in real time, while an individual performs a task. The fMRI technology can be combined with various behavioral exercises, and these performance tasks can entail highly controlled experiments of various aspects of thinking, remembering, feeling, and concentration. The fMRI uses a blood oxygen–dependent level signal to measure brain activation while participants perform various tasks. Different cognitive tasks will elicit different fMRI patterns of brain activation.

In the Sharot study, for the experimental task, participants viewed words that numerous prior studies have shown to be effective cues for memory. As you can see in Exhibit 8.1, some examples of the experimental stimuli were word cues, such as *morning, New York City, lunch, evening,* and *weather.* The researchers wanted to see if these words would cue different memories depending on the experimental condition in which they were presented. There were two experimental conditions: September 2001 and summer 2001. The same list of word cues was presented in both conditions. For example, in a trial in the September 2001 condition, a participant saw displayed on a screen "September 2001 morning." In a trial in the summer 2001 condition, a participant saw on a screen "summer 2001 morning." The same word cues were used across both conditions. That way, the researchers could compare word-cued 9/11 memories with word-cued summer 2001 memories.

To summarize, Sharot and colleagues used time of memory as a within-subjects variable with two levels: summer 2001 and September of 2001. All participants received the same word cues, presented one at a time for both conditions—summer 2001 and September 2001. As one of the dependent measures, the researchers recorded brain activity while the participants viewed cue words in both summer 2001 and September 2001 conditions.

## Ex Post Facto Variables and Comparison Groups

Sharot and colleagues found that their research participants differed considerably in their responses to their cued memories of 9/11. Wondering what might account for these differences, the researchers examined surveys that all participants had completed. Among the information surveyed included distance or proximity to the World Trade Center on the day the terrorists attacked. Curious, the researchers thought that proximity to the World Trade Center might be an important factor influencing their participants' responses. The researchers, thus, decided to divide their participants into two groups: (1) those who were closer to the World Trade Center, defined as a mean distance of 2.08 miles, labeled as the *Downtown* group, and (2) those farther away from the World Trade Center, defined as a mean distance of 4.53 miles, labeled as the *Midtown* group.

Here, we have an example of researchers creating comparison groups ex post facto, or after the fact, meaning, in this instance, after the fMRI data had been collected. In addition, they created a new subject variable based on participants' ratings of their memories. From these ratings, the researchers computed a new subject variable—a single score that they labeled "recollective experience enhancement." We can see that this quasi-experimental approach is very different from a factorial experiment in which groups are formed by random assignment and variables are defined conceptually and operationally a priori.

## Correlational Relationships

Sharot and colleagues wanted to examine whether being closer to the World Trade Center would be associated with more intense recollections of the 9/11 attacks. They found that indeed this was the case as participants who were closer to the World Trade Center had more intense recollections of the terrorist attacks. They plotted the statistically significant, negative correlation between distance from the World Trade Center and 9/11 memories ($r = -0.67$). The scatter diagram (see Chapter 4) used to plot the correlation is presented in Exhibit 8.8. As can be seen in Exhibit 8.8, on the horizontal x-axis is the *distance from World Trade Center* variable. On the vertical y-axis is the *recollective experience enhancement* variable. Each of the 24 participant scores on the distance and memory variables are plotted. Each point on the graph depicts a participant's score on these two variables. As you can see, the direction of the points on the graph tilts downward to the right. The imaginary line provided by all computer graphic programs clearly illustrated the right-downward tilt. This, then, is an example of a statistically significant negative correlation between World Trade Center distance and memory-rating scores. This scatterplot shows that the shorter the World Trade Center distance, meaning the closer to the site of the terrorist attacks, the more intense the personal recollection of 9/11.

Test your knowledge of this chapter so far by taking the mid-chapter quiz on the study site: www.sagepub.com/nestor2e

---

### STAT CORNER

#### Quasi-Experiment in Action

We have learned that quasi-experiments lack design features that improve internal validity, thus lessening confidence in causal conclusions. On the other hand, researchers are often interested in examining the relationship between variables; for example, Sharot and colleagues (2007) wanted to examine whether being closer to the World Trade Center would be associated with more intense recollections of the 9/11 attacks. As you know, the degree and direction of a relationship between two variables can be tested with a single statistic known as the correlation coefficient (the symbol for correlation is *r*). Correlation coefficients vary from −1.00 through 0.00 to +1.00. The number value of the correlation indicates the strength of the relationship between the two variables—a larger number indicates a stronger relationship. The sign, whether positive or negative, indicates the direction of the relationship. A positive correlation indicates that as one variable increases, so too does the other. A negative correlation indicates that as one variable increases, the other decreases.

Sharot et al. (2007) found a statistically significant, negative correlation between World Trade Center distance and 9/11 memories ($r = -0.67$). Remember that *statistically significant* means unlikely due to chance and *negative* refers to the direction of the relationship between the two variables. The negative direction means that participants who were closer to the World Trade Center (in this case, shorter distance, lower score on the distance variable) had higher ratings (in this case, higher scores on the recollective experience enhancement variable). Exhibit 8.8 plots the correlation between World Trade Center distance and 9/11 memories.

Recall that researchers often use scatter diagrams to graph correlations. A scatter diagram is a graph of a correlation. A correlation always involves two variables. Let's call one variable *x* and the other *y*. Let us say a participant had a score of 5 on one variable, labeled *x*, and a score of 10 on another variable, labeled *y*. Make a two-dimensional graph with a horizontal *x*-axis and a vertical *y*-axis. Now plot the participant's scores of 5, 10 (5 to the right and 10 up).

Each participant can be represented by a point on the graph, in this example, 5, 10, which represents scores on the *x* and *y* variables. So if there are 12 participants, there should be 12 points. The

*(Continued)*

(Continued)

direction of the points on the graph will signify whether the correlation between the two variables across all participants is either positive or negative. For a positive correlation, the graph will depict points that fall on an imaginary line that tilts upward to the right. For a negative correlation, the graph will depict points that fall on an imaginary line that tilts downward to the right. (See Activity Question 1 to practice drawing a scatter plot.)

| Exhibit 8.8 | Correlation Scatterplot Across All Groups for Enhancement in Recollective Experience, Defined as the Average Differential Scores on All Subjective Scales for 9/11 Memories Versus Summer Memories, With Participants' Distance From the WTC Defined by Ranking Participants From the Individual Closest to the WTC to the Individual Farthest From the WTC |
|---|---|

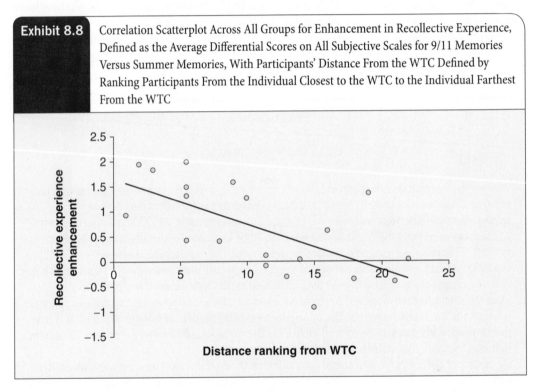

*Note:* WTC = World Trade Center.

Now consider the influence of distance from the World Trade Center on fMRI patterns of brain activation associated with 9/11 memories. Participants who were downtown and closest to the World Trade Center on that day showed a different pattern of brain activation from participants who were farther way from the World Trade Center. The Downtown group consisting of participants who were closest to the World Trade Center showed the greatest activation of the **amygdala**, an almond-shaped structure found deep in the brain that plays a key role in fusing memories with emotion. The amygdala, which is adjacent to the **hippocampus**, which is known to be crucial in remembering, thus played an important role in providing the emotional tone and intensity for the memories of those participants who were the closest to the World Trade Center on that day. The fMRI data showed the intense activation of the amygdala during retrieval of 9/11 memories relative to summer memories in the research participants.

Exhibit 8.9 provides a graphical representation of the different effects the two independent variables, memory (9/11, summer) and group (Midtown, Downtown), had on the dependent variable, fMRI response. This, as you will recall from Chapter 7, is referred to as a crossover two-way interaction because there are two

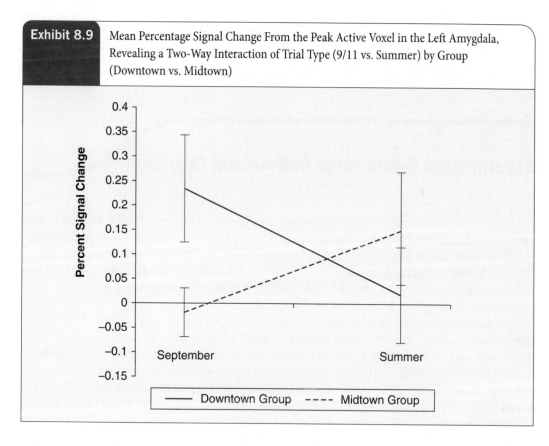

**Exhibit 8.9** Mean Percentage Signal Change From the Peak Active Voxel in the Left Amygdala, Revealing a Two-Way Interaction of Trial Type (9/11 vs. Summer) by Group (Downtown vs. Midtown)

independent variables (memory condition, group) that exert different effects on the dependent variable, which when plotted in a graph reveal lines that cross over each other.

## Quasi-Experimental Design Features

There are several notable design features of the Sharot et al. (2007) quasi-experiment. First, all their research participants viewed the cue words in both the September 2001 and the summer 2001 memory conditions. This within-subjects design feature offered some control over the well-known problem of individual differences in brain and behavioral responses. Second, Sharot and colleagues used a **control condition** of 2011 summer memories as a point of comparison for the 9/11 memories. This too represented strength in the research design for this quasi-experiment. Indeed, by using a baseline control measure, Sharot and colleagues could compare, within the same research participants, patterns of brain activation associated with 9/11 memories and those associated with the summer of 2001. Third, the design included two independent variables, memory condition and group, each with two levels. Thus, it would meet the criteria of a complex multifactorial design described in Chapter 7. However, because of the nature of the independent variables, it is further distinguished as a quasi-experimental design.

To summarize, such a sound and rigorous quasi-experimental design appeared eminently capable of answering the research question as to how 9/11 memories differ from regular memories. When evaluating research, ask yourself two simple questions: Can the experimental design provide an answer to the research question? Or is the experimental design doomed by uncontrolled or confounding variables such that any results would be suspect and leave the research question unanswered? Because we can answer yes to the first question and no to the second question, we can now look at the exciting findings of Sharot and colleagues (2007) with the confidence that they conducted a well-designed quasi-experimental study that, indeed, did reveal some very interesting and distinctive aspects of flashbulb memories of 9/11. While causality could not be established because of the quasi-experimental research design, the findings clearly suggest that closeness to the World Trade Center influenced the intensity of 9/11 memories.

# Quasi-Experimental Research of Culture and Cognition

In Chapter 1, we introduced you to the importance of culture for studying and understanding human behavior. And again in Chapter 4, we learned that culture figures prominently in our understanding of measurement of psychological constructs, especially in the psychometrics of assessing human intelligence. Culture is traditionally studied using nonexperimental research designs. Now in this section, we learn how researchers study culture, experimentally, and how these studies using simple but ingenious techniques have produced some rather interesting and powerful results.

You might ask why researchers would use an experimental approach to study culture. After all, culture is an important characteristic of individuals that would hardly seem suited to experimental studies. A very good point, we would reply, and you are indeed correct that culture cannot be directly manipulated; it cannot be randomly assigned. However, in defense of an experimental approach to culture, consider the following scenario: Many scholars and researchers have long been fascinated by differences in value orientations between Western (e.g., Europe and North America) and Eastern (e.g., East Asia and China) cultures. And in fact, converging lines of evidence reliably characterize Western culture as individualistic versus the collectivistic value orientation of the East (e.g., Nisbett et al., 2001).

An experimentally minded researcher takes these findings and asks the following questions: What are the processes and mechanisms underlying these robust cultural differences in value orientation? What effect do such cultural differences have on thinking, perception, and reasoning? Can these differences be manipulated? In other words, how can we uncover how these differences emerge, under what conditions they might be activated, and how they may affect individual psychology? We would argue for an experimental approach in studying these questions.

## Constructivist Theories of Culture

How then can we study these fascinating cultural differences experimentally? Enter the researchers Ying-yi Hong, Michael W. Morris, Chi-yue Chiu, and Veronica Benet-Martinez, who published an article in 2000 in the *American Psychologist* titled "Multicultural Minds: A Dynamic Constructivist Approach to Culture and Cognition." We use this article as a model to illustrate how quasi-experimental research can be effectively applied to the study of culture and cognition.

As we have emphasized throughout this book, sound research begins with theory. Accordingly, we note that Hong et al. (2000) framed their work in what is known as **constructivist theory**. In constructivist theory, culture is conceptualized as the rich blend of images, metaphors, practices, and discourses about human life that prevail in a given group or society (Shweder & Sullivan, 1993). This blend, likened to a "cultural menu," provides the raw materials from which people construct their own individual life stories or narratives. As McAdams and Pals (2006) write, "Culture then, provides each person with an extensive menu of stories about how to live, and each person chooses from the menu" (p. 212).

Two important implications follow from such a constructivist model of culture. First is that within the same person, there may exist two very different cultural menus. In fact, studies cited by Hong et al. (2000) have shown that many bicultural individuals often describe experiencing two internalized cultures that take turns in guiding their thoughts and perceptions. Second is that within any person, there is a dynamic ebb and flow to one's internalized culture; it is not relied on continuously for interpretation and meaning, but instead only a small subset of cultural knowledge may come to the fore at any given time. Of particular interest is that each of these implications can be tested experimentally. The first is rather straightforward: Recruit bicultural individuals as research participants.

The second is much more difficult. Hong et al.'s (2000) constructivist theory defines the process through which bicultural individuals alternate between two internalized cultural mental sets as **frame switching**. According to their model, bicultural individuals, when triggered by cues in the social environment, can switch between two interpretive frames rooted in their two different cultures. To test this model experimentally, then, requires techniques, tasks, and stimuli capable of eliciting certain cultural states of mind. In addition, these experimental procedures need to be nontransparent so that the intended induced cultural mental set is not apparent to the research participant.

## Experimental Tasks and Stimuli

We can thus see that constructivist theory requires methods that are not traditionally used in cultural studies. By the same token, however, it is important to incorporate interpretive tasks that have been well studied in traditional nonexperimental cultural psychology. Such tasks are important because they have an established track record of being sensitive to and influenced by cultural knowledge in a well-understood manner. In addition, constructivist theory would likely be best tested with an experimental task that would require participants to interpret some sort of ambiguous stimuli that could be viewed differently depending on one's cultural frame.

In light of these considerations, Hong et al. (2000) decided on films of animated fish in which it was ambiguous as to whether an individual fish was leading or being chased by the other fish (see Exhibit 8.10). In a prior study using these films, Morris and Peng (1994) showed that the Chinese and American participants provided different explanations for the individual fish's behavior. The Chinese participants were more likely than the American participants to attribute the behavior of the individual fish to external forces related to the group of fish as a whole. By contrast, the American participants explained the behavior in terms of the internal dispositions of the single fish. The researchers argued that how Americans and Chinese naturally explain ambiguous behaviors may be directly related to their culture. They reasoned that the weight accorded to internal dispositions resonates with the American culture of individualism, as does the weight accorded to external group factors with the collectivism of Chinese culture (Su et al., 1999).

Hong et al. (2000) sought to extend these findings by investigating whether they could experimentally induce frame switching in bicultural individuals. To do so, they adopted a well-known experimental technique from cognitive psychology called **priming.** Priming occurs when exposure to a stimulus facilitates responses to a subsequent event. Hong et al. theorized that *accessibility* of cultural knowledge would determine the extent to which such knowledge guides thinking, perceiving, and interpreting. They saw priming as a way to manipulate levels of accessibility of knowledge. For bicultural participants (e.g., Hong Kong Chinese undergraduate students), visual icons should prime switching between their American and Chinese cultural frames (see Exhibit 8.11). Hong et al. randomly assigned bicultural participants to either the American cultural priming condition or the Chinese cultural priming condition. Their results followed the same pattern as did the findings of the cross-national studies of Morris and Peng (1994). As predicted, bicultural participants primed by Chinese icons were more likely to provide contextual explanation for the fish's behavior than were bicultural participants primed by American icons.

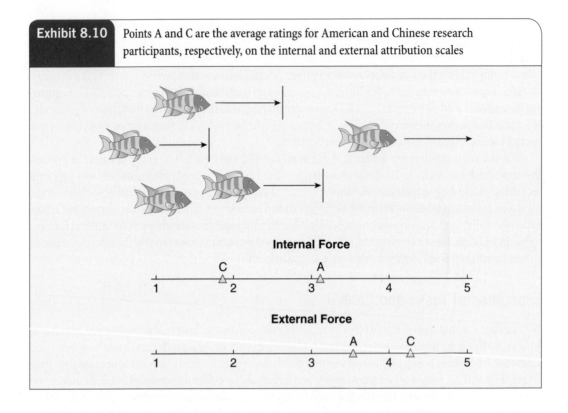

**Exhibit 8.10** Points A and C are the average ratings for American and Chinese research participants, respectively, on the internal and external attribution scales

We thus see how quasi-experimental research can be applied to cultural studies that have long been the province of nonexperimental and correlational approaches. In thinking about the experimental design used by Hong and colleagues, several points are worth keeping in mind. First, participants were selected on the basis of their biculturalism. As such, we can best classify these studies as quasi-experimental in nature. However, Hong and colleagues did also randomly assign participants to the cultural priming conditions. In this regard, then, cultural priming represented a true independent variable. Thus, the Hong study design combined the nonrandom selection of participants and their random assignment to priming conditions.

# Developmental Studies

Developmental psychology is defined as the scientific study of progressive psychological changes that unfold across the entire life span as human beings age. Key topics include the development of intelligence, personality, morality, problem solving, and language. Key questions focus on the principles that govern human development, whether, for example, children are *qualitatively* different from adults or simply have less experience than adults to draw on. Developmental psychologists conduct studies organized around the subject variable of age, as, for example, in investigations comparing learning styles of children of different ages. However, age as a quasi-independent variable is typically correlated with countless other variables, and these associations can complicate and confound our understanding of developmental changes or effects.

| Exhibit 8.11 | Examples of Iconic Images Used as Cultural Primes |

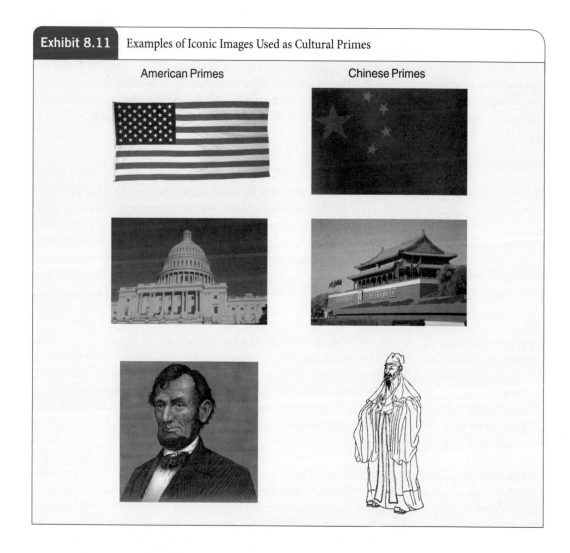

American Primes      Chinese Primes

## Cross-Sectional Design

Many developmental studies employ a **cross-sectional method** by taking groups of people of different ages (e.g., 6, 10, and 13 years) and then comparing these age-groups on psychological processes, such as moral reasoning, problem solving, or intelligence. A cross-sectional method is, however, confounded by **cohort effects** that result from comparing groups of persons who are at different ages at one point in time. A **cohort** is defined as a group of individuals sharing a certain characteristic, such as age, year of high school graduation, or locale. Different age-groups have different cohort effects that are the consequences of being born at different times. For example, compare the use of text messaging by people born in 1990 with those born in 1950. The 1990 cohort grew up with cell phones and text messaging, whereas the 1950 cohort was likely well into their 40s before these technologies even existed. This would likely translate into a large cohort effect, influencing any cross-sectional study of text messaging between these different age-groups.

A cross-sectional method is also confounded by **period effects** that are defined as historical influences that may affect responses to the dependent variable (see Schaie, 1977). As a hypothetical case, let us say we conducted studies in the 1960s on alcohol consumption and aging. We compared cohorts born in 1900 and 1940, and we found that the 1900 cohort consumed much less alcohol than the 1940 cohort. Based on our cross-sectional studies, we concluded that lower alcohol consumption by the elderly reflected an age effect. However, we discovered that other studies in the historical annals have shown that individuals born in 1900 consumed less alcohol even when compared with older cohorts born in the 1880s. We then recall from our American history classes that the 1900 cohort came of age during Prohibition. We now change our conclusion, realizing that these period effects in the form of historical differences between the 1900 and 1940 cohorts may have confounded our interpretation of reduced alcohol consumption in aging.

## Longitudinal Design

We can see that cohort effects and period effects are important limitations to keep in mind when using a cross-sectional method. To avoid cohort and period effects, developmental psychologists often use a **longitudinal method** in which the same research participants are followed over time, as for example, when the same child is tested at age 6, then at age 10, and then again at age 13. A longitudinal study can go on for decades, as participants might be followed over their life span. A well-known longitudinal study conducted by the psychiatrist George Vaillant followed 268 graduates from Harvard College classes of 1942, 1943, and 1944. A June 2009 *Atlantic Monthly* piece by Joshua Wolf Shenk captures the richness of a longitudinal method when he writes in describing Vaillant's work,

> Is there a formula—some mix of love, work, and psychological adaptation—for a good life? For 72 years, researchers at Harvard have been examining this question, following 268 men who entered college in the late 1930s through war, career, marriage and divorce, parenthood and grandparenthood, and old age. Here, for the first time, a journalist gains access to the archive of one of the most comprehensive longitudinal studies in history. Its contents, as much literature as science, offer profound insight into the human condition—and into the brilliant, complex mind of the study's longtime director, George Vaillant.

In a longitudinal study, samples all share the same age, and thus, there are no cohort effects. However, a longitudinal method is not without problems. In practical terms, following people over time is obviously very hard, and participant **attrition** or dropout can threaten sample size. A longitudinal study also may take decades to complete as the cohort ages. In addition, what are known as **secular trends** pose a main confound for longitudinal studies. Secular trends occur when a researcher cannot attribute longitudinal results to hypothesized age-related developmental processes, as, for example, to the age-related transition to adulthood. Rather, secular trends related to general changes that have taken place in society may have influenced or confounded the longitudinal study.

As a result, developmental researchers now often design studies that are able to distinguish longitudinal or age-related effects from secular trends. For example, Nelson, Neumark-Stzainer, Hannan, Sirard, and Story (2006) conducted a 5-year longitudinal study on weight-related health behavior in a sample of more than 2,500 adolescents. They collected observations of *longitudinal* changes in two age cohorts— early adolescence to midadolescence and midadolescence to late adolescence—as well as *secular* changes in physical activity, television video viewing, and leisure-time computer use.

Thus, as we can see, Nelson and colleagues were able to tease apart longitudinal trends from secular trends and to determine the extent to which changes in health-related behavior could be attributable to age versus secular trends. They found substantial longitudinal changes in physical activity, reflected by decreases of about 1 hour per week for the early- to midadolescent cohort and nearly 2 hours per week for the mid- to late-adolescent cohort. Their findings also showed dramatic secular trends in midadolescent computer use, reflected by increases of more than 2 hours per week for girls and nearly 5 hours per week for boys.

## Design Challenges

Researchers (e.g., Baltes, 1968; Schaie, 1965, 1977) have developed some ingenious designs to manage confounds that occur when age is used as a subject variable. Let us imagine that we want to examine the use of the highly popular social technology Facebook in four age cohorts consisting of participants born in 1960, 1962, 1964, and 1966. We interviewed our research participants at 2-year intervals, 2006, 2008, 2010, and 2012. Exhibit 8.12 presents some developmental research designs that we might consider for our study of Facebook use.

The most common method, cross-sectional, is presented in the first column of Exhibit 8.12. Here, we compare Facebook use across four different age-groups: 40-, 42-, 44-, and 46-year-old research participants. We know that this cross-sectional method is confounded by cohort and period (generational) effects that arise from comparing these different age-groups at one point in time, which in this example is the year of the interview, 2006.

The **time-lag design** is presented along the diagonal in Exhibit 8.12. This design allows us to examine participants of the same age interviewed at different times, in the years 2006, 2008, 2010, and 2012. Thus, with a time-lag design, the effects of time of testing can be investigated while holding age constant. As such, the time-lag design addresses cohort and period effects that confound a cross-sectional method.

The **cross-sequential design** is indicated by the central box in Exhibit 8.12. This design requires two or more age-groups evaluated at two or more time intervals. The advantage of a cross-sequential design is that it offers control for several potential confounds of age. For example, consider the 46-year-old age-group born in 1960. Longitudinal effects are measured by interviewing this age-group again in 2008, 2010, and 2012. Cross-sectional effects are measured by comparing the different age-groups tested in 2008. If both cross-sectional and longitudinal comparisons show the same effects of age, then we can be reasonable confident that our results are not confounded by cohort effects and time of interview effects. In addition, if time-lag comparisons of 46-year-old participants interviewed in 2006 with those interviewed in 2012 yield similar results to both cross-sectional and longitudinal analyses, then there would appear to be no evidence of secular trends confounding our results.

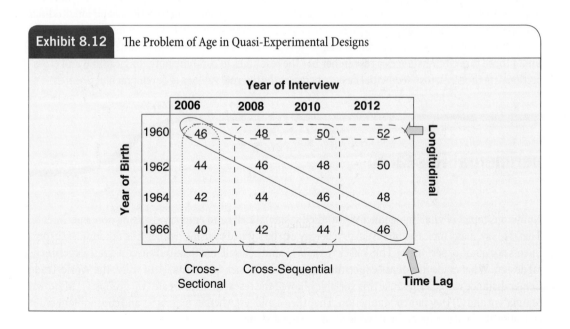

**Exhibit 8.12**  The Problem of Age in Quasi-Experimental Designs

## A Developmental Study of Brain Maturation

Attention deficit hyperactivity disorder (ADHD) is the most common psychiatric diagnosis given to children, occurring in approximately 3% to 5% of school-age children. Is ADHD due to a brain deficit or to a delay in brain development? In the Shaw et al. (2007) study titled "Attention-Deficit/Hyperactivity Disorder Is Characterized by a Delay in Cortical Maturation," two groups of children, those with and without ADHD—223 in each group—had repeated structural **magnetic resonance imaging (MRI)** exams of the brain from ages 6 to 16 years. By tracking these children over the course of 10 years and collecting multiple MRI scans on each child, the researchers were able to examine the developmental trajectories of brain regions and structures and their size, density, and thickness for both ADHD and control participants.

In a normally developing brain, the **cerebral cortex** (the brain's outer layer or "bark," which is thought to be the seat of higher thinking) thickens during early childhood but then reverses course and thins out, losing brain cells or neurons, as the brain matures through adolescence. Children differ considerably in the timing of these developmental or growth trajectories in brain maturation. We can think of these as maturational or developmental differences that children show in their schedules of peaks and troughs of thickening and thinning of the cerebral cortex.

Shaw measured these differences in children with ADHD and healthy controls who had been scanned (MRI) between two and five times within intervals of 2 or 3 years. The researchers examined cortical thickness using both cross-sectional and longitudinal analyses. For the cross-sectional analysis, they compared for each age (ages 6–16 years) the brain scans of children with ADHD and age-matched healthy controls. For the longitudinal analysis, the researchers examined changes in brain thickness measured over time in the repeated MRI scans for each child. Shaw et al. (2007) found a substantial delay of about 3 years in the age of reaching peak cortical thickness for the ADHD children. While the ADHD children showed the same sequence of brain development as the healthy control children, brain maturation occurred more slowly, on a delayed schedule.

Developmental studies require tremendous resources. Seldom does a study combine cross-sectional and longitudinal methods, as the Shaw study did. Shaw and colleagues (2007) also employed, as their dependent measure, MRI of brain anatomy. As a biological measure of the structure of the brain, MRI might arguably be free of the confounds of time and cohort that plague cross-sectional and longitudinal studies of psychological changes. As such, a cross-sequential design might have been unnecessary for the Shaw study. However, as we have seen in Exhibit 8.12, a cross-sequential design is rather straightforward under those rare circumstances a researcher has the resources to combine both longitudinal and cross-sectional methods. A cross-sequential design increases the internal validity of developmental research.

# Nonexperimental Research

Numerous topics of vital importance are studied systematically and empirically using nonexperiments. That is to say, many topics of interest in psychology can be studied by using neither true randomized experiments nor quasi-experiments. Think back to the 9/11 study. Recall that this study used a quasi-experimental design. What made this quasi-experimental instead of nonexperimental? In a word, the World Trade Center distance variable, because this variable allowed the researchers to create two groups: (1) Midtown Manhattan and (2) Downtown Manhattan. They then could test whether memories and concomitant brain activation differed as a function of World Trade Center distance.

Had they simply used as a control group subjects who lived on the West Coast and compared their 9/11 memories with those from Manhattan, then this design would be considered nonexperimental. The distinction between quasi-experiments and nonexperiments is not cut and dried. In both cases, the researcher selects independent variables that cannot be directly controlled and manipulated. In neither instance can causality be established.

However, quasi-experiments test the effects of natural treatments as quasi-independent variables. Different levels of quasi-independent variables can be established and even quantified, as in the case of the World Trade Center distance variable. By contrast, for nonexperiments, the researcher has even less control over the independent variable, and seldom can specific levels of the independent variable be precisely established or quantified. The bottom line is that both approaches have major limitations in terms of the internal validity needed for establishing causality, but quasi-experiments as a rule will allow us more confidence and greater precision in interpreting results.

## Ex Post Facto Control Group Designs

The **ex post facto control group design** is similar to the nonequivalent control group design and is often confused with it, but it does not meet the criteria for quasi-experimental designs. This design has experimental and comparison groups that are not created by random assignment, but unlike nonequivalent control group designs, individuals may decide themselves whether to enter the treatment or control group. As a result, in ex post facto (after the fact) designs, the people who join the treatment group may differ because of what attracted them to the group initially, not because of their experience in the group.

Susan Cohen and Gerald Ledford (1994) studied the effectiveness of self-managing teams in a telecommunications company with an ex post facto design (Exhibit 8.13). They compared work teams that they rated as self-managing with those that they found to be traditionally managed (meaning that a manager was responsible for the team's decisions). They found that the self-reported quality of work life was higher in the self-managed groups than in the traditionally managed groups.

What distinguishes this nonexperimental design from a quasi-experimental design is the fact that the teams themselves and their managers had some influence on how they were managed. As the researchers noted, "If the groups which were already high performers were the ones selected to be self-managing teams, then the findings could be due to a selection bias rather than any effects of self-management" (Cohen & Ledford, 1994, p. 34). Keep in mind that *selection bias* (see Chapter 6) is a source of internal invalidity that occurs when existing characteristics of participants may influence the formation of treatment and comparison groups. Thus, existing characteristics of employees and managers or their team composition might have influenced which "treatment" they received, as well as the outcomes achieved. This leaves us less certain about the effect of the treatment itself.

| Exhibit 8.13 | Ex Post Facto Control Group Design | | |
|---|---|---|---|
| *Self-Managing Work Teams* | | | |
| Treatment group | $O_1$ | X | $O_2$ |
| Comparison group | $O_1$ | | $O_2$ |
| Treatment group | Pretest: measures of satisfaction and productivity | Self-managing work team | Posttest: measures of satisfaction |
| Comparison group | Pretest: measures of satisfaction and productivity | | Posttest: measures of satisfaction |

*Note:* O = observation (present or posttest); X = experimental treatment.

# ▣ Conclusions

The critical advantage of quasi-experiments and nonexperiments is that they allow us to study topics of vital interest and also variables that would otherwise be unethical to manipulate directly. In this chapter, we have learned that carefully controlled and well-designed quasi-experiments and nonexperiments provide a powerful and valid research design to investigate topics that cannot be studied by randomized experiments.

There is always an implicit trade-off in experimental design between maximizing internal validity and external validity. Quasi-experimental and nonexperimental approaches cannot establish causality, as both approaches use quasi-independent variables that cannot be manipulated via random assignment. Associations between pairs of variables can be investigated and tested for statistical significance by computing a correlation coefficient. However, the temporal order of what came first cannot always be established. Likewise, questions regarding the validity of results can come into play if potentially extraneous influences could not be adequately controlled.

On the other hand, the more that assignment to treatments is randomized and all experimental conditions are controlled, the less likely it is that the research participants and setting will be representative of the large population. In this sense, then, quasi-experiments and nonexperiments may be viewed as earning higher grades on external validity, particularly ecological validity, than true experiments. That is to say, quasi-experiments and nonexperiments are used to study how a particular phenomenon may naturally occur over time and, in some instances for developmental studies, over the life span. The researcher cannot directly control or manipulate these so-called natural treatments, and this will generally add to the external validity of the results while limiting confidence in their internal validity.

# Key Terms

Aggregate matching
Amygdala
Attrition
Before-and-after design
Cerebral cortex
Cohort
Cohort effects
Constructivist theory
Control condition
Correlation coefficient
Cross-sectional method
Cross-sequential design

Ex post facto
Ex post facto control group design
Frame switching
Functional magnetic resonance imaging f(MRI)
Hippocampus
Individual matching
Interrupted-time-series design
Longitudinal method
Magnetic resonance imaging (MRI)
Multiple-group before-and-after design
Natural treatment

Nonequivalent control group design
Period effects
Priming
Quasi-experiment
Quasi-independent variable
Regression artifact
Regression to the mean
Repeated-measures panel design
Secular trends
Subject variable
Time-lag design
Time-series design

## Research in the News

The science writer Jonah Lehrer featured the work of the developmental and personality psychologist Walter Mischel in a piece in the *New Yorker*. In the article, Lehrer (2009a) describes the "marshmallow test," which Mischel invented to study the development of self-control in preschool children. Mischel's longitudinal studies showed that preschool children who could delay eating a second marshmallow experienced better outcomes in school, work, and health than did preschool children who failed to refrain from eating a second marshmallow. What confounds does the Mischel research present? How would a researcher use a cross-sequential design to study the development of self-control? Would the marshmallow test still predict outcome for preschool children today?

## Activity Questions

1. Each of our 5 research participants has a pair of scores, which we call $x$ and $y$:

   | $x$ | $y$ |
   |-----|-----|
   | 2   | 4   |
   | 6   | 8   |
   | 10  | 12  |
   | 14  | 16  |
   | 18  | 20  |

   a. Plot these scores in a scatter diagram. What do the points on the graph represent? What is the direction of the points on your graph? What does it signify? What is the direction of the relationship between the pairs of scores? Now reverse the scores.

   | $x$ | $y$ |
   |-----|-----|
   | 4   | 2   |
   | 8   | 6   |
   | 12  | 10  |
   | 16  | 14  |
   | 20  | 18  |

   b. Plot these scores in a scatter diagram. What is the direction of the points on the graph? How would you describe the relationship between the pairs of scores? Describe the difference between Scatter Diagram a and Scatter Diagram b.

2. As we learned in this chapter, Gibbons and colleagues examined the effect of public health warnings about the safety of antidepressant drugs issued by U.S. and European regulators in 2003 and 2004. The researchers wanted to know whether the policies that discouraged the use of antidepressants in treating children and adolescents had inadvertently led to untreated depression in the young, which in turn contributed to the jump in suicide rates. To answer this question, Gibbons et al. (2007), compared the suicide rates of children and adolescents before and after the regulators issued in 2003 and 2004 the warning discouraging antidepressants in young persons. Carefully review this study published in the *American Journal of Psychiatry*. How would you evaluate the research design? Would you consider this an example of a quasi-experiment that used an interrupted-time-series design? Why? What confounds should we consider? Explain your answers.

3. The work by Gibbons and others also illustrates the important role quasi-experimental research can play in social policy. Think of some other examples of high-impact quasi-experimental research. Discuss the pros and cons of quasi-experimental research in influencing public policy and social discourse. The discussion about intelligence from Chapter 4 might be a good starting point for a debate on quasi-experimental research in the world today.

# Review Questions

1. Explain why natural treatments and subject variables are considered quasi-independent variables. What are the experimental design implications when studying quasi-independent variables? What are the sources of invalidity in quasi-experimental research, and how might they be mitigated?

2. The three broad approaches to research design covered in this chapter and in Chapter 7 may be described as experimental, quasi-experimental, and nonexperimental. How would you rate these approaches (i.e., "+", strength/"−," weakness) on the following five criteria: (1) external validity, (2) internal validity, (3) random assignment, (4) use of control/comparison groups, and (5) ecological validity?

3. Compare and contrast before-and-after and nonequivalent control group designs. What kinds of research questions would be better studied with a before-and-after design than with a nonequivalent control group design? Explain your reasoning with examples taken from the scientific literature.

4. Describe individual matching and aggregate matching. What is the rationale for using these techniques, and what are their limitations?

5. Discuss the use of age as a subject variable in quasi-experimental research, particularly in developmental psychology. Compare the use of age as a quasi-independent variable in developmental psychology research with elderly versus child research participants. Why does age in geriatric research pose more problems in terms of potential confounds than it does in child developmental studies?

6. Compare and contrast longitudinal and cross-sectional designs. Describe the confounds related to a cross-sectional design, and how they are addressed in a longitudinal design. Describe the confounds related to a longitudinal design.

7. What is a cross-sequential design? How does a cross-sequential design incorporate features of longitudinal, cross-sectional, and time-lag designs? What are the advantages and disadvantages of a cross-sequential design?

8. What is an ex post facto control group design? What kind of research questions might be investigated with an ex post facto control group design? What are its limitations? What is a major source of invalidity with this design?

9. Describe how a quasi-experimental research approach can be used to study culture and cognition. What are some of the experimental techniques used to examine cultural effects on cognition? How would you describe the theoretical rationale underlying these techniques? How would you assess their external validity and ecological validity?

10. Describe a quasi-experimental research approach that uses a mixed-factorial design. What kinds of research questions might be studied using this approach? What are its advantages and disadvantages?

# Ethics in Action

1. Imagine that you are a developmental psychologist interested in studying age-related changes in moral reasoning in children (ages 8–12 years) and early adolescents (ages 13–17 years). As you likely know, to participate in research, minors (generally below the age of 18 years) require either parental consent or permission from a legally authorized person. Consult the APA (American Psychological Association) Ethics Code (Standard 3.10b Informed Consent, Standard 8.02a Informed Consent to Research). Explain the difference between informed consent and assent. Explain what ethical safeguards are necessary for research with minors as well as for other vulnerable populations.

2. In their book *Practical Ethics for Psychologists: A Positive Approach*, Knapp and VandeCreek cite Fisher (2000), who proposed that researchers adopt a "duty-based" perspective toward their participants and "treat them as moral agents with intrinsic worth and helpful perspectives, instead of simply the means by which investigators can reach their research goals" (Knapp & VandeCreek, 2006, p. 13). What is your position on a duty-based perspective toward research participants? How might researchers move toward achieving such a perspective? Are there some research approaches that are more suited for a duty-based perspective than others? Weigh the pros and cons of such a perspective in designing and conducting research.

# CHAPTER 9

# Small-*N* and Single-Subject Designs

---

## LEARNING OBJECTIVES: FAST FACTS

### Small-*N* and Single-Subject Designs

- Single-subject designs are tools for behavioral researchers to evaluate the impact of an intervention on an individual. Single-subject designs have four essential components: (1) the taking of repeated measurements, (2) a baseline phase (A), (3) a treatment phase (B), and (4) data analysis (often based on graphing).

*(Continued)*

(Continued)

- Single-subject A–B designs can be improved by adding a treatment withdrawal phase (A–B–A), by using multiple subjects at different baselines, or by trying multiple treatments. Repeated measurement controls for many of the potential threats to internal validity. The period between the last baseline measure and the first treatment measure is susceptible to the effect of history.

- Results of single-subject designs can be difficult to interpret due to discrepancies in baseline measures, delayed changes, improvements in the baseline period, and distortions due to graphing. Some researchers use statistical tests to lessen these problems. Generalizability from single-subject designs entails direct replication, systematic replication, and clinical replication.

## TESTING BEFORE LEARNING

Try your hand at these questions. Don't worry about not knowing the correct response, as you haven't read the chapter yet! But research shows that a pretest such as this can enhance learning (e.g., Kornell, Hays, & Bjork, 2009). So here is the answer. You come up with the question.

1. Repeated measurement of the dependent variable is a key component of this design.
   a. What is a between-subjects design?
   b. What is a Latin-square design?
   c. What are small-*N* and single-subject designs?
   d. What is a multifactorial design?

2. Typically abbreviated by using the letter "A" and represents the period in which the intervention is not offered to the subject
   a. What is repeated measurement of the dependent variable?
   b. What is baseline phase?
   c. What is treatment phase?
   d. What is a dependent variable?

3. Typically abbreviated by the letter "B" and represents the period in which the independent variable is repeatedly manipulated over successive trials or conditions
   a. What is a control variable?
   b. What is baseline phase?
   c. What is treatment phase?
   d. What is a dependent variable?

4. A desirable pattern for measurements taken in the baseline phase
   a. What is a flat line?
   b. What is a variable "flat" line?
   c. What is a linear trend?
   d. What is a curvilinear trend?

5. As a general rule, the more data points, the more certain you will be about the pattern prior to intervention.
   a. What is the treatment pattern?
   b. What is the intervention pattern?
   c. What is the causal pattern?
   d. What is the baseline pattern?

6. A severe problem for a single-subject design if baseline responses are not measured but reconstructed from memory
   a. What is a major threat to internal validity?
   b. What is a major threat to external validity?
   c. What is a major threat to ecological validity?
   d. What is a major threat to replication validity?

7. The concern or focus of the intervention in a single-subject design
   a. What is the independent variable?
   b. What is the dependent variable?
   c. What is the control variable?
   d. What is the subject variable?

8. A way to operationalize the outcome for the intervention in a single-subject design
   a. What is variability?
   b. What is cyclical?
   c. What is a trend?
   d. What is the frequency of the target behavior?

9. Addresses the issue of generalizability of findings from a single-subject design
   a. What is external validity?
   b. What is construct validity?
   c. What is internal validity?
   d. What is discriminant validity?

10. Direct replication, systematic replication, and clinical replication are ways to address this issue for a single-subject design.
    a. What is internal validity?
    b. What is statistical significance?
    c. What is external validity?
    d. What is statistical analysis?

# Modifying Behavior

Sam had not been an easy patient on the psychiatric hospital's inpatient ward. Although he was outgoing, friendly, and energetic, he also frequently chased, pushed, punched, and kicked peers and repeatedly hit himself on his forehead—to the point of causing abrasions. Those who knew his background were not terribly surprised by Sam's behavior: Sam had been diagnosed with schizoaffective disorder, bipolar type, mild mental retardation (his full-scale IQ was 58), and a seizure disorder, and he took a range of medications for these disorders. Yet the psychologists and others on Sam's treatment team focused on his behavior during their assessment, not on his psychiatric symptoms per se, for it was his aggressive and threatening behavior that endangered Sam and other patients on their ward and prevented him from living in the community.

The plan developed to modify Sam's behavior focused on reinforcers that Sam had identified himself. In their article about this case, Dr. Sarah W. Bisconer and her colleagues mentioned reinforcers ranging from having a diet soda or hot chocolate to receiving stickers, listening to a Walkman, helping staff with meals, walking with staff, or even going to a restaurant (Bisconer, Green, Mallon-Czajka, and Johnson, 2006). But would these reinforcers have the desired effect? To ensure delivery of the treatment program, the team psychologist trained the others in use of the reinforcers. To ensure maintenance of an objective behavioral record, the team psychologist developed a behavior checklist for the nurses to complete (see Exhibit 9.1). The combination of a treatment plan and a systematic scheme for observing target behaviors provides the basis for a single-subject design.

| **Exhibit 9.1** | Behavior Plan: Target Behavior Data Form | | | | |
|---|---|---|---|---|---|
| *Day* | *Shift* | *Aggression toward others* | *Aggression toward self* | *PRN* | *R* |
| Monday | Day | | | | |
| | Evening | | | | |
| | Night | | | | |
| Tuesday | Day | | | | |
| | Evening | | | | |
| | Night | | | | |

*(Continued)*

(Continued)

| Day | Shift | Aggression toward others | Aggression toward self | PRN | R |
|---|---|---|---|---|---|
| Wednesday | Day | | | | |
| | Evening | | | | |
| | Night | | | | |
| Thursday | Day | | | | |
| | Evening | | | | |
| | Night | | | | |
| Friday | Day | | | | |
| | Evening | | | | |
| | Night | | | | |
| Saturday | Day | | | | |
| | Evening | | | | |
| | Night | | | | |
| Sunday | Day | | | | |
| | Evening | | | | |
| | Night | | | | |

*Notes:* PRN = *pro re nata* medication, R = restraints. Place a vertical mark (I) in appropriate cell for each incident of target behavior or use of PRN medication or restraints.

As clinicians, we must often give our attention to the progress of a single case and consider the progress of that case. Too often, we think we "know" when a client is improving and are too quick to attribute that improvement to our own treatment efforts. Single-subject designs provide an alternative, more systematic procedure for testing for changes in a subject's behavior. They were also recommended by B. F. Skinner for the behavioral analysis required in operant conditioning experiments (Saville, 2003). In this chapter, you will learn how single-subject designs can be used to systematically test the effectiveness of a particular intervention as well as to monitor client progress.

Single-subject designs (sometimes referred to as single-case designs) offer an alternative to group designs. The very name suggests that the focus is on an $N = 1$, a single subject, although many researchers instead refer to this type of design as a "small-$N$ design" and apply it to between one and nine subjects. The structure of these designs makes them useful for research on interventions in behavior analysis and clinical practice, in which the focus is on a single individual (Saville, 2003; Yarnold, 1992). In particular, the clinical processes of assessment, establishing intervention goals and specific outcomes, providing the intervention, and evaluating progress have direct parallels to the structure of single-subject design, which depends on identifying target problems, taking preintervention measures, providing the intervention, taking additional measures, and making decisions about the efficacy of the intervention.

Contrast this design with group designs. In Chapters 6 through 8, we noted that group designs do not naturally conform to practice, particularly when the practice involves interventions with individuals. The analysis of group designs typically refers to the "group's average change score" or "the number of subjects altering their status." By describing the group, we miss each individual's experience with the intervention (Callahan & Barisa, 2005).

In this chapter, we first take you through the components of single-subject designs, including their basic features, measurement of the target problem, and interpretation of the findings. We then describe different designs and illustrate their roles in behavioral research, practice evaluation, and client monitoring. Finally, we discuss the generalizability of findings from single-subject designs and the ethical issues associated with single-subject designs.

## ▣ Foundations of Small-*N* Designs

The underlying principle of small-*N* and single-subject designs as a behavioral research tool is simple: If an intervention with a client, agency, or community is effective, there will be an improvement from the period prior to intervention to the period during and after the intervention. Formally, a small-*N* design is "an in-depth study of a single or relatively few subjects under tightly controlled experimental conditions in which the independent variable(s) is repeatedly manipulated over successive trials or conditions and in which the dependent variable(s) is repeatedly measured" (Saville & Buskist, 2003).

Small-*N* and single-subject designs typically have four components:

1. Repeated measurement of the dependent variable

2. Baseline phase

3. Treatment phase(s), with all subjects exposed to each phase

4. Graphic display, perhaps supplemented by statistical analysis

### Repeated Measurement

These designs require the repeated measurement of a dependent variable or, in other words, the target problem. So both prior to starting an intervention and during the intervention itself, you must be able to measure the subject's status on the target problem at regular time intervals, whether the intervals are hours, days, weeks, months, or the like. In the ideal research situation, measures of the target problem are taken with the client prior to actually implementing the intervention, for example, during the assessment process, and then continued during the course of the intervention. To gather information may mean withholding the intervention until the repeated measures can be taken. In the case of Sam, nursing staff assessed behavior three times daily for 3 months before the intervention began and then for 39 months afterward. Alternatively, repeated measures of the dependent variable can begin when the client is receiving an intervention for other problems. For example, a child may be seen for behavioral problems, but eventually, communication issues will be a concern. The repeated measurement of the communication issues could begin prior to that specific intervention focus.

There are times when it is not possible to delay the intervention, either because there is a crisis or because to delay intervention would not be ethically appropriate. Yet you may still be able to construct a set of preintervention measures by using data already collected or by asking about past experiences. Client records may have information from which a baseline can be produced. Some client records, such as report cards, may have very complete information, but other client records, such as case files, may or may not. When using client records, you are limited to the information that is available, and even that information may be missing. Another option is to ask clients about past behavior, such as how many drinks they had each week in the last several weeks. Similarly, if permission is granted, significant members of the client's network could be asked questions about the client's behaviors. Trying to construct measures by asking clients or family members depends on the client's or family member's memories or opinions and assumes that the information is both remembered and reported accurately. Generally, behaviors and events are easier to recall than moods or feelings. Even the recall of behaviors or events becomes more difficult with the passage of time and probably should be limited to the last month. Although recognizing the limits of these retrospective data collection methods is important, the limitations should not preclude using the information if that is all that is available, particularly for evaluating practice.

There are other times when using retrospective data is quite feasible and realistic. Agencies often collect quite a bit of data about their operations, and these data can be used to obtain repeated measurements. For example, if an agency director was trying to find an outreach method that would increase the number of referrals, previous monthly referral information could be used and the intervention begun immediately.

## Baseline Phase

The **baseline phase**, typically abbreviated by using the letter A, represents the period in which the intervention to be evaluated is not offered to the subject. During the baseline phase, repeated measurements of the dependent variable are taken or reconstructed. These measures reflect the status of the client on the dependent variable prior to the implementation of the intervention. The baseline phase measurements provide two aspects of control analogous to a control group in a group design. First, in a group design, we expect the treatment group to have different scores than the control group after the intervention. In a single-subject design, the subject serves as the control as the repeated baseline measurements establish the pattern of scores that we expect the intervention to change. Without the intervention, researchers assume that the baseline pattern of scores would continue its course. Second, in a control group design, random assignment controls for threats to internal validity. In a single-subject design, the repeated baseline measurements allow the researcher to discount some of the threats to the internal validity of the design.

In the baseline phase, measurements are taken until a pattern emerges. You know you have a pattern when you can predict with some certainty what might be the next score. To be able to predict the next score requires a minimum of three observations in the baseline stage. When there are only two measures, as in Exhibit 9.2a, "Can you predict the next score with any certainty?" The next data point could be higher, lower, or the same as the previous data points (see Exhibit 9.2b). With three measures, your certainty increases about the nature of the pattern. But even three measures might not be enough, depending on the pattern that is emerging. In Exhibit 9.2c, "Is the pattern predictable?" You probably should take at least two more baseline measures, but three or four additional measures may be necessary to see a pattern emerge. As a general rule, the more the data points, the more certain you will be about the pattern; it takes at least three consecutive measures that fall in some pattern for you to have confidence in the shape of the baseline pattern.

## Treatment Phase

The **treatment phase**, signified by a B, represents the time period during which the intervention is implemented. As during the baseline phase, repeated measurements of the same dependent variable using the same measures are obtained. Ultimately, the patterns and magnitude of the data points will be compared with the data points in the baseline phase to determine whether a change has occurred. Tony Tripodi (1994)

**Exhibit 9.2**   Predicting a Pattern

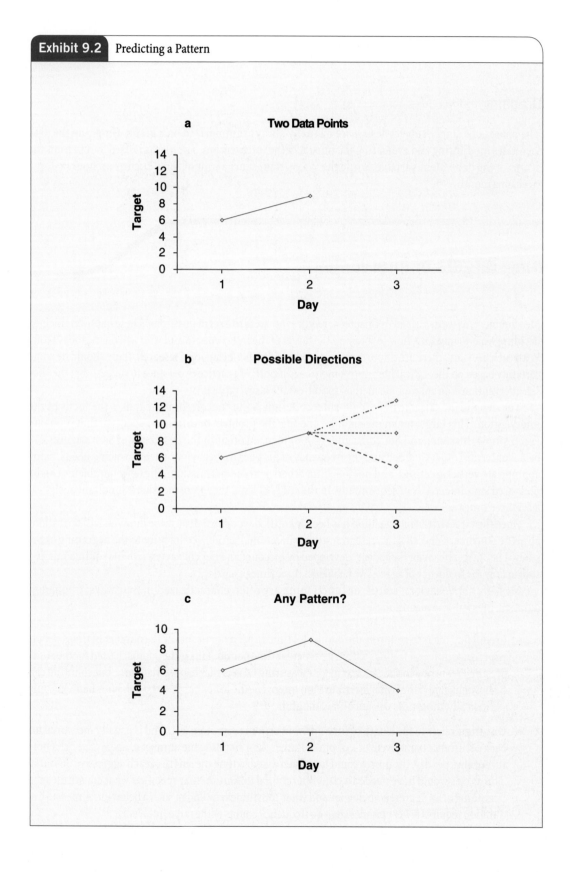

and David Barlow and Michel Hersen (1984) recommend that the length of the treatment phase be as long as the baseline phase.

## Graphing

The phases of a single-subject design are virtually always summarized on a graph. Graphing the data facilitates monitoring and evaluating the impact of the intervention. The *y*-axis is used to represent the scores of the dependent variable, while the *x*-axis represents a unit of time, such as an hour, a day, a week, or a month.

# Measuring Targets of Intervention

Measurement, as we described in Chapter 4, requires answers to a set of questions. These questions include deciding what to measure, how to measure the target of the intervention, and who will do the measuring. With each decision, there are important issues to consider. For behavioral research, there should be some certainty based on theoretical literature, empirical support, or practice experience to suggest that the chosen intervention is an appropriate method to address the target problem.

The dependent variable in a single-subject design is the concern or issue that is the focus of the intervention. This target for change may be one specific problem or different aspects of that problem. For example, Bisconer and her colleagues (2006) focused on both the frequency of Sam's aggressive behavior toward others and self and the frequency of his positive behaviors, such as voicing needs, using appropriate verbal greetings, and not touching others without permission. The target problems can be measured simultaneously or sequentially. In the study of Sam, they were measured simultaneously—at least three times daily.

Once the target of the intervention has been identified, you must determine how you will operationalize the outcome. Generally, in a research study, operationalization occurs prior to the beginning of the study. The "target behavior data form" developed by Bisconer and her colleagues (2006) required nursing staff to tally the frequency of aggressive behaviors three times each day.

Measures of behaviors, status, or functioning are often characterized in four ways: frequency, duration, interval, and magnitude.

- **Frequency** refers to counting the number of times a behavior occurs or the number of times people experience different feelings within a particular time period. This is the approach used for the study of Sam. Frequency counts are useful for measuring targets that happen regularly, but counting can be burdensome if the behavior occurs too often. On the other hand, if the behavior happens only periodically, the counts will not be meaningful.

- **Duration** refers to the length of time an event or some symptom lasts and is usually measured for each occurrence of the event or symptom. Rather than counting the number of aggressive behaviors three times per day, the nurses could have been asked to time the length of each aggressive outburst. The nurses would have needed a clear operational definition that specified what constitutes the beginning of an aggressive behavior and what constitutes the end of such a behavior. A measure of duration requires fewer episodes than do frequency counts of the target problem.

- Rather than look at the length of an event, we can examine the interval or the length of time between events. Using a measure of interval, the nurses would calculate the length of time between aggressive behaviors. Just as a clear operational definition was necessary for the duration measure, they would need a clear definition when measuring the interval between aggressive behaviors. This kind of measure may not be appropriate for events or symptoms that happen frequently unless the intent of the intervention is to delay their onset.

- Finally, the magnitude or the intensity of a particular behavior or psychological state can be measured. A scale might be developed by which the nurses rate or score the intensity of the aggressive behavior—how loud the screaming is, whether there is hitting that caused noticeable injury, and the like. Often, magnitude or intensity measures are applied to psychological symptoms or attitudes, such as measures of depressive symptoms, quality of peer interactions, or self-esteem.

It is important to consider who will gather the data and to understand the potential consequence of each choice. Participants or clients can be asked to keep logs and to record information in the logs. Participants can complete instruments at specified time points, either through self-administration or by an interview. Or the behavioral researcher may choose to observe the participant's behavior. In addition, the reliability and validity of the instruments should have been tested on subjects of the same age, gender, and ethnicity as the client who is the focus of the single-subject design (Nelson, 1994).

A particular problem in gathering the data is the issue of reactivity. In Chapter 4, we suggested that it is important to have measures that are nonreactive—that is, you want measures that do not influence the responses that people provide. The very process of measurement might change a subject's behavior. If you ask a subject to keep a log and to record each time a behavior occurred, the act of keeping the log may reduce the behavior. Staff, knowing that supervisors are looking for certain activities, may increase the number of those activities. Tripodi (1994) suggests that changes due to reactivity may be short in duration and observable in the baseline, so repeated measurements in the baseline might mitigate this problem. Nonetheless, it is important to recognize that there might be reactivity and to choose methods that limit reactivity.

An additional concern about measurement is the feasibility of the measurement process. Repeatedly taking measures can be cumbersome, inconvenient, and difficult. Is it going to be possible to use the method time and again? Is the method too time-consuming for the subject and/or the researcher or practitioner? Will continuous measurements reduce the incentive of the subject to participate in the research or treatment?

Finally, the choice of measurement must be sensitive enough to detect changes. If the measuring device is too global, it may be impossible to detect incremental or small changes, particularly in target problems, such as psychological status, feelings, emotions, and attitudes. In addition, whatever is measured must occur frequently enough or on a regular basis so that repeated measurements can be taken. If an event is a fairly rare occurrence, unless the research is designed to last a long time, it will be impractical to take repeated measures.

## Types of Small-*N* and Single-Subject Designs

You now have the different tools and components necessary to use a single-subject design. We will now describe the different types of these designs.

## Basic Design (A–B)

The *A–B design* is the basic single-subject design. It includes a baseline phase with repeated measurements and an intervention phase continuing the same measures (see Exhibit 9.3).

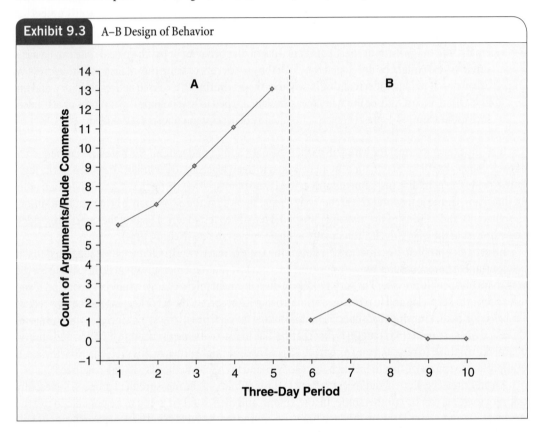

**Exhibit 9.3** A–B Design of Behavior

This is the type of design that Bisconer and colleagues (2006) used in their study of Sam: They assessed Sam's behavior for 3 months (the "A phase"), then they implemented their planned treatment and continued to assess his behavior (the "B phase"), which changed dramatically.

You can see some complexity in the details of Sam's behavior during the B phase in Exhibit 9.4, in which you can see some increases in staff injury in periods 4, 6, and 9. It is hard to know what to make of these fluctuations, since there was only one intervention and it was maintained throughout the B period. (And can you see how helpful it would have been to see what the trend was over a period of time during the baseline, "A," phase.)

The example points to the limits of the A–B design as a tool for research. The design cannot rule out other extraneous events, so it is impossible to conclude that the treatment *caused* the change. Perhaps the use of more psychotropic medication in periods 4, 6, and 9 (see Exhibit 9.4), not the treatment plan, was responsible for some of the reduction in aggressive behavior. More complicated single-subject designs can provide firmer answers to such questions.

## Withdrawal Designs

There are two withdrawal designs: the *A–B–A design* and the *A–B–A–B design*. By withdrawal, we mean that the intervention is concluded (A–B–A design) or is stopped for some period of time before the

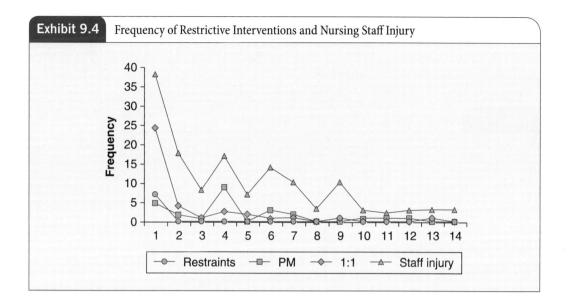

**Exhibit 9.4** Frequency of Restrictive Interventions and Nursing Staff Injury

intervention is begun again (A–B–A–B design). The premise is that if the intervention is effective, the target problem should be improved only during the course of intervention, and the target scores should worsen when the intervention is removed. If this assumption is correct, then the impact of an extraneous event (history) between the baseline and intervention phase would not explain the change.

This premise, however, poses a problem. Ideally, the point of intervention is to reduce or eliminate the target problem without the need for ongoing intervention. We would like the impact of the intervention to be felt long after the client has stopped the intervention itself. Practice theories, such as behavioral or cognitive behavioral treatment, are based on the idea that the therapeutic effects will persist. This concern, referred to as the carryover effect, may inhibit the use of these designs for research.

### A–B–A Designs

The A–B–A design builds on the A–B design by integrating a posttreatment follow-up that would typically include repeated measures. This design answers the question left unanswered by the A–B design: Does the effect of the intervention persist beyond the period in which treatment is provided? Depending on the length of the follow-up period, it may also be possible to learn how long the effect of the intervention persists.

The follow-up period should include multiple measures until a follow-up pattern emerges. The practicality of this depends on whether the relationship with the client extends beyond the period of the actual intervention. For example, the effect of an intervention designed to reduce problem behaviors in school might be amenable to repeated measurement after the end of the intervention, given that the client is likely still to be in school. On the other hand, a voluntary client who has come to a family service agency for treatment of depression might be more difficult to locate or might be unwilling to go through repeated follow-up measurements. In cases like this, consider simplifying and adapting the methods of collecting data to further reduce the burden on ex-clients, such as using phone interviews rather than face-to-face interviews.

Through replication and the aggregation of findings, the A–B–A design provides additional support for the effectiveness of an intervention. For example, Kirsten Ferguson and Margaret Rodway (1994) explored the effectiveness of cognitive–behavioral treatment on perfectionism by applying an *A–B–A design* to nine clients (Exhibit 9.5). They used two standardized scales to measure perfectionist thoughts and a nonstandardized client rating of perfectionist behaviors. In the baseline stage, clients completed the measurement twice a week (once a week at the beginning of an assessment with the practitioner and once a week at home, 3 days after the session). Data were collected over 4 weeks. The intervention stage lasted 8 weeks, with assessment prior to each counseling session, although only one follow-up measure was obtained, 3 weeks after the last counseling session.

| **Exhibit 9.5** | Graphic Display of the Burns Perfectionism Scale |

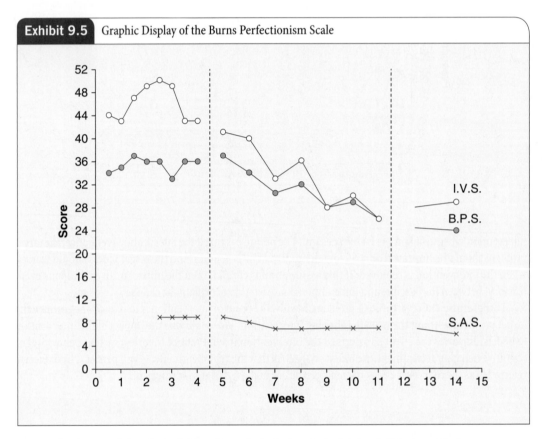

*Note:* I.V.S = Irrational Values Scale, B.P.S. = Burns Perfectionism Scale, S.A.S. = Self-Anchored Scale

## A–B–A–B Designs

The A–B–A–B design builds in a second intervention phase. The intervention in this phase is identical to the intervention used in the first B phase. The second intervention phase makes this design useful for behavioral research. The design replicates the intervention. For example, if during the follow-up phase the effects of the intervention begin to reverse (see Exhibit 9.6a), then the effects of the intervention can be established by doing it again. If there is a second improvement, the replication reduces the possibility that an event or history explains the change.

Just as with the A–B–A design, there is no guarantee that the effects will be reversed by withdrawing the intervention. If the practice theory holds, then it is unlikely that the effects will actually reverse themselves. So it may be that this first intervention period has to be short and end just as evidence of improvement appears. Even if the effect is not reversed during the follow-up, reintroducing the intervention may demonstrate a second period of additional improvement, as displayed in Exhibit 9.6b. This pattern suggests that the changes between the no-treatment and treatment phases are due to the intervention and not due to the result of history.

**Exhibit 9.6** A–B–A–B Designs

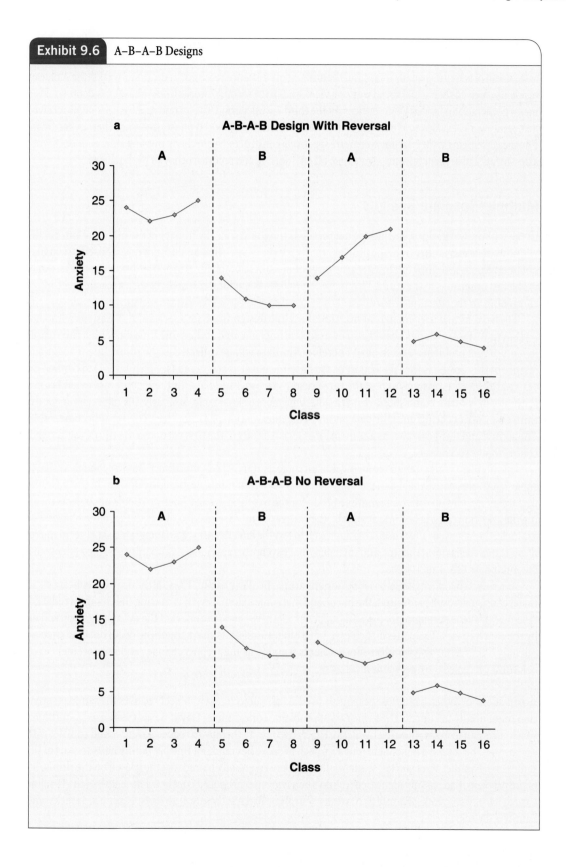

Kam-fong Monit Cheung (1999) used an A–B–A–B design to evaluate the effectiveness of a combination of massage therapy and social work treatment on six residents in three nursing homes. Measurements included an assessment of activities of daily living and the amount of assistance received. In the first 7 weeks (the A phase), residents received their usual social work services, and in the second 7 weeks (the B phase), residents received massage therapy and social work services. In the third 7-week period (the second A phase), residents received just social work services, and in the fourth 7-week period (the second B phase), massage therapy resumed. The measurements at the baseline were retrospectively constructed from client, nursing aide, and social work assessments. Subsequent measurements were taken from logs and reported behavior by the clients.

## Multiple-Baseline Designs

In the withdrawal designs, the individual serves as the control for the impact of the intervention. Yet the withdrawal designs suffer from the problem that often the target behavior does not reverse itself, and it may not be ethical to withdraw treatment early. A solution to these problems is to add additional subjects, target problems, or settings to the study. This method provides behavioral researchers with a feasible method of controlling for the effects of history.

The basic format is a **concurrent multiple-baseline design** in which a series of A–B designs (although A–B–A or A–B–A–B designs could also be used) are implemented at the same time for at least three cases (clients, target problems, or settings). Therefore, the data will be collected at the same time. The unique feature of this design is that the length of the baseline phase is staggered (see Exhibit 9.7) to control for external events (i.e., history) across the three cases. The baseline phase for the second case extends until the intervention data points for the first case become more or less stable. Similarly, the intervention for the third case does not begin until the data points in the intervention phase for the second case become stable. The second and third cases act as a control for external events in the first case, and the third case acts as a control for the second case.

One problem with a design requiring that all subjects start at the same time is having enough available subjects. An alternative that has been used is a **nonconcurrent multiple-baseline design**. In this case, the researcher decides on different lengths of time for the baseline period. Then as clients or subjects meeting the selection criteria become available, they are randomly assigned to one of the baseline phases. For example, Carla Jensen (1994) used this approach to test the effectiveness of an integrated short-term model of cognitive–behavioral therapy and interpersonal psychotherapy. Jensen randomly assigned clients to a baseline phase of 3, 4, or 5 weeks.

As a research tool, multiple-baseline designs are particularly useful. They introduce two replications so that if consistent results are found, the likelihood that some external event is causing the change is reduced. If some extraneous event might have an impact on all three cases, the effect of the event may be picked up by the control cases. The pattern of change in Exhibit 9.7 suggests that something occurred that affected not only Client A but also simultaneously Clients B and C, as they report changes and improvement even before they received the intervention.

*Across subjects.* When a multiple baseline is used across subjects, each subject receives the same intervention sequentially to address the same target problem. For example, David Besa (1994) used a multiple-baseline design to assess the effectiveness of narrative family therapy to reduce parent–child conflict with six families. Besa used a nonconcurrent approach because he could not find six family pairs to start at the same time. Families were started sequentially and were essentially paired together based on the similarity of the problem. Each family identified a child's behavior that produced conflict. The length of the baseline varied: Family 1, 7 weeks; Family 2, 10 weeks; Family 3, 10 days; Family 4, 15 days; Family 5, 3 weeks; and Family 6, 4 weeks.

## Exhibit 9.7 Multiple-Baseline Design

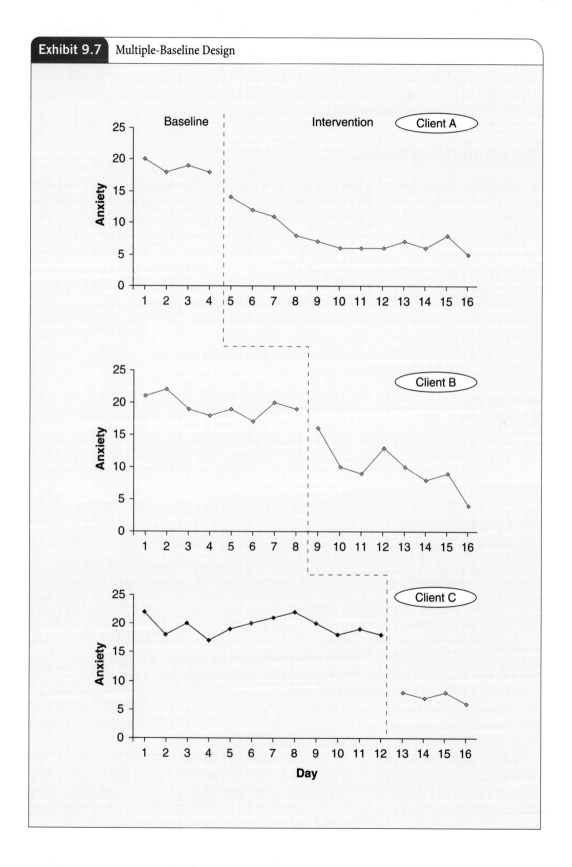

*Across different settings.* Multiple-baseline designs can be applied to test the effect of an intervention as it is applied to one client, dealing with one behavior but sequentially applied as the client moves to different settings. You might imagine a client with behavioral problems in school, at home, and at play with friends. A behavioral intervention might be used, with the application of rewards introduced sequentially across the three settings, starting with home, then school, then play.

## Multiple-Treatment Designs

In a multiple-treatment design, the nature of the intervention changes over time and each change represents a new phase of the design. This is the design used by Paul L. Beare, Susan Severson, and Patricia Brandt (2004) in a single-subject study of a long-term adult hospital resident they called "Ed." Ed was profoundly mentally retarded, with an IQ of 16, never initiated conversation, and made no eye contact with others. Ed had moved 4 years earlier into a group home and was working in a sheltered workshop where he folded precreased corner pads used for packing furniture. Three challenging behaviors interfered with Ed's functioning: self-injurious thigh slapping—so prolonged that it had led to a thick callous; vigorously tugging at his clothes—so vigorous that he destroyed some clothes each day; and restraining his own arms by crossing them under his legs. The treatment team developed a differential reinforcement plan in an attempt to reduce the self-injurious behavior. Preferred food was the chosen reinforcer. Ed's behavior was measured every 13 minutes throughout each 6-hour workday by a trained job coach. The specific measures are described in Exhibit 9.8 (Beare et al., 2004).

| **Exhibit 9.8** | Partial List of Challenging Behaviors |
| --- | --- |

- *Engagement on-task:* being physically involved with folding a corner pad, stacking completed pads, or moving an unfolded pad from the floor to the work surface. Consuming a reinforcer was counted as engaged. Ed was not on-task if he was away from the enclave. Data were not recorded during restroom breaks.

- *Self-injurious slapping:* striking any part of his body between the waist and knee, with either hand, irrespective of force.

- *Clothes manipulation:* pulling, tugging, or holding on to any article of his own clothes.

- *Self-restraint:* clasping one or both hands under the opposite arm pit, trapping one or both arms between legs, placing one or both hands down front of pants, clasping hands together behind back or in front of self.

Beare and his colleagues (2004) developed what they termed an A–B–BC–BCD–BCD design for the single-subject study of Ed. For the first intervention, Phase B, Ed received a food reward when he folded a pad. Ed's task engagement increased, but the slapping did not stop (Exhibit 9.9). Then, in Phase BC, Ed was given a food reward only when he folded a pad without slapping himself. In the BCD phase, reinforcement occurred only when both clothes manipulation and slapping were avoided. In the final BCD stage, Ed was moved to a community worksite and his behavior was observed there. Exhibit 9.9 displays the apparent effects of these various treatment phases on the different challenging behaviors.

Take a minute to inspect Exhibit 9.9. You can see that time on-task increased as soon as the food reinforcement started in Phase B, slapping declined sharply at the start of Phase C, and clothes manipulation dropped when Phase D began. This positive improvement was obtained in the community setting. However, the self-restraining behaviors, which were not the focus of a specific reinforcement strategy, decreased throughout the treatment period but then rose after movement to the community setting.

| Exhibit 9.9 | Percentage Scores for Engagement On-Task, Self-Slapping, Clothes Manipulation, and Self-Restraint Exhibited by a 46-Year-Old Worker With Severe Disabilities |
|---|---|

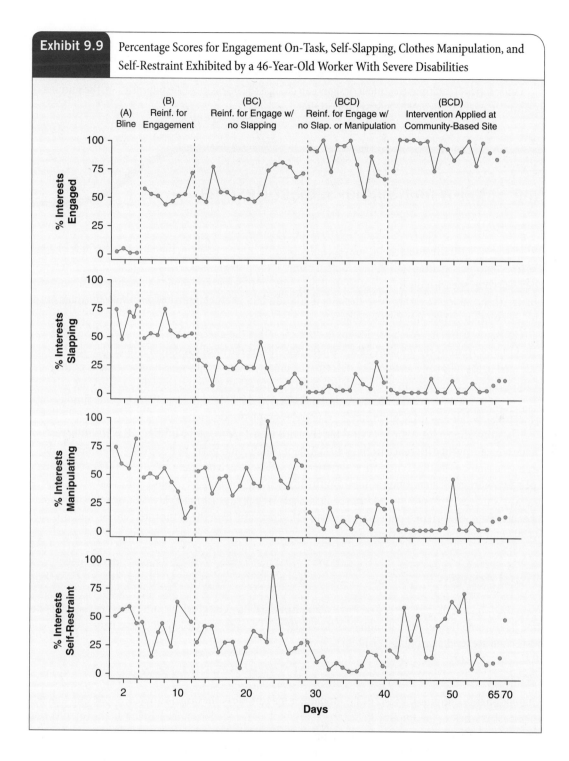

This complex research design yields a more convincing picture of the effect of the treatment program on Ed's behavior than would be possible with a simple A–B design. It also allows a more complete analysis of the effect of differential reinforcement: Ed's most challenging behaviors only changed when they were the focus of specific reinforcement; in general, reducing the rate of one challenging behavior did not also result in changing the rate of other challenging behaviors. However, it also appears that the frequency of self-restraining behavior might have varied in part in relation to the propensity to engage in the other behaviors. Thus, these rich findings also suggest the value of other lines of investigation.

Other types of multiple-treatment designs can change the *intensity* of the intervention, the number of treatments, or the nature of the intervention itself.

# Analyzing Small-*N* and Single-Subject Designs

Test your knowledge of this chapter so far by taking the mid-chapter quiz on the study site: www.sagepub.com/nestor2e

When you are engaged with a client, you typically are most concerned about the client's status and whether the intervention is making a difference for that client. If the intervention seems to be making a difference, then you continue with the intervention as it is needed; if the intervention is not leading to meaningful change, then you will likely abandon the intervention and try another intervention or vary the intensity of the intervention you are already providing.

How can we use single-subject designs to decide whether the intervention has been effective? One way is to visually examine the graphed data. Visual inspection is the most common method of evaluating the data, and in the following sections, we describe the presentation and possible interpretations of the data. Although you may make your graph by hand, both statistical software and spreadsheet software offer the tools to present data in graphs. For example, James Carr and Eric Burkholder (1998) provide simple, step-by-step instructions for using Microsoft Excel to create graphs for different types of single-subject designs.

The overriding issue is the **practical (or clinical) significance** of the findings. Has the intervention made a meaningful difference in the well-being of the subject, perhaps according to success criteria set by the client or by the community? Practical significance can be made more concrete by adopting a specific criterion for identifying a "meaningful difference." You may set a cutoff score that identifies the point at which a client is recovered from some malady—such as reaching a particular score on a measure of depression. Alternatively, you might measure the costs and benefits of the intervention and consider whether the benefits exceeded the costs.

## Visual Analysis

**Visual analysis** is the process of looking at a graph of the data points to determine whether the intervention has altered the subject's preintervention pattern of scores. Three concepts that help guide visual inspection are **level**, **trend**, and **variability**.

### Level

One option is to examine the level or the amount or magnitude of the target variable. A question that you might ask is whether the amount of the target variable has changed from the baseline to the intervention period. One option to describe the level is simply to inspect the actual data points, as illustrated in Exhibit 9.10a. It appears that the actual amount of the target variable—anxiety—has decreased.

Alternatively, the level of the phase scores may be summarized by drawing a line at the typical score for each phase separately. For example, the level may be summarized into a single observation using the mean (the average of the observations in the phase) or the median (the value at which 50% of the scores in the phase are higher and 50% are lower). The median is typically used in place of the mean when there are

**Exhibit 9.10** | Graphing Change: Levels, Means, and Trends

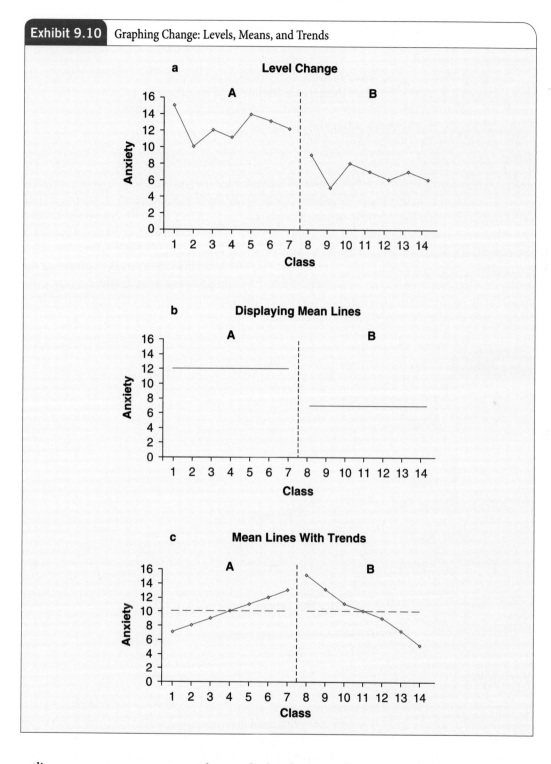

outliers or one or two extreme scores that greatly alter the mean. The mean of the baseline scores is calculated, and a horizontal line is drawn across the baseline phase at the mean. Then the mean of the intervention scores is calculated, and a horizontal line is drawn at the mean score across the intervention phase.

How these lines appear is displayed in Exhibit 9.10b. The summary line for the baseline phase can then be compared with the summary line for the intervention phase. You can see how this method simplifies the interpretation of the level.

Changes in level are typically used when the observations fall along relatively **stable lines**. Imagine the case, displayed in Exhibit 9.10c, where there is an ascending trend in the baseline phase and a descending trend in the intervention phase. As you can see, the direction has changed, but the mean for each phase may not have changed or may have changed only insignificantly.

### Trend

Another way to view the data is to compare trends in the baseline and intervention stages. As we have suggested earlier, a trend refers to the direction in the pattern of the data points and can be increasing, decreasing, or **cyclical**, or curvilinear. When there is a trend in the baseline, you might ask whether the intervention altered the direction of the trend. When the direction does not change, you may be interested in whether the rate of increase or decrease in the trend has changed. Does it alter the slope of the line? Because the published data from the study of Sam included only one data point to summarize behavior over the 3-month baseline period, we cannot use this method of comparing trend lines for the further analysis of these data. However, you can examine the reported trend after the baseline period to see if the behavior plan used by hospital staff to lessen Sam's aggressive behavior had any impact (see Exhibit 9.11). What would you conclude?

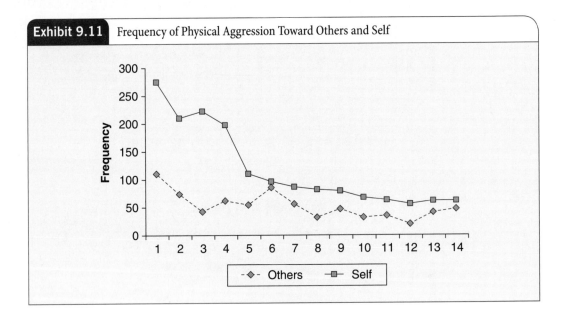

**Exhibit 9.11**  Frequency of Physical Aggression Toward Others and Self

## Variability

The interpretation of visually inspecting scores may depend on the stability or **variability** of the data points. By variability, we mean how different or divergent the scores are within a baseline or intervention phase. Widely divergent scores in the baseline make the assessment of the intervention more difficult, as do widely different scores in the intervention phase. One way to summarize variability with a visual analysis is to draw range lines, as was done in Exhibit 9.12. Whether the intervention had an effect depends on what goal was established with the client. As you can see in this graph, the only change has been a reduction in the spread of the points. But this does not mean that the intervention has not been effective, as it depends on the goal of the intervention. There are some conditions and concerns for which the lack of stability is the problem, and so creating stability may represent a positive change.

---

**Exhibit 9.12** Variability and Range Bars

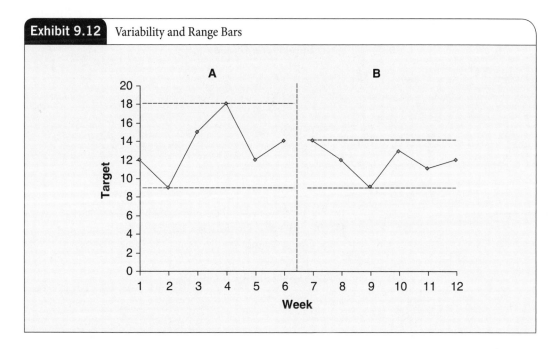

---

## Interpreting Visual Patterns

We next turn to patterns of level and trend that you are likely to encounter, although the patterns we present are a bit neater or more ideal than what actual data might look like. Exhibit 9.13a displays a situation in which there is a stable line (or a close approximation of a stable line), and so the level of the target problem is of interest. The target in this exhibit is the amount of anxiety, with lower scores being desired. For Outcome A, the intervention has only made the problem worse, for Outcome B, the intervention has had no effect, and Outcome C suggests that there has been an improvement.

In addition to the level–level comparisons, two other common patterns are displayed in Exhibit 9.13b, labeled Outcomes D and E. In both cases, there have been trend changes from no trend to a deteriorating trend, Outcome D, and an improving trend, Outcome E.

Exhibit 9.13c displays common patterns when there is a trend in the baseline. As you can see, the baseline phase is marked by an increase in anxiety from week to week. In the case of Outcome F, the intervention had no effect on the level of anxiety. For Outcome G, there was no change in the direction of the trend, but the rate of deterioration has slowed, suggesting that the intervention has been effective at least in slowing the increase of the problem but has not alleviated the problem. Outcome H represents the situation in which the intervention has improved the situation only to the extent that it is not getting worse. Finally, for Outcome I, the intervention has resulted in an improvement in the subject's status.

## Problems of Interpretation

Bisconer and colleagues' (2006) analysis of the case of Sam and the hypothetical examples presented earlier were quite neat, but the use of multiple treatments can complicate the analysis considerably—as can the complexity of the real world that you are studying. The results of Beare and colleagues' (2004) study of Ed

**Exhibit 9.13** Typical Baseline-Intervention Patterns

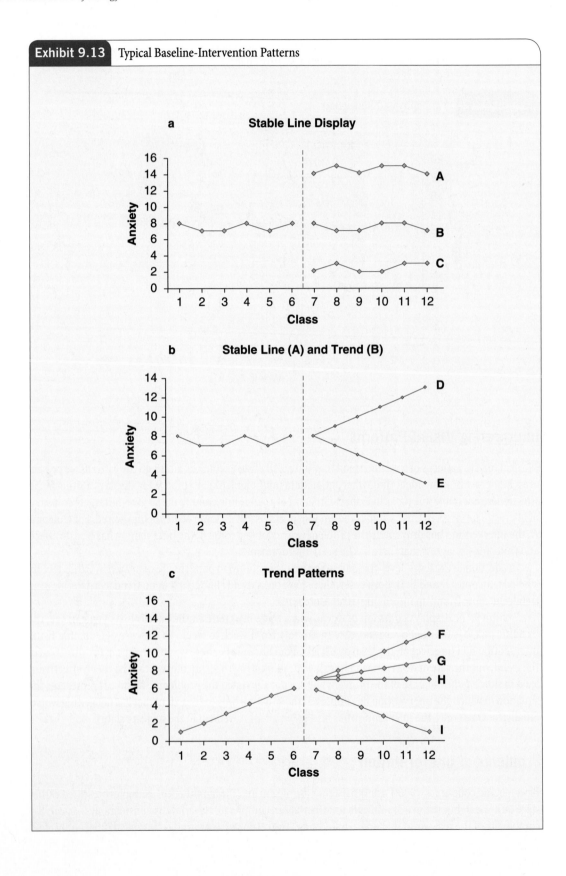

give some idea of the potential for such complications, even though the basic findings of that study were straightforward. It is possible, even likely, that you will encounter patterns that are much more ambiguous and that make conclusions from visual inspection less certain.

One problem occurs when there are widely discrepant scores in the baseline, as was the case in Exhibit 9.2c. When scores in the baseline differ, it becomes difficult to determine whether there is any pattern at the baseline, and measures of level or a typical score may not be representative of the data points at all. Therefore, judging whether the intervention has made a difference is more difficult.

### Delayed Change

A second problem is how to interpret changes in the intervention phase that are not immediately apparent. For example, the changes in anxiety displayed in Exhibit 9.14a and b took place several weeks into the

**Exhibit 9.14**  Delayed Change

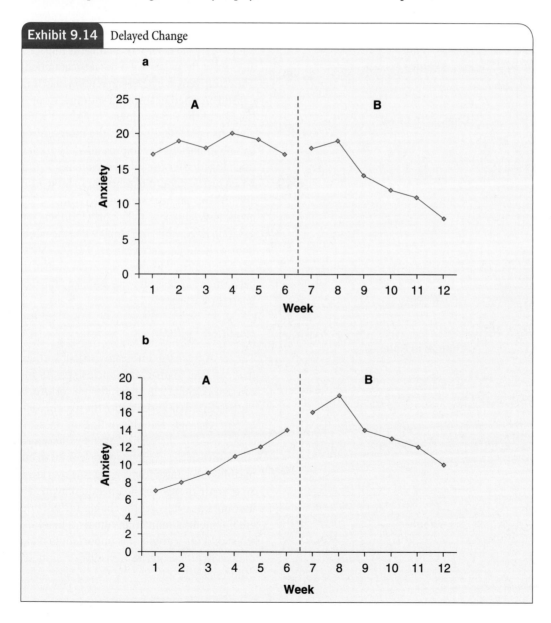

**Exhibit 9.15** Improvement in the Baseline

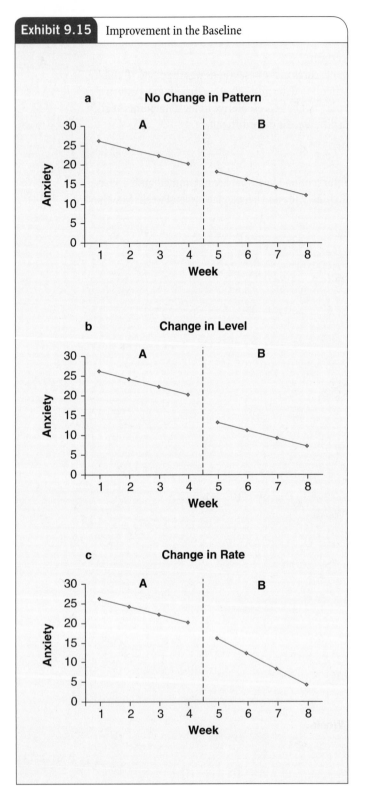

intervention. Is the change due to the intervention, or is it due to some extraneous event or factor unrelated to the intervention? There is no easy answer to this question. It may depend on the nature of the intervention and when it is hypothesized that change will occur. Not all treatment modalities will produce instantaneous improvement. On the other hand, the alternative interpretation—"something else happened" (i.e., history)—is equally plausible.

Another problem occurs when there is improvement in the target problem scores during the baseline phase, even prior to the onset of the intervention. This improvement may occur for a variety of reasons, including the impact of an event or the passage of time (i.e., maturation). The effectiveness of the intervention may then depend on whether there is a shift in level or in the rate of the improvement. In Exhibit 9.15a, you see a pattern in which the intervention had no impact, as the improvement continues unchanged after the intervention has begun. Based on the pattern of scores in Exhibit 9.15b and c, there may have been an intervention effect on the target problem. In Exhibit 9.15b, there was a shift in level, while in Exhibit 9.15c, the rate of improvement has accelerated. Of course, these changes may still be due to an event occurring between the last baseline measure and the first intervention measure.

### Distorted Pictures

The act of graphing can create visual distortions that can lead to different conclusions. As you can see in Exhibit 9.16, three different pictures of the baseline data appear, with the lines becoming increasingly flat, depending on the scale that is used on the vertical axis. Furthermore, the nature of the graph may prevent small but meaningful changes from being visually evident. So a small change in the unemployment rate may not be visible, yet the change includes the employment of many individuals. Therefore, when making a graph, it is important to make the axes as proportionate as possible to minimize distortions.

**Exhibit 9.16** Distorted Pictures

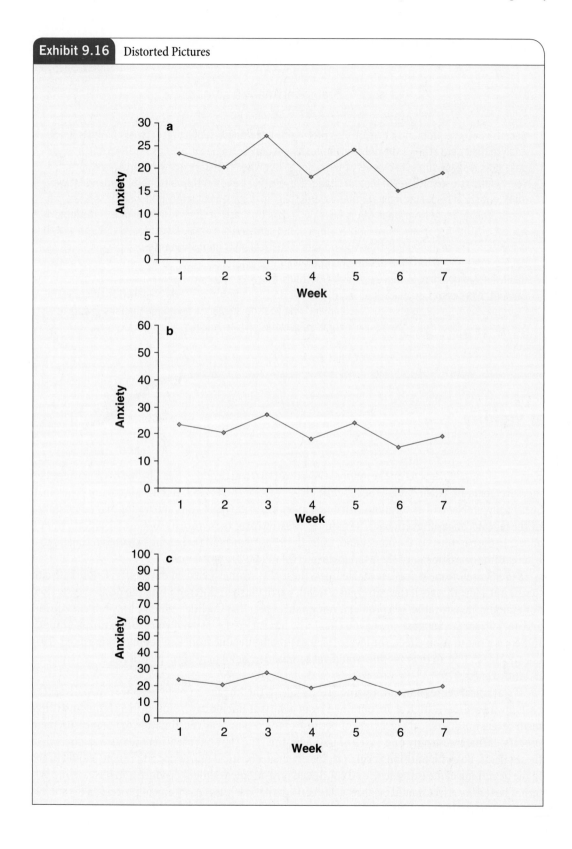

**STAT CORNER**

Statistical Analysis

Because of these problems of visual interpretation, some single-subject researchers have begun to analyze their data statistically. At first impression, it may seem peculiar to use statistics to analyze data from just one subject—or a very few subjects. But when there are many observations, it can be very helpful to use statistics to test for changes in levels or trends of the value of the dependent variable. Statistical tests may indicate that a trend that looks somewhat important when displayed in a graph is no different from what would be expected on the basis of chance. But in spite of the logical appeal of statistical tests, most single-subject (and small-*N*) data are still analyzed through visual inspection. The requirements that appropriate statistical tests impose on research design—such as having a prolonged baseline period or withdrawing the treatment at random intervals—can be difficult, if not impossible, to impose in clinical settings. Moreover, the particular statistics most appropriate for these designs, such as time-series analysis and randomization tests, can be difficult to learn (Kazdin, 1982). So for now, we just recommend that you should plan to review discussions of appropriate statistical tests if you plan to use a single-subject design (see Franklin, Allison, & Gorman, 1997).

# Internal Validity

Findings of causality depend on the internal validity of the research design (see Chapter 6). When repeated measurements are taken during the baseline phase, several threats to internal validity are controlled. Specifically, problems of maturation, instrumentation, statistical regression, and testing may be controlled by the repeated measurement because patterns illustrative of these threats to internal validity should appear in the baseline. On the other hand, when the measurement in the baseline phase is reconstructed from existing data or memory, these threats to internal validity are problematic.

When baseline measures are stable lines, these threats may be ruled out, but it is more difficult to rule out some threats if the pattern is a trend, particularly if the trend is in the desired direction. For example, if maturation is a problem, you would expect that the line would be linear or curvilinear and not horizontal. Suppose you have a client who has suffered a loss and you are measuring sadness. If there is a maturation effect, the level of sadness should decline from time point to time point. This does not mean that an intervention would not be effective, but it may be more difficult to demonstrate its effectiveness.

If statistical regression and testing effects occur, the impact is likely to appear initially in the baseline measures. A high score obtained from a measurement may be lower in a second measurement because of statistical regression or because of the respondent's acclimation to the measurement process. If there were only one baseline measure, then the first intervention measure might reflect these effects. But with multiple measures, the effect of statistical regression, if present, should occur in the beginning of measurement, and continued measurement should produce a stable baseline pattern. The testing effect should be observable early in the baseline measurement process as the subject adjusts to the testing requirements.

Repeated measurement in a baseline will not control for an extraneous event (history) that occurs between the last baseline measurement and the first intervention measurement. The longer the time period between the two measurement points, the greater the possibility that an event might influence the subject's scores. Later, we will describe single-subject designs that will control for the potential threat of history.

# Generalizability

Generalizability in the context of single-subject design—or group design, for that matter—is not an issue of representativeness or drawing generalizations to broader populations; rather, it is an issue of external validity. Therefore, the ideal is to take what has been tested in one research context and apply the findings to different settings, clients, or communities; to other providers; and even to other problems related to the target concern of the research. To do so when the sample consists of a single subject engaged in a particular intervention provided by a particular individual is challenging. To demonstrate the external validity of single-subject design requires replication both of the research conditions and beyond the research conditions.

Barlow and Hersen (1984) suggest that three sequential replication strategies be used to enhance the external validity of single-subject design. These are direct replication, systematic replication, and clinical replication.

*Direct replication.* **Direct replication** involves repeating the same procedures, by the same researchers, including the same providers of the treatment, in the same setting, and in the same situation, with different clients. Barlow and Hersen (1984) would add that even the clients should have similar characteristics. The strength of the findings is enhanced by having successful outcomes with these other clients. When the results are inconsistent, differences in the clients can be examined to identify characteristics that may be related to success or failure.

*Systematic replication.* From direct replication, the next step is **systematic replication**, which involves repeating the experiment in different settings using different providers and other related behaviors (Barlow & Hersen, 1984). Systematic replication also increases the number and type of clients exposed to the intervention. Through systematic replication, the applicability of the intervention to different conditions is evaluated. Like direct replication, systematic replication helps clarify conditions in which the intervention may be successful and conditions in which the intervention may not be successful.

*Clinical replication.* The last stage is **clinical replication**, which Barlow and Hersen (1984) define as combining different interventions into a clinical package to treat multiple problems. The actual replication takes place in the same setting and with clients who have the same types of problems. In many ways, findings from practice evaluation can enhance clinical replications.

For any replication effort to be successful, the treatment procedures must be clearly articulated, identified, and followed. Failing to adhere to the treatment procedures changes the intervention, and therefore, there is no true replication of the experiment.

## 回 Conclusions

Single-subject designs are useful for doing research, evaluating practice, and monitoring client progress. Single-subject designs have been underutilized as a research tool by behavioral researchers. Yet researchers using these designs can make a unique contribution to clinical practice knowledge because so much of practice is with individuals. Done systematically, the success or failure of different interventions can be evaluated with distinct clients and under differing conditions. Single-subject researchers can also use statistical analyses to achieve more explicit tests for effects than have been possible with graphic techniques (Callahan & Barisa, 2005; Huitema, 2002; Yarnold, 1992). Furthermore, single-subject designs may be useful in understanding the process of change and how it varies with particular clients.

## Key Terms

Baseline phase (A)
Clinical replication
Concurrent multiple-baseline design
Cyclical
Direct replication
Duration
Frequency

Interval
Level
Magnitude
Nonconcurrent multiple-baseline
  design
Practical (or clinical) significance
Rate

Stable line
Systematic replication
Treatment phase (B)
Trend
Variability
Visual analysis

## Research in the News

1. In "Exercise Your Brain, or Else You'll … Uh …," *The New York Times*, Katie Hafner (2008) reported on the many exercises that baby boomers are taking up to keep their brains active, to reduce forgetfulness, and, it is hoped, to lessen the risk of Alzheimer's disease. Design a single-subject experiment to test the impact of one of these brain exercise games on a friend. What indicators could you use to track the impact of the game?

2. "Exercise, the studies increasingly suggest, may be as good for your brain as it is for your body," according to research reviewed in a *Boston Globe* article by Carey Goldberg on April 21, 2008. Consider your friends and their exercise patterns. How could you design a single-subject study using an A–B–A–B design to investigate the effect of exercise on the mood of one of them? What challenges would you face in carrying out the study? What would be the advantages and disadvantages of carrying out this study if you were a therapist and your friend was a patient?

## STUDENT STUDY SITE

Please access the study site at **www.sagepub.com/nestor2e**, where you will find useful study materials such as mobile-friendly eFlashcards and mid-chapter and full chapter web quizzes for each chapter, along with carefully selected articles from research journals that illustrate the major concepts and techniques presented in the book.

# Activity Questions

1. Behavioral research seeks to confirm an intervention's effectiveness by observing scores when clients no longer receive the intervention. Yet the carryover effect may necessitate using a withdrawal design—ending a treatment prematurely—to do this successfully. Debate the merits of the withdrawal design in social work research. What are the advantages and disadvantages? Do the benefits outweigh the risks or vice versa?

2. Stress is a common occurrence in many students' lives. Measure the frequency, duration, interval, and magnitude of school-related stress in your life in a 1-week period of time. Take care to provide a clear operational definition of stress and construct a meaningful scale to rate magnitude. Did you notice any issues of reactivity? Which of the measurement processes did you find most feasible? Finally, do you believe that your operational definition was sufficient to capture your target problem and to detect changes?

# Review Questions

1. Visual analysis is used to communicate the impact of an intervention in visual form. What are the three primary ways that the pattern of scores established during a baseline or intervention stage may be viewed? When is each of them best used? What information is conveyed and what information may be omitted by choosing each one of them over the others?

2. Single-subject designs lack the inclusion of additional subjects serving as controls to demonstrate internal validity. How do the measurements during the baseline phase provide another form of control?

3. Behavioral research seeks to confirm an intervention's effectiveness by observing scores when clients no longer receive the intervention. Yet the carryover effect may necessitate using a withdrawal design—ending a treatment prematurely—to do this successfully. Debate the merits of the withdrawal design in social work research. What are the advantages and disadvantages? Do the benefits outweigh the risks or vice versa?

4. Use of single-subject methodology requires frequent measurement of symptoms or other outcomes. In their *American Psychologist* article introducing single-subject designs to the broader practitioner community, Jeffrey J. Borckardt and his colleagues (2008, p. 88) urge practitioners to discuss with patients before treatment begins the plan to use de-identified data in reports to the research community. Patients who do not consent still receive treatment—and data may still be recorded on their symptoms to evaluate treatment effects. Should the prospect of recording and publishing de-identified data on single subjects become a routine part of clinical practice? What would be the advantages and disadvantages of such a routine?

5. What are the weaknesses of single-subject designs when compared with true experimental designs? In what circumstances are single-subject designs useful? Which features add to single-subject designs more of the strengths of true experimental designs? Explain your reasoning.

# Ethics in Action

1. The relationship between the patient and therapist is the single most important factor in the therapeutic process. Do you think a therapist's use of a single-subject design to study the treatment process harms her relationship with the patient, presuming that she told the patient? Should she share her findings with the patient after the therapy is concluded? Or while it is in process? What if the patient abruptly announces that he is terminating? Should therapists in private practice have to have their single-subject study plans reviewed by some type of ethics board?

2. As you learned in this chapter, single-subject designs have been used to study behavior modification with patients who were not considered intellectually capable of providing informed consent. Do you think that it is ever permissible to include such patients in single-subject research? Who, if anyone, should be authorized to give consent in these cases? What special protections should be required? Now compare your answers with those you can find in the FAQ list at the website of the Office for Human Research Protections, U.S. Department of Health & Human Services: http://www.hhs.gov/ohrp/informconsfaq.html.

# Quantitative Data Analysis

## LEARNING OBJECTIVES: FAST FACTS

- Sample statistics are used to estimate population parameters. Mode, median, and mean are measures of central tendency. Range, variance, and standard deviation are measures of variability. Measures of central tendency and variability are used as descriptive statistics to characterize a sample.

- Inferential statistics are used to make inferences about the true difference in the population on the basis of sample data. The chi-square ($\chi^2$) test for independence is used to assess the statistical significance of frequency data for two variables measured at the nominal level. The *t* test can be used to test the difference in means between two groups or the difference in means for one group measured at two points in time. The *F* test can be used to test the differences in means for more than two groups or for two or more independent variables.

- Inferential statistics provide a direct test of the null hypothesis of no difference in population means. To select a critical value for a statistic, such as a *t* or *F* test, the researcher must specify the degrees of freedom, significance level, and directionality of the test (i.e., one-tailed or two-tailed). The significance level indicates the probability of a Type I error of mistakenly rejecting the null hypothesis of no difference in population means.

---

## TESTING BEFORE LEARNING

Try your hand at these questions. Don't worry about not knowing the correct response, as you haven't read the chapter yet! But research shows that a pretest such as this can enhance learning (e.g., Kornell, Hays, & Bjork, 2009). So here is the answer. You come up with the question.

1. The value that occurs the most frequently in a data set
   a. What is the mean?
   b. What is the median?
   c. What is the mode?
   d. What is the standard deviation?

2. A measure of central tendency that divides the distribution in half
   a. What is the median?
   b. What is the mode?
   c. What is the mean?
   d. What is the standard deviation?

3. The best measures of variability in a set of scores
   a. What are sample statistics and population parameters?
   b. What are mean and mode?
   c. What are mean and median?
   d. What are standard deviation and variance?

4. A statistic that indicates how far a particular score deviates from the mean
   a. What is the mean?
   b. What is the standard deviation?

   c. What is the median?
   d. What is the mode?

5. It is the most appropriate measure of central tendency for variables measured on an ordinal scale.
   a. What is the median?
   b. What is the mean?
   c. What is the mode?
   d. What is the standard deviation?

6. A measure of association between two variables that cannot demonstrate causation
   a. What is the mean?
   b. What is the correlation?
   c. What is the mode?
   d. What is the range?

7. It reflects the probability that an experimental result happened by chance.
   a. What is standard error of the mean?
   b. What is sampling error?
   c. What is statistical significance?
   d. What is the standard deviation?

8. Most values in a random population are distributed around the middle, with extreme values falling at either ends of the distribution.
   a. What is the power distribution?
   b. What is the sampling distribution?
   c. What is the chi-square distribution?
   d. What is the normal distribution?

*(Continued)*

(Continued)

9.  An inferential statistic that requires an interval or ratio scale of measurement and is used in comparing no more than two group means
    a.  What is a chi-square test?
    b.  What is a *t* test?
    c.  What is a correlation?
    d.  What is regression to the mean?

10. A statistical test of frequency data as to whether two or more categorical variables are related
    a.  What is the chi-square test of independence?
    b.  What is a *t* test?
    c.  What is an ANOVA *F* test?
    d.  What is a correlation?

**ANSWER KEY:** (1) c; (2) a; (3) d; (4) b; (5) a; (6) b; (7) c; (8) d; (9) b; (10) a

# Does Spending Money on Others Promote Happiness?

Can money buy happiness? Yes, but not in ways you might imagine. According to a March 2008 article in *Science*, the social psychologist Elizabeth Dunn and colleagues (2008) found an interesting association between increased happiness and spending money on others. How did they show this? Dunn and colleagues performed three different types of research: (1) a cross-sectional national representative survey, (2) a longitudinal field study, and (3) an experimental laboratory investigation. In each study, the researchers reported statistics that supported their hypothesis that spending money on other people has a more positive impact on happiness than spending money on oneself.

The Dunn experimental study provides a platform for us to introduce several common statistics used in psychological research. Following Dunn, we will imagine that we have 60 research participants rate their happiness in the morning, and then, we give each participant an envelope that contains either $5 or $20, which they are to spend by 5:00 p.m. that day. We randomly assign participants to either the *personal spending* condition, in which they are instructed to spend the money on a bill, an expense, or a gift for themselves, or the *prosocial spending* condition, in which they are instructed to spend the money on a gift for someone else or for a charity.

We thus have constructed two independent variables, each with two levels: (1) amount of money given ($5 vs. $20) and (2) spending (personal vs. prosocial). Now, we randomly assign 15 research participants to each of the resulting four conditions: (1) personal spending of $5, (2) personal spending of $20, (3) prosocial spending of $5, and (4) prosocial spending of $20. We call participants after 5:00 p.m. on that same day and ask them to rate their happiness from 1 to 10, with 1 = *very unhappy* and 10 = *very happy*. Thus, we have a 2 × 2 between-subjects factorial design. Our dependent measure is happiness rating.

How would you have rated your happiness if you had been in Treatment Condition 1? \_\_\_, 2? \_\_\_, 3? \_\_\_, 4? \_\_\_.

In this chapter, we use the Dunn experimental design to learn how statistics can be used to test the hypothesis that spending money on others can promote happiness. We also return to the 13-item maximizer/satisficer questionnaire from Chapter 2 to learn how to employ statistics to analyze percentages and correlational data. Here, we will imagine whether the percentages of maximizers and satisficers differ in young and older age-groups. We will also examine the correlation of age and maximizer/satisficer score.

Think of this chapter as a review of fundamental psychological statistics if you had completed a statistics course before you picked up *Research Methods in Psychology: Investigating Human Behavior* or as an introductory overview if your first exposure to statistics has been the statistics sections in our earlier chapters. Even though you can take a whole course on statistics for psychology (for good reason—there's a *lot* to learn), we don't want you to think of this chapter as something different from research methods. Rather, think of statistical analysis as flowing naturally from the design of a study and the method of observation or data collection.

# 回 Statistical Approach

As we learned in Chapter 2, there are two major types of statistics. Descriptive statistics are used to describe the variables in a study, both one at a time and in terms of their relations to each other. In our example of spending and happiness, we would report the composition of our sample with descriptive statistics about age, gender, socioeconomic status, and other such variables. We would also examine descriptive statistics for our dependent measure, happiness, and we would describe the relationship between the variables in our study using other descriptive statistics. Much important research is purely descriptive, ranging from reports on self-esteem among college students to the prevalence of mental illness in the general population.

Inferential statistics are used to estimate characteristics of a population from those we found in a random sample of that population (see Chapter 5). But inferential statistics can also be used for another purpose: to test hypotheses about the relationship between variables. How likely is it that the relationship we found between the independent and dependent variables in our experiment was due to chance? To put this inferential question another way, how confident can we be that the effect we observed was not simply due to chance? There are many different inferential statistical tests that help answer this question in particular circumstances; we will present the most commonly used in this chapter.

## The Level of Measurement Matters

Before we calculate statistics involving a variable, we must identify that variable's level of measurement. You may recall from Chapter 4 that there are four levels of measurement: (1) nominal, (2) ordinal, (3) interval, and (4) ratio. Each level has different arithmetic properties, and so different statistics are appropriate for variables measured at these different levels.

In the Dunn et al. (2008) example, the independent variable of spending (personal vs. prosocial) reflects a nominal scale of measurement. This represents a categorical variable in which participants are assigned either to spend on themselves or to spend on others. On the other hand, the dependent variable of happiness asks participants to rate their happiness on a 1 to 10 scale, with 1 = *very unhappy* and 10 = *very happy*. This happiness variable uses an ordinal scale of measurement. An ordinal scale involves minimal arithmetic distinctions. It allows us to rank responses from the lowest to highest, but it does not identify the numerical difference between responses of, say, 1 and 2 or 6 and 10. So even though we know that 1 is for *very unhappy* and 10 is for *very happy*, it does not really mean that a response of 10 is 9 units more happiness than a response of 1.

It is at the interval and ratio levels of measurement that the values of the variable reflect actual numbers on a scale with fixed intervals. In our study, we operationalized the independent variable, amount of money to spend, by providing participants with either $5 or $20. We know that $20 is $15 dollars more than $5 because we are using a scale with fixed intervals: dollars. In addition, that scale begins at an absolute zero point ($0), so the level of measurement is ratio. We can therefore calculate the ratio between the two values and conclude that $20 is four times greater than $5.

Although conceptually different, ratio and interval measures can be analyzed with the same statistical procedures. These procedures are more powerful than those that are allowable with an ordinal (or nominal) level of measurement. The levels of measurement of both independent and dependent variables are thus important factors to consider when designing experiments and other types of research and when planning statistical analyses of the resulting data. Now would be a good time to review our more complete discussion of levels of measurement in Chapter 4.

# 🔲 Univariate Distributions

Both frequency distributions and graphs are used to describe the distribution of variables one at a time. As we will see, a univariate distribution is a probability or frequency distribution of only one variable.

| Exhibit 10.1 | Frequency Distribution of Voting in the 2008 Presidential Election | |
|---|---|---|
| *Value* | *Frequency* | *Valid Percentage* |
| Voted | 1390 | 72.4 |
| Did not vote | 530 | 27.6 |
| Ineligible | 103 | |
| Don't know | 12 | |
| No answer | 9 | |
| Total | 2044 | 100.0 |
| *N* | | (1920) |

## Frequency Distributions

Often the first step in statistical analysis is to construct a frequency distribution for key variables. A frequency distribution shows the number of cases and/or the percentage of cases that receive each possible score on a variable. For many descriptive purposes, the analysis may go no further than a frequency distribution.

Constructing and reading frequency distributions for variables with few values is not difficult. For example, consider data from the 2010 General Social Survey (GSS) on voting. The frequency distribution of voting in Exhibit 10.1, for example, shows that 72.4% of the respondents eligible to vote said they voted, and 27.6% reported they did not vote. The total number of respondents to this question was 1,920, although 2,044 actually were interviewed. The rest were ineligible to vote, just refused to answer the question, said they did not know whether they had voted, or gave no answer.

Political ideology was measured with a question having seven response choices, resulting in a longer, but still relatively simple, frequency distribution (see Exhibit 10.2). The most common response was moderate, with 37.8% of the sample that responded choosing this label to represent their political ideology. The distribution has a symmetric shape, although somewhat more respondents identified themselves as conservative rather than liberal. About 4% of the respondents identified themselves as extremely conservative and about 4% as extremely liberal.

| Exhibit 10.2 | Frequency Distribution of Political Views | |
|---|---|---|
| *Value* | *Frequency* | *Valid Percentage* |
| Extremely liberal | 76 | 3.9% |
| Liberal | 259 | 13.1 |
| Slightly liberal | 232 | 11.8 |
| Moderate | 746 | 37.8 |
| Slightly conservative | 265 | 13.4 |
| Conservative | 315 | 16.0 |
| Extremely conservative | 80 | 4.1 |
| Total | 1973 | 100.0% |

Many frequency distributions (and graphs) require grouping of some values after the data are collected. There are two reasons for grouping:

1. There are more than 15 to 20 values to begin with, a number too large to be displayed in an easily readable table.

2. The distribution of the variable will be clearer or more meaningful if some of the values are combined.

Inspection of Exhibit 10.3 should clarify these reasons. In the first distribution, which is only a portion of the entire ungrouped GSS age distribution, it is very difficult to discern any shape, much less the central tendency. In the second distribution, age is grouped in the familiar 10-year intervals (except for the first, abbreviated category), and the distribution's shape is immediately clear.

**Exhibit 10.3** Grouped Versus Ungrouped Frequency Distributions

| Ungrouped | | Grouped | |
|---|---|---|---|
| Age (years) | Percentage | Age (years) | Percentage |
| 18 | 0.5 | 18–19 | 1.7 |
| 19 | 1.2 | 20–29 | 16.7 |
| 20 | 1.2 | 30–39 | 17.8 |
| 21 | 1.7 | 40–49 | 18.0 |
| 22 | 0.9 | 50–59 | 18.5 |
| 23 | 1.9 | 60–69 | 14.8 |
| 24 | 1.5 | 70–79 | 7.1 |
| 25 | 2.4 | 80–89 | 5.4 |
| 26 | 1.4 | | 100.0 |
| 27 | 2.1 | | (2041) |
| 28 | 1.5 | | |
| 29 | 2.2 | | |
| 30 | 2.0 | | |
| 31 | 2.1 | | |
| 32 | 1.6 | | |
| 33 | 1.8 | | |
| 34 | 1.6 | | |
| 35 | 2.2 | | |
| 36 | 1.5 | | |
| 37 | 1.9 | | |
| 38 | 1.5 | | |
| 39 | 1.7 | | |
| 40 | 1.8 | | |

*(Continued)*

(Continued)

| Ungrouped | | Grouped | |
|---|---|---|---|
| 41 | 1.9 | | |
| 42 | 1.7 | | |
| 43 | 2.1 | | |
| 44 | 1.9 | | |
| 45 | 1.8 | | |
| 46 | 1.9 | | |
| . . . | . . . | | |

Once we decide to group values, or categories, we have to be sure that we do not distort the distribution. Adhering to the following guidelines for combining values in a frequency distribution will prevent many problems:

- Categories should be logically defensible and preserve the distribution's shape.

- Categories should be mutually exclusive and exhaustive so that every case should be classifiable in one and only one category.

## Graphing

Several different types of graph are commonly used to depict frequency distributions. The most common and most useful are bar charts and histograms. For bar charts and histograms, each figure has two axes, the horizontal axis (the *x*-axis) and the vertical axis (the *y*-axis), and labels to identify the variables and the values, with tick marks showing where each indicated value falls along the axis.

A bar chart contains solid bars separated by spaces. It is a good tool for displaying the distribution of variables measured at the nominal level because there is, in effect, a gap between each of the categories. The bar chart of our 13-item maximizer/satisficer questionnaire, which we introduced in Chapter 2, is presented in Exhibit 10.4. This bar chart graphs how many students were classified as either maximizers or satisficers on the 13-item maximizer/satisficer questionnaire. Seven students were classified as maximizers (scores >61.75), and the remaining 22 students as satisficers (scores <61.75).

A histogram displays a frequency distribution of a quantitative variable. Exhibit 10.5 shows a histogram of scores on the maximizer/satisficer questionnaire for a sample of 29 college students. The figure shows that the most common score was 53.00.

Both graphs and frequency distributions allow the researcher to display the distribution of cases across the categories or scores of a variable. Graphs have the advantage of providing a picture that is easier to comprehend, although frequency distributions are preferable when exact numbers of cases having particular values must be reported and when many distributions must be displayed in a compact form.

## Beware of Deceptive Graphs

If graphs are misused, they can distort, rather than display, the shape of a distribution. Compare, for example, the two graphs in Exhibit 10.6. The first graph shows that high school seniors reported relatively stable rates of lifetime use of cocaine between 1980 and 1985. The second graph, using exactly the same numbers, appeared in a 1986 *Newsweek* article on the "coke plague" (Orcutt & Turner, 1993). To look at this graph, you would think that the rate of cocaine usage among high school seniors had increased dramatically during this period. But, in fact, the difference between the two graphs is due simply to changes in how the graphs are drawn. In the plague graph, the percentage scale on the vertical axis begins at 15 rather than at 0, making what was about a 1-percentage-point increase look very big indeed. In addition, omission from the plague graph of the more rapid increase in reported usage between 1975 and 1980 makes it look as if the tiny increase in 1985 were a new, and thus more newsworthy, crisis.

Adherence to several guidelines (Tufte, 1983; Wallgren, Wallgren, Persson, Jorner, & Haaland, 1996) will help you spot these problems and avoid them in your own work.

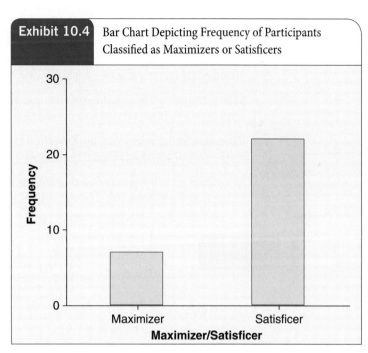

**Exhibit 10.4** Bar Chart Depicting Frequency of Participants Classified as Maximizers or Satisficers

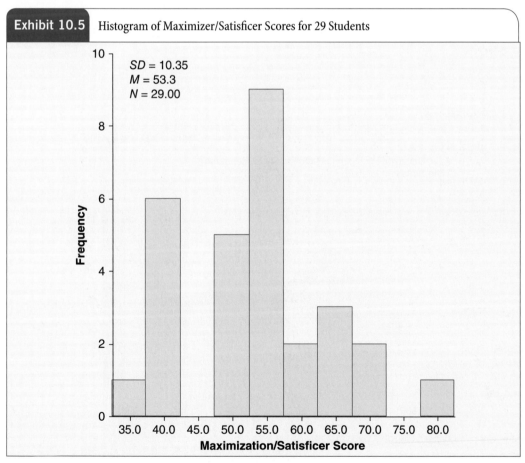

**Exhibit 10.5** Histogram of Maximizer/Satisficer Scores for 29 Students

- The difference between bars can be exaggerated by cutting off the bottom of the vertical axis and displaying less than the full height of the bars. Instead, begin the graph of a quantitative variable at 0 on both axes. It may be reasonable, at times, to violate this guideline, as when an age distribution is presented for a sample of adults, but in this case, be sure to mark the break clearly on the axis.

- Bars of unequal width, including pictures instead of bars, can make particular values look as if they carry more weight than their frequency warrants. Always use bars of equal width.

- Either shortening or lengthening the vertical axis will obscure or accentuate the differences in the number of cases between values. The two axes should be of approximately equal length.

- Avoid chart junk that can confuse the reader and obscure the distribution's shape (a lot of verbiage or umpteen marks, lines, lots of cross-hatching, etc.).

**Exhibit 10.6** Two Graphs of Cocaine Usage

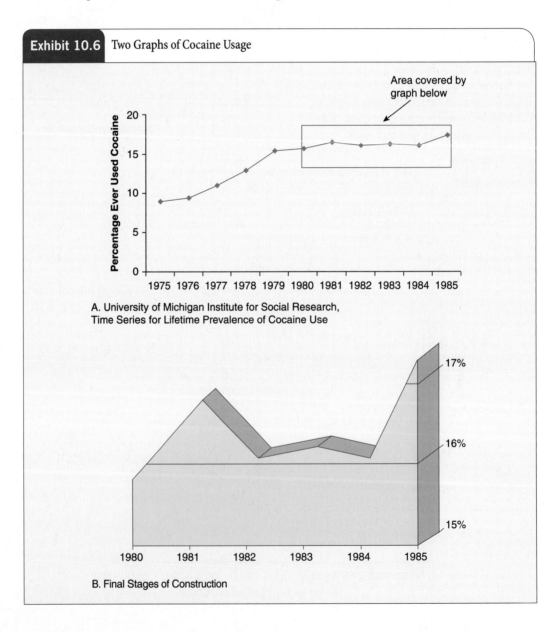

A. University of Michigan Institute for Social Research, Time Series for Lifetime Prevalence of Cocaine Use

B. Final Stages of Construction

## 🔲 Descriptive Statistics

Whichever type of display is used, the primary concern is to display accurately the distribution's shape, that is, to show how cases are distributed across the values of the variable. Three features of shape are important: **central tendency**, **variability**, and **skewness** (lack of symmetry). All three features are represented in a graph or in a frequency distribution.

Descriptive statistics involve mathematical calculations that allow us to make precise statements about these features of collected data, although the statistic used to characterize skewness is only appropriate for quantitative variables, is rarely used, and will not be considered here.

### Measures of Central Tendency

Central tendency is usually summarized with one of three statistics: (1) the mode, (2) the median, or (3) the mean. For any particular application, one of these statistics may be preferable, but each has a role to play in data analysis. To choose an appropriate measure of central tendency, the researcher must consider the level of measurement, the skewness of the distribution of the variable (if it is a quantitative variable), and the purpose for which the statistic is used.

### Mode

The **mode** is the most frequent value in a distribution. It is also termed the **probability average** because being the most frequent value, it is the most probable. For a nominal scale of measurement, the mode, defined as the most frequent score, is the only measure of central tendency. The mode indicates the most frequently occurring value. It is a simple count. It does not use the actual values of a scale, as we have seen in the gender example. The most frequent score or mode for our maximizer/satisficer questionnaire was 53 (see Exhibit 10.5).

The mode is used much less often than the other two measures of central tendency because it can so easily give a misleading impression of a distribution's central tendency. One problem with the mode occurs when a distribution is **bimodal**, in contrast to being **unimodal**. A bimodal (or trimodal, etc.) distribution has two or more categories with an equal number of cases and with more cases than any of the other categories. There is no single mode when a distribution is bimodal. Imagine that a particular distribution has two categories that have just about the same number of cases. Strictly speaking, the mode would be the category with more cases, even if the other frequent category had only slightly fewer cases. Another potential problem with the mode is that it might happen to fall far from the main clustering of cases in a distribution. With such a distribution, it would be misleading to say simply that the variable's central tendency was whatever the modal value was. However, when the issue is what the most probable value is, the mode is the appropriate statistic. Which ethnic group is the most common in a given school? The mode provides the answer.

### Median

The **median** is the position average or the point that divides the distribution in half (the 50th percentile). The median is inappropriate for variables measured at the nominal level because their values cannot be put in order, and so there is no meaningful middle position. To determine the median, we simply array the distribution of values in numerical order and find the value of the case that has an equal number of cases above and below it. If the median point falls between two cases (which happens if the distribution has an even number of cases), the median is defined as the average of the two middle values and is computed by adding the values of the two middle cases and dividing by 2. The median in a frequency distribution is determined by identifying the value corresponding to a cumulative percentage of 50. In our example, the median, abbreviated as *Mdn*, was 53 for our maximizer/satisficer questionnaire, which as you can see is identical to the mode.

## Mean

The **mean**, or arithmetic average, takes into account the value of each case in a distribution; it is a weighted average. The mean is computed by adding up the values of all the cases and dividing by the total number of cases, thereby taking into account the value of each case in the distribution:

$$\text{Mean} = \text{Sum of value of cases/Number of cases}$$

In algebraic notation, the equation is $\bar{Y} = \Sigma Y_i / N$. For example, to calculate the mean of eight cases, we add the values of all the cases $(\Sigma Y_i)$ and divide by the number of cases ($N$):

$$(28 + 117 + 42 + 10 + 77 + 51 + 64 + 55)/8 = 444/8 = 55.5.$$

Because computing the mean requires adding up the values of the cases, it makes sense to compute a mean only if the values of the cases can be treated as actual quantities—that is, if they reflect an interval or ratio level of measurement or if they are ordinal and we assume that ordinal measures can be treated as interval. It would make no sense to calculate the mean of a variable measured at the nominal level, such as religion. For example, imagine a group of four people in which there were two Protestants, one Catholic, and one Jew. To calculate the mean, you would need to solve the equation (Protestant + Protestant + Catholic + Jew)/4 = ? Even if you decide that Protestant = 1, Catholic = 2, and Jew = 3 for data entry purposes, it still doesn't make sense to add these numbers because they don't represent quantities of religion.

By contrast, it makes perfect sense to compute the mean score for the maximizer/satisficer questionnaire from Chapter 2 that we gave to our class of 29 students. We found a mean score of 53.28 for the maximizer/satisficer questionnaire, with scores ranging from a low of 36 to a high of 78. We can see that our three measures of central tendency are nearly identical. Three measures of central tendency all falling together characterizes a symmetric distribution of values for the maximizer/satisficer questionnaire. This can be seen in the histogram plotting the maximizer/satisficer scores in Exhibit 10.5.

## Median Versus Mean

Both the median and the mean are used to summarize the central tendency of quantitative variables, but their suitability for a particular application must be carefully assessed. The key issues to be considered in this assessment are the variable's level of measurement, the shape of its distribution, and the purpose of the statistical summary. Consideration of these issues will sometimes result in a decision to use both the median and the mean and will sometimes result in neither measure being seen as preferable. But in many other situations, the choice between the mean and median will be clear-cut as soon as the researcher takes the time to consider these three issues.

Level of measurement is a key concern because to calculate the mean, we must add up the values of all the cases—a procedure that assumes the variable is measured at the interval or ratio level. So even though we know that coding *Agree* as 2 and *Disagree* as 3 does not really mean that *Disagree* is 1 unit more of disagreement than

*Agree*, the mean assumes this evaluation to be true. Because calculation of the median requires only that we order the values of cases, we do not have to make this assumption. Technically speaking, then, the mean is simply an inappropriate statistic for variables measured at the ordinal level (and you already know that it is completely meaningless for variables measured at the nominal level). In practice, however, many social researchers use the mean to describe the central tendency of variables measured at the ordinal level.

The shape of the distribution of a variable should also be taken into account when deciding whether to use the median or mean. When a distribution is perfectly symmetric, so that the distribution of values below the median is a mirror image of the distribution of values above the median, the mean and median will be the same. But the values of the mean and median are affected differently by skewness, or the presence of cases with extreme values on one side of the distribution but not the other side. Because the median takes into account only the number of cases above and below the median point, not the value of these cases, it is not affected in any way by extreme values. Because the mean is based on adding the values of all the cases, it will be pulled in the direction of exceptionally high (or low) values. When the value of the mean is larger than the value of the median, we know that the distribution is skewed in a positive direction, with proportionately more cases with higher than lower values. When the mean is smaller than the median, the distribution is skewed in a negative direction.

This differential impact of skewness on the median and mean is illustrated in Exhibit 10.7. On the first balance beam, the cases (bags) are spread out equally, and the median and mean are in the same location.

**Exhibit 10.7** The Mean as a Balance Point

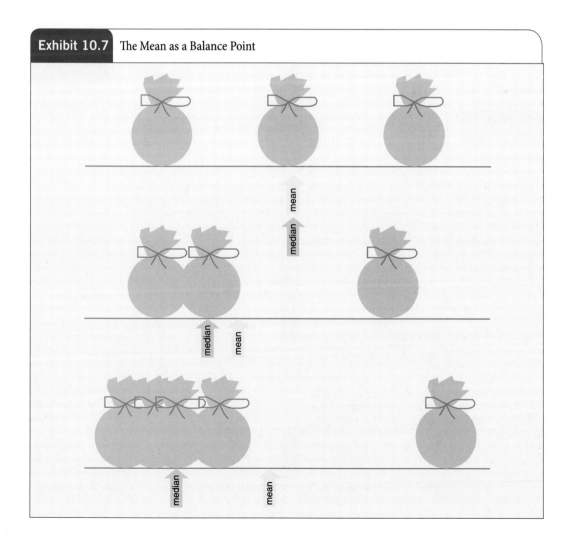

268 | *Research Methods in Psychology*

On the second and third balance beams, the median corresponds to the value of the middle case, but the mean is pulled toward the value of the one case with an extremely high value. For this reason, the mean age (47.97) for the 2,041 cases represented partially in the detailed age distribution in Exhibit 10.3 is higher than the median age (47). Although in the distribution represented in Exhibit 10.3, the difference is small, in some distributions, the two measures will have markedly different values, and in such instances, the median may be preferred.

The single most important influence on the choice of the median or the mean for summarizing the central tendency of quantitative variables should be the purpose of the statistical summary. If the purpose is to report the middle position in one or more distributions, then the median is the proper statistic, whether or not the distribution is skewed. For example, with respect to the age distribution from the GSS, you could expect that half the American population is younger than 46 years and half the population is older than that.

However, if the purpose of the research is to show how likely different groups are to have age-related health problems, the measure of central tendency for these groups should take into account people's ages, not just the number of people who are older and younger than a particular age. For this purpose, the median would be inappropriate, because it would not distinguish between two distributions like those presented in Exhibit 10.8. In the top distribution, everyone is between the ages of 35 and 45 years, with a median of 41. In the bottom distribution, the median is still 41, but almost half of the cases (4/9, 44%) have ages above 60 years. Here, in the second distribution, despite a median of 41, identical to the median of the first distribution, the higher mean captures the important fact that it has a greater number of older people.

Keep in mind that it is not appropriate to use either the median or the mean as a measure of central tendency for variables measured at the nominal level, because at this level of measurement the different

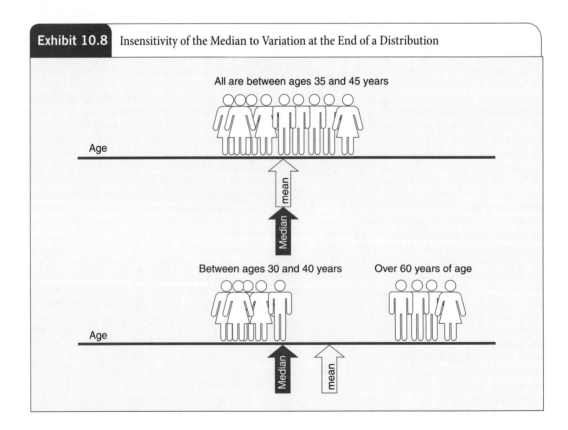

**Exhibit 10.8** Insensitivity of the Median to Variation at the End of a Distribution

attributes of a variable cannot be ordered as higher or lower (see Exhibit 10.9). Technically speaking, the mode should be used to assess the central tendency of variables measured at the nominal level (and it can be used with variables measured at the ordinal, interval, and ratio levels). The median is most suited to assess the central tendency of variables measured at the ordinal level (and it can also be used to measure the central tendency of variables at the interval and ratio levels). Finally, the mean is only suited to measuring the central tendency of variables measured at the interval and ratio levels.

| Exhibit 10.9 | Measures of Central Tendency (MCT) and Scales of Measurement | | |
|---|---|---|---|
| *Level of Measurement* | *Most Appropriate MCT* | *Potentially Useful MCT* | *Definitely Inappropriate MCT* |
| Nominal | Mode | None | Median, mean |
| Ordinal | Median | Mean, mode | None |
| Interval, ratio | Mean | Median, mode | None |

It is not entirely legitimate to represent the central tendency of a variable measured at the ordinal level with the mean: Calculation of the mean requires summing the values of all the cases, and at the ordinal level, these values indicate only order, not actual quantities. Nonetheless, many social scientists use the mean with ordinal-level variables and find that this is potentially useful for comparisons among variables and as a first step in more complex statistical analyses. As shown in Exhibit 10.9, the median and mode can also be useful as measures of central tendency for variables measured at the interval and ratio levels when the goal is to indicate the middle position (median) or the most frequent value.

In general, the mean is the most common measure of central tendency for quantitative variables, both because it takes into account the value of all cases in the distribution and because it is the foundation for many other advanced statistics. However, the mean's very popularity results in its use in situations for which it is inappropriate. Keep an eye out for this problem.

## Measures of Variation

You already have learned that central tendency is only one aspect of the shape of a distribution—the most important aspect for many purposes but still just a piece of the total picture. A summary of distributions based only on their central tendency can be very incomplete, even misleading. For example, three towns might have the same median income but still be very different in their social character due to the shape of their income distributions. As illustrated in Exhibit 10.10, Town A is a homogeneous middle-class community; Town B is very heterogeneous; and Town C has a polarized, bimodal income distribution, with mostly very poor and very rich people and few in between. However, all three towns have the same median income.

The way to capture these differences is with statistical measures of variation or variability. Three popular measures of variability in a set of data are the range, the variance, and the standard deviation (which is the most popular measure of variability). To calculate each of these measures, the variable must be at the interval or ratio level (but many would argue that, like the mean, they can be used with ordinal-level measures too). Statistical measures of variation are used infrequently with variables measured at the nominal level, so these other measures will not be presented here. It's important to realize that measures of variability are descriptive statistics that capture only part of what we need to be concerned with about the distribution of a variable. In particular, they do not tell us about the extent to which a distribution is skewed, which we've seen is very important for interpreting measures of central tendency. Researchers usually evaluate the skewness of distributions just by eyeballing them.

**Exhibit 10.10** Distributions Differing in Variability but Not Central Tendency

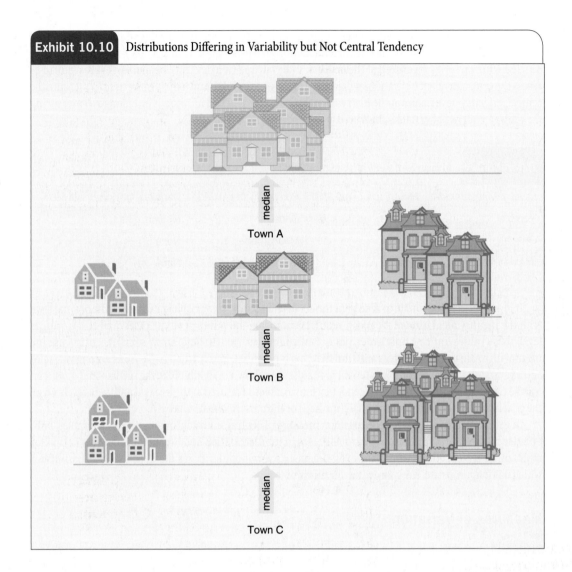

### Range

The **range** is a simple measure of variation, calculated as the highest value in a distribution minus the lowest value plus 1:

$$\text{Range} = \text{Highest value} - \text{Lowest value} + 1.$$

It often is important to report the range of a distribution to identify the whole range of possible values that might be encountered. However, because the range can be drastically altered by just one exceptionally high or low value (termed an **outlier**), it does not do an adequate job of summarizing the extent of variability in a distribution.

### Variance

The **variance** is the average squared deviation of each case from the mean, so it takes into account the amount by which each case differs from the mean. The variance is calculated using the following formula:

$$\sigma^2 = \frac{\Sigma\left(Y_i - \overline{Y}_i\right)^2}{N},$$

where $\overline{Y}$ = mean, $N$ = number of cases, $\Sigma$ = sum of all cases, $Y_i$ = value of case $i$ on variable $Y$, and $\sigma^2$ = variance.

Exhibit 10.11 shows an example of calculating the variance. The variance is used in many other statistics, although it is more conventional to measure variability with the closely related standard deviation than with the variance.

| Exhibit 10.11 | Calculation of the Variance | | |
|---|---|---|---|
| Case # | Score ($Y_i$) | $Y_i - \overline{Y}$(mean) | $(Y_i - \overline{Y})^2$ |
| 1 | 21 | −3.27 | 10.69 |
| 2 | 30 | 5.73 | 32.83 |
| 3 | 15 | −9.27 | 85.93 |
| 4 | 18 | −6.27 | 39.31 |
| 5 | 25 | 0.73 | 0.53 |
| 6 | 32 | 7.73 | 59.75 |
| 7 | 19 | −5.27 | 27.77 |
| 8 | 21 | −3.27 | 10.69 |
| 9 | 23 | −1.27 | 1.61 |
| 10 | 37 | 12.73 | 162.05 |
| 11 | 26 | 1.73 | 2.99 |
| Total | | | 434.15 |

*Note:* $\overline{Y}$ = 24.27, variance = 434.15, $SD$ = 20.81.

## Standard Deviation

The standard deviation is simply the square root of the variance. It is the square root of the average squared deviation of each case from the mean.

$$\sigma = \sqrt{\frac{\Sigma\left(Y_i - \overline{Y}_i\right)^2}{N}},$$

where $\overline{Y}$ = mean, $N$ = number of cases, $\Sigma$ = sum of all cases, $Y_i$ = value of case $i$ variable $Y$, $\sqrt{\phantom{x}}$ = square root, and $\sigma$ = standard deviation.

Standard deviation is thus the square root of the average squared deviation of each case from the mean. When the standard deviation is calculated from sample data, the denominator is supposed to be $N - 1$, rather than $N$, an adjustment that has no discernible effect when the number of cases is reasonably large. You also should note that the use of *squared* deviations in the formula accentuates the impact of relatively large deviations, because squaring a large number makes that number count much more.

The standard deviation can be used to answer two simple questions: (1) How much variation, dispersion, or spread is there in a set of scores, numbers, or data points? (2) How far from the average is a particular score? In our example using the maximizer/satisficer questionnaire, our group had a standard deviation of 10.35 on this test. As we will learn, this standard deviation value tells us that most of the students (approximately 68%) in our sample had scores on the questionnaire 10.35 points above or below the mean. That is, for the maximizer/satisficer questionnaire, our group had a mean of 53.28, with most scores falling between 42.93, that is, (53.28 − 10.35), and 63.63, that is, (53.28 + 10.35). We can also say that a student with a score of 65 falls "1 standard deviation unit above the mean." In the next section, you will learn the importance of a statement like this.

Test your knowledge of this chapter so far by taking the mid-chapter quiz on the study site: www.sagepub.com/nestor2e

# ▣ Inferential Statistics

We use inferential statistics to *infer* the characteristics of a population from the characteristics of a sample selected from that population.

By chance alone, any sample statistic, such as the mean, is very likely to be a little bit lower or a little bit higher than a hypothetical population parameter; sometimes the sample statistic will be quite a bit higher or lower than the population parameter. You can think of the mean for a particular sample as being one of the mean values we would obtain if we repeatedly drew new random samples from the population—in fact, we can imagine that we draw an infinite number of random samples from this population and calculate the mean of each. The distribution of the means of all these samples would be a sampling distribution (distribution of sample statistics). You may recall that we discussed sampling distributions in Chapter 5.

So the value of the mean or any other statistic we obtain for a random sample is not likely to equal exactly the population mean or, more generally, the population **parameter**. However, the mean of the distribution of sample means is the actual population mean. We can calculate a statistic called the **standard error of the mean** to indicate the degree to which the means of the samples vary from the population mean. You can think of the standard error as an estimate of the standard deviation of the sampling distribution.

You might wonder how we can calculate the mean and standard deviation of the sampling distribution when we can't possibly draw an infinite number of random samples from a population and calculate the means of all those samples. Well, the fact is that we can't. However, what we can do is determine how confident we can be that the mean (or some other statistic) of a random sample from a population is within a certain range of the population mean. This is the logic behind calculating confidence limits around the mean, as we did in Chapter 5.

Confidence limits around the mean assume a normal distribution of values. A **normal distribution** is a distribution that results from chance variation around a mean. It is symmetric and tapers off in a characteristic shape from its mean. If a variable is normally distributed (see Exhibit 10.12), 68% of the cases will be between ±1 standard deviation from the distribution's mean, and 95% of the cases will lie between ±1.96 standard deviations from the mean. This correspondence of the standard deviation to the normal distribution enables us to infer how confident we can be that the mean (or some other statistic) of a population sampled randomly is within a certain range of the hypothetical population mean. Now that you know how to compute the standard deviation, it is just a short additional step to compute the confidence limits around a mean.

There are just four more steps:

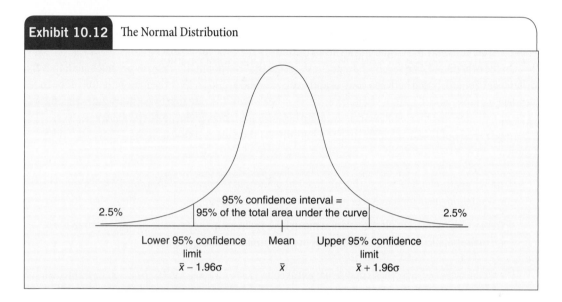

**Exhibit 10.12**   The Normal Distribution

1. Calculate the standard error (*SE*). This is the estimated value of the standard deviation of the sampling distribution (*s*) from which your sample was selected. It equals the standard deviation divided by the square root of the sample size minus 1: $SE = \sigma \sqrt{(n-1)}$.

2. Decide on the degree of confidence that you wish to have that the population parameter falls within the confidence interval you compute. It is conventional to calculate the 95%, 99%, or even 99.9% confidence limits around the mean. Most often, the 95% confidence limits are used, so we will just show the calculation for this estimate.

3. Multiply the value of the *SE* by 1.96. This is because 95% of the area under the normal curve falls within ±1.96 standard deviation units of the mean.

4. Add and subtract the number in Step 3 from the sample mean. The resulting numbers are the upper and lower confidence limits.

Recall that the standard deviation for the maximizer/satisficer questionnaire is 10.35 for our sample of 29 students. The standard error of the mean is the standard deviation of 10.35 divided by the square root of the sample size of 29 minus 1. This equals a standard error of the mean of 1.96 for the maximizer/satisficer questionnaire. Multiply the *SE* of 1.96 by 1.96 because 95% of the area under the normal curve falls within ±1.96 standard deviation units of the mean (Step 3). Thus, we can say with 95% certainty that the population mean is within ±3.84 of the obtained sample mean of 53.28 for the maximizer/satisficer questionnaire: The 95% confidence interval of the mean is 49.44 to 57.12.

This represents one use of inferential statistics: to estimate a population parameter from a sample statistic. We just inferred that the mean maximizer/satisficer score of the population is likely to be between 49.44 and 57.12.

## Hypothesis Testing

Inferential statistics are also used to test hypotheses. As we learned in Chapter 6, the logic of hypothesis testing centers on two hypotheses: (1) the null hypothesis and (2) the research (or alternative) hypothesis. In a test of the difference between two means, the null hypothesis states that the population means are equal; any differences observed in the study sample merely reflect random error. The null hypothesis predicts that the independent variable will have no effect on the dependent variable—the intervention will not work. The null hypothesis runs counter to the theory of the study—it's the reverse of what a researcher expects to demonstrate by conducting an investigation.

On the other hand, the **research hypothesis** states that the population means are not equal, that the differences demonstrated between control and experimental groups reflect the manipulation of the independent variable, as well as some random error. In other words, the research hypothesis states the investigator's prediction that there will be an association between the independent and dependent variables.

In our study of prosocial spending and happiness, the null and research hypotheses would be as follows:

$H_0$ (null hypothesis): The population mean for happiness in the *prosocial spending* group is *equal* to the population mean for happiness in the *personal spending* group.

$H_1$ (research hypothesis): The population mean for happiness in the *prosocial spending* group is *not equal* to the population mean for happiness in the *personal spending* group.

The notion of the null hypothesis may strike you as counterintuitive. Why, in essence, would you predict that your study would not work, that there would be no meaningful difference between the control and experimental groups, or that the independent variable will have no systematic effect on the dependent variable? There are two reasons why the null hypothesis is vital: First, it provides a precise statement—the population means are equal, and any observed differences are merely due to chance or normal variation. Second, it can be directly tested.

Note that the null hypothesis states that there is no difference between the means beyond what would be expected by normal variation—chance. The key term here is *normal variation*. How do we know what differences are simply due to normal variation? We do so by using inferential statistics to test the significance of the observed differences in the sample data. The extent to which an observed finding is merely due to normal variation can be determined by looking at the sampling distribution of a statistic.

As we have learned, when a result (such as a difference in means) is not likely due to chance, it is said to be statistically significant. Statistical significance is a function of where the obtained value or study result falls on the normal sampling distribution. This is measured in standard deviation units that are referred to as $z$ values and are provided in the $z$ table, which can be found in Appendix D as well as online (key search words: *normal distribution z-table*). In the normal sampling distribution, $z = 1$ standard deviation unit.

As shown in Exhibit 10.12, about 68% of the normal curve falls within $\pm 1$ standard deviation units ($z = 1$). About 95% of the normal curve falls within $\pm 1.96$ standard deviation units ($z = 1.96$), and about 99% of the normal curve falls within $\pm 2.58$ standard deviation units ($z = 2.58$). In testing for statistical significance, an obtained value that falls beyond $\pm 1.96$ standard deviation units is in an area of less than 5% of the normal curve (2.5% for each tail of the curve); this is considered unlikely due to chance. In statistical terms, the finding is statistically significant at the .05 level. This means that there is a 5% probability that the finding is due to chance (i.e., you are wrong!), and a 95% probability that the finding is reliable or statistically significant (i.e., you are right!).

It is conventional to reject null hypotheses only if we can be at least 95% confident that in doing so that the null hypothesis is truly false. But researchers who wish to be more confident before rejecting their null hypotheses will use the 99% or 99.9% level of confidence (corresponding to the .05, .01 and .001 "significance levels," respectively).

# The Dilemma of Type 1 and Type II Errors

Note that the researcher is faced with a decision: reject/accept the null hypothesis. In principle, inferential statistics allow *only* for the rejection/acceptance of a null hypothesis. However, recall from Chapter 6 that there is nothing in inferential statistics that directly tests the research hypothesis. That the null hypothesis is rejected does not necessarily lead to the automatic acceptance of the research hypothesis. The reason, simply stated, is that the null hypothesis could be rejected on the basis of a number of factors that might have nothing to do with the research hypothesis.

What, then, is a researcher to do? Recall from Chapter 2 the importance of design studies that allow for ruling out alternative explanations. This can be done by controlling for confounding factors. These are factors that might also influence the independent and dependent variable relationship, but through some extraneous, spurious process that is incidental to the theory being tested and evaluated. Also, state the research hypothesis as precisely as possible, such as the direction of the predicted group difference and the nature of the predicted relationship. As we have learned in factorial research designs, main and interaction effects can be statistically tested. A research hypothesis that is supported by a specifically predicted interaction effect is more difficult to attribute to extraneous, spurious factors.

As we know, because we are dealing with statistical probabilities rather than certainties, we can make one of two possible errors when testing the null hypothesis. A *Type I error* occurs when we reject the null hypothesis, but the null hypothesis is actually true. Here we decided that based on our sample statistics, the population means are not equal, but in fact they are. The statistical significance level indicates the chances of making a Type I error. A significance level of .05 means there is less than a 5% chance of making a Type I error, and a significance level of .01 means there is less than a 1% chance of making a Type I error. The significance level, also known as the alpha (signified by the Greek letter $\alpha$) level, indicates the probability of a Type I error.

*Type II error* occurs when we accept the null hypothesis as true when in fact it is false. You have mistakenly decided that the population means are equal when in fact they are not! Your failure to find statistically significant results means that you will conclude that your research hypothesis is unsupported. The probability of a Type II error, which is referred to as beta, $\beta$, is a function of three factors. First is the level of significance (Type I error) itself: Setting a very stringent significance level for making a Type I error increases the likelihood of making a Type II error. That is, if we make it very difficult to commit a Type I error of rejecting the null hypothesis of no difference, the likelihood of a Type II error of incorrectly accepting the null hypothesis must increase.

Second, the probability of committing a Type II error decreases with increasing sample size. Recall that another way to say this is that **statistical power** increases with larger sample size (see Chapter 6). A statistically underpowered study is one in which the probability of committing a Type II error is high. Third, effect size also influences the likelihood of committing a Type II error. Effect size is a measure of the magnitude of the effect of an independent variable on a dependent variable. Effect size differs from statistical significance, which indicates only the statistical probability that an observed finding is due to chance. An effect size indicates the magnitude of an observed finding, as for example how much improvement is associated with a significant treatment effect. In general, Type II error increases if the effect size is small. A small effect size is difficult to detect and therefore might result in our mistakenly accepting the null hypothesis (see also Chapter 6).

# *t* Test

Two of the most popular inferential statistics are used to test whether group means from a sample are statistically significant: (1) the *t* test for two groups and (2) the *F* test for more than two groups. The formulas for each require that you have the following information about the sample: sample size, means, and variance.

Each formula is a ratio: The numerator is simply the differences in group means, and the denominator is the total variance for the entire sample. Essentially, these numbers are plugged into a particular formula that generates a statistical value. The greater the obtained *t* value or *F* value, the less likely the obtained *t* value or *F* value is due to random variation and the more likely it is due to the effect of the independent variable.

The two-sample *t* test is commonly used to compare the means of two groups on a dependent variable measured using either an interval or a ratio scale. It provides a *t* statistic that has a known sampling distribution. The *t* test formula for equal-sized groups is as follows:

$$t = \frac{\bar{X}_1 - \bar{X}_2}{\sqrt{\dfrac{s_1^2}{N_1} + \dfrac{s_2^2}{N_2}}},$$

where $\bar{X}_1$ = mean of Sample 1, $\bar{X}_2$ = mean of Sample 2, $s_1^2$ = variance of Sample 1, $s_2^2$ = variance of Sample 2, and $N$ = total number of cases.

Thus, to calculate the value of the two-sample *t* test, divide the observed difference between the two group means by the total variation within each group (which is assumed to reflect error). This calculation provides a *t* statistic with an exact value. The value of *t* increases as the difference between the two group means increases. On the other hand, the more variation there is in the two samples, the smaller the value of *t*.

We must also take into account the **degrees of freedom**. Degrees of freedom (abbreviated as *df*) are determined on the basis of sample size. Degrees of freedom equal the total number of participants minus the number of groups.

One final piece of information needed pertains to the issue of a **one-tailed test** versus a **two-tailed test**. A one-tailed test is used when a research hypothesis specifies a direction of difference (e.g., the treatment group will perform better than the control group); otherwise, a two-tailed test is used. In practical terms, two-tailed tests are the convention for scientific publications in psychology.

The *t* value we calculate with our data can now be compared with a **critical *t* value** provided in the **Student's *t* table**. Exhibit 10.13 is an abbreviated *t* table of critical values for 5, 10, 18, and 20 degrees of freedom, an example provided by Lowry (2010). The full table of critical *t* values can be found in Appendix E. On each row, the numbers after the degrees of freedom indicate the critical value that +*t* or −*t* must equal or be greater than for the obtained result to be considered statistically significant. Each critical value is presented in the table columns for both one-tailed and two-tailed tests.

Exhibit 10.14 presents another example of a sampling distribution of *t* values with 18 degrees of freedom for one-tailed and two-tailed tests of significance, which is provided by Lowry (2010). Using a two-tailed test, the *t* value would have to equal or exceed +2.10 or −2.10 in order to be statistically significant at or beyond the .05 level. What this means is that when you obtain an absolute (unsigned) value of *t* equal to

**Exhibit 10.13** An Abbreviated *t* Table of Critical Values for 5, 10, 18, and 20 Degrees of Freedom (*df*)

| df | | Level of Significance | | | | |
|---|---|---|---|---|---|---|
| | One-tailed test | .05 | .025 | .01 | .005 | .0005 |
| | Two-tailed test | — | .05 | .02 | .01 | .001 |
| 5 | | 2.02 | 2.57 | 3.36 | 4.03 | 6.87 |
| 10 | | 1.81 | 2.23 | 2.76 | 3.17 | 4.59 |
| 18 | | 1.73 | 2.10 | 2.55 | 2.88 | 3.92 |
| 20 | | 1.72 | 2.09 | 2.53 | 2.85 | 3.85 |

or greater than 2.10, the result is statistically significant. And as you can also see in Exhibit 10.14, for a one-tailed test of significance, the obtained *t* statistic must be equal to or greater than +1.73 or −1.73 in order to be judged statistically significant at the .05 level.

| Exhibit 10.14 | Sampling Distribution of *t* Values With 18 Degrees of Freedom |
|---|---|

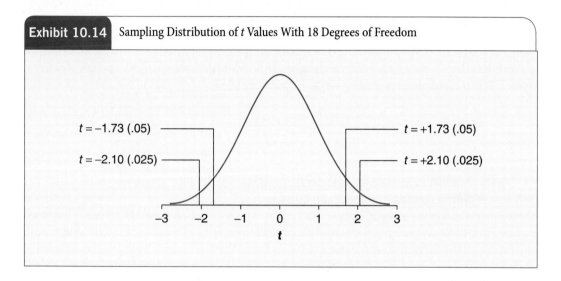

Now to return to our study and the pivotal question: Are happiness ratings for prosocial spending statistically or significantly different from those for personal spending? One way to address this question is to calculate a *paired t test* that compares pretest happiness and posttest happiness ratings for prosocial and personal spending groups. Prosocial spending had a mean happiness rating at pretest of 5.76 (standard deviation = 0.91) and at posttest of 7.10 (standard deviation = 0.87). A paired *t* test indicated that the pretest and posttest difference of 1.34 in happiness after prosocial spending achieved a very high level of statistical significance. This is reflected by a *t* value of −6.69, $df = 29$, $p < .001$. By contrast, a paired *t* test indicated that the pretest and posttest difference in happiness ratings for participants instructed to spend on themselves did not reach statistical significance, $t = .837$, $df = 29$, $p = .41$.

## Analysis of Variance

Whereas the *t* test is used to evaluate the results of an experiment with two groups, the analysis of variance (abbreviated ANOVA), also referred to as the *F* test, is used to evaluate the results of an experiment with more than two groups. As we learned in Chapter 6, researchers often have more than two groups in an experiment. For example, Merzenich and colleagues (Mahncke et al., 2006) compared three groups of research participants, some who received brain plasticity training, other participants who received an educational DVD, and still others who received no treatment (see Chapter 6). In this experimental design, Merzenich and colleagues had one factor or independent variable, which we can call treatment, with three levels or groups. To evaluate the results of an experiment such as the Merzenich study with more than two groups requires the ANOVA.

Following Elmes et al. (2006), we describe ANOVA as a set of *general* statistical procedures that can be applied to evaluate the results of findings generated from a much wider variety of experimental designs than the *t* test. The ANOVA comes in different flavors, so to speak, depending on the experimental design.

A **simple ANOVA** is used when one and only one factor is varied across more than two levels, such as in the Merzenich study of cognitive training. A simple ANOVA is also referred to as a **one-factor ANOVA**. However, as we learned in Chapters 7 and 8, experimenters often manipulate more than one factor or independent variable simultaneously. For these complex or multifactorial designs, the ANOVA is also appropriate, but this type of ANOVA is often referred to as a **multifactor ANOVA**. In comparison to the simple ANOVA, the multifactor ANOVA is much more computationally complex given that there are both main and interaction effects that need to be tested. The ANOVA formulas will also differ depending on whether a between-subjects or within-subjects design is used.

*Simple ANOVA.* The ANOVA procedure is essentially a comparison of variance estimates. As we learned earlier in this chapter, the variance of the population can be estimated from a particular sample of observations. That is, the formula for estimating variance presented earlier is

$$\sigma^2 = \frac{\sum (y_i - \bar{y}_i)^2}{N}.$$

The simple ANOVA calculates two independent estimates of variance. One measures the variability between the different groups—the greater the differences in the means of the different groups, the larger the estimate of variability between groups. This is referred to as the **between-groups variance**. It is based on how much the individual group means differ from the overall mean for all scores in the experiment; this overall mean is referred to as the *grand mean*. As the differences between each group mean and the grand mean increase, so too will the between-group variance. As you also recall from Chapter 7, for the simple ANOVA, the between-groups variance represents *systematic variance* due to the manipulation of the independent variable. Good experimental design seeks to maximize systematic variance by using powerful and effective independent variables that will distinguish the groups.

The other estimate of variance is the **within-groups variance**. The within-groups variance provides an estimate of how much the participants in each of the groups differ from one another. It reflects the deviation of the individual scores in each group from their respective group means. As you recall from Chapter 7, for the simple ANOVA, the within-groups variance is thought to represent in part *error variance*, which the researcher hopes to minimize through statistical control and experimental design features such as random assignment.

At the heart of calculating the ANOVA is the basic quantity known as **sums of squares**, which is shorthand for the *sum of squared deviations from the mean*. To understand sums of squares, we return to the above equation for estimating sample variance, $\sigma^2$. The sum of squares is the numerator in the above equation for estimating sample variance, $\sigma^2$. For the simple ANOVA, three sums of squares are important: First, the total sums of squares (SS Total) is the sum of squared deviations of each and every individual score from the grand mean, which is the mean of all scores in all groups in the study. Second is the sum of squares between groups (SS Between), which is the sum of squared deviations of the group means from the grand mean. Third is the sum of squares within groups (SS Within), which is the mean of the sum of squared deviations of the individual scores within groups, conditions, or level from their respective mean.

The formula for finding the total sums of squares is

$$\text{SS Total} = \sum \sum X^2 - \frac{T^2}{N}.$$

To calculate $\sum\sum X^2$ square each observation within each group, so $(X^2)$, and then sum together all these squared values, so $\sum X^2$. For the two summation signs, $\sum\sum$, one $\sum$ is for adding together the squared values within each group, and the other $\sum$ is for then adding together the $\sum X^2$ across the different groups. $T$ is the total for all observations, and $N$ is for total number of observations in the study.

The formula for finding the between-groups sums of squares is

$$\text{SS Between} = \frac{\Sigma(\Sigma X)^2}{n} - \frac{T^2}{N}.$$

First take the sum of values for each group, so ($\Sigma X$), next square the sum, so ($\Sigma X$)$^2$, and then divide by the number of observations on which it is based, so ($\Sigma X$)$^2$/$n$. For the second part of the formula, the $T^2$/$N$ term, $T$ is the total for all observations, and $N$ is the total number of observations in the study.

Finally, the sums of squares within groups is calculated by subtracting the value for SS Between from value for SS Total, so

$$\text{SS Within} = \text{SS Total} - \text{SS Between}.$$

Once you have calculated SS Between, SS Within, and SS Total, your next step is to compute the *mean squares* for between and within sums of squares. The mean square for the between sums of squares is calculated by dividing the value for the between sums of square by its corresponding degrees of freedom, which is simply the number of groups minus one. The mean square for the within sums of squares is calculated by dividing the value for the within sums of squares by its corresponding degrees of freedom, which is the number of groups multiplied by the number of observations per group minus 1. Each mean square provides an estimate of the population variance. The $F$ statistic is found by dividing the mean squares between by the mean squares within.

$$F = \frac{s_b^2}{s_w^2}$$

$$F = \frac{\text{Mean squares between}}{\text{Mean squares within}}$$

As with the $t$ statistic, this value is then compared with a critical $F$ value for particular degrees of freedom and level of statistical significance, usually set at a .05 level of probability. If the simple ANOVA yields an $F$ that exceeds the critical value that is provided in the critical values of the $F$ distribution table (see Appendix F), then the null hypothesis can be rejected. The ANOVA thus indicated that the groups differed significantly.

*Multifactor ANOVA.* We use the multifactor ANOVA when we have two or more independent variables within the same experiment. The simplest multifactor ANOVA is the 2 × 2 ANOVA, which is used for an experiment that simultaneously varies two factors each with two levels. As we know from Chapter 7, the advantage of the multifactor ANOVA is that the effects of all independent variables can be tested simultaneously. So instead of statically comparing each pair of conditions, levels, or groups, the multifactor ANOVA tests all of the effects simultaneously, thereby reducing the likelihood of chance findings. And as with the simple ANOVA, the multifactor ANOVA provides a statistical significance test ($F$ test) for each of the main effects of an experiment as well as their interactions. Thus, as we have just seen, like other statistical tests, the ANOVA/$F$ test allows us to determine whether each of these effects—main effects and interactions—are due to chance (see Appendix F).

For our purposes, returning to our study on spending and happiness, we have a 2 × 2 research design that allows us to test each of the two independent effects, spending and amount, as well as the interaction of the two. In other words, we want to know whether the spending effect differs as a function of the amount of money spent. Our dependent variable is the post-happiness rating score.

Our 2 × 2 ANOVA revealed a highly statistically significant main effect for type of spending (prosocial or personal). This is notated as follows: $F(1, 55) = 38.04$, $p < .001$. The (1, 55) is the degrees of freedom, and the 38.04 is the $F$ value. Like the $t$ value, the $F$ value increases as the difference between the means increases. The $p < .001$ indicates that the probability is less than one out of 1,000 that the effect of type of spending is due to chance. By contrast, the 2 × 2 ANOVA did not indicate a significant effect for amount of spending, since $F(1, 55) = .080$, $p = .779$. The telling value here is the $p$ value of 0.779, which means that there is about 78% probability that there is no true difference as a function of amount of money spent across personal and prosocial conditions. In addition, the interaction of spending and amount (signified as spending × amount) was not statistically significant: $F(1, 55) = .035$, $p = .852$.

In general, as we learned in Chapter 7, ANOVA results are examined by first evaluating the interaction of the independent variables and then looking at main effects of each independent variable. In our example, the two-way interaction of spending × amount was far from statistically significant. This indicated that happiness ratings did not vary as a function of whether the participants received either $5 or $20 for either prosocial or personal spending conditions. Likewise, the main effect of amount of money had no significant effect on happiness across both prosocial and personal spending conditions. However, the main effect of spending had a significant effect on happiness ratings across both money amounts. Regardless of whether participants received $5 or $20, they reported higher happiness ratings for prosocial spending than for personal spending.

## Chi-Square

The $t$ test and $F$ test are two of the inferential statistics that are most commonly used to test hypotheses in behavioral research, but they are by no means the only ones. Now that we have reviewed the basics of hypothesis testing, we will introduce two other popular statistics: chi-square ($\chi^2$) and Pearson's correlation coefficient ($r$). We will again present the formulas for each of these statistics.

Chi-square is most commonly used to test hypotheses involving two categorical variables whose relationship is displayed in a *contingency table* (also called a "crosstab" or a "percentage table"), which we had introduced in Chapter 5. Exhibit 10.15 displays a percentage table used in the 2006 *Science* article by Daniel Kahneman and his colleagues (p. 1908) about the relation between income and happiness.

To "read" the table, compare the percentages in each of the three happiness categories for the lowest income category (under $20,000) with the percentages in the next higher income category ($20,000–$49,999) and so on, continuing across the four columns of the table. Did the respondents tend to report more happiness the higher their family income?

Now let's focus on how the chi-square statistics is calculated with a contingency table. Recall the 13-item maximizer/satisficer questionnaire that we used in Chapter 2 to classify people as either

| Exhibit 10.15 | Self-Reported Global Happiness by Family Income | | |
|---|---|---|---|
| | *Percentage indicating global happiness at family income of* | | |
| *Response* | *Under $20,000* | *$20,000–$49,999* | *$50,000–$89,999* | *$90,000 and over* |
| Not too happy | 17.2 | 13.0 | 7.7 | 5.3 |
| Pretty happy | 60.5 | 56.8 | 50.3 | 51.8 |
| Very happy | 22.2 | 30.2 | 41.9 | 42.9 |

maximizers or satisficers. Let's imagine we want to test the hypothesis that the percentage of maximizers and satisficers differs between the young (18–35 years of age) and older (36–53 years of age) research participants.

The frequency data are presented in a 2 × 2 contingency table, with the young and older groups in the two rows and maximizers and satisficers along the two columns (see Exhibit 10.16). A contingency table presents frequencies or percentages for the dependent variable for all levels of an independent variable. For example, a 2 × 4 contingency table has two rows and four columns. The convention for notation is to present the number of rows and then the number of columns. It is called a contingency table because the idea is to test whether the numbers in the table are "contingent" or dependent on each other.

| Exhibit 10.16 | Determining the Value of Chi-Square (**Actual**/Expected Counts) | | |
|---|---|---|---|
| | *Age-Group* | | |
| | *Young* | *Older* | *Total* |
| Maximizers | **6**/4.5 | **3**/4.5 | **9** |
| Satisficers | **14**/15.5 | **17**/15.5 | **31** |
| Total | **20** | **20** | **40** |

As can be seen in Exhibit 10.16, for the young group, 6 of the 20 were classified as maximizers (30%) and 14 of the 20 as satisficers (70%); for the older group, 3 of the 20 were classified as maximizers (15%) and 17 of the 20 as satisficers (85%). While twice as many participants were classified as maximizers in the young group as in the older group, that alone does not indicate whether this group difference could have occurred by chance alone. Calculating the chi-square statistic allows us to determine the likelihood that we would have seen such a group difference when in the population we were sampling from there was actually no difference.

According to the null hypothesis, there would be no difference in maximization between the age-groups, meaning that these two variables are independent of each other. In this example, we would use the **two-variable chi-square** ($\chi^2$), also known as the **chi-square** ($\chi^2$) **test of independence**. Our two variables are age and maximizer/satisficer score, and our null hypothesis states that there is no relationship between age and percentages of maximizers/satisficers.

What would our table look like if the distribution of maximizer/satisficer scores was the same among young people as among old people? In this table, it would mean that for the 20 young people, the proportion who were maximizers would be 9/40—the same as for the overall distribution of maximizer/satisficer scores. The proportion of the 20 old people who were maximizers would be just the same: 9/40. The resulting four *expected frequencies* are in Exhibit 10.16 (for example, 4.5/20 is the same proportion as 9/40).

The formula for calculating the chi-square test of independence is as follows:

$$\chi^2 = \sum \frac{(O-E)^2}{E},$$

where $O$ is the observed frequency and $E$ is the expected frequency.

The degrees of freedom for the two-dimensional chi-square statistic is as follows:

$$df = (C-1)(R-1),$$

where $C$ is the number of columns or levels of the first variable and $R$ is the number of rows or levels of the second variable.

The greater the differences in frequencies between what is observed and what would be expected on the basis of chance, the larger the chi-square value and the less likely it is that the differences are due to chance. For our $2 \times 2$ table, the null hypothesis states that the expected frequencies for maximizers and satisficers should be the same for the young and the older groups. Statistical tables (see Appendix G) are available that provide the significance level of a chi-square value, taking into account the number of rows and columns in the table (the table's so-called degrees of freedom). Our present example (*using artificial data*) yielded a chi-square value of 1.29, with 1 degree of freedom, which is not statistically significant ($p > .05$). This lack of statistical significant level means that we fail to reject the null hypothesis that age and maximizers are independent with 95% confidence. The 15-percentage-point difference between young and old respondents in their distribution of maximization could thus have been due to chance. We cannot conclude that maximization and age are related.

## Correlation

The most commonly used statistic to measure the relationship between two quantitative variables is **Pearson's correlation coefficient, or *r***. The formula for computing the Pearson correlation coefficient is as follows:

$$r = \frac{\sum(X-\bar{X})(Y-\bar{Y})}{\sqrt{\sum(X-\bar{X})^2}\sqrt{\sum(Y-\bar{Y})^2}},$$

where $X$ = the score on one variable (the mean score has a bar over it), $Y$ = the score on the other variable, $\bar{Y}$ = mean, $\Sigma$ = sum, and $\sqrt{\phantom{x}}$ = square root.

We won't discuss the details of how to calculate the value of $r$ with this formula, but you can get an idea of how it works means from looking at just the numerator (the part of the formula above the horizontal line). The more the cases tend to have higher values of $X$ in relation to the mean value of $X$ at the same time as they have higher values of $Y$ in relation to the mean of $Y$, the higher the value of $r$ will be. When $r$ is high, we would say that $X$ tends to "covary" with $Y$. (If higher values of $X$ tend to be associated with lower values of $Y$, the value of $r$ would be negative, and we would say that they covary inversely with each other.)

You may recall that the correlation coefficient can vary from $-1.00$ through $.00$ to $+1.00$. The numerical value of the correlation indicates the strength of the relationship between the two variables—a larger number indicates a stronger relationship. The sign, whether positive or negative, indicates the direction of the relationship. A *positive* **correlation** indicates that as one variable increases, so too does the other. A *negative* correlation indicates that as one variable increases, the other decreases.

Kahneman et al. (2006, p. 1909) used Pearson correlations to assess the strength of the association between various respondent characteristics and three measures of happiness (Exhibit 10.17). You can see that household income was more related to life satisfaction ($r = .32$) than to the amount of the day the respondents said they were in a good mood ($r = .20$). The duration-weighted "happy" measure was not related to household income ($r = .06$) or to other respondent characteristics.

Kahneman et al. (2006, p. 1909) also reported the statistical significance of the correlation coefficients in Exhibit 10.17, using asterisks and footnotes. All the correlations in the first two columns were

| Exhibit 10.17 | Correlations Between Selected Life Circumstances and Subjective Well-Being Measures | | |
|---|---|---|---|
| Characteristic | Life Satisfaction | Amount of Day in Good Mood (%) | Duration-Weighted "Happy" |
| Household income | 0.32*** | 0.20*** | 0.06 |
| Married | 0.21*** | 0.15*** | 0.03 |
| Years of eduction | 0.16*** | 0.13*** | 0.03 |
| Employed | 0.14*** | 0.12** | 0.01 |
| Body mass index | −0.13*** | −0.08* | −0.06 |

$p$ values: $*p = .05$; $**p = .01$; $***p = .001$.

statistically significant at the $p < .05$ level; most were significant at the $p < .001$ level. None of the weak correlations in the last column were statistically significant; we cannot safely reject the likelihood that they were due to chance.

We know that our significant findings mean that we can reject the null hypothesis. And we can't emphasize enough the importance of rejecting the null hypothesis for only those findings that achieve statistical significance. The stringent level of significance required to reject the null hypothesis (at least .05) reminds us of the importance of not committing a Type I error. By the same token, however, when we must accept the null hypothesis because of statistically nonsignificant findings, we must consider the possibility of a Type II error. The problem, of course, is that our nonsignificant findings could be due to the limitations of the study design. For example, with a real data set, we might not have drawn a larger sample of students, so a significant correlation could not be achieved. The take-home message is that when we fail to reject the null hypothesis due to a nonsignificant finding, we have to recognize that this outcome could be due to limitations in our study design (of course, the same could be said when we obtain a statistically significant result).

# The Ethics of Statistics

We end this chapter by discussing some of the ethical issues that arise in reporting and analyzing data. As you recall from Chapter 3, the ethical principle most relevant to statistical analysis and reporting data is *integrity*, which is embodied in the APA Ethics Code, Standard 8.10b, *Reporting Research Results.*

Using statistics ethically means, first and foremost, being honest and open. Findings should be reported honestly, and researchers should be open about their thinking that guided their decisions to use particular statistics. Darrell Huff's (1954) little classic, *How to Lie With Statistics,* reminds us that it is possible to distort social reality with statistics, and it is unethical to do so knowingly, even when the error is due more to carelessness than to deceptive intent.

Summary or descriptive statistics can easily be used unethically, knowingly or not. When we summarize a distribution in a single number, even in two numbers, we are losing much information. Neither central tendency nor variation describes a distribution's overall shape. And taken separately, neither measure tells us about the other characteristic of the distribution (central tendency or variation). So reports using measures of central tendency should normally also include measures of variation. And we should also inspect the shape of any distribution for which we report descriptive statistics to ensure that the summary statistic does not mislead us (or anyone else) because of an unusual degree of skewness.

It is possible to mislead those who read statistical reports by choosing descriptive or summary statistics that accentuate a particular feature of a distribution. For example, imagine an unscrupulous realtor trying to convince a prospective home buyer in Community B that it is a community with very high property values when it actually has a positively skewed distribution of property values (see Exhibit 10.18). The realtor compares the mean price of homes in Community B with that for Community A (one with a homogeneous midpriced set of homes) and therefore makes Community B look pricier. In truth, the higher mean in Community B reflects a very skewed, lopsided distribution of property values—most residents own small, less pricey houses. A median would provide a better basis for comparison.

You can also easily see that an improperly constructed graph can distort the shape of a distribution. Recall how grouping data matter mightily. Whenever you need to group data in a frequency distribution or graph, you can reduce the potential for distortion by first looking at the entire data set, that is, the ungrouped distribution of raw numbers. You should then select a grouping procedure that does not distort the shape of the distribution of the original ungrouped set of raw numbers. When you create graphs, be

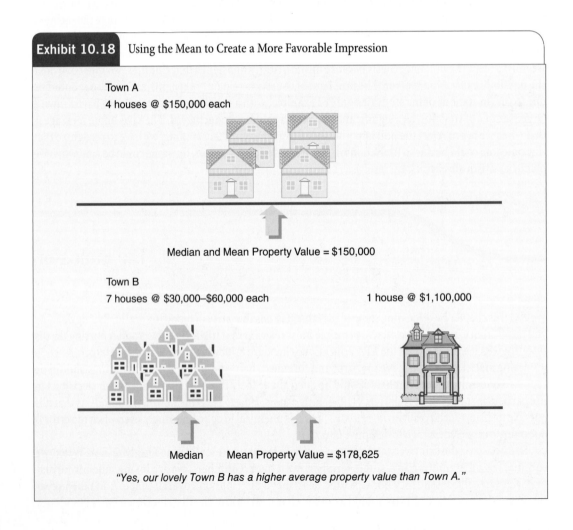

**Exhibit 10.18**   Using the Mean to Create a More Favorable Impression

Town A
4 houses @ $150,000 each

Median and Mean Property Value = $150,000

Town B
7 houses @ $30,000–$60,000 each          1 house @ $1,100,000

Median      Mean Property Value = $178,625

*"Yes, our lovely Town B has a higher average property value than Town A."*

sure to consider how the axes and their "tick" marks for grouping or scaling you choose may change the distribution's apparent shape.

Finally, when the data analyst begins to examine the relationships among variables in some real data, psychological research becomes most exciting. The moment of truth, it would seem, has arrived. Either the hypotheses are supported or they are not. But, in fact, this is also a time to proceed with caution and to evaluate the analyses of others with even more caution. This is especially true for large data sets, which often provide us with many opportunities to check out a great many relationships. Indeed, when relationships are examined among three or more variables at a time, the possibilities become almost endless.

However, this range of possibilities presents a great hazard for data analysis and for the accurate, truthful presentation of results. It becomes tempting to search around in the data until something emerges. Rejected hypotheses are forgotten in favor of highlighting what's going on in the data. It's not wrong to examine data for unanticipated relationships; the problem is that inevitably some relationships among variables will appear just on the basis of chance association alone. If you search hard and long enough, it will be possible to come up with something that really means nothing.

A reasonable balance, then, must be struck between deductive data analysis—inferential statistics to test hypotheses—and inductive analysis to explore the patterns in a data set. A priori hypotheses, meaning those formulated well in advance of data collection, must be tested as they were originally stated; any subsequently revised hypotheses are labeled post hoc (in Latin, "after this") and must be analyzed statistically using a more stringent level of significance. This adjustment in statistical significance is necessary to compensate for the increased probability of a Type I error that comes when exploring data and testing **post hoc hypotheses**. Unanticipated findings, often referred to as serendipitous results, need not be ignored and, in fact, can be very important discoveries, but they must be reported as a product of exploring post hoc hypotheses. Future researchers can try to test deductively, in the form of a priori hypotheses, serendipitous findings born of data exploration and post hoc statistical analyses.

# Conclusions

Statistics serve two important functions in research. First is to describe the distribution of scores on all variables of interest and the relations between some of those variables. Second, statistics are used to determine the likelihood that an observed finding is due to chance. Inferential statistics allow researchers to determine how confident they can be that a statistical description based on a random sample holds true in the population from which the sample was drawn. Inferential statistics also allow researchers to test the likelihood that a relationship between two (or more) variables occurred on the basis of chance.

To become proficient at using statistics, you will need to take a course devoted to statistics, with a textbook that is also focused on these techniques. If this appears to be an unsettling proposition, it may help you to know that the hard work of calculating statistics can be carried out easily with help of a statistical package. You can focus on understanding the meaning of statistics and leave the laborious calculations to a computer—as long as you spend some time learning about the calculations so that you understand what the statistics mean! If you are eager to start, we have provided on the study site of this book several tutorials that will help you learn how to use one of the most popular statistical packages: IBM SPSS (the Statistical Package for the Social Sciences; SPSS was acquired by IBM in October 2009).

# Key Terms

Between-groups variance
Bimodal
Central tendency
Chi-square ($\chi^2$) test of independence
Correlation
Critical *t* value
Degrees of freedom
*F* test
Mean
Median
Mode
Multifactor ANOVA

Normal distribution
One-factor ANOVA
One-tailed test
Outlier
Parameter
Pearson's correlation coefficient or *r*
Post hoc hypotheses
Probability average
Range
Research hypothesis
Simple ANOVA
Skewness

Standard error of the mean
Statistical power
Student's *t* table
Sums of squares
*t* test
Two-tailed test
Two-variable chi-square ($\chi^2$)
Unimodal
Variability
Variance
Within-groups variance

# Research in the News

1. The controversy around a major study of National Football League (NFL) retirees has prompted Congressional hearings. At issue is the design of the study, which examines concussions sustained while playing professional football and dementia in later life. In a piece in the *New York Times* (December 20, 2009), which nicely amplifies the meaning of statistical power, the reporter Alan Schwartz quoted Amy Borenstein, an epidemiologist testifying before the Congressional hearing, as saying, "The design suffers from a total lack of statistical power to detect an effect if one truly exists." Imagine that you have been hired to design a better study of NFL retirees, one that has sufficient statistical power to detect an effect, if one truly exists, between football concussions and later diagnosis of dementia. Explain statistical power and how you might design a better study. What would be an appropriate comparison group for NFL retirees?

2. In a piece appearing in the *Wall Street Journal*, April 24, 2007, "Shattering the Bell Curve," David A. Shaywitz reviews two books by Nassim Taleb, titled *Fooled by Randomness* (2001) and *The Black Swan* (2007). In both these books,

Taleb, Shaywitz writes, provides a provocative critique of the normal distribution, arguing in effect that most important things in life are not normally distributed. This, of course, runs counter to the central idea presented in this chapter that places the normal distribution front and center in any statistical testing of a hypothesis. Taleb, as Shaywitz describes, contends that

> Height follows the bell curve in its distribution. Wealth does not: It follows an asymmetric, L-shaped pattern known as a "power law," where most values are below average and a few far above. In the realm of the power law, rare and extreme events dominate the action.

Debate the pros and cons of the normal distribution versus the power law. How does the power law present a countervailing force to the normal distribution? Does the power law pose a threat to statistical reasoning in psychological research? What advantages/disadvantages do you see in normal distribution versus power law?

## STUDENT STUDY SITE

Please access the study site at **www.sagepub.com/nestor2e,** where you will find useful study materials such as mobile-friendly eFlashcards and mid-chapter and full chapter web quizzes for each chapter, along with carefully selected articles from research journals that illustrate the major concepts and techniques presented in the book.

## Activity Questions

1. You have two groups of research participants. One group ($n = 35$) receives SAT (Scholastic Assessment Test) coaching, and the other group ($n = 35$) does not. You want to compare actual SAT scores between the coached and uncoached groups.

   a. What is the scale of measurement of your dependent variable?

   b. What statistical test would you use to compare the two groups on SAT scores?

   c. What level of statistical significance would you use? What are the degrees of freedom, and what is the critical value?

   d. What is the null hypothesis, and what is the research hypothesis?

   e. What is the Type I error, and what is the Type II error?

   f. What is the probability of making a Type I error?

   g. What are some of the study confounds? What control variables would you recommend?

2. You want to examine the effects of age on scores on the maximizer/satisficer questionnaire. You have three age-groups: 20 young (ages 18–35 years), 20 middle-aged (50–65 years), and 20 old (66–80 years). You calculate the percentages of maximizers and satisficers for each age-group. You want to know whether the percentage of maximizers and satisficers differs for the three age-groups.

   a. What is the scale of measurement of your dependent variable?

   b. What statistical test would you use to compare the three age-groups?

   c. What level of statistical significance would you use? What are the degrees of freedom, and what is the critical value?

   d. What is the null hypothesis, and what is the research hypothesis?

   e. What is the Type I error, and what is the Type II error?

   f. What is the probability of making a Type I error?

   g. What is the best tabular format for presenting your data?

   h. What are some of the study confounds? What control variables would you recommend?

3. You want to examine the effects of age on scores on the maximizer/satisficer questionnaire. You collected a sample of 600 research participants that is composed of equal proportions of young (ages 18–35 years), middle-aged (50–65 years), and old (66–80 years) people. You want to know whether there is an association between age and score on the maximizer/satisficer questionnaire.

   a. What is the scale of measurement for age? What is the scale of measurement for the maximizer/satisficer questionnaire?

   b. What statistical test would you use to examine the association of age and maximizer/satisficer score?

   c. What level of statistical significance would you use? What are the degrees of freedom, and what is the critical value?

d. What is the null hypothesis, and what is the research hypothesis?

e. What is the Type I error, and what is the Type II error?

f. What is the probability of making a Type II error?

g. What are some of the study confounds? What control variables would you recommend?

4. Recall from Chapter 7 the Adams and Kleck (2003) study, which examined the processing of facial displays of emotions. In this study, research participants judged faces that varied in expression (anger/sad) and eye gaze (direct/averted). The study aimed to separate the influences of expression and eye gaze on reaction time for labeling faces as either sad or angry.

a. What is the scale of measurement for the dependent variable?

b. What are the independent variables, and how many levels are there for each independent variable?

c. What statistical test would you use? What are the main effects and the interaction effects?

d. What is the null hypothesis, and what is the research hypothesis?

e. What is the Type I error, and what is the Type II error?

f. What is the probability of making a Type I error?

g. What are some of the study confounds? What control variables would you recommend?

# Review Questions

1. Explain why "levels of measurement matter" in statistics.

2. Discuss the considerations that come into play in choosing the mean versus the median.

3. Discuss the relationship of statistical power to sample size and effect size.

4. What descriptive statistic is used for summarizing data measured using a nominal scale? Why?

5. What is the best descriptive statistic of central tendency for data measured using an ordinal scale? Why?

6. What are two popular types of graphic displays for frequency distributions? Describe them in relation to the level of measurement of the variables to be graphed.

7. What is the difference between a sample statistic and a population parameter? Why is this difference so important in statistical reasoning?

8. Discuss the difference between descriptive and inferential statistics.

9. What is the standard error? What does it measure, and why is it used?

10. How do you select a critical value for a statistic, such as a *t* test or an *F* test? What does a critical value for a statistic mean? Why is it important?

# Ethics in Action

1. *How to Lie With Statistics* is a small but classic book by Darrell Huff (1954) with a timeless and vital message for all researchers, which is echoed in the APA Ethics Code for reporting data accurately. How would you guard against distorting data in both graphic presentation and statistical description and analyses?

2. Actual falsification of data is fraudulent and always unethical. Unfortunately, when it does occur, it is always incalculably harmful to the research enterprise and abjectly deceitful to participants and to the public at large. It can involve completely fabricating data or omitting participant responses to skew the data. Why do you think cheating occurs in research, and how might teachers, courses, and textbooks (like this one) better address this ethical challenge?

3. Honest mistakes in reporting data can also occur. When these occur, the APA Ethics Code (Standard 8.10b, *Reporting Research Results*) states that researchers should take steps to correct the errors. Describe some honest mistakes that can occur in recording data and in using and reporting statistics. How might you safeguard against them?

# CHAPTER 11

# Qualitative Methods

## LEARNING OBJECTIVES: FAST FACTS

### Qualitative Methods

- Qualitative methods are most useful in exploring new issues, investigating hard-to-study groups, and determining the meaning people give to their lives and actions. They rely primarily on participant observation, intensive interviewing, and, in recent years, focus groups.

- Field researchers must develop strategies for entering the field, developing and maintaining relations in the field, and sampling, recording, and analyzing data. Selection of sites or other units to study may reflect an emphasis on typical cases, deviant cases, and/or critical cases that can provide more information than others. Sampling techniques commonly used within sites or in

*(Continued)*

(Continued)

selecting interviewees in field research include theoretical sampling, purposive sampling, snowball sampling, quota sampling, and, in special circumstances, random selection with the experience sampling method.

- Four ethical issues that should be given particular attention in field research concern (1) voluntary participation, (2) subject well-being, (3) identity disclosure, and (4) confidentiality.

## TESTING BEFORE LEARNING

Try your hand at these questions. Don't worry about not knowing the correct response, as you haven't read the chapter yet! But research shows that a pretest such as this can enhance learning (e.g., Kornell, Hays, & Bjork, 2009). So here is the answer. You come up with the question.

1. Emphasizes observations about natural behavior, attitudes, and artifacts that capture life as it is experienced by the participants rather than in categories predetermined by the researcher
   a. What are quantitative methods?
   b. What are qualitative methods?
   c. What is a saturation point?
   d. What are participant-observers?

2. This research develops ideas inductively, seeks to understand the social context and sequential nature of attitudes and actions, and explores the subjective meanings that participants attach to events.
   a. What is quantitative research?
   b. What is experimental research?
   c. What is survey research?
   d. What is qualitative research?

3. Open-ended, relatively unstructured questioning in which the interviewer seeks in-depth information on the interviewee's feelings, experiences, and perceptions
   a. What is qualitative interviewing?
   b. What is a focus group?
   c. What is participant observation?
   d. What is rapport?

4. A qualitative method for gathering data that involves developing a sustained relationship with people while they go about their normal activities
   a. What is qualitative interviewing?
   b. What is a focus group?
   c. What is participant observation?
   d. What is rapport?

5. A qualitative method that involves unstructured group interviews in which the focus group leader actively encourages discussion among participants on the topics of interest
   a. What is qualitative interviewing?
   b. What is a focus group?
   c. What is participant observation?
   d. What is rapport?

6. Primary means of recording participant observation data
   a. What are test scores?
   b. What are coded data?
   c. What are notes?
   d. What are reactive effects?

7. Always remember to evaluate how your actions in the setting and your purposes for being there may affect the actions of others and your own interpretations.
   a. What are saturation points?
   b. What are participant observations?
   c. What are field notes?
   d. What are reactive effects?

8. Memory joggers used for writing the actual field notes
   a. What are jottings?
   b. What are participant observations?
   c. What are field notes?
   d. What are systematic observations?

9. A qualitative focus group may identify issues to be included in a quantitative survey.
   a. What are participant-observers?
   b. What is a mixed method?
   c. What is a qualitative method?
   d. What is a quantitative method?

10. The goal is to establish an authentic, or credible, description of what was observed.
    a. What is qualitative data analysis?
    b. What is statistical significance?
    c. What is survey research?
    d. What is participant observation?

# When School and Family Commitments Conflict

*There is a nurse that asked me if I was still in school and I told her no . . . I have to help my mom for her to raise up this house and she told me that that was not my responsibility. That my responsibility was to be in school, not helping her. And I didn't like that because I know that it is my responsibility for the simple fact that [she] is my mother and she is the only person I have.*

—Sánchez, Esparza, Colón, & Davis, 2010, p. 870

"Maribel," the young woman who made these comments, worked full-time in a nursing home instead of going to college so that she could help her mother. Her coworker's statement that she shouldn't give her mother's needs priority over her own upset her. What would you say this is an example of? What is the basic issue or "theme" about orientation to higher education that this quote illustrates? Write your answer here:

_____. Don't worry; there is no single correct answer.

"Maribel" (a fictitious name) was one of 32 Latino young adults who were interviewed at length about their transition from high school. In many respects, there was nothing unusual about her comments—if you are familiar with the family orientations common in Latino culture. But because Maribel had given her consent to participate in a study of the educational orientations of young graduates of a Chicago high school, her comments were elicited by a trained interviewer, they were recorded and transcribed (after identifying information was removed), and they were analyzed by a research team. After this analysis was completed, the research team wrote up the results in an article that was published in the *Journal of Adolescent Research* (Sánchez et al., 2010). As a result, we can learn about educational orientations and transitions after high school from the comments of Maribel and the other young people who were interviewed.

For us, Maribel's statement also introduces qualitative methods, in which psychologists learn about human behavior by listening to people speak naturally or by observing their behavior in a natural setting. Her statement also reminds us that some aspects of human orientations and behaviors are ill suited to investigation with experiments or surveys. In this chapter, you will learn how Sánchez et al. (2010) and others used qualitative methods to illuminate the orientations and actions of young people and others going through transitional periods. You will also learn, from a variety of examples, that some of our greatest insights into human behavior can result from what appear to be very ordinary activities: listening, talking, participating, observing.

But qualitative research is much more than just doing what comes naturally. Qualitative researchers must question respondents strategically, observe keenly, take notes systematically, and prepare to spend more time and invest more of their whole selves in data collection than often occurs with experiments or surveys. So studying qualitative methods requires learning specific techniques that go beyond everyday practices. Moreover, you will learn how to review carefully each element of qualitative research designs so that you can estimate how much confidence you can have in the validity of conclusions based on qualitative methods.

The chapter begins with an overview of the major features of qualitative research as reflected in the research on educational orientations. The next section discusses the different ways of collecting qualitative data, ranging from intensive interviewing to observations and group discussions. We will use research on some other types of transitions to illustrate some of these techniques. We also discuss techniques for analyzing qualitative data. A special section focuses on ways that qualitative methods can be combined with quantitative methods so that research can benefit from the strengths of both. We conclude with a discussion of ethical issues in qualitative research. By the chapter's end, you should appreciate the hard work required to translate "doing what comes naturally" into systematic research, be able to recognize strong and weak points in qualitative studies, and be ready to do some of it yourself.

# Fundamentals of Qualitative Research

You have seen in the excerpt from Sánchez et al. (2010) that the "data" used in qualitative research can be ordinary speech. You will see in this chapter other examples of qualitative research in which the data are observations of human behavior as it occurs in a natural setting. More generally, qualitative methods involve "an interpretive, naturalistic approach to the world" in which things are studied "in their natural settings, attempting to make sense of, or interpret, phenomena in terms of the meanings people bring to them" (Denzin & Lincoln, 2005, p. 3). Attitudes are assessed by listening to people talk, not by requesting answers to a series of questions with fixed response choices. Behavior is observed as it happens, not based on responses to planned treatments delivered to randomly assigned groups.

There are many different types of qualitative methods, but we will begin by pointing out several common features that distinguish these methods from experimental and survey research designs (Denzin & Lincoln, 2000; Maxwell, 1996; Wolcott, 1995).

*Collection primarily of qualitative rather than quantitative data.* Any research design may collect both qualitative and quantitative data, but qualitative methods emphasize observations about natural behavior, attitudes, and artifacts that capture life as it is experienced by the participants rather than in categories predetermined by the researcher. As Sánchez et al. (2010) explained,

> A qualitative approach allowed us to examine the texture and nuances of the transition from high school in an understudied population. (p. 864)

*Exploratory research questions, with a commitment to inductive reasoning.* Qualitative researchers typically begin their projects seeking not to test preformulated hypotheses but to discover what people think, how they act, and why, in some setting. Only after many observations do qualitative researchers try to develop general principles to account for their observations (Levitt, Butler, & Hill, 2006). Sánchez et al. (2010) described the rationale for their exploratory approach after reviewing the relevant research literature.

> Research reveals mixed findings concerning the effects of multiple responsibilities on individuals' pursuit and performance in college . . . the literature has not parceled out the influence of family obligation attitudes and SES on Latino youth's decisions, adoption of multiple responsibilities, and pathways toward adulthood. (p. 863)

*A focus on previously unstudied processes and unanticipated phenomena.* Previously unstudied attitudes and actions can't adequately be understood with a structured set of questions or within a highly controlled experiment. So qualitative methods have their greatest appeal when we need to explore new issues, investigate hard-to-study groups, or determine the meaning people give to their lives and actions.

Of course, this does not mean that qualitative research should or must begin with a completely blank slate. As Brinegar, Salvi, Stiles, and Greenberg (2006) explained, theory guided their analysis of psychotherapy experiences,

> The theory is not considered a rigid treatise to be voted up or down in light of supporting or disconfirming evidence. Rather, theory is a flexible (permeable) account that was constructed as a way of understanding previous observations and now must be elaborated, extended, qualified, and modified to encompass the observations at hand. (p. 165)

*A focus on human subjectivity, on the meanings that participants attach to events and that people give to their lives.* Unlike quantitative methods, in which the researcher attempts to measure attitudes and behavior "objectively" with standardized instruments, the qualitative researcher tries to learn how people make sense of what is happening to them. In their qualitative research about the transition of urban, low-income Latinos from high school, Sánchez and her coauthors (2010) define their approach as "phenomenological,"

> which involves capturing the meaning of the lived experiences of several individuals about a particular phenomenon (Reitz, 1999)... in-depth interviews with individuals who have lived the phenomenon of interest to explore their everyday lived experiences. (p. 864)

*Reflexive research design, in which the design develops as the research progresses.* Qualitative research is sensitive to how "the activity of studying something will always change it, will affect it" (Banister, Burman, Parker, Taylor, & Tindall, 1994, p. 14). Each component of the design may need to be reconsidered or modified in response to new developments or to changes in some other component. (Maxwell, 1996). The reflexive feature of qualitative methods appeared in the way that Sánchez and her colleagues (2010) approached the analysis of their in-depth interviews.

> The interview protocol was revised as data were collected and analyzed to ensure that we came as close as possible to the phenomena of interest. (p. 867)

*Sensitivity to the researcher's subjectivity.* Many qualitative researchers question the possibility of achieving an objective perspective on human behavior—coming to conclusions about the data that any psychologist would see as valid—and instead focus attention on how their own backgrounds might influence their observations. Sarah Knox, Alan W. Burkard, Adanna J. Johnson, Lisa A. Suzuki, and Joseph G. Ponterotto (2003) explain how they "explored their potential biases and expectations" prior to interviewing African American and European American therapists about their experiences of addressing race in research on psychotherapy:

> Two researchers indicated that they had been supervised by someone of a different race than their own. . . . In terms of personal experiences, three authors stated that the time they spent living in a culturally diverse area had affected them. . . . When discussing their approach to or experience of addressing race in therapy, one researcher indicated having had only positive experiences with addressing race. . . . One researcher was struggling with whether she should address race with clients of her same racial background. (p. 468)

What do these fundamental features of qualitative methods add up to? When these features are specified and combined in different ways, they provide a rich array of useful techniques for investigating human behavior. These qualitative techniques can be used as supplements or as alternatives to experimental or survey designs when investigations focus on previously unstudied issues, on how people interpret their experiences, or on the broader social context of behavior. Qualitative methods may be the only reasonable choice for some people or settings where controlled designs and systematic measures are not feasible.

# Methods for Collecting Qualitative Data

There are several distinctive approaches to collecting qualitative data. We will focus on three of them: **qualitative interviewing, participant observation**, and **focus groups**. Participant observation and intensive interviewing are often used in the same project; focus groups are a unique data collection strategy that combines some elements of these two approaches.

*Qualitative interviewing:* A qualitative method that involves open-ended, relatively unstructured questioning in which the interviewer seeks in-depth information on the interviewee's feelings, experiences, and perceptions (Lofland & Lofland, 1984).

*Participant observation:* A qualitative method for gathering data that involves developing a sustained relationship with people while they go about their normal activities.

*Focus groups:* A qualitative method that involves unstructured group interviews in which the focus group leader actively encourages discussion among participants on the topics of interest.

# Qualitative Interviewing

Qualitative interviewing is used to find out about people's experiences, thoughts, and feelings, often with a goal of understanding how they make sense of their experiences. Qualitative interviewing can be used by itself or combined with the participant observation approach that you will learn about next (Wolcott, 1995).

Unlike the more structured interviewing that may be used in survey research (discussed in Chapter 5), qualitative interviewing relies on open-ended questions. Rather than asking standard questions in a fixed order, qualitative interviewers may allow the specific content and order of questions to vary from one interviewee to another. Rather than presenting fixed responses, qualitative interviewers expect respondents to answer questions in their own words (Banister et al., 1994).

What distinguishes qualitative interviewing from less planned forms of questioning is consistency and thoroughness. For example, Levitt et al. (2006) used qualitative interviews "as one path through which researchers can develop understandings of this interpersonal process of change [in psychotherapy]" (p. 314). The researchers' description of their 1.5-hour interviews captures the logic of intensive interviewing:

The main questions asked clients to describe whatever was significant or important to them about their general psychotherapy, specific psychotherapy moments, and therapeutic relationship. Additional probes were used to further clarify the meanings in their responses. . . . Interview questions were designed to promote discussion in a nonleading manner. (Levitt et al., 2006, p. 315)

So qualitative interviewing engages researchers more actively with subjects than standard survey research does. The researchers must listen to lengthy explanations, ask follow-up questions tailored to the preceding answers, and seek to learn about interrelated belief systems or personal approaches to things rather than measure a limited set of variables. As a result, qualitative interviews are often much longer than standardized interviews, sometimes as long as 15 hours, conducted in several different sessions. The qualitative interview becomes more like a conversation between partners than an interview between a researcher and a subject (Kaufman, 1986). Some call it "a conversation with a purpose" (Rossman & Rallis, 1998).

The qualitative interview follows a preplanned outline of topics. It may begin with a few simple questions that gather background information while building rapport. These are often followed by a few general **"grand tour" questions** that are meant to elicit lengthy narratives (Miller & Crabtree, 1999). Some projects may use semistructured interviews with a standard set of questions asked in a predefined order, particularly when the focus is on developing knowledge about prior events, standard processes, or some narrowly defined topic. But more exploratory projects, particularly those aiming to learn about interviewees' interpretations of the world, may let each interview flow in a unique direction in response to the interviewee's experiences and interests (Kvale, 1996; Rubin & Rubin, 1995; Wolcott, 1995). In either case, qualitative interviewers must adapt nimbly throughout the interview, paying attention to nonverbal cues, expressions with symbolic value, and the ebb and flow of the interviewee's feelings and interests. "You have to be free to follow your data where they lead" (Rubin & Rubin, 1995, p. 64).

A few of the early questions from the interview schedule of Sánchez et al. (2010) provide a good example of the flow of a qualitative interview, from general questions to those more focused on the topic of concern, with probes to encourage respondents to go into some depth about their feelings and experiences.

A. *Introductory questions: I am going to start by asking you, generally, about your life.*

1. How do you define yourself, ethnically? OR If someone were to ask you, what would you say your race or ethnicity is?

2. Can you tell me about what you are doing now in your life (e.g., going to school, working, volunteering)? (*inquire about job responsibilities, job title, major, etc.*)

   a. Are you involved in any extracurricular activities (could be on-campus or outside of school, e.g., church activities)?

   b. What is your typical day like (ask everyone, including those who "aren't doing anything")?

3. Where are you living (e.g., living at home, living independently)?

   a. Who are you living with (make sure they tell you who every individual is)?

B. *Pretransition influences: Now I am going to ask you about influences and experiences in high school that led you to where you are now.*

1. Tell me about what your experiences were like at Kelvyn Park?

   a. What kind of student were you?

   b. What was it like being a student there?

   c. In what kind of academic track were you? (*regular, remedial, honors*)

    d. Were you involved in extracurricular activities? If so, which activities?

    e. How did you feel about your high school?

    f. Did you enjoy being a student there? Why or why not?

2. How do you make decisions in general? (e.g., Do you mostly rely on feelings? Do you think decisions through slowly and carefully? Do you decide quickly and jump in? Do you talk to a lot of other people before deciding?)

## Selecting Interviewees

Random selection is rarely used to select respondents for intensive interviews, but the selection method must still be considered carefully. Sánchez et al. (2010) recruited students for their interview project from classes that were included in a larger survey of seniors at a high school. The methods section of their article includes a careful description of their selection procedures.

> A total of 150 students participated in the survey, and they were asked if they were interested in a follow-up interview that focused on their transition from high school. Eighty (53%) participants indicated an interest and were asked to provide their contact information. In March 2004 [one year later] we attempted to contact all 80 participants. However, 22 (28%) of these participants' phone numbers were disconnected, 16 (20%) participants were unable to be reached, 5 (6%) declined to be interviewed, 1 (1%) was ineligible because he was still in high school and 3 (4%) did not provide phone numbers. We scheduled appointments with 33 participants who were interested. One participant's interview was excluded from their study because she was African American and our focus was on Latinos. Thus the remaining 32 interview transcripts were analyzed for this study. (p. 867)

When interviews are planned with members of a population defined by some special experiences or knowledge, researchers should try to select interviewees who are knowledgeable about the subject of the interview, who are open to talking, and who represent the range of perspectives (Rubin & Rubin, 1995). Grossman, Sorsoli, and Kia-Keating (2006) explained their screening procedures for interviews with men who had been abused as children:

> Participants were recruited through letters written to clinicians in the community and by posted flyers seeking resilient men with histories of childhood sexual abuse. . . . Brief telephone screenings were conducted to ascertain whether participants had a history of childhood sexual abuse that met the criteria of being perpetrated by a member of the immediate or extended family. . . . Participants were also screened for resiliency; specifically . . . if they had never been sexually abusive to anyone and were functioning well. (p. 435)

Selection of new interviewees should continue, if possible, at least until the **saturation point** is reached, the point when new interviews seem to yield little additional information (so some call it the "point of redundancy") (see Exhibit 11.1). As new issues are uncovered, additional interviewees may be selected to represent different opinions about these issues.

Whatever the selection process used, it must be carefully described and its limitations noted when the research is reported. Sánchez and colleagues (2010) included the following acknowledgment of possible sampling bias in their article:

> A limitation of this study is sampling bias given that we were unable to reach everyone who indicated an interest in participating in the interviews. Those who participated in this study are

likely to be those living in more stable households compared to those who were not reached due to change of address or disconnected phone numbers. Therefore, this sample may not represent individuals from a greater range of disadvantaged situations. Despite the sampling bias, study participants do reflect a range of paths following high school, including college, work, and those not attending college and unemployed. (p. 880)

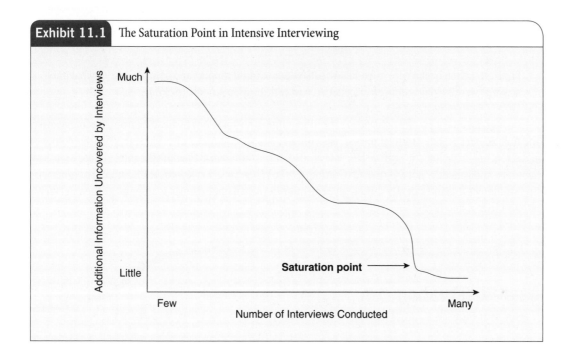

**Exhibit 11.1**  The Saturation Point in Intensive Interviewing

## Asking Questions and Recording Answers

Qualitative interviewers must plan their main questions around an outline of the interview topic. For example, the semistructured interview protocol used by Sánchez and her colleagues (2010, p. 867) included four main sections:

1. Present status

2. Role of various participants in decision making about post–high school plans

3. Adjustment to life after high school

4. Aspirations and expectations for their future

The questions should generally be short and to the point. More details can then be elicited through nondirective probes (e.g., "Can you tell me more about that?" or "uh-huh," echoing the respondent's comment, or just maintaining a moment of silence). Follow-up questions can then be tailored to answer the main questions.

Tape recorders are commonly used to record intensive and focus group interviews. Most researchers who have tape recorded interviews feel that they do not inhibit most interviewees and, in fact, are routinely ignored. The occasional respondent is very concerned with his or her public image and may therefore speak "for the tape recorder," but such individuals are unlikely to speak frankly in any research interview. In any case, constant note taking during an interview prevents adequate displays of interest and appreciation by the interviewer and hinders the degree of concentration that results in the best interviews.

## Developing Rapport

In the first few minutes of the interview, the goal is to show interest in the interviewee and to explain clearly what the purpose of the interview is (Kvale, 1996). Sánchez and her coauthors (2010) explained how they used the start of their interviews to build rapport:

> The first section began with introductory questions to build rapport and gain of sense of what participants were currently doing (e.g., whether are working or in school). (p. 867)

During the interview, the interviewer should maintain an appropriate distance from the interviewee, one that doesn't violate cultural norms; the interviewer should maintain eye contact and not engage in distracting behavior. An appropriate pace is also important; pause to allow the interviewee to reflect, elaborate, and generally not feel rushed (Gordon, 1992). When an interview covers emotional or otherwise stressful topics, the interviewer should give the interviewee an opportunity to unwind at the interview's end (Rubin & Rubin, 1995).

# Participant Observation

Participant observation is a qualitative method in which natural social processes are studied as they happen (in "the field" rather than in the laboratory) and are left relatively undisturbed. It is the seminal qualitative research method—a means for observing human behavior as the research subjects experience it, in its totality, and for understanding subjects' interpretations of their behavior and that of others (Wolcott, 1995). By observing people and interacting with them in the course of their normal activities, **participant-observers** seek to avoid the artificiality of experimental designs and the unnatural structured questioning of survey research (Koegel, 1987). This method encourages consideration of the context in which human behavior occurs, of the complex and interconnected nature of interpersonal relations, and of the sequencing of events (Bogdewic, 1999).

Based on this description, you can understand why participant observation was the method used to study the process of change among homeless persons diagnosed with severe mental illness who had transitioned from living in shelters to living in group homes in the Boston McKinney Project (Schutt, 2011). This project was funded by the National Institute of Mental Health in 1990 to test the value for homeless mentally ill persons living in group homes or independent apartments. The research design included random assignment to group or independent living (after an initial screen for eligibility and safety) and standard measures that were administered to subjects.

The group homes that the principal investigator Stephen M. Goldfinger, MD; one of the authors of this book (R.K.S.), and several other coinvestigators developed for this study were different from the traditional group homes used by most mental health agencies (Schutt, 2011). The McKinney group homes were termed *Evolving Consumer Households*, and they were supposed to shift from staff management to resident control over the 1.5-year study period. But how would this occur?

We knew that the development of consumer-managed collective households was a sufficiently novel and unprecedented approach that we could not guarantee that all Evolving Consumer Households would move systematically and uniformly toward the goal of independence and tenant control. Studying the process of housing evolution of each of these "micro-cultures" became the responsibility of a team of three anthropologists. Each ethnographer spent several days per week speaking with and observing tenants and staff in at least two group households. (Goldfinger et al., 1997, pp. 34–35)

The first concern of every participant-observer is to decide what balance to strike between observing and participating. This decision must take into account the specifics of the situation being studied, the researcher's own background and personality, the larger sociopolitical context, and ethical concerns. Consider the "mix" of participating and observing in the Boston McKinney Project's group homes:

Data collection consisted principally of participant observation, the hallmark of the anthropological method. Participant observation involves spending time with people in their own settings, talking with them about their lives, and following events as they develop over time. In this instance, it involved both attending formal events and joining in more informal activities, such as grocery shopping, sports, walks, card games, watching TV, cooking, or just "hanging out." Informal interviews with residents and staff were also part of the data collection process. (Ware, 1999, p. 5)

The balance of participating and observing that is most appropriate also changes, often many times, during most projects. In public settings involving other people, in which observing while standing or sitting does not attract attention, your activities as an observer may be no different from those of others who are simply observing others to pass the time. However, when you take notes, when you systematically check out the different areas of a public space or different people in a crowd, when you arrive and leave at particular times, you are acting differently in important respects than others in the setting. If you observe in this way in a public place, you should always remember to evaluate how your actions in the setting and your purposes for being there may affect the actions of others and your own interpretations.

This is the problem of **reactive effects**. It is not "natural" in most social situations for someone to be present who will record her or his observations for research and publication purposes, and so individuals may alter their behavior. The observer is even more likely to have an impact when the social setting involves few people or if observing is unlike the usual activities in the setting. Observable differences between the observer and those being observed also increase the likelihood of reactive effects. A McKinney ethnographer (unpublished notes) described how she tried to overcome her "unusual" status in a group home:

I finally try to explain who I am and what I'm doing there. I allude to the fact that everyone has been "very polite," and not asked, but that they must have been wondering. I say that I am an anthropologist. [A resident asks] "What's that?" [I say] That's someone who studies social processes, and my job here is to study this experiment that we're all involved in together and try to explain what works and doesn't work and why . . . by being with people and talking to people.

Observers in the Boston McKinney Project (unpublished notes) visited each group home for several hours each week and so did not simply "blend" into the setting as if they were residents.

[A resident] tried to explain further who I was to [another]. "She's not staff, she just comes and visits us there—she's with the housing project."

Most **field researchers** adopt a role that involves some active participation in the setting. Usually, they participate in enough group activities to develop rapport with members and to gain a direct sense of what group members experience. Notes from the medical anthropology team in the Boston McKinney Project (Schutt, 2011) provide a good example of the rapport-building function of participation. On different occasions, over the 18 months that they observed in a particular house, a team member might play cards with house residents, help out in the yard, walk or even drive to a store, or meet for lunch or a local show. Such active participation in resident activities often led to more feelings of trust and to lengthy conversations about a range of issues. As a McKinney ethnographer noted, after being introduced by a resident to a staff member:

> There have been a lot of indications recently from various tenants of my acceptance on the "inside," but this one definitely felt the nicest.

But being a participant as well as an observer inevitably creates some boundary issues: Participants in the setting can simply forget about the researcher's role and the researcher can start to function simply as a participant. McKinney observers were at times asked by residents for cash, offered food, solicited for advice, and considered as possible romantic partners.

Experienced participant-observers try to lessen some of the resulting problems by evaluating both their effect on others in the setting and the effect of others on their observations. Participant-observers write about these effects throughout the time they are in the field and while they analyze their data. They also try to preserve some physical space and regular time when they can concentrate on their research, and they schedule occasional meetings with other researchers to review the fieldwork. The McKinney observers often commented on these issues in their notes:

> I think I overreacted, because I was so pleased with the way that things had worked out at the meeting and I could not have left [the resident this ethnographer was talking to] thinking that it was otherwise.... I showed him the minutes.... I felt like I had gone too far.

## Entering the Field

Entering the field, the setting under investigation, is a critical stage in a participant observation project because it can shape many subsequent experiences. Researchers must learn in advance how participants dress and what their typical activities are so as to avoid being caught completely unprepared. Finding a participant who can make introductions is often critical (Rossman & Rallis, 1998), and formal permission may be needed in an organizational setting (Bogdewic, 1999). It can take weeks or even months until entry is possible.

In the following **field notes**, one McKinney ethnographer describes how two of them introduced themselves to staff at a meeting:

> I started in with a brief description of our responsibilities: ... We were going to hang out and take notes and help out and sometimes do formal interviews in order to get an overall sense of how this group home was another stage in the unfolding of treatment programs for the mentally ill and the homeless in MA.... Except for situations of danger or self-destruction, we weren't there to judge anyone's performance but simply to record how everyone worked together to make the program a success. We also mentioned that if anyone felt uncomfortable with anything we were doing to please discuss it.... There were quite a few questions on the nature of anthropology and our role and "what, specifically, we are looking for." [We] talked about how looking for specifics would be biasing ... about us trying to treat the house as a different culture, to try to make sense of what we

all normally take for granted as normal and ordinary. . . . We left, with many assurances of how glad they were to meet with us and how they were looking forward to seeing us again. I remember warm smiles and enthusiastic goodbyes.

## Managing Relationships

Researchers must be careful to manage their relationships in the research setting so they can continue to observe and interview diverse members of the social setting throughout the long period typical of participant observation (Maxwell, 1996). Every action the researcher takes can develop or undermine this relationship. Interaction early in the research process is particularly sensitive, because participants don't know the researcher, and the researcher doesn't know the routines. You can sense the tension in a McKinney ethnographer's note about comments directed to her by a staff member who had just criticized some other staff who had just left:

> [Referring to the ethnographer] . . . don't put that down! On second thought, maybe you should!! No, really, go ahead. They gotta find out somehow!

As the observers established rapport with house residents, interaction became more natural.

Experienced participant-observers have developed some sound advice for others seeking to maintain relationships in the field (Bogdewic, 1999; Rossman & Rallis, 1998; Whyte, 1955; Wolcott, 1995):

- Develop a plausible (and honest) explanation for yourself and your study.

- Maintain the support of key individuals in groups or organizations under study.

- Be unobtrusive and unassuming. Don't "show off" your expertise.

- Don't be too aggressive in questioning others (e.g., don't violate implicit norms that preclude discussion of illegal activity with outsiders). Being a researcher requires that you do not simultaneously try to be the guardian of law and order. Instead, be a reflective listener.

- Ask very sensitive questions only of informants with whom your relationship is good.

- Be self-revealing, but only up to a point. Let participants learn about you as a person, but without making too much of yourself.

- Don't fake your social similarity with your subjects. Taking a friendly interest in them should be an adequate basis for developing trust.

- Avoid giving or receiving monetary or other tangible gifts but without violating norms of reciprocity. You can't be a participant-observer without occasionally helping others, but you will lose your ability to function as a researcher if you come to be seen as someone who gives away money or other favors.

- Be prepared for special difficulties and tensions if multiple groups are involved. It is hard to avoid taking sides or being used in situations of intergroup conflict.

## Taking Notes

Notes are the primary means of recording participant observation data (Emerson, Fretz, & Shaw, 1995). It is almost always a mistake to try to take comprehensive notes while engaged in the field—the process of writing extensively is just too disruptive. The usual procedure is to jot down brief notes about highlights of the observation period. These brief notes (called **jottings**) can then serve as memory joggers when writing the actual field notes at a later session. It will also help maintain a daily log and to record in it each day's activities (Bogdewic, 1999). With the aid of the jottings and some practice, researchers usually remember a great deal of what happened—as long as the comprehensive field notes are written immediately afterward, or at least within the next 24 hours, and before they have been discussed with anyone else.

Although there is no fixed formula to guide note taking, observers try to identify the who, what, when, where, why, and how of activities in the setting. Their observations will usually become more focused over time as the observer develops a sense of the important categories of people and activities and gradually develops a theory that accounts for what is observed (Bogdewic, 1999). Banister et al. (1994) suggest writing notes to address each of the following issues:

1. *Describe the context*, including the physical setting.

2. *Describe the participants*, including potentially important variables, such as age, gender, and clothing.

3. *Describe who the observer is*, including links to the context being observed.

4. *Describe the actions of participants*, including both verbal and nonverbal behavior and action sequences.

5. *Consider alternative interpretations of the situation*, including giving some rationale for them.

6. *Explore your feelings in being an observer*, including your experience of the observation.

Usually, writing up notes takes much longer—at least three times longer—than observing does. Field notes must be as complete, detailed, and true as possible to what was observed and heard. Direct quotes should be distinguished clearly from paraphrased quotes, and both should be set off from the researcher's observations and reflections. Pauses and interruptions should be indicated. The surrounding context should receive as much attention as possible, and a map of the setting always should be included, with indications of where individuals were at different times.

Careful note taking yields a big payoff. On page after page, field notes will suggest new concepts, causal connections, and theoretical propositions. Social processes and settings can be described in rich detail, with ample illustrations. Exhibit 11.2 contains field notes recorded by Norma Ware, the lead anthropologist studying group homes in the Boston McKinney Project (Schutt, 2011). The notes contain observations of the setting, the questions the anthropologist asked, the answers she received, and her analytic thoughts about one of the residents. What can be learned from just this one page of field notes? The mood of the house at this time is evident, with joking, casual conversation, and close friendships. We see how a few questions and a private conversation provide the foundation for a more complete picture of one resident, describing "Jim's" relationships with others, his personal history, his interests and personality, and his orientation to the future. We can see analytic concepts emerge in the notes, such as the concept of "pulling himself together." You can imagine how researchers can go on to develop a theoretical framework for understanding the setting and a set of concepts and questions to inform subsequent observations.

Complete field notes must provide even more than a record of what was observed or heard. Notes also should include descriptions of the methodology: where the researchers were standing or sitting while they observed, how they chose people for conversation or observation, what counts of people or events they made and why. Sprinkled throughout the notes also should be a record of the researchers' feelings and thoughts while observing: when they were disgusted by some statement or act, when they felt threatened or intimidated, why their attention shifted from one group to another, and what ethical concerns arose. Notes like these provide a foundation for later review of the likelihood of bias or of inattention to some salient features of the situation.

```
┌─────────────────────────────────────────────────────────────────────────┐
```

**Exhibit 11.2**    Field Notes From an Evolving Consumer Household (ECH)

I arrive around 4:30 p.m. and walk into a conversation between Jim and somebody else as to what color jeans he should buy. There is quite a lot of joking going on between Jim and Susan.
. . .
     I return to the living room and sit down on the couch with Jim and Susan. Susan teases Jim and he jokes back. Susan is eating a T.V. dinner with M & M's for dessert. There is joking about working off the calories from the M & M's by doing sit-ups, which she proceeds to demonstrate. This leads to a conversation about exercise during which Jim declares his intention to get back into exercise by doing sports, like basketball.

     Jim seems to have his mind on pulling himself together, which he characterizes as "getting my old self back." When I ask him what he's been doing since I saw him last, he says, "Working on my appearance." And in fact, he has had a haircut, a shave, and washed his clothes. When I ask him what his old self was like, he says, "You mean before I lost everything?" I learn that he used to work two jobs, had "a family" and was into "religion." This seems to have been when he was quite young, around eighteen. He tells me he was on the street for 7–8 years, from 1978–1985, drinking the whole time. I ask him whether he thinks living at [the ECH] will help him to get his "old self back" and he says that it will "help motivate me." I observe that he seems pretty motivated already. He says yes, "but this will motivate me more."

     Jim has a warm personality, likes to joke and laugh. He also speaks up—in meetings he is among the first to say what he thinks and he talks among the most. His "team" relationship with Bill is also important to him—"me and Bill, we work together."

Notes may, in some situations, be supplemented by still pictures, videotapes, and printed material circulated or posted in the research setting. Such visual material can bring an entirely differently qualitative dimension into the analysis and call attention to some features of the social situation and actors within it that were missed in the notes (Grady, 1996). Commentary on this material can be integrated with the written notes (Bogdewic, 1999).

## Managing the Personal Dimensions

Our overview of participant observation would not be complete without considering its personal dimensions. Because field researchers become a part of the social situation they are studying, they cannot help but be affected on a personal, emotional level. At the same time, those being studied react to researchers not just as researchers but as personal acquaintances—often as friends, sometimes as personal rivals. Managing and learning from this personal side of field research is an important part of any project.

    The impact of personal issues varies with the depth of researchers' involvement in the setting. The more involved researchers are in multiple aspects of the ongoing social situation, the more important personal issues become, and the greater the risk of "going native." In a moment of intense interaction, a McKinney ethnographer reported giving some advice to a staff member:

[She] asked [a resident] and I what she should do. I told her that it probably should be up to [another resident] to make sure he takes his meds sometime in the evening.

    There is no formula for successfully managing the personal dimension of field research. It is much more art than science and flows more from the researcher's own personality and natural approach to other people than from formal training.

If you plan a field research project, follow these guidelines (Whyte, 1955):

- Take the time to consider how you want to relate to your potential subjects as people.

- Speculate about what personal problems might arise and how you will respond to them.

- Keep in touch with other researchers and personal friends outside the research setting.

- Maintain standards of conduct that make you comfortable as a person and that respect the integrity of your subjects.

When you evaluate participant-observers' reports, pay attention to how they defined their role in the setting and dealt with personal problems. Don't place too much confidence in such research unless the report provides this information. The primary strengths of participant observation—learning about the social world from the participants' perspectives, as they experience it, and minimizing the distortion of these perspectives by the methods used to measure them—should not blind us to its primary weaknesses—the lack of consistency in the data collected, particularly when different observers are used, and the many opportunities for direct influence of the researchers perspective on what is observed. Whenever we consider using the method of participant observation, we also must realize that the need to focus so much attention on each setting studied will severely restrict the possible number of settings or people we can study.

# Systematic Observation

Observations can be made in a more systematic, quantitative design that allows systematic comparisons and more confident generalizations. A researcher using **systematic observation** develops a standard form on which to record variation within the observed setting in terms of variables of interest. Such variables might include the frequency of some behavior(s), the particular people observed, the weather or other environmental conditions, and the number and state of repair of physical structures. In some systematic observation studies, records will be obtained from a random sample of places or times.

Antonio Pascual-Leone and Leslie S. Greenberg (2007) used a systematic observation strategy to investigate emotional processing in experiential therapy. Therapy clients gave their informed consent, and their therapy sessions were videotaped. The researchers reviewed a total of 102 sessions, rated each one with their Classification of Affective-Meaning States (CAMS) form, and identified 34 sessions in which clients exhibited global distress. These sessions were then coded systematically.

Ratings began with a confirmation of the preselected global distress marker, which served as the rater's first code. Using the CAMS, the rater then coded emotion event continuously for the presence of any one of the given possible emotion codes. Raters were instructed to make codes as they saw them unfold sequentially and indicated the time at which they initiated a change in code. . . . Raters using the Experiencing Scale were operationally independent from raters using the CAMS. High experiencing in the last 15% of each event was used as an indicator of good within-session outcome. (Pascual-Leone & Greenberg, 2007, p. 881)

The systematic observations give us greater confidence in the measurement of emotional processing than we would have based on unstructured descriptive reports by observers or self-reports by patients to survey questions. However, for some purposes, it might be more important to know how emotional the patient felt during the therapy session, so interviews or perhaps just general observational reports on the videotaped sessions might be preferred.

## 🔲 Focus Groups

Focus groups are groups of unrelated people that are formed by a researcher and then led in group discussion of a topic for 1 to 2 hours. The researcher asks specific questions and guides the discussion to ensure that group members address these questions, but the resulting information is qualitative and relatively unstructured. Focus groups do not involve representative samples; instead, individuals are recruited who have the time to participate, have some knowledge pertinent to the focus group topic, and share key characteristics with the target population.

Test your knowledge of this chapter so far by taking the mid-chapter quiz on the study site: www.sagepub.com/nestor2e

Yalda Uhls and Patricia Greenfield (2011) at the University of California, Los Angeles, used focus groups to explore the way in which media exposure was related to the future aspirations of preadolescents:

> Focus group methodology explored whether preadolescent children (a) perceive a relationship between the value of fame and popular TV programs, (b) connect fame and future aspirations, (c) relate social networking sites to the fame motive, and (d) use YouTube or other platforms for posting videos as tools for achieving fame. Because this was new territory, a qualitative in-depth method was chosen to begin exploring these issues. (p. 317)

Most focus groups involve 5 to 10 people, a number that facilitates discussion by all in attendance (Krueger & Casey, 2009, p. 6). Participants usually do not know one another, although some studies in organized settings may include friends or coworkers. Opinions differ on the value of using homogeneous versus heterogeneous participants. Homogeneous groups may be more convivial and willing to share feelings, but heterogeneous groups may stimulate more ideas (Brown, 1999, pp. 115–117). In any case, it is important to avoid having some participants who have supervisory or other forms of authority over other participants (Krueger & Casey, 2009, p. 22).

Uhls and Greenfield's (2011) focus group study began with recruitment of 20 children (9 girls and 11 boys) between 10 and 12 years old, each of whom participated in one small same-sex group (see Exhibit 11.3). Each child had to bring a signed parental consent form that explained the research before the child could participate; the children also had to sign a consent form.

Focus group moderators must begin the discussion by creating the expectation that all will participate and that the researcher will not favor any particular perspective or participant. It is not a good idea to use focus groups when dealing with emotionally charged issues, when sensitive information is needed and when confidentiality cannot be ensured, or when the goal is to reach consensus (Krueger & Casey, 2009, p. 20). All questions should be clear, simple, and straightforward. The moderator should begin with easy-to-answer general factual questions and then, about one quarter to halfway through the allotted time, shift to key questions on specific issues. In some cases, discussion may be stimulated by asking participants to make a list of concerns or experiences, to rate predefined items, or to choose among alternatives.

| Exhibit 11.3 | Characteristics of Focus Group Participants |
|---|---|

*Gender, Number, Age, Ethnic Composition, and First-Choice Values of Each Focus Group*

| Group | Gender | N | Age and grade | Ethnicity | First-choice value[a] |
|---|---|---|---|---|---|
| I. Elementary school | Female | 4 | Three 10-yr-olds (4th grade), one 11-yr-old (5th grade) | Two European Americans, two Latinos | Fame (2) |
| | | | | | Benevolence |
| | | | | | Community feeling |
| II. Elementary school | Male | 4 | Three 10-yr-olds (4th grade), one 11-yr-old (5th grade) | Three European Americans, one Latino | Fame |
| | | | | | Achievement |
| | | | | | Benevolence |
| | | | | | Have a lot of fun[b] |
| III. Middle school | Female | 5 | Three 11-yr-olds, two 12-yr-olds (all 6th grade) | Four European Americans, one Middle-Eastern American | Fame (2) |
| | | | | | Community feeling |
| | | | | | Kindness[c] |
| | | | | | Achievement |
| IV. Middle school | Male | 4 | Three 11-yr-olds, one 12-yr-old (all 6th grade) | One European American, one African American, two Asian Americans | Fame (2) |
| | | | | | Benevolence |
| | | | | | Achievement |
| V. Middle school | Male | 3 | One 11-yr-old, two 12-yr-olds (all 6th grade) | Three European Americans | Fame |
| | | | | | Financial success |
| | | | | | Kindness[c] |

*Note:* When more than one child selected the same first-choice value in a group, the numeral in parentheses represents the number who selected that value. yr = year.

a. Because the "votes" on values were anonymous, first-choice values cannot be lined back to particular participants.

b. One child produced this response, even though it was not in the list of seven values.

c. The focus group leader defined benevolence using the word *kindness*. Two of the children used this word on their slips of paper; these responses were aggregated with "benevolence."

Although the researcher, or group moderator, uses an interview guide, the dynamics of group discussion often require changes in the order and manner in which different topics are addressed (Brown, 1999). If the question flow is successful, the participants should experience the focus group as an engaging and friendly discussion, and the moderator should spend more time after the introductory period listening and guiding the discussion than asking questions. The moderator may conclude the group discussion by asking participants for recommendations to policymakers or their further thoughts that have not had a chance to express (Krueger & Casey, 2009, pp. 36–48). The issue of impact of interviewer style and questioning on intensive interview findings, which was discussed in the previous section, also must be considered when evaluating the results of focus groups.

In their study of preadolescents, Uhls and Greenfield (2011) conducted their focus groups in a classroom after school. The moderator, the research assistants, and the children all sat on chairs in a circle. They selected a video from one of three and watched its first 5 minutes. Then, they

> discussed their interpretation of the themes and characters. After this discussion, the moderator wrote on the whiteboard the children's ideas about how they felt one might prepare for the kinds of activities in which the characters participated. The discussion flowed in a more open direction for the next 5–10 min. (p. 318)

No formal procedure exists for determining the generalizability of focus group answers, but the careful researcher should conduct at least several focus groups on the same topic and check for consistency in the findings. Some focus group experts advise on conducting enough focus groups to reach the point of "saturation," when an additional focus group adds little new information to that which already has been generated (Brown, 1999). In any case, it is always important to consider how recruitment procedures have shaped the generalizability of focus group findings. Uhls and Greenfield (2011) also took into account the unique location of their focus group study.

> We cannot conclude that our findings are representative of American youth: Besides being small, our sample was in Los Angeles, a city in which fame is more apparent, given that it is home to many Hollywood stars and studios. Because trends beginning in media-saturated Los Angeles subsequently go national . . . , the logical next step is to conduct a survey with a large sample of preadolescents in diverse socioeconomic and geographical settings. (p. 320)

Focus group methods share with other field research techniques an emphasis on discovering unanticipated findings and exploring hidden meanings. They can be an indispensable aid for developing hypotheses and survey questions, for investigating the meaning of survey results, and for quickly assessing the range of opinion about an issue.

> Focus groups provided an in-depth portrait of preadolescents' interpretations of fame portrayed in favourite programs and their use of interactive media tools to search for an audience for themselves. (Uhls & Greenfield, 2011, p. 324)

## 🖻 Mixed Methods

In simplest terms, mixed methods combine the strengths of different approaches to improve a research investigation. There are different ways of combining methods (Creswell, Plano Clark, Gutmann, & Hanson, 2008). Often, some qualitative methods are combined with some quantitative methods, but particular types of qualitative or quantitative methods can also be "mixed" (Tashakkori & Teddlie, 2003). For example, a qualitative focus group may identify issues to be included in a quantitative survey. Alternatively, a quantitative experimental study may be followed by qualitative interviews that explore the process by which a treatment had an effect. Some mixed-methods designs may have a dominant method, with supplementary methods used to focus attention on some specific questions. For example, Stanley Milgram supplemented his experiment on obedience to authority with qualitative observations about participants' subjective reactions to the experimental treatment (see Chapter 3). Other mixed-methods designs may give equal attention to different methods.

Cresswell (2010) popularized a simple notational system for distinguishing different ways of mixing quantitative and qualitative methods. This system distinguishes the priority given to one method over the other and the sequence in which they are used in a research project. For example,

- QUAL + QUAN: equal importance of the two approaches and their concurrent use

- QUAL → quan: sequenced use, with qualitative methods given priority

- QUAN(qual): qualitative methods embedded within a primarily quantitative project

Uhls and Greenfield's (2011) study of preadolescents' aspirations used mixed methods in a design that Cresswell's system would characterize as QUAL(quan)—a qualitative project that had some quantitative methods embedded within it. The quantitative data consisted of children's ratings of life goals, which were collected just before each focus group began.

Deborah Gioia and John S. Brekke (2009) used mixed methods to investigate the impact of neurocognition on daily living in the community for individuals with schizophrenia. It is an important question for behavioral scientists, since there is a very large gap between the sophistication of neurocognitive tests and the limited knowledge about how, or whether, performance on cognitive tests is related to community functioning. They used a QUAN + QUAL strategy.

The mixed-methods study began with the selection of 10 individuals with schizophrenia and who had been scored as high or low in neuropsychological functioning based on tests administered to a large sample. Gioia then spent 3 to 5 hours on each of 3 days with each of these 10 individuals. She observed them as they engaged in community activities such as shopping, managing money, or ordering a meal in a restaurant. Gioia wrote detailed field notes after each observational session and then categorized the behavioral strategies of each person as "rote," "instrumental," "facilitative social," or "independent social." Exhibit 11.4 includes the definition of one category—"rote tasks"—and some of the information provided about a participant who exemplified this behavioral strategy.

Among their 10 participants, Gioia and Brekke (2009) found that differences in observed functioning paralleled neuropsychological scores: "The low NP group showed a restricted range of rote and instrumental behavior, with rote behavior predominant in the ratings" (p. 102). Although their conclusions can only be tentative due to the limited size of their sample, Gioia and Brekke's research helps give us more confidence

| **Exhibit 11.4** | Definition of Rote Behavioral Strategy | |
|---|---|---|
| *Task* | *Definition* | *Participant Example* |
| Rote tasks | Tasks that are generally purposeful and productive, but are done repeatedly in a repetitive or scripted fashion—folding clothes, putting away groceries, cleaning, sweeping—and are often directed by others. | RL is a single white male is [sic] his 50s living in supported housing. He does not work or attend school and is most comfortable doing assigned chores. He sweeps the courtyard daily, helps with lifting and unloading supplies. He is seen by the staff as dependable and helpful. He does not venture beyond these daily tasks and sometimes needs reminders. RL keeps a box with every receipt and check-stub from his social security checks dating back at least a decade. . . . |

in the generalizability of neuropsychological tests to community functioning. A behavioral researcher should always consider whether data of another type should be collected in research designed with a single method in mind and whether additional research using different methods is needed before a research question can be answered with sufficient confidence. The ability to apply diverse techniques to address different aspects of a complex research question is one mark of a sophisticated behavioral researcher.

# Qualitative Data Analysis

The focus on text—on qualitative data rather than on numbers—is the most important feature of qualitative analysis. The "text" that qualitative researchers analyze is most often transcripts of interviews or notes from participant observation sessions, but text can also refer to pictures or other images that the researcher examines. Qualitative data analysts often seek to describe their textual data in ways that capture the setting or people who produced this text on their own terms rather than in terms of predefined measures and hypotheses. In this way, qualitative data analysis tends to be inductive: The analyst identifies important categories in the data, as well as patterns and relationships, through a process of discovery. There are often no predefined measures or hypotheses.

Good qualitative data analyses are also distinguished by their focus on the interrelated aspects of the setting, group, or person under investigation—the case—rather than breaking the whole into separate parts. The whole is always understood to be greater than the sum of its parts, and so the social context of events, thoughts, and actions becomes essential for interpretation. Within this framework, it doesn't really make sense to focus on two variables out of an interacting set of influences and test the relationship between just those two.

Qualitative data analysis is an iterative and reflexive process that begins as data are being collected rather than after data collection has ceased (Stake, 1995). Next to his or her field notes or interview transcripts, the qualitative analyst jots down ideas about the meaning of the text and how it might relate to other issues. This process of reading through the data and interpreting them continues throughout the project. The analyst adjusts the data collection process itself when it begins to appear that additional concepts need to be investigated or new relationships explored.

## Documentation

The data for a qualitative study most often are notes jotted down in the field or during an interview—from which the original comments, observations, and feelings are reconstructed—or text transcribed from audiotapes. What to do with all this material? Many field research projects have slowed to a halt because a novice researcher becomes overwhelmed by the quantity of information that has been collected. A 1-hour interview can generate 20 to 25 pages of single-spaced text (Kvale, 1996).

The first formal analytical step is documentation. The various contacts, interviews, written documents, and whatever it is that preserves a record of what happened all need to be saved and listed. Documentation is critical to qualitative research for several reasons: It is essential for keeping track of what will be a rapidly growing volume of notes, tapes, and documents; it provides a way of developing an outline for the analytic process; and it encourages ongoing conceptualizing and strategizing about the text. You can see in Exhibit 11.5 how Grossman et al. (2006) documented their interviews in their study of victims of sexual abuse.

| Exhibit 11.5 | | Reported Perpetrators and Approximate Age Range Over Which Sexual Abuse Occurred |
|---|---|---|
| *Participant* | *Approximate age range* | *Perpetrators* |
| Earl | 7–13 | uncle, male friend of father's |
| Brad | 4–12 | older sister, female babysitter, male stranger |
| Ron | 4–10 | grandfather, older brother |
| Morgan | 2–11 | mother, older brother |
| Will | 2–13 | stepfather, older sister, other men and women in group |
| Paul | 4–6 | grandfather |
| Martín | 7–8 | school principal and wife |
| Uhan | 5–7 | female babysitter, male neighbor |
| Malcolm | 7 | sister |
| Burt | 2–13 | father, mother, male church camp director, other men |
| Web | 2–14 | father, mother |
| Bill | 2–17 | mother, older sister, older foster sister, male boarder, female babysitter |
| Amhad | 11–12 | Big brother |
| Christos | 3–15 | uncle, male and female cousins, older neighborhood boy, older male and female children of friends of mother |
| Tomas | 7–10 | adult male cousin |
| Alejandro | 4–15 | two uncles |

## Conceptualizing, Coding, and Categorizing

Identifying and refining important concepts is a key part of the iterative process of qualitative research. The goal is to establish an authentic, or credible, description of what was observed. The process is very inductive, with codes emerging from careful reading of the interview transcripts or observation notes. Careful attention to developing codes that identify instances of the same attitude or behavior and then categorizing observations with these codes is an important step in achieving this goal, with multiple participants cross-checking their codes to maximize reliability.

Sánchez and her collaborators (2010) provide a detailed description of the process:

The research team members individually coded interviews and met weekly to discuss the development of codes. During this stage, we allowed new codes to emerge from the data, the definitions of codes were revised, redundant codes were collapsed or discarded, and subcategories of codes were developed.... Once a solid code list was generated, we conducted the second phase of analysis. This phase consisted of a team of four coders who alternated in pairs, with each pair coding two transcripts individually per week. The pairs met weekly to discuss the coded transcripts and to resolve any discrepancies and inconsistencies in coding. Any discrepancies that could not be resolved by the pair were discussed by the larger groups until they were resolved. The discussions with the larger group also allowed us to conduct cross-case analyses to determine the similarities and differences across interview transcripts regarding the relevant themes. (p. 868)

This process of creating codes led to the identification of three major themes into which the text could be classified.

*The role of family obligation attitudes in decision making and behaviors.* For example,

My father passed away so, he left us with a house to pay and bills like crazy so . . . since I'm coming from Mexico . . . Mexico is still very conservative so since my father is away, I am the man of the house okay. (p. 870)

*Juggling multiple responsibilities during the transition from high school.* As an example,

When [my brother] was born, [my parents] worked odd hours. We had a family business, my dad worked there. My mom, she would work a lot of . . . double shifts and they were 8 hours, . . . So, when my brother was born, I . . . would be the one getting up in the middle of the night to feed him, to change his diaper. (p. 873)

*The transition from high school as stressful.*

Work takes me away from studying and doing my homework 'cause I get home late and I do paperwork. I take my work home, doing paperwork and stuff. (p. 876)

Grossman and her colleagues (2006) provide an example of a more detailed categorization scheme that emerged in their qualitative study of male survivors of child abuse (Exhibit 11.6).

**Exhibit 11.6**  Categories of Meaning Making

| Type of Meaning Making | Narrative Example |
|---|---|
| Meaning making through actions | |
| Altruistic behaviors | "Certain kids when I was in school, I'd defend them if I could. Like, if they were kind of outcast, I was like 'I know how that feels.' So I would try to help them out." |
| Creative expressions | "Create characters. Fantasize. That was the safe space." |
| Meaning making by developing cognitive frameworks | |
| Finding ways to understand the abuser's psychology | "He was gang-raped when he was about 6 years old. When he would abuse me, it was a replication of what had happened to him." |
| Finding ways to understand the role of the self | "I blamed my neediness for what got me into the situation." |

*(Continued)*

(Continued)

| Type of Meaning Making | Narrative Example |
|---|---|
| Using a socio-cultural framework | "Many women of that generation had none of their needs met. . . . There she is in the suburbs; she's supposed to be a housewife. The women were forced to be like that at that time. It was a horrible mess." |
| Developing a philosophical view | "When I was 4 or 5, I was convinced that there was another world below where we were [where] things would be much better for me." |
| Meaning making through spirituality | "I've been forgiven for a lot of things that I've done in my life. And because of that, there is really nothing that anyone does to me that I shouldn't be able to forgive. So whatever my sister has done, whatever anyone has done to me, it all pales in comparison to what I've done to God, from a religious viewpoint." |

Researchers should check their coding with others to establish reliability. Analytic insights are tested against new observations, the initial statement of problems and concepts is refined, the researcher then collects more data, interacts with the data again, and the process continues. The process of coding and categorizing that Sánchez et al. (2010) used (above) provides a good example.

## Examining Relationships and Displaying Data

Examining relationships is the centerpiece of the analytic process, because it allows the researcher to move from simple description of the people and settings to explanations of why things happened as they did it with those people in that setting. For example, Sánchez et al. (2010) found that family and work obligations led to stress for youth transitioning from high school.

> It's really tough. I usually try to spend my mornings with my sister, or nighttimes we'll watch TV together. I try to spend some time on Saturday with my father. . . . And then church, . . . school, I can't miss it. (p. 875)

Financial responsibilities also created stress.

> Just paying for everything. I want to go shopping. I want to go out more, but it's like I know I have to save up the money for next semester and then when next semester comes up, I have to save up for next semester. (p. 877)

The process of examining relationships can be captured in a **matrix** that shows how different concepts are connected or perhaps what causes are linked with what effects. Exhibit 11.7 displays a matrix used by Knox et al. (2003) to capture the relationship between therapists' race and the way that they discussed race in a cross-racial dyad.

| Exhibit 11.7 | Domains, Categories, and Frequencies of Therapists' Discussion of a Specific Cross-Racial Dyad: Discussing Race Had Positive Effect | | |
|---|---|---|---|
| *Domain* | *Category* | *Frequency: AA* | *Frequency: EA* |
| 1. When therapists addressed race | Early in therapy | Variant | Typical |
| | Middle of therapy | Variant | Variant |
| 2. Why therapists addressed race | Perceived discomfort in client | Typical | Variant |
| | Because client raised race | Variant | Variant |
| | Because client struggled with personal vs. community expectations | — | Variant |
| 3. Therapists' comfort addressing race | Felt comfortable | Typical | Variant |
| | Felt discomfort | — | Typical |
| 4. How therapists addressed race | Directly (e.g., questions, confrontations) | Typical | Typical |
| | Followed client's lead | Variant | Variant |
| 5. Perceived effect of addressing race | Positive | General | General |
| | Increased trust/security m relationship | Typical | Typical |

AA = African American: EA = European American: dashes indicate that the category did not emerge for these participants.

## Authenticating Conclusions

No set standards exist for evaluating the validity or "authenticity" of conclusions in a qualitative study, but the need to consider carefully the evidence and methods on which conclusions are based is just as great as with other types of research. Individual items of information can be assessed in terms of at least three criteria (Becker, 1958):

- *How credible was the informant?* Were statements made by someone with whom the researcher had a relationship of trust or by someone the researcher had just met? Did the informant have reason to lie? If the statements do not seem to be trustworthy as indicators of actual events, can they at least be used to help understand the informant's perspective?

- *Were statements made in response to the researcher's questions, or were they spontaneous?* Spontaneous statements are more likely to indicate what would have been said had the researcher not been present.

- *How does the presence or absence of the researcher or the researcher's informant influence the actions and statements of other group members?* Reactivity to being observed can never be ruled out as a possible explanation for some directly observed social phenomenon. However, if the researcher carefully compares what the informant says goes on when the researcher is not present, what the researcher observes directly, and what other group members say about their normal practices, the extent of reactivity can be assessed to some extent. Confidence in the conclusions from a field research study is also strengthened by an honest and informative account about how the researcher interacted with subjects in the field, what problems he or she encountered, and how these problems were or were not resolved.

Sánchez et al. (2010) extended the process of authenticating their conclusions by involving some of their participants and also by cross-checking decisions across the research team:

Credibility was enhanced through the use of member checking, triangulation, and peer debriefing. Member checking involved sharing findings with 4 participants after data collection and analysis to ensure participants' perspectives and experiences were captured accurately. Triangulation in this study involved cross-checking data by using multiple investigators throughout data collection and analyses. We conducted peer debriefing by discussing findings with two researchers outside our research team. (p. 868)

## STAT CORNER

### Computer-Assisted Qualitative Data Analysis

The analysis process can be enhanced in various ways by using a computer. Programs designed for qualitative data can speed up the analysis process, make it easier for researchers to experiment with different codes, test different hypotheses about relationships, and facilitate diagrams of emerging theories and preparation of research reports (Coffey & Atkinson, 1996; Richards & Richards, 1994). The steps involved in computer-assisted qualitative data analysis parallel those used traditionally to analyze text, such as notes, documents, or interview transcripts: preparation, coding, analyzing, and reporting. We use QSR International's NVivo to illustrate these steps; it is one of the most popular programs and was used by Sánchez et al. (2010).

> ***Computer-assisted qualitative data analysis*** *uses special computer software to assist qualitative analyses through creating, applying, and refining categories; tracing linkages between concepts; and making comparisons between cases and events.*

Text preparation begins with typing or scanning text in a word processor or, with NVivo, directly into the program's rich text editor. Computer-assisted qualitative data analysis programs also allow other types of files, including pictures and videos. Coding the text involves categorizing particular text segments, and each program allows you to assign a code to any segment of text (in NVivo, you drag through the characters to select them). You can make up codes as you go through a document and also assign codes that you have already developed to text segments. Exhibit 11.8 shows the screen that appears in NVivo at the coding stage, when a particular text segment is assigned a code. NVivo also lets you examine the coded text "in context"—embedded in its place in the original document.

| Exhibit 11.8 | NVivo Coding Stage |
|---|---|

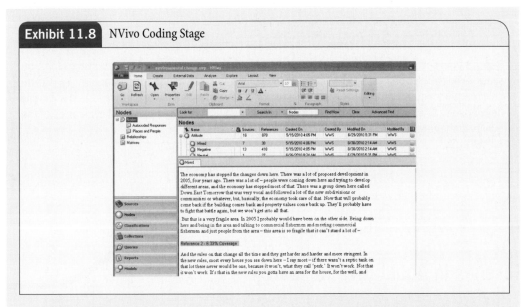

In qualitative data analysis, coding is not a one-time-only or one-code-only procedure. Each program allows you to be inductive and holistic in your coding: You can revise codes as you go along, assign multiple codes to text segments, and link your own comments ("memos") to text segments. You can work "live" with the coded text to alter coding or create new, more subtle categories. You can also place hyperlinks to other documents in the project or any multimedia files outside it.

Analysis focuses on reviewing cases or text segments with similar codes and examining relationships among different codes. You may decide to combine codes into larger concepts. You may specify additional codes to capture more fully the variation among cases. You can test hypotheses about relationships among codes and develop more free-form models (see Exhibit 11.9). You can specify combinations of codes that identify cases that you want to examine.

| Exhibit 11.9 | A Free-Form Model in NVivo |
|---|---|

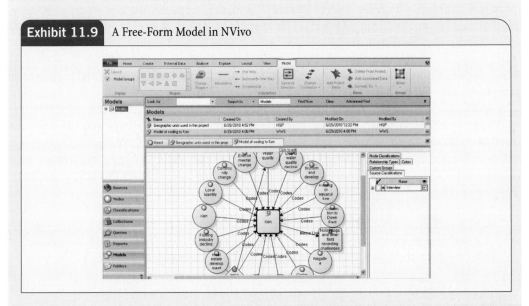

*(Continued)*

(Continued)

Reports from each program can include text to illustrate the cases, codes, and relationships that you specify. You can also generate counts of code frequencies and then import these counts into a statistical program for quantitative analysis. However, the many types of analyses and reports that can be developed with qualitative analysis software do not lessen the need for a careful evaluation of the quality of the data on which conclusions are based.

# 🔲 Ethical Issues in Qualitative Research

No matter how hard the qualitative researcher strives to study the social world naturally, leaving no traces, the very act of research itself imposes something "unnatural" on the situation, so the qualitative researcher may have an impact that has ethical implications. Four ethical issues should be given particular attention.

*Voluntary participation.* Ensuring that subjects are participating in a study voluntarily is not often a problem with intensive interviewing and focus group research, but it often is a point of contention in participant observation studies. Practically, much field research would be impossible if the participant-observer were required to request permission of everyone having some contact, no matter how minimal, with a group or setting being observed. And should the requirement of voluntary participation apply equally to every member of an organization being observed? What if the manager consents, the workers are ambivalent, and the union says no? Requiring everyone's consent would limit participant observation research to settings without serious conflicts of interest.

*Subject well-being.* Every field researcher should consider carefully before beginning a project how to avoid harm to subjects. It is not possible to avoid every theoretical possibility of harm nor to be sure that any project will cause no adverse consequences whatsoever to any individual. Direct harm to the reputations or feelings of particular individuals is what researchers must carefully avoid. They can do so, in part, by maintaining the confidentiality of research subjects. They also must avoid adversely affecting the course of events while engaged in a setting. The ethical problem becomes more difficult when subjects appear to be in harm's way, and the researcher must decide whether to take some action to lessen the likelihood of harm. A McKinney ethnographer's notes included an instructive example:

> I took his statements about cutting himself quite seriously, though I did not consider it a direct suicide threat since he was smiling when he said it. I told him that I thought he should talk to someone besides me about it because it sounded very serious and that he needed professional help.

These problems are rare in qualitative interviewing and focus groups, but researchers using these methods should try to identify negative feelings and help distressed subjects cope with their feelings through debriefing or referrals for professional help.

*Identity disclosure.* Current ethical standards require informed consent of research subjects, and most would argue that this standard cannot be met in any meaningful way if researchers do not disclose fully their identity. But how much disclosure about the study is necessary, and how hard should researchers try to make sure that their research purposes are understood? In field research on Co-Dependents Anonymous, Leslie Irvine (1998) found that the emphasis on anonymity and expectations for group discussion made it difficult to disclose her identity. Less-educated subjects may not readily comprehend what research is or be able to weigh the possible consequences of the research for themselves. Should researchers inform subjects if the study's interests and foci change while it is in progress? What balance do you think should be struck between the disclosure of critical facts and a coherent research strategy?

*Confidentiality.* Field researchers normally use fictitious names for the characters in their reports, but doing so does not always guarantee confidentiality to their research subjects. Individuals in the setting studied may be able to identify those whose actions are described and thus may become privy to some knowledge about their colleagues or neighbors that had formerly been kept from them. Therefore, researchers should make every effort to expunge possible identifying material from published information and to alter unimportant aspects of a description when necessary to prevent identity disclosure. In any case, no field research project should begin if some participants clearly will suffer serious harm by being identified in project publications. Procedures for protecting privacy and maintaining confidentiality should be negotiated with participants early in the study if at all possible.

These ethical issues cannot be evaluated independently. The final decision to proceed must be made after weighing the relative benefits and risks to participants. Few qualitative research projects will be barred by consideration of these ethical issues. The more important concern for researchers is to identify the ethically troublesome aspects of their proposed research and resolve them before the project begins and to act on new ethical issues as they come up during the project.

# 🖾 Conclusions

Qualitative research allows the careful investigator to obtain a richer and more intimate view of human behavior than is possible with more structured methods. And the emphases in qualitative research on inductive reasoning and incremental understanding help stimulate and inform other research approaches. Exploratory research to chart the dimensions of previously unstudied behaviors and intensive investigations of the subjective meanings that motivate individual action are particularly well served by the techniques of participant observation, intensive interviewing, and focus groups.

The very characteristics that make qualitative research techniques so appealing restrict their use to a limited set of research problems. It is not possible to draw representative samples for study using participant observation, and for this reason, the generalizability of any particular field study's results cannot really be known. Only the accumulation of findings from numerous qualitative studies permits confident generalization, but here again, the time and effort required to collect and analyze the data make it unlikely that many field research studies will be replicated.

In the final analysis, qualitative research involves a mode of thinking and investigating different from that used in experimental and survey research. As a research methodologist, you must be ready to mix and match the methods as required by the research problem to be investigated and the setting in which it is to be studied.

# Chapter Highlights

- Qualitative methods are most useful in exploring new issues, investigating hard-to-study groups, and determining the meaning people give to their lives and actions. In addition, many behavioral research projects can be improved, in some respects, by taking advantage of qualitative techniques.

- Qualitative researchers tend to develop ideas inductively, try to understand the social context and sequential nature of attitudes and actions, and explore the subjective meanings that participants attach to events. They rely primarily on participant observation, intensive interviewing, and, in recent years, focus groups.

- Intensive interviews involve open-ended questions and follow-up probes, with specific question content and order varying from one interview to another. Intensive interviews can supplement participant observation data.

- Field researchers must develop strategies for entering the field, developing and maintaining relations in the field, and sampling, recording, and analyzing data. Selection of sites or other units to study may reflect an emphasis on typical cases, deviant cases, and/or critical cases that can provide more information than others. Sampling techniques commonly used within sites or in selecting interviewees in field research include theoretical sampling, purposive sampling, snowball sampling, quota sampling, and, in special circumstances, random selection with the experience sampling method.

- Recording and analyzing notes is a crucial step in field research. Jottings are used as brief reminders about events in the field, while daily logs are useful for chronicling the researcher's activities. Detailed field notes should be recorded and analyzed daily. Analysis of the notes can guide refinement of methods used in the field and of the concepts, indicators, and models developed to explain what has been observed.

- Systematic observation techniques quantify the observational process to allow more systematic comparison between cases and greater generalizability.

- Focus groups combine elements of participant observation and intensive interviewing. They can increase the validity of attitude measurement by revealing what people say when they present their opinions in a group context instead of in the artificial one-on-one interview setting.

- Four ethical issues that should be given particular attention in field research concern voluntary participation, subject well-being, identity disclosure, and confidentiality.

# Key Terms

| | | |
|---|---|---|
| Field notes | Jottings | Qualitative interviewing |
| Field researcher | Matrix | Reactive effects |
| Focus groups | Participant observation | Saturation point |
| "Grand tour" question | Participant-observer | Systematic observation |

# Research in the News

1. Williams syndrome results from a genetic error that leads to social gregariousness combined with poor comprehension of social dynamics. In a *New York Times* story about the syndrome, the reporter David Dobbs (2007) described the experience of two teenage twins with Williams who spoke to a motorcycle club about their problems, leaving club members in tears. How would you have planned a participant observation study to learn about the sociability

of "bikers" in a situation like this? What behaviors would you have looked for?

2. What a *New York Times* article termed "the grim neurology of teenage drinking" (Butler, 2006) often begins with a very

social process. What questions would you ask a focus group of teens about social occasions at which some engage in binge drinking? What follow-up questions could encourage discussion about social pressure to drink?

## Activity Questions

1. Conduct a brief observational study in a public location on campus where students congregate. A cafeteria, a building lobby, or a lounge would be ideal. You can sit and observe, taking occasional notes unobtrusively, without violating any expectations of privacy. Observe for 30 minutes. Write up field notes, being sure to include a description of the setting and a commentary on your own behavior and your reactions to what you observed.

2. Devise a plan for using a focus group to explore and explain student perspectives on some current event. How would you recruit students for the group? What types of students would you try to include? How would you introduce the topic and the method to the group? What questions would you ask? What problems would you anticipate, such as discord

between focus group members or digressions from the chosen topic? How would you respond to these problems?

3. Conduct a three-question qualitative interview with a classmate about her first date, car, college course, or something else that you and your classmates agree on. Then collect all the responses and analyze them in a "committee of the whole." Follow the procedures discussed in the section on qualitative analysis.

4. Using any of the major search engines, search the Web for the topic "Freud" and "psychoanalysis," keeping field notes on what you find. Categorize each site and write a brief report based on the data you have collected. What are the different views of Freudian psychoanalysis and who holds these views?

## Review Questions

1. The variable extent to which a researcher participates in a situation being observed allows qualitative researchers to adapt to very different social situations but also creates some difficult challenges. Identify a social situation in which different levels of participation would be appropriate and identify the unique challenges they would create.

2. You read in this chapter a quote from an ethnographer in the McKinney housing study who learned that a house resident

was talking seriously about cutting himself. If you were the ethnographer, would you have immediately informed house staff about this? Would you have told anyone? What if the resident asked you not to tell anyone? In what circumstances would you feel it is ethical to take action to prevent the likelihood of a subject harming him or herself or others?

3. Compare the method of qualitative interviewing with the design of structured surveys described in Chapter 5. What

are the comparative advantages and disadvantages of qualitative interviewing?

4. Devise a plan for using a focus group to explore and explain student perspectives on some current event. How would you recruit students for the group? What types of students would you try to include? How would you introduce the topic and the method to the group? What questions would you ask? What problems would you anticipate, such as discord between focus group members or digressions from the chosen topic? How would you respond to these problems?

# Ethics in Action

1. The McKinney ethnographers observed a variety of problems in the group homes, ranging from arguments between tenants, conflicts with staff over chores, and incoherent speech due to drug use. Do you think the ethnographers should ever have intervened in these problems? Notified staff about them? Called police? What ethical standards do your answers suggest you would favor in ethnographic research?

2. Would it ever be ethical for participant-observers to conduct their observations covertly, without revealing their identity as a researcher to the group or individuals they are observing? Do you believe that social scientists should simply avoid conducting research on groups or individuals who refuse to admit researchers into their lives? Would there be any advantages to a strategy of covert observation? Might there be practical problems with this approach?

3. Should any requirements be imposed on researchers who seek to study other cultures, to ensure that procedures are appropriate and interpretations are culturally sensitive? What practices would you suggest for cross-cultural researchers to ensure that ethical guidelines are followed? (Consider the wording of consent forms and the procedures for gaining voluntary cooperation.)

CHAPTER 12

# Essentials of APA Report Writing

Written or print communication is the primary medium by which research is disseminated. Without a written report, the most groundbreaking findings will go undocumented, the perfect experiment will remain unknown, and new theoretical perspectives will be unrealized. How then should we go about composing a written report of research findings? What format are we to follow? Are there habits and practices that lead to effective report writing?

Let's begin with an illustrative case of writing a report of an empirical study. As a class exercise, students in our research methods course answered two questions, each of which we presented and handed out on separate sheets of paper. One question asked students to rate their current happiness on a 1 to 10 scale with 1 = *very unhappy* and 10 = *very happy*. The other question asked students how many dates they had in the past 30 days. We manipulated the order in which we presented the two questions. Half the class received the happiness question first, followed by the dating question, and the other half received the dating question followed by the happiness question. Our research question asked, Would the order of the presentation of questions influence answers?

For the purpose of this illustration, we use artificial data. On the basis of these artificial data, we calculate the correlation of the two questions for each of the orders of presentation. Our results indicate no statistically significant correlation between answers when students responded to the happiness question first, followed by the dating question. However, answers did correlate significantly when students responded to the dating question first, followed by the happiness question. Our task is now to write up these results. Below we will learn how to compose a written report of this empirical study.

# The APA Format

The American Psychological Association (APA) format provides us with a blueprint for report writing. The format is presented in clear and precise detail in the *Publication Manual of the American Psychological Association* (APA, 2010c). This is the most up-to-date version of the *Publication Manual* (sixth edition). We will present the general guidelines for using the *Publication Manual*, outlining both style and organization of report writing.

For additional information, there are several other sources that you may find helpful in learning about report writing using the APA format. These include *APA: The Easy Way!* by Houghton and Houghton (2007), *The APA Pocket Handbook* by Jill Rossiter (2007), *The Psychologist's Companion* by R. J. Sternberg (2003), *Concise Rules of APA Style* (APA, 2005), and a computer program called *APA-Style Helper*, which can be used with most word processors to make sure that your paper is formatted in APA style. The *Publication Manual, Concise Rules of APA Style*, and *APA-Style Helper* can be purchased directly from the APA websites at http://www.apa.org and http://www.apastyle.org.

As we learned in Chapter 2, the APA format for organization of a written report of an empirical study is rather straightforward: title, abstract, introduction, method, results, discussion, references, author notes, footnotes, tables, figure captions, and figures. Becoming familiar with APA writing style, on the other hand, is much more difficult. *Concise, clear,* and *interesting* are adjectives that frequently describe APA writing style. These terms, however, are not intended to intimidate. For beginners as well as for seasoned veterans of APA writing style, clarity, brevity, and felicitous phrasing are aspirational. In other words, live with imperfection, remember there is no good writing, there is only good rewriting, and it is better to write and to rewrite than to have never written at all!

APA style emphasizes written language that is sensitive to racial and ethnic identity, gender, age, sexual orientation, and disabilities. The goal is to eliminate sexism and ethnic bias in writing. For example, *gender* is the correct term to describe males and females as social groups, as in the phrase "gender differences evidently in average income." The term *sex* is the correct term to describe biological features of men and women, as in "sex chromosomes" or "sex-determining gene." However, gender pronouns can often be sexist. Other biased terms are *he, his, man, men, mankind,* and so forth, in representing both men and women. In describing people, a general rule is to refer to people in terms as they prefer.

Often the best policy is not to assume but rather to inquire politely and respectfully so that you will be sensitive to any terms or labels that might be offensive. In research reports of studies of persons with disabilities, be very mindful of the stigmatizing effects of diagnostic labels. For example, do not use the term *schizophrenic* as a noun, but rather use the phrase "a person with the diagnosis of schizophrenia." Similarly, when comparing a group of people with a disability, such as a diagnosis of schizophrenia, with a control group, do not describe the control group as the "normal group." Instead, write "We compared people with the disorder and without the disorder." Also, people in a research study are referred to as *participants*. This term is used to distinguish human and animal subjects.

APA style also emphasizes the importance of proper documentation and citation. Consider the following statement: "The prevalence of schizophrenia in the general population is 1%" (Gottesman, 1991). Note that the statement is substantiated by the Gottesman (1991) study that empirically demonstrated the 1% prevalence rate of schizophrenia in the general population.

In report writing, any written statement or claim, such as the example citing the prevalence of schizophrenia, needs to be documented. Documentation in the form of citing a reference allows the reader to know that the statement is supported and substantiated by evidence. In addition, it allows the reader to check the reference to determine the accuracy of the statement and learn the details of the cited study.

You should only cite references or sources that you have read firsthand. For references that you have not read yourself, use a secondary citation for the work. For example, imagine that you read in your textbook the following: "Aristotle emphasized the importance of distinguishing in moral reasoning actions that are bad and criminal versus those that are mad and insane." You would write, "Aristotle as cited by Nestor and Schutt (2015) emphasized the importance of distinguishing bad and criminal acts from mad and insane acts in moral reasoning."

Here our textbook, Nestor and Schutt (2015), is a secondary source for the reference citing Aristotle. In general, however, use secondary sources sparingly, as mistakes in describing and understanding ideas can be perpetuated in secondary sources when authors fail to read the original or primary work. The mechanics of APA style of documentation are covered below in the reference section in the organization of report writing.

Proper documentation is essential—an ethical imperative. Your ideas, thoughts, sentences, phrases, and words must be clearly separated from those from other sources. Always err on the side of crediting others. Even for what you may believe to be your truly original ideas and insights, there are almost always others who have had similar thoughts published in the literature. Citing these helps also to place ideas and thoughts in context as well as to show how ideas of others may have influenced your work. Never present another person's published work or parts of published work as your own. In other words, do not plagiarize.

**Plagiarism** is a serious ethical as well as legal problem that can result in expulsion, grade failure, job loss, and litigation for violating copyright laws (Hard, Conway, & Moran, 2006). Directly quoting another author with the proper reference is a must. However, filling a paper with many direct quotes or with very lengthy quotes is self-defeating and counterproductive—why bother reading a paper filled with quotes?

As a result, good writing requires paraphrasing with proper citation of the author(s). When paraphrasing, you put into your own words another cited or referenced author's own ideas. It is not easy finding different words for the same idea. In general, do not use three or more consecutive words in a sentence that are the same as those written in the original source. Use quotes with citation if you do, or better still, revise your sentence. In the following sections, we will examine six essential parts of an APA written report of an empirical study: abstract, introduction, method, results, discussion, and references.

# Report Organization in the APA Format

APA style requires that all reports be typed, entirely double-spaced, in 12-point serif font with at least 1-inch margins for right and left and top and bottom. The alignment of the text is set to the left margin; do not right justify. All pages are numbered consecutively, beginning with the title page. Page numbers are placed in the top margin, 1 inch from the right side of the paper. The number appears by itself with no punctuation.

## Title

Appearing as the first page of your report is the title page. It contains the title of the report, author's name and school affiliation, a running head, page header, and page number. A running head is a short title of the paper that should be no more than 50 characters in length. A good title conveys specific information as to the major thrust of the study. Typically, the title of the paper describes the relationships between independent and dependent variables of the study.

Consider the title of a 2004 published paper in the APA journal *Neuropsychology* by the first author of this book (P.G.N.) and his colleagues, "Neuropsychological Correlates of Diffusion Tensor Imaging in Schizophrenia." The title indicates that the study examined the relationship of neuropsychological performance and diffusion tensor imaging (structural brain imaging of white matter) in schizophrenia.

In general, when choosing a title, look to your research question and hypothesis. The title we chose for our in-class exercise described above is "Focusing Illusion in College Students." Here the theoretical construct of the paper, focusing illusion, is placed front and center in the title. This informs the reader of the topic and rationale for the study in a way that the study variables for our in-class exercise—order of questions and their answers—could not.

## Abstract

The abstract is presented on the second page, following the title page. It comes at the beginning of the paper, but the abstract is the last section that the author writes. The **abstract** is a brief paragraph, no more than 120 words, that states what was done to whom and the major results or findings. The abstract parallels the structure and organization of the paper: Begin with a sentence or two that summarizes the introduction, followed by a sentence or two for the method, then the results, and finally the discussion. Expect your earlier drafts of the abstract to be too long, and then, you can start to whittle it down to size. This is the best approach, as editing works best for shortening rather than lengthening.

## Introduction

In the **introduction**, we describe what our plan is and the reason our study needs to be done. We begin by providing a theoretical description of our research question or principal problem. So for our in-class exercise, the concept of focusing illusion is pivotal. Our first order of business, then, is to whet the appetite of the reader. Borrowing from Kahneman et al. (2006), consider the following as our opening sentence:

> *When people are led to think about the influence of any single thing on their happiness, such as money, they tend to overstate its importance.*

Our initial statement, both general and nontechnical, leads to a more specific description of the key phenomenon under study—focusing illusion (Kahneman et al., 2006).

> *Exaggerating the impact of any one factor can lead to a particular form of cognitive bias, known as a focusing illusion.*

We then present a simple example used in previous research studying focusing illusion.

> *For example, consider two simple questions: (1) How happy are you? (2) How many dates did you have last month?*

We now draw connections with previous research.

*Previous studies (Kahneman et al., 2006; Strack, Martin, & Schwartz, 1988), have shown a strong correlation in responses to these two questions when participants are presented with the dating question first, followed by the happiness question. However, the correlation disappeared when participants answered the happiness question first followed by the dating question (Strack et al., 1988).*

In your own words, elaborate on the meaning of these studies.

*The dating question (coming first) may have drawn attention to that part of life, leading people to exaggerate its importance in their responses to the more general question regarding their happiness.*

Now tell the reader how you plan to study the focusing illusion.

*The purpose of this study is to examine whether the order of presentation of these two simple questions to be answered by college students in a research methods class would induce a focusing illusion.*

Notice that this simple sentence reports two important facts about our study. First is that focusing illusion will be studied by manipulating the order of presentation of two simple questions, and, second, our sample consists of college students who will answer the two questions.

Our next and often final step in the introduction is to present our main hypothesis. Setting the stage for the method, the hypothesis, as outlined in Kahneman et al. (2006), reported here is intended to focus the reader on the primary reason for the study.

*It is hypothesized that when college students are asked first about the number of dates they had in the past 30 days, that aspect of life will influence their responses to the second question about their overall level of happiness. By contrast, for students who are presented the happiness question first, followed by the dating question, their answers to these two questions will be unrelated.*

This text tells the reader our principal prediction, essentially why we are doing the study. The focusing illusion is expected to be induced by the order of presentation of our two questions. When respondents first answer the question as to how many dates they have had in the past 30 days, this factor becomes exaggerated, creating, we predict, a focusing illusion that unduly influences participants' answers to the second general question regarding their overall level of happiness. By contrast, when we present the dating question second, after the general question of happiness, no focusing illusion will be induced, and there will be no relationship between answers to these two questions.

These sentences are meant to engage you in the process of writing an introduction. Each sentence helps the reader understand why the study is needed and how it is conducted. An introduction must thus provide background and context for the study. This is done by reporting a brief history of the topic followed by a balanced summary of previous research that is relevant to the topic. In researching a topic, searching a database such as PsycINFO or Google Scholar is an important first step (see Chapter 2).

## Method

The **method** section is the most straightforward section of the report. It is often written first and in fact while the study is being conducted so as to serve as an official record to document procedures, measures, and actions of participants. It is written in the past tense. The method section must be presented clearly so that another researcher should be able to repeat or reproduce the study exactly.

Also of critical importance to keep in mind is that the validity of a study's findings will be judged largely on the extent to which its method provided variables that adequately captured the phenomena under study. For example, Does presenting the dating question first constitute a valid means to induce a focusing illusion? The take-home message is that evaluating and critiquing any research begins by carefully examining the study method. Unlike the introduction, results, and discussion, the method section is divided into the following subsections: participants, materials, design, and procedure.

*Participants.* Report how many participants were in the study, and how they were recruited. Parenthetically, recall that we have learned that the number of participants or the size of a study sample represents an important piece of information that you should consider in evaluating and critiquing a study. Likewise, how participants were recruited, with *random sampling* as the gold standard for research, is yet another piece of information included in all method sections that is essential for evaluating and critiquing a study. In addition, present in your method age, gender, education, student status, and any other important characteristics, such as whether participants were compensated, received course credit, or volunteered for no material benefit. Again, describe your participants so that a reader can evaluate the *generalizability* of your sample. Also include in the participant subsection of the method that your study was approved by the institutional review board and was in accordance with APA ethical guidelines (see Chapter 3).

*Materials.* Describe measures, variables, and type of apparatus or stimuli used in the study. If your study only used a survey, then in the material subsection, you would describe the survey, such as the number of items and the nature of the questions. For example, in our focusing illusion study, you could present the two-item questionnaire:

- On a scale of 1 to 10, with 1 = *very unhappy* and 10 = *very happy*, rate how happy you are with your life in general.

- How many dates did you have last month?

*Design.* Report the type of design used in the study. Specify the independent and dependent variables. Indicate whether your study employs within-groups or between-groups design or a mixed-group design. For example, the focusing illusion study used a between-groups comparison of participants' responses as a function of the order of presentation of a two-item questionnaire. The order of presentation is the independent variable and the dependent variable is the answers to the two questions.

*Procedure.* Here, specify the sequence of steps of the study, essentially what you had the participants do and how you collected their data. For example, in our focusing illusion study, we would write the following:

> *We manipulated the order of presentation of a two-item questionnaire. Participants were randomly assigned to either one of two orders of presentation. Thirty participants answered the happiness item first followed by the dating item and 30 participants answered the dating item first followed by the happiness item.*

## Results

In the **results** section, summarize your findings and the statistical tests you performed. Report your findings in sufficient detail, but do not overwhelm the reader with such detail that the most relevant findings in regard to the study hypotheses are lost in a sea of numbers. Report all relevant findings, including those that run counter to your hypotheses and expectations, such as findings that are statistically nonsignificant or much smaller in magnitude (effect size) than predicted by your theory. Individual scores or raw data are not reported, with the exception of single-subject designs that by definition focus on one or a small number of participants. Do not hide unexpected, disappointing, or uncomfortable results by omission.

You typically begin the results section by providing descriptive statistics of your study sample. Often descriptive statistics are presented in a table with means and standard deviations. Exhibit 12.1 is taken from a publication by us (Nestor et al., 2010) in *Neuropsychology*. This is a typical table that provides descriptive data in the form of means and standard deviations for both patient and control groups. Note that uppercase and italicized *N* refers to the total number of cases, whereas lowercase and italicized *n* refers to the number of cases of a group or subsample, as for instance, when you may want to report scores separately for males and females, or, as in Exhibit 12.1, patients and controls.

**Exhibit 12.1**   Neuropsychological Scores for Patients With Schizophrenia for WAIS-III ($n = 22$) and IGT ($n = 23$) and for Control Participants for WAIS-III ($n = 23$) and IGT ($n = 24$)

| Demographic Information | Patients | Controls |
|---|---|---|
| Age | 38.78 ± 9.90 | 41.5 ± 7.35 |
| Education | 12.83 ± 1.99 | 15.00 ± 1.98 |
| SES | 3.75 ± 1.22 | 2.42 ± 1.06 |
| Parental SES | 2.83 ± 1.11 | 2.71 ± 1.27 |
| WAIS-III IQ | | |
| Full scale | 91.83 ± 13.74 | 105.22 ± 16.24 |
| Verbal | 95.35 ± 14.78 | 104.22 ± 14.16 |
| Performance | 88.87 ± 12.20 | 105.30 ± 18.07 |
| WAIS-III Index | | |
| Verbal comprehension | 99.96 ± 15.88 | 103.13 ± 14.47 |
| Perceptual organization | 94.74 ± 16.05 | 107.48 ± 17.56 |
| Working memory | 91.91 ± 13.54 | 105.75 ± 15.68 |
| Processing speed | 81.04 ± 10.1 | 101.87 ± 14.48 |
| Iowa Gambling Task | | |
| Block 1 | −2.17 ± 12.02 | −1.17 ± 10.87 |
| Block 2 | −1.25 ± 10.01 | 4.33 ± 9.08 |
| Block 3 | 1.25 ± 9.97 | 6.91 ± 9.65 |
| Block 4 | −1.58 ± 9.55 | 3.83 ± 10.30 |
| Block 5 | −0.08 ± 9.16 | 4.67 ± 11.31 |

*Notes:* Values are means plus or minus standard deviations. SES = socioeconomic status, WAIS-III = Wechsler Adult Intelligence Scale–Third Edition, IGT = Iowa Gambling Test.

In our illustrative study, let us present in text (as opposed to in a table) means (*M*) and standard deviations (*SD*) for responses to each of the two questions for our entire sample of 60 (*N* = 60) participants:

*The entire sample of 60 participants had a mean happiness rating of 6.75 with a standard deviation of 1.34 and a mean number of dates for the past 30 days of 6.63 with a standard deviation of 2.35.*

In writing the results, we assume that the reader has a professional knowledge of statistics. We therefore would not need to indicate in our report that one standard deviation unit indicates that about two thirds of the entire sample responses fall between ± one standard deviation unit of the mean. The reader will likely know this, just as the reader will likely know the arithmetic mean. (Of course, for class exercises and assignments, you may very well need to show that you understand these concepts!)

There are numerous approaches to the analysis of data, including both quantitative (Chapter 10) and qualitative (Chapter 11). In the results section, we want to clearly present our data analytic approach. For our illustrative study on focusing illusion, this means that we specify the statistics used to test our hypothesis. This will allow the reader to judge whether we used the most direct and powerful statistical test of the theory and hypothesis of the study. First, let us make clear our statistic test used to test the hypothesis. For example,

*The focusing illusion predicted that answers to the two questions should be correlated only when the dating question came first, followed by the happiness question. To test this hypothesis, we computed the Pearson correlation (symbol for Pearson correlation is* r*) between the responses of the two questions for each of the two orders of presentation. The results indicated a significant correlation for answers when the dating question came first, followed by the happiness question (*r = .493*, *p = .006*). By contrast, when the happiness question came first, followed by the dating question, the results indicated no significant correlation (*r = .031*, ns). Thus, as predicted, and in support for the theory of focusing illusion, answers to these two questions correlated significantly only when participants responded to the dating question first followed by the happiness question.*

Several points of both substance and style are important to keep in mind. First, notice that the text specifically links the statistical test, Pearson correlation, to the main theory and hypothesis of the study, that being under what conditions does a focusing illusion occur. Second, without being repetitious or redundant, we remind the reader that we manipulated the order of presentation of the two questions, which served as the independent variable of our study.

Third, we report the quantitative results of our statistical analyses, and we present the Pearson correlation as a three-decimal number. Because a correlation statistic cannot be greater than 1, we do not use a zero before the decimal fraction. The same principle for recording holds for significance level. Note that we present the exact *p* value for a statistically significant result. For a nonstatistically significant result, we do not present the exact *p* value, which we know by definition is greater than .05; instead, use the symbol *ns* to indicate a nonsignificant value. Fourth, we make a simple declarative statement as to whether the obtained results either supported or failed to support the hypothesis and theory of focusing illusion of the study. Any additional interpretive statements and conclusions are not appropriate for the results section and are addressed more fully in the discussion section that follows the results section.

## Discussion

Now, having reported the results, you are ready to evaluate and interpret their implications, particularly in relation to your original hypothesis. Keep in mind that the culture of scientific report writing favors a modest, conservative, careful, and cautious style. Even when significant results are obtained in favor of the research hypothesis, you as a writer of the research report should always avoid sweeping generalizations and inflated pronouncements. Keep in mind that your findings still represent the results only of one study. Emphasize the importance of independent replication of any obtained significant finding. Present clearly and forthrightly aspects of the findings that may not fit with the results and that may raise questions and problems of interpretation and meaning. Qualify results to the specific conditions of the study.

Content of the **discussion** section begins with a clear statement as to whether the obtained results either supported or did not support the research hypothesis. If the results failed to support the hypothesis, offer explanations; these are typically referred to as post hoc, meaning that they occur "after the fact." Here, consider similarities and differences between your study and the work of others. Oftentimes you might return to the method section and look to see how your study conditions and participants aligned with the work of others.

The *Publication Manual* (APA, 2010c) emphasizes critical factors that need to be accounted for when interpreting results in the discussion section. First, consider sources of potential bias and other threats to both internal validity of the study design and external validity of the study sample of participants. Consideration of internal validity is relatively straightforward and transparent and can be largely done by carefully reviewing the method and results sections.

External validity is trickier. Here, be mindful of cultural and ethical sensitivities: Research studies that produce empirical results about groups of people can be misused prejudicially. Second, in interpreting results, always make sure to account for the imprecision of measurements: There are no perfect measurements in psychology. Third, take into account the number of tests used and the extent to which they overlap or are redundant. For example, a correlation can be artificially inflated between two tests that use the same form of measurement, such as pencil-and-paper. That is why researchers often use a multimethod approach with different forms of measurements (e.g., behavior observation, pencil-and-paper) of the same trait (see Chapter 4).

Also, when interpreting results, be mindful of the inherent nature of statistical analysis of data collected across several measures. The number of statistical tests, such as the number of correlations computed, can lead to chance findings. For example, imagine you have a set of 10 test scores that you correlated with a set of 10 brain volume measures. A $10 \times 10$ correlation matrix will have a total of 100 values, each test score correlated with each brain volume measure. By chance alone, five of these correlations are expected to be significant.

Let's say these significant correlations coincided with those that you had predicted beforehand. How, then, would you know for certain whether the obtained correlations represented genuine statistical support for the hypothesis or, conversely, were simply due to chance that comes with computing a large number of statistical tests or correlations? This is a rather complicated problem. The important point to remember is that any written discussion about data interpretation needs to be mindful of the inherent limitations of statistical testing. Finally, in the discussion section, you may want to address any other weaknesses or limitations of your study.

The discussion section concludes with a commentary on the meaning and importance of your findings. Here, make sure your interpretations are well reasoned and based on the empirical evidence from your results section. Again, a common mistake is to overstate the impact of your study and to over interpret the significance and meaning of your results. Whether brief or extensive, your closing commentary must be tightly reasoned and crystal clear. It revisits why the research problem is important (as presented in the introduction) and carefully addresses implications beyond the particulars of your study. It comments on the theoretical, clinical, or practical significance of your results. As stated in the *Publication Manual* (APA, 2010c), in this concluding section, you might also touch on the extent to which any real-life applications are warranted on the basis of your research and what problems remain unresolved or newly emerged because of your findings.

For our illustrative case, we begin our discussion by restating our major findings:

*The study examined whether a focusing illusion could be induced by manipulating the order of presentation of two simple questions. In support of the hypothesis, the results indicated that responses to the two test items correlated significantly but only when participants answered the dating question first, followed by the happiness question. These results suggested that presenting the dating question first created a focusing illusion whereby participants exaggerated the specific impact of their current level of dating when considering the second, more global question of how happy they are with their lives in general. In stark contrast, and also consistent with the hypothesis, participants showed no evidence of a focusing illusion when presented with the happiness question first, followed by the dating question. That is, the responses to the two questions did not correlate when participants answered the happiness question first, followed by the dating question.*

Next, we need to place our findings in context. How do our results relate to previous research? Revisit the literature review of your introduction. In a real full-length paper, you would have a fairly extensive literature review. For our illustration, our introduction does include two important sources, the Kahneman et al. (2006) review and Strack et al. (1988) experiment, and we would therefore make sure we address our findings in relation to these two key works. In addition, in a real full-length paper, in the introduction section, you would have cast the phenomenon of focusing illusion within a wider theoretical framework. For example,

*Research on focusing illusion emanates from a school of cognitive psychology that studies how our thinking can be deceived or distorted by heuristic biases or mistakes of reasoning. These errors of thinking have been likened to curious blind spots or mental tunnels in our minds (Piatelli-Palmarini, 1994). Focusing illusion is just one type of heuristic bias but one that may be a source of error in significant decisions that people make.*

Most important is to emphasize the limitations of our study. Indeed, even though our artificial results supported the hypothesis and conformed to previous research, our study (i.e., class exercise) on focusing illusion had several major limitations and flaws. How do you report these? First, be straightforward and open: Do not hide them or hope that they will be overlooked. Second, carefully explain the limitations, and comment as to the degree of importance in relation to your study. How much of a threat to internal validity do they pose? How much of a threat to external validity? In other words, simply listing limitations and flaws will not be well received but rather will come across as rote and dull. Instead, explain clearly and thoroughly, make sure the reader knows not only the limitations but also the relative importance of these for the current study.

In our example, two important limitations come immediately to mind. One might be classified as a threat to external validity and the other to internal validity. The external validity of our findings is clearly threatened by the simple fact that all participants were enrolled in a research methods class and answered the two-item questionnaire as part of an in-class exercise. The limited generalizability of this sample is clearly a major point to emphasize in your discussion. Likewise, for internal validity, we failed to control for any number of variables, such as age, education, relationship/marital status, depression, or other mental status conditions, all of which could have influenced our results.

## References

Two important "must knows" regarding **references**: First, for references cited in the body of the text, whether in the introduction, method, results, or discussion, list the last names of the authors of the work followed by the date of publication. For example,

Strack, Martin, and Schwartz (1988) reported that . . .

Or you could write,

Previous work (Strack, Martin, & Schwartz, 1988) demonstrated that ...

Note that when the authors' last names appear outside the parentheses, use the word *and*, but use an ampersand (&) when they appear inside the parentheses. For two authors, always list in your text both names in the order that they appear on the referenced publication. For referenced works by three or more authors, list all names the first time you cite the work as in the above example. Thereafter, list only the first author, followed by *et al.* and the year of publication:

Strack et al. (1988) suggested that...

Second, following the discussion and beginning on a separate page under the label *References* that is centered at the top of the page is the reference section of your report. Here, you list the reference for each work cited in your paper. Only references contained in the body of your text are included in the reference section. There should be no entries on your list of references that have not been cited in the body of your text. Likewise, there should be no reference cited in the body of your text that is not also included in your reference list.

A reference to a journal article contains the following: author(s), date, title, journal (italicized), volume (italicized), and page range:

Nestor, P. G., Kubicki, M., Gurrera, R. J., Niznikiewicz, M., Frumin, M., McCarley, R. W., & Shenton, M. E. (2004). Neuropsychological correlates of diffusion tensor imaging in schizophrenia. *Neuropsychology, 18,* 629–637.

For a reference to a book cited in the text and listed in the reference, you need the following information: author(s) date, title (italicized), city in which book was published, and publisher. From an example taken from Houghton and Houghton (2007):

Shotton, M. A. (1989). *Computer addiction? A study of computer dependency.* London, England: Taylor & Francis.

For a reference to a journal article read on the Internet that was originally in print, list the author(s), publication date, article title [Electronic version], journal title, volume, issue, and pages. From an example taken from Houghton and Houghton (2007):

Ostroff, C. (1998). The relationship between satisfaction, attitudes, and performance: An organizational level analysis [Electronic version]. *Journal of Applied Psychology, 12*(2), 963–974.

Test your knowledge of this chapter so far by taking the mid-chapter quiz on the study site: www.sagepub.com/nestor2e

## Literature Review

Now let's imagine that you have been assigned to write a literature review. What is a literature review and how would you go about completing such a task? Literature reviews are critical examinations of empirical studies that have already been published (see Chapter 2). In a literature review, you evaluate published studies in terms of their methods as well as their conceptual foundation. Consider, for example, the methods employed in terms of samples studied, measurements, and operational definitions of critical independent and dependent variables. Also consider the ideas and concepts that have inspired the various studies.

But perhaps what makes a literature review so challenging is that you, as the author, need to abstract common themes and weave together theories and results from a number of studies to describe the "big picture" of your topic of research. The emphasis is on analyses, critique, and evaluation of both theories and empirical work conducted to test these theories. Do not simply summarize studies but rather draw connections, abstract common themes, and identify gaps, inconsistencies, and contradictions in the literature. Develop a case for the steps that are needed to advance research and to solve these problems.

Selecting a topic is the first and most important step in writing a good literature review (see Chapter 2). In our earlier example of writing a report on an empirical study, the paper by Kahneman and colleagues served as a pivotal article for us. We found the article to be especially well written, with clear, concise, and engaging prose, containing a number of valuable citations, including the Strack et al. (1988) study that served as the foundation for our in-class exercise.

We found fascinating the overall theme cultivated by Kahneman and colleagues of how our minds can deceive us and can lead to erroneous decisions. The eye-catching title alone, "Would You Be Happier If You Were Richer? A Focusing Illusion," resonated with intrigue and fun and, published in the prestigious international journal *Science*, underscored the relevance and impact of the topic. Also adding to the luster of the article is the fact that the lead author, the psychologist Daniel Kahneman, won the 2002 Nobel Prize in Economic Sciences for his pioneering studies on decision making under uncertainty! (see Chapter 1).

Once you have finalized your topic, you will read and review a number of articles. How many studies should you review? For published reviews, 100 or more studies may be cited. Luckily, most professors will require you to review between 5 and 15 articles. Fewer articles mean that your literature review will not be exhaustive. You will have to be especially discriminating in selecting the most useful and representative articles.

Often helpful are index cards, a summary sheet, or even a table that lists the following key features of each article: What is the research question or problem (introduction), how was it studied (method), what were the findings (results), and how were they understood and interpreted (discussion)? Answers to each of these key questions can be found in the body of the text in particular sections of the paper (presented in parentheses), and all will be contained in the abstract, which will give you a helpful overview of the study.

Read for content and depth. Examine the articles to see how previous works are described and how much emphasis is given to any particular study. For example, key works are given more attention with respect to both methodological detail and theoretical contribution. Less important studies may be cited but not described in detail.

In reading an article, think about the principles of construct validity that we covered in Chapter 4. As you may recall, constructs are synonymous with ideas or theories. For example, let's imagine that you are writing a review paper on the topic of false memory. In reviewing the literature, you would want to identify the methods used to study false memory. You would look to see whether different methods to assess false memory, such as psychological studies and brain imaging, converge to reveal a consistent pattern of evidence. Studies using different methods of the same construct should agree, so this would be a critical point for you to develop in your literature review.

A literature review does not follow the same organization and structure as an article reporting an empirical study. You will have an abstract that appears on the first page that summarizes your review. But you will not have prescribed method and results sections for a literature review. Nevertheless, you will identify headings for major sections that will help you organize the structure of the paper. Try to make headings as specific as possible. For clues, look at published literature reviews to see how authors typically use headers to delineate major sections of their articles. Outline your paper with sections, some of which will correspond to the headers that you will use in the final written product.

Here are a set of steps that might be helpful to keep in mind when writing a literature review (APA, 2010c; University of Washington Psychology Writing Center, 1997–2005):

- Introduce and define research question or problem, and explain its importance and meaning.

- Focus research question to the studies reviewed.

- Describe studies, explain their methods and results.

- Identify relationships, gaps, inconsistencies across studies.

- Discuss how the research area may be advanced and improved.

Consider a literature review published by one of us (P.G.N.), "Mental Disorder and Violence: Personality Dimensions and Clinical Features" (Nestor, 2002). First, I introduced the research question, identifying what it is and why it is worth examining: For example, my research question asked, How do some mental disorders increase the risk of violence?

I then explained why this research question is worth examining. To wit, understanding of these factors may lead to prevention of violence for at-risk individuals. Next, I narrowed the research topic to the studies reviewed. I distinguished between two approaches, actuarial and clinical, each of which has been used to study mental disorders and violence. I then described how these two approaches had until recently revealed divergent and inconsistent findings, with age and past history serving as strong actuarial predictors of violence in contrast to the failure of clinical variables, such as symptoms and diagnoses, to predict violence. Last, I presented a model generated from my review of these studies for understanding violence and mental disorders:

> The risk of violence may be understood in terms of four fundamental personality dimensions: 1) impulse control; 2) affect regulation; 3) narcissism; and 4) paranoid cognitive personality style.... This review supports the hypothesis that these four fundamental personality dimensions operate jointly, and in varying degrees, as clinical risk factors for violence among groups with these classes of mental disorders. (Nestor, 2002, p. 1973)

## Poster Presentation

A poster is a very effective and economical way to communicate results of your research. In fact, many research studies that will be eventually published in peer-reviewed scientific journals are first presented in what are referred to as poster sessions at national or regional conferences. Most, if not all, psychological conventions include poster sessions in which the bulk of new research is presented. A poster includes the same major sections that are found in a published article: title, abstract, introduction, method, results, discussion, and references. However, a poster contains much less detail than an article, and information is often presented in bulleted lists of major points. The amount of space a conference provides for each poster varies, but dimensions of 3 to 4 feet high and 5 to 6 feet wide are common. Exhibit 12.2 provides an example of a common poster layout adapted from Cozby (2009) and the 2010 website of Psi Chi The International Honor Society in Psychology: http://www .psichi.org/.

Posters can be constructed using large-format printing technology that is often made available through your psychology department. Or, if a poster printer is not available, a series of separate pages can be laid out following the example presented in Exhibit 12.2. Each page corresponds to a particular section, such as abstract or introduction, and each section is printed on letter-sized paper, numbered, and tacked to the poster board in the proper sequence.

In general, you may want to construct your poster so that one or two important points can be easily gleaned. A simple figure and an easy-to-read table are generally included in a poster. Try to make your poster as visually friendly as possible. Text should be presented in a large font along with simple figures and

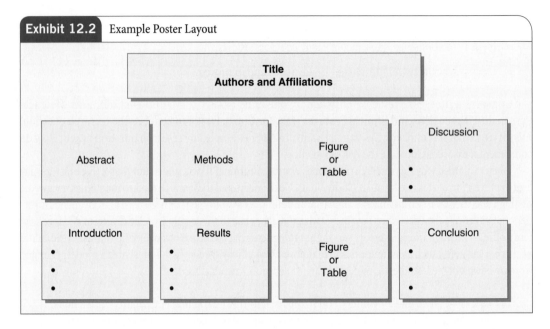

**Exhibit 12.2**  Example Poster Layout

tables. The idea is to keep it concise and visually pleasing. Finally, make sure to have printed handouts summarizing your poster available for viewers. The handouts must include presenters' (authors') names, the title of the poster, name of the organization or conference where the poster was presented, and date (year, month). This information is necessary to cite a poster in the APA format:

Presenters, A. A. (Year, Month). Title of poster. Poster session presented at the meeting of the Organization Name, Location.

You can see how easily our report on the focusing illusion exercise with artificial data could be presented in a poster. Look back at the text (italics) for the introduction, method, results, and discussion sections of our report. Note that text for each of these sections is sufficiently concise and brief for a poster presentation.

As you can also see in Exhibits 12.3 and 12.4, we present a table and figure that would be well suited for a poster presentation of our artificial data. You can see that the table and figure visually depict the two major points of the study. That is, Exhibit 12.4a depicts a scatter diagram (see Chapter 8) plotting the significant correlation between responses to the dating and happiness questions when the dating question came first followed by the happiness question. By contrast, Exhibit 12.4b depicts a scatter diagram (see Chapter 8) plotting the nonsignificant correlation between responses to the happiness and dating questions when the happiness question came first followed by the dating question.

**Exhibit 12.3**  Happiness Ratings and Number of Dates for Participants Who Answered the Dating Question Followed by Happiness Question ($n = 30$) Versus Participants Who Answered the Happiness Question Followed by the Dating Question ($n = 30$)

|  | *Happiness* | *Number of Dates* |
|---|---|---|
| Date question followed by happiness question | $6.57 \pm 1.17$ | $6.93 \pm 1.48$ |
| Happiness question followed by date question | $6.93 \pm 1.48$ | $6.13 \pm 2.47$ |

*Note:* Values are means plus or minus standard deviations (based on artificial data; see text).

| Exhibit 12.4a | Scatter Diagram Plotting the Significant Correlation Between Responses to the Dating and Happiness Questions When the Dating Question Came First Followed by the Happiness Question |
|---|---|

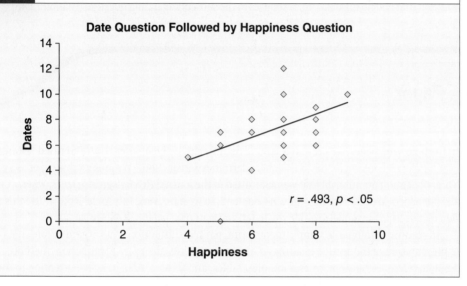

| Exhibit 12.4b | Scatter Diagram Plotting the Nonsignificant Correlation Between Responses to the Dating and Happiness Questions When the Happiness Question Came First Followed by the Dating Question |
|---|---|

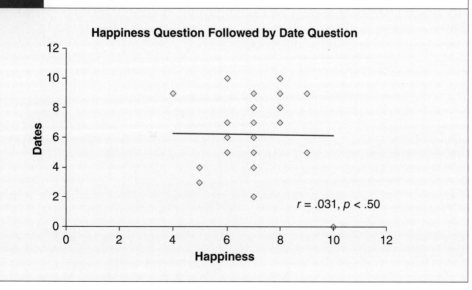

Thus, a viewer of the poster can see that your data showed clear evidence of a focusing illusion: When college students were asked first about the number of dates they had in the past 30 days, that aspect of their life became exaggerated, influencing their responses when they encountered the more general second question about their overall level of happiness (Exhibit 12.4a). By contrast, presenting the happiness question first had no influence on responses to the subsequent dating question (Exhibit 12.4b).

# Sample Paper

In the following pages, we present a sample manuscript by Iyengar et al. (2006) titled "Doing Better but Feeling Worse: Looking for the 'Best' Job Undermines Satisfaction." We present this paper as an example of a prepublication manuscript that was submitted to the journal *Psychological Science*, where it was eventually published. We covered this study in Chapter 2, so we have come full circle! Now we use this prepublication manuscript as a model to guide you in writing your own papers in APA style.

In reading through the sample manuscript, pay close attention to its organization, that is, the order of presentation of the section headings of the report—title, abstract, introduction, method, results, discussion, references, author notes, footnotes, tables, and figures. Also pay close attention to the APA style requirements for page numbering, reference citations, and the format of figures and tables.

Writing is not easy, and writing in APA style can be overwhelming. It is important therefore to think of the APA format as providing a general organization for your papers. It is meant to be helpful to you in structuring and ordering your ideas, providing a format to follow in reporting results of your psychological studies. You may want to master the general APA format for organization as well as the general rules for citations and references. For more specific questions, such as citations for different kinds of sources, whether newspaper articles or online documents, consult the *Publication Manual*. Remember, even the most seasoned authors or researchers will make errors in APA style. Fortunately, editorial offices of journal articles are equipped with experts who can correct these errors. So the take-home message is do not be discouraged and afraid to make mistakes. For your papers, just make sure to follow the general APA format for organization and referencing. This, we hope, will help rather than hinder you in presenting your research results.

# Doing Better but Feeling Worse:
# Looking for the "Best" Job Undermines Satisfaction

*Sheena S. Iyengar*
*Columbia University*

*Rachael E. Wells*
*Columbia University*

*Barry Schwartz*
*Swarthmore College*

KEYWORDS: Maximizing, job search, satisfaction

Word Count: 3,917, excluding title page, abstract, references, and tables

*Source:* Sample Paper. Reprinted with permission from the authors.

## Abstract

Expanding on Simon's (1955) seminal theory, this investigation compares the choice-making strategies of maximizers with those of satisficers and finds that maximizing tendencies, while positively correlated with objectively better decision outcomes, are also associated with more negative subjective evaluations of these decision outcomes. Specifically, graduating university students were administered a scale that measured maximizing tendencies, and then followed over the course of the year as they searched for jobs. Students with high maximizing tendencies secured jobs with 20% higher starting salaries. However, maximizers were less satisfied than satisficers with the jobs they obtained, and experienced more negative affect throughout the job search process. These effects were mediated by maximizers' greater reliance on external sources of information, and their fixation on realized and unrealized options during the choice search and selection process.

## Introduction

> "Success is getting what you want. Happiness is wanting what you get."

> —Attributed to Dale Carnegie circa 1944

Half a century ago, Simon (1955, 1956, 1957) introduced an important distinction between "maximizing" and "satisficing" as choice-making strategies. To maximize is to seek the best, requiring an exhaustive search of all possibilities. To satisfice is to seek "good enough," searching until an option is encountered that crosses the threshold of acceptability. For example, compare the strategies of a maximizer versus a satisficer selecting a TV show from one of 400 cable channels. The maximizer would channel surf, exploring *all* the channels, spending so much time deciding on a show that little time would be left for viewing. The satisficer would most likely channel surf until he or she encounters the first acceptable show, put down the remote, and actually watch the show. Simon based his distinction on the idea that the limited information-processing capacities of organisms made maximizing impossible.

In the modern world of almost unimaginable choice, this distinction is even more pertinent (see Iyengar & Lepper, 2000; Schwartz, 2004a, 2004b).

Expanding on Simon's classic theory, recent studies by Schwartz et al. (2002) comparing the decision-making processes of maximizers and satisficers revealed that those exhibiting maximizing tendencies, like the channel surfer described above, were less satisfied with their decision outcomes than their satisficing counterparts. Researchers asked participants about recent purchasing decisions and used a "maximization scale" to measure individual differences in maximizing tendencies. Their findings suggested that the experiences of maximizers differed from those of satisficers both during the decision-making process and when evaluating their final decision outcome. Specifically, while they were involved in the decision-making process, maximizers were more likely to engage in an exhaustive search of all available options and compare their decisions with those of others (Schwartz et al., 2002). Even though maximizers invested more time and effort during the decision-making process and explored more options than satisficers—presumably to achieve greater satisfaction—they nonetheless felt worse about the outcome that they achieved. Results showed that maximizing tendencies were positively correlated with regret, depression, and decision difficulty, and negatively correlated with happiness, life satisfaction, optimism, and satisfaction with decision outcomes (Schwartz et al., 2002).

Such differences in the subjective choice-making experiences between maximizers and satisficers are attributed to the fact that maximizers create a more onerous choice-making process for themselves. Initially, maximizers focus on increasing their choice sets by exploring multiple options, presumably because expanded choice sets allow for greater possibilities to seek out and find the elusive "best." Yet as the number of options proliferates, cognitive limitations prevent decision makers from evaluating and comparing all options (Iyengar & Jiang, 2004; Iyengar & Lepper, 2000; Miller, 1956). Identifying the "best" becomes increasingly difficult, compelling maximizers to rely on external (often social) rather than internal standards to evaluate and select outcomes (Lyubomirsky & Ross, 1997). In addition, the inevitability of trade-offs among attractive options intensifies the sting of passing up one attractive alternative when choosing a more attractive one, and increases expectations about the quality and utility of the chosen alternative.

But do the very strategies that render maximizers less happy with their decision outcomes also enable them to achieve better objective decision outcomes? Perhaps there is utility associated with the strategic pursuit of real and imagined options, and the careful observation of others' choice-making experiences—utility that may be reflected in the form of more effective deliberations and objectively better outcomes. Unlike prior investigations of the relationship between maximizing tendencies and decision outcomes, the current investigation examines the effects of maximizing tendencies on both the objective outcome associated with the decision as well as the subjective experience of the decision maker throughout the process.

Thus, expanding on this nascent literature, the present study allows us to test the hypotheses that during the choice search and selection process, maximizers will invest more heavily in gathering information from external sources (thereby incurring search costs and perhaps prioritizing externally valued criteria) and will fixate more on realized and unrealized options (thereby incurring opportunity costs), both of which together will contribute to more successful decision outcomes, yet also result in greater negative affect and reduced subjective well-being. We chose to test these predictions within the consequential domain of graduating college students' job search processes, which allowed us to examine the influence of maximizing tendencies on both actual and perceived decision outcomes and afforded us the opportunity to examine reactions to the decision process as decisions were being made. Regardless of the finite number of offers made to job seekers, during the search process itself, maximizers face both the search costs and the raised expectations associated with contemplating an almost limitless set of employment possibilities. To determine how a maximizing orientation affects both the *affective* experiences and the *objective* outcomes of the job search process, we measured the maximizing tendencies of participants from multiple institutions during the fall of their final year and subsequently followed them throughout their job search. Specifically, the longitudinal questionnaire study measured both how well applicants actually did and how well they thought they did. This methodology allowed us to test the following predictions: that compared with satisficers, maximizers would desire more options, plan to apply for more jobs, rely more on social comparison and other external sources of information, obtain jobs with higher expected returns (i.e., salary), but also experience greater negative affect than satisficers throughout the process and at the conclusion of their job search.

# Method

## Participants

Graduating students (predominantly undergraduate seniors) were recruited from 11 colleges and universities that varied in geographical region, university rank, and school size. Females constituted 69.7% of the sample. The median age of participants was 21 (range: 20 to 57), and 64% of participants were Caucasian, 26% Asian, and 10% Other. Participants majored in the social sciences (36%), arts/humanities (25%), engineering (16%), natural sciences and math (11%), and business (15%). At T1, 548 participants responded, followed by response rates of 69.5% and 56% at T2 and T3, respectively. Five $200 prizes were raffled off among participants who completed all three surveys.

## Procedures

Career services from 11 participating institutions directed students who were just beginning their job searches in November 2001 (T1) to our survey website. T1 participants were notified via e-mail of our follow-up online surveys in February 2002, as they were completing applications, interviewing, and getting offers (T2), and in May 2002, as they were accepting offers (T3). While it is difficult to calculate the percentage of students who, on encountering the online advertisement, chose to participate in the survey, consultations with career services staff provided us with numerical estimates of the total number of students who utilized career services in their job search within the given academic year. Since the advertisement was available only to those students who were affiliated with career services between the months of September and November (approximately 25%), we calculated that response rates ranged from 17.4% to 53.2% across a sampling of participating institutions.

## Measures

*Maximizing tendencies.* At T1, participants completed 11 maximization items drawn from Schwartz et al. (2002), each of which were rated on a scale from 1 (*Strongly disagree*) to 9 (*Strongly agree*) ($\alpha = .6$). Two sample items are as follows: "When I am in the car listening to the radio, I often check other stations to see if something better is playing, even if I am relatively satisfied with what I'm listening to" and "When shopping, I have a hard time finding clothes that I really love." Individual item scores were averaged to create a composite maximizing score. Overall, men ($N = 166$, $M = 5.48$) and women ($N = 382$, $M = 5.10$) from our sample population showed significantly higher maximizing tendencies than those in a recent national adult sample (Kliger & Schwartz, 2005) [men: $N = 3,261$, $M = 4.9$, $t(165) = 7.03$, $p < .0001$; women: $N = 4,692$, $M = 4.77$, $t(381) = 6.28$, $p < .0001$], a difference which may be at least partly attributable to the age difference between the two samples, as maximization tendencies have found to be negatively correlated with age (Kliger & Schwartz, 2005).

*Option fixation.* We used three measures to examine option fixation. At T1, we measured the number of options that participants pursued: "For approximately how many jobs do you anticipate applying?" Participants provided responses in numerical form. Note that the number of anticipated applications ranged from 1 to 1,000, exhibiting extreme right skewness (skew = 7.5) and kurtosis (69.0) and was therefore log transformed. At T2, we measured participants' fixation on unrealized options on a scale from 1 (*Strongly* disagree) to 9 (*Strongly agree*): "I often fantasize about jobs that are quite different from the actual job(s) that I am pursuing." At T3, we measured participants' regret with their choice set size on a scale from 1 (*Not at all*) to 9 (*To a large extent*): "I wish I had pursued more options in my job search process."

*Reliance on external influences.* We created a single composite measure of five items ($\alpha$ = .70) to test reliance on external influences. At T1, participants were asked, "How much have you been using the services offered by the career services office at your school during the job search?" "To what extent have you consulted experts' ranking such as 'top companies,' 'fastest growing fields,' etc.?" "How much do you seek advice from your family regarding the job search (i.e., input, suggestions, etc.)?" and "To what extent do you compare your own job search process and results to those of your peers?" The question regarding peer comparison was repeated at T2. Participants responded on a scale from 1 (*Very little*) to 9 (*Very much*).

*Job market performance.* Participants were asked how many interviews they had received at T2 and T3, how many job offers they had received at T3, and their annual salary (in dollars/year/hour) when they accepted a full-time job offer at T3. In the case of jobs with hourly wages, we determined how many hours per week participants were required to work and converted this information into an estimated annual salary.

*Negative affect.* Participants' negative affect with the job search process was measured at all three time periods. At T1 and T2, participants were asked "To what extent does each of the following describe how you are generally feeling about the job search process?" rating each of seven emotions from 1 (*Not at all*) to 9 (*Extremely*) (T1 $\alpha$ = .86; T2 $\alpha$ = .89): "pessimistic," "stressed," "tired," "anxious," "worried," "overwhelmed," and "depressed." At T3, the same question was repeated, however, for those who had accepted job offers, it was modified to read "To what extent does each of the following describe how you are feeling about the offer you accepted and your upcoming new job?" and three emotions were added (T3 $\alpha$ = .92): "regretful," "disappointed," and "frustrated." Composite measures for T1, T2, and T3 were constructed.

*Outcome satisfaction.* We measured participants' satisfaction with their accepted job offers by averaging their responses [on a scale from 1 (*Not at all*) to 9 (*Very satisfied*)/(*Very confident*)] on two items: (1) "How satisfied are you with the offer you have accepted?" and (2) "How confident are you that you made the right choice about where to work next year?" ($\alpha$ = .88).

### Demographics and Other Control Variables

We gathered information on age, sex, ethnicity, family income level, university affiliation, and rank (as measured by *U.S. News & World Report*, "Best National Universities," 2001), geographic location, and information on academic standing, including major, overall GPA, and job-related activities (i.e., current stage in the job search process).

## Results

### Preliminary Analysis

Table 1 reports the means and standard deviations for all hypothesized variables, with maximizers and satisficers separated by a median split. Attrition analyses demonstrate that our initial sample differed from T2 and T3 samples in terms of demographics: East Asians, children of foreign-born parents, and older students constituted less of the later samples, while those who did not identify themselves with one specific ethnicity constituted greater portion of the sample at T3. However, T1, T2, and T3 samples did not differ as a function of our hypothesized variables (including maximizing score, number of logged anticipated applications, fixation on unrealized options, and reliance on external influences). Further analyses reveal that the subsample of participants who reported having completed the job search at T3 comprised significantly more business majors and fewer arts/humanities majors, younger job seekers, and those with higher GPAs, socioeconomic backgrounds, and a heavier reliance on external influences. All regression analyses reported below controlled for gender, university rank, age, academic major, cumulative GPA (collected at T2), and whether a job offer had been accepted. See Table 2 for full regression models including control variables. Note that, following Killeen (2005), as we report our regression results, we provide the probabilities of replicating our effects (denoted by $p_{rep}$) in addition to reporting standard $p$ values.

| Table 1 | Mean Differences Between Maximizers and Satisficers* | |
|---|---|---|
| | *Maximizers' Mean* | *Satisficers' Mean* |
| Anticipated applications | 20+ | 10 |
| Fixation on unrealized options | 5.17 (2.55) | 4.02 (2.47) |
| Regret with choice set size | 5.09 (2.39) | 4.52 (2.20) |
| Reliance on external influences | 5.02 (1.65) | 4.65 (1.62) |
| Salary (in $10K) | 4.45 (1.34) | 3.71 (1.35) |
| Negative affect (T1) | 5.54 (1.56) | 4.81 (1.59) |
| Negative affect (T2) | 5.40 (1.67) | 4.81 (1.83) |
| Negative affect (T3) | 4.50 (1.82) | 3.91 (1.78) |
| Outcome satisfaction | 7.02 (1.78) | 7.58 (1.55) |

*Standard deviations are provided in parentheses.

+The scores reported for anticipated applications are medians, rather than means, and are only for students from universities not ranked within the top 15 as university rank significantly interacted with maximizing tendencies university rank.

*Note:* T1, T2, and T3 = first, second, and third assessments, respectively.

## Main Effects for Maximizing Tendencies

As illustrated in Table 2, maximizing tendencies were observed to be positively correlated with increased option fixation, greater reliance on external influences, improved job market performance, and more negative affective experiences. At T1, those with greater maximizing tendencies anticipated applying for more jobs [$\beta = .13$, $t(537) = 2.35$, $p < .05$, $p_{rep} = .93$]; however, this effect was attenuated among those attending high ranked universities [$\beta = -.50$, $t(537) = -2.33$, $p < .05$, $p_{rep} = .93$]. Among students in top-15 ranked universities, the median for both maximizers and satisficers was 30, while in lower ranked universities, the median was 20 for maximizers and 10 for satisficers. At T2, those with greater maximizing tendencies fantasized more about jobs that they were not pursuing [$\beta = .23$, $t(372) = 4.48$, $p < .001$, $p_{rep} = .99$], such that every one-unit increase in maximizing was associated with a 0.59 increase in this measure. At T3, those with greater maximizing tendencies reported that they "wished that they had pursued still more options" [$\beta = .18$, $t(263) = 2.96$, $p < .01$, $p_{rep} = .97$], such that every one-unit increase in maximizing was associated with a 0.40 increase in this measure. Additionally, those with greater maximizing tendencies were more reliant on external influences during T1 and T2 of the job search process [$\beta = .17$, $t(366) = 3.63$, $p < .001$, $p_{rep} = .99$]. Every one-unit increase in maximizing was associated with a 0.27 increase in this measure.

**Table 2**  Regression Analyses Betas

| | 1 | 2 | 3 | 4 | 5 | 6 | 7 | 8 |
|---|---|---|---|---|---|---|---|---|
| | Logged Anticipated Applications | Fixation on Unrealized Options | Regret with Choice Set Size | Reliance on External Influences | Salary-Initial Model | Salary-Mediator Model | Negative Affect (T1)-Initial Model | Negative Affect (T1)-Mediator Model |
| **Control Variables** | | | | | | | | |
| Female sex (0-M; 1-F) | .03 | .00 | .04 | -.07 | -.16* | -.11 | .04 | .04 |
| Top 15-ranked university | .73** | .01 | .02 | .05 | .29** | .27** | .11* | .03 |
| Age | .11* | -.00 | .13* | -.17** | .06 | .10 | -.05 | -.08† |
| Business major | .25** | -.06 | .05 | .33** | .11 | .03 | .08 | .01 |
| Social sciences major | .24** | -.08 | .02 | .18 | -.00 | .02 | .08 | .01 |
| Science/math major | .03 | -.16* | -.05 | -.01 | .08 | .06 | -.01 | -.02 |
| Engineering major | .21** | -.12 | -.06 | .11 | .32† | .36* | .06 | .00 |
| Education major | -.01 | -.04 | .00 | -.04 | – | -.20 | -.03 | -.03 |
| Arts/humanities major | .12 | -.08 | .08 | -.04 | -.28† | .20** | .08 | .04 |
| Cumulative GPA | | -.09 | -.18** | .02 | .19* | .15* | – | – |
| S had already accepted an offer by point of DV measurement | -0.09* | -.01 | -.18** | .21** | | | -.19** | -.16** |
| Salary (in $10K) | | | | | | | | |

| | Logged Anticipated Applications | Fixation on Unrealized Options | Regret with Choice Set Size | Reliance on External Influences | Salary-Initial Model | Salary-Mediator Model | Negative Affect (T1)-Initial Model | Negative Affect (T1)-Mediator Model |
|---|---|---|---|---|---|---|---|---|
| **Maximizing Variables** | | | | | | | | |
| Maximizing score | .13* | .23** | .18** | .17** | .20** | .15* | .26** | .25** |
| Maximizing score*Top-15 ranked university | −.50* | | | | | | | |
| **Proposed Mediators** | | | | | | | | |
| Logged anticipated applications | | | | | | — | | .29** |
| Fixation on unrealized options | | | | | | — | | |
| Regret with choice set size | | | | | | — | | |
| Reliance on external influence | | | | | | .27** | | |
| Full Model $R^2$ | .14 | .08 | .14 | .28 | .49 | .54 | .13 | .20 |
| $\Delta R^2$ vs. Control Model | .01 | .05 | .03 | .03 | .04 | .09 | .07 | .14 |
| $\Delta R^2$ vs. Previous Model of Same DV | | | | | | .05 | | .07 |
| Model $F$-Ratio | 7.06 | 2.60 | 3.34 | 11.28 | 10.22 | 11.29 | 6.98 | 10.97 |
| Degrees of freedom | 537 | 372 | 263 | 366 | 115 | 115 | 535 | 535 |
| $p_{rep}$ | .99 | .98 | .99 | .99 | .99 | .99 | .99 | .99 |

*(Continued)*

**Table 2** (Continued)

| Control Variables | 9 Negative Affect T2-Initial Model | 10 Negative Affect T2-Mediator Model | 11 Negative Affect T2-Ctrl for Neg. Affect T1 | 12 Negative Affect T3-Initial Model | 13 Negative Affect T3-Mediator Model | 14 Negative Affect T3 – Ctrl for Neg. Affect T1 | 13 Outcome Satisfaction – Initial Model | 14 Outcome Satisfaction-Ctrl for Neg. Affect T1 | 15 Outcome Satisfaction-Ctrl for Neg. Affect T1 |
|---|---|---|---|---|---|---|---|---|---|
| Female sex (0-M; 1-F) | −.01 | −.01 | −.02 | −.04 | −.04 | −.07 | .05 | .08 | .10 |
| Top 15-ranked university | .09† | .01 | .01 | −.03 | −.05 | −.08 | −.05 | −.04 | −.02 |
| Age | −.10* | −.13** | −.06 | .00 | −.00 | .01 | −.08 | −.10 | −.10 |
| Business major | −.00 | −.02 | −.02 | .05 | −.02 | .02 | −.08 | −.20 | −.21 |
| Social sciences major | .02 | .00 | −.01 | .12 | .09 | .08 | −.04 | −.17 | −.16 |
| Science/math major | .01 | .06 | .06 | −.08 | −.04 | −.02 | .09 | .02 | .03 |
| Engineering major | .05 | .05 | .05 | .07 | .09 | .09 | .04 | −.14 | −.14 |
| Education major | .05 | .05 | .03 | .09 | .10† | .06 | – | | |
| Arts/humanities major | .04 | .04 | .01 | .06 | .07 | .06 | −.02 | −.02 | −.02 |
| Cumulative GPA | −.03 | .01 | .01 | −.08 | −.02 | −.00 | .20* | .02 | .01 |
| S had already accepted an offer by point of DV measurement | −.31** | −.30** | −.24** | −.53** | −.53** | −.52** | – | | |
| Salary (in $10K) | | | | | | | .12 | .22† | .19 |

| | Negative Affect T2- Initial Model | Negative Affect T2- Mediator Model | Negative Affect T2- Ctrl for Neg. Affect T1 | Negative Affect T3 – Initial Model | Negative Affect T3 – Mediator Model | Negative Affect T3 – Ctrl for Neg. Affect T1 | Outcome Satisfaction – Initial Model | Outcome Satisfaction- Ctrl for Neg. Affect T1 | Outcome Satisfaction- Ctrl for Neg. Affect T1 |
|---|---|---|---|---|---|---|---|---|---|
| **Maximizing Variables** | | | | | | | | | |
| Maximizing score | .18** | .11* | .01 | .16** | .06 | .03 | −.28** | −.14 | −.10 |
| Maximizing score* Top-15 ranked university | | | | | | | | | |
| **Proposed Mediators** | | | | | | | | | |
| Logged anticipated applications | | .21** | .04 | | | | | | |
| Fixation on unrealized options | | .25** | .15** | | .10† | .04 | | −.27** | −.21* |
| Regret with choice set size | | | | | .21** | .16** | | −.34** | −.31** |
| Reliance on external influence | | | | | .18** | .11* | | | |
| Negative Affect T1 | | | .59** | | | .31** | | | −.23* |
| Full Model $R^2$ | .14 | .24 | .52 | .35 | .42 | .50 | .16 | .34 | .38 |
| $\Delta R^2$ vs. Control Model | .03 | .13 | .41 | .02 | .09 | .17 | .07 | .25 | .29 |
| $\Delta R^2$ vs. Previous Model of Same DV | | .10 | .28 | | .07 | .08 | | .18 | .03 |
| Model F-Ratio | 4.70 | 8.07 | 25.75 | 11.18 | 11.85 | 15.16 | 1.75 | 4.05 | 4.46 |
| Degrees of freedom | 365 | 365 | 365 | 257 | 257 | 257 | 115 | 115 | 115 |
| $p_{rep}$ | .99 | .99 | .99 | .99 | .99 | .99 | .85 | .99 | .99 |

Note: DV = dependent variable; GPA = grade point average; T1, T2, and T3 = first, second, and third assessments, respectively.

*$p < .05$. **$p < .01$. †$p < .10$.

345

Indeed, job seekers with greater maximizing tendencies were offered an average of $7,430 more in salary than their satisficing counterparts [$\beta = .20$, $t(115) = 2.83$, $p < .01$, $p_{rep} = .96$], such that every one-unit increase in the maximizing composite score was associated with a $2,630 increase in the annual salary obtained. Based on a median split of the maximizing scale, the mean salary of maximizing job seekers was $44,515, while that of satisficing job seekers was $37,085. This difference in salary between maximizing and satisficing job seekers was unaccounted for by the number of interviews or job offers received, as maximizing tendencies did not prove to be a significant predictor of either number of interviews (T2 poisson regression $\beta = .09$, $C^2 = 1.43$, ns; T3 poisson $\beta = .05$, $C^2 = .55$, ns) or offers attained (T3 poisson regression $\beta = .09$, $C^2 = 1.80$, ns).

Greater maximizing tendencies were also associated with experiences of greater negative affect at all three times of the job search process [T1: $\beta = .26$, $t(535) = 6.32$, $p < .001$, $p_{rep} = .99$; T2: $\beta = .18$, $t(365) = 3.56$, $p < .001$, $p_{rep} = .99$; T3: $\beta = .16$, $t(257) = 2.98$, $p < .01$, $p_{rep} = .97$]. Every one-unit increase in maximizing was associated with 0.40, 0.31, and 0.28 increases in negative affect at T1, T2, and T3, respectively. Those with greater maximizing tendencies also reported less satisfaction with their accepted job offers even when controlling for annual salary achieved [$\beta = -.28$, $t(115) = -2.92$, $p < .01$, $p_{rep} = .97$], such that every one-unit increase in maximizing was associated with a 0.43 decrease in reported satisfaction.

### Mediators of Maximizing Tendencies

As illustrated in Table 2, results suggest that the relationship of maximizing tendencies with job market performance and negative affective experience was mediated by a combination of reliance on external influences and option fixation. Reliance on external influences [$\beta = .27$, $t(115) = 3.41$, $p < .01$, $p_{rep} = .98$] acted as a partial mediator of the effect of maximizing on job market performance. The positive correlational relationship between maximizing and negative affect was observed to be partially mediated at T2 by logged anticipated applications [$\beta = .21$, $t(365) = 4.14$, $p < .001$, $p_{rep} = .99$] and fixation on unrealized options [$\beta = .25$, $t(365) = 5.15$, $p < .001$, $p_{rep} = .99$], and fully mediated at T3 by fixation on unrealized options [$\beta = .10$, $t(257) = 1.81$, $p < .10$, $p_{rep} = .85$], regret with choice set size [$\beta = .21$, $t(257) = 3.82$, $p < .001$, $p_{rep} = .99$], and reliance on external influence [$\beta = .18$, $t(257) = 3.01$, $p < .01$, $p_{rep} = .97$]. In fact, the relationship between maximizing tendencies and outcome satisfaction was also fully mediated by fixation on unrealized options [$\beta = -.27$, $t(115) = -2.81$, $p < .01$, $p_{rep} = .96$] and regret with choice set size [$\beta = -.34$, $t(257) = -3.80$, $p < .001$, $p_{rep} = .99$]. Even when T1 negative affective experience is included as a control in the regression models, similar results emerge.

## Discussion

Maximizers do better financially in their job search but feel worse. In their quest for placement after graduation, those with greater maximizing tendencies not only pursue and fixate on realized and unrealized options to a greater degree, but they also rely on more external sources of information than do more satisficing job seekers. These efforts result in higher payoffs; maximizers earn starting salaries that are 20% higher than those of satisficers. Yet, despite their relative success, they are less satisfied with the outcomes of their job search and more "pessimistic," "stressed," "tired," "anxious," "worried," "overwhelmed," and "depressed" throughout the process. Why?

Perhaps maximizers are merely high achievers with more past successes and superior credentials who have rightly learned to expect more of themselves. No matter how well they do, maximizers feel worse because they fail to match these high expectations. Certainly there is evidence to suggest that maximizers have histories of past success; we find significantly more maximizers within top-ranked universities. However, there is also evidence to suggest that equating maximizing tendencies with capability oversimplifies the story. After all, we do not find a significant relationship between maximizing and another marker of academic success, GPA. Furthermore, if one assumed maximizers' success on the job market to simply be about better credentials, one would expect proxies for high qualifications such as university rank and GPA to mediate the effects of maximizing on job market performance. Yet we find that even when controlling for these two indices, maximizing tendencies are still predictive of salary. Thus, whatever the relationship between maximizing and high achievement, past achievement in and of itself seems inadequate to explain high expectations as the putative source of maximizers' negative affect. Why, then, do maximizers feel worse when they do better?

Perhaps the fact that maximizers start the job search process at T1 feeling worse suggests that they are simply dispositionally less happy than satisficers and, therefore, less satisfied with the outcome of *any* decision. Contrary to this "dispositional unhappiness" prediction, even after accounting for initial negative affect at T1, we observe that option fixation and regret with choice set size mediate the effect of maximizing on outcome satisfaction at T2 and T3. Our findings support earlier research by Schwartz et al. (2002) that suggest that even when controlling for dispositional happiness, maximizing tendencies make an independent contribution to subjective evaluations.

Instead, we suggest that maximizers may be less satisfied and experience greater negative affect with their resulting jobs because their pursuit of the elusive "best" induces them to consider a large number of possibilities, thereby increasing their potential for regret and/or anticipated regret, engendering unrealistically high expectations, and creating mounting opportunity costs. Such effects may be integral to identifying maximizing as a goal, and may detract from the satisfaction that maximizers ultimately derive from their decisions.

Although we treat maximizing tendencies as a global individual difference measure, it may well be that maximizing strategies to find the "best" are simply a set of learned behaviors or search strategies designed specifically for decision-making tasks, and not necessarily even *all* decision-making tasks. In fact, mediation analyses demonstrate that individual differences in maximizing tendencies are explained by differences in option fixation and reliance on external sources of information. Nonetheless, whether global or specific, maximizing tendencies seem to cast a long shadow on people's evaluations of their decision and search outcomes.

Of course, the findings from this investigation are limited in that salary is merely one measure of objective success in the job search process. Our present investigation does not allow us to assess whether maximizers' lesser job satisfaction stems from other measures of job search success, such as working conditions, colleagues, organizational commitment, and opportunities for advancement. Additionally, our affective measures allow us to assess decision makers' experiences with the process and their *expected* satisfaction with their impending employment but are limited in that they do not assess job seekers' affective experience with their resulting employment.

Psychologists and economists alike have assumed the provision of choice to be beneficial, as it allows decision makers more opportunities for preference matching, and more generally enables utility maximization. However, the present investigation is part of a growing body of literature that posits that decision makers' appraisals of their decision outcomes may have less to do with their ability to preference match or increase the expected value of their decision outcomes than it does with the decision makers' social values (Iyengar & Lepper, 1999), mispredicted expectations during the decision process (Frederick & Loewenstein, 1999; Kahneman, 1999; Loewenstein & Schkade, 1999; Wilson, 2002; Wilson & Gilbert, 2003), and the affect experienced during the decision process itself (Botti & Iyengar, 2004). Maximizers, then, epitomize the type of decision maker who may overestimate the affective benefits that result from pursuing the best objective outcome, and underestimate the affective costs of a process that involves evaluating as many options as possible and fixating on choices that may be nonexistent. Even when they get what they want, maximizers may not always want what they get. Individual decision makers as well as policymakers are thus confronted by a dilemma: If the subjective well-being of the decision maker and the objective value of the decision outcome are at odds, which should be prioritized? What should people do when "doing better" makes them feel worse?

# References

Best National Universities. (2001, September 17). *U.S. News & World Report, 131,* 106.

Botti, S., & Iyengar, S. S. (2004). The psychological pleasure and pain of choosing: When people prefer choosing at the cost of subsequent outcome satisfaction. *Journal of Personality and Social Psychology, 87,* 312–326.

Frederick, S., & Loewenstein, G. (1999). Hedonic adaptation. In D. Kahneman, E. Diener, & N. Schwarz (Eds.), *Well-being: The foundations of hedonic psychology* (pp. 302–329). New York, NY: Russell Sage.

Iyengar, S. S., & Jiang, W. (2004). *Choosing not to choose: The effect of more choices on retirement savings decisions.* Manuscript submitted for publication, Columbia University.

Iyengar, S. S., & Lepper, M. R. (1999). Rethinking the value of choice: A cultural perspective on intrinsic motivation. *Journal of Personality and Social Psychology, 76,* 349–366.

Iyengar, S. S., & Lepper, M. R. (2000). When choice is demotivating: Can one desire too much of a good thing? *Journal of Personality and Social Psychology, 79,* 995–1006.

Kahneman, D. (1999). Objective happiness. In D. Kahneman, E. Diener, & N. Schwarz (Eds.), *Well-being: The foundations of hedonic psychology* (pp. 3–25). New York, NY: Russell Sage.

Killeen, P. R. (2005). An alternative to null-hypothesis significance tests. *Psychological Science, 16,* 345–353.

Kliger, M., & Schwartz, B. (2005). *Maximizing tendencies: Evidence from a national sample.* Unpublished raw data, Simmons Company.

Loewenstein, G., & Schkade, D. (1999). Wouldn't it be nice? Predicting future feelings. In D. Kahneman, E. Diener, & N. Schwarz (Eds.), *Well-being: The foundations of hedonic psychology* (pp. 85–108). New York, NY: Russell Sage.

Lyubomirsky, S., & Ross, L. (1997). Hedonic consequences of social comparison: A contrast of happy and unhappy people. *Journal of Personality and Social Psychology, 73,* 1141–1157.

Miller, G. A. (1956). The magic number seven plus or minus two: Some limits in our capacity for processing information. *Psychological Review, 63,* 81–97.

Schwartz, B. (2004a). *The paradox of choice: Why more is less.* New York, NY: Ecco.

Schwartz, B. (2004b, April). The tyranny of choice. *Scientific American,* 71–75.

Schwartz, B., Ward, A., Monterosso, J., Lyubomirsky, S., White, K., & Lehman, D. R. (2002). Maximizing versus satisficing: Happiness is a matter of choice. *Journal of Personality and Social Psychology, 83,* 1178–1197.

Simon, H. A. (1955). A behavioral model of rational choice. *Quarterly Journal of Economics, 59,* 99–118.

Simon, H. A. (1956). Rational choice and the structure of the environment. *Psychological Review, 63,* 129–138.

Simon, H. A. (1957). *Models of man, social and rational: Mathematical essays on rational human behavior.* New York, NY: Wiley.

Wilson, T. D. (2002). *Strangers to ourselves: Discovering the adaptive unconscious.* Cambridge, MA: Harvard University Press.

Wilson, T. D., & Gilbert, D. T. (2003). Affective forecasting. In M. P. Zanna (Ed.), *Advances in experimental social psychology* (Vol. 35, pp. 345–411). San Diego, CA: Academic Press.

## Authors' Note

Sheena S. Iyengar, Management Division, Graduate School of Business, Columbia University; Rachael E. Wells, Management Division, Graduate School of Business, Columbia University; Barry Schwartz, Psychology Department, Swarthmore College.

This research was supported by a National Science Foundation Young Investigator Career Award.

Correspondence can be addressed to: Sheena S. Iyengar, Management Division, Columbia University Business School, by e-mail ss957@columbia.edu, or telephone (212) 854–8308. Detailed statistical information yielded by analyses of differences in subsample characteristics is also available on request.

## 回 Conclusions

The APA format provides us with a blueprint for report writing. Two of the most common types of reports are empirical studies and literature reviews. The APA format for organization of a written report of an empirical study is rather straightforward: title, abstract, method, results, discussion, references, author notes, footnotes, tables, and figures with captions. Literature reviews are critical examinations of empirical studies that have already been published. In a literature review, you evaluate published studies in terms of their methods as well as their conceptual foundation. A literature review does not follow the same organization and structure as an article reporting an empirical study. You will have an abstract that appears on the first page that summarizes your review. But you will not have the prescribed method and results sections for a report on an empirical study. Instead, you will identify headings for major sections that will help you organize the structure of the paper. Try to make headings as specific as possible. For clues, look at published literature reviews to see how authors typically use headings to delineate major sections of their articles.

In summary, writing in psychology is both a communal and a learning process. We read the works of others. We can learn how to structure a report, organize ideas, and develop a line of argument by outlining and diagramming a work that we find to be especially well written. We can ask peers and teachers to provide feedback on our own written work. We might also ask our instructor to identify key ingredients of a text that make a particular article well written. And as we stated at the outset, stay positive and open, and remember it's better to have rewritten than to have never written!

## Chapter Highlights

- Our psychological knowledge advances through written research.

- The APA format provides us with a blueprint for report writing.

- APA style emphasizes written language that is sensitive to racial and ethnic identity, gender, age, sexual orientation, and disabilities.

- APA style also emphasizes the importance of proper documentation and citation.

- Plagiarism is a serious ethical as well as legal problem that can result in expulsion, grade failure, job loss, and litigation for violating copyright laws.

- Two common types of research articles are empirical studies and literature reviews.

- Empirical studies are reports of original research, and literature reviews are critical evaluations of works that have already been published.

- The 13 parts of a written report are as follows: (1) title, (2) title and affiliations of authors, (3) abstract, (4) introduction, (5) method, (6) results, (7) discussion, (8) references, (9) author notes, (10) footnotes, (11) tables, (12) figure captions, and (13) figures.

- We examined in detail how to write six essential sections of an empirical study: (1) abstract, (2) introduction, (3) method, (4) results, (5) discussion, and (6) references.

- Four steps that might be helpful to keep in mind when writing a literature review are as follows: (1) introduce and define research question or problem; (2) narrow research question to the studies reviewed; (3) describe studies in detail and identify relationships, gaps, and inconsistencies in the literature; and (4) discuss how the research problem may be ameliorated or rectified.

# Key Terms

| | | |
|---|---|---|
| Abstract | Discussion | Plagiarism |
| APA | Introduction | References |
| APA format | Method | Results |

# Research in the News

In Chapter 2, we learned about meta-analyses as a type of literature review that has become widely used by researchers over the past 15 years. In meta-analyses, researchers use quantitative procedures to statistically combine the results of numerous studies. As a form of a literature review, meta-analyses are, however, not without controversy. Consider a January 12, 2010, nytimes.com article by Richard A. Friedman, MD, titled "Before You Quit Antidepressants. . . ."

In his commentary, Friedman takes issue with a recent meta-analysis appearing in the *Journal of the American Medical Association (JAMA)* authored by Fournier and colleagues (2010) that questioned the effectiveness of antidepressant drugs. The *JAMA* article, based on a meta-analysis of six studies of 718 patients, indicated that antidepressant medication is no more effective than a placebo pill for the treatment of mild to moderate forms of depression. Disputing these findings, Friedman (2010) wrote,

> The study is a so-called meta-analysis—not a fresh clinical trial, but a combined analysis of previous studies.

A common reason for doing this kind of analysis is to discover potential drug effects that might have been missed in smaller studies. By aggregating the data from many studies, researchers gain the statistical power to detect broad patterns that may have not been evident before. . . . But meta-analyses can be tricky. First, they are only as good as the smaller studies they analyze. And then there are hundreds of studies out there, how to decide which ones to include.

Debate the issue of meta-analysis as a valid form of literature review. How would you compare and contrast meta-analysis with the traditional form of literature review we covered here in this chapter? How would you evaluate the selection of studies included in the Fournier article? How would you respond to criticism leveled by Friedman? Would you have reported the results differently? How might you have reported the results to avoid this ensuing controversy?

## STUDENT STUDY SITE

Please access the study site at **www.sagepub.com/nestor2e,** where you will find useful study materials such as mobile-friendly eFlashcards and mid-chapter and full chapter web quizzes for each chapter, along with carefully selected articles from research journals that illustrate the major concepts and techniques presented in the book.

# Activity Questions

1. Plagiarism is no joke. What are the regulations on plagiarism in class papers at your school? What do you think the ideal policy would be? Should this policy take into account cultural differences in teaching practices and learning styles? Do you think this ideal policy is likely to be implemented? Why or why not? Based on your experiences, do you believe that most student plagiarism is the result of misunderstanding about proper citation practices, or is it the result of dishonesty? Do

you think that students who plagiarize while in school are less likely to be honest as researchers?

2. The National Academies of Sciences wrote a lengthy report on ethics issues in scientific research. Visit the site and read the free executive summary you can obtain at http://www. nap.edu/catalog.php?record_id=10430. Summarize the information and guidelines in the report.

3. Write an abstract of no more than 120 words describing our in-class exercise that investigated focusing illusion in college students.

4. Read the Kahneman et al. (2006) article. Outline the paper so that you can understand the structure and organization of ideas presented. Identify the major thesis of the paper, its background, and evidence in favor of and against the research question.

# Review Questions

1. Describe how you would, according to APA style, organize a report of an empirical study. Describe the content you must include for each of the major sections of your report.
2. Describe how you would, according to APA style, organize a written literature review. What is the rationale for your literature review and how would you go about accomplishing your objective or aim?

3. What are the pros and cons of a scientific poster? How does a scientific poster differ from a written manuscript or article? How would you describe the relationship between a poster and a written manuscript?

# Ethics in Action

1. The APA Ethics Code (Standard 8.10b, *Reporting Research Results*) indicates that when mistakes in reporting data occur and are published, the researchers should take steps to correct the errors. How would a researcher go about making corrections to data already published? How might errors be avoided?

2. As we noted in Chapter 3, in a July 2010 *Scientific American* piece, "When Scientists Lie," the essayist Michael Shermer comments on the book by vice provost of California Institute of Technology David Goodstein titled *On Fact and Fraud: Cautionary Tales From the Front Lines of Science* (2010). Both the Shermer essay and the Goodstein book resonate with the thrust of this chapter devoted to the topic of reporting

research results. In his book, Goodstein writes, as reported by Shermer, "Injecting falsehoods into the body of science is rarely, if ever, the purpose of those who perpetuate fraud. They almost always believe that they are injecting a truth into the scientific record" (p. 2). In other words, in many instances of scientific fraud and deceit, the perpetrators fool themselves into believing that their finding or discovery will turn out to be true when subsequent investigators perform the proper studies. What do you make of this? Comment on these apparent acts of conscious and unconscious self-deception, that is, how scientists might fool themselves into believing and defending "research lies." What are the ethical and practical implications of these costly misrepresentations?

# Appendix A

## Summaries of Frequently Cited Research Articles

Actual research studies are used throughout the text to illustrate particular research approaches and issues. You can use the following summaries at any point to review the design of these studies. The chapter number in brackets indicates the text chapter in which the study is introduced.

Aronson, E., & Mills, J. (1959). The effect of severity of initiation on liking for a group. *Journal of Abnormal and Social Psychology, 59*, 177–181. [Chapter 3]. A classic experimental study of students at an all-women's college in the 1950s. The students were assigned randomly to either read embarrassing words or listen to a boring, taped discussion prior to being allowed to join a group in order to determine the effect of severity of initiation on liking for the group.

Beare, P. L., Severson, S., & Brandt, P. (2004). The use of a positive procedure to increase engagement on-task and decrease challenging behavior. *Behavior Modification, 28*, 28–44. [Chapter 9]. A single-subject study of a long-term adult hospital resident with profound mental retardation to determine whether a differential reinforcement plan could reduce his self-injurious behavior.

Bisconer, S. W., Green, M., Mallon-Czajka, J., & Johnson, J. S. (2006). Managing aggression in a psychiatric hospital using a behaviour plan: A case study. *Journal of Psychiatric and Mental Health Nursing, 13*, 515–521. [Chapter 9]. A single-subject study of a psychiatric hospital inpatient to determine whether a treatment program based on reinforcers could reduce his aggressive and threatening behavior.

Brinegar, M. G., Salvi, L. M., Stiles, W. B., & Greenberg, L. S. (2006). Building a meaning bridge: Therapeutic progress from problem formulation to understanding. *Journal of Counseling Psychology, 53*, 165–180. [Chapter 11]. A qualitative study of brief client-centered therapy in the York University Depression Project, using recordings of actual therapy sessions.

Cohen, S. G., & Ledford, G. E., Jr. (1994). The effectiveness of self-managing teams: A quasi-experiment. *Human Relations, 47*, 13–43. [Chapter 8]. A study of the effectiveness of self-managing teams in a telecommunications company, using an ex post facto design. Each work group identified as self-managing was matched with a traditionally managed work group that produced the same product or service.

Dunn, E. W., Aknin, L. B., & Norton, M. I. (2008). Spending money on others promotes happiness. *Science, 319*, 1687–1688. [Chapter 10]. A multimethod research using cross-sectional and longitudinal surveys and a laboratory experiment to test the hypothesis that spending money on other people has a more positive impact on happiness than does spending money on oneself.

Haney, C., Banks, C., & Zimbardo, P. G. (1973). Interpersonal dynamics in a simulated prison. *International Journal for Criminology and Penology, 1*, 69–97. [Chapter 3]. A classic study of the impact of social position—being a prisoner or a prison guard—on behavior. The male volunteers signed a contract to participate for 2 weeks in a simulated prison. The prisoners became passive and disorganized, whereas the guards became verbally and physically aggressive and the experiment was terminated after 6 days.

Hard, S. F., Conway, J. M., & Moran, A. C. (2006). Faculty and college student beliefs about the frequency of student academic misconduct. *Journal of Higher Education, 77*, 1058–1080. [Chapter 12]. A group-based survey about plagiarism and other misconduct in classes within one university.

Humphreys, L. (1970). *Tearoom trade: Impersonal sex in public places.* Chicago, IL: Aldine de Gruyter. [Chapter 3]. A two-part study of men who participate in anonymous homosexual encounters. First, Humphreys worked as a covert participant by serving as a lookout (a "watch queen") in a public bathroom (and copying down the license plate numbers of participants); second, he surveyed the men in their homes, without revealing how he had obtained their names.

Iyengar, S. S., Wells, R. E., & Schwartz, B. (2006). Doing better but feeling worse. Looking for the "best" job undermines satisfaction. *Current Directions in Psychological Science, 17,* 143–150. [Chapters 1 and 12]. A survey of graduating students early and late in their initial job search. Contrasts starting salaries and feelings of satisfaction between students classified as maximizers and satisficers.

Keyes, C. L. M. (2007). Promoting and protecting mental health as flourishing: A complementary strategy for improving national mental health. *American Psychologist, 62,* 95–108. [Chapter 4]. A conceptualization of mental health and mental illness as on a continuum, with measures used in survey research to identify prevalence.

Levitt, H., Butler, M., & Hill, T. (2006). What clients find helpful in psychotherapy: Developing principles for facilitating moment-to-moment change. *Journal of Counseling Psychology, 53,* 314–324. [Chapter 11]. A study of the process of change in psychotherapy based on 1.5-hour intensive qualitative interviews.

Levitt, H. M., Swanger, R. T., & Butler, J. B. (2008). Male perpetrators' perspectives on intimate partner violence, religion, and masculinity. *Sex Roles, 58,* 435–448. [Chapter 11]. An exploration of perspectives of intimate partner violence perpetrators in the southern U.S. semistructured interviews analyzed using the grounded theory method.

Mahncke, H. W., Connor, B. B., Appelman, J., Ahsanuddin, O. N., Hardy, J. L., Wood, R. A., . . . Merzenich, M. M. (2006). Memory enhancement in healthy older adults using a brain plasticity-based training program: A randomized controlled study. *Proceedings of the National Academy of Sciences of the United States of America, 103,* 12523–12528. [Chapter 6]. A randomized experiment to determine whether healthy participants 60 years or older would show improved mental abilities following brain plasticity training that involved "working out"—performing a prescribed 5-day-a-week regimen of cognitive exercises on their home computers.

Meyers, D. G., & Diener, E. (1996). Most people are happy. *Psychological Science, 7,* 181–185. [Chapter 5]. The comparison of findings about happiness ("subjective well-being") from surveys in 43 nations in which nationally representative samples were selected.

Milgram, S. (1965). Some conditions of obedience and disobedience to authority. *Human Relations, 18,* 57–75. [Chapter 3]. An attempt to identify through laboratory experiments the conditions under which ordinary citizens would resist instructions from authority figures to inflict pain on others. Men were recruited through local newspaper ads, told that they were to participate in a study of learning, and instructed to help a "student" memorize words by administering an electric shock (with a phony machine).

Nakonezny, P. A., Reddick, R., & Rodgers, J. L. (2004). Did divorces decline after the Oklahoma City bombing? *Journal of Marriage and Family, 66,* 90–100. [Chapter 8]. A time-series design to identify the impact of the Oklahoma City terrorist bombing in April 1995 on the divorce rate in Oklahoma. The average rate of change in divorce rates in Oklahoma's 77 counties in the 10 years prior to the bombing compared with that 5 years after the bombing.

Nestor, P. G., Klein, K., Pomplun, M., Niznikiewicz, M., & McCarley, R. W. (2010). Gaze cueing of attention in schizophrenia: Individual differences in neuropsychological functioning and symptoms. *Journal of Clinical and Experimental Neuropsychology, 32,* 281–288. [Chapter 8]. A quasi-experimental study comparing the experimentally manipulated effect of social and nonsocial attention as measured by speeded target detection in persons with schizophrenia and in a control group of healthy volunteers.

Phillips, D. P. (1982). The impact of fictional television stories on U.S. adult fatalities: New evidence on the effect of the mass media on violence. *American Journal of Sociology, 87,* 1340–1359. [Chapter 7]. A quasi-experimental study of the effect of TV soap opera suicides on the number of actual suicides in the United States, using a multiple-group before-and-after design. The soap opera suicides in 1977 were identified, and then the suicide rates in the week prior to and during the week of each suicide story were compared. Deaths due to suicide increased from the control period to the experimental period in 12 of the 13 comparisons.

Rowe, G., Hirsh, J. B., & Anderson, A. K. (2007). Positive affect increases the breadth of attentional selection. *Proceedings of the National Academy of Sciences, 104,* 383–388. [Chapter 7]. A multifactorial experimental study of how emotions may broaden attentional allocation to both external visual and internal conceptual space.

Schutt, R. K. (2011). *Homelessness, housing and mental illness.* With Stephen M. Goldfinger. Cambridge, MA: Harvard University Press. [Chapter 11]. A comprehensive analysis of group and independent living alternatives for homeless persons with severe mental illness. A multimethod study using experimental design, surveys, and participant-observation (ethnography).

Strack, F., Martin, L. L., & Stepper, S. (1988). Inhibiting and facilitating conditions of the human smile: A nonobtrusive test of the facial feedback hypothesis. *Journal of Personality and Social Psychology, 54,* 766–777. [Chapters 2, 5]. An experimental study of students to test the hypothesis that induced involuntary smiling would increase happiness.

Wageman, R. (1995). Interdependence and group effectiveness. *Administrative Science Quarterly, 40,* 145–180. [Chapter 8]. A quasi-experimental study of the effect of task design and reward allocation on work team functioning, with 800 Xerox service technicians in 152 teams. Team performance was influenced positively by management that stressed either interdependence or autonomy, but hybrid management models were associated with poorer team performance.

# Appendix B

## Questions to Ask About a Research Article

1. What is the basic research question or problem? Try to state it in just one sentence. (Chapter 1)

2. How would you classify the methods and design of the study? (Chapter 1)

3. Describe the theoretical framework of the study. How did the theoretical framework influence the design and methods of the study? How did the theoretical framework provide a rationale for the study? (Chapters 2, 6, 7)

4. Did the theoretical framework seem appropriate for the research question addressed? Can you think of a different theoretical perspective that might have been used? (Chapters 1, 7)

5. What prior literature was reviewed? Was it relevant to the research problem? To the theoretical framework? Does the literature review appear to be adequate? Are you aware of (or can you locate) any important studies that have been omitted? (Chapter 2)

6. What is the research hypothesis of the study? How is it linked to the theoretical framework of the study? How does the research hypothesis translate theoretical constructs into operational procedures? (Chapters 2, 4)

7. Identify the independent variable(s). How many independent variables and how many levels for each independent variable exist? Describe whether the researchers used random assignment in allocating participants to the different levels of the independent variable(s). Discuss the implications of independent variables created by random assignment versus those selected on the basis of preexisting characteristics. (Chapters 2, 6, 7, 8)

8. Identify the dependent variable. What level of measurement does the dependent variable incorporate? How does the level of measurement of the dependent variable affect the kinds of statistical tests employed? What are the advantages/disadvantages of using parametric versus nonparametric statistics? (Chapters 4, 10)

9. How was the study sample recruited? How would you define the sampling methods? How representative is the study sample of the targeted population? How do these considerations affect the generalizability of the results? How do these considerations affect the external validity of the study? (Chapter 5)

10. Comment on the sample size of the study. How did the sample size affect the statistical power of the study? Do you think the study had adequate statistical power? What about the effect sizes? (Chapters 2, 6, 10)

11. Did the researchers vary the independent variable(s) between subjects or within subjects? Do you think the design was optimal? What threats to internal validity need to be considered in relation to how participants were assigned to the conditions of the experiment? (Chapters 6, 7)

12. State the research hypothesis and null hypothesis for the study. State the Type I error for this study. State the Type II error. What level of statistical significance was used? What does this mean for this study? (Chapters 2, 6, 10)

13. Would you describe the study as a single-factor or multifactor experiment? Why? What are the statistical implications? (Chapters 6, 7, 10)

14. What were the main results? What statistical tests were used to analyze the data? Were they appropriate, especially with regard to the level of measurement of the dependent variable? What statistical effects did the research design allow to be tested? Did the design allow for testing of statistical interactions? If so, what interactions were tested? If not, explain why the design did not allow for testing of statistical interactions. (Chapters 6, 7, 10)

15. Can you think of a different research approach for studying this topic? How might a qualitative research approach investigate the theory and the hypothesis? Would a small-$N$ design be worth considering? (Chapters 9, 11)

16. Did the discussion carefully weigh the evidence and pay sufficient attention to the limitations of the study in reference to external and internal validity? (Chapters 2, 4, and 6)

17. Did the study seem consistent with current ethical standards? Were any trade-offs made between different ethical guidelines? Was an appropriate balance struck between adherence to ethical standards and use of the most rigorous scientific practices? (Chapter 3)

18. Did the author(s) adequately represent the findings in the discussion and/or conclusion sections? Were the conclusions well-grounded in the findings? Are any other interpretations possible? (Chapters 2, 6, 7, 8, 12)

19. Compare the study with others addressing the same research question. Did the study yield additional insights? In what ways was the study design more or less adequate than the design of previous research? (Chapters 2, 6, 7, 8, 12)

20. What additional research questions and hypotheses are suggested by the study's results? What light did the study shed on the theoretical framework used? (Chapters 2, 6, 7, 8, 12)

# Appendix C

## How to Read a Research Article

The discussions of research articles throughout the text may provide all the guidance you need to read and critique research on your own. But reading about an article in bits and pieces to learn about particular methodologies is not quite the same as reading an article in its entirety to learn what the researcher found out. The goal of this appendix is to walk you through an entire research article, answering the review questions introduced in Appendix B. Of course, this is only one article and our "walk" will take different turns than would a review of other articles, but after this review you should feel more confident when reading other research articles on your own.

We will use for this example the study by Adams and Kleck (2003) published in *Psychological Science* titled "Perceived Gaze Direction and the Processing of Facial Displays" reprinted on pages 360–365 of this appendix. As you recall, Adams and Kleck used a complex experimental design to study how facial expression of emotions and eye gaze direction influence how we perceive others. We have reproduced below each of the article review questions from Appendix B, followed by our answers to them. After each question, we indicate the chapter where the question was discussed. You can also follow our review by reading through the article itself and noting our comments (also refer to Chapter 7).

1. What is the basic research question or problem? Try to state it in just one sentence. (Chapter 1)

How do facial expressions of emotions and gaze direction operate as social signals telling us whether to approach or to avoid a person? This is essentially the question that inspired Adams and Kleck (2003) to experimentally investigate how we naturally and automatically perceive facial expressions of emotion holistically as messages (e.g., "that person is mad about something").

2. How would you classify the methods and design of the study? (Chapter 1)

According to our research toolbox, we would classify the Adams and Kleck (2003) study as using an experimental design. As we will see below, Adams and Kleck created photos of faces in which they varied two independent variables—eye gaze direction (direct/averted) and expression (anger/fear).

3. Describe the theoretical framework of the study. How did the theoretical framework influence the design and methods of the study? How did the theoretical framework provide a rationale for the study? (Chapters 2, 6, 7)

Theories of *embodied cognition* provide the conceptual framework for the Adams and Kleck (2003) study. These researchers theorized that when a research participant views a photo display of a facial emotion, he or she automatically reenacts or reexperiences its perceptual, somato-visceral, and motoric features (which are collectively referred to as "embodiment"). This reenactment influences to a large degree how emotions are perceived and communicated. Thus, emotions as embodied experiences provided Adams and Kleck a rationale for understanding how facial features serve as key signals in emotion perception and communication.

4. Did the theoretical framework seem appropriate for the research question addressed? Can you think of a different theoretical perspective that might have been used? (Chapters 1, 7)

Yes, the theoretical framework provided a strong basis for investigating the research question and for designing the experiment. First, the theory specified a mechanism through which perceived emotions may influence our behavior, that is, whether we approach or avoid a stimulus. The mechanism is one of embodiment—when we view an emotional stimulus, such as facial expression of anger, we reenact its perceptual, somatovisceral, and motoric features, and these experiences influence our subsequent perceptions and actions.

5. What prior literature was reviewed? Was it relevant to the research problem? Does the literature review appear to be adequate? Are you aware of (or can you locate) any important studies that have been omitted? (Chapters 2, 7)

As is often the case for empirical articles appearing in *Psychological Science*, literature reviews are brief and to the point. However, it is clear from the literature review that the article is well-grounded in theory and builds on prior studies of social communication. Indeed, as Adams and Kleck (2003) stated, "Surprisingly, the interaction between gaze direction and facial expression of emotion in human perception has remained a virtually uncharted inquiry in the analysis of social communication" (p. 644).

6. What is the research hypothesis of the study? How is it linked to the theoretical framework of the study? How does the research hypothesis translate theoretical constructs into operational procedures? (Chapters 2, 4, 7)

Their literature review indicated that different emotional expressions can be perceived more readily if associated with certain directions of the eyes. Adams and Kleck (2003) were particularly interested in studies that showed anger expression to be more quickly perceived when accompanied by a direct gaze, in contrast to fear faces being more quickly perceived when coupled with an averted gaze. Based on these studies, Adams and Kleck formulated a two-pronged hypothesis: (1) anger faces with direct gaze would be more readily perceived than anger faces with averted gaze and (2) fear faces with averted gaze would be more readily perceived than fear faces with direct gaze.

7. Identify the independent variable(s). How many independent variables and how many levels for each independent variable exist? Describe whether the researchers used random assignment in allocating participants to the different levels of the independent variable(s). Discuss the implications of independent variables created by random assignment versus those selected on the basis of preexisting characteristics. (Chapters 2, 6, 7, 8)

The experiment manipulated two independent variables: (1) emotional expression and (2) gaze direction. Each independent variable had two levels: anger or fear faces, the two levels of emotional expression and direct or averted, the two levels of gaze direction. In other words, each face varied in expression (anger or fear) and gaze direction (direct or averted). The $2 \times 2$ factorial design produced four combinations of conditions: (1) anger/direct gaze faces, (2) anger/averted gaze faces, (3) fear/direct gaze faces, and (4) fear/averted gaze faces. They used a within-subjects design. What this meant is that all participants received all four types of faces. This allowed for the comparison of participants' response times in emotional judgment for the four different kinds of faces—(1) anger and direct gaze, (2) anger and averted gaze, (3) fear and direct gaze, and (4) fear and averted gaze.

8. Identify the dependent variable. What level of measurement does the dependent variable incorporate? How does the level of measurement of the dependent variable affect the kinds of statistical tests employed? What are the advantages/disadvantages of using parametric versus nonparametric statistics? (Chapters 4, 7, 10)

The dependent measure was response time in milliseconds for judging faces as expressions of either anger or fear. Response time reflects a ratio level of measurement that allows for the most powerful data analytic techniques—parametric statistics.

9. How was the study sample recruited? How would you define the sampling methods? How representative is the study sample of the targeted population? How do these considerations affect the generalizability of the results? How do these considerations affect the external validity of the study? (Chapter 5)

The researchers recruited 13 male and 19 female undergraduate students. As in many psychological studies using undergraduates as research participants, the sampling method here would be defined as one of convenience. As such, it is unclear as to the representativeness of the study sample. The sample of convenience detracts from both the generalizability of the results and the overall external validity of the study.

10. Comment on the sample size of the study. How did the sample size affect the statistical power of the study? Do you think the study had adequate statistical power? What about the effect sizes? (Chapters 2, 6, 7, 10)

The sample size of 32 college students is small. However, because the researchers used a within-subjects design, fewer research participants were needed. Their significant findings (see below and also Chapter 7) indicated sufficient statistical power. However, the effect sizes were in milliseconds, but this is consistent with prior studies of emotional influences on human perception.

11. Did the researchers vary the independent variable(s) between subjects or within subjects? Do you think the design was optimal? What threats to internal validity need to be considered in relation to how the participants were assigned to the conditions of the experiment? (Chapters 6, 7)

The researchers varied the independent variables within subjects. The within-subjects design was

optimal. What this meant is that all participants received all four types of faces. This allowed for the comparison of participants' response times in emotional judgment for the four different kinds of faces—(1) those with anger and direct gaze, (2) those with anger and averted gaze, (3) those with fear and direct gaze, and (4) those with fear and averted gaze. In so doing, with a within-subjects design, individual differences that could figure very prominently in processing emotions are automatically controlled. In other words, people may vary greatly in their responses to emotional faces. Because in a within-subjects design each participant serves as his or her own control, these individual differences are effectively held constant.

The second advantage is that within-subject designs are more economical than between-subjects designs. That is, fewer participants are needed to perform the experimental task. However, having fewer participants require that you collect more observations per participant. Here for a point of clarification, let us suppose that observations are analogous to the items of a test. The reliability of a test can often be increased by simply adding more items. The same principle is good to keep in mind in light of the reduced number of participants commonly used in within-subjects designs. For example, Adams and Kleck (2003) had a sample size of 32 participants. Yet their experimental task had 240 slides consisting of 60 anger/direct gaze, 60 anger/averted gaze, 60 fear/direct gaze, and 60 fear/averted gaze slides. The 240 slides were presented in a random order. The large number of items or slides in their experimental task provided a sufficient number of observations to measure emotional perception reliably.

12. State the research hypothesis and null hypothesis for the study. State the Type I error for this study. State the Type II error. What level of statistical significance was used? What does this mean for this study? (Chapters 2, 6, 7, 10)

The research hypothesis predicted that anger faces with direct gaze would be more readily perceived than anger faces with averted gaze, whereas fear faces with averted gaze would be more readily perceived than fear faces with direct gaze. The null hypothesis stated that there would be no difference in responses to faces as a function of expression (anger/fear) and eye gaze (direct/averted).

The Type I error would occur if we wrongly rejected the null hypothesis of no difference in responses to faces as a function of expression (anger/fear) and eye gaze (direct/averted) as false when in fact it was true. The Type II error would occur if we wrongly accepted the null hypothesis of no difference in responses to faces as a function of expression (anger/fear) and eye gaze (direct/averted) as true when in fact it was false. Per convention, the researchers set a .05 level of statistical significance. This means that there is a 5% chance that their findings could be attributed to chance. Or there is a 95% chance that the null hypothesis is false and therefore should be rejected in favor of the research hypothesis.

13. Would you describe the study as a single-factor or multifactor experiment? Why? What are the statistical implications? (Chapters 6, 7, 10)

A multifactor experiment by definition must have two or more independent variables. The current study design manipulated two independent variables and therefore would be properly described as a multifactor experiment. The principal statistical implication and advantage are that a multifactor experimental design is required to test the interactions of two or more independent variables. Recall the research hypothesis, which essentially states faster responses to both anger faces with direct gaze and fear faces with indirect gaze. Thus, the research hypothesis here predicts an interaction of facial expression and eye gaze. That is, the effect of facial expression on response times differs depending on direction of eye gaze. Or the effect of eye-gaze direction on responses times differs depending on the type of facial expression. We know that these two statements are identical, and each illustrates the meaning of the statistical interaction: The influence of an independent variable differs depending on the level of a second independent variable.

14. What were the main results? What statistical tests were used to analyze the data? Were they appropriate, especially with regard to the level of measurement of the dependent variable? What statistical effects did the research design allow to be tested? Did the design allow for testing of statistical interactions? If so, what interactions were tested? If not, explain why the design did not allow for testing of statistical interactions. (Chapters 6, 7, 10)

The main results pointed to an interaction whereby direct gaze led to faster judgment of anger faces but slower judgment of fear faces. On the other hand, averted gaze led to faster judgment of fear faces but slower judgment of anger faces. The proper statistical test was the 2 × 2 ANOVA (see Chapter 10), as the dependent variable of response times to judge faces represented a ratio level of measurement.

15. Can you think of a different research approach for studying this topic? How might a qualitative research approach investigate the theory and the hypothesis? Would a small-$N$ design be worth considering? (Chapters 9, 11)

The Adams and Kleck (2003) study presented an example of a classic 2 × 2 factorial design, which was ideally suited for testing the research hypothesis. Given the theoretical framework of emotional embodiment along with their hypothesis, neither a qualitative research approach nor a small-$N$ design would be worth considering.

16. Did the discussion carefully weigh the evidence and pay sufficient attention to the limitations of the study in reference to external and internal validity? (Chapters 2, 4, and 6)

Yes, the discussion carefully weighed the evidence of both experiments and placed their current findings within the context of prior studies. As is the case in most published scientific articles, issues of external validity and internal validity are not directly and explicitly addressed (except in instances when these are very much related to the central topic under investigation). As a research consumer and as a student in this course, it is essential to keep issues of internal validity and external validity in the forefront when evaluating a published study.

17. Did the study seem consistent with current ethical standards? Were any trade-offs made between different ethical guidelines? Was an appropriate balance struck between adherence to ethical standards and use of the most rigorous scientific practices? (Chapter 3)

The study was consistent with ethical standards. All studies must be approved by the host institutional review board, as was the case for the current investigation. Participants were either paid for their time or received course credit.

18. Did the author(s) adequately represent the findings in the discussion and/or conclusion sections? Were the conclusions well-grounded in the findings? Are any other interpretations possible? (Chapters 2, 6, 7, 8, 12)

Yes, the authors adequately represented their findings in the discussion section. The data clearly favored their interpretation, which was well-grounded in their theoretical framework.

19. Compare the study with others addressing the same research question. Did the study yield additional insights? In what ways was the study design more or less adequate than the design of previous research? (Chapters 2, 6, 7, 8, 12)

Yes, as the authors wrote,

Although many aspects of facial information appear to be independently processed (e.g., lip reading, emotional expression, gender, and age: Bruce & Young, 1986; Young, 1988), the current findings suggest that gaze direction and facial expressions of emotions are not. By merging the study of facial expressions with the perception of gaze direction, the current research confirms that these cues interact meaningfully in the perceptual processing of emotionally relevant facial information. (p. 646)

20. What additional research questions and hypotheses are suggested by the study's results? What light did the study shed on the theoretical framework used? (Chapters 2, 6, 7, 8, 12)

One important question raised by the current findings is this: How do gaze direction and facial expression influence perceptual judgments for other kinds of facial expressions, such as surprise, sadness, or joy? With respect to the importance of the current finding of the interactive effects of gaze direction and facial expressions on perceptual judgment, Adams and Kleck (2003) wrote,

This finding is important for a number of reasons. It suggests that gaze direction is an important cue in perceptual processing of facial displays of emotion, which has not been previously demonstrated in the research literature. It also suggests that the effects of gaze direction on the processing of emotion depend on the specific type of emotion displayed by the face. An understanding of the precise nature of this interaction and the brain mechanisms that support it await further research developments. (p. 646)

---

## RESEARCH REPORT

## Perceived Gaze Direction and the Processing of Facial Displays of Emotion

*Reginald B. Adams Jr. and Robert E. Kleck*

*Dartmouth College*

*Source:* Research Report from "Perceived Gaze Direction and the Processing of Facial Displays of Emotion," by Reginald B. Adams, Jr., and Robert E. Kleck in *Psychological Science*, Vol. 14, No. 6, November 2003, pp. 644–647.

Address correspondence to Reginald B. Adams, Jr., Department of Psychological and Brain Sciences, Dartmouth College, 6207 Moore Hall, Hanover, NH 03755; e-mail: rba@alum.dartmouth.org.

**Abstract—**There is good reason to believe that gaze direction and facial displays of emotion share an information value as signals of approach or avoidance. The combination of these cues in the analysis of social communication, however, has been a virtually neglected area of inquiry. Two studies were conducted to test the prediction that direct gaze would facilitate the processing of facially communicated approach-oriented emotions (e.g., anger and joy), whereas averted gaze would facilitate the processing of facially communicated avoidance-oriented emotions (e.g., fear and sadness). The results of both studies confirmed the central hypothesis and suggest that gaze direction and facial expression are combined in the processing of emotionally relevant facial information.

An attraction to the eye region of the face may be innately prepared (e.g., Baron-Cohen, 1997; Driver et al., 1999; Hess & Petrovich, 1987). Compelling cross-species evidence for this contention is apparent in the eyespot configurations that appear on lower-order animals such as birds, reptiles, fish, and insects (Argyle & Cook, 1976). These spots are thought to mimic the eyes of larger animals, thereby warding off potential predators. In humans, both adults and infants prefer to look at the eyes compared with other facial features (Janik, Wellens, Goldberg, & Dell'Osso, 1978; Morton & Johnson, 1991), and they are particularly sensitive to the gaze direction displayed by others (Baron-Cohen, 1997; Driver et al., 1999; Macrae, Hood, Milne, Rowe, & Mason, 2002).

The ability to detect the direction of gaze displayed by another is believed to play a pivotal role in the development of person and affective construal processes (Baron-Cohen, 1997; Macrae et al., 2002; Perrett & Emery, 1994). A particular direction of gaze, however, can convey multiple social meanings. Direct gaze in both humans and nonhuman primates, for example, can communicate threat (Argyle & Cook, 1976; Redican, 1982) or friendliness (Kleinke, 1986; Van Hoof, 1972). Thus, other contextual cues must be utilized when reading social meaning into the behavior of the eyes. Argyle and Cook (1976) have noted that "if the suitable experimental situations could be devised . . . [subjects] who are exposed to the same gaze, but with different context cues, would react differently, and evaluate the looker and the looker's intentions quite differently" (p. 96).

Facial expressions can offer critical contextual information that is either consistent or inconsistent with the behavioral intentions communicated by a specific gaze behavior. Fundamentally, the behavioral intentions to approach and avoid drive biological behavior (e.g., Baron-Cohen, 1997; Brothers & Ring, 1992; Davidson & Hugdahl, 1995). Both gaze behavior and emotion have been found to be associated with the behavioral motivations to approach or avoid (see Argyle & Cook, 1976; Davidson & Hugdahl, 1995; Harmon-Jones & Segilman, 2001). Positive emotions, anger, and direct gaze, for example, are associated with approach motivation. Negative emotions (other than anger) and averted gaze are associated with avoidance motivation. Thus, as a signaling system, facial expressions of emotion and gaze behavior may combine to signal these basic behavioral tendencies. Given the importance of perception of gaze direction in the affective construal process, the perceptual primacy of the eyes over other facial cues, and the shared signal value of gaze direction and facial expressions of emotion (approach/avoidance), there is good reason to believe that gaze direction might influence how efficiently facial expressions of emotion are processed by perceivers.

Surprisingly, the interaction between gaze direction and facial expressions of emotion in human perception has remained a virtually uncharted area of inquiry in the analysis of social communication. Ample evidence supports the contention that certain patterns of gaze behavior and facial expressions of emotion co-occur in both humans (e.g., Argyle & Cook, 1976; Fehr & Exline, 1987) and nonhuman primates (e.g., Hinde & Rowell, 1962; Redican, 1982) in a manner consistent with a shared underlying approach-avoidance signal value. Showing that behaviors generally co-occur, however, does not establish their mutual effect on perceptual processing. In the current research, we aimed to clarify the role of gaze direction in emotion perception by investigating its influence on how efficiently emotion information is recognized in the face. Direct gaze was predicted to facilitate the processing of facially communicated approach-oriented emotions (e.g., anger and joy), whereas averted gaze was predicted to facilitate the processing of facially communicated avoidance-oriented emotions (e.g., fear and sadness).

## STUDY 1

## Method

### Participants

Thirteen male and 19 female undergraduate students were recruited. The participants received $10 and came to the laboratory in small groups of no more than 6 people.

### Materials

*Pure expressions.* Facial photographs of 15 male and 15 female stimulus persons showing highly recognizable expressions of anger and fear (referred to here as "pure" expressions) were presented. For each stimulus person, we included one photograph showing a pure expression of anger and one photograph showing a pure expression of fear. These photographs were selected from the Pictures of Facial Affect (Ekman & Friesen, 1978), a set developed by Kirouac and Doré (1984), the Montreal Set of Facial Displays of Emotion (Beaupré, Cheung, & Hess, 2000), and a set developed by us (Adams & Kleck, 2001). All stimulus persons were of European descent. Because each face was presented twice in the averted-gaze condition (left and right), each was also presented twice in the direct-gaze condition to balance out the design. Thus, a total of 240 pure expressions of anger and fear were included in this study. Gaze direction was manipulated using Adobe Photoshop™.

*Blended expressions.* Eight male and 8 female "blended" target faces were also used in this study. Each face displayed anger and fear, which were blended using a morphing algorithm included in the Morph 2.5™ software for the Macintosh. Exemplar faces were selected from the Pictures of Facial Affect (Ekman & Friesen, 1978) and the Montreal Set of Facial Displays of Emotion (Beaupré et al., 2000). The anger and fear expressions for each stimulus person were blended at approximately equal levels. The resulting images were inspected by an expert in the Facial Action Coding System (FACS; see Ekman & Friesen, 1978) and were verified to be physically viable, ecologically valid expressions. Each blended expression was presented in three gaze conditions (left, right, and direct), and the direct-gaze face for each stimulus person appeared twice to balance out the design. Thus, 64 presentations of blended expressions were randomly intermingled among the presentations of the 240 pure emotional expressions.

All pure and blended expressions were digitized, cropped to display only the head and neck of each individual, and presented in black and white on a computer screen at an approximate size of 4 × 3 in.

### Procedure

Each participant was seated approximately 24 in. in front of a 15-in. monitor with a serial mouse for data acquisition with millisecond precision. Stimulus trials were presented using Superlab Pro™ (see Haxby, Parasuraman, Lalonde, & Abboud, 1993). The participants were instructed to indicate via a right or left mouse click whether each face displayed anger or fear. Each face was presented in the center of the computer screen. Each trial began with a 500-ms fixation point, which was immediately replaced by a blank screen for 50 ms before the onset of the stimulus face. The face remained on the screen until a response was made. The participants were asked to label each face as quickly and as accurately as possible.

## Results

### Pure expressions

Prior to analysis, the data were trimmed and log-transformed. Responses more than 3 standard deviations above or below the mean were excluded from analysis (0.76%), as were trials resulting in incorrect responses (10.1%). For ease of interpretation, we converted data back into milliseconds for reporting the means and standard errors.

The central hypothesis was tested with a 2 (anger vs. fear expression) × 2 (direct vs. averted gaze) repeated-measures analysis of variance. A significant main effect of emotion emerged, $F(1, 31) = 8.05$, $p = .01$, $r = .45$; anger faces were correctly labeled more quickly ($M = 888.2$ ms, $SE = 23.9$ ms) than were fear faces ($M = 917.9$ ms, $SE = 25.5$ ms). This main effect was qualified by the predicted interaction between emotion and gaze direction, $F(1, 31) = 40.37$, $p < .0001$, $r = .75$ (see Table 1). As expected, anger expressions were more quickly decoded when displayed in conjunction with direct than with averted gaze, $t(31) = 4.88$, $p < .0001$, $r = .66$. Fear expressions, in contrast, were more quickly decoded when displayed in conjunction with averted than with direct gaze, $t(31) = -5.27$, $p < .0001$, $r = .69$.

### Blended expressions

The use of emotion-blended expressions allowed us to test whether gaze direction could shift the relative perceptual dominance of one emotion over the other. Using the proportion of fear-versus-anger labels as the dependent variable of interest, we computed a direct $t$-test comparison. Blended expressions were given approximately equal numbers of fear labels and anger labels when displaying direct gaze ($M = .51$, $SE = .025$), whereas they were given more fear labels than anger labels when displaying averted gaze ($M = .68$, $SE = .028$), $t(31) = 5.86$, $p < .0001$, $r = .72$.

## Discussion

Study 1 offers preliminary evidence for the role of gaze direction in facilitating the processing of facial displays of emotion. The reaction time data for labeling pure anger and fear expressions showed that gaze directly influences the time it takes to make correct emotion judgments. The categorical index for the blended expressions showed that gaze direction can shift the relative perceptual dominance of one emotion over another. These findings suggest that gaze direction influences the processing of facial anger and fear displays, in terms of both processing speed and perceptual interpretation. To replicate these findings and firmly establish that these processing differences are not restricted to threat-related emotional expressions (perhaps as part of an early-warning mechanism), we conducted Study 2 using different approach- and avoidance-oriented emotional expressions, joy and sadness.

| Table 1 | Mean Response Latencies (in Milliseconds) to Correctly Label Anger and Fear Expressions, as a Function of Gaze Direction | | | |
|---|---|---|---|---|
| | Response Latency | | Standard Error | |
| Type of emotional expression | Direct Gaze | Averted Gaze | Direct Gaze | Averted Gaze |
| Anger | 862.3 | 914.1 | 23.5 | 25.6 |
| Fear | 944.5 | 891.2 | 27.5 | 24.4 |

## STUDY 2

## Method

### Participants

Seventeen male and 11 female undergraduate students were recruited. Participants received either partial course credit or $7. They came to the laboratory in small groups of no more than 6 people.

### Materials

As in Study 1, facial stimuli displaying pure facial expressions (in this case, joy or sadness) were used. All stimuli were selected from the same facial sets and prepared according to the same parameters as described for Study 1. Blended expressions combining joy and sadness expressions, however, did not yield suitable stimuli, and therefore were not included in this study. Notably, researchers have historically had difficulty blending expressions of positive and negative emotions (Nummenmaa, 1990).

### Procedure

The task was identical to the task in Study 1, except that joy and sadness emotion judgments were made and participants saw a total of 240 rather than 304 stimuli.

## Results

The dependent measure of interest was the mean latency of response for correctly labeling faces as displaying either joy or sadness. Prior to analyses, the data were trimmed and log-transformed. Outliers (1.2%) and incorrect responses (5.1%) were dropped from the analyses. As for Study 1, the means and standard errors reported here were transformed back to milliseconds.

To test the hypothesis that gaze would influence the speed with which facial expressions were labeled, we computed a 2 (joy vs. sadness expression) × 2 (direct vs. averted gaze) repeated measures analysis of variance. A main effect for emotion emerged, $F(1, 27) = 15.26$, $p < .0001$, $r = .6$; joyous faces ($M = 609.5$ ms, $SE = 16.0$ ms) were correctly labeled more quickly than sad faces

($M$ = 633.9 ms, $SE$ = 15.2 ms). The predicted interaction between emotion and gaze direction was found, $F(1, 27)$ = 20.97, $p$ <.0001, $r$ = .66 (see Table 2). As expected, joy expressions were more quickly decoded when displayed with direct than with averted gaze, $t(27)$ = 3.51, $p$ <.01, $r$ = .56. Sadness expressions were more quickly decoded when displayed with averted than with direct gaze, $t(27)$ = –2.63, $p$ <.02, $r$ = .45.

## Discussion

The results for joy and sadness expressions are consistent with those for anger and fear expressions, reported in Study 1. The latencies to correctly label the emotional expressions varied as a joint function of gaze direction and whether the facial display in question represented an approach- or avoidance-oriented emotion.

## GENERAL DISCUSSION

In the current studies, anger and joy expressions (which are approach oriented) were more quickly labeled when presented with direct than with averted gaze, whereas fear and sadness expressions (which are avoidance oriented) were more quickly labeled when presented with averted than with direct gaze. The finding that gaze and facial expressions are combined in the perceptual processing and interpretation of emotion suggests a process that is potentially highly evolved. As noted, a fundamental dimension of behavioral intention is approach and avoidance. The ability to detect another's intention to either approach or avoid is seen by many researchers as a principal mediating factor governing social interaction. Given that both emotion expression and gaze behavior reflect these underlying approach-avoidance motivational intentions, the integration of these cues in social perception likely subserves an adaptive function.

The present findings might seem counterintuitive given recent research on gaze direction. For instance, Macrae et al. (2002) used a gender detection task to test the effects of gaze direction on the processing efficiency of person construal. They found that the participants were quicker in correctly labelling the gender of faces displaying direct gaze than faces displaying averted or closed eyes. In addition, Driver et al. (1999) used a letter discrimination task to test the effects of gaze direction as an attentional cuing device. They found that the gaze direction of a stimulus face triggers a reflexive shift of attention in the same direction in the observer. From these studies, one might conclude that direct gaze ought to facilitate the processing of all facial displays of emotion as a function of where the observer's attentional resources are allocated; direct gaze seems to shift attentional resources toward the face, whereas averted gaze appears to shift attentional resources away. The current studies, however, demonstrate that the influence of gaze direction on the perception of facial displays of emotion varies depending on the motivational orientation associated with the emotion being expressed.

Although many aspects of facial information appear to be independently processed (e.g., lip reading, emotional expression, gender, and age; Bruce & Young, 1986; Young, 1998), the current findings suggest that gaze direction and facial expressions of emotion are not. By merging the study of facial expressions with the study of perception of gaze direction, the current research confirms that these cues interact meaningfully in the perceptual processing of emotionally relevant facial information. This finding is important for a number of reasons. It suggests that gaze direction is an important cue in the perceptual processing of facial displays of emotion, which has not been previously demonstrated in the research literature. It also suggests that the effects of gaze direction on the processing of emotion depend on the specific type of emotion displayed by the face. An understanding of the precise nature of this interaction and the brain mechanisms that support it awaits further research developments.

**Table 2**  Mean Response Latencies (in milliseconds) to Correctly Label Joy and Sadness Expressions, as a Function of Gaze Direction

| Type of Emotional Expression | Response Latency | | Standard Error | |
|---|---|---|---|---|
| | Direct Gaze | Averted Gaze | Direct Gaze | Averted Gaze |
| Joy | 600.8 | 618.3 | 15.5 | 17.0 |
| Sadness | 641.4 | 626.4 | 15.2 | 15.8 |

Acknowledgments: The authors would like to thank Katharine D. Adams and Abigail A. Marsh for helpful comments on an earlier draft; Brent F. Jones for help in creating the stimuli and implementing the studies; and Punam A. Keller, C. Neil Macrae, Jennifer A. Richeson, and George L. Wolford for suggestions regarding experimental design and data analysis. This research was supported in part by a Doctoral Dissertation Improvement Grant from the National Science Foundation (Award No. 0121947) to Reginald B. Adams Jr. and a Rockefeller Reiss Family Senior Faculty grant to Robert E. Kleck.

## REFERENCES

Adams, R. B., Jr., & Kleck, R. E. (2001). [Young adult facial displays]. Unpublished set of photographs.

Argyle, M., & Cook, M. (1976). *Gaze and mutual gaze.* New York, NY: Cambridge University Press.

Baron-Cohen, S. (1997). *Mindblindness: An essay on autism and theory of mind.* Cambridge, MA: MIT Press.

Beaupré, M., Cheung, N., & Hess, U. (2000, October). *La reconnaissance des expressions émotionnelles faciales par des décodeurs africains, asiatiques et caucasiens.* Poster presented at the annual meeting of the Société Québécoise pour la Recherche en Psychologie, Hull, Quebec, Canada.

Brothers, L., & Ring, B. (1992). A neuroethological framework for the representation of minds. *Journal of Cognitive Neuroscience, 4,* 107–118.

Bruce, V., & Young, A. (1986). Understanding face recognition. *British Journal of Psychology, 77,* 305–327.

Davidson, R. J., & Hugdahl, K. (Eds.). (1995). *Brain asymmetry.* Cambridge, MA: MIT Press.

Driver, J., Davis, G., Ricciardelli, P., Kidd, P., Maxwell, E., & Baron-Cohen, S. (1999). Gaze perception triggers reflexive visuospatial orienting. *Visual Cognition, 6,* 509–540.

Ekman, P. F., & Friesen, W. V. (1978). *The Facial Action Coding System: A technique for the measurement of facial movement.* Palo Alto, CA: Consulting Psychologists Press.

Fehr, B. J., & Exline, R. V. (1987). Social visual interaction: A conceptual and literature review. In A. W. Siegman & S. Feldstein (Eds.), *Nonverbal behavior and communication* (pp. 225–325). Hillsdale, NJ: Erlbaum.

Harmon-Jones, E., & Segilman, J. (2001). State anger and prefrontal brain activity: Evidence that insult-related relative left-prefrontal activation is associated with experienced anger and aggression. *Journal of Personality and Social Psychology, 80,* 797–803.

Haxby, J. V., Parasuraman, R., Lalonde, F., & Abboud, H. (1993). SuperLab: General-purpose Macintosh software for human experimental psychology and psychological testing. *Behavior Research Methods, Instruments, & Computers, 25,* 400–405.

Hess, E. H., & Petrovich, S. B. (1987). *Pupillary behavior in communication.* Hillsdale, NJ: Erlbaum.

Hinde, R. A., & Rowell, T. E. (1962). Communication by posture and facial expression in the rhesus monkey. *Proceedings of the Zoological Society of London, 138,* 1–21.

Janik, S. W., Wellens, A. R., Goldberg, M. L., & Dell'Osso, L. F. (1978). Eyes as the center of focus in the visual examination of human faces. *Perceptual & Motor Skills, 47,* 857–858.

Kirouac, G., & Doré, F. Y. (1984). Judgment of facial expressions of emotion as a function of exposure time. *Perceptual & Motor Skills, 59,* 147–150.

Kleinke, C. L. (1986). Gaze and eye contact: A research review. *Psychological Bulletin, 100,* 78–100.

Macrae, C. N., Hood, B. M., Milne, A. B., Rowe, A. C., & Mason, M. F. (2002). Are you looking at me? Gaze and person perception. *Psychological Science, 13,* 460–464.

Morton, J., & Johnson, M. (1991). CONSPEC and CONLEARN: A two-process theory of infant face recognition. *Psychological Review, 98,* 164–181.

Nummenmaa, T. (1990). Sender repertoires of pure and blended facial expressions of emotion. *Scandinavian Journal of Psychology, 31,* 161–180.

Perrett, D. I., & Emery, N. J. (1994). Understanding the intentions of others from visual signals: Neurophysiological evidence. *Cognitive/Current Psychology of Cognition, 13,* 683–694.

Redican, W. K. (1982). An evolutionary perspective on human facial displays. In P. Ekman (Ed.), *Emotion in the human face* (pp. 212–280). New York: Cambridge University Press.

van Hoof, J. A. R. A. M. (1972). A comparative approach to the phylogeny of laughter and smiling. In R. A. Hinde (Ed.), *Nonverbal communication* (pp. 209–241). New York: Cambridge University Press.

Young, A. W. (1998). *Face and mind.* Oxford, England: Oxford University Press.

# Appendix D

## Proportions of Area Under Standard Normal Curve

| A | B | C | A | B | C | A | B | C |
|---|---|---|---|---|---|---|---|---|
| Z | | | Z | | | Z | | |
| 0.00 | .0000 | .5000 | 0.30 | .1179 | .3821 | 0.60 | .2257 | .2743 |
| 0.01 | .0040 | .4960 | 0.31 | .1271 | .3783 | 0.61 | .2291 | .2709 |
| 0.02 | .0080 | .4920 | 0.32 | .1255 | .3745 | 0.62 | .2324 | .2676 |
| 0.03 | .0120 | .4880 | 0.33 | .1293 | .3707 | 0.63 | .2357 | .2643 |
| 0.04 | .0160 | .4840 | 0.34 | .1331 | .3669 | 0.64 | .2389 | .2611 |
| 0.05 | .0199 | .4801 | 0.35 | .1368 | .3632 | 0.65 | .2422 | .2578 |
| 0.06 | .0239 | .4761 | 0.36 | .1406 | .3594 | 0.66 | .2454 | .2546 |
| 0.07 | .0279 | .4721 | 0.37 | .1443 | .3557 | 0.67 | .2486 | .2514 |
| 0.08 | .0319 | .4681 | 0.38 | .1480 | .3520 | 0.68 | .2517 | .2483 |
| 0.09 | .0359 | .4641 | 0.39 | .1517 | .3483 | 0.69 | .2549 | .2451 |
| 0.10 | .0398 | .4602 | 0.40 | .1554 | .3446 | 0.70 | .2580 | .2420 |
| 0.11 | .0438 | .4562 | 0.41 | .1591 | .3409 | 0.71 | .2611 | .2389 |
| 0.12 | .0478 | .4522 | 0.42 | .1628 | .3372 | 0.72 | .2642 | .2358 |
| 0.13 | .0517 | .4483 | 0.43 | .1664 | .3336 | 0.73 | .2673 | .2327 |
| 0.14 | .0557 | .4443 | 0.44 | .1700 | .3300 | 0.74 | .2704 | .2296 |
| 0.15 | .0596 | .4404 | 0.45 | .1736 | .3264 | 0.75 | .2734 | .2266 |
| 0.16 | .0636 | .4364 | 0.46 | .1772 | .3228 | 0.76 | .2764 | .2236 |
| 0.17 | .0675 | .4325 | 0.47 | .1808 | .3192 | 0.77 | .2794 | .2206 |
| 0.18 | .0714 | .4286 | 0.48 | .1844 | .3156 | 0.78 | .2823 | .2177 |
| 0.19 | .0753 | .4247 | 0.49 | .1879 | .3121 | 0.79 | .2852 | .2148 |
| A | B | C | A | B | C | A | B | C |
| −Z | | | −Z | | | −Z | | |

| A | B | C | A | B | C | A | B | C |
|---|---|---|---|---|---|---|---|---|
| Z | | | Z | | | Z | | |
| 0.20 | .0793 | .4207 | 0.50 | .1915 | .3085 | 0.80 | .2881 | .2119 |
| 0.21 | .0832 | .4168 | 0.51 | .1950 | .3050 | 0.81 | .2910 | .2090 |
| 0.22 | .0871 | .4129 | 0.52 | .1985 | .3015 | 0.82 | .2939 | .2061 |
| 0.23 | .0910 | .4090 | 0.53 | .2019 | .2981 | 0.83 | .2967 | .2033 |
| 0.24 | .0948 | .4052 | 0.54 | .2054 | .2946 | 0.84 | .2995 | .2005 |
| 0.25 | .0987 | .4013 | 0.55 | .2088 | .2912 | 0.85 | .3023 | .1977 |
| 0.26 | .1026 | .3974 | 0.56 | .2123 | .2877 | 0.86 | .3051 | .1949 |
| 0.27 | .1064 | .3936 | 0.57 | .2157 | .2843 | 0.87 | .3078 | .1922 |
| 0.28 | .1103 | .3897 | 0.58 | .2190 | .2810 | 0.88 | .3106 | .1894 |
| 0.29 | .1141 | .3859 | 0.59 | .2224 | .2776 | 0.89 | .3133 | .1867 |
| 0.90 | .3159 | .1841 | 1.21 | .3869 | .1131 | 1.52 | .4357 | .0643 |
| 0.91 | .3186 | .1814 | 1.22 | .3888 | .1112 | 1.53 | .4370 | .0630 |
| 0.92 | .3212 | .1788 | 1.23 | .3907 | .1093 | 1.54 | .4382 | .0618 |
| 0.93 | .3238 | .1772 | 1.24 | .3925 | .1075 | 1.55 | .4394 | .0606 |
| 0.94 | .3264 | .1736 | 1.25 | .3944 | .1056 | 1.56 | .4406 | .0594 |
| 0.95 | .3289 | .1711 | 1.26 | .3962 | .1038 | 1.57 | .4418 | .0582 |
| 0.96 | .3315 | .1685 | 1.27 | .3980 | .1020 | 1.58 | .4429 | .0571 |
| 0.97 | .3340 | .1660 | 1.28 | .3997 | .1003 | 1.59 | .4441 | .0559 |
| 0.98 | .3365 | .1635 | 1.29 | .4015 | .0985 | 1.60 | .4452 | .0548 |
| 0.99 | .3389 | .1611 | 1.30 | .4032 | .0968 | 1.61 | .4463 | .0537 |
| 1.00 | .3413 | .1587 | 1.31 | .4049 | .0951 | 1.62 | .4474 | .0526 |
| 1.01 | .3438 | .1562 | 1.32 | .4066 | .0934 | 1.63 | .4484 | .0516 |
| 1.02 | .3461 | .1539 | 1.33 | .4082 | .0918 | 1.64 | .4495 | .0505 |
| 1.03 | .3485 | .1515 | 1.34 | .4099 | .0901 | 1.65 | .4505 | .0495 |
| 1.04 | .3508 | .1492 | 1.35 | .4115 | .0885 | 1.66 | .4515 | .0485 |
| 1.05 | .3531 | .1469 | 1.36 | .4131 | .0869 | 1.67 | .4525 | .0475 |
| 1.06 | .3554 | .1446 | 1.37 | .4147 | .0853 | 1.68 | .4535 | .0465 |
| 1.07 | .3577 | .1423 | 1.38 | .4162 | .0838 | 1.69 | .4545 | .0455 |
| 1.08 | .3599 | .1401 | 1.39 | .4177 | .0823 | 1.70 | .4554 | .0446 |
| 1.09 | .3621 | .1379 | 1.40 | .4192 | .0808 | 1.71 | .4564 | .0436 |
| 1.10 | .3643 | .1357 | 1.41 | .4207 | .0793 | 1.72 | .4573 | .0427 |
| 1.11 | .3665 | .1335 | 1.42 | .4222 | .0778 | 1.73 | .4582 | .0418 |
| 1.12 | .3686 | .1314 | 1.43 | .4236 | .0764 | 1.74 | .4591 | .0409 |
| 1.13 | .3708 | .1292 | 1.44 | .4251 | .0749 | 1.75 | .4599 | .0401 |
| 1.14 | .3729 | .1271 | 1.45 | .4265 | .0735 | 1.76 | .4608 | .0392 |
| A | B | C | A | B | C | A | B | C |
| −Z | | | −Z | | | −Z | | |

*(Continued)*

(Continued)

| A (Z) | B | C | A (Z) | B | C | A (Z) | B | C |
|---|---|---|---|---|---|---|---|---|
| 1.15 | .3749 | .1251 | 1.46 | .4279 | .0721 | 1.77 | .4616 | .0384 |
| 1.16 | .3770 | .1230 | 1.47 | .4292 | .0708 | 1.78 | .4625 | .0375 |
| 1.17 | .3790 | .1210 | 1.48 | .4306 | .0694 | 1.79 | .4633 | .0367 |
| 1.18 | .3810 | .1190 | 1.49 | .4319 | .0681 | 1.80 | .4641 | .0359 |
| 1.19 | .3830 | .1170 | 1.50 | .4332 | .0668 | 1.81 | .4649 | .0351 |
| 1.20 | .3849 | .1151 | 1.51 | .4345 | .0655 | 1.82 | .4656 | .0344 |
| 1.83 | .4664 | .0336 | 2.13 | .4834 | .0166 | 2.43 | .4925 | .0075 |
| 1.84 | .4671 | .0329 | 2.14 | .4838 | .0162 | 2.44 | .4927 | .0073 |
| 1.85 | .4678 | .0322 | 2.15 | .4842 | .0158 | 2.45 | .4929 | .0071 |
| 1.86 | .4686 | .0314 | 2.16 | .4846 | .0154 | 2.46 | .4931 | .0069 |
| 1.87 | .4693 | .0307 | 2.17 | .4850 | .0150 | 2.47 | .4932 | .0068 |
| 1.88 | .4699 | .0301 | 2.18 | .4854 | .0146 | 2.48 | .4934 | .0066 |
| 1.89 | .4706 | .0294 | 2.19 | .4857 | .0143 | 2.49 | .4936 | .0064 |
| 1.90 | .4713 | .0287 | 2.20 | .4861 | .0139 | 2.50 | .4938 | .0062 |
| 1.91 | .4719 | .0281 | 2.21 | .4864 | .0136 | 2.51 | .4940 | .0060 |
| 1.92 | .4726 | .0274 | 2.22 | .4868 | .0132 | 2.52 | .4941 | .0059 |
| 1.93 | .4732 | .0268 | 2.23 | .4871 | .0129 | 2.53 | .4943 | .0057 |
| 1.94 | .4738 | .0262 | 2.24 | .4875 | .0125 | 2.54 | .4945 | .0055 |
| 1.95 | .4744 | .0256 | 2.25 | .4878 | .0122 | 2.55 | .4946 | .0054 |
| 1.96 | .4750 | .0250 | 2.26 | .4881 | .0119 | 2.56 | .4948 | .0052 |
| 1.97 | .4756 | .0244 | 2.27 | .4884 | .0116 | 2.57 | .4949 | .0051 |
| 1.98 | .4761 | .0239 | 2.28 | .4887 | .0113 | 2.58 | .4951 | .0049 |
| 1.99 | .4767 | .0233 | 2.29 | .4890 | .0110 | 2.59 | .4952 | .0048 |
| 2.00 | .4772 | .0228 | 2.30 | .4893 | .0107 | 2.60 | .4953 | .0047 |
| 2.01 | .4778 | .0222 | 2.31 | .4896 | .0104 | 2.61 | .4955 | .0045 |
| 2.02 | .4783 | .0217 | 2.32 | .4898 | .0102 | 2.62 | .4956 | .0044 |
| 2.03 | .4788 | .0212 | 2.33 | .4901 | .0099 | 2.63 | .4957 | .0043 |
| 2.04 | .4793 | .0207 | 2.34 | .4904 | .0096 | 2.64 | .4959 | .0041 |
| 2.05 | .4798 | .0202 | 2.35 | .4906 | .0094 | 2.65 | .4960 | .0040 |
| 2.06 | .4803 | .0197 | 2.36 | .4909 | .0091 | 2.66 | .4961 | .0039 |
| 2.07 | .4808 | .0192 | 2.37 | .4911 | .0089 | 2.67 | .4962 | .0038 |
| 2.08 | .4812 | .0188 | 2.38 | .4913 | .0087 | 2.68 | .4963 | .0037 |
| 2.09 | .4817 | .0183 | 2.39 | .4916 | .0084 | 2.69 | .4964 | .0036 |
| 2.10 | .4821 | .0179 | 2.40 | .4918 | .0082 | 2.70 | .4965 | .0035 |
| 2.11 | .4826 | .0174 | 2.41 | .4920 | .0080 | 2.71 | .4966 | .0034 |
| 2.12 | .4830 | .0170 | 2.42 | .4922 | .0078 | 2.72 | .4967 | .0033 |
| 2.73 | .4968 | .0032 | 2.94 | .4984 | .0016 | 3.15 | .4992 | .0008 |
| 2.74 | .4969 | .0031 | 2.95 | .4984 | .0016 | 3.16 | .4992 | .0008 |
| 2.75 | .4970 | .0030 | 2.96 | .4985 | .0015 | 3.17 | .4992 | .0008 |
| 2.76 | .4971 | .0029 | 2.97 | .4985 | .0015 | 3.18 | .4993 | .0007 |
| 2.77 | .4972 | .0028 | 2.98 | .4986 | .0014 | 3.19 | .4993 | .0007 |
| A (−Z) | B | C | A (−Z) | B | C | A (−Z) | B | C |

| A | B | C | A | B | C | A | B | C |
|---|---|---|---|---|---|---|---|---|
| Z | | | Z | | | Z | | |
| 2.78 | .4973 | .0027 | 2.99 | .4986 | .0014 | 3.20 | .4993 | .0007 |
| 2.79 | .4974 | .0026 | 3.00 | .4987 | .0013 | 3.21 | .4993 | .0007 |
| 2.80 | .4974 | .0026 | 3.01 | .4987 | .0013 | 3.22 | .4994 | .0006 |
| 2.81 | .4975 | .0025 | 3.02 | .4987 | .0013 | 3.23 | .4994 | .0006 |
| 2.82 | .4976 | .0024 | 3.03 | .4988 | .0012 | 3.24 | .4994 | .0006 |
| 2.83 | .4977 | .0023 | 3.04 | .4988 | .0012 | 3.25 | .4994 | .0006 |
| 2.84 | .4977 | .0023 | 3.05 | .4989 | .0011 | 3.30 | .4995 | .0005 |
| 2.85 | .4978 | .0022 | 3.06 | .4989 | .0011 | 3.35 | .4996 | .0004 |
| 2.86 | .4979 | .0021 | 3.07 | .4989 | .0011 | 3.40 | .4997 | .0003 |
| 2.87 | .4979 | .0021 | 3.08 | .4990 | .0010 | 3.45 | .4997 | .0003 |
| 2.88 | .4980 | .0020 | 3.09 | .4990 | .0010 | 3.50 | .4998 | .0002 |
| 2.89 | .4981 | .0019 | 3.10 | .4990 | .0010 | 3.60 | .4998 | .0002 |
| 2.90 | .4981 | .0019 | 3.11 | .4991 | .0009 | 3.70 | .4999 | .0001 |
| 2.91 | .4982 | .0018 | 3.12 | .4991 | .0009 | 3.80 | .4999 | .0001 |
| 2.92 | .4982 | .0018 | 3.13 | .4991 | .0009 | 3.90 | .4999 | .0000 |
| 2.93 | .4983 | .0017 | 3.14 | .4992 | .0008 | 4.00 | .4999 | .0000 |
| A | B | C | A | B | C | A | B | C |
| −Z | | | −Z | | | −Z | | |

*Source:* Abridged from Fisher and Yates (1974).

# Appendix E

## Critical Values for *t* Distribution

| | Confidence Intervals (%) | | | | | |
|---|---|---|---|---|---|---|
| | 80 | 90 | 95 | 98 | 99 | 99.9 |
| | Level of Significance for One-Tailed Test | | | | | |
| | .10 | .05 | .025 | .01 | .005 | .0005 |
| | Level of Significance for Two-Tailed Test | | | | | |
| df | .20 | .10 | .05 | .02 | .01 | .001 |
| 1 | 3.078 | 6.314 | 12.706 | 31.821 | 63.657 | 636.619 |
| 2 | 1.886 | 2.920 | 4.303 | 6.965 | 9.925 | 31.598 |
| 3 | 1.638 | 2.353 | 3.182 | 4.541 | 5.841 | 12.941 |
| 4 | 1.533 | 2.132 | 2.776 | 3.747 | 4.604 | 8.610 |
| 5 | 1.476 | 2.015 | 2.571 | 3.365 | 4.032 | 6.859 |
| 6 | 1.440 | 1.943 | 2.447 | 3.143 | 3.707 | 5.959 |
| 7 | 1.415 | 1.895 | 2.365 | 2.998 | 3.499 | 5.405 |
| 8 | 1.397 | 1.860 | 2.306 | 2.896 | 3.355 | 5.041 |
| 9 | 1.383 | 1.833 | 2.262 | 2.821 | 3.250 | 4.781 |
| 10 | 1.372 | 1.812 | 2.228 | 2.764 | 3.169 | 4.587 |
| 11 | 1.363 | 1.796 | 2.201 | 2.718 | 3.106 | 4.437 |
| 12 | 1.356 | 1.782 | 2.179 | 2.681 | 3.055 | 4.318 |
| 13 | 1.350 | 1.771 | 2.160 | 2.650 | 3.012 | 4.221 |
| 14 | 1.345 | 1.761 | 2.145 | 2.624 | 2.977 | 4.140 |
| 15 | 1.341 | 1.753 | 2.131 | 2.602 | 2.947 | 4.073 |

| df | .20 | .10 | .05 | .02 | .01 | .001 |
|----|-----|-----|-----|-----|-----|------|
| 16 | 1.337 | 1.746 | 2.120 | 2.583 | 2.921 | 4.015 |
| 17 | 1.333 | 1.740 | 2.110 | 2.567 | 2.898 | 3.965 |
| 18 | 1.330 | 1.734 | 2.101 | 2.552 | 2.878 | 3.922 |
| 19 | 1.328 | 1.729 | 2.093 | 2.539 | 2.861 | 3.883 |
| 20 | 1.325 | 1.725 | 2.086 | 2.528 | 2.845 | 3.850 |
| 21 | 1.323 | 1.721 | 2.080 | 2.518 | 2.831 | 3.819 |
| 22 | 1.321 | 1.717 | 2.074 | 2.508 | 2.819 | 3.792 |
| 23 | 1.319 | 1.714 | 2.069 | 2.500 | 2.807 | 3.767 |
| 24 | 1.318 | 1.711 | 2.064 | 2.492 | 2.797 | 3.745 |
| 25 | 1.316 | 1.708 | 2.060 | 2.485 | 2.787 | 3.725 |
| 26 | 1.315 | 1.706 | 2.056 | 2.479 | 2.779 | 3.707 |
| 27 | 1.314 | 1.703 | 2.052 | 2.473 | 2.771 | 3.690 |
| 28 | 1.313 | 1.701 | 2.048 | 2.467 | 2.763 | 3.674 |
| 29 | 1.311 | 1.699 | 2.045 | 2.462 | 2.756 | 3.659 |
| 30 | 1.310 | 1.697 | 2.042 | 2.457 | 2.750 | 3.646 |
| 40 | 1.303 | 1.684 | 2.021 | 2.423 | 2.704 | 3.551 |
| 60 | 1.296 | 1.671 | 2.000 | 2.390 | 2.660 | 3.460 |
| 120 | 1.289 | 1.658 | 1.980 | 2.358 | 2.617 | 3.373 |
| ¥ | 1.282 | 1.645 | 1.960 | 2.326 | 2.576 | 3.291 |

*Source:* Abridged from Fisher and Yates (1974, Table V).

# Appendix F

## Critical Values of *F*

Critical values of *F* for $a = .05$.

| $df_{denominator}$ | \multicolumn{10}{c}{$df_{numerator}$} | | | | | | | | | |
| --- | --- | --- | --- | --- | --- | --- | --- | --- | --- | --- |
| | 1 | 2 | 3 | 4 | 5 | 6 | 8 | 12 | 24 | ¥ |
| 1 | 161.40 | 199.50 | 215.70 | 224.60 | 230.20 | 234.00 | 238.90 | 243.90 | 249.00 | 254.30 |
| 2 | 18.51 | 19.00 | 19.16 | 19.25 | 19.30 | 19.33 | 19.37 | 19.41 | 19.45 | 19.50 |
| 3 | 10.13 | 9.55 | 9.28 | 9.12 | 9.01 | 8.94 | 8.84 | 8.74 | 8.64 | 8.53 |
| 4 | 7.71 | 6.94 | 6.59 | 6.39 | 6.26 | 6.16 | 6.04 | 5.91 | 5.77 | 5.63 |
| 5 | 6.61 | 5.79 | 5.41 | 5.19 | 5.05 | 4.95 | 4.82 | 4.68 | 4.53 | 4.36 |
| 6 | 5.99 | 5.14 | 4.76 | 4.53 | 4.39 | 4.28 | 4.15 | 4.00 | 3.84 | 3.67 |
| 7 | 5.59 | 4.74 | 4.35 | 4.12 | 3.97 | 3.87 | 3.73 | 3.57 | 3.41 | 3.23 |
| 8 | 5.32 | 4.46 | 4.07 | 3.84 | 3.69 | 3.58 | 3.44 | 3.28 | 3.12 | 2.93 |
| 9 | 5.12 | 4.26 | 3.86 | 3.63 | 3.48 | 3.37 | 3.23 | 3.07 | 2.90 | 2.71 |
| 10 | 4.96 | 4.10 | 3.71 | 3.48 | 3.33 | 3.22 | 3.07 | 2.91 | 2.74 | 2.54 |
| 11 | 4.84 | 3.98 | 3.59 | 3.36 | 3.20 | 3.09 | 2.95 | 2.79 | 2.61 | 2.40 |
| 12 | 4.75 | 3.88 | 3.49 | 3.26 | 3.11 | 3.00 | 2.85 | 2.69 | 2.50 | 2.30 |
| 13 | 4.67 | 3.80 | 3.41 | 3.18 | 3.02 | 2.92 | 2.77 | 2.60 | 2.42 | 2.21 |
| 14 | 4.60 | 3.74 | 3.34 | 3.11 | 2.96 | 2.85 | 2.70 | 2.53 | 2.35 | 2.13 |
| 15 | 4.54 | 3.68 | 3.29 | 3.06 | 2.90 | 2.79 | 2.64 | 2.48 | 2.29 | 2.07 |
| 16 | 4.49 | 3.63 | 3.24 | 3.01 | 2.85 | 2.74 | 2.59 | 2.42 | 2.24 | 2.01 |

|  | $df_{numerator}$ | | | | | | | | | |
|---|---|---|---|---|---|---|---|---|---|---|
| $df_{denominator}$ | 1 | 2 | 3 | 4 | 5 | 6 | 8 | 12 | 24 | ¥ |
| 17 | 4.45 | 3.59 | 3.20 | 2.96 | 2.81 | 2.70 | 2.55 | 2.38 | 2.19 | 1.96 |
| 18 | 4.41 | 3.55 | 3.16 | 2.93 | 2.77 | 2.66 | 2.51 | 2.34 | 2.15 | 1.92 |
| 19 | 4.38 | 3.52 | 3.13 | 2.90 | 2.74 | 2.63 | 2.48 | 2.31 | 2.11 | 1.88 |
| 20 | 4.35 | 3.49 | 3.10 | 2.87 | 2.71 | 2.60 | 2.45 | 2.28 | 2.08 | 1.84 |
| 21 | 4.32 | 3.47 | 3.07 | 2.84 | 2.68 | 2.57 | 2.42 | 2.25 | 2.05 | 1.81 |
| 22 | 4.30 | 3.44 | 3.05 | 2.82 | 2.66 | 2.55 | 2.40 | 2.23 | 2.03 | 1.78 |
| 23 | 4.28 | 3.42 | 3.03 | 2.80 | 2.64 | 2.53 | 2.38 | 2.20 | 2.00 | 1.76 |
| 24 | 4.26 | 3.40 | 3.01 | 2.78 | 2.62 | 2.51 | 2.36 | 2.18 | 1.98 | 1.73 |
| 25 | 4.24 | 3.38 | 2.99 | 2.76 | 2.60 | 2.49 | 2.34 | 2.16 | 1.96 | 1.71 |
| 26 | 4.22 | 3.37 | 2.98 | 2.74 | 2.59 | 2.47 | 2.32 | 2.15 | 1.95 | 1.69 |
| 27 | 4.21 | 3.35 | 2.96 | 2.73 | 2.57 | 2.46 | 2.30 | 2.13 | 1.93 | 1.67 |
| 28 | 4.20 | 3.34 | 2.95 | 2.71 | 2.56 | 2.44 | 2.29 | 2.12 | 1.91 | 1.65 |
| 29 | 4.18 | 3.33 | 2.93 | 2.70 | 2.54 | 2.43 | 2.28 | 2.10 | 1.90 | 1.64 |
| 30 | 4.17 | 3.32 | 2.92 | 2.69 | 2.53 | 2.42 | 2.27 | 2.09 | 1.89 | 1.62 |
| 40 | 4.08 | 3.23 | 2.84 | 2.61 | 2.45 | 2.34 | 2.18 | 2.00 | 1.79 | 1.51 |
| 60 | 4.00 | 3.15 | 2.76 | 2.52 | 2.37 | 2.25 | 2.10 | 1.92 | 1.70 | 1.39 |
| 120 | 3.92 | 3.07 | 2.68 | 2.45 | 2.29 | 2.17 | 2.02 | 1.83 | 1.61 | 1.25 |
| ¥ | 3.84 | 2.99 | 2.60 | 2.37 | 2.21 | 2.09 | 1.94 | 1.75 | 1.52 | 1.00 |

*Source:* Abridged from Fisher and Yates (1974, Table V).

*Note:* In ANOVA, $df_{numerator} = df_{between}$; $df_{denominator} = df_{within}$. In regression, $df_{numerator} = df_{regression}$; $df_{denominator} = df_{residual}$.

Critical values of $F$ for $a = .01$.

|  | $df_{numerator}$ | | | | | | | | | |
|---|---|---|---|---|---|---|---|---|---|---|
| $df_{denominator}$ | 1 | 2 | 3 | 4 | 5 | 6 | 8 | 12 | 24 | ¥ |
| 1 | 4052 | 4999 | 5403 | 5625 | 5764 | 5859 | 5981 | 6106 | 6234 | 366 |
| 2 | 98.49 | 99.01 | 99.17 | 99.2 | 99.3 | 99.3 | 99.3 | 99.4 | 99.4 | 9.50 |
| 3 | 34.12 | 30.81 | 29.46 | 28.71 | 28.24 | 27.91 | 27.49 | 27.05 | 26.60 | 26.12 |
| 4 | 21.20 | 18.00 | 16.69 | 15.98 | 15.52 | 15.21 | 14.80 | 14.37 | 13.93 | 13.46 |

*(Continued)*

(Continued)

| $df_{denominator}$ | $df_{numerator}$ | | | | | | | | | |
|---|---|---|---|---|---|---|---|---|---|---|
| | 1 | 2 | 3 | 4 | 5 | 6 | 8 | 12 | 14 | ¥ |
| 5 | 16.26 | 13.27 | 12.06 | 11.39 | 10.97 | 10.67 | 10.27 | 9.89 | 9.47 | 9.02 |
| 6 | 13.74 | 10.92 | 9.78 | 9.15 | 8.75 | 8.47 | 8.10 | 7.72 | 7.31 | 6.88 |
| 7 | 12.25 | 9.55 | 8.45 | 7.85 | 7.46 | 7.19 | 6.84 | 6.47 | 6.07 | 5.65 |
| 8 | 11.26 | 8.65 | 7.59 | 7.0 | 6.63 | 6.37 | 6.03 | 5.67 | 5.28 | 4.86 |
| 9 | 10.56 | 8.02 | 6.99 | 6.42 | 6.06 | 5.80 | 5.47 | 5.11 | 4.73 | 4.31 |
| 10 | 10.04 | 7.56 | 6.55 | 5.99 | 5.64 | 5.39 | 5.06 | 4.71 | 4.33 | 3.91 |
| 11 | 9.65 | 7.20 | 6.22 | 5.67 | 5.32 | 5.07 | 4.74 | 4.40 | 4.02 | 3.60 |
| 12 | 9.33 | 6.93 | 5.95 | 5.41 | 5.06 | 4.82 | 4.50 | 4.16 | 3.78 | 3.36 |
| 13 | 9.07 | 6.70 | 5.74 | 5.20 | 4.86 | 4.62 | 4.30 | 3.96 | 3.59 | 3.16 |
| 14 | 8.86 | 6.51 | 5.56 | 5.03 | 4.69 | 4.46 | 4.14 | 3.80 | 3.43 | 3.00 |
| 15 | 8.68 | 6.36 | 5.42 | 4.89 | 4.56 | 4.32 | 4.00 | 3.67 | 3.29 | 2.87 |
| 16 | 8.53 | 6.23 | 5.29 | 4.77 | 4.44 | 4.20 | 3.89 | 3.55 | 3.18 | 2.75 |
| 17 | 8.40 | 6.11 | 5.18 | 4.67 | 4.34 | 4.10 | 3.79 | 3.45 | 3.08 | 2.65 |
| 18 | 8.28 | 6.01 | 5.09 | 4.58 | 4.25 | 4.01 | 3.71 | 3.37 | 3.00 | 2.57 |
| 19 | 8.18 | 5.93 | 5.01 | 4.50 | 4.17 | 3.94 | 3.63 | 3.30 | 2.92 | 2.49 |
| 20 | 8.10 | 5.85 | 4.94 | 4.43 | 4.10 | 3.87 | 3.56 | 3.23 | 2.86 | 2.42 |
| 21 | 8.02 | 5.78 | 4.87 | 4.37 | 4.04 | 3.81 | 3.51 | 3.17 | 2.80 | 2.36 |
| 22 | 7.94 | 5.72 | 4.82 | 4.31 | 3.99 | 3.76 | 3.45 | 3.12 | 2.75 | 2.31 |
| 23 | 7.88 | 5.66 | 4.76 | 4.26 | 3.94 | 3.71 | 3.41 | 3.07 | 2.70 | 2.26 |
| 24 | 7.82 | 5.61 | 4.72 | 4.22 | 3.90 | 3.67 | 3.36 | 3.03 | 2.66 | 2.21 |
| 25 | 7.77 | 5.57 | 4.68 | 4.18 | 3.86 | 3.63 | 3.32 | 2.99 | 2.62 | 2.17 |
| 26 | 7.72 | 5.53 | 4.64 | 4.14 | 3.82 | 3.59 | 3.29 | 2.96 | 2.58 | 2.13 |
| 27 | 7.68 | 5.49 | 4.60 | 4.11 | 3.78 | 3.56 | 3.26 | 2.93 | 2.55 | 2.10 |
| 28 | 7.64 | 5.45 | 4.57 | 4.07 | 3.75 | 3.53 | 3.23 | 2.90 | 2.52 | 2.06 |
| 29 | 7.60 | 5.42 | 4.54 | 4.04 | 3.73 | 3.50 | 3.20 | 2.87 | 2.49 | 2.03 |
| 30 | 7.56 | 5.39 | 4.51 | 4.02 | 3.70 | 3.47 | 3.17 | 2.84 | 2.47 | 2.01 |
| 40 | 7.31 | 5.18 | 4.31 | 3.83 | 3.51 | 3.29 | 2.99 | 2.66 | 2.29 | 1.80 |
| 60 | 7.08 | 4.98 | 4.13 | 3.65 | 3.34 | 3.12 | 2.82 | 2.50 | 2.12 | 1.60 |
| 120 | 6.85 | 4.79 | 3.95 | 3.48 | 3.17 | 2.96 | 2.66 | 2.34 | 1.95 | 1.38 |
| ¥ | 6.64 | 4.60 | 3.78 | 3.32 | 3.02 | 2.80 | 2.51 | 2.18 | 1.79 | 1.00 |

*Source:* Abridged from Fisher and Yates (1974, Table V).

*Note:* In ANOVA, $df_{numerator} = df_{between}$; $df_{denominator} = df_{within}$. In regression, $df_{numerator} = df_{regression}$; $df_{denominator} = df_{residual}$.

Critical values of $F$ for $a = .001$.

| $df_{denominator}$ | \multicolumn{10}{c}{$df_{numerator}$} |
|---|---|---|---|---|---|---|---|---|---|---|
| | 1 | 2 | 3 | 4 | 5 | 6 | 8 | 12 | 24 | ¥ |
| 1 | 405284 | 500000 | 540379 | 562500 | 576405 | 585937 | 598144 | 610667 | 623497 | 636619 |
| 2 | 998.5 | 999.0 | 999.2 | 999.2 | 999.3 | 999.3 | 999.4 | 999.4 | 999.5 | 999.5 |
| 3 | 167.5 | 148.5 | 141.1 | 137.1 | 134.6 | 132.8 | 130.6 | 128.3 | 125.9 | 123.5 |
| 4 | 74.14 | 61.25 | 56.18 | 53.44 | 51.71 | 50.53 | 49.00 | 47.41 | 45.77 | 44.05 |
| 5 | 47.04 | 36.61 | 33.20 | 31.09 | 29.75 | 28.84 | 27.64 | 26.42 | 25.14 | 23.78 |
| 6 | 35.51 | 27.00 | 23.70 | 21.90 | 20.81 | 20.03 | 19.03 | 17.99 | 16.89 | 15.75 |
| 7 | 29.22 | 21.69 | 18.77 | 17.19 | 16.21 | 15.52 | 14.63 | 13.71 | 12.73 | 11.69 |
| 8 | 25.42 | 18.49 | 15.83 | 14.39 | 13.49 | 12.86 | 12.04 | 11.19 | 10.30 | 9.34 |
| 9 | 22.86 | 16.39 | 13.90 | 12.56 | 11.71 | 11.13 | 10.37 | 9.57 | 8.72 | 7.81 |
| 10 | 21.04 | 14.91 | 12.55 | 11.28 | 10.48 | 9.92 | 9.20 | 8.45 | 7.64 | 6.76 |
| 11 | 19.69 | 13.81 | 11.56 | 10.35 | 9.58 | 9.05 | 8.35 | 7.63 | 6.85 | 6.00 |
| 12 | 18.64 | 12.97 | 10.80 | 9.63 | 8.89 | 8.38 | 7.71 | 7.00 | 6.25 | 5.42 |
| 13 | 17.81 | 12.31 | 10.21 | 9.07 | 8.35 | 7.86 | 7.21 | 6.52 | 5.78 | 4.97 |
| 14 | 17.14 | 11.78 | 9.73 | 8.62 | 7.92 | 7.43 | 6.80 | 6.13 | 5.41 | 4.60 |
| 15 | 16.59 | 11.34 | 9.34 | 8.25 | 7.57 | 7.09 | 6.47 | 5.81 | 5.10 | 4.31 |
| 16 | 16.12 | 10.97 | 9.00 | 7.94 | 7.27 | 6.81 | 6.19 | 5.55 | 4.85 | 4.06 |
| 17 | 15.72 | 10.66 | 8.73 | 7.68 | 7.02 | 6.56 | 5.96 | 5.32 | 4.63 | 3.85 |
| 18 | 15.38 | 10.39 | 8.49 | 7.46 | 6.81 | 6.35 | 5.76 | 5.13 | 4.45 | 3.67 |
| 19 | 15.08 | 10.16 | 8.28 | 7.26 | 6.61 | 6.18 | 5.59 | 4.97 | 4.29 | 3.52 |
| 20 | 14.82 | 9.95 | 8.10 | 7.10 | 6.46 | 6.02 | 5.44 | 4.82 | 4.15 | 3.38 |
| 21 | 14.59 | 9.77 | 7.94 | 6.95 | 6.32 | 5.88 | 5.31 | 4.70 | 4.03 | 3.26 |
| 22 | 14.38 | 9.61 | 7.80 | 6.81 | 6.19 | 5.76 | 5.19 | 4.58 | 3.92 | 3.15 |
| 23 | 14.19 | 9.47 | 7.67 | 6.69 | 6.08 | 5.65 | 5.09 | 4.48 | 3.82 | 3.05 |
| 24 | 14.03 | 9.34 | 7.55 | 6.59 | 5.98 | 5.55 | 4.99 | 4.39 | 3.74 | 2.97 |
| 25 | 13.88 | 9.22 | 7.45 | 6.49 | 5.88 | 5.46 | 4.91 | 4.31 | 3.66 | 2.89 |
| 26 | 13.74 | 9.12 | 7.36 | 6.41 | 5.80 | 5.38 | 4.83 | 4.24 | 3.59 | 2.82 |
| 27 | 13.61 | 9.02 | 7.27 | 6.33 | 5.73 | 5.31 | 4.76 | 4.17 | 3.52 | 2.75 |
| 28 | 13.50 | 8.93 | 7.19 | 6.25 | 5.66 | 5.24 | 4.69 | 4.11 | 3.46 | 2.70 |
| 29 | 13.39 | 8.85 | 7.12 | 6.19 | 5.59 | 5.18 | 4.64 | 4.05 | 3.41 | 2.64 |
| 30 | 13.29 | 8.77 | 7.05 | 6.12 | 5.53 | 5.12 | 4.58 | 4.00 | 3.36 | 2.59 |
| 40 | 12.61 | 8.25 | 6.60 | 5.70 | 5.13 | 4.73 | 4.21 | 3.64 | 3.01 | 2.23 |
| 60 | 11.97 | 7.76 | 6.17 | 5.31 | 4.76 | 4.37 | 3.87 | 3.31 | 2.69 | 1.90 |
| 120 | 11.38 | 7.31 | 5.79 | 4.95 | 4.42 | 4.04 | 3.55 | 3.02 | 2.40 | 1.56 |
| ¥ | 10.83 | 6.91 | 5.42 | 4.62 | 4.10 | 3.74 | 3.27 | 2.74 | 2.13 | 1.00 |

*Source:* Abridged from Fisher and Yates (1974, Table V).

*Note:* In ANOVA, $df_{numerator} = df_{between}$; $df_{denominator} = df_{within}$. In regression, $df_{numerator} = df_{regression}$; $df_{denominator} = df_{residual}$.

# Appendix G

## Critical Values of Chi-Square

| df | .10 | .05 | .01 | .001 |
|----|-----|-----|-----|------|
| 1 | 2.71 | 3.84 | 6.64 | 10.83 |
| 2 | 4.60 | 5.99 | 9.21 | 13.82 |
| 3 | 6.25 | 7.81 | 11.34 | 16.27 |
| 4 | 7.78 | 9.49 | 13.28 | 18.47 |
| 5 | 9.24 | 11.07 | 15.09 | 20.52 |
| 6 | 10.64 | 12.59 | 16.81 | 22.46 |
| 7 | 12.02 | 14.07 | 18.48 | 24.32 |
| 8 | 13.36 | 15.51 | 20.09 | 26.12 |
| 9 | 14.68 | 16.92 | 21.67 | 27.88 |
| 10 | 15.99 | 18.31 | 23.21 | 29.59 |
| 11 | 17.28 | 19.68 | 24.72 | 31.26 |
| 12 | 18.55 | 21.03 | 26.22 | 32.91 |
| 13 | 19.81 | 22.36 | 27.69 | 34.53 |
| 14 | 21.06 | 23.68 | 29.14 | 36.12 |
| 15 | 22.31 | 25.00 | 30.58 | 37.70 |
| 16 | 23.54 | 26.30 | 32.00 | 39.25 |
| 17 | 24.77 | 27.59 | 33.41 | 40.79 |
| 18 | 25.99 | 28.87 | 34.80 | 42.31 |
| 19 | 27.20 | 30.14 | 36.19 | 43.82 |

| df | .10 | .05 | .01 | .001 |
|----|-----|-----|-----|------|
| 20 | 28.41 | 31.41 | 37.57 | 45.32 |
| 21 | 29.62 | 32.67 | 38.93 | 46.80 |
| 22 | 30.81 | 33.92 | 40.29 | 48.27 |
| 23 | 32.01 | 35.17 | 41.64 | 49.73 |
| 24 | 33.20 | 36.42 | 42.98 | 51.18 |
| 25 | 34.38 | 37.65 | 44.31 | 52.62 |
| 26 | 35.56 | 38.88 | 45.64 | 54.05 |
| 27 | 36.74 | 40.11 | 46.96 | 55.48 |
| 28 | 37.92 | 41.34 | 48.28 | 56.89 |
| 29 | 39.09 | 42.56 | 49.59 | 58.30 |
| 30 | 40.26 | 43.77 | 50.89 | 59.70 |
| 40 | 51.80 | 55.76 | 63.69 | 73.40 |
| 50 | 63.17 | 67.50 | 76.15 | 86.66 |
| 60 | 74.40 | 79.08 | 88.38 | 99.61 |
| 70 | 85.53 | 90.53 | 100.42 | 112.32 |

*Source:* Abridged from Fisher and Yates (1974).

# Appendix H

## Critical Values of the Correlation Coefficient

| | Level of Significance for One-Tailed Test | | | |
|---|---|---|---|---|
| | .05 | .025 | .01 | .005 |
| | Level of Significance for Two-Tailed Test | | | |
| df | .10 | .05 | .02 | .01 |
| 1 | .988 | .997 | .9995 | .9999 |
| 2 | .900 | .950 | .980 | .990 |
| 3 | .805 | .878 | .934 | .959 |
| 4 | .729 | .811 | .882 | .917 |
| 5 | .669 | .754 | .833 | .874 |
| 6 | .622 | .707 | .789 | .834 |
| 7 | .582 | .666 | .750 | .798 |
| 8 | .549 | .632 | .716 | .765 |
| 9 | .521 | .602 | .685 | .735 |
| 10 | .497 | .576 | .658 | .708 |
| 11 | .476 | .553 | .634 | .684 |
| 12 | .458 | .532 | .612 | .661 |
| 13 | .441 | .514 | .592 | .641 |
| 14 | .426 | .497 | .574 | .623 |
| 15 | .412 | .482 | .558 | .606 |
| 16 | .400 | .468 | .542 | .590 |

| df | .10 | .05 | .02 | .01 |
|----|-----|-----|-----|-----|
| 17 | .389 | .456 | .528 | .575 |
| 18 | .378 | .444 | .516 | .561 |
| 19 | .369 | .433 | .503 | .549 |
| 20 | .360 | .423 | .492 | .537 |
| 21 | .352 | .413 | .482 | .526 |
| 22 | .344 | .404 | .472 | .515 |
| 23 | .337 | .396 | .462 | .505 |
| 24 | .330 | .388 | .453 | .496 |
| 25 | .323 | .381 | .445 | .487 |
| 26 | .317 | .374 | .437 | .479 |
| 27 | .311 | .367 | .430 | .471 |
| 28 | .306 | .361 | .423 | .463 |
| 29 | .301 | .355 | .416 | .456 |
| 30 | .296 | .349 | .409 | .449 |
| 35 | .275 | .325 | .381 | .418 |
| 40 | .257 | .304 | .358 | .393 |
| 45 | .243 | .288 | .338 | .372 |
| 50 | .231 | .273 | .322 | .354 |
| 60 | .211 | .250 | .295 | .325 |
| 70 | .195 | .232 | .274 | .303 |
| 80 | .183 | .217 | .256 | .283 |
| 90 | .173 | .205 | .242 | .267 |
| 100 | .164 | .195 | .230 | .254 |

*Source:* Abridged from Fisher and Yates (1974, Table VII).

# Appendix I

## Table of Random Numbers

| Line/Col. | (1) | (2) | (3) | (4) | (5) | (6) | (7) | (8) | (9) | (10) | (11) | (12) | (13) | (14) |
|---|---|---|---|---|---|---|---|---|---|---|---|---|---|---|
| 1 | 10480 | 15011 | 01536 | 02011 | 81647 | 91646 | 69179 | 14194 | 62590 | 36207 | 20969 | 99570 | 91291 | 90700 |
| 2 | 22368 | 46573 | 25595 | 85393 | 30995 | 89198 | 27982 | 53402 | 93965 | 34095 | 52666 | 19174 | 39615 | 99505 |
| 3 | 24130 | 48360 | 22527 | 97265 | 76393 | 64809 | 15179 | 24830 | 49340 | 32081 | 30680 | 19655 | 63348 | 58629 |
| 4 | 42167 | 93093 | 06243 | 61680 | 07856 | 16376 | 39440 | 53537 | 71341 | 57004 | 00849 | 74917 | 97758 | 16379 |
| 5 | 37570 | 39975 | 81837 | 16656 | 06121 | 91782 | 60468 | 81305 | 49684 | 60672 | 14110 | 06927 | 01263 | 54613 |
| 6 | 77921 | 06907 | 11008 | 42751 | 27756 | 53498 | 18602 | 70659 | 90655 | 15053 | 21916 | 81825 | 44394 | 42880 |
| 7 | 99562 | 72905 | 56420 | 69994 | 98872 | 31016 | 71194 | 18738 | 44013 | 48840 | 63213 | 21069 | 10634 | 12952 |
| 8 | 96301 | 91977 | 05463 | 07972 | 18876 | 20922 | 94595 | 56869 | 69014 | 60045 | 18425 | 84903 | 42508 | 32307 |
| 9 | 89579 | 14342 | 63661 | 10281 | 17453 | 18103 | 57740 | 84378 | 25331 | 12566 | 58678 | 44947 | 05585 | 56941 |
| 10 | 85475 | 36857 | 43342 | 53988 | 53060 | 59533 | 38867 | 62300 | 08158 | 17983 | 16439 | 11458 | 18593 | 64952 |
| 11 | 28918 | 69578 | 88231 | 33276 | 70997 | 79936 | 56865 | 05859 | 90106 | 31595 | 01547 | 85590 | 91610 | 78188 |
| 12 | 63553 | 40961 | 48235 | 03427 | 49626 | 69445 | 18663 | 72695 | 52180 | 20847 | 12234 | 90511 | 33703 | 90322 |
| 13 | 09429 | 93969 | 52636 | 92737 | 88974 | 33488 | 36320 | 17617 | 30015 | 08272 | 84115 | 27156 | 30613 | 74952 |
| 14 | 10365 | 61129 | 87529 | 85689 | 48237 | 52267 | 67689 | 93394 | 01511 | 26358 | 85104 | 20285 | 29975 | 89868 |
| 15 | 07119 | 97336 | 71048 | 08178 | 77233 | 13916 | 47564 | 81056 | 97735 | 85977 | 29372 | 74461 | 28551 | 90707 |
| 16 | 51085 | 12765 | 51821 | 51259 | 77452 | 16308 | 60756 | 92144 | 49442 | 53900 | 70960 | 63990 | 75601 | 40719 |
| 17 | 02368 | 21382 | 52404 | 60268 | 89368 | 19885 | 55322 | 44819 | 01188 | 65255 | 64835 | 44919 | 05944 | 55157 |
| 18 | 01011 | 54092 | 33362 | 94904 | 31273 | 04146 | 18594 | 29852 | 71585 | 85030 | 51132 | 01915 | 92747 | 64951 |
| 19 | 52162 | 53916 | 46369 | 58586 | 23216 | 14513 | 83149 | 98736 | 23495 | 64350 | 94738 | 17752 | 35156 | 35749 |
| 20 | 07056 | 97628 | 33787 | 09998 | 42698 | 06691 | 76988 | 13602 | 51851 | 46104 | 88916 | 19509 | 25625 | 58104 |
| 21 | 48663 | 91245 | 85828 | 14346 | 09172 | 30168 | 90229 | 04734 | 59193 | 22178 | 30421 | 61666 | 99904 | 32812 |

*(Continued)*

(Continued)

| Line/Col. | (1) | (2) | (3) | (4) | (5) | (6) | (7) | (8) | (9) | (10) | (11) | (12) | (13) | (14) |
|---|---|---|---|---|---|---|---|---|---|---|---|---|---|---|
| 22 | 54164 | 58492 | 22421 | 74103 | 47070 | 25306 | 76468 | 26384 | 58151 | 06646 | 21524 | 15227 | 96909 | 44592 |
| 23 | 32639 | 32363 | 05597 | 24200 | 13363 | 38005 | 94342 | 28728 | 35806 | 06912 | 17012 | 64161 | 18296 | 22851 |
| 24 | 29334 | 27001 | 87637 | 87308 | 58731 | 00256 | 45834 | 15398 | 46557 | 41135 | 10367 | 07684 | 36188 | 18510 |
| 25 | 02488 | 33062 | 28834 | 07351 | 19731 | 92420 | 60952 | 61280 | 50001 | 67658 | 32586 | 86679 | 50720 | 94953 |
| 26 | 81525 | 72295 | 04839 | 96423 | 24878 | 82651 | 66566 | 14778 | 76797 | 14780 | 13300 | 87074 | 79666 | 95725 |
| 27 | 29676 | 20591 | 68086 | 26432 | 46901 | 20849 | 89768 | 81536 | 86645 | 12659 | 92259 | 57102 | 80428 | 25280 |
| 28 | 00742 | 57392 | 39064 | 66432 | 84673 | 40027 | 32832 | 61362 | 98947 | 96067 | 64760 | 64584 | 96096 | 98253 |
| 29 | 05366 | 04213 | 25669 | 26422 | 44407 | 44048 | 37937 | 63904 | 45766 | 66134 | 75470 | 66520 | 34693 | 90449 |
| 30 | 91921 | 26418 | 64117 | 94305 | 26766 | 25940 | 39972 | 22209 | 71500 | 64568 | 91402 | 42416 | 07844 | 69618 |
| 31 | 00582 | 04711 | 87917 | 77341 | 42206 | 35126 | 74087 | 99547 | 81817 | 42607 | 43808 | 76655 | 62028 | 76630 |
| 32 | 00725 | 69884 | 62797 | 56170 | 86324 | 88072 | 76222 | 36086 | 84637 | 93161 | 76038 | 65855 | 77919 | 88006 |
| 33 | 69011 | 65797 | 95876 | 55293 | 18988 | 27354 | 26575 | 08625 | 40801 | 59920 | 29841 | 80150 | 12777 | 48501 |
| 34 | 25976 | 57948 | 29888 | 88604 | 67917 | 48708 | 18912 | 82271 | 65424 | 69774 | 33611 | 54262 | 85963 | 03547 |
| 35 | 09763 | 83473 | 73577 | 12908 | 30883 | 18317 | 28290 | 35797 | 05998 | 41688 | 34952 | 37888 | 38917 | 88050 |
| 36 | 91567 | 42595 | 27958 | 30134 | 04024 | 86385 | 29880 | 99730 | 55536 | 84855 | 29080 | 09250 | 79656 | 73211 |
| 37 | 17955 | 56349 | 90999 | 49127 | 20044 | 59931 | 06115 | 20542 | 18059 | 02008 | 73708 | 83317 | 36103 | 42791 |
| 38 | 46503 | 18584 | 18845 | 49618 | 02304 | 51038 | 20655 | 58727 | 28168 | 15475 | 56942 | 53389 | 20562 | 87338 |
| 39 | 92157 | 89634 | 94824 | 78171 | 84610 | 82834 | 09922 | 25417 | 44137 | 48413 | 25555 | 21246 | 35509 | 20468 |
| 40 | 14577 | 62765 | 35605 | 81263 | 39667 | 47358 | 56873 | 56307 | 61607 | 49518 | 89656 | 20103 | 77490 | 18062 |
| 41 | 98427 | 07523 | 33362 | 64270 | 01638 | 92477 | 66969 | 98420 | 04880 | 45585 | 46565 | 04102 | 46880 | 45709 |

| Line/Col. | (1) | (2) | (3) | (4) | (5) | (6) | (7) | (8) | (9) | (10) | (11) | (12) | (13) | (14) |
|---|---|---|---|---|---|---|---|---|---|---|---|---|---|---|
| 42 | 34914 | 63976 | 88720 | 82765 | 34476 | 17032 | 87589 | 40836 | 32427 | 70002 | 70663 | 88863 | 77775 | 69348 |
| 43 | 70060 | 28277 | 39475 | 46473 | 23219 | 53416 | 94970 | 25832 | 69975 | 94884 | 19661 | 72828 | 00102 | 66794 |
| 44 | 53976 | 54914 | 06990 | 67245 | 68350 | 82948 | 11398 | 42878 | 80287 | 88267 | 47363 | 46634 | 06541 | 97809 |
| 45 | 76072 | 29515 | 40980 | 07391 | 58745 | 25774 | 22987 | 80059 | 39911 | 96189 | 41151 | 14222 | 60697 | 59583 |
| 46 | 90725 | 52210 | 83974 | 29992 | 65831 | 38857 | 50490 | 83765 | 55657 | 14361 | 31720 | 57375 | 56228 | 41546 |
| 47 | 64364 | 67412 | 33339 | 31926 | 14883 | 24413 | 59744 | 92351 | 97473 | 89286 | 35931 | 04110 | 23726 | 51900 |
| 48 | 08962 | 00358 | 31662 | 25388 | 61642 | 34072 | 81249 | 35648 | 56891 | 69352 | 48373 | 45578 | 78547 | 81788 |
| 49 | 95012 | 68379 | 93526 | 70765 | 10593 | 04542 | 76463 | 54328 | 02349 | 17247 | 28865 | 14777 | 62730 | 92277 |
| 50 | 15664 | 10493 | 20492 | 38391 | 91132 | 21999 | 59516 | 81652 | 27195 | 48223 | 46751 | 22923 | 32261 | 85653 |
| 51 | 16408 | 81899 | 04153 | 53381 | 79401 | 21438 | 83035 | 92350 | 36693 | 31238 | 59649 | 91754 | 72772 | 02338 |
| 52 | 18629 | 81953 | 05520 | 91962 | 04739 | 13092 | 97662 | 24822 | 94730 | 06496 | 35090 | 04822 | 86772 | 98289 |
| 53 | 73115 | 35101 | 47498 | 87637 | 99016 | 71060 | 88824 | 71013 | 18735 | 20286 | 23153 | 72924 | 35165 | 43040 |
| 54 | 57491 | 16703 | 23167 | 49323 | 45021 | 33132 | 12544 | 41035 | 80780 | 45393 | 44812 | 12515 | 98931 | 91202 |
| 55 | 30405 | 83946 | 23792 | 14422 | 15059 | 45799 | 22716 | 19792 | 09983 | 74353 | 68668 | 30429 | 70735 | 25499 |
| 56 | 16631 | 35006 | 85900 | 98275 | 32388 | 52390 | 16815 | 69298 | 82732 | 38480 | 73817 | 32523 | 41961 | 44437 |
| 57 | 96773 | 20206 | 42559 | 78985 | 05300 | 22164 | 24369 | 54224 | 35083 | 19687 | 11052 | 91491 | 60383 | 19746 |
| 58 | 38935 | 64202 | 14349 | 82674 | 66523 | 44133 | 00697 | 35552 | 35970 | 19124 | 63318 | 29686 | 03387 | 59846 |
| 59 | 31624 | 76384 | 17403 | 53363 | 44167 | 64486 | 64758 | 75366 | 76554 | 31601 | 12614 | 33072 | 60332 | 92325 |
| 60 | 78919 | 19474 | 23632 | 27889 | 47914 | 02584 | 37680 | 20801 | 72152 | 39339 | 34806 | 08930 | 85001 | 87820 |
| 61 | 03931 | 33309 | 57047 | 74211 | 63445 | 17361 | 62825 | 39908 | 05607 | 91284 | 68833 | 25570 | 38818 | 46920 |
| 62 | 74426 | 33278 | 43972 | 10119 | 89917 | 15665 | 52872 | 73823 | 73144 | 88662 | 88970 | 74492 | 51805 | 99378 |

*(Continued)*

(Continued)

| Line/Col. | (1) | (2) | (3) | (4) | (5) | (6) | (7) | (8) | (9) | (10) | (11) | (12) | (13) | (14) |
|---|---|---|---|---|---|---|---|---|---|---|---|---|---|---|
| 63 | 09066 | 00903 | 20795 | 95452 | 92648 | 45454 | 09552 | 88815 | 16553 | 51125 | 79375 | 97596 | 16296 | 66092 |
| 64 | 42238 | 12426 | 87025 | 14267 | 20979 | 04508 | 64535 | 31355 | 86064 | 29472 | 47689 | 05974 | 52468 | 16834 |
| 65 | 16153 | 08002 | 26504 | 41744 | 81959 | 65642 | 74240 | 56302 | 00033 | 67107 | 77510 | 70625 | 28725 | 34191 |
| 66 | 21457 | 40742 | 29820 | 96783 | 29400 | 21840 | 15035 | 34537 | 33310 | 06116 | 95240 | 15957 | 16572 | 06004 |
| 67 | 21581 | 57802 | 02050 | 89728 | 17937 | 37621 | 47075 | 42080 | 97403 | 48626 | 68995 | 43805 | 33386 | 21597 |
| 68 | 55612 | 78095 | 83197 | 33732 | 05810 | 24813 | 86902 | 60397 | 16489 | 03264 | 88525 | 42786 | 05269 | 92532 |
| 69 | 44657 | 66999 | 99324 | 51281 | 84463 | 60563 | 79312 | 93454 | 68876 | 25471 | 93911 | 25650 | 12682 | 73572 |
| 70 | 91340 | 84979 | 46949 | 81973 | 37949 | 61023 | 43997 | 15263 | 80644 | 43942 | 89203 | 71795 | 99533 | 50501 |
| 71 | 91227 | 21199 | 31935 | 27022 | 84067 | 05462 | 35216 | 14486 | 29891 | 68607 | 41867 | 14951 | 91696 | 85065 |
| 72 | 50001 | 38140 | 66321 | 19924 | 72163 | 09538 | 12151 | 06878 | 91903 | 18749 | 34405 | 56087 | 82790 | 70925 |
| 73 | 65390 | 05224 | 72958 | 28609 | 81406 | 39147 | 25549 | 48542 | 42627 | 45233 | 57202 | 94617 | 23772 | 07896 |
| 74 | 27504 | 96131 | 83944 | 41575 | 10573 | 08619 | 64482 | 73923 | 36152 | 05184 | 94142 | 25299 | 84387 | 34925 |
| 75 | 37169 | 94851 | 39117 | 89632 | 00959 | 16487 | 65536 | 49071 | 39782 | 17095 | 02330 | 74301 | 00275 | 48280 |
| 76 | 11508 | 70225 | 51111 | 38351 | 19444 | 66499 | 71945 | 05422 | 13442 | 78675 | 84081 | 66938 | 93654 | 59894 |
| 77 | 37449 | 30362 | 06694 | 54690 | 04052 | 53115 | 62757 | 95348 | 78662 | 11163 | 81651 | 50245 | 34971 | 52924 |
| 78 | 46515 | 70331 | 85922 | 38329 | 57015 | 15765 | 97161 | 17869 | 45349 | 61796 | 66345 | 81073 | 49106 | 79860 |
| 79 | 30986 | 81223 | 42416 | 58353 | 21532 | 30502 | 32305 | 86482 | 05174 | 07901 | 54339 | 58861 | 74818 | 46942 |
| 80 | 63798 | 64995 | 46583 | 09765 | 44160 | 78128 | 83991 | 42865 | 92520 | 83531 | 80377 | 35909 | 81250 | 54238 |
| 81 | 82486 | 84846 | 99254 | 67632 | 43218 | 50076 | 21361 | 64816 | 51202 | 88124 | 41870 | 52689 | 51275 | 83556 |
| 82 | 21885 | 32906 | 92431 | 09060 | 64297 | 51674 | 64126 | 62570 | 26123 | 05155 | 59194 | 52799 | 28225 | 85762 |
| 83 | 60336 | 98782 | 07408 | 53458 | 13564 | 59089 | 26445 | 29789 | 85205 | 41001 | 12535 | 12133 | 14645 | 23541 |

| Line/Col. | (1) | (2) | (3) | (4) | (5) | (6) | (7) | (8) | (9) | (10) | (11) | (12) | (13) | (14) |
|---|---|---|---|---|---|---|---|---|---|---|---|---|---|---|
| 84 | 43937 | 46891 | 24010 | 25560 | 86355 | 33941 | 25786 | 54990 | 71899 | 15475 | 95434 | 98227 | 21824 | 19585 |
| 85 | 97656 | 63175 | 89303 | 16275 | 07100 | 92063 | 21942 | 18611 | 47348 | 20203 | 18534 | 03862 | 78095 | 50136 |
| 86 | 03299 | 01221 | 05418 | 38982 | 55758 | 92237 | 26759 | 86367 | 21216 | 98442 | 08303 | 56613 | 91511 | 75928 |
| 87 | 79626 | 06486 | 03574 | 17668 | 07785 | 76020 | 79924 | 25651 | 83325 | 88428 | 85076 | 72811 | 22717 | 50585 |
| 88 | 85636 | 68335 | 47539 | 03129 | 65651 | 11977 | 02510 | 26113 | 99447 | 68645 | 34327 | 15152 | 55230 | 93448 |
| 89 | 18039 | 14367 | 61337 | 06177 | 12143 | 46609 | 32989 | 74014 | 64708 | 00533 | 35398 | 58408 | 13261 | 47908 |
| 90 | 08362 | 15656 | 60627 | 36478 | 65648 | 16764 | 53412 | 09013 | 07832 | 41574 | 17639 | 82163 | 60859 | 75567 |
| 91 | 79556 | 29068 | 04142 | 16268 | 15387 | 12856 | 66227 | 38358 | 22478 | 73373 | 88732 | 09443 | 82558 | 05250 |
| 92 | 92608 | 82674 | 27072 | 32534 | 17075 | 27698 | 98204 | 63863 | 11951 | 34648 | 88022 | 56148 | 34925 | 57031 |
| 93 | 23982 | 25835 | 40055 | 67006 | 12293 | 02753 | 14827 | 22235 | 35071 | 99704 | 37543 | 11601 | 35503 | 85171 |
| 94 | 09915 | 96306 | 05908 | 97901 | 28395 | 14186 | 00821 | 80703 | 70426 | 75647 | 76310 | 88717 | 37890 | 40129 |
| 95 | 50937 | 33300 | 26695 | 62247 | 69927 | 76123 | 50842 | 43834 | 86654 | 70959 | 79725 | 93872 | 28117 | 19233 |
| 96 | 42488 | 78077 | 69882 | 61657 | 34136 | 79180 | 97526 | 43092 | 04098 | 73571 | 80799 | 76536 | 71255 | 64239 |
| 97 | 46764 | 86273 | 63003 | 93017 | 31204 | 36692 | 40202 | 35275 | 57306 | 55543 | 53203 | 18098 | 47625 | 88684 |
| 98 | 03237 | 45430 | 55417 | 63282 | 90816 | 17349 | 88298 | 90183 | 36600 | 78406 | 06216 | 95787 | 42579 | 90730 |
| 99 | 86591 | 81482 | 52667 | 61583 | 14972 | 90053 | 89534 | 76036 | 49199 | 43716 | 97548 | 04379 | 46370 | 28672 |
| 100 | 38534 | 01715 | 94964 | 87288 | 65680 | 43772 | 39560 | 12918 | 86537 | 62738 | 19636 | 51132 | 25739 | 56947 |

# Glossary

**2 × 2 factorial design:** An experimental design that has two independent variables, each with two levels, resulting in four conditions.

**A priori:** A term that means to come before, as in a testable hypothesis should be formulated before experimentation or observation.

**Abstract:** A section of a written report that summarizes the major points of the study.

**Additivity:** In a factorial design, additivity is the term used when there is no interaction between independent variables.

**Aggregate matching:** A comparison group is selected that has similar distributions on key variables as the treatment group, such as the same average age, the same percentage female, and so on.

**Alternate-forms reliability:** A procedure for testing the reliability of responses to questions in which participants' answers are compared after the test takers have been asked slightly different versions of the questions or when randomly selected halves of the sample have been administered slightly different versions of the questions.

**Alternative explanation:** To establish causality, other plausible explanations for the observed relationship must be eliminated.

**Amygdala:** An almond shaped structure found deep in the brain that plays a key role in fusing memories with emotion.

**Analysis of covariance:** A statistical technique to test whether a difference on a dependent measure exists, even after controlling or covarying for the effects of specific control variables.

**Analysis of variance (ANOVA):** Also known as the *F* test, it is a general statistical procedure used when there are more than two levels of an independent variable, or for complex experimental designs with two or more independent variables.

**Antagonistic interaction:** See Crossover interaction.

**APA:** American Psychological Association.

**APA format:** Organization and style of writing specified by the APA.

**Applied research:** Research focus is on important questions of immediate relevance in solving practical problems.

**Approach avoidance motivation:** A psychological theory that states that behavioral cues share informational value as signals of approach, propelling behavior forward, or conversely, they may fuel avoidance, triggering inhibition.

**Attrition:** When research participants drop out, often a major problem in longitudinal studies.

**Availability sampling:** Sampling in which elements are selected on the basis of convenience.

**Bar chart:** A graphic for qualitative variables in which the variable's distribution is displayed with solid bars separated by spaces.

**Baseline:** Used as a comparison condition for assessing the effect of a treatment.

**Baseline phase (A):** The period in a single-subject design during which the intervention to be evaluated is not offered to the subject and repeated measurements of the dependent variable are taken or reconstructed.

**Basic research:** Studies that focus on understanding the nature of abstract psychological processes and ideas, rather than on the immediate solution to a problem.

**Before-and-after design:** A quasi-experimental design consisting of several before-after comparisons involving the same variables but different groups.

**Belmont Report:** Developed in 1979 by a national commission to specify ethical standards for the protection of human subjects.

**Beneficence:** The Belmont Report principle that requires minimizing possible harms and maximizing benefits.

**Between-groups variance:** Calculated by comparing the difference of each of the means of the individual groups with the overall or grand mean for all scores in the experiment; the between-groups variance represents systematic variance due to the manipulation of the independent variable.

**Between-subjects design:** In an experiment, independent groups of participants receive the different levels of the independent variable.

**Bimodal:** A distribution that has two nonadjacent categories with about the same number of cases, and these categories have more cases than any others.

**Carryover effects:** An important source of experimental error for a within-subjects design, this problem occurs when the effects from one treatment condition are carried over to the next.

**Case studies:** Investigations that involve systematic investigation of a single case or a small set of very similar cases.

**Cases:** See Elements.

**Ceiling effect:** A problem that detracts from the sensitivity of a research design can occur when a dependent variable is seriously restricted in range by very high scores.

**Census:** Research in which information is obtained through the responses that all available members of an entire population give to questions.

**Central tendency:** The most common value (for variables measured at the nominal level) or the value around which cases tend to center (for a quantitative variable).

**Cerebral cortex:** The brain's outer layer or "bark," thought to be the seat of higher thinking.

**Certificate of Confidentiality:** A certificate that can be issued by the National Institutes of Health to protect a researcher studying high-risk populations or behaviors from being legally required to disclose confidential information.

**Chi-square ($\chi^2$):** An inferential statistic used to test hypotheses about the relationships between variables in a contingency table.

**Chi-square ($\chi^2$) test of independence:** An inferential statistic used to test hypotheses about the relationships between two or more categorical variables in a contingency table.

**Clinical replication:** Used to enhance generalizability of single-subject designs, clinical replication involves combining different interventions into a clinical package to treat multiple problems.

**Cluster:** A naturally occurring, mixed aggregate of elements of the population.

**Cluster sampling:** Sampling in which elements are selected in two or more stages, with the first stage being the random selection of naturally occurring clusters and the last stage being the random selection of elements within clusters.

**Code of Conduct, American Psychological Association:** Eighty-three standards adopted (updated) in 2002 to guide psychologists' clinical and research practice.

**Cognitive illusions:** Mistakes of reasoning that occur when our thinking deceives us; often referred to as curious blind spots, or mental tunnels.

**Cognitive psychology:** School of psychology that focuses on the study of mental processes, such as attention, perception, memory, and language.

**Cohort:** A group of individuals sharing a certain characteristic, such as age, year of high school graduation, or locale.

**Cohort effects:** A confound that occurs in a cross-sectional method when comparing groups of persons who are at different ages at one point in time.

**Comparison group:** In an experiment, a group that has been exposed to a different treatment (or value of the independent variable) than the experimental group.

**Computer-assisted personal interview (CAPI):** A personal interview in which the laptop computer is used to display interview questions and to process responses that the interviewer types in, as well as to check that these responses fall within allowed ranges.

**Conceptual definition:** It provides the meaning, often rather broad in scope, of an abstract term, such as intelligence, anxiety or emotion. Like a dictionary definition, it demarcates a semantic or linguistic meaning of a psychological term, that is, its usage in words, texts, and language.

**Concurrent multiple-baseline design:** A series of A–B designs (although A–B–A or A–B–A–B designs could also be used) are implemented at the same time for at least three cases (clients, target problems, or settings).

**Concurrent validity:** The type of validity that exists when scores on a measure are closely related to scores on a criterion measured at the same time.

**Condition:** A particular way in which participants are treated; a group or treatment in an experiment.

**Confirmatory bias:** A natural tendency of the human mind to actively seek out and assign more weight to any kind of evidence that favors existing beliefs, expectations, or a hypothesis in hand.

**Confirmatory factor analysis:** A statistical technique that is used to determine whether the same set of factors underlying a construct in study sample can be replicated in a new independent sample.

**Confounding variables:** The researcher fails to control for unwanted sources of influences. These factors subsequently cannot be ruled out as viable alternative explanations.

**Confounds:** The researcher fails to control for unwanted sources of influences. These factors subsequently cannot be ruled out as viable alternative explanations.

**Construct:** An abstraction or concept that is specified in a theory to describe, explain, and predict a wide range of related empirical findings. Constructs that are studied in psychology, such as intelligence, personality, memory, anxiety, or attention, are not directly observable material entities.

**Construct validity:** Established by showing that the same traits measured by different methods are related (convergent validity), whereas different traits measured by the same methods are unrelated (discriminant validity).

**Constructivist theory:** Psychological theory that emphasizes general cognitive processes such as categorizing, storytelling, and persuasion as tools by which the mind creates cultural meaning.

**Content validity:** The extent to which test items have sufficient breadth to capture the full range of a construct intended to be measured.

**Context effects (also called priming effects):** Occur in a survey when one or more questions influence how subsequent questions are interpreted.

**Contingency table:** Often used with chi-square ($\chi^2$) test of independence to tabulate and analyze relationship between two or more categorical variables.

**Contingent question:** A question that is asked of only a subset of survey respondents.

**Control condition:** Serves as a comparison condition in a within-subjects design.

**Control group:** A comparison group that receives no treatment.

**Control variable:** A variable that is either held constant in an experiment or its effects are statistically controlled.

**Convergent validity:** An important aspect of construct validity, convergent validity measures the extent to which the same trait measured by two different methods yields similar results.

**Correlation:** A statistic that measures the extent to which two variables are associated but not necessarily causally related.

**Correlation coefficient:** A number varying from −1.00 through 0.00 to + 1.00 that indicates the strength of the relationship between the two variables.

**Counterbalancing:** For a within-subjects design, a commonly used technique to control for the potentially confounding effects of order of treatments.

**Covariation of the cause and effect:** In establishing causality, evidence that shows that when the cause is present, the effect occurs and when the cause is absent, the effect does not occur.

**Cover letter:** The letter sent with a mailed questionnaire. It explains the survey's purpose and auspices and encourages the respondent to participate.

**Criterion validity:** The extent to which test scores agree with an objective criterion that follows logically from the measured variable.

**Critical *t* value:** The value that the *t* statistic must exceed to reject the null hypothesis at a certain level of probability.

**Cronbach's alpha:** A statistic commonly used to measure interitem reliability.

**Cross-cultural psychology:** This field of study investigates the universality of psychological processes across different cultures.

**Crossover interaction:** In a $2 \times 2$ design, a type of interaction in which the effects of one independent variable on a dependent variable are reversed at different levels of the other independent variable.

**Cross-population generalizability:** Exists when findings about one group, population, or setting hold true for other groups, populations, or settings.

**Cross-sectional method:** Taking a large group of participants of various ages at one time and testing them.

**Cross-sequential design:** A quasi-experimental design used in developmental psychology in which several different ages are sampled at several different time periods.

**Cultural psychology:** An area in psychology that studies how culture shapes our thinking, and how our thinking shapes culture.

**Culture:** The rich and intricate melding of shared meanings, communal practices and rituals, and collective discourses and beliefs about human life that prevail in a given group or society.

**Cyclical** A baseline phase pattern in a single-subject design reflecting ups and downs depending on the time of measurement.

**Data:** Information that is gained objectively from observation or experimentation that can be measured and evaluated statistically.

**Debriefing:** A researcher's informing subjects after an experiment about the experiment's purposes and methods and evaluating subjects' personal reactions to the experiment.

**Deductive research:** The type of research in which a specific expectation is deduced from a general premise and is then tested.

**Degrees of freedom:** In tests of statistical significance, the number of observations that are free to vary in estimating a population parameter.

**Demand characteristics:** Cues available that tip off participants to the scientific hypothesis of the researcher and influence how participants respond to study stimuli.

**Dependent variable:** The observed effect, result, or outcome that is measured in response to a systematic change in the independent variable.

**Descriptive statistics:** Statistics used to describe the distribution of and relationship among variables usually in the form of averages and standard deviations (a statistical measure of variability).

Design sensitivity: The extent to which a researcher has constructed the best possible study to evaluate the topic under investigation.

Dichotomy: Variable having only two values.

Direct replication: Used to enhance the generalizability of a single-subject design, it involves repeating the single-subject design using the same procedures, by the same researchers, including the same providers of the treatment, in the same setting, and in the same situation, with different clients.

Direction of association: A pattern in a relationship between two variables—the values of variables tend to change consistently in relation to change on the other variable. The direction of association can be either positive or negative.

Discriminant validity: An approach to construct validation, established by showing evidence that different traits measured by the same methods are unrelated.

Discussion: A section of a written report in which the author provides theoretical interpretation for the findings of the study.

Disproportionate stratified sampling: Sampling in which elements are selected from strata in different proportions from those that appear in the population.

Doctrine of falsification: Scientists should aim to falsify their theories rather than confirm them.

Double-barreled question: A single survey question that actually asks two questions but allows only one answer.

Double blind: A procedure often used in randomized clinical trials whereby both the researcher and the participants are "blind" to who receives the "real" drug/treatment and who receives the placebo.

Double negative: A question or statement that contains two negatives, which can muddy the meaning of the question.

Duration: The length of time an event or some symptom lasts; usually is measured for each occurrence of the event or symptom in a single-subject design.

Ecological fallacy: An error in reasoning in which incorrect conclusions about individual-level processes are drawn from group-level data.

Ecological validity: The extent to which a study or experiment approximates the actual real-life phenomena under investigation.

Effect size: A standardized measure of association; often the difference between the mean of the experimental group and the mean of the control group on the dependent variable, adjusted for the average variability in the two groups. The effect size measures the strength of the relationship between the independent and dependent variables.

Electronic survey: A survey that is sent and answered by computer, either through e-mail or on the Web.

Elements: The individual members of the population whose characteristics are to be measured.

E-mail survey: A survey that is sent and answered through e-mail.

Empirical article: A report on a particular study, written in a certain format that is divided into sections, with an Abstract, Introduction, Method, Results, and Discussion.

Empirical generalization: A statement that describes patterns found in data.

Empiricism: A school of philosophy that holds that knowledge is gained through experience, observation, and experiment.

Epistemology: A branch of philosophy that studies how knowledge is gained or acquired.

Error variance: The deviation of individual scores in each group or condition from its respective mean.

Ethnography: A naturalistic observation method that studies people in their natural settings so that their behaviors and words can be put into their proper context.

Ex post facto: Means literally "after the fact" and refers to investigations in which conditions of a study are determined *after* rather than *before* (a priori) some variation or event has naturally occurred.

Ex post facto control group design: A nonexperimental design in which comparison groups are selected after the treatment program or other variation in the independent variable has occurred.

Exhaustive: Every case can be classified as having at least one attribute (or value) for the variable.

Experimental: A researcher is able to exercise control over the variable or variables that are assumed to be the causal agent producing the predicted effect.

Experimental control: Holding constant as many extraneous variables as possible so that any effect on the dependent variable can be attributed to changes in the independent variable.

Experimental error: Any influence on the dependent variable that is not due solely to the systematic change in the independent variable.

Experimental group: In an experiment, the group of research participants that receives the treatment or experimental manipulation.

Experimental stimuli: Materials that are used in constructing an independent variable.

Experimental task: A task that participants perform that is used as an independent variable.

External validity: The extent to which the results of a study generalize to other situations or populations.

*F* test: Analysis of variance (ANOVA) computes an *F* statistic, which is the ratio of two types of variance: systematic and error variance.

Face validity: The type of validity that exists when an inspection of items used to measure a concept suggests that they are appropriate "on their face."

**Facial feedback hypothesis:** Originating from the James-Lange theory of emotion, the facial feedback hypothesis now falls under the embodiment theory of emotion. The idea is that facial movements by themselves can reenact particular emotional feelings and that these emotional feelings can be created by simply "tricking" a person into making specific facial contractions.

**Factor analysis:** A set of data-analytic techniques used to reduce correlational data to a smaller number of dimensions.

**Factorial design:** An experimental design in which all conditions of the independent variable are combined with all conditions of the other independent variable. The main effects of each independent variable as well as the interaction effects between and among the independent variables can be statistically tested.

**Factors:** Another term for the independent variables in an experiment.

**Federal Policy for the Protection of Human Subjects:** Specific regulations based on the Belmont Report principles that were adopted in 1991 by the Department of Health and Human Services and the Food and Drug Administration.

**Fence-sitters:** Survey respondents who see themselves as being neutral on an issue and choose a middle (neutral) response that is offered.

**Field notes:** Notes that describe what has been observed, heard, or otherwise experienced in a participant observation study. These notes usually are written after the observational session.

**Field researcher:** A researcher who uses qualitative methods to conduct research in the field developing and maintaining relationships.

**Filter question:** A survey question used to identify a subset of respondents who then are asked other questions.

**Floaters:** Survey respondents who provide an opinion on a topic in response to a closed-ended question that does not include a "Don't know" option, but who will choose "Don't know" if it is available.

**Floor effect:** A problem that detracts from the sensitivity of a research design can occur when a dependent variable fails to discriminate various degrees of poor performance, meaning that all scores are confined to the very low end of the range.

**Focus groups:** A qualitative method that involves unstructured group interviews in which the focus group leader actively encourages discussion among participants on the topics of interest.

**Frame switching:** In constructivist theory, when a person alternates between two internalized mental sets, as when a bicultural individual moves back and forth between two internalized cultural mental sets.

**Frequency:** In a single-subject design, counting the number of times a behavior occurs or the number of times people experience different feelings within a particular time period.

**Frequency distribution:** Numerical display showing the number of cases, and usually the percentage of cases (the relative frequencies) corresponding to each value or group of values of a variable.

**Functional magnetic resonance imaging f(MRI):** A widely used technique that records the brain at work, in real time, while an individual performs a task.

**Generalizability:** The extent to which findings derived from a sample can be applied to a wider population.

**Generalization:** A broad statement that cannot be directly tested, but rather needs to be translated into one or more hypotheses.

**"Grand tour" question:** A broad question at the start of an interview that seeks to engage the respondent in the topic of interest; used in intensive (depth) interviewing.

**Group-administered survey:** A survey that is completed by individual respondents who are assembled in a group.

**Health Insurance Portability and Accountability Act (HIPAA):** Rule adopted by the U.S. Congress in 1996 requiring researchers to have valid authorization for any use or disclosure of "protected health information" (PHI) from a health care provider.

**Heuristic:** A simplifying mental shortcut that people use to make a difficult judgment.

**Heuristic biases:** Mistakes in reasoning due to our natural propensity to favor subjective impressions and personal anecdotes over cold, hard, statistics.

**Hippocampus:** Key memory center of the brain.

**Histogram:** A graphic for quantitative variables in which the variable's distribution is displayed with adjacent bars.

**Hypothesis:** A statement that is derived from a theory that usually specifies a relationship between two or more variables.

**Idiosyncratic variation:** Variation in responses to questions that is caused by individuals' reactions to particular words or ideas in the question instead of by variation in the concept that the question is intended to measure.

**Independent variable:** An element of the study that is systematically manipulated, changed, or selected.

**Independent-groups design:** Also known as between-groups design; in an experiment, independent groups of participants receive different levels of the independent variable.

**Index:** The sum or average of responses to a set of questions about a concept.

**Individual differences:** In a between-subjects design, peoples' differences can confound results, and thus, random assignment in forming experimental and control groups can be used to help neutralize these differences.

**Individual matching:** Individual cases in the treatment and control groups are matched on some variables.

**Inductive research:** The type of research in which general conclusions are drawn from specific data.

**Inferential statistics:** A mathematical tool for estimating how likely it is that a statistical result based on data from a random sample is representative of the population from which the sample is assumed to have been selected.

**In-person interview:** A survey in which an interviewer questions respondents face-to-face and records their answers.

**Institutional review board (IRB):** A group of organizational and community representatives required by federal law to review the ethical issues in all proposed research that is federally funded, involves human subjects, or has any potential for harm to subjects.

**Interaction:** An interaction occurs when the effects of one level of the independent variable depend on the particular level of the other independent variable.

**Interitem reliability:** An approach that calculates reliability based on the correlation among multiple items used to measure a single concept; also known as internal consistency.

**Internal validity:** Speaks to the logic of experimental design—the extent to which procedures and methods are optimally arranged so that the effects of the independent variable on the dependent variable can be "evaluated unambiguously."

**Interobserver reliability:** When similar measurements are obtained by different observers rating the same persons, events, or places.

**Interrupted-time-series design:** In quasi-experiments, examines the effects of a naturally occurring treatment on the behavior of a large group of people.

**Interval level of measurement:** A measurement of a variable in which the numbers indicating a variable's values represent fixed measurement units but have no absolute, or fixed, zero point.

**Interval:** In a single-subject design, measuring the length of time between events, behaviors, or symptoms.

**Interview schedule:** The survey instrument contains the questions asked by the interviewer in an in-person or phone survey.

**Introduction:** The section of a written report that identifies the problem to be investigated and why it is important.

**Is/ought:** In philosophy of science, "is" questions can be best addressed by facts, empirical data, or scientific research whereas "ought" questions call on cultural values and ethical considerations but cannot be answered solely on the basis of scientific evidence.

**Jottings:** Brief notes written in the field about highlights of an observation period.

**Journals:** Peer-reviewed scientific periodicals such as *Psychological Science*.

**Justice:** The Belmont Report principle that requires distributing benefits and risks of research fairly.

**Latent variable models:** Specialized statistical techniques that are used to evaluate constructs and to develop models of possible relationships among a set of variables.

**Latin-square design:** To combat confounds of carryover effect in within-subjects experiments, a Latin-square design is an *incomplete* counterbalancing arrangement, in which each possible order of treatments occurs equally often across research participants.

**Level:** Flat lines reflecting the amount or magnitude of the target variable in a single-subject design.

**Level of measurement:** The mathematical precision with which the values of a variable can be expressed. The nominal level of measurement, which is qualitative, has no mathematical interpretation; the quantitative levels of measurement—ordinal, interval, and ratio—are progressively more precise mathematically.

**Likert scale:** An ordinal level of measurement that often involves a question about attitude or opinions that asks for a numerical rating of the extent of agreement or disagreement.

**Longitudinal method:** The same research participants are followed over time; avoids cohort and period effects that confound the cross-sectional method.

**Longitudinal research design:** A study in which data are collected that can be ordered in time; also defined as research in which data are collected at two or more points in time.

**Magnetic resonance imaging (MRI):** Provides a measure of the structural anatomy of the brain.

**Magnitude:** In a single-subject design, the intensity of a particular behavior or psychological state may be measured.

**Mailed survey:** A survey involving a mailed questionnaire to be completed by the respondent.

**Main effect:** In a factorial experiment, the effects of one independent variable on a dependent variable are averaged over all levels of another independent variable.

**Manipulation check:** A pilot or "dry run" to assess whether the independent variable manipulation creates the intended effect. IRB approval is required before conducting a manipulation check.

**Matched-pairs design:** Pairs of participants that are matched on a variable that is strongly related to the dependent variable, and then, one of the pairs is randomly assigned to the experimental condition and the other to the control condition; that is, each member of the pair is assigned to *different* levels of the independent variable. An effective matched-pairs design provides a degree of experimental control of between-subjects individual differences that are comparable with that of a within-subjects design.

**Matching:** It is a procedure for equating the characteristics of individuals in different comparison groups in an experiment. Matching can be done on either an individual or an aggregate basis. For individual matching, individuals who are similar in terms of key characteristics are paired prior to assignment, and then, the two members of each pair are assigned to the two groups. For aggregate matching, groups are chosen for comparisons that are similar in terms of the distribution of key characteristics.

**Matrix:** A form on which can be recorded systematically particular features of multiple cases or instances that a qualitative data analyst needs to examine.

**Mean:** The arithmetic, or weighted, average, computed by adding up the value of all the cases and dividing by the total number of cases.

**Measurement:** The assignment of numerals to objects or events according to some objective rule.

**Median:** The position average, or the point that divides a distribution in half (the 50th percentile).

**Meta-analysis:** A method that provides a more unbiased evaluation of the literature than a conventional review article by using objective statistics to weigh the strength of results from individual studies.

**Method:** The section of a written report that details the operations and procedures used in the study.

**Milgram's obedience experiments:** Experimental laboratory-based study of obedience to authority in which subjects recruited at Yale University in the 1960s were told that they were to administer shocks when supposed "learners" failed to answer questions correctly.

**Mixed-factorial design:** An experimental design in which one independent is varied between subjects and the other independent variable is varied within subjects.

**Mixed-mode survey:** A survey that is conducted by more than one method, allowing the strengths of one survey design to compensate for the weaknesses of another and maximizing the likelihood of securing data from different types of respondents; for example, nonrespondents in a mailed survey may be interviewed in person or over the phone.

**Mode:** The most frequent value in a distribution.

**Multifactor ANOVA:** Used for experimental designs with more than one factor or independent variable varied simultaneously. Compared with the simple ANOVA, the multifactor ANOVA is much more computationally complex given that there are both main and interaction effects that need to be tested.

**Multifactorial designs:** Experiments that allow for the testing of effects of all possible combinations of the levels of the independent variables on the dependent variable. These provide information as to the main effect of each independent variable as well as any interactions between and among independent variables.

**Multiple-group before-and-after design:** A type of quasi-experimental design in which several before-and-after comparisons are made involving the same independent and dependent variables but different groups.

**Multitrait–multimethod matrix:** In evaluating construct validity, a correlation matrix composed of at least two methods of measurement of two different constructs.

**Mutually exclusive:** A variable's attributes (or values) are mutually exclusive when every case can be classified as having only one attribute (or value).

**Natural treatment:** A naturally occurring event is treated as a quasi-independent variable, which can be measured but cannot be manipulated.

**Naturalistic observation:** A type of research method used to collect behavioral data in natural environments as opposed to laboratory or other controlled settings.

**Nominal level of measurement:** Variables whose values have no mathematical interpretation; they vary in kind or quality but not in amount (also called the categorical or qualitative level).

**Nonconcurrent multiple-baseline design:** A multiple baseline design in which subjects are randomly assigned into A–B designs with different baseline phase lengths.

**Nonequivalent control group design:** A quasi-experimental design in which experimental and comparison groups are designated before the treatment occurs but are not created by random assignment.

**Nonexperimental:** Actions and events are carefully measured and catalogued but independent variables cannot be directly manipulated.

**Nonparametric statistics:** Mathematical procedures used for variables that are measured on a nominal or ordinal scale.

**Nonprobability sampling method:** Sampling method in which the probability of selection of population elements is unknown.

**Nonrespondents:** People or other entities who do not participate in a study although they are selected for the sample.

**Normal curve:** When the distribution of scores approximates a normal curve, most scores fall near the center, with gradually fewer scores as you move toward either extreme.

**Normal distribution:** See Normal curve.

**Norms:** The mean and standard deviation used to characterize the distribution of test scores for a standardization sample.

**Null hypothesis:** The hypothesis of no difference or no relationship, which the researcher tries to reject, nullify, or disprove.

**Null result:** When an independent variable fails to produce any effect on the dependent variable.

**Nuremberg War Crime Trials:** In 1946, exposed horrific medical experiments conducted by Nazi doctors and others in the name of "science."

Office for Protection from Research Risks, National Institutes of Health: Monitors IRBs, with the exception of research involving drugs (which is the responsibility of the federal Food and Drug Administration).

One-factor ANOVA: See Simple ANOVA.

One-tailed test: To reject the null hypothesis, the value of the test statistic must fall in either the upper or the lower end of its sampling distribution. The null hypothesis can only be rejected by a higher value of the test statistic falling in the upper end of the sampling distribution or by a lower value of the test statistic falling in the lower end of the sampling distribution but not by a value falling in both ends of the distribution.

Operational definition: Indicates how a concept is coded, measured, or quantified. An operational definition is among several possible objective and measurable indicators of a concept.

Ordinal level of measurement: A measurement of a variable in which the numbers indicating a variable's values specify only the order of the cases, permitting "greater than" and "less than" distinctions.

Outcome bias: When a test consistently produces lowers scores for an identifiable class of people defined by race, gender, or ethnicity, such results reflect outcome bias.

Outlier: An exceptionally high or low value in a distribution.

Paired-sample t test: A statistical test used in a within-subjects design to determine whether means vary over two test conditions; often used to compare scores from a group before and after a treatment or intervention.

Parameter: A numerical characteristic of a population that is estimated on the basis of a sample statistic, such as the sample mean or sample standard deviation.

Parametric statistics: Mathematical procedures that require variables to be measured on either an interval or a ratio scale.

Participant observation: A qualitative method for gathering data that involves developing a sustained relationship with people while they go about their normal activities.

Participant-observer: A researcher who gathers data through participating and observing in a setting where he or she develops a sustained relationship with people while they go about their normal activities. The term *participant-observer* is often used to refer to a continuum of possible roles, from complete observation, in which the researcher does not participate along with others in group activities, to complete participation, in which the researcher participates without publicly acknowledging being an observer.

Pearson's correlation coefficient, or r: The most commonly used statistic to measure the relationship between two quantitative variables.

Peer review: The process by which other independent reviewers (meaning no relationship with the researchers whose work is under review) evaluate the scientific merit of the work.

Period effects: An inherent confound for a cross-sectional method when historical influences may affect responses to the dependent variable.

Periodicity: A sequence of elements (in a list to be sampled) that varies in some regular, periodic pattern.

Phone survey: A survey in which interviewers question respondents over the phone and then record their answers.

Phrenology: A now-defunct field of study, which was once considered a science in the 18th century, which held that bumps and fissures of the skull determined the character and personality of a person.

Pilot study: The experimenter collects pilot data to test out the procedures and measures before formally running the study.

Placebo: Often used in treatment outcome research, an inert substance or sham procedure employed to assess the psychological effects of expecting and receiving a treatment.

Plagiarism: The act of copying portions of materials written by somebody else and not identifying the original author.

Popular science: Literature often written by eminent scientists who aim to explain science to a general audience.

Population: Any entire collection of people, animals, plants or things, all of which can be referred to as units, from which information is collected.

Population parameter: The value of a statistic, such as a mean, computed using the data for the entire population; a sample statistic is an estimate of a population parameter.

Positive psychology: A relatively new school of psychology that seeks to learn about human thriving, flourishing, optimism, resilience, joy, and capabilities.

Post hoc: In Latin "after this" and refers to hypotheses that are formulated after data are collected and analyzed.

Post hoc hypotheses: Hypotheses that are formulated after data have been collected and analyzed.

Posttest: In experimental research, the measurement of an outcome (dependent) variable after an experimental intervention or after a presumed independent variable has changed for some other reason.

Power analysis: The power of a study refers to its ability to find a significant difference when a real difference exists. Power analysis is determined by sample size, statistical significance level, and effect size.

Practical (or clinical) significance: When evaluating the impact of an intervention in a single-subject design, whether the intervention made a meaningful difference in the well-being of the subject.

Predictive validity: The ability of a measure to predict scores on a criterion measured in the future.

Pretest: In experimental research, the measurement of an outcome (dependent) variable prior to an experimental intervention or change in a presumed independent variable for some other reason. The pretest is exactly the same "test" as the posttest, but it is administered at a different time.

Pretest–posttest control group design: See Randomized comparative change design.

**Primary source:** Firsthand empirical report published in a peer-review journal.

**Priming:** Exposure to a stimulus facilitates responses to a subsequent event.

**Probability:** The likelihood that a given event will occur.

**Probability average:** See Mode.

**Probability of selection:** The likelihood that an element will be selected from the population for inclusion in the sample. In a census of all elements of a population, the probability that any particular element will be selected is 1.0. If half of the elements in the population are sampled on the basis of chance (say by tossing a coin), the probability of selection for each element is one half, or .5. As the size of the sample decreases as a proportion of the population, so does the probability of selection.

**Probability sampling method:** A sampling method that relies on a random, or chance, selection method so that the probability of selection of population elements is known.

**Program evaluation:** This research studies the effects on behavior of large-scale policy changes as well as social reforms and innovations occurring in government, schools, courts, prisons, businesses, health care, housing, and so on.

**Proportionate stratified sampling:** Sampling method in which elements are selected from strata in exact proportion to their representation in the population.

**Proprietary:** A privately owned entity that is open only to subscribers, usually for a fee.

**Pseudoscience:** Dubious but fascinating claims that are touted as "scientifically proven" and bolstered by fervent, public testimonials of believers who have experienced, first hand, or who have claimed to have witnessed the phenomenon; however, such evidence is not based on the principles of the scientific method.

**Psychological traits:** Presumed enduring and stable dispositions such as intelligence, personality characteristics, or attitudes that can be measured by objective tests.

**Psychology:** Broadly defined as the scientific study of people, the mind and behavior that focuses attention on virtually endless questions about how we feel, think, behave, believe, and interact.

**Psychometrics:** A school of psychology that studies the application of psychological tests as objective measures of the mind and mental processes.

**PsycINFO:** Specialized, noncommercial search engines sponsored by the American Psychological Association to serve as databases for citations and abstracts of the world's literature in psychology and related fields.

**PsycLIT:** See PsycINFO.

**Publication bias:** A bias that can occur due to the fact that most literature reviews include only studies that have been published. Studies that are often unpublished because of negative findings are not considered, creating a bias toward published studies that typically report positive findings.

**Purposive sampling:** A nonprobability sampling method in which elements are selected for a purpose, usually because of their unique position.

**Qualitative interviewing:** A method that involves open-ended, relatively unstructured questioning in which the interviewer seeks in-depth information on the interviewee's feelings, experiences, and perceptions. Also called *intensive interviewing*.

**Qualitative research:** Emphasis is placed on understanding context—the what, how, when, and where of an event or action. It yields data regarding meanings, concepts, definitions, characteristics, metaphors, symbols, and descriptions of events or actions.

**Quasi-experiment:** Employed to investigate the effects of a quasi-independent variable on a dependent variable.

**Quasi-independent variable:** A distinct type of independent variable that can be measured and varied but cannot be directly controlled by the experiment and therefore cannot be manipulated. Subject variables and natural treatments are examples of quasi-independent variables.

**Questionnaire:** The survey instrument contains the questions in a self-administered survey.

**Quota sampling:** A nonprobability sampling method in which elements are selected to ensure that the sample represents certain characteristics in proportion to their prevalence in the population.

**Random assignment:** A procedure that is used to control for bias that ensures that each participant has an equal likelihood of being placed in either control or experimental groups. That is, the assignment of cases is done by a chance procedure, as by tossing a coin.

**Random-digit dialing:** The random dialing by a machine of numbers within designated phone prefixes, which creates a random sample for phone surveys.

**Random error of measurement:** Variation due to multiple little factors that have nothing to do with the construct you are trying to measure.

**Random sample:** A sample in which a random process was used to select the members from a population.

**Random sampling:** A method of sampling that relies on a random, or chance, selection method so that every element of the sampling frame has a known probability of being selected.

**Random sampling error (chance sampling error):** Differences between the population and the sample that are due only to chance factors (random error), not to systematic sampling error. Random sampling error may or may not result in an unrepresentative sample. The magnitude of sampling error due to chance factors can be estimated statistically.

**Randomization:** Procedures that are used to counteract bias; whether randomizing order of presentation of test stimuli or randomly assigning participants to different study conditions.

**Randomized clinical trials:** A type of specific experiment that is considered the gold standard for a clinical trial in which participants are randomly assigned to separate groups that compare different treatments.

**Randomized comparative change design:** The classic true experimental design in which subjects are assigned randomly to two groups; both these groups receive a pretest, one group then receives the experimental intervention, and then both groups receive a posttest. Also called the posttest-only control group design.

**Randomness:** The state of being influenced by nothing but a chance process.

**Range:** The true upper limit in a distribution minus the true lower limit (or the highest rounded value minus the lowest rounded value plus 1).

**Rate:** In a single-subject design, refers to the increase in the trend line of the behavior or other outcome over time.

**Ratio level of measurement:** A measurement of a variable in which the numbers indicating a variable's values represent fixed measuring units and an absolute zero point.

**Reactive effects:** The changes in an individual or group behavior that are due to being observed or otherwise studied.

**Reductionist fallacy:** An error in reasoning that occurs when incorrect conclusions about group-level processes are based on individual-level data.

**References:** The last section of an APA report, which follows the discussion section and begins on a separate page under the label *References*; lists the reference for each work cited in the body of the text.

**Regression artifact:** A threat to internal validity that occurs when subjects who are chosen for a study because of their extreme scores on the dependent variable become less extreme on the posttest due to natural cyclical or episodic change in the variable.

**Regression to the mean:** The tendency for extreme scores on a measure to move closer to the group average when retested due to the inherent unreliability of measurement.

**Reliability:** The degree to which a measure or a set of data is consistent.

**Reliability measure:** Statistics that summarize the consistency among a set of measures. Cronbach's alpha is the most common measure of the reliability of a set of items included in an index.

**Repeated-measures design:** The term often used to describe the design when the same participant can be tested repeatedly over time.

**Repeated-measures panel design:** A quasi-experimental design consisting of several pretest and posttest observations of the same group.

**Replication:** Repeating a previous research study to determine whether its findings can be duplicated.

**Replicated:** Reproducing the results of a previous study.

**Replication validity:** Underscores the importance of multiple, independent replications of a scientific finding before it can be considered a valid discovery.

**Representative sample:** A sample that "looks like" the population from which it was selected in all respects potentially relevant to the study. The distribution of characteristics among the elements of a representative sample is the same as the distribution of those characteristics among the total population. In an unrepresentative sample, some characteristics are overrepresented or underrepresented.

**Research circle:** A diagram of the elements of the research process, including theories, hypotheses, data collection, and data analysis.

**Research hypothesis:** A statement derived from theory that predicts that the variables under investigation are statistically related in the population; in other words, the obtained results in the study sample are true for the general population.

**Respect for persons:** The Belmont Report principle that requires treating persons as autonomous agents and protecting those with diminished autonomy.

**Results:** Section of a written report that presents the major statistical findings of the study.

**Review articles:** Critical examinations of empirical studies that have already been published.

**Robust:** The extent to which findings of a study are reproducible or replicable given different conditions, settings, and samples.

**Sample:** A group of units selected from a larger group that is known as the population.

**Sample bias:** A particular form of bias when some members of the population are less likely to be included than others in the study.

**Sample generalizability:** The extent to which findings derived from a sample can be applied to a wider population.

**Sample statistic:** A quantitative value such as an average that is calculated on a subset of observations or data selected from a larger population.

**Sampling distribution:** The hypothetical distribution of a statistic across all random samples that could be drawn from a population.

**Sampling error:** Any difference between the characteristics of a sample and the characteristics of a population. The larger the sampling error, the less representative the sample.

**Sampling frame:** A list of all elements in a population.

**Sampling interval:** The number of cases from one sampled case to another in a systematic random sample.

**Saturation point:** The point at which subject selection is ended in intensive interviewing, when new interviews seem to yield little additional information.

**Scale:** The level of measurement of a variable, as in nominal, ordinal, interval, or ratio.

**Scatter diagram:** A graph that is used to depict the degree of correlation between a pair of variables. It is made by plotting the scores of individuals on the two variables.

**Science journalism:** Reports appearing in media outlets that focus on recent developments in science that are judged newsworthy.

**Scientific method:** A formal way of knowing that is exclusively reliant on objective, empirical investigation.

**Secondary source:** Secondhand accounts of scientific work that can appear in various outlets, such as review articles, textbooks, and newspapers.

**Secular trends:** A potential confound for longitudinal studies occurs when results cannot be attributed to hypothesized age-related developmental processes but rather to general changes that have taken place in society.

**Selection bias:** A source of internal invalidity that occurs when research participants are not randomly selected.

**Self-correcting:** A key defining feature of science that relies on empirical evidence for evaluating whether theories and beliefs should be discarded.

**Serendipity:** An accidental discovery of something that is highly useful and beneficial.

**Simple ANOVA:** Analysis of variance used for experimental designs in which one and only one factor is varied across more than two levels; also referred to as one-factor ANOVA.

**Simple main effect:** A simple main effect compares the influence of one level of an independent variable at a given level of another independent variable.

**Simple random sampling:** A method of sampling in which every sample element is selected only on the basis of chance, through a random process.

**Single-factor experiment:** An experiment with one independent variable.

**Skewness:** The extent to which cases are clustered more at one or the other end of the distribution of a quantitative variable rather than in a symmetric pattern around its center. Skew can be positive (a right skew), with the number of cases tapering off in the positive direction, or negative (a left skew), with the number of cases tapering off in the negative direction.

**Skip patterns:** The unique combination of questions created in a survey by filter questions and contingent questions.

**Snowball sampling:** A method of sampling in which sample elements are selected as they are identified by successive informants or interviewees.

**Social brain hypothesis:** According to this theoretical perspective, intelligent thought is shaped by our "social connectivity"—the degree to which we enjoy friendships, love, companionship, and intimacy.

**Social desirability bias:** A validity threat in testing in which examinees respond defensively to test items based on how they wish to be perceived rather than openly and genuinely.

**Social Sciences Citation Index (SSCI):** A citation database that consists of world-leading social science journals across more than 50 fields of study.

**Split-half reliability:** Reliability achieved when responses to the same questions by two randomly selected halves of a sample are about the same.

**Spurious relationship:** A relationship between two variables that is due to variation in a third variable.

**Stable line:** A line in the baseline phase of a single-subject design that is relatively flat, with little variability in the scores so that the scores fall in a narrow band.

**Staged manipulations:** When a confederate who typically is presented as another participant, but is actually an accomplice of the researcher; the accomplice or confederate is used to help create the psychological state or social situation that is the topic of investigation.

**Standard deviation:** A statistic used to measure variability in a sample and calculated by taking the square root of the average squared deviation of each case from the mean.

**Standard error of the mean:** Indicates the degree to which the means of the samples vary from the population mean.

**Standardization:** Procedures to ensure that testing, scoring, and interpretation are uniform across all administrations of a test.

**Standardization sample:** A random selection of people drawn from a carefully defined population.

**Statistical control:** To increase internal validity, mathematical procedures can be employed to quantify the effects of variables that cannot be randomized but are known to be strongly related to the dependent variable, independent variable, or both.

**Statistical power:** The probability that a statistical test will correctly reject the null hypothesis, that is, when the null hypothesis is in fact false.

**Statistical significance:** The mathematical likelihood that an association is not due to chance, judged by a criterion set by the analyst (often that the probability is less than 5 out of 100, or $p < .05$).

**Stereotype threat:** Performance on a test is lowered by the fear that one's behavior will confirm an existing stereotype of a group with which one identifies.

**Stratified random sampling:** A method of sampling in which sample elements are selected separately from population strata that are identified in advance by the researcher.

**Stratified sample:** In this method of sampling, sample elements are selected separately from population strata that are identified in advance by the researcher.

**Student's *t* table:** Provides the critical value a *t*-statistic needs to exceed in order to reject the null hypothesis at a certain level of probability.

**Subject variable:** In a quasi-experimental design, selection of participants on the basis of some characteristic that can be measured or described but cannot be directly manipulated, such as intelligence, gender, height, weight.

**Sums of squares:** Shorthand for the *sum of squared deviations from the mean.* Each score is subtracted from the mean and squared, and then all these values are summed.

**Survey pretest:** A method of evaluating survey questions and procedures by testing them out on a small sample of individuals like those to be included in the actual survey and then reviewing responses to the questions and reactions to the survey procedures.

**Survey research:** Research in which information is obtained from a sample of individuals through their responses to questions about themselves or others.

**Systematic bias:** Overrepresentation or underrepresentation of some population characteristics in a sample due to the method used to select the sample. A sample shaped by systematic sampling error is a biased sample.

**Systematic observation:** A strategy that increases the reliability of observational data by using explicit rules that standardize coding practices across observers.

**Systematic random sampling:** A method of sampling in which sample elements are selected from a list or from sequential files, with every *n*th element being selected after the first element is selected randomly within the first interval.

**Systematic replication:** Repeating a single-subject design in different settings using different providers and other related behaviors to increase generalizability.

**Systematic variance:** The sum of the deviation of the means for each experimental condition from the grand mean (the mean of the mean of all conditions of an experiment). The goal is to design experiments that will maximize systematic variance.

***t* test:** An inferential statistic to test whether a pair of group means from a sample are statistically significant.

***Tearoom Trade*:** The book by the sociologist Laud Humphreys that raised ethical questions about his covert observation and subsequent interviewing of men engaging in homosexual acts in public bathrooms.

**Temporal precedence:** In establishing causality, evidence that demonstrates that the cause comes before the effect.

**Testable hypothesis:** A statement often in the form of a prediction that is made prior to the actual collection of data.

**Test–retest reliability:** The extent to which scores remain consistent on the same test administered on two different occasions to the same group of examinees.

**Theory:** A coherent set of propositions that are used as principles to describe, understand, and explain psychological or behavioral phenomena.

**Third variable:** A problem in describing the relationship between two variables when a third variable that is extraneous to the two variables may account for the observed relationship.

**Time-lag design:** Used to determine the effects of time of testing while holding age constant by comparing only those participants who were of the same age but who were tested in different years—for example, comparing 20-year-olds tested in 1990 with 20-years-olds tested in 1995.

**Time-series design:** A quasi-experimental design consisting of many pretests and posttests observations of the same group.

**Treatment:** Another term for condition of an experiment.

**Treatment group:** The group that receives the treatment under investigation.

**Treatment phase (B):** The intervention phase of a single-subject design.

**Trend:** Repeated measurement scores that are either ascending or descending in magnitude in a single-subject design.

**True experiment:** In a true experiment, a researcher has complete control over the manipulation of the independent variable. Such experimental control allows for testing whether systematically varying the independent variable causes changes in the dependent variable.

**Tuskegee syphilis study:** Researchers funded by the U.S. Public Health Service followed 399 low-income African American men with syphilis in the 1930s, collecting data to study the "natural" course of the illness, without informing all participants of their illness or of the discovery of a cure (penicillin) developed in the 1950s.

**Two-tailed test:** The null hypothesis can be rejected by high or low values of a test statistic falling in both ends of its sampling distribution.

**Two-variable chi-square ($\chi^2$):** A nonparametric statistical test that is used to investigate the association between two categorical variables.

**Type I error:** The probability that the null hypothesis is rejected when it is in fact true; equals the significance level. In other words, a researcher makes an incorrect decision to reject the null hypothesis when it is in fact true.

**Type II error:** This incorrect decision indicates the failure to reject the null hypothesis when it is in fact false. In other words, a researcher makes an incorrect decision to accept the null hypothesis when it is in fact false.

**Unimodal:** A distribution of a variable in which there is only one value that is the most frequent.

**Validity:** The extent to which a study provides a true measure of what it is *meant* to investigate.

**Variable:** Any characteristic that can take on different values or can vary across research participants.

**Variability:** In a single-subject design, the extent to which cases are spread out through the distribution or clustered in just one location.

**Variance:** The average squared deviation of each case from the mean; so it takes into account the amount by which each case differs from the mean.

**Visual analysis:** The process of looking at a graph of the data points in a single-subject design to determine whether the intervention has altered the subject's preintervention pattern of scores.

**Web survey:** A survey that is accessed and responded to on the World Wide Web.

**Within-groups variance:** An estimate of the degree to which the participants in each of the groups differ from one another. Reflects the deviation of the individual scores in each group from their respective group means; it is also referred to as error variance.

**Within-subjects design:** In an experiment, all research participants receive all levels of the independent variable.

**Zimbardo's prison simulation study:** A simulated prison was created and volunteers were assigned the role of guards or prisoners. Reactions to playing these roles were so extreme that the experiment was terminated after 6 days.

# References

Abel, D. (2000, March 26). Census may fall short at colleges. *The Boston Sunday Globe*, pp. B1, B4.

Abel, E. L., & Kruger, M. (2010). Smile intensity in photographs predicts longevity. *Current Directions in Psychological Science, 21*(4), 541–542.

Adair, G., Dushenko, T. W., & Lindsay, R. C. L. (1985). Ethical regulations and their impact on research practice. *American Psychologist, 40*, 59–72.

Adams, R. B., Jr., Gordon, H. L., Baird, A. A., Ambady, N., & Kleck, R. E. (2003). Effects of gaze on amygdala sensitivity to anger and fear faces. *Science, 300*(5625), 1536. doi:10.1126/science.1082244

Adams, R. B., & Kleck, R. E. (2003). Perceived gaze direction and processing of facial displays of emotion. *Psychological Science, 14*, 644–647.

Adler, P. A., & Adler, P. (1994). Observational techniques. In N. K. Denzin & Y. S. Lincoln (Eds.), *Handbook of qualitative research* (pp. 377–392). Thousand Oaks, CA: Sage.

Aknin, L. B., Barrington-Leigh, C. P., Dunn, E. W., Helliwell, J. F., Burns, J., Biswas-Diener, R., . . . Norton, M. I. (2013). Prosocial spending and well-being: Cross-cultural evidence for a psychological universal. *Journal of Personality and Social Psychology, 99*, 52–61.

Alfonso, V. C., & Allison, D. B. (1992). Further development of the Extended Satisfaction With Life Scale. Manuscript submitted for publication.

Altman, L. K. (1987, March 31). U.S. and France end rift on AIDS. *The New York Times*. Retrieved from http://www.nytimes.com/1987/04/01/us/us-and-france-end-rift-on-aids.html?pagewanted=all&src=pm

American Psychological Association. (2005). *Concise rules of APA style*. Washington, DC: Author.

American Psychological Association. (2009). APA *publication style manual*. Washington, DC: Author.

American Psychological Association. (2010a). *APA-style helper* [Computer software]. Washington, DC: Author.

American Psychological Association. (2010b). *Ethical principles of psychologists and code of conduct*. Retrieved from http://www.apa.org/ethics/code/principles.pdf

American Psychological Association. (2010c). *Publication manual of the American Psychological Association* (6th ed.). Washington, DC: Author.

American Psychological Association. (n.d.). *Psychological bulletin description*. Retrieved from http://www.apa.org/pubs/journals/bul/

Anastasi, A. (1988). *Psychological testing*. New York, NY: Macmillan.

Andrews, F. M., & Whithey, S. B. (1976). *Social indicators of well-being: Americans' perception of life quality*. New York, NY: Plenum Press.

Armas, G. C. (2002, November 23). Government won't file appeal in census case. *The Boston Globe*, p. A1.

Aronson, E., & Mills, J. (1959). The effect of severity of initiation on liking for a group. *Journal of Abnormal and Social Psychology, 59*, 177–181.

Aronson, J., Steele, C. M., Salinas, M. F., & Lustina, M. J. (1998). The effects of stereotype threat on the standardized test performance of college students. In E. Aronson (Ed.), *Readings about the social animal* (8th ed.). New York, NY: Freeman.

Arwood, T., & Panicker, S. (2007). *Assessing risk in social and behavioral sciences: Collaborative Institutional Training Initiative*. Coral Gables, FL: University of Miami. Retrieved from https://www.citiprogram.org/rcrpage.asp?language=english&affiliation=100

Baltes, P. B. (1968). Longitudinal and cross-sectional sequences in the study of age and generation effects. *Human Development, 11*, 145–171.

Banister, P., Burman, E., Parker, I., Taylor, M., & Tindall, C. (1994). *Qualitative methods in psychology: A research guide*. Philadelphia, PA: Open University Press.

Barlow, D., & Hersen, M. (1984). *Single-case experimental designs: Strategies for studying behavior change* (2nd ed.). New York, NY: Pergamon.

Baumeister, R. F., Twenge, J. M., & Nuss, C. K. (2002). Effects of social exclusion on cognitive processes: Anticipated aloneness reduces intelligent thought. *Journal of Personality and Social Psychology, 83,* 817–827.

Baumrind, D. (1964). Some thoughts on ethics of research: After reading Milgram's "Behavioral study of obedience." *American Psychologist, 19,* 421–423.

Baumrind, D. (1985). Research using intentional deception: Ethical issues revisited. *American Psychologist, 40,* 165–174.

Beare, P. L., Severson, S., & Brandt, P. (2004). The use of a positive procedure to increase engagement on-task and decrease challenging behavior. *Behavior Modification, 28,* 28–44.

Becker, H. S. (1958). Problems of inference and proof in participant observation. *American Sociological Review, 23,* 652–660.

Belluck, P. (2009, January 18). Test subjects who call the scientist Mom or Dad. *The New York Times,* pp. 1, 14.

Bem, D. J. (2003). Writing the empirical journal article. In J. M. Darley, M. P. Zanna, & H. L Roediger, III (Eds.), *The compleat academic: A career guide* (2nd ed., pp. 185–219). Washington, DC: American Psychological Association.

Berg, B. (2004). *Qualitative research methods for the social sciences* (5th ed.). Boston, MA: Pearson.

Besa, D. (1994). Evaluating narrative family therapy using single-system research designs. *Research on Social Work Practice, 4,* 309–325.

Binder, A., & Meeker, J. W. (1993). Implications of the failure to replicate the Minneapolis experimental findings. *American Sociological Review, 58,* 886–888.

Bisconer, S. W., Green, M., Mallon-Czajka, J., & Johnson, J. S. (2006). Managing aggression in a psychiatric hospital using a behaviour plan: A case study. *Journal of Psychiatric and Mental Health Nursing, 13,* 515–521.

Biswas-Diener, R., Vitterso, J., & Diener, E. (2005). Most people are pretty happy, but there is cultural variation: The Inughuit, the Amish, and the Maasai. *Journal of Happiness Studies, 6,* 205–226.

Blais, M. R., Vallerand, R. J., Pelletier, L. G., & Briere, N. M. (1989). L'Echelle de satisfaction de vie: Validation Canadienne-Francais du "Satisfaction With Life Scale [French-Canadian Validation of the Satisfaction With Life Scale]. *Canadian Journal of Behavioral Science, 21,* 210–223.

Block, N. (1995). How heritability misleads about race. *Cognition, 56,* 99–128.

Bloom, P., & Weisberg, D. S. (2007). Childhood origins of adult resistance to science. *Science, 316,* 996–997.

Bogdewic, S. P. (1999). Participant observation. In B. F. Crabtree & W. L. Miller (Eds.), *Doing qualitative research* (pp. 33–45). Thousand Oaks, CA: Sage.

Borckardt, J. J., Nash, M. R., Murphy, M. D., Moore, M., Shaw, D., & O'Neil, P. (2008). Clinical practice as natural laboratory for psychotherapy research: A guide to case-based time-series analysis. *American Psychologist, 63,* 77–95.

Bouchard, T. J., Jr., & McGue, M. (1981). Familial studies of intelligence: A review. *Science, 212,* 1055–1059.

Bramness, J. G., Walby, F. A., & Tverdal, A. (2007). The sales of antidepressants and suicide rates in Norway and its counties, 1980–2004. *Journal of Affective Disorders, 102,* 1–9.

Brinegar, M. G., Salvi, L. M., Stiles, W. B., & Greenberg, L. S. (2006). Building a meaning bridge: Therapeutic progress from problem formulation to understanding. *Journal of Counseling Psychology, 53(2),* 165–180.

Brown, J. (1992). *The definition of a profession: The authority of metaphor in the history of intelligence testing, 1890–1930.* Princeton, NJ: Princeton University Press.

Brown, J. B. (1999). The use of focus groups in clinical research. In B. F. Crabtree & W. L. Miller (Eds.), *Doing qualitative research* (2nd ed., pp. 109–124). Thousand Oaks, CA: Sage.

Brown, R., & Kulik, J. (1977). Flashbulb memories. *Cognition, 5,* 73–99.

Bushman, B. J., & Baumeister, R. F. (1998). Threatened egotism, narcissism, self-esteem, and direct and displaced aggression. *Journal of Personality and Social Psychology, 75,* 219–229.

Butler, K. (2006, July 4). The grim neurology of teenage drinking. *The New York Times,* pp. D1, D6.

Byrne, R. (2006). *The secret.* New York, NY: Atria Books.

Callahan, C. C., & Barisa, M. T. (2005). Statistical process control and rehabilitation outcome: The single-subject design reconsidered. *Rehabilitation Psychology, 50,* 24–33.

Campbell, D. T., & Fiske, D. W. (1959). Convergent and discriminant validation by the multitrait-multimethod matrix. *Psychological Bulletin, 56,* 81–105.

Campbell, D. T., & Stanley, J. C. (1966). *Experimental and quasi-experimental designs for research.* Chicago, IL: Rand McNally.

Cantril, H. (1965). *The patterns of human concerns.* New Brunswick, NJ: Rutgers University Press.

Carey, B. (2012, November 2). Fraud case seen as a red flag for psychology research. *The New York Times.* Retrieved from http://www.nytimes.com/2011/11/03/health/research/noted-dutch-psychologist-stapel-accused-of-research-fraud.html

Carey, S. (2000). Science education as conceptual change. *Journal of Applied Developmental Psychology, 21*(1), 13–19.

Carmazza, A. (1996). The brain's dictionary. *Nature, 380,* 485–486.

Carr, J. E., & Burkholder, E. O. (1998). Creating single-subject design graphs with Microsoft Excel™. *Journal of Applied Behavior Analysis, 31,* 245–251.

Carson, S. H., Fama, J., & Clancy, K. (2008). *Writing for psychology: A guide for psychology concentrators.* Cambridge, MA:

Department of Psychology, Faculty of Arts and Sciences, Harvard University.

Cava, A., Cushman, R., & Goodman, K. (2007). *HIPAA and human subjects research: Collaborative Institutional Training Initiative.* Coral Gables, FL: University of Miami. Retrieved from https://www.citiprogram.org/members/learners

Cheung, K. M. (1999). Effectiveness of social work treatment and massage therapy for nursing home clients. *Research on Social Work Practice, 9,* 229–247.

Cloud, J. (2009, January 16). How to lift your mood? Try smiling. *Time Magazine.* Retrieved from http://www.time.com/time/health/article/0,8599,1871687,00.html

Coffey, A., & Atkinson, P. (1996). *Making sense of qualitative data: Complementary research strategies.* Thousand Oaks, CA: Sage.

Cohen, S. G., & Ledford, G. E., Jr. (1994). The effectiveness of self-managing teams: A quasi-experiment. *Human Relations, 47,* 13–43.

Cook, T. D., & Campbell, D. T. (1979). *Quasi-experiments: Design and analysis for field settings.* Chicago, IL: Rand McNally.

Cooper, K. B., & Victory, N. J. (2002). *A nation online: How Americans are expanding their use of the Internet.* Washington, DC: National Telecommunications and Information Administration, Economics and Statistics Administration, U.S. Department of Commerce. Retrieved from http://www.ntia.doc.gov/legacy/ntiahome/dn/anationonline2.pdf

Costa, P. T., Jr., & McCrae, R. R. (1985). *The NEO Personality Inventory Manual.* Odessa, FL: Psychological Assessment Resources.

Couper, M. P., Baker, R. P., Bethlehem, J., Clark, C. Z. F., Martin, J., Nicholls W. L., II, & O'Reilly, J. M. (Eds.). (1998). *Computer-assisted survey information collection.* New York, NY: Wiley.

Cozby, P. C. (2009). *Methods in behavioral research* (10th ed.). New York, NY: McGraw-Hill.

Creswell, J. W. (2010). Mapping the developing landscape of mixed methods research. In A. Tashakkori & C. Teddlie (Eds.), *SAGE handbook of mixed methods in social & behavioral research* (2nd ed., pp. 45–68). Thousand Oaks, CA: Sage.

Creswell, J. W., Plano Clark, V. L., Gutmann, M. L., & Hanson, W. E. (2008). Advanced mixed methods research designs. In V. L. Plano Clark & J. W. Creswell (Eds.), *The mixed methods reader* (pp. 161–198). Thousand Oaks, CA: Sage.

Crowne, D. P., & Marlowe, D. (1960). A new scale of social desirability independent of psychopathology. *Journal of Consulting Psychology, 24*(4), 349–354. doi:10.1037/h0047358

Csikszentmihalyi, M., & Csikszentmihalyi, I. S. (1988). *Optimal experiences: Psychological studies of flow in consciousness.* Cambridge, MA: Cambridge University Press.

Csikszentmihalyi, M., & Larson, R. (1987). Validity and reliability of the experience-sampling method. *Journal of Nervous and Mental Disease, 175,* 526–536.

Currie, J., & Thomas, D. (1995). Does Head Start make a difference? *American Economic Review, 85,* 341–365.

Czopp, A. M., Monteith, M. J., & Mark, A. Y. (2006). Standing up for a change: Reducing bias through interpersonal confrontation. *Journal of Personality and Social Psychology, 90,* 784–803.

Darwin, C. (1859). *On the origin of species by means of natural selection, or the preservation of favoured races in the struggle for life.* London, England: John Murray.

Darwin, C. (1988). *The expression of the emotions in man and animals.* New York, NY: Oxford University Press. (Original work published 1872)

DeCoster, J. (1998). *Overview of factor analysis.* Retrieved from http://www.stat-help.com/factor.pdf

Denzin, N. K., & Lincoln, Y. S. (Eds.). (2000). Introduction: *The discipline and practice of qualitative research.* In The handbook of qualitative research (2nd ed., pp. 1–29). Thousand Oaks, CA: Sage.

Denzin, N. K., & Lincoln, Y. S. (Eds.). (2005). Introduction: The discipline and practice of qualitative research. In *The SAGE handbook of qualitative research* (3rd ed., pp. 1–32). Thousand Oaks, CA: Sage.

Diener, E. (2000). Subjective well-being: The science of happiness and a proposal for a national index. *American Psychologist, 55,* 34–43.

Diener, E., & Diener, C. (1996). Most people are happy. *Psychological Science, 7,* 181–185.

Diener, E., Diener, M., & Diener, C. (1995). Factors predicting the subjective well-being of nations. *Journal of Personality and Social Psychology, 69,* 851–864.

Diener, E., Emmons, R. A., Larson, R. J., & Griffin, S. (1985). The satisfaction with life scale. *Journal of Personality Assessment, 49,* 71–75.

Diener, E., Ng, W., Harter, J., & Arora, R. (2010). Wealth and happiness across the world: Material prosperity predicts life evaluation, whereas psychosocial prosperity predicts positive feelings. *Journal of Personality and Social Psychology, 104,* 635–652.

Dillman, D. A. (1978). *Mail and telephone surveys: The total design method.* New York, NY: Wiley.

Dillman, D. A. (2000). *Mail and Internet surveys: The tailored design method* (2nd ed.). New York, NY: Wiley.

Dillman, D. A., Christenson, J. A., Carpenter, E. H., & Brooks, R. M. (1974). Increasing mail questionnaire response: A four-state comparison. *American Sociological Review, 39,* 744–756.

Dobbs, D. (2007, July 8). The gregarious brain. *The New York Times.* Retrieved from http://www.nytimes.com/2007/07/08/magazine/08sociability-t.html?_

r=1&scp=1&sq=the%20grega rious%20 brain&st=cse

Duenwald, M. (2005, January 2). The physiology of … facial expressions: A self-conscious look of fear, anger, or happiness can reveal more than a lie detector. *Discover*. Retrieved from http://discover-magazine.com/2005/jan/physiology-of-facial-expressions/#.UnQNAVNptn4

Dunn, E. W., Aknin, L. B., & Norton, M. I. (2008). Spending money on others promotes happiness. *Science, 319*, 1687–1688.

Eid, M., & Diener, E. (2004). Global judgments of subjective well-being: Situational variability and long-term stability. *Social Indicators Research, 65*, 244–277.

Eisenberg, D., Gollust, S. E., Golberstein, E., & Hefner, J. L. (2007). Prevalence and correlates of depression, anxiety, and suicidality among university students. *American Journal of Orthopsychiatry, 77*, 534–542.

Ekman, P. (1992). Facial expressions of emotion. *Current Directions in Psychological Science, 3*, 34–38.

Ekman, P. (2003). *Emotions revealed*. New York, NY: Owl Books.

Elliot, A. J. (2006). The hierarchical model of approach-avoidance motivation. *Motivation and Emotion, 30*, 111–116.

Elmes, D. G., Kantowitz, B. H., & Roedinger, H. L., III. (2006). *Research methods in psychology* (8th ed.). Belmont, CA: Wadsworth.

Emerson, R. M., Fretz, R. I., & Shaw, L. L. (1995). *Writing ethnographic fieldnotes*. Chicago, IL: University of Chicago Press.

Enserink, M. (2008, February 27). The problem with Prozac. *ScienceNOW*. Retrieved from http://news.sciencemag.org/2008/02/problem-prozac

Evans, J. A. (2008). Electronic publishing and narrowing of science and scholarship. *Science, 321*, 395–399.

Ewbank, M. P., Jennings, C., & Calder, A. J. (2009). Why are you angry with me? Facial expressions of threat influence perception of gaze direction. *Journal of Vision, 9*, 1–7.

Exercise for your aging brain. (2006, December 26). *The New York Times*. Retrieved from http://www.nytimes.com/2006/12/26/opinion/26tue4.html

Ferguson, K., & Rodway, M. (1994). Cognitive behavioral treatment of perfectionism: Initial evaluation studies. *Research on Social Work Practice, 4*, 283–308.

Fisher, C. B. (2000). Relational ethics in psychological research: One feminist's journey. In M. Brabek (Ed.), *Practicing feminist ethics in psychology* (pp. 125–142). Washington, DC: American Psychological Association.

Fisher, C. B. (2003). *Decoding the ethics code: A practical guide for psychologists*. Thousand Oaks, CA: Sage.

Fisher, R. A., & Yates, F. (1974). *Statistical tables for biological, agricultural, and medical research* (6th ed.). London, England: Longman.

Fournier, J. C., DeRubeis, R. J., Hollon, S. D., Dimidjian, S., Amsterdam, J. D., Shelton, R. C., & Fawcett, J. (2010). Antidepressant drug effects and depression severity: A patient-level meta-analysis. *Journal of the American Medical Association, 303*(1), 47–53.

Fowler, F. J. (1988). *Survey research methods* (Rev. ed.). Newbury Park, CA: Sage.

Fram, A., & Tompson, T. (2008, March 19). Many college students stressed out, poll finds. *Boston Globe*. Retrieved from http://www.boston.com/news/nation/articles/2008/03/19/many_college_students_stressed_out_poll_finds/

Frank, M. C., & Saxe, R. (2012). Teaching replication. *Perspectives on Psychological Science, 7*, 600–604.

Franklin, R. D., Allison, D. B., & Gorman, B. S. (Eds.). (1997). *Design and analysis of single-case research*. Mahwah, NJ: Erlbaum.

Friedman, R. A. (2010, January 11). Before you quit antidepressants … *The New York Times*. Retrieved from http://www.nytimes.com/2010/01/12/health/12mind.html

Gallup World Poll. Retrieved from http://www.gallup.com/home.aspx

Gardner, H. (1983). Frames of mind: *The theory of multiple intelligences*. New York, NY: Basic Books.

Gardner, H. (1993). *Multiple intelligences: The theory in practice*. New York, NY: Basic Books.

Geer, J. G. (Ed.). (2004). *Public opinion and polling around the world: A historical encyclopedia*. Santa Barbara, CA: ABC-CLIO.

Gibbons, R. D., Hur, K., Bhaumik, D. K., & Mann, J. J. (2005). The relationship between antidepressant medication use and rate of suicide. *Archives of General Psychiatry, 62*, 165–172.

Gibbons, R. G., Brown Hendricks, C., Hur, K., Marcus, S., Bhaumik, D., Erkens, J. A., . . . Mann, J. J. (2007). Early evidence on the effects of regulator's suicidality warning on SSRI prescriptions and suicide in children and adolescents. *American Journal of Psychiatry, 164*(9), 1356–1363.

Gilbert, D. T. (1991). How mental systems believe. *American Psychologist, 46*, 107–119.

Gioia, D., & Brekke, J. S. (2009). Neurocognition, ecological validity, and daily living in the community for individuals with schizophrenia: A mixed methods study. *Psychiatry: Interpersonal and Biological Processes, 72*(1), 94–107.

Gladwell, M. (2002, August 5). The naked face. *The New Yorker, 78*(2), 38–49.

Goldberg, C. (2008, April 21). Mood lifting. *The Boston Globe*, pp. C1, C3.

Goldfinger, S. M., Schutt, R. K., Tolomiczenko, G. S., Turner, W., Ware, N., Penk, W. E., . . . Seidman, L. J. (1997). Housing persons who are homeless and mentally ill: Independent living or evolving consumer households? In W. R. Breakey & J. W. Thompson (Eds.), *Mentally ill and homeless: Special programs for special needs* (pp. 29–49). Amsterdam, Netherlands: Harwood.

Goodstein, D. (2010). *On fact and fraud: Cautionary tales from the front lines of science*. Princeton, NJ: Princeton University Press.

Gordon, R. (1992). *Basic interviewing skills*. Itasca, IL: Peacock.

Gotlib, I. H., & McCann, C. D. (1984). Construct accessibility and depression: An examination of cognitive and affective factors. *Journal of Personality and Social Psychology, 47*(2), 427–439. doi:10.1037/0022-3514.47.2.427

Gottesman, I. I. (1991). *Schizophrenia genesis: The origins of madness.* New York, NY: W. H. Freeman.

Grady, J. (1996). The scope of visual sociology. *Visual Sociology, 11,* 10–24.

Gray, J. R., & Thompson, P. M. (2004). Neurobiology of intelligence: Science and ethics. *Nature Reviews Neuroscience, 5,* 471–482.

Greely, H., Sahakian, B., Harris, J., Kessler, R. C., Gazzaniga, M., Campbell, P., & Farah, M. J. (2008). Towards responsible use of cognitive enhancing drugs by the healthy. *Nature, 456,* 702–705.

Greene, R. L. (1996). The influence of experimental design: The example of the Brown-Peterson paradigm. *Canadian Journal of Experimental Psychology, 50,* 240–242.

Gross, C. (2012, January 9). Disgrace on Marc Hauser. *The Nation.* Retrieved from http://www.thenation.com/article/165313/disgrace-marc-hauser?page=0,0#axzz2d5mxMDmi

Grossfeld, S. M. (2007, December 15). There are very, very many others. *The Boston Globe.* Retrieved from http://www.boston.com/sports/baseball/articles/2007/12/15/mitchell_there_are_very_very_many_others/

Grossman, F. K., Sorsoli, L., & Kia-Keating, M. (2006). A gale force wind: Meaning making by male survivors of childhood sexual abuse. *American Journal of Orthopsychiatry, 76*(4), 434–443.

Groves, R. M. (1989). *Survey errors and survey costs.* New York, NY: Wiley.

Groves, R. M., & Couper, M. P. (1998). *Nonresponse in household interview surveys.* New York, NY: Wiley.

Grunebaum, M. F., Ellis, S. P., Li, S., Oquendo, M. A., & Mann, J. J. (2004). Antidepressants and suicide risk in the United States, 1985–1999. *Journal of Clinical Psychiatry, 65,* 1456–1462.

Hafner, K. (2008, May 3). Exercise your brain, or else you'll . . . uh . . . *The New York Times.* Retrieved from http://www.nytimes.com/2008/05/03/technology/03brain.html?_r=0

Haney, C., Banks, C., & Zimbardo, P. G. (1973). Interpersonal dynamics in a simulated prison. *International Journal of Criminology and Penology, 1,* 69–97.

Hard, S. F., Conway, J. M., & Moran, A. C. (2006). Faculty and college student beliefs about the frequency of student academic misconduct. *Journal of Higher Education, 77,* 1058–1080.

Harmon, A. (2010, April 21). Tribe wins fight to limit research on its DNA. *The New York Times.* Retrieved from http://www.nytimes.com/2010/04/22/us/22dna.html?pagewanted=all

Heinen, T. (1996). *Latent class and discrete latent trait models: Similarities and differences.* Thousand Oaks, CA: Sage.

Hines, T. (2003). *Pseudoscience and the paranormal: A critical examination of the evidence.* Buffalo, NY: Prometheus.

Holmes, S. A. (2001, February 12). Census officials ponder adjustments crucial to redistricting. *The New York Times,* p. A17.

Holt, J. (2011, November 25). Two brains running. *New York Times Book Review,* p. BR16.

Hong, Y.-Y., Morris, M. W., Chiu, C.-Y, & Benet-Martinez, V. (2000). Multicultural minds: A dynamic constructivist approach to culture and cognition. *American Psychologist, 55,* 709–720.

Houghton, P. M., & Houghton, T. J. (2007). *APA: The easy way!* Flint, MI: Baker College.

Huff, D. (1954). *How to lie with statistics.* New York, NY: W. W. Norton.

Huitema, B. E. (2002). Statistical analysis and single-subject designs: Some misunderstandings. In J. S. Bailey & M. R. Burch (Eds.), *Research methods in applied behavior analysis* (pp. 209–232). Thousand Oaks, CA: Sage.

Humphreys, L. (1970). *Tearoom trade: Impersonal sex in public places.* Chicago, IL: Aldine de Gruyter.

Hussain, Z., & Griffiths, M. D. (2009). The attitudes, feelings, and experiences of online gamers: A qualitative analysis. *CyberPsychology & Behavior, 12,* 747–753.

Ioannidis, J. P. A. (2005). Why most published research findings are false. *PLoS Medicine, 2,* e124.

Irvine, L. (1998). Organizational ethics and fieldwork realities: Negotiating ethical boundaries in codependents anonymous. In S. Grills (Ed.), *Doing ethnographic research: Fieldwork settings* (pp. 167–183). Thousand Oaks, CA: Sage.

Isacsson, G. (2001). Suicide prevention: A medical breakthrough. *Acta Psychiatrica Scandinavica, 102,* 113–117.

Iyengar, S. S., Wells, R. E., & Schwartz, B. (2006). Doing better but feeling worse. Looking for the "best" job undermines satisfaction. *Current Directions in Psychological Science, 17,* 143–150.

James, W. (1890). *The principles of psychology.* New York, NY: Henry Holt.

Jarrett, C. (2006, March 3). Are you a grumpy maximizer or a happy satisficer? *British Psychological Society Research Digest.* Retrieved from http://bps-research-digest.blogspot.com/2006/03/are-you-grumpy-maximiser-or-happy.html

Jensen, C. (1994). Psychosocial treatment of depression in women: Nine single-subject evaluations. *Research on Social Work Practice, 4,* 267–282.

Kagay, M. R. (with Elder, J.). (1992, October 9). Numbers are no problem for pollsters. Words are. *The New York Times,* p. E5.

Kahneman, D. (2011). *Thinking, fast and slow.* New York, NY: Farrar, Straus, & Giroux.

Kahneman, D., & Klein, G. (2009). Conditions for intuitive expertise: A failure to disagree. *American Psychologist, 64,* 515–526.

Kahneman, D., Krueger, A. B., Schkade, D. A., Schwartz, N., & Stone, A. A. (2004). A survey method for characterizing daily life experiences: The day reconstruction method. *Science, 306,* 1776–1780.

Kahneman, D., Krueger, A. B., Schkade, D., Schwarz, N., & Stone, A. A. (2006). Would you be happier if you were richer? A focusing illusion. *Science, 30,* 1908–1910.

Kahneman, D., & Tversky, A. (1973). On the psychology of prediction. *Psychology Review, 80,* 237–251.

Kammann, R., & Flett, R. (1983). Affectometer 2: A scale to measure current level of happiness. *Australian Journal of Psychology, 35,* 259–265.

Kandel, E. (2006). *In search of memory: The emergence of a new science of mind.* New York, NY: W. W. Norton.

Kaufman, S. R. (1986). *The ageless self: Sources of meaning in late life.* Madison: University of Wisconsin Press.

Kazdin, A. E. (1982). *Single-case research designs: Methods for clinical and applied settings.* New York, NY: Oxford.

Keeter, S. (2008, May). *Survey research and cell phones: Is there a problem?* Paper presented at the Harvard Program on Survey Research Spring Conference, New Technologies and Survey Research. Cambridge, MA: Institute of Quantitative Social Science, Harvard University.

Kershaw, S. (2000, May 16). In a black community, mistrust of government hinders census. *The New York Times,* p. A20.

Keyes, C. L. M. (2007). Promoting and protecting mental health as flourishing: A complementary strategy for improving national mental health. *American Psychologist, 62,* 95–108.

Kidder, L. H. (1981). *Research methods in social relations.* New York, NY: Holt, Reinhart & Winston.

Killingsworth, M. A., & Gilbert, D. T. (2010). A wandering mind is an unhappy mind. *Science, 330,* 932.

Kilpatrick, D. G., Ruggiero, K. J., Acierno, R., Saunders, B. E., Resnick, H. S., & Best, C. L. (2003). Violence and risk of PTSD, major depression, substance abuse/dependence, and comorbidity: Results from the National Survey of Adolescents. *Journal of Consulting and Clinical Psychology, 1,* 692–700.

Kirk, E. E. (2002). *Evaluating information on the Internet.* Baltimore, MD: Sheridian Libraries, Johns Hopkins. Retrieved from http://guides.library.jhu.edu/evaluatinginformation

Kirk, R. E. (1994). *Experimental design: Procedures for behavioral sciences* (3rd ed.). Pacific Grove, CA: Wadsworth.

Kline, P. (1986). *A handbook of test construction: Introduction to psychometric design.* New York, NY: Methuen.

Knapp, S. J., & VandeCreek, L. D. (2006). *Practical ethics for psychologists: A positive approach.* Washington, DC: American Psychological Association.

Kniffin, K. M., & Wilson, D. S. (2004). The effect of nonphysical traits on the perception of physical attractiveness: Three naturalistic studies. *Evolution and Human Behavior, 25,* 88–101.

Knox, S., Burkard, A. W., Johnson, A. J., Suzuki, L. A., & Ponterotto, J. G. (2003). African American and European American therapists' experiences of addressing race in cross-racial psychotherapy dyads. *Journal of Counseling Psychology, 50*(4), 466–481.

Koegel, P. (1987). *Ethnographic perspectives on homeless and homeless mentally ill women.* Washington, DC: Alcohol, Drug Abuse, and Mental Health Administration, Public Health Service, U.S. Department of Health and Human Services.

Korn, J. H. (1997). *Illusions of reality: A history of deception in social psychology.* Albany: State University of New York Press.

Kornell, N., Hays, M. J., & Bjork, R. A. (2009). Unsuccessful retrieval attempts enhance subsequent learning. *Journal of Experimental Psychology: Learning, Memory, and Cognition, 35,* 989–998.

Kosslyn, S. M., & Rosenberg, R. S. (2001). *Psychology: The brain, the person, the world.* Needham Heights, MA: Allyn & Bacon.

Krueger, R. A., & Casey, M. A. (2009). *Focus groups: A practical guide for applied research* (4th ed.). Thousand Oaks, CA: Sage.

Krueger, A. B., & Schkade, D. A. (2008). The reliability of subjective well-being measures. *Journal of Public Economics, 92,* 1833–1845.

Kuhn, T. S. (1962). *The structure of scientific revolutions.* Chicago, IL: University of Chicago Press.

Kvale, S. (1996). *Interviews: An introduction to qualitative research interviewing.* Thousand Oaks, CA: Sage.

Labaw, P. J. (1980). *Advanced questionnaire design.* Cambridge, MA: ABT Books.

Langford, T. (2000, June 1). Census workers in Dallas find the well-off hard to count. *The Boston Globe,* p. A24.

Larson, C. J. (1993). *Pure and applied sociological theory: Problems and issues.* New York, NY: Harcourt Brace Jovanovich.

Lavrakas, P. J. (1987). *Telephone survey methods: Sampling, selection, and supervision.* Newbury Park, CA: Sage.

Lehrer, J. (2009a, May 18). Don't! The secret of self-control. *The New Yorker,* pp. 26–32.

Lehrer, J. (2009b, April 26). Inside the baby mind. *The Boston Sunday Globe.* Retrieved http://www.boston.com/bostonglobe/ideas/articles/2009/04/26/inside_the_baby_mind/?page=4

Lemann, N. (1999). *The big test: The secret history of American meritocracy.* New York, NY: Farrar, Straus & Giroux.

Lempert, R. (1989). Humility is a virtue: On the politicization of policy-relevant research. *Law & Society Review, 23,* 146–161.

Leppanen, J. M., & Nelson, C. A. (2009). Tuning the developing brain to social signals of emotions. *Nature Review Neuroscience, 1,* 37–47.

Levitt, H., Butler, M., & Hill, T. (2006). What clients find helpful in psychotherapy: Developing principles for facilitating moment-to-moment change. *Journal of Counseling Psychology, 53*(3), 314–324.

Levy, P. S., & Lemeshow, S. (1999). *Sampling of populations: Methods and applications* (3rd ed.). New York, NY: Wiley.

Lewontin, R. (1976). Race and intelligence. In J. Block & G. Dworkin (Eds.), *The IQ controversy: Critical readings* (pp. 78–92). New York, NY: Pantheon Books.

Likert, R. (1932). A technique for the measurement of attitudes. *Archives of Psychology, 140,* 1–55.

Lilienfeld, S. O. (2005). The 10 commandments of helping students distinguish science from pseudoscience in psychology. *Observer, 18,* 9. Retrieved from http://www.psychologicalscience.org/index.php/publications/observer/2005/september-05/the-10-commandments-of-helping-students-distinguish-science-from-pseudoscience-in-psychology.html

Lofland, J., & Lofland, L. H. (1984). *Analyzing social settings: A guide to qualitative observation and analysis* (2nd ed.). Belmont, CA: Wadsworth.

Lowry, R. (2010). Concepts & applications of inferential statistics. Retrieved from http://vassarstats.net/textbook/

Ludwig, J., & Marcotte, D. E. (2005). Antidepressants, suicide, and drug regulation. *Journal of Policy, Analysis and Management, 24,* 249–272.

Magnus, K., Diener, E., Fujita, F., & Pavot, W. (1993). Extraversion and neuroticism as predictors of object life events: A longitudinal analysis. *Journal of Personality and Social Psychology, 65,* 1046–1053.

Mahncke, H. W., Connor, B. B., Appelman, J., Ahsanuddin, O. N., Hardy, J. L., Wood, R. A., . . . Merzenich, M. M. (2006). Memory enhancement in healthy older adults using a brain plasticity-based training program: A randomized, controlled study. *Proceedings of the National Academy of Sciences of the United States of America, 103,* 12523–12528.

Mandal, M. K., & Ambady, N. (2004). Laterality of facial expression of emotion: Universal and culture-specific influences. *Behavioral Neuroscience, 15,* 23–34.

Marshall, G. D., & Zimbardo, P. G. (1979). Affective consequences of inadequately explained physiological arousal. *Journal of Personality and Social Psychology, 37,* 970–988.

Martin, L. L., & Kettner, P. M. (1996). *Measuring the performance of human service programs.* Thousand Oaks, CA: Sage.

Matsumoto, D., & Willingham, B. (2009). Spontaneous facial expression of emotion of congenitally and noncongenitally blind individuals. *Journal of Personality and Social Psychology, 96,* 2–10.

Maxwell, J. A. (1996). *Qualitative research design: An interactive approach.* Thousand Oaks, CA: Sage.

McAdams, D. P., & Pals, J. L. (2006). A new Big Five: Fundamental principles for an integrative science of personality. *American Psychologist, 61,* 204–217.

McKenna, F. P., & Sharma, D. (2004). Reversing the emotional Stroop effect reveals that it is not what it seems: The role of fast and slow components. *Journal of Experimental Psychology: Learning, Memory, and Cognition, 30*(2), 382–392. doi:10.1037/0278-7393.30.2.382

Milgram, S. (1963). Behavioral study of obedience. *Journal of Abnormal and Social Psychology, 67,* 371–478.

Milgram, S. (1964). Issues in the study of obedience: A reply to Baumrind. *American Psychologist, 19,* 848–852.

Milgram, S. (1965). Some conditions of obedience and disobedience to authority. *Human Relations, 18,* 57–76.

Milgram, S. (1974). *Obedience to authority: An experimental view.* New York, NY: Harper & Row.

Milgram, S. (1977). Subject reaction: The neglected factor in the ethics of experimentation. *Hastings Law Review, October,* 19–23.

Milgram, S. (1992). *The individual in a social world: Essays and experiments* (2nd ed.). New York, NY: McGraw-Hill.

Miller, A. G. (1986). *The obedience experiments: A case study of controversy in social science.* New York, NY: Praeger.

Miller, W. L., & Crabtree, B. F. (1999). Depth interviewing. In B. F. Crabtree & W. L. Miller (Eds.), *Doing qualitative research* (pp. 89–107). Thousand Oaks, CA: Sage.

Mohr, L. B. (1992). *Impact analysis for program evaluation.* Newbury Park, CA: Sage.

Morris, M. W., & Peng, K. (1994). Culture and cause: American and Chinese attributions for social physical events. *Journal of Personality and Social Psychology, 67,* 949–971.

Myers, D., & Diener, E. (1995). Who is happy? *Psychological Science, 6,* 10–19.

Na, J., Grossmann, I., Varnum, M. E. W., Kitayama, S., Gonzalez, R., & Nisbett, R. E. (2010). Cultural differences are not always reducible to individual differences. *Proceedings of the National Academy of Sciences of the United States of America, 107,* 6192–6197.

Nagourney, A. (2002, November 5). Cellphones and caller ID are making it harder for pollsters to pick a winner. *The New York Times,* p. A20.

Nakonezny, P. A., Reddick, R., & Rodgers, J. L. (2004). Did divorces decline after the Oklahoma City bombing? *Journal of Marriage and Family, 66,* 90–100.

Neisser, U., Boodoo, G., Bouchard, T. J., Boykin, A. W., Brody, N., Ceci, S. J., . . . Urbina, S. (1996). Intelligence: Knowns and unknowns. *American Psychologist, 51,* 77–101.

Nelson, D. L., Schrieber, T. A., & McEvoy, C. L. (1992). Processing implicit and explicit representations. *Psychological Review, 99,* 322–348.

Nelson, J. C. (1994). Ethics, gender, and ethnicity in single-case research and evaluation. *Journal of Social Service Research, 18,* 139–152.

Nelson, M., Neumark-Stzainer, D., Hannan, P. J., Sirard, J. R., & Story, M. (2006). Longitudinal and secular trends in physical activity and sedentary behavior during adolescence. *Pediatrics, 118,* e1627–e16343.

Nestor, P. G. (2002). Mental disorder and violence: Personality dimensions and clinical features. *American Journal of Psychiatry, 159*(12), 1973–1978.

Nestor, P. G., Akdag, S. J., O'Donnell, B. F., Niznikiewicz, M. A., Law, S., Shenton,

M. E., & McCarley, R. W. (1998). Word recall in schizophrenia: A connectionist model. *American Journal of Psychiatry, 155,* 1685–1690.

Nestor, P. G., Kubicki, M., Gurrera, R. J., Niznikiewicz, M., Frumin, M., McCarley, R. W., & Shenton, M. E. (2004). Neuropsychological correlates of diffusion tensor imaging in schizophrenia. *Neuropsychology, 18,* 629–637.

Nestor, P. G., Kubicki, M., Nakamura, M., Niznikiewicz, M., McCarley, R. W., & Shenton, M. E. (2010). Comparing prefrontal gray and white matter contributions to intelligence and decision making in schizophrenia and healthy controls. *Neuropsychology, 1,* 121–129.

Nestor, P. G., & O'Donnell, B. F. (1998). The mind adrift: Attentional dysregulation in schizophrenia. In R. Parasuraman (Ed.), *The attentive brain* (pp. 527–546). Cambridge: MIT Press.

Nickerson, R. S. (1998). Confirmatory bias: A ubiquitous phenomenon in many guises. *Review of General Psychology, 2,* 175–220.

Niedenthal, P. M. (2007). Embodying emotion. *Science, 316,* 1002–1005.

Nisbett, R. E. (2009). *Intelligence and how to get it: Why schools and culture count.* New York, NY: W. W. Norton.

Nisbett, R. E., Aronson, J., Blair, C., Dickens, W., Flynn, J., Halpern, D. F., & Turkheimer, E. (2012). Intelligence: New findings and theoretical developments. *American Psychologist, 67,* 130–159.

Nisbett, R. E., Fong, G. T., Lehman, D. R., & Cheng, P. W. (1987). Teaching reasoning. *Science, 238,* 625–631.

Nisbett, R. E., Peng, K., Choi, I., & Norenzayan, A. (2001). Culture and systems of thought: Holistic vs. analytic cognition. *Psychological Review, 108,* 291–310.

Orcutt, J. D., & Turner, J. B. (1993). Shocking numbers and graphic accounts: Quantified images of drug problems in the print media. *Social Problems, 49,* 190–206.

Parasuraman, R. (Ed.). (1998). *The attentive brain.* Cambridge: MIT Press.

Pascual-Leone, A., & Greenberg, L. S. (2007). Emotional processing in experiential therapy: Why "the only out is through." *Journal of Consulting and Clinical Psychology, 75*(6), 875–887.

Paulos, J. A. (2010a, May 13). Metric mania. *The New York Times Magazine,* pp. 11–12.

Paulos, J. A. (2010b, Oct 24). Stories vs. statistics. *The New York Times.* Retrieved from http://opinionator.blogs.nytimes.com/2010/10/24/stories-vs-statistics/?_r=0

Pavot, W., & Diener, E. (1993). Review of the satisfaction with life scale. *Psychological Assessment, 5,* 164–172.

Pavot, W., Diener, E., Colvin, C. R., & Sandvik, E. (1991). Further validation of Satisfaction with Life Scale: Evidence for cross-method convergence of well-being measures. *Journal of Personality Assessment, 57,* 149–161.

Perry, G. (2013). *Behind the shock machine: The untold story of the notorious Milgram experiments.* New York, NY: The New Press.

Peterson, R. A. (2000). *Constructing effective questionnaires.* Thousand Oaks, CA: Sage.

Phillips, D. P. (1982). The impact of fictional television stories on U.S. adult fatalities: New evidence on the effect of mass media on violence. *American Journal of Sociology, 87,* 1340–1359.

Piattelli-Palmarini, M. (1994). *Inevitable illusions: How mistakes of reasons rule our minds.* New York, NY: Wiley.

Piliavin, J. A., & Piliavin, I. M. (1972). Effect of blood on reactions to a victim. *Journal of Personality and Social Psychology, 23,* 353–361.

Popper, K. R. (1959). *The logic of scientific discovery.* New York, NY: Basic Books.

Rees, G., Frackowiak, R., & Frith, C. (1997). Two modulatory effects of attention that mediate object categorization in human cortex. *Science, 275,* 835–838.

Reynolds, P. D. (1979). *Ethical dilemmas and social science research.* San Francisco, CA: Jossey-Bass.

Richards, T. J., & Richards, L. (1994). Using computers in qualitative research. In N. K. Denzin & Y. S. Lincoln (Eds.), *Handbook of qualitative research* (pp. 445–462). Thousand Oaks, CA: Sage.

Roediger, H. L. (2012). Psychology's woes and a partial cure: The value of replication. *APS Observer, 25*(2). Retrieved from http://www.psychologicalscience.org/index.php/advocacy/observer/2012/february-12

Roediger, H. L., & Finn, B. (2010). The plusses of getting it wrong. *Scientific American Mind, March/April,* 39–41.

Roman, A. (2005). *Women's health network client survey: Field report.* Unpublished report, Center for Survey Research, University of Massachusetts, Boston.

Ross, C. E. (1990). *Work, family, and the sense of control: Implications for the psychological well-being of women and men.* Proposal submitted to the National Science Foundation, University of Illinois at Urbana.

Rossi, P. H., & Freeman, H. E. (1989). *Evaluation: A systematic approach* (4th ed.). Newbury Park, CA: Sage.

Rossiter, J. (2007). *The APA pocket handbook.* Grand Blanc, MI: DW Publishing.

Rossman, G. B., & Rallis, S. F. (1998). *Learning in the field: An introduction to qualitative research.* Thousand Oaks, CA: Sage.

Rowe, G., Hirsh, J. B., & Anderson, A. K. (2007). Positive affect increases the breadth of attentional selection. *Proceedings of the National Academy of Sciences of the United States of America, 104,* 383–388.

Rubin, H. J., & Rubin, I. S. (1995). *Qualitative interviewing: The art of hearing data.* Thousand Oaks, CA: Sage.

Sánchez, B., Esparza, P., Colón, Y., & Davis, K. E. (2010). Tryin' to make it during the transition from high school: The role of family obligation attitudes and economic context for Latino-emerging adults. *Journal of Adolescent Research, 25,* 858–885.

Saville, B. K. (2003). Single-subject designs. In S. F. Davis (Ed.), *Handbook of research methods in experimental psychology* (Vol. 1., pp. 80–92). Malden, MA: Blackwell.

Saville, B. K., & Buskist, W. (2003). Traditional idiographic approaches: Small-*N* research designs. In S. F. Davis (Ed.), *Handbook of research methods in experimental psychology* (Vol. 1., pp. 66–82). Malden, MA: Blackwell.

Schaie, K. W. (1965). A general model for the study of developmental problems. *Psychological Bulletin, 64,* 92–107.

Schaie, K. W. (1977). Quasi-experimental designs in the psychology of aging. In J. E. Birren & K. W. Schaie (Eds.), *Handbook of the psychology of aging* (pp. 39–58). New York, NY: Van Nostrand.

Schober, M. F. (1999). Making sense of survey questions. In M. G. Sirken, D. J. Herrmann, S. Schechter, N. Schwartz, J. M. Tanur, & R. Tourangeau (Eds.), *Cognition and survey research* (pp. 77–94). New York, NY: Wiley.

Schuman, H., & Presser, S. (1981). *Questions and answers in attitude surveys: Experiments on question form, wording, and context.* New York, NY: Academic Press.

Schutt, R. K. (with S. M. Goldfinger). (2011). *Homelessness, housing and mental illness.* Cambridge, MA: Harvard University Press.

Schutt, R. K. (2012). *Investigating the social world: The process and practice of research* (7th ed.). Thousand Oaks, CA: Pine Forge Press.

Schutt, R. K., Cruz, E. R., & Woodford, M. L. (2008). Client satisfaction in a breast and cervical cancer early detection program: The influence of ethnicity and language, health, resources and barriers. *Women & Health, 48,* 283–302.

Schwartz, A. (2009, December 20). NFL acknowledges long term concussion effects. *The New York Times.* Retrieved from http://www.nytimes.com/2009/12/21/sports/football/21concussions.html

Schwartz, B. (2004, April). The tyranny of choice. *Scientific American,* 70–75.

Seligman, M. E. P. (1991). *Learned optimism: How to change your mind and your life.* New York, NY: Knopf.

Sharot, T., Martorella, E. A., Delgado, M. R., & Phelps, E. A. (2007). How personal experience modulates the neural circuitry of memories of September 11. *Proceedings of the National Academy of Science of the United States of America, 104,* 389–394.

Shaw, P., Eckstrand, K., Sharp, W., Blumental, J., Lerch, J. P., Greenstein, D., . . . Rapoport, J. L. (2007). Attention-deficit/hyperactivity disorder is characterized by a delay in cortical maturation. *Proceedings of the National Academy of Sciences of the United States of America, 104,* 19649–19654.

Shaywitz, D. A. (2007, April 24). Shattering the bell curve. *The Wall Street Journal.* Retrieved from http://online.wsj.com/article/SB117736979316179649-search.html

Sheldon, K. M., & King, L. (2001). Why positive psychology is necessary. *American Psychologist, 56,* 216–217.

Shenk, J. W. (2009, June). What makes us happy? *Atlantic Monthly.* Retrieved from http://www.theatlantic.com/magazine/archive/2009/06/what-makes-us-happy/7439/

Shepard, R. (1990). *Mind sights.* New York, NY: W. H. Freeman.

Shepherd, J., Hill, D., Bristor, J., & Montalvan, P. (1996). Converting an ongoing health study to CAPI: Findings from the National Health and Nutrition Study. In R. B. Warnecke (Ed.), *Health survey research methods conference proceedings* (pp. 159–164). Hyattsville, MD: U.S. Department of Health and Human Services.

Sherman, L. W. (1992). *Policing domestic violence: Experiments and dilemmas.* New York, NY: Free Press.

Sherman, L. W. (1993). Implications of a failure to read the literature. *American Sociological Review, 58,* 888–889.

Sherman, L. W., & Berk, R. A. (1984). The specific deterrent effects of arrest for domestic assault. *American Sociological Review, 49,* 261–272.

Shermer, M. (2008). A new phrenology? *Scientific American, 298*(5), 42.

Shermer, M. (2010). When scientists lie: Fraud, deception, and lies in research reveal how science is (mostly) self-correcting. *Scientific American, 303*(1), 34.

Shrout, P. E., & Fleiss, J. L. (1979). Intraclass correlation: Uses in assessing rater reliability. *Psychological Bulletin, 2,* 420–428.

Shweder, R., & Sullivan, M. A. (1993). Cultural psychology: Who needs it? *Annual Review of Psychology, 44,* 497–523.

Sieber, J. E. (1992). *Planning ethically responsible research: A guide for students and institutional review boards.* Newbury Park, CA: Sage.

Simon, H. A. (1956). Rational choice and the structure of the environment. *Psychological Review, 63,* 129–138.

Singham, M. (2010, May 9). The new war between science and religion. *Chronicle of Higher Education.* Retrieved from http://chronicle.com/article/The-New-War-Between-Science/65400/

Sjoberg, G. (Ed.). (1967). *Ethics, politics, and social research.* Cambridge, MA: Schenkman.

Smyth, J. D., Dillman, D. A., Christian, L. M., & Stern, M. J. (2004, May 13). *How visual grouping influences answers to Internet surveys.* Paper presented at the annual meeting of the American Association for Public Opinion Research, Phoenix, AZ. Retrieved from http://www.sesrc.wsu.edu/dillman/papers/2007/ContextEffects.pdf

Stake, R. E. (1995). *The art of case study research.* Thousand Oaks, CA: Sage.

Stanovich, K. (1997). *How to think straight about psychology* (4th ed.). New York, NY: HarperCollins.

Steele, C. M., & Aronson, J. (1995). Stereotype threat and the intellectual test performance of African Americans. *Journal of Personality and Social Psychology, 69,* 797–811.

Steptoe, A., Wardle, J., & Marmot, M. (2005). Positive affect and health-related neuroendocrine, cardiovascular, and inflammatory processes. *Proceedings of the National Academy of Sciences of the United States of America, 102,* 6508–6512.

Sternberg, R. J. (2003). *The psychologist's companion: A guide to scientific writing for students and researchers* (4th ed.). New York, NY: Cambridge University Press.

Strack, F., Martin, L. L., & Schwartz, N. (1988). Priming and communication: Social determinants of information use in judgments of life satisfaction. *European Journal of Social Psychology, 18,* 429–442.

Strack, F., Martin, L. L., & Stepper, S. (1988). Inhibiting and facilitating conditions of the human smile: A nonobtrusive test of the facial feedback hypothesis. *Journal of Personality and Social Psychology, 54,* 768–777.

Su, S. K., Chiu, C.-Y., Hong, Y.-Y., Leung, K., Peng, K., & Morris, M. W. (1999). Self-organization and social organization: American and Chinese constructions. In T. R. Tyler, R. Kramer, & O. John (Eds.), *The psychology of social self* (pp. 193–222). Mahwah, NJ: Erlbaum.

Sudman, S. (1976). *Applied sampling.* New York, NY: Academic Press.

Talbot, M. (2009, April 27). Brain gain: The underground world of "neuroenhancing" drugs. *The New Yorker.* Retrieved from http://www.newyorker.com/reporting/2009/04/27/090427fa_fact_talbot

Taleb, N. N. (2001). *Fooled by randomness: The hidden role of chance in the markets and in life.* New York, NY: Texere LLC.

Taleb, N. N. (2007). *The Black Swan: The impact of the highly improbable.* New York, NY: Random House.

Tashakkori, A., & Teddlie, C. (2003). *Handbook of mixed methods in social and behavioral research.* Thousand Oaks, CA: Sage.

Thaiss, C., & Sanford, J. (2000). *Writing for psychology.* Needham Heights, MA: Allyn & Bacon.

Tourangeau, R. (2004). Survey research and societal change. *Annual Review of Psychology, 55,* 775–801.

Tripodi, T. (1994). *A primer on single-subject design for clinical social workers.* Washington, DC: National Association of Social Workers.

Trochim, W. M. (2006). *The research methods knowledge base* (2nd ed.). Retrieved from http://www.socialresearchmethods.net/kb/

Tufte, E. (1983). *The visual display of quantitative information.* Cheshire, CT: Graphics Press.

Tuhus-Dubrow, R. (2008, November 29). Group think. *The Boston Sunday Globe.* Retrieved from http://www.boston.com/bostonglobe/ideas/articles/2008/11/23/group_think/

Tversky, A., & Kahneman, D. (1974). Judgment under uncertainty: Heuristics and biases. *Science, 185,* 1124–1131.

Uhls, Y. T., & Greenfield, P. M. (2011). The value of fame: Preadolescent perceptions of popular media and their relationship to future aspirations. *Developmental Psychology, 48,* 315–326.

Underwood, B. (1957). *Psychological research.* New York, NY: Appleton.

University of Maryland. (2013). *Stress: University of Maryland Medical Center.* Baltimore, MD: Author. Retrieved from http://umm.edu/health/medical/reports/articles/stress

University of Washington Psychology Writing Center. (1997). *Writing a psychology literature review.* Retrieved from http://www.psych.uw.edu/writingcenter/writingguides/pdf/litrev.pdf

U.S. Bureau of the Census. (2001, July 13). *Statement by William G. Barron Jr. on the Current Status of Results of Census 2000 Accuracy and Coverage Evaluation Survey.* Washington, DC: U.S. Department of Commerce, Bureau of the Census. Retrieved from www.census.gov/pressRelease/www/2001/cb01cs06.html

U.S. Bureau of the Census. (2010a, August 10). *1.6 billion in 2010 census savings returned.* Washington, DC: U.S. Department of Commerce, Bureau of the Census. Retrieved from http://2010.census.gov/news/releases/operations/

U.S. Bureau of the Census. (2010b, April 30). *Door-to-door visits begin for 2010 census.* Washington, DC: U.S. Department of Commerce, Bureau of the Census. Retrieved from http://2010.census.gov/news/releases/operations/

U.S. Bureau of the Census. (2010c, March 15). *2010 census forms arrive in 120 million mailboxes across nation.* Washington, DC: U.S. Department of Commerce, Bureau of the Census. Retrieved from http://2010.census.gov/news/releases/operations/

U.S. Bureau of the Census. (2010d, March 17). *Questions and answers: Real people, real questions, real answers.* Washington, DC: U.S. Department of Commerce, Bureau of the Census. Retrieved from http://2010.census.gov/2010census/about/answers.php

U.S. Department of Health, Education, and Welfare. (1979). *The Belmont report: Ethical principles and guidelines for the protection of human subjects of research.* Washington, DC: National Commission for the Protection of Human Subjects of Biomedical and Behavioral Research, Office of the Secretary, Department of Health, Education, and Welfare. Retrieved from http://www.hhs.gov/ohrp/humansubjects/guidance/belmont.html

U.S. Department of Health and Human Services, Office of Research Integrity. (2012, September 6). Findings of research misconduct. *Federal Register, 77*(177). Retrieved from https://www.federalregister.gov/articles/2012/09/06/2012-21992/findings-of-research-misconduct.

U.S. Public Health Service. (1999). *Mental health: A report of the Surgeon General.* Rockville, MD: Author.

Van Hoye, G., & Lievens, F. (2003). The effects of sexual orientation on hirability ratings: An experimental study. *Journal of Business and Psychology, 18,* 15–30.

Varkevisser, C. M., Pathmanathan, I., & Brownlee, A. (1991). *Designing and conducting health systems research projects: Volume 1. Proposal development and fieldwork.* Ottawa, Ontario, Canada: Canada's International Development Research Centre.

Wageman, R. (1995). Interdependence and group effectiveness. *Administrative Science Quarterly, 40,* 145–180.

Wallgren, A., Wallgren, B., Persson, R., Jorner, U., & Haaland, J. (1996). *Graphing statistics and data: Creating better charts.* Thousand Oaks, CA: Sage.

Ware, N. C. (1999). Evolving consumer households: An experiment in community living for people with severe psychiatric disorders. *Psychiatric Rehabilitation Journal, 23*(1), 3–10.

Wechsler, D. (1944). *The measurement of adult intelligence* (3rd ed.). Baltimore, MD: Williams & Wilkins.

Wechsler, D. (1997). *WAIS-III administration and scoring manual.* San Antonio, TX: Psychological Corporation.

Wechsler, D. (2008). *WAIS-IV administration and scoring manual.* San Antonio, TX: Psychological Corporation.

Whalen, P. J. (1998). Fear, vigilance, and ambiguity: Initial neuroimaging studies of the amygdala. *Current Directions in Psychological Science, 7,* 177–188.

Whalen, P. J., Kagan, J., Cook, R. G., Davis, F. C., Kim, H., Polis, S., . . . Johnstone, T. (2004). Human amygdala responsivity to masked fearful eye whites. *Science, 306,* 2061.

Whyte, W. F. (1955). *Street corner society.* Chicago, IL: University of Chicago Press.

Willis, S. L., Tennstedt, S. L., Marsiske, M., Ball, K., Elias, J., Koepke, K. M., . . . Wright, E. (2006). Long-term effects of cognitive training on everyday functional outcomes in older adults. *JAMA, 296,* 2805–2814.

Wolcott, H. F. (1995). *The art of fieldwork.* Walnut Creek, CA: AltaMira Press.

Yang, Y. (2008). Social inequalities in happiness in the United States, 1972 to 2004: An age-period-cohort analysis. *American Sociological Review, 703,* 204–226.

Yardley, J. K., & Rice, R. W. (1991). The relationship between mood and subjective well-being. *Social Indicators Research, 24,* 101–111.

Yarnold, P. R. (1992). Statistical analysis for single-case designs. In F. B. Bryant, J. Edwards, R. S. Tindale, E. J. Posavac, L. Hath, E. Henderson, & Y. Suarez-Bakazar (Eds.), *Methodological issues in applied social psychology* (pp. 177–197). New York, NY: Plenum Press.

Zarracina, J. (2010, April 4). A life lesson from the majors. Smile, you'll live longer. *The Boston Sunday Globe,* p. C10.

Zielbauer, P. (2000, April 21). 2 cities lag far behind the U.S. in heeding the call of the census. *The New York Times,* p. A21.

Zimbardo, P. G. (2007). *The Lucifer effect: Understanding how good people turn evil.* New York, NY: Random House.

# Exhibit Credits

Exhibit 1.1: Shepard (1990). Copyright © 1990 Roger Shepard. Reprinted by permission of the author.

Exhibit 1.3: Varkevisser, Pathmanathan, and Brownlee (1991).

Exhibit 1.4: Photo taken by Cecil Greek.

Exhibit 1.5: Stockbyte/Thinkstock.

Exhibit 2.3: Retrieved from http://www.theepochtimes.com/n2/images/stories/large/2012/08/28/97426195.jpg

Exhibit 2.7: Paul Ekman, PhD/Paul Ekman Group, LLC.

Exhibit 2.8: Retrieved from http://www.uni.edu/commstudies/researchmethods/images/chapterfour/hourglass.png

Exhibit 3.1: From the film *OBEDIENCE* © 1968 by Stanley Milgram; © renewed 1993 by Alexandra Milgram; distributed by Penn State, Media Sales.

Exhibit 3.2: From the film *OBEDIENCE* © 1968 by Stanley Milgram; © renewed 1993 by Alexandra Milgram; distributed by Penn State, Media Sales.

Exhibit 3.7: Zimbardo (2007). Copyright © 2007 by Phillip G. Zimbardo Inc. Used by permission of Random House, Inc.

Exhibit 4.1: Adapted from "Levels of Measurement," Research Assessment Adviser, http://www.research-assessment-adviser.com/levels-of-measurement.html.

Exhibit 4.2: From "Data Collection and Analysis," *Neuroscience for Kids*, by Dr. Eric H. Chudler, Department of Bioengineering, University of Washington. Reprinted with permission.

Exhibit 4.6: © Comstock/Thinkstock.

Exhibit 4.7: From "Data Collection and Analysis," *Neuroscience for Kids*, by Dr. Eric H. Chudler, Department of Bioengineering, University of Washington. Reprinted with permission.

Exhibit 4.9: Adapted from "Data Classification," Six Sigma Material, http://www.six-sigma-material.com/Data-Classification.html.

Exhibit 4.10: © Comstock/Thinkstock.

Exhibit 4.11: Created by Kevin Murray based on data from Aronson, Steele, Salinas, and Lustina (1998).

Exhibit 4.12: Adapted from Krueger and Schkade (2008) and Pavot and Diener (1993).

Exhibit 4.14: Adapted from Kidder (1981).

Exhibit 4.15: Adapted from Kidder (1981).

Exhibit 4.16: Created by Kevin Murray based on data from Aronson et al. (1998).

Exhibit 4.17: Block (1995). Copyright © 1995, Elsevier. Reprinted with permission.

Exhibit 5.10: Data from Schuman and Presser (1981, p. 121).

Exhibit 5.14: Dillman (1978). Copyright © 1978 Don A. Dillman.

# Index

*Note:* Page numbers referring to exhibits and tables are followed by (exhibit) and (table), respectively.

# About the Authors

**Paul G. Nestor, PhD,** is a Professor of Psychology at the University of Massachusetts Boston and Assistant Professor in Psychology in the Department of Psychiatry at the Harvard Medical School. A summa cum laude and Phi Beta Kappa graduate of Boston University, he earned his MA and PhD in clinical psychology from The Catholic University of America and was a postdoctoral fellow in the National Institute of Mental Health Clinical Research Training Program at Harvard Medical School. His peer-reviewed publications cover a variety of areas of behavioral science, including neuropsychology, structural and functional neuroimaging, attention, memory, personality, forensic psychology, and schizophrenia. He has authored or coauthored more than 100 peer-reviewed articles in journals such as *Journal of Abnormal Psychology, Neuropsychology, American Journal of Psychiatry, Archives of General Psychiatry, Biological Psychiatry, NeuroImage, Neuropsychologia, Cortex, Schizophrenia Research, Journal of Nervous and Mental Disease, Journal of Neuroscience, Proceedings of the National Academy of Science,* and *Law and Human Behavior.* His research has been federally supported by competitive grants from both the National Institute of Mental Health and the Department of Veterans Affairs, and he is a past recipient of a Veterans Administration Merit Review Award, "Cognitive Neuroscience Studies of Schizophrenia." He is also the past recipient of the University of Massachusetts Boston Chancellor's Award for Distinguished Scholarship (2003) for his research in psychology. His article "Neuropsychological Correlates of Diffusion Tensor Imaging in Schizophrenia" was one of the top 50 downloaded from the APA website during 2005, with an annualized adjusted rate of 2,238 downloads. His teaching has been recognized by the College of Arts and Sciences Outstanding Faculty Achievement Award, University of Massachusetts Boston (1999). He also has experience in media presentation for both television and radio, including having his research featured on the Discovery Channel series, "Most Evil" (August 2006) and WUMB "Commonwealth Journal" (January 2003). He is a licensed psychologist in Massachusetts, specializing in clinical psychology, neuropsychology, and forensic psychology.

**Russell K. Schutt, PhD,** is Professor and Chair of Sociology at the University of Massachusetts Boston and Lecturer on Sociology in the Department of Psychiatry (Beth Israel-Deaconess Medical Center) at the Harvard Medical School. He completed his BA, MA, and PhD degrees at the University of Illinois at Chicago and was a postdoctoral fellow in the National Institute of Mental Health–Funded Sociology of Social Control Training Program at Yale University (1977–1979). In addition to *Investigating Human Behavior,* he is the author or coauthor of other SAGE research methods texts for sociology, social work, and criminology/criminal justice and author of *Homelessness, Housing, and Mental Illness* (2011), as well as other books and more than 60 peer-reviewed articles, book chapters, and other publications appearing in journals such as *Psychiatric Services, Schizophrenia Bulletin, Schizophrenia Research, Journal of Nervous and Mental Disease, Journal of Health and Social Behavior; Evaluation and Program Planning* and *American Journal of Sociology* on topics including homelessness, service preferences and satisfaction, mental health, cognitive functioning, service systems and organizations, law, and teaching research methods. His funded research experience includes a National Cancer Institute–funded study of community health workers and recruitment for cancer clinical trials, a large translational research project for the Massachusetts Department of Public Health's Women's Health Network, a National Institute of Mental Health–funded study of housing alternatives for homeless persons diagnosed with severe mental illness and evaluations of service programs in the Massachusetts Department of Public Health, the Massachusetts Department of Mental Health, and the Veterans Administration. He has received the Chancellor's Award for Distinguished Service and the College of Arts and Sciences Outstanding Achievement Award at the University of Massachusetts Boston.

# SAGE researchmethods

The essential online tool for researchers from the world's leading methods publisher

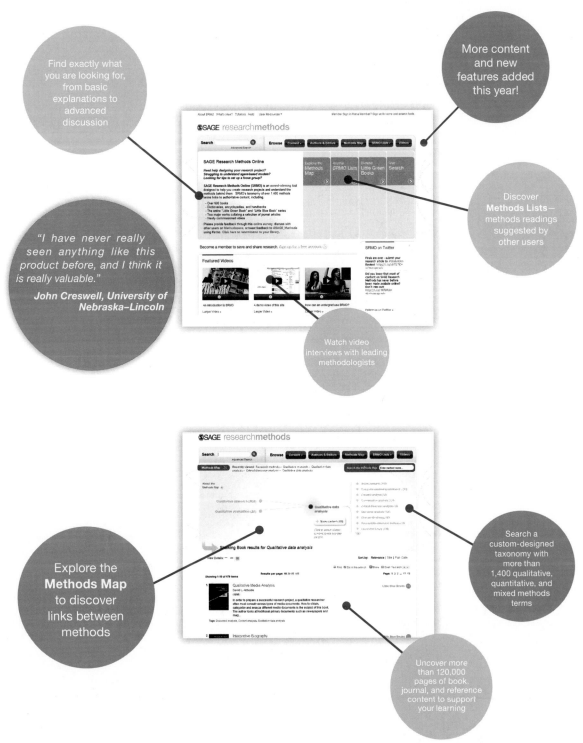

Find exactly what you are looking for, from basic explanations to advanced discussion

More content and new features added this year!

*"I have never really seen anything like this product before, and I think it is really valuable."*

**John Creswell, University of Nebraska–Lincoln**

Discover **Methods Lists**— methods readings suggested by other users

Watch video interviews with leading methodologists

Explore the **Methods Map** to discover links between methods

Search a custom-designed taxonomy with more than 1,400 qualitative, quantitative, and mixed methods terms

Uncover more than 120,000 pages of book, journal, and reference content to support your learning

Find out more at
www.sageresearchmethods.com